32

# UNITY AND DIVERSITY IN THE CHURCH

# UNITY AND DIVERSITY IN THE CHURCH

PAPERS READ AT
THE 1994 SUMMER MEETING AND
THE 1995 WINTER MEETING OF
THE ECCLESIASTICAL HISTORY SOCIETY

EDITED BY

## R. N. SWANSON

PUBLISHED FOR
THE ECCLESIASTICAL HISTORY SOCIETY
BY
BLACKWELL PUBLISHERS LTD
1996

Copyright © Ecclesiastical History Society 1996

First published 1996

2 4 6 8 10 9 7 5 3 1

Blackwell Publishers Ltd
108 Cowley Road
Oxford OX4 1 JF
UK

Blackwell Publishers Inc.
238 Main Street
Cambridge, Massachusetts 02142
USA
*British Library Cataloguing in Publication Data*

A CIP catalogue record for this book is available from the
British Library.

*Library of Congress Cataloging-in-Publication Data*

Ecclesiastical History Society. Summer Meeting (1994: University of Nottingham)
    Unity and diversity in the church: papers read at the 1994 Summer Meeting and the 1995
  Winter Meeting of the Ecclesiastical History Society / edited by R. N. Swanson.
        540 pp. (Studies in church history; 32)
    Includes bibliographical refrences and index.
    ISBN 0–631–19892-X
    1. Church history—Congresses.   2. Church—Unity—History of doctrines—Congresses.
  3. Religious pluralism—Christianity—History of doctrines—Congresses.
  4. Multiculturalism—Religious aspects—Christianity—History of doctrines—Congresses.
  5. Schism—History—Congresses.   6. Christian union—History—Congresses.
  I. Swanson, R. N. (Robert Norman) II. Ecclesiastical History Society. Winter Meeting (1995:
  King's College, London)
  III. Title. IV. Series.
  BR148.E23   1994                                                               95–33575
  270—dc20                                                                       CIP

Typeset in 11 on 12 pt Bembo
by Pure Tech India Ltd., Pondicherry
Printed in Great Britain by Hartnolls Limited, Bodmin, Cornwall
This book is printed on acid-free paper

# CONTENTS

v

# CONTENTS

# CONTENTS

# PREFACE

As might be expected, 'Unity and Diversity in the Church', the theme chosen by Dr David Thompson for his Presidency of the Ecclesiastical History Society in 1994–5, stimulated considerable interest. Some sixty communications were offered at the Summer Conference; unfortunately, not all could be published. The papers printed here comprise the seven main papers delivered at the summer conference of 1994 and the January meeting in 1995, and a minority of the communications offered in the summer. The editorial decisions taken to reduce the number of papers to the published few were inevitably extremely hard, and harsh. Several highly competent essays had to be excluded to ensure a reasonable chronological balance and a volume which can stand as a coherent reflection of current research. It is to be hoped that those not accommodated here will soon find publication elsewhere.

The Society wishes to thank the University of Nottingham, and especially the staff of Hugh Stewart Hall, for tolerating the presence of a gaggle of ecclesiastical historians during an exceptionally hot three days. Alison McHardy, assisted by assorted postgraduates, deserves deepest thanks for acting as local liaison and organizing a wide-ranging series of outings. Once again, we thank King's College, London, for hospitality at the January gathering. As ever, Ann McCall and the production staff at Blackwell Publishers have provided constant support to ensure that the volume has gone through as smoothly as possible.

It would be improper for a new editor not to use the opportunity to pay tribute to the stalwart work of Diana Wood in maintaining the high standards of *Studies in Church History* over the past years. The Society owes her a great debt of thanks for her work as co-editor with Bill Sheils for volumes 23–7, and sole editor for volumes 28–31 (not to mention her work overseeing the subsidia, including editing Subsidia 9, and all the attendant administration involved in being Editor for the Society). Only a successor can appreciate how great the debt really is: it is a hard act to follow.

Robert Swanson

# LIST OF CONTRIBUTORS

DAVID BAGCHI
Lecturer in Theology, University of Hull

CLYDE BINFIELD
Reader in History, University of Sheffield

SIMON BRIGHT
University of Keele

RICHARD CARWARDINE
Professor of History, University of Sheffield

CATHERINE CUBITT
Lecturer in History, University of York

JOHN DORAN
Research Student, Royal Holloway and Bedford New College, University of London

MARTIN DUDLEY
Rector of St Bartholomew the Great, Smithfield, London

EAMON DUFFY
Fellow of Magdalene College and Reader in Church History, University of Cambridge

KEITH A. FRANCIS
Assistant Professor of History, Pacific Union College, Angwin, California

EILEEN L. GROTH
Assistant Professor of History, Florida State University, Tallahassee, Florida

SARAH HAMILTON
Research Student, King's College, London

RICHARD D. HARRISON
Research Student, University of Lancaster

MARGARET HARVEY
Lecturer in History, University of Durham

YITZHAK HEN
Post-doctoral Research Fellow, University of Haifa, Israel

ANDREW JOTISCHKY
Lecturer in Medieval History, University of Lancaster

FRANCES KNIGHT
Lecturer in Christian Theology, University of Wales, Lampeter

ANDREW LOUTH
Professor of Cultural History, Goldsmiths' College, University of London

ROSAMOND McKITTERICK
Fellow of Newnham College and Reader in Early Medieval European History, University of Cambridge

GARY MACY
Professor of Religious Studies, University of San Diego, California

ROB MEENS
Postdoc-medewerker, Department of History, University of Utrecht

SUSAN HARDMAN MOORE
Lecturer in Reformation Studies, King's College London

DOUGLAS M. MURRAY
Lecturer in Ecclesiastical History, University of Glasgow

W. B. PATTERSON
Professor of History, University of the South, Sewanee, Tennessee

DAMIAN J. SMITH
Research Student, University of Birmingham

JOKE SPAANS
Lecturer, Fryske Akademy, Ljouwert, The Netherlands

BRIAN STANLEY
Lecturer in Church History, Trinity College, Bristol

TIMOTHY C. F. STUNT
Stowe School, Buckingham

DAVID M. THOMPSON (*President*)
Fellow of Fitzwilliam College and Lecturer in Modern Church History, University of Cambridge

STEPHEN TURNBULL
Research Student, University of Leeds

JONATHAN WESTAWAY
Research Student, University of Lancaster

ROBERT S. M. WITHYCOMBE
Senior Fellow, St Mark's National Theological Centre, Canberra, ACT, Australia

JOHN WOLFFE
Lecturer in Religious Studies, The Open University

DAVID L. WYKES
Research Lecturer, Department of History, University of Leicester

# ABBREVIATIONS

Abbreviated titles are adopted within each paper after the first full citation. In addition, the following abbreviations are used throughout the volume.

| | |
|---|---|
| *AHP* | *Archivum historiae pontificiae* (Rome, 1963–) |
| *AnBoll* | *Analecta Bollandiana* (Brussels, 1882–) |
| AV | Authorized [King James] Version |
| *BJRL* | *Bulletin of the John Rylands Library* (Manchester, 1903–) |
| BL | British Library, London |
| BM | British Museum, London |
| BN | Bibliothèque nationale, Paris |
| *CChr* | *Corpus Christianorum* (Turnhout, 1953–) |
| *CChr.CM* | *Corpus Christianorum, continuatio medievalis* (1966–) |
| *CChr.SL* | *Corpus Christianorum, series Latina* (1953–) |
| *ChH* | *Church History* (New York/Chicago, 1932–) |
| *CQR* | *Church Quarterly Review* (London, 1875–) |
| CUL | Cambridge, University Library |
| *DEC* | *Decrees of the Ecumenical Councils*, ed. Norman P. Tanner, 2 vols (London and Washington DC, 1990) |
| *EETS* | *Early English Text Society* (London, 1864–) |
| *EHR* | *English Historical Review* (London, 1886–) |
| *HistJ* | *Historical Journal* (Cambridge, 1958–) |
| *HR* | *Historical Research* (London, 1986–) |
| *HThR* | *Harvard Theological Review* (New York/ Cambridge, Mass., 1908–) |
| *HZ* | *Historische Zeitschrift* (Munich, 1859–) |
| *JBS* | *Journal of British Studies* (Hartford, Conn., 1961–) |
| *JEH* | *Journal of Ecclesiastical History* (Cambridge, 1950–) |
| *JHI* | *Journal of the History of Ideas* (London, 1940–) |
| *JMH* | *Journal of Modern History* (Chicago, 1929–) |
| *JThS* | *Journal of Theological Studies* (London, 1899–) |
| Mansi | J. D. Mansi, ed., *Sacrorum conciliorum nova et amplissima collectio*, 31 vols (Florence and Venice, 1757–98) |
| *MGH* | *Monumenta Germaniae Historica inde ab a. c.500 usque ad a. 1500*, ed. G. H. Pertz *et al.* (Hanover, Berlin, etc., 1826–) |
| *MGH. Cap* | *Capitularia regnum Francorum* (1883–97) |
| *MGH. Conc* | *Concilia* (1893–) |

# ABBREVIATIONS

| | |
|---|---|
| *MGH. SRG* | *Scriptores rerum Germanicarum in usum scholarum* . . . (1826–32), ns (1922–) |
| *MGH. SS* | *SS Scriptores* (in folio) (1826–1934) |
| nd | no date |
| *NH* | *Northern History* (Leeds, 1966–) |
| ns | new series |
| *OMT* | *Oxford Medieval Texts* (Oxford, 1971–) |
| *PaP* | *Past and Present: A Journal of Scientific History* (London, 1952–) |
| *PG* | *Patrologia Graeca*, ed. J. P. Migne, 161 vols (Paris, 1857–66) |
| *PL* | *Patrologia Latina*, ed. J. P. Migne, 217 vols + 4 index vols (Paris, 1841–61) |
| PRO | London, Public Record Office |
| *PS* | *Parker Society* (Cambridge, 1841–55) |
| *RB* | *Révue Bénédictine de critique, d'histoire et de littéraire religieuses* (Maredsous, 1884–) |
| *SCH* | *Studies in Church History* (London/Oxford, 1964–) |
| *SCH.S* | *Studies in Church History, Subsidia* (Oxford, 1978–) |
| *TRHS* | *Transactions of the Royal Historical Society* (London, 1871–) |
| *VCH* | *Victoria County History* (London, 1900–) |

# INTRODUCTION

Since the Ecclesiastical History Society began to choose themes for its conferences in 1966 the unity of the Church has never been included among them – though schism, heresy and religious protest have! When I was elected President I immediately decided that this was the theme which I should choose; and to avoid misunderstanding, I linked the theme of diversity to that of unity. This I did for two reasons: first, because unity has often been confused with uniformity, particularly in England; and secondly, because the nature of the unity of the Church is inseparable from an understanding of its diversity.

The papers contained in this volume illustrate the richness of this theme, and several communications were excluded with great reluctance through lack of space. The opening paper by Andrew Louth shows how the way in which the Church could understand its unity changed in the fourth century as a result of its assimilation to imperial political structures; but at the same time a challenge to such an understanding came from the ascetic movement which inherited the role of the martyrs in linking the earthly Church to the heavenly one, thereby providing an alternative model of unity.

The link between earth and heaven is most obviously reflected in worship, and several papers discuss the significance of liturgical diversity. Yitzhak Hen demonstrates the liturgigal variety that existed in Frankish Gaul under the Merovingians and Catherine Cubitt illustrates a similar diversity in the Anglo-Saxon Church, despite the rhetoric of unity. Rosamond McKitterick extends the discussion to biblical and legal texts in the Carolingian dominions, suggesting by musical analogy that unison rather than unity is the key to understanding the period. The legal discussion is also illustrated in a fascinating paper by Rob Meens, which shows that rules on ritual purity tended to be interpreted strictly in the early Middle Ages, despite the liberalism of Gregory the Great on the subject and the veneration in which he was held. Damian Smith shows that it was not easy to eliminate the Spanish rite from eleventh-century Spain in favour of the Roman, and in a much later period Martin Dudley illustrates the diversification of Anglican liturgy in Britain and North America in the twentieth century.

Worship and devotion are the points at which the religion of the clergy and the religion of the people meet. Eamon Duffy discusses the fear that religious division would destroy the social and political fabric of the nation in Tudor England, but also shows that at the level of private devotion there was a striking similarity between Roman Catholic and Protestant forms until the end of the sixteenth century. Diversity in devotional practice can, however, be turned into a matter of faith and this is illustrated from two very different periods and places. David Bagchi shows how the question of giving the chalice to the laity became a doctrinal question in the Reformation period because the claim for communion in both kinds was seen as a challenge to the authority of the Church. Stephen Turnbull tells the story of the 'hidden Christians' of Japan who survived 250 years of official suppression from the seventeenth century, only to find themselves increasingly regarded as apostate by the newly admitted Roman Catholic missionaries in the nineteenth century.

The long-standing divisions of the Church receive considerable attention. The differences between the Greek and Latin traditions are considered in three very different essays. Sarah Hamilton discusses the different ways in which the story of Otto III's penances is recounted in Greek and Latin sources from eleventh-century Italy. Andrew Jotischky looks at the way in which the history of the Carmelite order was represented in the West so as to limit the sense of its Greek Orthodox origins. John Doran examines the Latin mission to Nicaea of 1234, suggesting that the Greek Church was impeded by the inherently backward-looking nature of its dependence on the ecumenical councils, whereas the Roman Church had the ability to endorse or initiate change through the authority entrusted to the papacy.

The position of the papacy in the later Middle Ages is discussed in an important paper by Margaret Harvey. She argues that there is no evidence that faith in the papacy as an institution was lastingly undermined by the Great Schism, and that before the Reformation belief in the papal office was compatible with serious disagreement with the pope. The institutional problem, however, was a familiar one: the unwillingness of those who affirmed the necessity of a particular institution to provide the financial means for it to continue in the way they expected. Another paper which raises fascinating questions on a related theme is Gary Macy's discussion of whether there was a 'the Church' in the Middle Ages. He rightly notes that until one has decided whether there is agreement as to what constituted 'the Church', the issues of unity or disunity cannot be meaningfully discussed. Assumptions of the necessary priority of canonical, theological or institutional criteria for identifying the Church beg the question which requires consideration, and the widespread belief that the Church consisted of the faithful in all places has to be taken more seriously.

Inevitably a large number of papers deal with various attempts to restore unity after the Reformation, and the diversity that existed within the churches from the sixteenth century onwards. Joke Spaans offers an interesting discussion of the religious diversity of seventeenth- and eighteenth-century Holland, pointing out that in the end the government divided the population into religious groups by making the churches responsible for poor relief. Brown Patterson explains why Pierre du Moulin in the years preceding the Synod of Dort urged a plan to reunite the Calvinist, Lutheran and Anglican churches, culminating in an unsuccesful scheme for reconciliation with Rome. Susan Hardman Moore shows how an English Puritan returning from New England to an Essex parish in the 1640s could justify different patterns of church life on either side of the Atlantic, particularly in relation to the operation of the parish.

From 1662 Protestant Dissenters were formally divided from the Church of England. Jonathan Westaway and Richard Harrison contribute an interesting paper on the way in which attitudes to exorcism were used to define relations between Anglicans, Roman Catholics and Dissenters in Lancashire at the end of the seventeenth century. David Wykes shows that although the 'happy union' of 1690 between Presbyterians and Congregationalists may have been short-lived in London, it lasted much longer in the provinces. Simon Bright illustrates the diversity of belief among early nineteenth-century Quakers as a result of the evangelical revival. The significance of that revival for Christian unity is also the topic of Timothy Stunt's paper on the effects of the *Réveil* in Switzerland at the same time. Another illustration of the same problem is found in John Wolffe's paper on evangelical attempts on both sides of the Atlantic to realize the ideal of unity in diversity through the foundation of the Evangelical Alliance in 1845–6.

The fluidity of denominational boundaries in political action is demonstrated by Eileen Groth's paper on the way in which Christians of different traditions were able to co-operate in the Birmingham Political Union. From a rather different point of view, Frances Knight suggests that the practical outworking of internal reform of the Church of England in the mid-nineteenth century, particularly through the enforcement of clerical residence, may have sharpened the local divisions between Anglicans and non-Anglicans and to that extent may have forged a new, denominational Anglican identity. The Church of England was also expanding overseas in the nineteenth century, and discovered that colonial situations did not fit easily into its domestic established status. Robert Withycombe opens up a relatively untouched field of research in considering the effects that this had on conceptions of Anglican unity and diversity.

There is always a tendency for church history to be dominated by consideration of Europe. Fortunately in this volume there are several contributions about the non-European world. Richard Carwardine contributes a seminal paper on unity and pluralism in the early history of the USA. Despite the common evangelical heritage there were persistent conflicts between Methodists and Baptists, something which has tended to be neglected because the traditional historiographical emphasis is on the long-established northeast rather than the rapidly expanding south and west. Brian Stanley takes that discussion one stage further by examining the way in which denominational identity was reshaped and, in its traditional forms, questioned in the context of missionary activity in both Asia and Africa. Keith Francis offers an interesting account of the response of one new nineteenth-century church with a strong missionary emphasis, the Seventh Day Adventists, to the World Missionary Conference at Edinburgh in 1910.

The Edinburgh Conference is usually regarded as marking the beginning of the modern ecumenical movement. The last group of papers touch on different aspects of that movement. Douglas Murray considers the deployment of the precedent of 1610 for consecrating bishops who had not been episcopally ordained as presbyters in the discussion of Anglican-Presbyterian union in the first decade of the twentieth century. Clyde Binfield writes with characteristic verve on the way in which the Second Vatican Council offered an opportunity for the traditionally pan-protestant YMCA to welcome and be accepted by the Roman Catholic Church. Finally, in looking again at the origins of the Appeal to All Christian People framed by the Lambeth Conference of 1920, I have tried to explain why there was apparently rapid progress in relations between the Church of England and the Free Churches in the period 1920–4, only then to reach a position of deadlock from which it has not been possible so far to escape.

My hopes for this year have been more than fulfilled in this volume. So often division in the Church is regarded as inevitable, and those who work for unity as hopeless idealists. What these historical studies show is that the concepts of unity and diversity are not as alien to each other as the rhetoric sometimes suggests. Once that is acknowledged, the practical question becomes not whether but how they can be brought together in a way which will be mutually enriching and reinforcing. At that point the historian hands over the task to those with responsibility for leadership in the churches. A more visible expression of the unity of the Church need not be a pleasing dream.

David M. Thompson

# UNITY AND DIVERSITY IN THE CHURCH OF THE FOURTH CENTURY

by ANDREW LOUTH

To look back to the early Church as a theologian and historian, and ask questions about her unity, is to enter on a long tradition, which goes back at least to the Reformation, if not to the Great Schism of 1054 itself. Once the Church had split, the various separated Christians looked back to justify their position in that tragedy. They scoured the early sources for evidence for and against episcopacy, papacy, authority confided to tradition or to Scripture alone: they questioned the form in which these early sources have come down to us – the sixteenth century saw reserves of scholarly genius poured into the problem, for instance, of the genuineness of the Ignatian correspondence, and what fired all that, apart from scholarly curiosity, was the burning question of the authenticity of episcopal authority on which Ignatius speaks so decisively. Out of that the critical discipline of patristics emerged. It was, in fact, rather later that the fourth century became the focus of the debate about the unity, authority, and identity of the Church – Newman obviously springs to mind and his *Arians of the Fourth Century* (London, 1833) and his *Essay on the Development of Doctrine* (London, 1845). Later on, the fourth century attracted the attention of scholars such as Professor H. M. Gwatkin and his *Studies in Arianism* (Cambridge, 1882), and Professor S. L. Greenslade and his *Schism in the Early Church* (London, 1953), and in quite modern times Arianism, in particular, has remained a mirror in which scholars have seen reflected the problems of the modern Church (a good example is the third part of Rowan Williams's *Arius: Heresy and Tradition* [London, 1987], though there are plenty of others). Continental scholars such as Adolf von Harnack also studied the past, informed by theological perspectives derived from the present; in a different and striking way Erik Peterson turned to the fourth century to find the roots of an ideology of unity that was fuelling the murderous policies of Nazism.[1] In all these cases the

---

[1] Erik Peterson, *Der Monotheismus als politisches Problem*, reprinted in *Theologische Traktate* (Munich, 1951), pp. 45–147. See also A. Schindler, ed., *Monotheismus als Politisches Problem? Erik Peterson und die Kritik der politischen Theologie* (Gütersloh, 1978).

1

fourth century seemed to be a test case – for questions of *modern* ecclesiology: Rome defended by development in the case of Newman, the justification for the ecumenical movement in the case of Greenslade. As scholars looked back they had various ideas as to how the unity of the Church could be expressed, in what it consisted – Newman was concerned to argue that without the living authority of the papacy none of these add up to very much, Greenslade on the contrary pointed to the very varied ways in which the Church has articulated a sense of its unity and identity and wanted to insist that nothing is a *sine qua non*. There are of course dangers in looking back over the centuries, and I do not wish to suggest that scholars in the past were not aware of them. The main danger is, it seems to me, that things that are obvious to us may never have occurred to those who lived in the past, and contrariwise what seemed pressing to them may be ignored by us because it is not crucial for us. But, conscious, I hope, of the warning of one of my Cambridge professors that one cannot jump out of one's epistemological skin, what I want to do in this paper is to try and recapture something of what unity and diversity in the Church meant to Christians in the fourth century.

But let us begin in the present century. In a survey carried out in Moscow and Pskov in 1992, people were asked where they got their religious and philosophical ideas from. Overall the most influential source of such ideas was newspapers and TV (thirty-nine per cent); even among believers this was still an important source (twenty-seven per cent), running close to relatives and friends (twenty-nine per cent), and the Gospels or other religious literature (thirty-three per cent). The Church, sermons, conversations with clergy were pretty low down the scale (nine per cent overall, only nineteen per cent among believers).[2] What is interesting about these statistics is that they demonstrate the existence of what we could call 'organs of ecumenicity' that the early Church would not even have dreamt of. The 'media' make possible a common pool of ideas, and also a common sense of belonging, that was not there in the fourth century. Many people, even believers, derive their notion of what Christianity is about from the media, and even derive something of their sense

[2] Lyudmila Vorontsova and Sergei Filatov, 'The changing pattern of religious belief: *perestroika* and beyond', *Religion, State and Society*, 22.1 (1994), pp. 89–96, table on p. 92.

of identity as religious believers from the same source. And this is clearly something new. It is, of course, the printing press that forms the crucial turning-point in making available ideas in a way that transcends the physical reach of the human communities which originated or fostered them. What that made available was new 'organs of ecumenicity' – a common Bible, printed catechisms, a uniform liturgy – all of these used by religious communities in Western Europe from the early modern period onwards as ways of expressing and nurturing their unity and identity. And none of this was available in that way to the Church of the fourth century: 'would that we were so lucky' must be the view of many in the modern Russian Orthodox Church! It is here that I would locate one of the greatest differences between ourselves and people of the fourth century, differences that have caused our 'world' to shrink, so that our immediate consciousness has expanded to embrace virtually the whole of the globe, and is no longer restricted to the local communities to which we belong.

At this point I think wewneed to remind ourselves just how diverse and disparate the communities of the fourth century – and not just the Christian communities – were. The basic unit was the city – πόλις, *civitas* – with its surrounding countryside. Except in the case of a few great cities, especially Rome and Constantinople, the city and its surroundings were a self-contained economic unit. They were also self-governing, governed by local notables. Their loyalties were primarily local, which found expression in the local religious cults that Christians were to call 'pagan'. The Roman Empire made no attempt to erase this prevailing sense of locality. A variety of languages were spoken but we have little idea about them except when they attained literary expression – something that had already happened to Latin and Greek, and was to happen in the fourth century, largely under Christian auspices, in the cases of Syriac, Coptic, and Gothic. This sense of locality was reinforced by distance, and slowness and difficulty in travelling: we hear of quite a bit of travelling, but it was the preserve of a tiny class. We know, and Peter Brown has recently given eloquent expression to,[3] the problems caused to those who were responsible for governing

---

[3] See P. Brown, *Power and Persuasion in Late Antiquity. Towards a Christian Empire* (Wisconsin, 1992), pp. 3–34.

the empire by poor communications and powerful local interests: a governor could be months away from any confirmation from the Imperial court, and in many cases it would be safer to collude with the power of local notables than to risk confrontation in such a vacuum of clear imperial support. There was, of course, a unified system of public office imposed from above, of which the governors were the lowest rank. Cities were grouped into provinces, each subject to a governor appointed for about two years, provinces into dioceses under *vicarii*, dioceses into prefectures governed by praetorian prefects, themselves subject to the emperor (or Imperial college). Emperors often spoke in their edicts of the empire as a single whole and issued decrees in respect of it, but recent studies of the fourth century have emphasized the distance we must recognize between the rhetoric of imperial decree and political reality: the language may be that of a 'command economy', but there was not the administrative machinery for that to be an attainable reality.[4]

It was such a world that the fourth-century Church inhabited, and whatever unity it experienced had to be something achievable within such a world. The Church's own rhetoric of unity was considerable. The New Testament fuelled such language and made it inevitable: the great high-priestly prayer placed on the lips of Jesus in John 17, the frequent exhortations to unity found in Saint Paul's epistles, ,together with the powerful imagery he uses to express it, especially that of the Church as the body of Christ – all this makes unity an inexorable part of Christian self-consciousness. There were other pressures behind such rhetoric of unity. Philosophical thinking – both profound, as with Plotinus, and popular, say in the Hermetic literature – laid great store by unity. Everything came from unity and was destined for unity. Division was seen as fragmentation, multiplicity as attenuation.

> The One remains, the many change and pass;
> Heaven's light forever shines, Earth's shadows fly;
> Life, like a dome of many-coloured glass,
> Stains the white radiance of Eternity . . .[5]

---

[4] See, for instance, summarizing much modern research, Averil Cameron, *The Later Roman Empire* (London, 1993), pp. 113ff., and on Diocletian's 'Price Edict' (301), p. 38.

[5] P. B. Shelley, 'Adonais', stanza 52 (ed. T. Hutchinson, 1904; 1952 edition, Oxford, p. 443).

Morality was defined in terms of unity; singleness – i.e., celibacy – became an ideal that reached beyond the confusing multiplicity of the present. All that only made the Christian rhetoric of the unity of the Church even more compelling. To what, in the real world of the fourth-century Roman Empire, did that rhetoric of unity correspond?

The first thing to be mentioned is, I think, obvious: it is that in the course of the fourth century what was meant by the unity of the Church changed, or rather that the ways in which the Church could express its unity changed – it became 'ecumenical' in the sense that it became an important part of the *oikoumene*, the inhabited world over which the emperor ruled as God's representative. But what did the Church bring into the fourth century? What organs of unity did it already possess, before it had thrust upon it, or found itself thrust into, the imperial structures of unity?

Long before the beginning of the fourth century, the primary, empirical expression of the unity of the Church had emerged. The Christian Church had spread throughout the Roman Empire as an urban phenomenon: it was in the city that the Church flourished. By the end of the second century, at the latest, the unity of the Church in each place had found expression in the fact that each local community, each 'church' in one of the senses of the word *ecclesia*, was led by a bishop, an *episcopus*. It is still not clear what the *essential* role of the bishop was: it is confused by the fact that from the fourth century onwards the bishop became the obvious spokesman for and representative of the local church for almost all purposes in the new 'ecumenical' Church. Dom Gregory Dix has argued,[6] convincingly I think, that the primary and essential role of the bishop in the Christian community was liturgical: he presided over the celebration of the Christian liturgy, nothing took place without his authority, though certainly in larger cities much must have been delegated.

---

[6] In his *Jurisdiction in the Early Church* (London, 1975). For a full, but concise, account of the role of the Christian bishop in late antiquity (mainly, of course, from the fourth century onwards), see H. Chadwick, 'The role of the Christian bishop in ancient society', in *Center for Hermeneutical Studies, Protocol of the 35th Colloquy* (February 1979), 35 (Berkeley, Cal., 1979), pp. 1–14 (reprinted in idem, *Heresy and Orthodoxy in the Early Church* [London, 1991], no. 3).

This principle of 'one city, one bishop' seems to have been adhered to quite strictly: even a huge city like Rome had only one bishop – we know from Eusebius that already by the middle of the third century the single bishop (Cornelius) presided over an establishment of forty-six presbyters, seven deacons, seven sub-deacons, forty-two acolytes, fifty-two exorcists, readers, and doorkeepers, and more than fifteen hundred widows and distressed persons.[7] More than one bishop meant schism, a divided Church (or rather division from the Church): an uncompromising assertion of precisely that by Pope Cornelius is the point of the letter just quoted from Eusebius.

In what other ways was the unity of the Church expressed? The next point that needs to be stressed is something that flows from the liturgical function of the bishop. The celebration of the eucharist itself is an expression of unity – such an idea goes right back to Paul (see I Cor. 10.16–17). But the unity of what – the universal Church, or the local community gathered together with its bishop? One of the earliest eucharistic prayers makes it clear that more is meant than the unity of the local community: 'Be mindful of your Church, O Lord; deliver it from all evil, perfect it in your love, sanctify it, and gather it from the four winds into the kingdom that you have prepared for it.'[8] But as the eucharistic prayers become more expansive, it becomes clear that more is meant than the unity of all Christians who are alive. The Liturgy of St Basil, immediately after the invocation of the Holy Spirit over the worshippers and the holy gifts, prays:

> and unite us all one with another who partake of the one bread and the cup in the communion of the One Holy Spirit . . . that we may find mercy and grace with all the saints who have been pleasing to you from eternity, forefathers, fathers, patriarchs, prophets, apostles, preachers, evangelists, martyrs, confessors, teachers, and every just spirit, all made perfect in faith, and especially our most holy,

[7] Cited in Eusebius, *Ecclesiastical History*, VI, xliii, 11 (ed. E. Schwartz, *Die Griechischen Christlichen Schriftsteller der ersten drei Jahrhunderte*, Eusebius Werke, 2 [3 parts, Berlin, 1903–9], p. 618).

[8] *Didache* 10 (F. X. Funk and K. Bihlmeyer, eds, *Die Apostolischen Väter*, 3rd edn [Tübingen, 1970], p. 6).

most pure and ever-blessed Lady, Mother of God and ever-Virgin, Mary . . ."[9]

The one Church into the unity of which we are gathered in the eucharist is primarily the communion of those 'made perfect in faith', secondly it is those gathered together at any particular celebration of the eucharist within that deeper unity, and thirdly (or perhaps: second equal) it is everyone everywhere embraced by that deeper unity. I emphasize this, because the impression is often given that *ecclesia* means either the universal Church (in the sense of geographically universal) or the local Christian community or both: it does indeed mean both, but because first of all it has the meaning just suggested, of unity with the Church already gathered together before the heavenly throne. One might perhaps object that this sense of the Church as embracing those 'beyond the veil' is hardly a sense in which the rhetoric of unity is cashed in terms of the *real* world of the Roman Empire. But I do not think it would have seemed so to Christians of this period. That other world was very real: the Christian cult of saints did not expand into a vacuum, it expanded into another world of whose contours Christians were much more confident than either their modern brothers and sisters in the faith or their pagan contemporaries. And, I might add, they often give the impression that they were more confident of the contours of the realm beyond, inhabited by the saints and patriarchs, and opened up by Christ's resurrection, than of many parts of the Mediterranean world beyond their own immediate locality. The local church, with its growing number of local saints, came to do at least as good a job of defining and expressing local loyalties and local identity as the local pagan cults had done, while at the same time expressing a sense of belonging that transcended the merely local.

In what other ways did the rhetoric of unity find expression? As well as giving expression to a sense of unity with the heavenly courts in the way I have just sketched, the liturgy has historically been used as a way of imposing uniformity and therefore a sense of common unity: one thinks of the place of the Tridentine mass

---

[9] F. E. Brightman, *Liturgies Eastern and Western* (Oxford, 1896), pp. 330f. [my translation].

between Trent and Vatican II,[10] or of the place of the Book of Common Prayer within Anglicanism. In both cases it is widely felt that unity has been made less tangible with the loss of uniformity of liturgical rite. The Church as it embarked on the fourth century had nothing approaching liturgical uniformity: the liturgical variety that becomes manifest with the evidence in the fourth and fifth centuries clearly has deep roots. And yet – sometime towards the end of the second century a Christian bishop, Abercius, whose see was probably Hieropolis in Phrygia (often confused with Hierapolis in the valley of the Maeander), had an inscription set up in which he spoke of his travels to Rome in the West and as far as Nisibis in the East, in which he says,

> He [the pure Shepherd whose disciple Abercius is] also sent me to royal Rome to behold it and to see the golden-robed, golden-slippered Queen. And there I saw a people bearing the splendid seal. And I saw the plain of Syria and all the cities, even Nisibis, crossing over the Euphrates. And everywhere I had associates. In company with Paul I followed, while everywhere faith led the way, and set before me for food the fish from the fountain, mighty and stainless (whom a pure virgin grasped), and gave this to friends to eat always, having good wine and giving the mixed cup with bread.[11]

This text, resplendent with symbolism – the 'splendid seal' is clearly the baptismal seal, the fish a eucharistic reference to Christ (perhaps the earliest) – bears witness to the fact that wherever he was Abercius felt himself at one with other Christians in the celebration of the eucharist. Reading this inscription one might wonder what linguistic diversity Abercius had to cope with in his travels. Greek was clearly the language of his own Church, though it was not the original language of the region.

---

[10] It was pointed out to me that my rhetoric has led me into exaggeration: in many parts of Europe, even by the nineteenth century, the Tridentine mass had only made slow progress in becoming accepted.

[11] Translation taken from J. Lightfoot, *The Apostolic Fathers*, Part II, 1 (London, 1885), p. 480. For his discussion of Abercius, whom he identifies with Eusebius' Avircius Marcellus (see Eusebius, *Ecclesiastical History*, V, xvi; ed. Schwartz, pp. 458–68), see pp. 476–85. A substantial fragment of the inscription survives and was discovered by W. M. Ramsay in 1883.

In the West he travelled as far as Rome, where his Greek would have stood him in good stead: some evidence suggests that Christianity in Rome was Greek-speaking until the beginning of the third century, though other evidence seems to point to Latin Christianity (Hermas refers to a kind of Roman fast as *statio*, a Latin word,[12] and the discovery of the ROTAS-SATOR square at Pompeii is evidence for Latin-speaking Christianity on the Italian mainland by the middle of the first century.)[13] In the East he reached Nisibis, recently (under Verus in the 160s) restored to the Roman Empire: it was presumably Hellenistic, it did not become a centre for Christian Syriac culture until the fourth century.

But the point of this digression is that another way of articulating unity – that of linguistic culture – does not seem to have had any great importance for the early Church. All the original documents of Christianity – the apostolic letters, the Gospels – are, of course, in Greek and the Church was greatly assisted by the widespread use of Greek throughout the Roman Empire. But in the early centuries, where Latin was the local language, Christianity clothed itself in Latin dress. Later on, Christianity adopted the linguistic dress of Syriac, CoCtic, and Gothic: in each case a literature was created, for Christianity was a literary religion, needing at least some of the Scriptures to be available in any language it adopted. Later still, in the ninth century, an alphabet and the basic linguistic structures were created for Slavonic, enabling it to become yet another Christian language. These points seem to me to be worth recalling, since later on various forms of Christianity did identify themselves very closely with a literary culture: Byzantine Christianity for a century or so before the conversion of the Slavs, and Roman Christianity for more than a millenium (though even as late as the ninth century neither Pope Nicholas I nor his successor Pope Hadrian II identified Roman Christianity exclusively with Latin, as their attitude to the Moravian mission of St Cyril and St Methodius makes clear). But there seems to have been no attempt to use

---

[12] Hermas, *Pastor*, *Simil.*, 5.1.1 and 2 (ed. M. Whittaker, *Die Griechischen Christlichen Schriftsteller der ersten Jahrhunderte*, Die Apostolischen Väter, I. Der Hirt des Hermas [Berlin, 1967], p. 52).

[13] On the Rotas-Sator square, see H. Last, 'The Rotas-Sator Square: present position and future prospects', *JThS*, ns 3 (1952), pp. 92–7.

linguistic culture to express the universality of Christianity in the early centuries, and especially not in the fourth century, when on the contrary the Church seems to have presided over linguistic diversification.

There are also two perhaps more prosaic ways of trying to express the unity of the Church that had been developed before the fourth century. The first is the council or synod (synod is the Christian name, as Ammianus Marcellinus tells us).[14] On several occasions in Eusebius' *Church History* we read of synods of bishops gathered together to deal with some problem. For instance in the 260s several synods seem to have met in Antioch to deal with the problem of Paul of Samosata, who had succeeded Demetrian as Bishop of Antioch. Eusebius' account is confused, and scholarly discussion has probably compounded the confusion. Eusebius at any rate regarded Paul as a heretic whose Christology was inadequate. A synod was required to deal with the problem, since Paul was himself a bishop. We also hear of synods in connection with the problems raised by the Decian persecution and the mass apostasy it occasioned. The synods in Carthage we know from the surviving correspondence of Cyprian, Bishop of Carthage: they met under the chairmanship of Cyprian and reached binding decisions as to how to meet the various problems raised. The Decian persecution also provoked the Novatianist schism in Rome, dealt with by Pope Cornelius by means of a synod with representatives from Italy, Africa and elsewhere. Eusebius tells us of synods from the second century, dealing with issues such as the date of Easter, and the heresy of Montanism. The issues raised vary: sometimes they concern matters of practice – moral or liturgical, sometimes matters of faith. They are concerned with defining the limits of belonging: the sanction is exclusion from communion. Communion is a pre-eminently episcopal matter: it is the bishop who celebrates (or presides over) the eucharist, it is he who baptizes and cate-chizes (something that remains an episcopal duty until at least the fifth century), and so ultimately decides who shall be admitted to catechesis and baptism. It is not surprising, then, that these

---

[14] See Ammianus Marcellinus, *Res gestae*, XV, xvii, 7 (ed. J. C. Rolfe, Loeb Classical Library, 3 vols, 1964 edn, 1, p. 162) [*synodus ut appellant*]; cf. XXI, xvi, 18 (Loeb Classical Library, 2, p. 184).

synods appear, from the evidence Eusebius gives us, as predominantly episcopal: they are exercises in what is nowadays known as episcopal 'collegiality'. Cyprian, in his *De ecclesiae catholicae unitate*, provides the germ of a theological justification of such episcopal collegiality. Episcopacy is a unity, each bishop holds his part in its totality ('episcopatus unus est cuius a singulis in solidum pars tenetur'). 'So the Church forms a unity, however far she spreads . . . just as the sun's rays are many, yet the light is one.'[15] Synods are a formal expression of such collegiality: Eusebius' *Church History* also reveals informal expressions of such collegiality, exercised through letters, for instance through the letters written by Cornelius of Rome and Dionysius of Alexandria to Fabius of Antioch, who was inclined to take Novatian's part over apostasy.[16] With the synods at Carthage, we have already seen them being used to generate what was to be called canon law, laws concerned with the life of the Church: by the beginning of the fourth century that process had moved a step further, as the canons of the Council of Elvira indicate.[17]

The papacy was another expression of the unity of the church. Because it was later to develop such clearly defined features there has been a tendency to read them back into the earliest period, and a corresponding tendency to refuse to do anything of the sort. But it is difficult not to see Rome already exercising a ministry of unity in the letter Clement wrote, on behalf of the Roman Church, to the Christians of Corinth at the end of the first century, nor to see Rome being conceded some kind of special role when Ignatius addresses the Roman Church as the one who 'presides in love' – προκαθημένη τῆς ἀγάπης.[18] What this amounted to, what it could amount to, is much less clear. One thing, though, I think is certain: Rome neither made nor was conceded any such kind of claim on the grounds that it was the capital of the Roman Empire. There is no evidence either way, but it seems to me unlikely that persecuted Christians

[15] Cyprian, *De unitate*, 5 (Cyprian, *De lapsis* and *De ecclesiae catholicae unitate*, ed. and trans. M. Bevenot, SJ, Oxford Early Christian Texts [Oxford, 1971], p. 64).

[16] *Ecclesiastical History*, VI, xlii–xliii (ed. Schwartz, pp. 610–24).

[17] For the canons of Elvira, see M. J. Routh, *Reliquiae Sacrae*, 2nd edn (Oxford, 1846), 4, pp. 255–74.

[18] Ignatius, *Ad Rom.*, prologue (Funk and Bihlmeyer, eds, p. 97).

would have regarded the seat of the persecuting power (which they called 'Babylon') with any religious reverence for that reason – the Church there might have been venerated because of the multitude of Christians who had suffered there, but that is something different. And on the question of Rome's claims, it is striking that Rome always makes a claim on the basis of something that makes some kind of Christian sense – the pope as successor of Peter (already by Pope Stephen's time), as the guardian of the relics of the Roman martyrs, especially Peter and Paul (Pope Damasus' best claim to fame). All I want to claim is that by the beginning of the fourth century the church of Rome, and even the bishop of Rome, have already seen that church, or that office, as exercising a peculiar ministry of unity for the Church as a whole.

So far I have explored – or sketched – various ways in which the unity of the Church was articulated or expressed by the beginning of the fourth century. The points I have made do not constitute any kind of exclusive list: a case can be made (though it is speculative) that until the fourth century various forms of Christian identity existed side-by-side, and in particular that alongside the model of episcopally-defined communion, there existed the model of membership of a doctrinally-defined school. But if that is so then the history of the fourth century is the history of the victory (or final victory) of the bishops.

The fourth century, as everyone knows (though students are constantly tempted to foreshorten the process), saw a dramatic transition in the fortunes of the Church. As the century began, the Church was on the brink of the so-called 'Great Persecution'. That ended with the conversion of Constantine and the beginning of imperial favour for the Christian Church. By the end of the century and the reign of Theodosius, who died in 395, it can be said that the Christian Church had become the official religion of the Roman Empire. The status as object of imperial favour – and even more its final status as official leligion – gave the question of Christian unity a new dimension. If there was schism, if there were rival claimants to an episcopal see, for instance in Carthage, as there were, who was going to receive the imperial bounty? It is not surprising, from what we have seen already, that this question rises in a local context. The attempts to deal with this problem, the problem of Donatism, are a

12

curious mixture of imperial measures – the bishop of Rome appointed as head of an imperial commission – and the traditional methods of the Christian Church – Pope Miltiades inviting other bishops to join him and thus turning the commission into a synod. Although Constantine was able to reach an unambiguous conclusion as to which claimant in Carthage was the real one, the Donatists did not vanish by imperial decree, could not be compelled by anything less than unacceptable force to give up their churches, nor prevented from seizing churches repaired by imperial funds. The schism, as we know, dragged on and on. More serious was the Arian controversy, which reached the attention of the emperor just after he had attained sole control of the Empire with the defeat of Licinius in 324. This, as everyone knows, was dealt with by the calling of the first 'ecumenical' council at Nicaea in 325. Although it w s not called 'ecumenical' for another dozen years (or if it was, that most likely has something to do with the Church's plea for exemption from tax, as Professor Henry Chadwick has suggested),[19] it is not wrong in retrospect to see it as 'ecumenical' and as marking a turning-point. This is not primarily because of its decision about Arianism, though that came to have almost paradigmatic significance too, but because of what was decided in the canons it passed, especially canon 6.[20] 'Let the ancient customs continue' begins the canon, and then goes on to spell them out: the authority customarily exercised by the bishop of Alexandria over Egypt, Libya, and Pentapolis, the 'similar' authority exercised by the bishop of Rome, and finally, 'similarly in Antioch and the other provinces the prerogatives of the metropolises over the churches are to be preserved'.[21] This confirms what has already been affirmed in canon 4 that the right of confirming episcopal appointments lies with the metropolitan bishop. This is seen as the continuation of 'the ancient customs – τὰ ἀρχαῖα ἔθη – but it also conforms the organization of the Church to the existing (and changing) norms of the administration of the Empire: the metropolitans correspond to the governors of the provinces, and

---

[19] See H. Chadwick, 'The origin of the title "Oecumenical Council" ', *JThS*, ns, 23 (1972), pp. 132–5, esp. p. 135 and note.
[20] On canon 6 see H. Chadwick, 'Faith and order at the Council of Nicaea: a note on the background of the sixth canon', *HThR* 53 (1960), pp. 171–95.
[21] Following the text defended by Chadwick, 'Faith and order', pp. 180–1.

their see is the seat of the governor. It seems that something like this had already emerged by the beginning of the fourth century, but this formalized it, and it meant that as the division of the provinces changed, so did the area subject to a metropolitan – as was to happen in Cappadocia in 371/2 to the distress of St Basil of Caesarea.[22] The power of the metropolitan bishop was magnified – bishops become more and more his suffragans – as also emerges from St Basil's reaction to the events of the 370s. In the cases of Alexandria, Rome and Antioch, their jurisdiction extended beyond that of the civil province (though this is stated very unclearly in the case of Antioch, which is perhaps why the original text is no longer preserved in the Greek MSS), corresponding in some way to that of the *vicarii* or even the praetorian prefects. The structure of the Church mirrors that of the Empire, and vice versa: there is more than a suggestion that they are interdependent. What then of the unity of the Church: does it simply reflect the unity of the Empire? There is a good deal of evidence to support such an idea: Christianity, both in the West and the East, identifies itself with the Empire, and has little interest in extending beyond the (old) boundaries (St Patrick, who preached Christianity in Ireland beyond the traditional frontier, seems to have regarded the terms *Romanus* and *Christianus* as synonymous).[23] The idea that the Church reflects the Empire seems to be the reasoning behind canon 3 of the Council of Constantinople (381) – 'because it is new Rome, the bishop of Constantinople is to enjoy privileges of honour after the bishop of Rome' – reaffirmed in canon 28 of the Council of Chalcedon (451), where the parallelism between Church and Empire is expressed in greater detail.[24] This symbiosis between Church and Empire was further deepened by other developments in the fourth century, especially the way in which Constantine's concession to Christian consciences in allowing bishops to function as magistrates[25] had the long-term effect of

[22] See B. Gaïn, *L'Église de Cappadoce au iv<sup>e</sup> siècle d'après la correspondance de Basile de Césarée (330–379)*, Orientalia Christiana Analecta, 225 (Rome, 1985), pp. 306–9, with literature cited there.

[23] See St Patrick, *Ep.* 2, and L. Bieler's note in *The Works of St Patrick*, Ancient Christian Writers, 17 (London, 1953), pp. 90f.

[24] For the texts of the canons, see *DEC*, 1, pp. 32, 99–100.

[25] See A. H. M. Jones, *The Later Roman Empire, 284–602*, 3 vols (Oxford, 1964), 1, p. 480 and n.21 [3, p. 134].

making the bishop an important local figure, exercising imperial authority, at least in his legal capacity, in the city – something that had a profound effect on the daily life of St Augustine, for instance. The Church's own perceptions of unity were being drawn into, perhaps even swallowed up by, the needs of the Christian *oikoumene*.

That is, however, only part of the story of the fourth century. Many Christians were clearly seduced by the tangible importance they acquired from these changes. One recalls Ammianus' acid words on the benefits of the papal throne: 'once they have reached it they are assured of rich gifts from ladies of quality; they can ride in carriages, dress splendidly, and outdo kings in the lavishness of their table'.[26] But it was, perhaps curiously, from the bishop of Rome that there emerged resistance to the growing symbiosis of Church and Empire (of course, individual bishops protested and proclaimed the independence of what were to be called priesthood and empire when the imperial embrace sought to constrain them to adopt policies they rejected – one thinks of Athanasius and Ambrose – but that is something different). Rome – whether bishop or church – had never accepted that its authority reflected the authority of the capital, and the canons of Constantinople and Chalcedon, mentioned above, that implied such an argument was never accepted by the pope. Increasingly, from the fourth century onwards, Rome developed a sense of its own authority. The shambles of conciliar ecumenicity in the reign of Constantius, especially – bishops travelling from synod to synod, 'hamstringing the post service', as Ammianus puts it,[27] to devise under imperial pressure one unacceptable doctrinal compromise after another – must have done wonders for Rome's claim to be arbiter of orthodoxy.

But resistance to the growing symbiosis of Church and Empire came from another direction, too. I stressed earlier how important was the sense of unity with the Church 'beyond the veil', and illustrated it from a liturgical text which very likely belongs to the fourth century. The 'local' members of the heavenly court had been the martyrs, and bishops had been able to moderate

[26] Ammianus Marcellinus, *Res gestae*, XXVII, iii, 14 (ed. Rolfe, 3, p. 20). Trans. W. Hamilton in Ammianus Marcellinus, *The Later Roman Empire*, Penguin Classics (Harmondsworth, 1986), p. 336.

[27] Ammianus Marcellinus, *Res gestae*, XXI, xvi, 18 (ed. Rolfe, 2, p. 184).

their acknowledged authority by their control of liturgical celebration, though, especially in the heat of persecution, the tensions between bishop and martyr could come into the open, as we know from the case of Cyprian. But normally martyrs were dead, and bishops could c ntrol their cult and their influence. In the fourth century, however, as we know, the mantle of the martyr passed to the ascetic: these men and women stood on the frontier between this world and the next and exercised powers of intercession and healing that were widely acknowledged. They secured their place on the frontier by their rejection of this world, and when they recognized the importance of the Christian emperor, as from the time of St Antony onwards they often did, it was as a servant of the true God to whose court they, the ascetics, had privileged access: think for instance of St Daniel the Stylite's visit to Constantinople, concluding with the emperor, the faithless Basiliscus, and the patriarch prostrate on the ground at the feet of the holy man.[28]

What I have suggested is that in the course of the fourth century there was an attempt to develop an 'ecumenical' understanding of the unity of the Church by assimilating it to the imperial institutions. This was a considerable success: such a church is recognizable in the Church of the Byzantine Empire, and even in the West the Church played a part in the preservation of many of the elements of public order that the successor barbarian states owed to the Roman Empire. But it is only part of the story: the powerful rhetoric of unity had meant something tangible in the pre-Nicene Church, something articulated through the bishop and the liturgy. It is also the case that the attempt to enlist the pope as an imperial servant met with only limited success, though it would be a long time before the papacy was able to offer a ministry of unity in anything other than a piecemeal way – suitable 'organs of ecumenicity' needed to be developed and were only adequately provided by the growth of the new monastic orders of the tenth and eleventh centuries. But what had been most tangible about the unity of the Church – a felt communion through the Eucharist with the

---

[28] *Life of St Daniel the Stylite*, LXXXIII, trans. Ed. Dawes and N. H. Baynes, *Three Byzantine Saints* (London and Oxford, 1948), pp. 57–8.

heavenly court – was something that imperial ecumenicity could not provide, and I have suggested that the ascetics could and did. So, too, could the growing cult of the saints and their relics. The centuries that follow the fourth century see a complex power struggle taking place for the heart of the *Una sancta*. The challenge to a fundamentally secular understanding of unity came from both the pope's growing sense of his Petrine ministry of unity, which resisted assimilation of ecclesiastical authority to state authority, and from the ascetics. One can discern, as one often thinks one can at the end of Late Antiquity, different tracks leading out of Late Antiquity – to Western and Eastern Christendom respectively. If the ascetic challenge differs from the papal challenge in that it preserves the tangible sense of a unity that embraces the heavenly court, whereas the papal challenge simply offers a different understanding of the same kind of coercive authority, that may also suggest something about the differences that emerge as Late Antiquity gives way to the Middle Ages.

Goldsmiths' College, University of London

# UNITY IN DIVERSITY: THE LITURGY OF FRANKISH GAUL BEFORE THE CAROLINGIANS*

by YITZHAK HEN

Uniformity was at the heart of the Carolingian reforms, and it is apparent more than anywhere else in the liturgical reforms pursued by the Carolingians.[1] It is logical to assume that the early Carolingian reformers' stress on liturgical uniformity was, at least in part, a reaction to the diversity of Merovingian practice. This paper offers some preliminary observations on liturgical diversity and attitudes towards unified liturgical practices in Merovingian Gaul.

On 19 March 416, Pope Innocent I wrote to Bishop Decentius of Gubbio that 'if the priests of the Lord really wished to preserve ecclesiastical uses intact, as received from the Holy Apostles, no diversity and no variation would be found in the ritual and ceremonial'.[2] He strengthened this statement by urging all the churches of the West to follow the liturgical practice of Rome.[3] The situation in Gaul, however, seems never to have

* I am grateful to Rosamond McKitterick, Julia Smith and Mary Garrison for their perceptive and stimulating criticism of an earlier draft of this paper. Thanks are also due to the president and members of the Ecclesiastical History Society for their generous grant that enabled me to attend the conference at Nottingham.

[1] On the liturgical reforms of Pippin III and Charlemagne see R. McKitterick, *The Frankish Church and the Carolingian Reforms, 789–895* (London, 1977), pp. 115–54; C. Vogel, 'La réforme liturgique sous Charlemagne', in W. Braunfels, ed., *Karl der Große. Lebenswerk und Nachleben*, 2 vols (Düsseldorf, 1965), 2, pp. 217–32; and 'Les motifs de la romanisation du culte sous Pépin le Bref (751–768) et Charlemagne (774–814)', in *Culto cristiano politica imperiale carolingia. Atti del XVIII Convegni di Studi sulla spiritualità medievale, 9–12 octobre 1977* (Todi, 1979), pp. 13–41. On the issue of unity and diversity in the Carolingian Church see R. Kottje, 'Einheit und Vielfalt des kirchlichen Lebens in der Karolingerzeit', *Zeitschrift für Kirchengeschichte*, 76 (1965), pp. 323–42.

[2] Innocent I, Ep. 25, *PL* 20, cols 551–2. I cite the translation of G. Ellard, 'How fifth-century Rome administered sacraments', *Texts and Studies*, 9 (1948), p. 5. On the letter itself see R. Cabié, *La lettre du Pape Innocent I à Decentius de Gubbio* (Louvain, 1973).

[3] Although Innocent I is often cited to illustrate papal intolerance of diversity and craving for uniformity in liturgical matters, his attempt to standardize Western liturgy according to Roman practice is, in fact, unique and very unrepresentative of the views held by many leading figures of the early Church. An examination of the various papal and patristic views on the matter is far beyond the scope of this chapter. For some general references see C. Vogel, *Medieval Liturgy: An Introduction to the Sources*, rev. and trans. W. G. Storey and N. K. Rasmussen (Washington DC, 1986), pp. 372–3; see also P. Meyvaert, 'Diversity within unity, a Gregorian theme', *The Heythrop Journal*, 4 (1963), pp. 141–62; R. A. Markus, 'Gregory the Great and a Papal missionary strategy', *SCH*, 6 (1970), pp. 29–38.

19

fallen into line with Innocent I's objectives, and liturgical diversity was the case throughout the Merovingian period. This, I would argue, derived from a long tradition of liturgical composition which, inevitably, promoted the notion of diversity within unity in liturgical practices.

Despite the prevailing theme of literary decline in the sources from late antique Gaul, the late fourth and fifth century was a significant period of intellectual activity in Gaul as far as the aristocracy was concerned.[4] Local literary circles sprang up throughout southern Gaul, the stronghold of the Gallo-Roman senatorial aristocracy. Such groups provided those aristocrats with 'additional opportunities to socialise and demonstrate their unity of spirit'.[5] At the same time, religious, clerical, and especially episcopal status came to be a crucial element in the aristocratic world view, and high offices within the Church were in great demand among members of the Gallo-Roman aristocracy.[6] The widening spread and the growing influence of Christianity among the aristocracy of late antique Gaul gave rise to an increasing interest in Christianity's theology, ethics, and rituals. It is, then, not at all surprising that some of these aristocrats turned to liturgical composition, and that even from the little evidence which survives, Gaul emerges as a prolific centre for liturgical production long before the Merovingian age. Hilary of Poitiers (d. 367), for example, is said to have written a book of hymns,[7] and Gennadius relates in his *Liber de viris illustribus* how Musaeus, a presbyter from Marseilles (d. *c*.460), composed *lectiones totius anni, responsoria psalmorum capitula*, and to the request

---

[4] See, for example, R. W. Matthisen, 'The theme of literary decline in late Roman Gaul', *Classical Philology*, 83 (1988), pp. 45–52; I. N. Wood, 'Continuity or calamity?: the constraints of literary models', in J. Drinkwater and H. Elton, eds, *Fifth-Century Gaul: A Crisis of Identity?* (Cambridge, 1992), pp. 9–18.

[5] See R. Matthisen, *Roman Aristocrats in Barbarian Gaul: Strategies for Survival in an Age of Transition* (Austin, Texas, 1993), pp. 105–18; the citation is from p. 111. See also idem, *Ecclesiastical Factionalism and Religious Controversy in Fifth-Century Gaul: A Regional Analysis* (Washington DC, 1989), pp. 83–5, 235–42, 251–3.

[6] See M. Heinzelmann, 'L'aristocratie et les évêchés entre Loire et Rhin jusqu'à la fin du VIIᵉ siècle', *Revue d'histoire de l'église de France*, 62 (1976), pp. 75–90, and *Bischofsherrschaft in Gallien* (Sigmaringen, 1976); F. Prinz, 'Die bischöfliche Stadtherrschaft im Frankenreich vom 5. bis zum 7. Jahrhundert', *HZ*, 217 (1973), pp. 1–35; Matthisen, *Roman Aristocrats*, pp. 89–103.

[7] Jerome, *Liber de viris illustribus*, 100, ed. E. C. Richardson, *Text und Untersuchungen zur Geschichte der altchristlichen Literatur*, 14 (Leipzig, 1896), p. 48. See also A. Wilmart, 'Le *de Mysteriis* de St Hilaire au Monte-Cassin', *RB*, 27 (1910), pp. 12–21, who thinks it was actually a treatise on mysticism.

of Bishop Eustachius a *sacramentarium egregium et non parvum volumen*. The latter included a section for the temporal feasts, a collection of reading passages from biblical sources, and a series of chants and psalms.[8] Sidonius Apollinaris reports that Claudianus Mamertus, the Bishop of Vienne, composed a lectionary,[9] and Sidonius himself, we are told, composed *contestatiunculae*, which were probably prefaces to the mass,[10] and an entire sacramentary.[11] Unfortunately, none of these works has survived.

Turning to the evidence from the Merovingian period, it seems that the interest in composing new liturgical material did not die out. Indeed Gregory of Tours, in his own conservative way, continued to use Sidonius' compositions, for which he even provided a new introduction.[12] Moreover, he also refers to two attempts made in his lifetime to compose new prayers. One was made by Bishop Praetextatus of Rouen, who composed various prayers while in exile in Jersey. He recited these in front the bishops who gathered at the Council of Mâcon (585), and was criticized because of their inadequate literary form.[13] Another attempt was made by King Chilperic who composed *opuscula vel ymnus sive missas* which, not surprisingly, were greeted with disdain by Gregory of Tours.[14]

The best evidence for the prolific liturgical productivity of Merovingian Gaul is provided by the manuscripts. Apart from many fragments of liturgical manuscripts, there are six (more or less) complete liturgical compositions which survive from Merovingian Gaul. It is on these manuscripts that one should concentrate in order to examine the question of liturgical diversity

---

[8] Gennadius, *Liber de viris illustribus*, 79, ed. Richardson, *Text und Untersuchungen*, pp. 88–9. On various fragments which were attributed to Musaeus see G. Morin, 'Fragments inédits et jusqu'à present uniques d'Antiphonaire gallican', *RB*, 22 (1905), pp. 329–56, and 'Le plus ancient monument qui existe da la liturgie gallicane', *Ephemerides liturgicae*, 51 (1937), pp. 3–12.

[9] Sidonius Apollinaris, *Ep.* 4:11:6 (carm. 11. 16–17), ed. and trans W. B. Anderson, *Sidonius: Poems and Letters*, 2 vols (Cambridge, Mass., and London, 1936–65), 2, p. 108. On Musaeus' compositions see G. Morin, 'Le plus ancien *Comes* ou lectionaire de l'église romain', *RB*, 27 (1910), pp. 41–74 and 'La lettre-préface du *Comes ad Constantium* se rapporterait au lectionaire de Claudien Mamert?', *RB*, 30 (1913), pp. 228–31.

[10] Sidonius Apollinaris, *Ep.* 7:3, p. 302.

[11] Gregory of Tours, *Libri Historiarum X* [hereafter *LH* ], II, 22, B. Krusch and W. Levison, eds, *MGH Scriptores Rerum Merovingicarum* I:1 (Hanover, 1951), p. 67.

[12] *LH*, II, 22, p. 67.

[13] *LH*, VIII, 20, p. 387.

[14] *LH*, VI, 46, p. 320.

in Merovingian Gaul.[15] These liturgical manuscripts are the Old Gelasian Sacramentary,[16] the Gothic Missal,[17] the Old Gallican Missal,[18] the Frankish Missal,[19] the Bobbio Missal,[20] and the Lectionary of Luxeuil.[21]

These compositions, representing the Merovingian-Gallican branch of Western liturgy, were compiled, partially composed for the first time, and later re-copied by men and women in religious communities throughout Gaul, mainly in the regions of Neustria and Burgundy, during the late seventh and early eighth centuries.[22] That active *scriptoria* were operating in the regions of Neustria and Burgundy throughout the Merovingian period is well known.[23] These centres, whose book production and libraries were the culmination of intellectual life in Merovingian Gaul, were perceived by their contemporaries as authoritative

---

[15] On the liturgy of early medieval Gaul the best introduction is Vogel, *Medieval Liturgy*. All manuscripts cited in this chapter will include the number assigned to them in *Codices latini antiquiores: a Palaeographical Guide to Latin Manuscripts prior to the Ninth Century*, ed. E. A. Lowe, 11 vols and supplement (Oxford, 1934–71) [hereafter *CLA*].

[16] Vatican, MS reg. lat. 316+ BN, MS latin: 7193, fols 41–56 (*CLA* I:105). *Liber sacramentorum Romanae aeclesiae ordinis anni circuli* (*Sacramentarium Gelasianum*), ed. L. C. Mohlberg (Rome, 1960) [hereafter *Gelasianum*].

[17] Vatican, MS reg. lat. 317 (*CLA*, I, 106). *Missale Gothicum*, ed. L. C. Mohlberg (Rome, 1961) [hereafter *Gothicum*].

[18] Vatican, MS pal. lat. 493 (*CLA* I, 92–4). *Missale Gallicanum vetus*, ed. L. C. Mohlberg (Rome, 1958).

[19] Vatican, MS reg. lat. 257 (*CLA* I, 103). *Missale Francorum*, ed. L. C. Mohlberg (Rome, 1957) [hereafter *Francorum*].

[20] BN, MS latin 13246 (*CLA* V, 653). *The Bobbio Missal: A Gallican Mass Book*, ed. E. A. Lowe, Henry Bradshaw Society, 58 (London, 1920) [hereafter *Bobbio*].

[21] BN, MS latin 9427 (*CLA* V, 579). *Le Lectionnaire de Luxeuil*, ed. P. Salmon (Rome, 1944) [hereafter *Luxeuil*].

[22] The standard guide to early medieval liturgical manuscripts is still K. Gamber, *Codices liturgici latini antiquiores*, Spicilegium Friburgensis Subsidia 1, 2nd edn (Fribourg, 1968), yet Gamber's analysis and typology is in many cases out of date and in need of revision according to modern scholarship. Also useful is V. Leroquais, *Les Sacramentaires et les missals manuscrits des bibliothèques publiques de France*, 4 vols (Paris, 1924). For more details on the Merovingian liturgical manuscripts see Y. Hen, 'Popular Culture in Merovingian Gaul, A.D. 481–751' (Cambridge, Ph.D. thesis, 1994), and see there for further bibliography.

[23] See, for example, J. Vezin, 'Les scriptoria de Neustrie, 650–850', in H. Atsma, ed., *La Neustrie: les pays au nord de la Loire de 650 à 850*, 2 vols (Sigmaringen, 1989), 2, pp. 307–18; R. McKitterick, 'The scriptoria of Merovingian Gaul: a survey of the evidence', in H. B. Clarke and M. Brennan, eds, *Columbanus and Merovingian Monasticism*, British Archaeological Reports 113 (Oxford, 1981), pp. 173–207; 'The diffusion of insular culture in Neustria between 650 and 850: the implications of the manuscript evidence', in Atsma, *La Neustrie*, 2, pp. 395–432, and 'Nuns' scriptoria in England and Francia in the eighth century', *Francia*, 19 (1992), pp. 1–35.

religious centres,[24] and thus it is no wonder they showed a distinctive interest in liturgy.

Yet, although their place of production is fairly clear, the origins and the development of these liturgical compositions is very difficult to trace.[25] We do not know the circumstances which inspired their composition, nor can we identify the liturgical sources which the compilers used in their work. It is clear, however, that all these manuscripts are based on earlier liturgical compositions, now lost, which were partly composed in Gaul, and partly adapted, paraphrased, or simply copied from non-Gaulish liturgical traditions, such as the Roman or the Visigothic (Mozarabic). No single liturgical source can be identified as the exemplar of the Merovingian liturgical books, and indeed no such hypothetical source can be reconstructed from the manuscripts we possess.[26] This is in sharp contrast to what would have been expected, had Innocent I's attitude prevailed throughout the West. Juxtaposing the Merovingian sacramentaries, missals, and lectionaries, one can clearly see how strikingly they differ from one another, and how diverse is the liturgical practice they represent.

To start with, one can list the difference in their content. The Old Gelasian Sacramentary contains a total of 289 masses, which are divided into three books each dedicated to a different cycle of liturgical prayers (that is, one to the temporal cycle, one to the sanctoral cycle, and one book of votive masses). The Gothic Missal contains seventy-nine masses which are dedicated to temporal and sanctoral feasts only. The Old Gallican Missal contains forty-nine masses most of which are for Easter and the Paschaltide. The Frankish Missal contains only twenty-three masses,

---

[24] See, for example, D. Ganz, 'The Merovingian library of Corbie', in Clarke and Brennan, *Columbanus*, pp. 153–72; and 'Corbie and Neustrian monastic culture', in Atsma, *La Neustrie*, 2, pp. 339–47.

[25] On the development of liturgical books see D. M. Hope and G. Woolfenden, 'Liturgical books', in C. Jones, G. Wainwright, E. Yarnold and P. Bradshaw, eds, *The Study of Liturgy*, rev. edn (London and New York, 1992), pp. 96–101.

[26] Chavasse's attempt to reconstruct the supposed Roman book on which the Old Gelasian is based has not been generally accepted and is often criticized. See A. Chavasse, *Le Sacramentaire Gélasien* (Paris, 1957); and see his critics J. Janini, *Analecta Tarraconensia*, 31 (1958), pp. 196–8; C. Coebergh, 'Le Sacramentaire gélasien ancien', *Archiv für Liturgiewissenschaft*, 7 (1961), pp. 45–88; and J. D. Thompson, 'The contribution of *Vaticanus Reginensis* 316 to the history of western service books', *Studia patristica*, 13 (1975), pp. 425–9.

mainly for various ordinations and saints' feasts, but with none for the temporal cycle. Finally, the Bobbio Missal contains in one book the masses for all three cycles together with three reading passages from the Bible for each of these masses. By contrast, the Lectionary of Luxeuil contains only the readings for the masses, without the celebrant's prayers and benedictions.[27]

Further, the saints commemorated in each of these liturgical compositions are different. The Lectionary of Luxeuil, for instance, mentions Stephen, Mary, Peter, Paul and John the Apostles, John the Baptist, Julian, the Holy Innocents, and Geneviève.[28] The Bobbio Missal, on the other hand, omits Julian and Geneviève but adds Michael, Martin, and Sigismund.[29] The Gothic Missal chose to commemorate days in honour of more than twenty saints, and the Old Gelasian dedicates prayers to more than fifty.[30] The significant difference in the sanctoral cycle of each of these manuscripts is a direct outcome of the scope and nature of the cult of the saints in Merovingian Gaul. Unlike the temporal cycle, whose feasts were fixed and dictated universally, the cult of the saints was a very local activity. Different churches venerated different saints, and different dioceses enlarged their sanctoral cycle by absorbing different new saints, many of whom were local inhabitants of the region.[31] It is, therefore, not at all surprising to find different masses for different saints in each of the Merovingian sacramentaries, not to mention the various prayers which they include to unspecified martyrs and confessors.[32]

The flexibility in use of the prayers themselves is another element which points to the lack of any binding liturgical form. For example, the reading passages which were listed by the Lectionary of Luxeuil for a mass *de uno confessorem* (II Tim. 3.16–4.8; Matt. 25.14–21),[33] were assigned by the Bobbio Missal

---

[27] On the Gallican reading system see Salmon, *Le Lectionnaire*, pp. lxxxvii–xcii.

[28] *Luxeuil*, chs, 9–10, 29, 23, 63, 11, 62, 18, 12–13 and 16 respectively.

[29] *Bobbio*, chs 393–7, 360–7 and 334–8 respectively.

[30] *Gothicum*, chs 5–7, 12–20, 44, 51–72; *Gelasianum*, I, chs 6–8; II, chs 1–79.

[31] An excellent introduction on the cult of the saints in Merovingian Gaul is given by R. Van Dam, *Saints and their Miracles in Late Antique Gaul* (Princeton, 1993). See also F. Graus, *Volk, Herrscher und Heiliger im Reich der Merowinger. Studien zur Hagiographie der Merowingerzeit* (Prague, 1965).

[32] See for example: *Gelasianum*, II, chs, 1, 72–9; *Francorum*, chs 15–18; *Bobbio*, chs 339–59; *Luxeuil*, chs 66–9; *Gothicum*, chs 64–72.

[33] *Luxeuil*, ch. 68.

to a mass *in depositione Sancti Martini*,[34] while the Bobbio prayer assigned to the very same feast of St Martin under the title *ad pacem*[35] is incorporated both in the Gothic Missal as the *collectio sequitur* for a mass in honour of one confessor,[36] and as the preface to the mass *in natale Sancti Marceli confessoris* in the Old Gelasian Sacramentary.[37] Even more confusing is the difference between the Merovingian lectionaries in assigning the reading passages to each of the temporal and sanctoral feasts. While the Lectionary of Luxeuil and the Bobbio Missal agree in most cases about the biblical passages to be assigned to each occasion, they are completely different from the palimpsest lectionaries of Wolfenbüttel or Paris,[38] and from the marginal notes to the Gospel Book of St Kilian.[39] Thus, for example, passages from Genesis, I Corinthians, and the Gospel of John were assigned by the Lectionary of Luxeuil and the Bobbio Missal to the mass *in dedicatione ecclesiae*,[40] while passages from Isaiah, Haggai, the Epistle to the Ephesians, and the Gospel of Matthew were assigned by the Wolfenbüttel lectionary to the very same mass.[41] Many more similar examples of such versatility in using and recycling existing prayers can be found in the Merovingian sacramentaries.[42]

Against the background of the evidence adduced above there is little doubt that considerable diversity in liturgical celebration did exist in Merovingian Gaul. This diversity is apparent on two

[34] *Bobbio*, chs. 360–2.

[35] *Bobbio*, ch. 366.

[36] *Gothicum*, ch. 463.

[37] *Gelasianum*, II, ch. 3:810.

[38] These are Wolfenbüttel, Herzog-August Bibliothek, MS 4160, ed. A. Dold, *Das älteste Liturgiebuch der lateinischen Kirche*, Texte und Arbeiten 26–8 (Beuron, 1936) [hereafter Wolfenbüttel]; and BN, MS latin 10863, ed. E. Chatelain, 'Fragments palimpsestes d'un lectionnaire mérovingienne', *Revue d'histoire et de littérature religieuse*, 5 (1900), pp. 193–9.

[39] Würzburg, Universitätsbibliothek, MS M.p.th.Q.1a; and see G. Morin, 'Liturgie de la basilique de Rome au VIIᵉ siècle', *RB*, 28 (1911), pp. 328–30; P. Salmon, 'Le système des lectures liturgiques contenues dans les notes marginales du MS M.p.th.Q.la de Wurzbourg', *RB*, 61 (1951), pp. 38–53, and 62 (1952), pp. 294–6.

[40] *Luxeuil*, ch. 73; *Bobbio*, chs 384–6.

[41] Wolfenbüttel, pp. 57–8; Salmon, *Le Lectionnaire*, p. cxviii. A leaf in the script of Luxeuil (Chicago, Newberry Library, frag. 1) from what appears to be a fragmentary volume of the prophetic books (*CLA* IX, 1337) contains the passages from Haggai and is also marked *ad dedicatione*. On this leaf see D. Ganz, 'The Luxeuil prophets and Merovingian missionary strategy', in R. G. Babcock, ed., *Beinecke Studies in Early Manuscripts, Yale University Library Gazette*, supplement to vol. 66 (1991), pp. 105–17, especially pp. 110–11; and see also R. G. Babcock, 'The Luxeuil prophets and the Gallican liturgy', *Scriptorium*, 47 (1993), pp. 52–5.

[42] See, for example, the first Sunday of Advent in Salmon, *Le Lectionnaire*, pp. civ–cv.

different levels of the liturgical practice. On the first level, different feasts for different saints were celebrated in different places around Gaul, and thus turned the liturgical calendar into a very local one. Furthermore, different votive and private masses were dedicated by each of the sacramentaries we possess, probably in response to local demand and the personal inclinations of the bishop who commissioned the book.[43] On the second level are the different prayers and reading passages that were assigned to the same masses by different sacramentaries and missals. These reflect not only a diversity in local customs and usages, but also different ideals and standards on the part of the composers. Although commissioned by churches and monasteries throughout Gaul, these volumes enshrined the local usages of the centres in which they were copied.

Notwithstanding this diversity, there are some voices in Merovingian Gaul which call for a standardized liturgical rite and which, if taken at face value, might give the impression that liturgical unity was a burning issue and even the absolute goal of several Merovingian Church councils. The first is canon 27 of the first Council of Épaon (517) which declares that in celebrating the divine office, the provincial bishops must observe the *ordo* which their metropolitan follows.[44] The second is the third canon of the second Council of Vaison (529) which introduced the *Kyrie eleison* and the *Sanctus* into Gaul, and demanded their incorporation into every mass.[45] And finally, the first canon of the fifth Council of Arles (554) which repeats the resolution of Épaon nt a provincial level, by asking all the co-provincial bishops to celebrate the mass *ad formam Arelatensis*, that is, a diocesan uniformity and conformity with the metropolitan.[46]

Although they may seem to call for uniformity, these conciliar decrees had a different primary purpose in actuality. A clear distinction has to be made here between the mass as a series of

[43] On private masses see A. Angenendt, 'Missa specialis. Zugleich ein Beitrag zur Entstehung der Privatemessen', *Frühmittelalterliche Studien*, 17 (1983), pp. 153–221; see also H. Mayr-Harting, *The Coming of Christianity to Anglo-Saxon England*, 3rd edn (London, 1991), pp. 182–90.

[44] *Concilium Epaonense* (517), ch. 27. C. De Clercq, ed., *Concilia Galliae. A. 511 – A. 695, CChr. SL*, 148A (1963), p. 30.

[45] *Concilium Vasense* (529), ch. 3, De Clercq, ed., *Concilia*, p. 79.

[46] *Concilium Arelatense* (554), ch. 1, De Clercq, ed., *Concilia*, p. 171. On all these councils see O. Pontal, *Historie des conciles mérovingiens* (Paris, 1989), pp. 58–71, 82–4 and 137–9 respectively.

acts and gestures, and the prayers that were recited during the celebration, a distinction between the ritual and the text.[47] The main aim of the Merovingian church councils was to regularize the procedure for celebrating the mass. They are not concerned with texts and words. Thus, the Council of Épaon stresses the *ordo*, the Council of Arles the *forma*, and the Council of Vaison introduces two new components into the sequence of the rite. These decrees, it seems, call neither for complete uniformity in liturgical matters, as did the Council of Toledo (633),[48] nor for the adoption of the Roman rite, as did the Councils of Gerona (517) or Braga (561).[49] The only intention of the Merovingian councils in these three canons was to standardize the celebration of the mass in its acts and gestures, that is, to ensure that a common basic structure would be followed throughout the kingdom, and that no part of the rite would be neglected or even missed out by the celebrant. In other words, they simply reveal a desire for the ritual and the form of the mass to be less diverse, at least within an ecclesiastical province or diocese. Furthermore, the idea of adopting the Roman rite stood in sharp contrast to the practice of liturgical composition in Gaul, and consequently to the prevailing liturgical diversity which had evolved within the Frankish Church.

Thus, in referring to unity and diversity in the liturgy of Merovingian Gaul, one must distinguish between the actual structure and procedure of celebrating the mass on the one hand, and the content of the prayers themselves on the other. While some efforts to standardize the form of the mass were indeed made by the Merovingian Church, the content of the prayers, the various benedictions, and the readings themselves enjoyed an apparently unlimited freedom. Each celebrant had to follow strictly the general pattern of a mass and to ensure that no part of it was omitted or forgotten. But as to the content of these parts, like the three readings, the prayer of the deacon for the people,

[47] See J.-C. Schmitt, *La Raison des gestes dans l'occident médiéval* (Paris, 1990), pp. 13–92, especially pp. 57–84.

[48] *Concilium Toletanum IV* (633), ch. 2, J. Vives, ed., *Concilios Visigóticos e Hispano Romanos* (Madrid, 1963), p. 188.

[49] *Concilium Gerundense* (517), ch. 1; *Concilium Baracense* (561), chs 4 and 5, Vives, ed., *Concilios Visigóticos*, pp. 39 and 72 respectively. On all these Councils see J. Orlandis and D. Ramos Lissón, *Die Synoden auf der iberische Halbisel bis zum Einbruch des Islam (711)* (Paderborn, 1981).

or the collects of the celebrant after the deacon's prayer, the celebrant was free to choose whatever he deemed appropriate for the occasion, and even to compose some prayers of his own if he were capable of doing so.

The tendency to standardize the ceremony and gestures of the mass celebration can be seen, not only in these church councils' decrees, but also in the masses provided by the Merovingian sacramentaries which, with small variations and changes, reflect the same basic structure of the celebration. That tendency further accords with the step-by-step guide to celebrating the mass also known as the *Expositio antiquae liturgiae gallicanae.*[50] This treatise, written especially for the instruction of the clergy, is a technical exposition on how to perform the mass, and what every part of it signifies. This detailed commentary on the mass, traditionally attributed to Bishop Germanus of Paris (d. 576),[51] together with the church councils, reflects a Merovingian preoccupation with authority, orthodoxy and correctness, and thus again attests a prevailing attempt to stanaardize the mass in terms of acts and gestures.

To sum up, the prolific liturgical productivity and creativity which characterized Merovingian Gaul goes back at least to the fourth century, and from then it was never bound by any rule or regulation concerning the style or content of the liturgical text. By examining the liturgical manuscripts themselves, one can see quite clearly how strikingly they differ from one another not only in their content (that is, the events and days they chose to celebrate), but also in their style, length of prayers, and use of

---

[50] *Expositio antiquae liturgiae gallicanae*, E. A. Ratcliff, ed., Henry Bradshaw Society, 98 (London, 1971).

[51] This attribution has been questioned in the past. See for example E. Bishop, *Liturgica historica* (Oxford, 1918), p. 131, n. 1; A. Wilmart, 'Germain de Paris; Lettres attribuées à Saint', *Dictionnaire d'archéologie chrétienne et de liturgie*, 6:i (Paris, 1928), cols 1049–62; and introduction to J. Quasten, ed., *Expositio antiquae liturgiae gallicanae* (Münster, 1934). It was basically the allegorical interpretations offered by this small treatise that lead McKitterick to deny its Merovingian origin, and to attribute it to liturgical preoccupations and reforms of the Carolingian age; see McKitterick, *The Frankish Church*, p. 216. Yet, I would submit that the *Expositio* is more likely to be a Merovingian composition, not only because of linguistic and literary peculiarities which it demonstrates, but primarily because it describes the pure Gallican rite, characteristic of Merovingian Gaul. See A. Van der Mensbrugghe, 'L'expositio missae gallicanae est-elle de St Germain de Paris?', *Messager de l'exarchat du patriarche russe en Europe occidental*, 8 (1959), pp. 217–49, and 'Pseudo-Germanus reconsidered', *Studia patristica*, 5 (1962), pp. 172–84.

biblical and patristic quotations. Yet, one has to bear in mind that despite the great diversity and freedom in liturgical production and practice which characterized Merovingian Gaul, there were some basic structures and conventions which the liturgists had to obey, and which were common to all Merovingian mass celebrations. These formed guidelines within which the possibilities for diversity were nevertheless still immense.

The liturgical reforms of Pippin III and his son Charlemagne aimed at unifying the Frankish liturgy and standardizing it according to what were understood or claimed to be Roman practices. By implication they suppressed the diversity of practice which had resulted from the liturgical productivity of Merovingian Gaul. A series of new sacramentaries, known as the eighth-century Gelasians, was compiled as a result of the efforts to Romanize the Frankish liturgy.[52] Although based on earlier Frankish exemplars and using Merovingian prayers extensively, these sacramentaries show a strong tendency towards the Roman rite, not only in their content, which is closely related to a Roman sacramentary similar to the Sacramentary of Padua,[53] but also in their structure which follows the Roman practice of a single volume arranged according to the liturgical calendar. The great similarity between these sacramentaries and the fact that a single archetype can be postulated, the so-called Sacramentary of Flavigny, demonstrate a degree of standardization alien to the prevailing Merovingian diversity of practice. Even if uniformity as Innocent I or the Carolingian reformers perceived it was still far away, Frankish liturgical creativity suffered extremely.[54] Another blow was still to come in the form of the *Hadrianum*, whose arrival at the court of Charlemagne marked a new stage in the growth of liturgical uniformity. It basically called into question the pluralism which characterized Merovingian liturgy, and inaugurated a new age of rigorous attempts at standardization and Romanization.

---

[52] On these sacramentaries see B. Moreton, *The Eighth-Century Gelasian Sacramentary: A Study in Tradition* (Oxford, 1976); Vogel, *Medieval Liturgy*, pp. 70–8.

[53] Padua, Biblioteca Capitolare, MS D47, fols 11r–100r.

[54] This must not be taken to imply that Frankish liturgical creativity disappeared altogether. Carolingian control was insufficient to enforce unity to that extent. A good example of continuous creativity can be seen in liturgical music: see S. Rankin, 'Carolingian music', in R. McKitterick, ed., *Carolingian Culture: Emulation and Innovation* (Cambridge, 1994), pp. 274–316.

The Carolingian reforms were, as many contemporary sources emphasize, the result of Pippin III's and Charlemagne's personal involvement and extensive intervention in Church affairs.[55] This interest, however, is emphatically not the consequence of arbitrary aesthetic concern. It is, rather, a systematic deployment of political power and resources to accomplish specific aims and objectives. As far as the early Carolingian craving for liturgical uniformity is concerned, these aims and objectives originated from grave doubts about either the ability of the clergy to carry out the liturgical rite, or the authenticity and correctness of the rite itself. In both cases the move towards standardization does not represent a higher stage of maturity, as Pierre Salmon would have argued,[56] but rather a higher degree of centralization of power and control which enabled the authorities, religious and secular, to take drastic precautionary moves in order to overcome incapacity at the local level, and to ensure the correctness of the rite in a more global sense.

From the evidence adduced above, there are strong arguments to associate the question of liturgical uniformity with the political background. This correlation can be witnessed elsewhere. In Visigothic Spain, for instance, the political unification of most of the peninsula by Leovigild and the intensive co-operation between the bishops and the monarch, once the conversion to Catholicism was accomplished under Reccared, facilitated the active participation of the secular ruler in religious matters,[57] and thus gave rise to the attempts at liturgical uniformity attested by the Council of Toledo. Similar conditions characterized the Frankish kingdom under Pippin III and Charlemagne. Yet, in Merovingian Gaul there had been no political mechanism which could have enforced similar liturgical unity, and despite the proclaimed desire for unity of liturgical practice, diversity was unavoidable.

University of Haifa

---

[55] Such tendencies can also be seen in the activities of several Merovingians, and especially in the activities of Queen Balthild.

[56] P. Salmon, *Le Lectionnaire de Luxeuil: études paléographiques et liturgiques* (Rome, 1953), p. 76.

[57] See R. Collins, *Early Medieval Spain: Unity in Diversity, 400–1000* (London, 1983), especially pp. 32–87.

# RITUAL PURITY AND THE INFLUENCE OF GREGORY THE GREAT IN THE EARLY MIDDLE AGES*

*by* ROB MEENS

Unity and diversity form a theme which Gregory the Great addressed in his famous set of answers to Augustine of Canterbury. Augustine had asked the Pope:

> Even though the faith is one, are there varying customs in the churches? and is there one form of mass in the Holy Roman Church and another in the Churches of Gaul?

To this, the Pope replied:

> My brother, you know the customs of the Roman Church in which, of course, you were brought up. But it is my wish that if you have found any customs in the Roman or the Gaulish church or any other church which may be more pleasing to Almighty God, you should make a careful selection of them and sedulously teach the Church of the English, which is still new in the faith, what you have been able to gather from other churches. For things are not to be loved for the sake of a place, but places are to be loved for the sake of their good things. Therefore choose from every individual Church whatever things are devout, religious, and right. And when you have collected these as it were into one pot, put them on the English table for their use.[1]

In an attempt to question the authenticity of the *Libellus responsionum* Dom Suso Brechter discredited this passage by Gregory as being out of line with papal policy. Paul Meyvaert, however, has

---

*I would like to thank Mary Garrison and Mayke de Jong for their comments on an earlier version of this paper.

[1] Translation taken from *Bede's Ecclesiastical History of the English People*, ed. Bertram Colgrave and R. A. B. Mynors, rev. ed. (Oxford, 1992) [hereafter Bede, *HE*], pp. 81–3. The last sentence reads differently in Bede, who incorporates this text in bk i, 27. The original text of the *Libellus* with translation is given ibid., p. 82, n.1; cf. J. M. Wallace-Hadrill, *Bede's Ecclesiastical History of the English People. A Historical Commentary* (Oxford, 1988), p. 40.

demonstrated the centrality of the theme of diversity and unity in Gregory's thought.[2] In the *Libellus responsionum* the Pope advised Augustine on questions of ecclesiastical organization and ritual purity. On the latter issue he dismissed certain views which were apparently inspired by a literal interpretation of the text of the Bible, and especially the book of Leviticus.

In this paper I will explore the different attitudes towards questions of purity and impurity in the early medieval period through the lens of the history of Gregory's *Libellus responsionum*. It is often supposed that Gregory's work did not eliminate older 'archaic' attitudes towards questions of purity. Although this is true to a certain extent, early medieval attitudes prove to be much more diverse than historians tend to admit.[3] For Gregory, diverging attitudes toward these questions were no hindrance for the unity of the Church. His tolerance seems to have paved the way for a great diversity in practice.

The authenticity of the *Libellus responsionum* has been questioned not only by modern scholars, among whom Suso Brechter was the most formidable, but also by St Boniface in the eighth century.[4] Though we are still eagerly awaiting a new edition of this text that could finally settle the question of its authenticity,

[2] S. Brechter, *Die Quellen zur Angelsachsenmission Gregors des Grossen: eine historiographische Studie*, Beiträge zur Geschichte des alten Mönchtums und des Benediktinerordens, 22 (Münster, 1941); Paul Meyvaert, 'Diversity within unity, a Gregorian theme', in his *Benedict, Gregory, Bede and others* (London, 1977), no. 6 [originally in *Heythrop Journal*, 4 (1963), pp. 141–62], cf. Henry Chadwick, 'Gregory the Great and the mission to the Anglo-Saxons', in *Gregorio Magno e il suo tempo: XIX Incontro di studiosi dell'antichità cristiana in collaborazione con l'École Française de Rome, 9–12 maggio 1990, Studio Ephemeridis 'Augustinianum'*, 33, 2 vols (Rome, 1991), 1, pp. 199–212, esp. pp. 207–12.
[3] Arnold Angenendt, *Das Frühmittelalter. Die abendländische Christenheit von 400 bis 900* (Stuttgart, Berlin, Cologne, 1990), p. 346: 'Die Auskunft der "Responsa" galt offenbar als zu lax und fand bei nicht einem einzigen frühmittelalterlichen Autor Gehör'; cf. idem, ' "Mit reinen Händen". Das Motiv der kultischen Reinheit in der abendländischen Askese', in Georg Jenal, ed., *Herrschaft, Kirche, Kultur. Beiträge zur Geschichte des Mittelalters. Festschrift für Friedrich Prinz zu seinem 65. Geburtstag* (Stuttgart, 1993), pp. 297–316, esp. p. 304; Jean-Louis Flandrin, *Un temps pour embrasser. Aux origines de la morale sexuelle occidentale (VI–XI siècle)* (Paris, 1983), p. 81: 'la doctrine de Grégoire le Grand n'apparaît guère dans nos pénitentiels'. The continuing tension between the two poles is noticed by Franz Kohlschein, 'Die Vorstellung der kultischen Unreinheit der Frau. Das weiterwirkende Motiv für eine zwiespältige Situation?' in Teresa Berger and Albert Gerhards, eds., *Liturgie und Frauenfrage. Ein Beitrag zur Frauenforschung aus liturgiewissenschaftlicher Sicht* (St Ottilien, 1990), pp. 269–88, esp. pp. 277–9. See p. 279: 'Die Spannung zwischen beiden Polen bleibt erhalten, und in den Quellen liegt der Akzent mal auf der einen, mal auf der anderen Auffassung.'
[4] See letter 33, *Briefe des Bonifatius, Willibalds Leben des Bonifatius, nebst einigen zeitgenössischen Dokumenten*, ed. Reinhold Rau, Ausgewählte Quellen zur deutschen Geschichte des Mittelalters: Freiherr vom Stein-Gedächtnisausgabe, 4b (Darmstadt, 1968), p. 110.

the document is now generally regarded as genuine. Indeed, Paul Meyvaert showed that the manuscript tradition suggests that Bede used a late recension of the *Libellus* when writing his *Ecclesiastical History*.[5] So there is no reason to assume that the document is a forgery concocted at the time Bede wrote his work. Unfortunately, historical discussion has been focused on the document's authenticity. Its background has only received attention insofar as it could shed light on this question. In itself, however, the *Libellus* has some interesting implications for the earliest history of the Christianization of the Anglo-Saxons; for it suggests that, contrary to Bede's famous statement, the British did make an effort to convert the Anglo-Saxon population.[6]

In his answers Gregory made it clear that the Old Testament rules concerning ritual purity were not to be interpreted literally, but rather had to be understood in a spiritual way. Augustine's questions had referred to the impurity inherent in the sexual act, in giving birth, and in menstruation. Apparently these three areas of behaviour made people unclean and hence unfit for approaching a church, an altar, or the holy sacraments. It makes more sense to assume that these ideas about impurity, which Gregory argued against, were held by Christians rather than by pagan Anglo-Saxons. They bear some resemblance to ideas expressed in texts written in Britain and Ireland in the sixth and seventh centuries. Therefore, they should be viewed as a reaction to British and Irish forms of Christianity influencing the Anglo-Saxon populace.[7]

In his answers Gregory opts for a spiritual interpretation of the Old Testament texts concerned with ritual purity.[8] When

[5] Paul Meyvaert, 'Bede's text of the *Libellus Responsionum* of Gregory the Great to Augustine of Canterbury', in his *Benedict, Gregory, Bede and others*, no. 10 [originally in P. Clemoes and K. Hughes, eds, *England before the Conquest: Studies in Primary Sources Presented to Dorothy Whitelock* (Cambridge, 1971), pp. 15–33]. The same author is preparing a critical edition of the *Libellus*: see his 'Le *Libellus Responsionum* à Augustin de Cantorbéry: une oeuvre authentique de Saint Grégoire le Grand', in J. Fontaine et al., eds, *Grégoire le Grand. Colloques internationaux du C.N.R.S.: Chantilly, Centre culturel Les Fontaines, 15–19 september 1982* (Paris, 1986), pp. 543–9, esp. p. 543, n. 1.

[6] Bede, *HE*, i, 22, ed. Colgrave and Mynors, p. 68: 'Qui inter alia inenarrabilium scelerum facta, quae historicus eorum Gildas flebili sermone describit, et hoc addebant, ut numquam genti Saxonum siue Anglorum, secum Brittaniam incolenti, uerbum fidei praedicando committerent.' Cf. T. M. Charles-Edwards, 'Bede, the Irish and the Britons', *Celtica*, 15 (1983), pp. 42–52.

[7] Rob Meens, 'A Background to Augustine's mission to Anglo-Saxon England', *Anglo-Saxon England*, 22 (1994), pp. 5–17.

[8] He takes the same stance concerning the observance of Sunday, see D. Norberg, ed., *S. Gregorii Magni. Registrum Epistularum Libri VIII–XIV, Appendix*, CChr. SL 140A (1982), XIII, 1, pp. 991–3.

discussing Augustine's question about how soon after childbirth a woman could enter church, Gregory says:

> You know by the teaching of the Old Testament that she should keep away for thirty-three days if the child is a boy and sixty-six days if it is a girl [Lev. 12.4–5]. This, however, must be understood figuratively [*in mysterio accipitur*]. For if she enters the church even at the very hour of her delivery, for the purposes of giving thanks, she is not guilty of any sin.[9]

Concerning the Old Testament rule that a man who has had sexual intercourse with his wife should not enter the temple before sunset (Lev. 15.16), Gregory says this can be understood in a spiritual sense (*intellegi spiritaliter potest*).[10] In the ninth response Gregory declares that spiritual people will accept the Old Testament law that a man having had a nocturnal illusion must not enter church until evening, but that they will interpret it differently (*aliter populus spiritalis intellegens sub eodem intellectu*).[11] For Gregory there is an important distinction between the letter and the spirit, the outward and the inward, the Old Testament and the New: 'In the Old Testament it is the outward deeds that are observed, . . . in the New Testament careful heed is paid not so much to what is done outwardly as to what is thought inwardly.'[12]

While Gregory wants to interpret the Old Testament precepts in a spiritual way and not apply them in a legalistic manner, he does not dismiss them out of hand. He leaves room for diversity. A woman ought not to be forbidden to receive Holy Communion during her menstruation, but if out of deep reverence she stays away from it, that is to be praised. If she wants to receive it, she is not to be judged.[13] A man having had sexual intercourse with his wife should wash himself and stay away from church for some time. For even lawful intercourse cannot take place with-

---

[9] Bede, *HE*, i, 27, resp. VIII, pp. 90–1.

[10] Ibid., pp. 94–5.

[11] Resp. IX, ibid., pp. 98–9.

[12] Resp. VIII, ibid. pp. 94–5: 'Sicut enim in Testamento ueteri exteriora opera obseruantur, ita in Testamento nouo non tam quod exterius agitur quam id quod interius cogitatur.'

[13] Resp. VIII, ibid., pp. 92–3.

out desire of the flesh, which is sinful in itself. But if a man succeede in having intercourse without feeling of desire and only for the sake of getting children, he has to decide himself if he wants to enter church and receive Holy Communion or not.[14] Even so, in the case of a man defiled by a nocturnal illusion, he should consider the reason why he was overcome by this impurity. When it happened because of a natural superfluity or weakness, it is not to be feared. If it is caused by gluttony, there is some guilt, though not enough to prevent him from partaking in mass or the eucharist. However, if other priests are present, a priest in these circumstances should humbly abstain from offering the sacrifice of the holy mystery. By adding 'in my opinion' (*ut arbitror*), here, Gregory makes it clear that he is not offering binding rules, but rather spiritual advice.[15]

So, although Gregory in general objects to a legalistic, literal interpretation of the Old Testament rules, he does share the view that bodily states can be polluting. Augustine's questions suggest, however, a much stricter obedience to the Old Testament precepts. This apparently worried the Archbishop and so he sought advice from the Pope who had sent him on his mission. Gregory makes it very clear that he does not support any legalistic obedience to the Old Testament rules. It is the inward attitude that counts, not outward behaviour.

Gregory seems to have argued against attitudes in Anglo-Saxon England that were influenced by British and Irish forms of Christianity. His answers, however, did not settle the question. Theodore of Tarsus, sent to Canterbury in the year 668 to be the new archbishop of the English, still encountered the legalistic view. In several instances he had to argue against such views, which were probably propagated by Irish penitentials. For example, he insists that a woman should abstain from sexual intercourse for forty days after giving birth to a child, whether it is a boy or a girl.[16] This seems to be a reaction against the view

---

[14] Resp. VIII, ibid., pp. 94–6.

[15] Resp. IX, ibid., pp. 98–103.

[16] *Paenitentiale Theodori. Discipulus Umbrensium* [hereafter *P. Theod. U*] II, xii, 3, ed. Paul Willem Finsterwalder, *Die Canones Theodori Cantuariensis und ihre Überlieferungsformen* (Weimar, 1929) [hereafter Finsterwalder], p. 326. On the penitential of Theodore and its complicated textual transmission, see R. Kottje, 'Paenitentiale Theodori', in *Handwörterbuch zur deutschen Rechtsgeschichte*, 3 (Berlin, 1984), cols 1413–16, to be supplemented with M. M. Woesthuis, 'A note on two manuscripts of the "Penitentiale Theodori" from the library of De Thou', *Sacris Erudiri* 34 (1994), pp. 175–84.

that the impurity resulting from the birth of a girl lasted longer than from the birth of a boy.[17] It is peculiar that Theodore did not refer to the *Libellus* sent by Gregory to his predecessor Augustine. It is even more remarkable that Theodore endorsed the principle that giving birth causes impurity, implying not only a taboo on sexual intercourse, but also a taboo on entering church. For, contrary to Gregory's advice, he assigns a three week period of penance for a woman entering church during her period of uncleaness after delivery, which was reckoned to last for forty days.[18] Theodore also forbids women to enter church or to receive Holy Communion during menstruation, whether they are laywomen or nuns.[19] So, contrary to Gregory's spiritual interpretation of the Old Testament purity rules, Theodore seems to accept them in a more literal sense, though he is prepared to adapt the literal text according to his own inclination, for example, by omitting the distinction between the birth of a girl and a boy.

The same attitude can be inferred from Theodore's treatment of dietary prescriptions. In the *Libellus responsionum* Gregory had casually rejected the distinction between pure and impure food. Theodore, in contrast, explicitly responds to some prescriptions from Irish sources by contradicting or altering these. And, although he rejects some of these dietary prescriptions, Theodore does, in principle, accept the distinction between pure and impure food, which Gregory had rejected.[20] Theodore's attitude towards ideas of pollution and purity seems to have been influenced by two elements. The first is the persistence of ideas

[17] See *Paenitentiale Cummeani*, II, 31, in Ludwig Bieler, ed., *The Irish Penitentials, with an appendix by D. A. Binchy*, Scriptores Latini Hiberniae, 5 (Dublin, 1963) [hereafter Bieler], p. 116; the *Collectio Hibernensis*, XLVI, 11, ed. F. W. H. Wasserschleben, *Die irische Kanonensammlung*, 2nd edn (Leipzig, 1885), pp. 187–8; and for the *Liber ex Lege Moysis*, see Raymund Kottje, *Studien zum Einfluss des Alten Testamentes auf Recht und Liturgie des früheren Mittelalters (6.–8. Jahrhundert)*, Bonner Historische Forschungen 23, 2nd edn (Bonn, 1970), p. 78.

[18] *P. Theod. U*, I, xiv, 18, ed. Finsterwalder, p. 309.

[19] *P. Theod. U*, I, xiv, 17–18, ed. Finsterwalder, p. 308. Cf. *P. Theodori. Canones Gregorii*, cc. 125–6, ibid., p. 265; *P. Theodori. Capitula Dacheriana*, cc. 42 and 122, ibid., pp. 243 and 249; *P. Theodori. Canones Cottoniani*, cc. 106–6, ibid., p. 278; *P. Theodori. Canones Basilienses*, c. 43a–b, ed. Franz Bernd Asbach, *Das Poenitentiale Remense und der sogen. Excarpsus Cummeani: Überlieferung, Quellen und Entwicklung zweier kontinentaler Bußbücher aus der 1. Hälfte des 8. Jahrhunderts* (Regensburg, 1975), 'Anhang', p. 83.

[20] See Rob Meens, 'Pollution in the early Middle Ages: the case of the food regulations in penitentials', *Early Medieval Europe*, 4 (1995), pp. 3–19, esp. 9.

about purity and impurity in the Anglo-Saxon world, in spite of Gregory's letter. This persistence may result from the continuing influx of Irish missionaries among the Anglo-Saxons, while, at the same time, it seems likely that these ideas were also approved of by the indigenous population. The second element influencing Theodore's position is his Greek background. Greek attitudes toward ritual impurity seem to have been more in line with the Old Testament prescriptions. And while Gregory the Great did not have much sympathy for the Greeks, Vitalian, the Pope who sent Theodore to Canterbury, was 'amongst the most instrumental in exposing Rome to Eastern influences'.[21]

So, despite Gregory's replies to Augustine of Canterbury, his views do not seem to have taken root among the Anglo-Saxons. This is all the more surprising since Gregory was held in great veneration by the English.[22] His authority was even invoked to enhance the prestige of one of the traditions of the Penitential of Theodore: the *Canones Gregorii*.[23] Moreover, the manuscript tradition of the Penitential of Theodore is linked closely to that of the *Libellus responsionum*. This seems to be no coincidence, but the product of deliberate compilation.[24] If we look at the manuscript tradition of Theodore's Penitential, we can observe that of the two manuscripts containing the *Capitula Dacherianaa (one of the versiono of Theodore's penitential), one also contains the Libellus responsionum.*[25] Of the Theodorian tradition called after Gregory the Great, the *Canones Gregorii*, five out of seventeen manuscripts also include the *Libellus*. In one of these the *Libellus* follows directly on Theodore's Penitential, while in another both texts are intertwined in the sense that first the tables of contents of both works are given followed by the texts themselves.[26] The

---

[21] H. Mayr-Harting, *The Coming of Christianity to Anglo-Saxon England*, 3rd edn (London, 1991), p. 122. Cf. pp. 169–70 for the growth of Byzantine influence in Rome after the period of Gregory the Great and footnote 3 for the role Vitalian played in this process.

[22] The earliest Life of Gregory, for example, was written in England; see Bertram Colgrave, 'The earliest Life of St. Gregory the Great, written by a Whitby monk', in Kenneth Jackson and others, *Celt and Saxon: Studies in the Early British Border* (Cambridge, 1963), pp. 119–37.

[23] Finsterwalder, pp. 253–70.

[24] Finsterwalder, p. 217: 'Nicht durch Zufall, sondern mit voller Absicht ist daher die ganze Theodorüberlieferung mit diesen *Interrogationes Augustini* eng verknüpft bis zur direkten Aufnahme in eine Überlieferungsform [= Vienna, Österreichische Nationalbibliothek, MS lat. 2195] hinein.'

[25] BN, MS latin 3182, see Finsterwalder, p. 13, and the recent description of the MS in Reinhold Haggenmüller, *Die Überlieferung der Beda und Egbert zugeschriebenen Bußbücher* (Frankfurt a. M. and Berne, etc., 1991), p. 92.

connection between the *Discipulus Umbrensium*-version of Theodore's Penitential and the *Libellus responsionum* is even stronger. Of twenty-five medieval manuscripts containing this version of Theodore, at least twelve also contain the *Libellus*.[27] Here too, the two texts sometimes immediately follow upon each other, which suggests a deliberate connection between the two.

The close connection between these two texts owes a lot to the editor of the *Collectio Vetus Gallica*, working in Corbie in the second quarter of the eighth century, who incorporated both texts into his appendix to this collection of canon law.[28] Though he did not adopt the first book of Theodore's Penitential, which contains the passages contrary to Gregory's *Libellus*, these passages were included in the *Excarpsus Cummeani*.[29] And this eighth-century penitential was alao included by the Corbie editor in his appendix to the *Collectio Vetus Gallica*. The difference between Theodore and Gregory must, therefore, have been visible for everyone using these manuscripts.

---

[26] *Libellus* in: BL, MS Add. 16413 (see Letha Mahadevan, 'Überlieferung und Verbreitung des Bussbuchs "Capitula Iudiciorum" ', *Zeitschrift der Savigny-Stiftung für Rechtsgeschichte, Kan. Abt.* 72 [1986], pp. 17–75, esp. pp. 24–8); BN, MS latin 3848 B (ibid., p. 31); and Prague, Knihovna pražké kapituly, MS O LXXXIII (Hubert Mordek, *Kirchenrecht und Reform im Frankenreich. Die Collectio Vetus Gallica, die älteste systematische Kanonessammlung des fränkischen Gallien. Studien und Edition* [Berlin and New York, 1975], p. 223, n. 38); the *Libellus* follows directly on Theodore in Munich, Bayerische Staatsbibliothek, Clm 14780 (Finsterwalder, p. 30); both texts are intertwined in Oxford, Bodleian Library, MS Bodl. 311 (see Ludger Körntgen, *Studien zu den Quellen der frühmittelalterlichen Bußbücher*, Quellen und Forschungen zum Recht im Mittelalter, 7 [Sigmaringen, 1993], p. 91).

[27] For the manuscript tradition of *P. Theod. U*, see Rob Meens, *Het tripartite boeteboek. Overlevering en betekenis van vroegmiddeleeuwse biechtvoorschriften (met editie en vertaling van vier 'tripartita')* (Hilversum, 1994), p. 34, n.49. The following MSS contain *P. Theod. U* and the *Libellus*: Berlin, Staatsbibliothek Preuss. Kulturbesitz, Hamilton 132 (H) (s. IX in., Corbie); Brussels, Koninklijke Bibliotheek, 10127–44 (s. VIII/IX, northeastern part of France or Belgium); Cambridge, Corpus Christi College 320 (s. XI–XII, England); Cologne, Dombibliothek, 91 (C) (s. VIII/IX, Burgundy or near Corbie); London, BL, MS Add. 16413 (s. XI in., southern Italy); Munich, Bayerische Staatsbibliothek, Clm 22288 (s. XII[1], Windberg near Straubing); Paris, BN, MS latin 1603 (s. VIII–IX, northern France); Stuttgart, Württembergische Landesbibliothek, HB VI, 109 (s. IX 1/3, southwest Germany, maybe Constanz); Stuttgart, Württembergische Landesbibliothek, HB VI, 112 (s. X, near Bodensee); Vesoul, Bibliothèque Municipale, MS 73 (s. X/XI); Vienna, Österreichische Nationalbibliothek, latin 2195 (s. VIII ex., Salzburg); Vienna, Österreichische Nationalbibliothek, latin 2223 (s. IX 1/3, from a 'mainfränkisches' scriptorium).

[28] Mordek, *Kirchenrecht*, p. 217; for the Corbie redaction, see pp. 86–94.

[29] *Excarpsus Cummeani*, III, 14–15, ed. H. J. Schmitz, *Die Bussbücher und das kanonische Bussverfahren* (Düsseldorf, 1898) [reprint: Graz, 1958] (hereafter Schmitz II), p. 614. The canons are explicitly attributed to Theodore.

Theodore's sentences prohibiting unclean women from entering church were adopted in a number of later penitentials. Apart from the *Excarpsus Cummeani*, they were included in the *Paenitentiale Floriacense* (57), the *Paenitentiale Bigotianum* (II, viii, 1), the *Paenitentiale Remense* (V, 55–6), the *Paenitentiale Vindobonense B* (XXIX, 13–14), the *Paenitentiale Parisiense compositum* (123), the *Paenitentiale Martenianum* (LXXVII, 9) and in the *Paenitentiale Pseudo-Theodori* (II (17), 2 and 8).[30] The *Libellus responsionum* is not only transmitted together with the Penitential of Theodore and the *Excarpsus Cummeani*, but also with the *Vindobonense B*, the *Paenitentiale Capitula Iudiciorum*, the Penitential of Halitgar of Cambrai, and the penitentials attributed to Bede or Egbert.[31] We may, therefore, suppose that the *Libellus* provided a counterweight to the legalistic view advocated by Theodore. The elaborate argumentation of such an authority as Gregory the Great, transmitted in over 200 manuscripts, was probably more influential than Theodore's short penitential rules.

Yet we do not know how people dealt with these texts when both occurred in the same manuscript. What happened is suggested by the *Paenitentiale Capitula Iudiciorum*. Here Theodore's sentence on menstruating women is adopted, probably from the *Excarpsus Cummeani*.[32] But the compiler of this text added that the blessed Gregory, Roman Pope, conceded both things to menstruating women that are prohibited here, that is to enter church and to receive Holy Communion. But, so the *Capitula*

---

[30] For the *Floriacense*, see Raymund dottje, ed., *Paenitentialia minora Franciae et Italiae saeculi VIII–IX*, *CChr. SL* 156 (1994), p. 102; for the *Bigotianum*, Bieler, p. 222; for *Remense*, Asbach, *Das Poenitentiale Remense*, 'Anhang', p. 37; for the *Vindobonense B* and the *Parisiense compositum*, Meens, *Het tripartite boeteboek*, pp. 398, 502; for the *Martenianum*, see W. von Hörmann, 'Bußbücherstudien IV', *Zeitschrift der Savigny-Stiftung für Rechtsgeschichte: Kan. Abt.*, 4 (1914), pp. 358–483, at pp. 468–9; for 'Pseudo-Theodore', see F. W. H. Wasserschleben, *Die Bussordnungen der abendländischen Kirche* (Halle, 1851) [hereafter Wasserschleben], p. 577.

[31] Together with the *Vindobonense B* in Vienna, Österreichische Nationalbibliothek, MS Latin 2233, see Meens, *Het tripartite boeteboek*, p. 109. With the *P. Capitula Iudiciorum* in BL, MS Add. 16413 (s. XI in., southern Italy), St Gall, Stiftsbibliothek, cod. 150 (pp. 273–322) (s. VIII/IX or IX in., St Gall), and Vienna, Österreichische Nationalbibliothek, MS Latin 2223 (*olim iur. can.* 116) (s. IX in., 'Maingebied'), see Mahadevan, 'Überlieferung', pp. 25–8, 35, 44–5. For the connection with Halitgar and the penitentials attributed to Bede and Egbert, see R. Kottje, *Die Bussbücher Halitgars von Cambrai und des Hrabanus Maurus. Ihre Überlieferung und ihre Quellen*, Beiträge zur Geschichte und Quellenkunde des Mittelalters, 8 (Berlin and New York, 1980), pp. 14–83 and Haggenmüller, *Die Überlieferung*, pp. 51–116.

[32] On the relationship between these two penitentials, see Meens, *Het tripartite boeteboek*, pp. 157–75.

*Iudiciorum* continues, he praised the women who out of humility abstained from doing this. It is remarkable that Theodore's sentence, although clearly recognizable as such in the *Excarpsus Cummeani* (probably the direct source of this passage), is here attributed to the Irish (*Scotorum Judicium*).[33]

Although it uses Theodore's Penitential, the *Paenitentiale Merseburgense A* does not adopt Theodore's sentences prohibiting women from entering church when in a state of impurity. Instead, it explicitly allows menstruating women to enter church and to receive holy communion by including the fragment from the *Libellus* concerning this question. It also includes the part in which Gregory praises women who abstain in these circumstances, but it concludes that if they do approach the altar, they are not to be judged.[34]

A similar attitude towards the same question is to be found in the *Paenitentiale Pseudo-Gregorii*. Here Theodore's sentence on women entering church during menstruation is cited, but it is followed directly by a much longer extract from the *Libellus responsionum*, with a similar import to that in the *Paenitentiale Merseburgense A*. This chapter in the *Paenitentiale Pseudo-Gregorii* concludes with the remark that menstruation is to be considered as carrying no guilt because it happens naturally. This lenient Gregorian approach was apparently not accepted by all, for one manuscript of this text, written in the second half of the ninth century, omits all material from Gregory and only adopts the Theodorian view.[35]

The same tension can be observed in the *Paenitentiale Pseudo-Theodori*, although the *Libellus* is not used here. Pseudo-Theodore adopts the sentences forbidding menstruating women to enter church from Theodore. To the Theodorian sentence that man and wife should abstain after delivery, he adds that after

---

[33] *P. Capitula Iudicorum* X, 5, ed. Meens, *Het tripartite boeteboek*, p. 450.

[34] *P. Merseburgense A*, c.89–90, in Kottje, *Paenitentialia minora*, pp. 152–3; in the Vienna MS of this text (Österreichische Nationalbibliothek, Latin 2225) the text is changed in such a way that it says exactly the opposite of what the other MSS say.

[35] *P. Ps.-Gregorii*, c. XXV, ed. Franz Kerff, 'Das Paenitentiale Pseudo-Gregorii. Eine kritische Edition', in Hubert Mordek, ed., *Aus Archiven und Bibliotheken. Festschrift für Raymund Kottje zum 65. Geburtstag* (Frankfurt a. M., Berne, etc., 1992), pp. 161–88. esp. pp. 182–3. Gent, Bibliotheek der Rijksuniversiteit, MS 506, omits the Gregorian material. This section of the *P. Ps.-Gregorii* was adopted in the canonical collection in nine books (Vat. latin 1349); see Pierre J. Payer, *Sex and the Penitentials. The Development of a Sexual Code, 550–1150* (Toronto, 1984), pp. 96–7.

forty days the woman should enter church with lanterns and offerings.[36] In other words, he is on the literal side. Among the sentences concerning dietary rules in which all sorts of food are declared taboo, the author suddenly cites the biblical passages in which the Jewish dietary rules are explicitly criticized (Matt. 15.11, Col. 2.16–17 and I Tim. 4.4). Yet from these he does not conclude that the dietary rules should be discarded. For this ancient religious tradition, transmitted and protected by the Fathers, should not be abolished because it does not deviate from the true faith. He then cites St Paul, defending the existing diversity in early Christian communities, regarding food and holy days (Rom. 14.5). So here diversity acts as a justification for understanding the Old Testament rules in a literal way.[37]

Jonas of Orléans in the ninth century knew the *Libellus responsionum* when he wrote his *Mirror for the Laity* (*De institutione laicali*) but he also chose to perceive the Old Testament rules in a literal way. While admitting that the law is to be understood spiritually, texts from the Fathers, that is from Jerome and Caesarius of Arles (the latter mistakenly identified by Jonas as Augustine of Hippo), and an ancient tradition show that in the case of the ban on sexual activity during menstruation the Old Testament rules are to be followed according to the letter. But the spiritual meaning has also to be saved (*salvo spiritali intellectu*). Jonas comes back to the spiritual meaning of the Old Testament rules when dealing with the topic of visiting a church after delivery or during menstruation. Though again the mystical meaning of the Old Testament is to be saved, some follow the Christian custom that keeps to the letter of the law. Jonas praises women who abstain from entering a church during their menstruation because of their uncleanness. Finally, he insists that people have to enter church and receive Holy Communion with a clean body and a pure mind.[38]

Jonas reveals the existence of a diversity of practice when he says that *some* keep to the letter of the law and that in *some* provinces women refrain from entering church during menstruation. This diversity is confirmed by the texts analysed above.

---

[36] *P. Ps.-Theodori*, II (17), 2, ed. Wasserchleben, p. 577.

[37] *Ibid.*, XVI (31), 14, ed. Wasserschleben, pp. 602–3.

[38] Jonas of Orléans, *De institutione laicali*, II, x–xi, *PL* 106, cols 186–8.

Gregory's *Libellus* did not put an end to the persistent idea that menstruation and giving birth were polluting and that women in these states should avoid contact with the sacred. The ritual of churching women should be seen as a legacy of this concept of impurity.[39] Ideas about impurity were fed by textual traditions, from the Old Testament and from Roman authors, but they seem to have found a fruitful breeding ground in the insular and Frankish world. This suggests that they were not concepts adopted from another culture, but were congenial to early medieval culture. Ideas of purity and impurity seem to have formed important elements in the early medieval world view and this seems to have accorded well with that in which the Jewish purity rules first originated.[40]

If Gregory's influence could not abolish these notions about impurity, it did nonetheless succeed in altering them. For through the incorporation of the *Libellus* in penitential texts and manuscripts, the strict adherence to purity rules evolved into a custom in which giving thanks became more central. The motive changed from community-based rules of impurity to the personal motive of thanksgiving; from the outward to the inward. It is this tension in early medieval religion between concepts of purity and impurity on the one hand and ideas of personal responsibility on the other, that has often confused modern historians.[41]

The tension between the outward and the inward led to a diversity in practice. This would not have bothered Gregory the Great. In the *Libellus responsionum* in general, as in his specific answer on the question about ritual purity, he leaves room for diversity. Jonas of Orléans seems to have understood this well when he defended the literal understanding of the Old Testament rules by saying that this old Christian custom was neither

---

[39] Although in practice the ritual could express a variety of meanings; see David Cressy, 'Purification, thanksgiving and the churching of women in post-reformation England', *PaP*, 141 (1993), pp. 106–46, esp. pp. 111 and 144–6.

[40] Cf. Flandrin, *Un temps pour embrasser*, p. 81; Angenendt, *Das Frühmittelalter*, p. 346; Meens, 'Pollution'.

[41] See the remarks on the confusion of modern historians in Pierre J. Payer, 'The humanism of the penitentials and the continuity of the penitential tradition', *Mediaeval Studies*, 46 (1984), pp. 340–54; and Alexander Murray, 'Confession before 1215', *TRHS*, ser. 6, 3 (1993), pp. 51–81, at p. 62. I cannot agree, however, with Murray's pessimistic view on the frequency of auricular confession in the early medieval period.

indecent, nor improper, nor contrary to a spiritual interpretation of the text. If notions of purity and impurity indeed had a native background, Gregory would not have objected either. After all, it was he who advocated an accommodation to pagan practices in his famous instruction to Abbot Mellitus in the early years of the English mission, again distinguishing between the outward and the inward: 'while some outward rejoicings are preserved, they [the Anglo-Saxons] will be able more easily to share in inward rejoicings'.[42]

University of Utrecht

---

[42] Bede, *HE*, i, 30, ed. Colgrave and Mynors, pp. 106–8. See R. A. Markus, 'Gregory the Great and a papal missionary strategy', *SCH* 6 (1970), pp. 29–38.

# UNITY AND DIVERSITY IN THE EARLY ANGLO-SAXON LITURGY

by CATHERINE CUBITT

The early Anglo-Saxon Church felt that it possessed a special relationship with the papacy and Rome, going back (according to Bede) to the Gregorian mission of 597. Despite setbacks to this mission, unity with the Church of Rome triumphed over Irish traditions to become the keystone in the identity of the English Church. Imitation of Roman liturgical customs was a significant element in this union. In the early days of the Gregorian mission, liturgical uniformity had been unimportant, indeed Gregory specifically instructed Augustine to create a liturgy of mixed ancestry, taking the best from what he had experienced.[1] But by the late seventh century, indifference had been overtaken by enthusiasm for the Roman chant: Bede tells us of the efforts of, for example, Benedict Biscop and Bishop Wilfrid to introduce Roman liturgical customs into their foundations.[2] In 747, the Southumbrian Council of *Clofesho* decreed that the feasts of the Christian calendar and the monastic office should be performed in accordance with Roman texts and practices.[3]

This paper explores the nature and extent of liturgical conformity to Roman practices up to the time of the Council of *Clofesho*. It examines how far this desire for unity had permeated Anglo-Saxon liturgy and looks particularly at the means of transmission of liturgical texts. But first it is necessary briefly to consider the role of the liturgy in the life of the Anglo-Saxon Church, both as a bearer of symbolic unity and as an agent of unity within the monastic community.

---

[1] Bede, *Historia ecclesiastica gentis Anglorum* [hereafter *HE* ],ed. and trans. B. Colgrave and R. A. B. Mynors, *Bede's Ecclesiastical History of the English People* (Oxford, 1969), i, 27. This passage is discussed by P. Meyvaert, 'Diversity within unity, a Gregorian theme', in his *Benedict, Gregory, Bede and others* (London, 1977), 6, pp. 141–62. See also the contribution by Rob Meens to the present volume (pp. 31–43).

[2] *HE*, iv, 8 and iv, 2.

[3] *Councils and Ecclesiastical Documents Relating to Great Britain and Ireland*, ed. A. W. Haddan and W. Stubbs [hereafter *HS*], 3 vols (Oxford, 1869–79), 3, pp. 367–8, cc. 13, 15, 18. These liturgical provisions are discussed in my book, *Anglo-Saxon Church Councils, c.650–c.850* (Leicester, 1995)ch. 5.

The liturgical life of an Anglo-Saxon monastery was central to its sense of identity and community: participation in the daily routine of music and prayer was the essential backbone of the religious life, involving the whole community. It acted as a potent force in the creation of a common identity. Descriptions of contemporary monastic life illustrate this well: Æthelwulf, who wrote in the ninth century a verse account of his monastery, *De abbatibus*, provided vivid pictures of the night office, with dramatic contrasts between the darkness outside and the rich and radiant interior of the church.[4] The identity between a monastic community at prayer and its members is seen in a remarkable episode in the anonymous life of Ceolfrith, who had been abbot of Bede's monastery of Jarrow. Jarrow had been devastated by plague, leaving only Ceolfrith and one small boy (possibly Bede himself) to maintain the office. Reluctantly, Ceolfrith decided to reduce the burden of the services, but after only a week he broke down and reinstated his cuts, unable to bear any longer this impoverishment of the liturgical life.[5]

The intensely emotional account of Ceolfrith's sudden and unexpected departure from Wearmouth-Jarrow also underscores the centrality of corporate worship to a monastery's sense of community. A poignant contrast can be felt in the account of Ceolfrith's leave-taking between the community's participation in the services of the day – which were much disrupted by tears – and Ceolfrith's withdrawal from his flock.[6] The words and music of the services were important vehicles of emotional expression: Bede's resignation in the face of death was expressed through his persistence in the chant, but early in his illness he broke down when singing the words, 'O King of glory, Lord of might, who didst this day ascend in triumph above all the heavens, leave us not comfortless.' The author of the account of Bede's last days commented: 'it was an hour before he tried to repeat what he had left unfinished, and so it was every day. And

---

[4] Æthelwulf, *De abbatibus*, ed. A. Campbell (Oxford, 1967), c. 20.

[5] Anonymous, *Vita Ceolfrithi*, c. 14, in *Venerabilis Baedae opera historica*, ed. C. Plummer, 2 vols (Oxford, 1896), 1, p. 393. Discussed by D. Whitelock, 'Bede and his teachers and friends', and P. Wormald, 'Bede and Benedict Biscop', in G. Bonner, ed., *Famulus Christi. Essays in Commemoration of the Thirteenth Centenary of the Birth of the Venerable Bede* (London, 1976), pp. 20–2, 143–4.

[6] Anonymous, *Vita Ceolfrithi*, cc. 23–7; *Historia abbatum* in *Venerabilis Baedae opera historica*, 1, pp. 364–87.

when we heard it, we shared his sorrow; we read and wept by turns, or rather, we wept continually as we read.'[7]

The chronological framework of monastic life was provided by the liturgical year and by the daily office. Church festivals and the monastic hours are frequently used in ecclesiastical literature to mark the temporal location of events: the account of Bede's death, for example, places his final illness between Easter and Pentecost, and his demise is very precisely remembered by reference to the liturgical divisions of the day. Since the commemoration of the feasts and fasts of the Church created the essential rhythm of monastic life, the deviant Irish reckoning of Easter was indeed a powerful threat to the unity of the Anglo-Saxon Church.

In Bede's *Historia ecclesiastica gentis Anglorum*, knowledge of Roman liturgy is presented as a symbol of the tenuous survival of Roman identity despite the vicissitudes of paganism and apostasy, and its near eclipse by the Irish mission with its heretical deviation from papal norms. The practice of Roman chant waxed and waned with the fortunes of the Gregorian mission. After the flight of the Roman evangelist, Paulinus, from Northumbria, the thread of continuity there survived in the person of James the Deacon, who, according to Bede, 'was very skilful in church music'. Bede continues, 'when peace was restored to the kingdom and the number of believers grew, he also began to instruct many in singing, after the manner of Rome and the Kentish people.'[8] The despatch of Theodore of Tarsus to Canterbury by Pope Vitalian represented a much-needed injection of Roman order and unity which, in Bede's account, coincided with a renewed interest in Roman liturgy:

From that time also the knowledge of sacred music, which had hitherto been known only in Kent, began to be taught in all the English churches. With the exception of James already mentioned, the first singing master in the Northum-

---

[7] The account is edited and translated in *HE*, pp. 582–3. See also B. Ward, *Bede and the Psalter*, Jarrow Lecture 1991 (Jarrow, 1991), pp. 1–3, on this moment and on the emotional power of liturgical use of the psalter, and, further, M. Berry, 'What the monks sang: music in Winchester in the late tenth century', in B. Yorke, ed., *Bishop Æthelwold: his Career and Influence* (Woodbridge, 1988), pp. 149–54, emphasizing the importance of the liturgy in a tenth-century monastic context.

[8] *HE*, ii. 20.

brian churches was Æddi surnamed Stephanus, who was invited from Kent by the most worthy Wilfrid, who was the first bishop of the English race to introduce the catholic way of life to the English churches.[9]

Notice how in this passage, Wilfrid's championing of Roman liturgy is paired with his allegiance to papal orthodoxy. The visit of John the Archcantor, precentor of St Peter's, Rome, represented a reinforcement of England's bond with the papacy, just as the despatch of Theodore did; it also combined Bede's twin obsessions of liturgical and doctrinal correctness, since John was a papal delegate with responsibility for an enquiry into the island's orthodoxy.[10]

The liturgical tradition of the Anglo-Saxon Church acted as a powerful embodiment of its Roman roots. It was above all a living and lived tradition: the skills of the Roman chant had been maintained by human links in a chain stretching back to Gregory and Augustine.[11] To those monks, nuns, and clerks trained in these techniques, their participation in the daily office and mass must have acted as an almost tangible manifestation of the union of their Church with Rome. In this way the rhetoric of Roman unity and liturgical continuity rested upon the actual experience of the Anglo-Saxon churchmen and women.

Bede was not the only Anglo-Saxon writer to proclaim the Roman roots of English liturgical practice. Aldhelm, writing in his prose treatise, *De virginitate*, stated that Pope Gregory had been responsible for the order of the women saints read out in the canon of the mass.[12] Another text, attributed to the eighth-century archbishop of York, Ecgberht, claimed that Gregory had given Augustine a missal and antiphonary, in which he had fixed the dates of the Ember Fasts for the Anglo-Saxon Church.[13] However both authors had got their facts wrong. The particular sequence cited by Aldhelm was probably not ordered by Gregory at all but can be paralleled by Irish and Frankish mass books (the

[9] *HE*, iv, 2

[10] *HE*, iv, 18.

[11] See, for example, Bede's comments on Putta and Maban, *HE*, iv, 2 and v, 20.

[12] From *Aldhelm, The Prose Works*, trans. M. Lapidge and M. Herren (Ipswich, 1979), p. 108; D. A. Manser, 'Le témoinage d'Aldhelm de Sherborne sur une particularité du canon Grégorien de la messe romaine', *RB*, 28 (1911), pp. 90–5; E. Bishop, *Liturgica historica* (Oxford, 1918), pp. 104–5.

[13] Ecgberht, *Dialogus ecclesiasticae institutionis, Interrogatio* 16, *HS*, 3, pp. 410–13.

Stowe and Bobbio Missals) and may belong to a more ancient Roman tradition.[14] The dates of the Ember Fasts mentioned in Ecgberht's Dialogues are more likely to derive from later Roman practices.[15] These assertions are manifestations of a created tradition, which validated the customs of the Anglo-Saxon Church by claiming their Roman descent.

This Gregorian origin myth had been made necessary by the recent divisions in English ecclesiastical history. The rejection of the Irish method of dating Easter at the Synod of Whitby had divorced the Church from its Irish roots: the chain of human authority reaching back through Aidan to Columba had been severed, and Roman authority substituted. The English Church needed to invoke the figures of Augustine and Gregory to legitimate the introduction of new customs in the late seventh and early eighth centuries by men like Benedict Biscop and Wilfrid.[16]

The modern agenda for the study of Anglo-Saxon liturgy has largely been set by Bede and the Romanists. Questions like the nature of the liturgical texts brought over by Augustine and the links between Anglo-Saxon and Roman liturgy have tended to preoccupy its students.[17] Evidence for the use of Roman liturgy in England is certainly strong and derives from a variety of sources. The writings of Bede, for example, suggest that he was familiar with Gelasian prayers and ceremonies. In his biblical commentaries, *De tabernaculo* and *In Ezram et Neemiam*, he described the Gelasian baptismal ceremony, the *Apertione aurium*, to

---

[14] K. Gamber, 'Das Regensburg Fragment eines Bonifatius-Sakramentars. Ein neuer Zeuge des vorgregorianischen Messkanon', *RB*, 85 (1975), pp.p266–302.

[15] G. G. Willis, *Essays in Early Roman Liturgy*, Alcuin Club Collections, 46 (London, 1964), pp. 49–97; Bullough, 'Roman books and the Carolingian *renovatio*', in his *Carolingian Renewal: Sources and Heritage* (Manchester, 1991), pp. 5–6 (reprinted from *SCH*, 14 [1977]). Bullough suggests that this passage in the Dialogues may be later than Ecgberht's pontificate.

[16] This argument is developed in Cubitt, *Anglo-Saxon Church Councils*, ch. 5.

[17] See, for example, H. Ashworth, 'Did St Augustine bring the "Gregorianum" to England?', *Ephemerides liturgicae*, 72 (1958), pp. 39–43; C. Hohler, 'Some service books of the later Saxon church', in *Tenth-Century Studies. Essays in Commemoration of the Millennium of the Council of Winchester and Regularis Concordia*, ed. D. Parsons (Chichester, 1975), pp. 60–4; G. G. Willis, *Further Essays in Early Roman Liturgy*, Alcuin Club Collections, 50 (London, 1968), pp. 192–8, 201. On early Anglo-Saxon liturgy see Bullough, 'Roman books', pp. 1–7; H. Mayr-Harting, *The Coming of Christianity to Anglo-Saxon England* (London, 1972), pp. 168–90, and H. Gneuss, 'Liturgical books in Anglo-Saxon England and their Old English terminology', in M. Lapidge and H. Gneuss, eds., *Learning and Literature: Studies presented to Peter Clemoes on the Occasion of his Sixty-Fifth Birthday* (Cambridge, 1985), pp. 91–141.

take but one instance.[18] Prayers quoted or echoed in letters of Boniface have been identified with those in Roman sources.[19] The earliest witness to the Roman lectionary system is an Anglo-Saxon manuscript now in Würzburg copied in the mid-eighth century, containing a list of Roman stations and the feasts celebrated at them, as well as the pericopes for Epistle and Gospel readings.[20] These few examples from a weighty body of evidence indicate that Roman liturgy was well established in a number of Anglo-Saxon centres.

However, such evidence does not necessarily point to unified liturgical services. Practices in the Holy See itself were not monolithic and unchanging: the goalposts in any contest to replicate Roman usage were apt to move.[21] The Epistle and Gospel pericopes copied into the Würzburg manuscript would have been out of date by the time that it was copied since they can be dated to c.500 and c.645 respectively.

Bede's monastery of Wearmouth-Jarrow might be regarded as a flagship of Roman liturgy; but the series of homilies composed by Bede reveals that a Neapolitan rather than a Roman pericope list was the basis for readings in the church at Jarrow.[22] It includes local Neapolitan feasts, for example, that of St Januarius, and seems to have been derived from an ancient Gospel book which also served as the exemplar for the Lindisfarne Gospels and other books.[23]

---

[18] Bede, *In Ezram et Neemiam* and *De tabernaculo* in *Bedae venerabilis opera II: opera exegetica*, ed. D. Hurst (Turnhout, 1969), pp. 310–11, 89, compare with *Le sacramentaire grégorien, ses principales formes d'après les plus anciens manuscrits, I: Le sacramentaire, le supplément d'Aniane*, ed. J. Deshusses (Fribourg, 1971), p. 46, xxxiiii.

[19] H. Frank, 'Die Briefe das heiligen Bonifatius und das von ihm benutze Sakramentar', in *Sankt Bonifatius. Gedenkgabe zum zwölfhundertsten Todestag* (Fulda, 1954), pp. 58–88.

[20] Würzburg Universitätsbibliothek, M. p. th. f. 62, see T. Klauser, *Des römische Capitulare Evangeliorum: Texte und Untersuchungen zu seiner ältesten Geschichte, I Typen*, Liturgiegeschichtliche Quellen und Forschungen 28, 2nd edn, (Munster, 1972), p. xxxiii, no. 21; J. Chapman, *Notes on the Early History of the Vulgate Gospels* (Oxford, 1908), pp. 191–9.

[21] Though note that E. O'Carragain, 'Liturgical innovations associated with Pope Sergius and the iconography of the Ruthwell and Bewcastle crosses', in R. T. Farrell, ed., *Bede and Anglo-Saxon England. Papers in Honour of the 1300th Anniversary of the Birth of Bede given at Cornell University in 1973 and 1974*, British Archaeological Reports, 46 (Oxford, 1978), pp. 131–47, argues that liturgical innovations introduced by Pope Sergius were very quickly absorbed by the Anglo-Saxons.

[22] G. Morin, 'Le recueil primitif des homélies de Bede sur l'Evangile', *RB*, 9 (1892), pp. 316–26.

[23] G. Morin, 'Le liturgie de Naples au temps de saint Grégoire', *RB*, 8(1891), pp. 481–93 and 529–37; idem, 'Les notes liturgiques de l'évangelaire de Burchard', *RB*, 10 (1893), pp. 113–26; Chapman, *Notes on the Early History*; T. J. Brown in T. D. Kendrick et al., *Evangelorum Quattuor Codex Lindisfarnensis*, 2 vols (Oltun and Lausanne, 1960), 2, pp. 34–7, 47–50.

The impact of South Italian customs can be seen in a number of Anglo-Saxon liturgical documents. The Neapolitan saints of Bede's homilies also partially resurface in the main body of entries in Willibrord's Calendar, where two later hands added saints native to Capua, probably from the sanctoral of a sacramentary.[24] All three layers of Roman, Neapolitan, and Capuan saints come together in an important but very fragmentary manuscript, the Regensberg Sacramentary, copied in a mid-eighth-century Northumbrian script.[25] A further testimony to the South Italian influence on Anglo-Saxon liturgy is provided by the *Old English Martyrology*, a ninth-century Mercian compilation, which refers in some entries to 'old' and 'new' mass books. The entries to 'old mass books' include the southern and central Italian saints found in the calendar of the Regensburg Sacramentary.

Frankish and Irish prayers also left their mark upon Anglo-Saxon texts. Mayr-Harting has shown that the Romanist, Wilfrid, probably used a Gallican service for the consecration of the altar at Ripon,[26] and a number of manuscript fragments in Anglo-Saxon hands point to a fondness for the elaborate episcopal blessings of the Franks.[27] Irish influence on the spirituality

---

[24] BN, MS latin 10837, facsimile by H. Wilson, *The Calendar of St Willibrord from Ms Paris Lat. 10837*, Henry Bradshaw Society, 55 (London, 1918).

[25] Berlin, Öffentl. Wissenschaftl. Bibliothek, MS Latin fol. 877², and Regensburg, Walderdorff Samml. and Regensburg, Bischöflichen Zentralbibl. Clm. 1. P. Siffrin, 'Zwei Blätter eines Sakramentars in irischer Schrift des 8. Jahrh. aus Regensburg', *Jahrbuch für Liturgiewissenchaft*, 10 (1930), pp. 1–39. See also the discussion of D. A. Bullough, 'Alcuin and the kingdom of heaven: liturgy, theology and the Carolingian age', in *Carolingian Renewal*, p. 168 (reprinted from U. R. Blumenthal, ed, *Carolingian Essays: Andrew W. Mellon Lectures in Early Christian Studies*, [Washington DC, 1983]).

[26] *Vita sancti Wilfridi*, c. 17, ed. B. Colgrave, in *The Life of Bishop Wilfrid by Eddius Stephanus* (Cambridge, 1927); noted by Mayr-Harting, *Coming of Christianity*, pp. 180–1. For the Gallican service, see *Liber sacramentorum Romanae aecclesiae ordinis anni circuli*. (*Cod. Vat. Reg. lat. 316/Paris Bibl. Nat. 7193, 41/56*), ed. L. C. Mohlberg (Rome, 1960), pp. lxxxviii, 107–10; *Missale Francorum* (*Cod. Vat. Reg. lat. 257*), ed. L. C. Mohlberg (Rome, 1957), no. 12, pp. 17–19. See also the discussion of A. Chavasse, *Le Sacramentaire Gélasien* (*Vaticanus Reginensis 316*). *Sacramentaire presbytéral en usage dans les titres romains au viiᵉ siècle* (Tournai, 1957), pp. 36–49.

[27] Insular fragments of Gallican blessings are: the Rualand fragment (now lost: see *Missale Gallicanum Vetus*: (*Cod. Vat. Palat. lat. 493*), ed. L. C. Mohlberg [Rome, 1958], pp. 93–4); Cambridge, Trinity Hall College Library, MS 24, fols 78–83; BN MS latin 9488, fols 3–4. See H. M. Bannister, 'Liturgical fragments', *JThS*, 9 (1908), pp. 398–403, and further discussion in Cubitt, *Anglo-Saxon Church Councils*, ch. 5.

of English prayer is clearly indicated by the content of Anglo-Saxon books of private prayer.[28]

Diversity rather than uniformity may therefore be the real keynote of early Anglo-Saxon liturgy. This is hardly surprising when one examines the substance of contemporary accounts of the Christianization of England rather than their pro-Roman rhetoric. These suggest that the contribution of Irish and Frankish evangelists far outweighed that of the Roman mission and it is unlikely that their efforts were entirely superseded by the enthusiasm for all things Roman which predominated after the Synod of Whitby. Recent scholarship has also emphasized the significance of the links between Anglo-Saxon monasteries and those Frankish foundations associated with Columbanus.[29] Do these hold any clues to the origins and transmission of liturgical texts in Anglo-Saxon England?

Bede reported that before the monastic life took root in England, Anglo-Saxon nobles joined Frankish houses, and also sent their daughters to them.[30] Bede singled out the monasteries of Faremoutiers, Chelles, and Andelys-sur-Seine, which all enjoyed Columbanian associations.[31] Faremoutiers was a daughter-house of Columbanus's own foundation of Luxeuil; Chelles had been refounded from Jouarre by the former Anglo-Saxon slave, Queen Balthild; and Jouarre itself was set up by a noble, Ado, under the Irish monk's influence. Possible links with Jouarre can also be traced through Bishop Agilbert, the erstwhile Bishop of

[28] See A. B. Kuypers, *The Prayer Book of Aedeluald the Bishop, Commonly Called the Book of Cerne* (Cambridge, 1902); K. Hughes, 'Some aspects of Irish influence on early English private prayer', *Studia Celtica*, 5 (1970), pp. 48–61; see also P. Sims-Williams, 'Thought, word and deed: an Irish triad', *Eriu*, 29 (1978), pp. 99–105.

[29] J. Campbell, 'The first century of Christianity in England', in his *Essays in Anglo-Saxon History* (London, 1986), pp. 49–67; I. N. Wood, 'Ripon, Francia and the Franks Casket in the early Middle Ages', *NH*, 26 (1990), pp. 1–19; 'The Franks and Sutton Hoo', in I. N. Wood and N. Lund, eds, *People and Places in Northern Europe 500–1600: Essays in Honour of Peter Hayes Sawyer* (Woodbridge, 1991), pp. 1–14, idem, 'Frankish hegemony in England', in *The Age of Sutton Hoo*, ed. M. Carver (Woodbridge, 1992), pp. 235–41.

[30] *HE*, iii, 8.

[31] *HE*, iii, 8. On Columbanian foundations see A. Dierkens, 'Prolégomènes à une histoire des relations culturelles entre les îles britanniques et le continent pendant le Haut Moyen Age. La diffusion du monachisme dit columbanien ou iro-franc dans quelques monastères de la région parisienne au VII<sup>e</sup> siècle et la politique religieuse de la reine Bathilde', in H. Atsma, ed., *La Neustrie. Les pays du nord de la Loire de 650 à 850. Colloque historique international*, Beihefte der Francia, 16, 2 vols (Sigmaringen, 1989), 2, pp. 371–94; and I. N. Wood, *The Merovingian Kingdoms 450–751* (Harlow, 1994), pp. 184–9.

Wessex. He was probably related to Ado and was buried at Jouarre. Agilbert also leads us to Bishop Wilfrid, whom he consecrated priest and with whom he collaborated at the Synod of Whitby. Wood has argued that Wilfrid's houses of Ripon and Hexham should be seen as outliers of Columbanian monasticism. There are also reasons to add the double monastery of Barking to this list through the possible Merovingian connections of its founder, Bishop Eorcenwald of London.

These contacts all date to the second half of the seventh century, a formative period when renewed interest in Roman chants and prayers was manifest. There are, unfortunately, few manuscript remains to identify the nature of this activity. In the eighth century, the nunneries of the Paris basin so favoured by seventh-century Anglo-Saxon ladies became important and active scriptoria. McKitterick has identified a number of groups of manuscripts of related script type and decoration which should probably be linked with the monasteries of Jouarre, Faremoutiers, Andelys-sur-Seine, and Rebais. The script, orthography, and membrane preparation of some of the manuscripts linked with these houses reveal insular symptoms, perhaps a sign of continuing links with Anglo-Saxon houses.[32]

Liturgical books form a surprisingly high proportion of the total corpus and they number some of the most important witnesses to Roman and Gallican liturgy. For example, the only surviving complete sacramentary of the 'Old Gelasian' type was probably copied at Jouarre in the mid-eighth century. This manuscript is now partially preserved in the Vatican Library.[33] Other Seine basin liturgica include the manuscripts of the *Missale Francorum* and the *Missale Gallicanum vetus*.[34] Moreover, there are links between the Vatican Gelasian book and the *Missale Francorum* – the ritual for ordinations in both derives from a common source, while the *Missale Francorum* drew upon a prayer collection like the 'Old Gelasian', but richer and fuller.[35]

---

[32] R. McKitterick, 'Nuns' scriptoria in England and Francia in the eighth century', *Francia*, 19, i (1992), pp. 1–35; idem, 'The diffusion of insular culture in Neustria between 650 and 850: the implications of the manuscript evidence', in Atsma, *La Neustrie*, 2, pp. 395–434.

[33] Vatican Library, MS Reg. Lat. 316 and BN, MS latin 7193, fols 41–56.

[34] Vatican Library, MSS Reg. 257 and Pal. 493. These are usefully discussed by Y. Hen, 'Popular culture in Merovingian Gaul A. D. 481–751' (Cambridge, Ph.D. thesis, 1994), pp. 59–61.

[35] Chavasse, *Le Sacramentaire Gélasien*, pp. 5–27; *Missale Francorum*, ed. Mohlberg, pp. 59–63.

Some late literary evidence points to the reception of books from these Frankish monasteries in England. The *Life of Bertila*, the seventh-century abbess of Jouarre (and, later, of Chelles), states that she sent relics, books, and teachers to England.[36] The textual evidence of the fragmentary Regensburg Sacramentary may also be suggestive in this context.[37] The fragments of this sacramentary consist of mass prayers and parts of the canon of the mass and leaves from a calendar. Siffrin's analysis revealed significant correspondences with the Vatican Gelasian book, including the southern and central Italian saints in its sanctoral. But Siffrin was also anxious to highlight the similarities in the structuring and selection of material between the Regensburg fragments and the *Missale Francorum*, going so far as to suggest that the Regensburg texts might give some idea of the appearance of the lost temporal of the latter. The emphasis he placed upon the similarities between these two books anticipated Gamber's conclusions concerning the canon of the mass, based on leaves not discovered until forty years after Siffrin had written. For the text these contain belongs to the same ancient Roman family as that quoted by Aldhelm (also extant in the Stowe and Bobbio Missals) and found in the *Missale Francorum* where it stands closest to the textual tradition of the Regensburg fragment. It is worth noting that Aldhelm may also have Columbanian links since he enjoyed warm relations with the double house of Barking.[38]

There are problems in linking this eighth-century liturgical evidence with the well-documented seventh-century contacts discussed above, since it is impossible to say what relevance texts attested at centres in the eighth century may have had for liturgy fifty or a hundred years earlier. The caveat is an important one, but the links are suggestive and the substantial evidence for regular traffic between England and the continent provides numerous contexts for the passage of mass prayers and other texts to England. One can, for example, speculate that Bishop Agilbert gave his protégé, Wilfrid, a sacramentary or collection of prayers

[36] *Vita Bertilae abbatissae Calensis*, ed. W. Levison, *MGH Scriptores rerum Merovingicarum* (Berlin, 1913), pp. 101–9.
[37] P. Siffrin, 'Das Walderdorffer Kalendarfragment saec. viii und die Berliner Blätter eines Sacramentars aus Regensburg', *Ephemerides liturgicae*, 47 (1933), pp. 201–24, idem, 'Zwei Blätter in irischer Schrift', pp. 1–39; Gamber, 'Das Regensburg Fragment', pp. 266–302.
[38] See the discussion in Lapidge and Herren, *Aldhelm*, pp. 51, 59–132.

when he consecrated him bishop in Compiègne.[39] The Gallican dedicatory rite probably used by Wilfrid at Ripon can be found in both the Vatican Gelasian sacramentary and in the *Missale Francorum*. On the other hand, did liturgical texts travel the other way, from England to Francia? Hohler has suggested, for example, that the Gelasian sacramentary was put together for Augustine and the Anglo-Saxon mission.[40] The corpus of liturgical evidence in early Anglo-Saxon England is meagre in the extreme, and yet it is frequently characterized by influences from the south of Italy. The variety of provenances for this material is also noteworthy. It is a remarkable coincidence, therefore, that the Vatican Gelasian book also includes saints and feasts from Naples, Capua, and other places in South Italy.[41] Does the ubiquity of southern and central Italian influence in Anglo-Saxon material point to its dissemination from England? We know, for example, that Abbot Hadrian journeyed to England from *Niridanum* in Campania via Rome (where he picked up the future Archbishop of Canterbury, Theodore) and via Paris and Meaux (whose bishops, Agilbert and Faro, had Columbanian connections).[42] The links of Theodore and Hadrian are suggestive of how the southern and central Italian influence in the liturgy might have been carried, but one should be aware, as Chavasse has rightly cautioned, that refugees from southern Italy were by no means rare in Rome in the sixth and seventh centuries.[43]

Connections like these provide models of transmission but not precise contexts. They are suggestive of the sorts of per-

[39] *HE*, iii, 28. For the possibility that in the tenth and eleventh centuries, archbishops of Canterbury may have given pontificals to newly consecrated suffragans, see D. Dumville, *Liturgy and the Ecclesiastical History of Late Anglo-Saxon England* (Woodbridge, 1992), p. 94.

[40] Hohler, 'Some service books', pp. 60–2.

[41] Chavasse, *Le Sacramentaire Gélasien*, pp. 340–4. Dr Hen informs me that southern Italian influence is otherwise unknown in Merovingian liturgical books.

[42] *HE*, iv, 1. The possible connection between Theodore and Hadrian and the southern Italian element in the Anglo-Saxon liturgy has been much commented on; see D. Rollason, *Saints and Relics in Anglo-Saxon England* (Oxford, 1989), pp. 68–9, for example. For evidence of book traffic from England to Francia, see, for example, Lapidge and Herren, *Aldhelm*, pp. 149 and 167, correspondence showing that Aldhelm's works were known at Péronne in his lifetime. See Hohler, 'Some service books', pp. 60–2, who favours Augustine as the bearer of the Gelasian sacramentary to England and Bishop Agilbert as its carrier to the continent. See M. Lapidge, ed., *Anglo-Saxon Litanies of the Saints*, Henry Bradshaw Society, 106 (London, 1991), pp. 13–25, for Theodore's influence on Anglo-Saxon liturgy.

[43] Chavasse, *Le Sacramentaire Gélasien.*, pp. 342–3; an explanation favoured by Mayr-Harting, *Coming of Christianity*, pp. 176–7.

sonal networks within which knowledge, skills, and texts could circulate. Such images stimulate the historical imagination, which perhaps works more happily with known and knowable figures than with shadowy and anonymous possibilities. Yet speculation on such concrete lines can hinder as well as facilitate research: the invention of traditions, according to which every development is linked to a great personage, has dominated liturgical scholarship since at least the time of Aldhelm (witness the now discredited attributions of mass books to Popes Leo, Gelasius, and Gregory).[44] The latest in this hallowed line of liturgical red herrings is Boniface who, although a West Saxon, is credited with the ownership of the Northumbrian Regensburg Sacramentary.[45] Columbanus, alas, has never made it into such august circles;[46] he has been one of historiography's losers. Although the monasteries founded under his influence are coming increasingly to occupy centre stage in studies of early medieval religious history, Columbanus never succeeded in creating an order which survived into modern times and could produce scholars devoted to chronicling his achievements and those of his foundations. The Benedictine reforms of the ninth century not only covered Columbanus' traces but also set the tone for subsequent historiography. Columbanus, when remembered at all, was commemorated as a missionary.[47] The purpose of this article is not, however, to substitute one great man for another but rather to highlight the possible role of anonymous but influential women in the transmission of liturgical texts.

Did monasteries which owed their foundation to Columbanus and his circle favour a distinctive liturgy? This is a question which might be probed further, but a superficial glance at the

[44] C. Vogel, *Medieval Liturgy: An Introduction to the Sources*, rev. and trans. W. G. Storey and N. K. Rasmussen (Washington DC, 1986), pp. 39, 68, 79.

[45] The Boniface attribution was put forward by Siffrin, 'Das Walderdorffer Kalendarfragment', pp. 212–13, and used regularly as the name of the sacramentary by Gamber, who would also like to attribute the southern Italian element in the Vatican Gelasian book to Paulinus of Nola; see 'Das kampanische Messbuch als Vorläufer des Gelasianum: ist der hl. Paulinus von Nola der Verfasser?', *Sacris erudiri*, 12 (1961), pp. 2–111. See also Bullough, 'Alcuin and the kingdom of heaven', p. 168, on the supposed Boniface connection.

[46] A hymn in the Antiphonary of Bangor has been attributed to Columbanus' pen by M. Lapidge; see 'Columbanus and the "Antiphonary of Bangor" ', *Peritia*, 4 (1985), pp. 104–16.

[47] See, for example, P. O'Connor, 'St Columbanus' Society. The modern disciples of the saint', in *Mélanges Columbaniens. Actes du congrès international de Luxeuil 20–23 juillet 1950*, Associations des amis de St Columban de Luxeuil (Paris, nd), pp. 413–16.

evidence suggests not.[48] Three different mass books were produced in approximately the first half of the eighth century by the Paris basin affinity – the Vatican Gelasian, the *Missale Francorum*, and *Missale Gallicanum vetus* – which does not suggest the promotion of any one usage. Books like these, which all contain Roman material and Frankish prayers and rituals, probably provide a better guide to Anglo-Saxon practice than the more purely Roman Gregorian sacramentary.

These Frankish books date from a period of liturgical creativity before the circulation of standardized mass books. Moreton has argued that liturgical handbooks did not take the form of sacramentaries before the second half of the eighth century, but collections of prayers and individual mass-sets were circulated. The three 'Roman' sacramentaries – the Leonine, Gelasian, and so-called Eighth-Century Gelasian books – draw upon these in different ways, their redactors re-editing gtheir source-material to suit their own purposes.[49]

Liturgical uniformity is a will o' the wisp, much sought after but vanishing before it can be grasped. The untidiness of much of the Anglo-Saxon evidence would accord nicely with Moreton's model since the extant manuscript fragments contain prayers which cannot be sourced and formulae in unique combinations.[50] Did unity with Rome lie only in the eyes of its Anglo-Saxon beholders? Or did it lie not so much in the texts which preoccupy modern scholars, but elsewhere, in other aspects of liturgical celebration,[51] for example, in the chronological synchronism of the liturgical year with that celebrated in Rome?

University of York

---

[48] J. Guérout, 'S. Fare', and 'Faremoutiers', in *Dictionnaire d'histoire et de géographie ecclésiastiques*, 16 (Paris, 1967), pp. 505–31, 534–5. J. Guérout, in *L'abbaye royale Notre Dame de Jouarre*, 2 vols (Paris, 1961), 1, pp. 1–67; Dierkens, 'Prolégomenes', pp. 381–2.

[49] M. B. Moreton, 'Roman sacramentaries and ancient prayer traditions', *Studia patristica*, 15 (1984), pp. 577–80.

[50] See, for example, Siffrin's analysis of the Christmas and St Stephen masses in the Regensburg Fragment, 'Zwei Blätter', pp. 11–14.

[51] See the extremely valuable comments in Hen's chapter (pp. 19–30) on uniformity of practice in liturgical matters.

# UNITY AND DIVERSITY IN THE CAROLINGIAN CHURCH

by ROSAMOND McKITTERICK

With their steady series of conquests during the eighth century, adding Alemannia, Frisia, Aquitaine, the Lombard kingdom in northern Italy, Septimania, Bavaria, Saxony, and Brittany to the Frankish heartlands in Gaul, the Carolingians created what Ganshof regarded as an unwieldy empire.[1] Was the Carolingian Church unwieldy too? Recent work, notably that of Janet Nelson, has underlined not only the political ideologies that helped to hold the Frankish realms together, but also the practical institutions and actions of individuals in government and administration.[2] Can the same be done for the Church? Despite the extraordinary diversity of the Carolingian world and its ecclesiastical traditions, can it be described as a unity? What sense of a 'Frankish Church' or of 'Frankish ecclesiastical institutions' can be detected in the sources?

One possibility might be within a missionary context. What did Frankish missionaries offer to new converts? Would Christian evangelists preaching the Gospel and establishing the faith in pagan regions also bring the particular versions of texts approved at home? In the eighth century, there were no prescribed approved texts. Anglo-Saxon missionaries such as Boniface and Willibrord, working in areas already Christianized, appeared simply to have used what was to hand, though the texts they provided for their own work, as we shall see, may have been influential at a local level. In the Christianization of Moravia, on the other hand, we might be able to observe the introduction of either the approved Carolingian reform texts or, at the least, liturgical texts perceived to be Frankish and western. The subject is still being debated, but the philological indications are in

---

[1] F. L. Ganshof, *Frankish Institutions under Charlemagne*, trans. Bryce and Mary Lyon (New York, 1968).

[2] For example, Janet L. Nelson, *Politics and Ritual in the Early Middle Ages* (London, 1986); *Charles the Bald* (London, 1992); 'Literacy in Carolingian government', in Rosamond McKitterick, ed., *The Uses of Literacy in Early Mediaeval Europe* (Cambridge, 1990), pp. 258–96; and 'Kingship and empire in the Carolingian world', in Rosamond McKitterick, ed., *Carolingian Culture: Emulation and Innovation* (Cambridge, 1994), pp. 52–87.

favour of some Frankish input in the early ninth century, with 'Old Church Slavonic' translations, before the creative period under the Byzantine missionaries Cyril and MeMhodius from the 860s onwards.[3] The earliest remnant of Old Church Slavonic in the 'Kiev leaflets', for example, gives some indication that the original Sacramentary on which the prayers in the surviving fragments were based was a text similar to Padua, Biblioteca Capitolare, MS D47, namely the priest's Sacramentary of the old Gregorian type favoured by the Emperor Lothar in his palace chapel, rather than the *Hadrianum* with Supplement promoted by Charlemagne and his advisers. Thus, although it is impossible to demonstrate direct Frankish or insular influence on the earliest Slavic manuscripts, it does look as if the early Christianization of Moravia introduced texts in use in parts of the Frankish empire even if they were not necessarily those politically approved. When the Byzantine missionaries Cyril and Methodius arrived they did not at first wish, as far as one can judge, to make too radical a departure from existing, western and Frankish, Christian practice in the areas in which they worked. Only gradually was a recognizably eastern and Byzantine liturgy introduced, translated into Old Church Slavonic and written in the new Glagolitic alphabet created for the purpose. Nevertheless, the outcome was that the Moravian Church was thereafter oriented eastwards in its liturgy and ritual and ceased to have any ecclesiastical association with the West. The turning away from the political influence of the Franks on the part of the Moravian rulers Rastislav and Svatopluk complemented this.[4]

---

[3] A clear statement of the issues is to be found in A. P. Vlasto, *The Entry of the Slavs into Christendom* (Cambridge, 1970), but the important discussions of the detail are A. Dostál, 'The origins of the Slavonic liturgy', *Dumbarton Oaks Papers*, 19 (1965), pp. 67–88, and an assessment of Dostál's paper in light of the subsequent two decades' investigations in Dostál's *Festschrift* by Henrik Birnbaum: 'On the eastern and western components of the earliest Slavic liturgy: the evidence of the *Euchologium Sinaiticum* and related texts', in T. G. Winner, ed., *Essays in the Area of Slavic Languages, Linguistics, and Byzantology: A Festschrift in Honor of Antonin Dostál on the Occasion of his Seventy-Fifth Birthday, Byzantine Studies/Études Byzantines*, 8, 11, 12 (1981, 1984–5), pp. 25–44. See also Ihor Ševčenko, 'Report on the Glagolitic fragments (of the Euchologium Sinaiticum?) discovered on Sinai in 1975 and some thoughts on the models for the make up of the earliest Glagolitic manuscripts', in Ihor Ševčenko, *Byzantium and the Slavs in Letters and Culture* (Cambridge, Mass., 1991), pp. 617–50.

[4] See Jonathan Shepard, 'Slavs and Bulgars', in Rosamond McKitterick, ed., *The New Cambridge Medieval History, II: 700–900* (Cambridge, 1995), pp. 228–48. I am very grateful to Jonathan Shepard for his guidance on the Moravian mission.

Liturgy in this context becomes a symbol of unity and affiliation. It is for this reason that I propose to look at the question of
the liturgy, and especially the mass, more closely as a means of
determining the degree to which there may have been unity
within the apparent diversity of the Carolingian church.[5]

From the reign of Pippin III, king of the Franks (741–68), onwards,
statements concerning the organization and ritual of the church
within the Frankish realms of western Europe reveal a preoccupation with correctness, authority, and concord with the holy see. In
the *Admonitio generalis* of 789, for example, it is stressed how terrible
is the sentence of anathema which strikes those who dare presumptuously to contravene the decrees of the universal councils; the
bishops are warned to guard themselves against it, and, conforming
to the provisions of the canons, may rather be thought worthy to
attain the eternal joys of peace.[6] Only the canonical books and
catholic treatises, and the words of holy authors, are to be read and
expounded.[7] The bishops are to make sure that the priests preach
rightly and worthily, and are not to be allowed to invent anything,
or preach to the people new or non-canonical things which come
from their own imagining and are not in conformity with sacred
scriptures.[8] Sunday observance is enjoined upon all the people: 'As
my father of noble memory also ordered in his conciliar edicts,
manual labour is not to be carried out on the Lord's day. . . .
Rather, people are to assemble from all quarters at the church for
the solemnities of the Mass, and to praise God for all the good
things which he rendered us on that day.'[9]
    Further, Charlemagne and his advisers stressed that chant
should be in accordance with what 'our father of blessed memory, King Pippin, strove to bring to pass when he abolished the
Gallican chant for the sake of harmony (*unanimitas*) with the
apostolic see and the peaceful concord (*concordia*) of God's holy
church'.[10]

---

[5] I also hope to provide a wider context for the important contributions to the subject of the liturgy
in the early Middle Ages made by Yitzhak Hen and Catherine Cubitt, above, pp. 19–30 and 45–57.
[6] *MGH Cap*, I, no. 22, c. 60, p. 57; translation by P. D. King, *Charlemagne. Translated Sources* (Kendal,
1986), p. 214.
[7] Ibid., c. 78, p. 60; trans. King, p. 218.
[8] Ibid., c. 82, p. 61; trans. King, p. 219.
[9] Ibid., c. 81, p. 61; trans. King, pp. 218–19.
[10] Ibid., c. 80, p. 61; trans. King (I have modified it slightly), p. 218.

The wide diffusion of the *Admonitio generalis* and related decrees, the sending out of royal *missi* to inspect whether notice was being taken of all matters concerning Christian conduct covered by the capitularies,[11] and the ample evidence for successful efforts on the part of bishops, abbots, clergy, and lay magnates to consolidate the Christian faith, reorganize the administration of the church, and enforce seemly clerical behaviour among the clergy,[12] might appear to indicate that unity of law, administration, and ritual was not only required but also swiftly established within the Frankish Church. Certainly the calls in Carolingian royal legislation as well as synodal decrees for conformity to authoritative texts can actually be balanced, both by the recording of the provision of such texts as were recommended, and by surviving manuscripts witnessing to their production and dissemination.

It is in the examination of the detail of the production and dissemination of the new recommended and authorized texts, however, set beside the continued production of older works, that we rapidly become disabused of the notion that any uniformity of canonical and monastic observance, liturgical rites, or Bible texts was attained in the Frankish kingdoms in the eighth and ninth centuries.

The recommendation of the Rule of St Benedict in the reforming councils of both Carloman and Pippin III, and its subsequent reiteration in the 'Reform Councils of 813',[13] for example, is associated with the request by Charlemagne to the abbot of Monte Cassino for a copy of Benedict's autograph version of the Rule and the sending of the so-called *Aachener Urexemplar* from which the earliest surviving copy of the original text of the Rule, St Gallen, Stiftsbibliothek, MS 914, was made.[14] Despite the promotion of the Rule of Benedict by the Emperor

[11] *MGH Cap*, I, no. 33 ( 02), c. 40, p. 98.

[12] R. McKitterick, *The Frankish Church and the Carolingian Reforms, 789–895* (London, 1977).

[13] *MGH Conc*, II. 1, no. 1, c. 7, p. 4; no. 2 c. 1 p. 7; no. 11, p. 60, lines 19–20.

[14] Ludwig Traube, *Textgeschichte der Regula Sancti Benedicti*, Abhandlungen der Königlichen Akademie der Wissenschaften, philo.-philol.-, und hist.- Klasse, 25 (Munich, 1910), and *Theodemari abbatis Casinensis epistula ad Karolum regem*, ed. Kassius Hallinger and Maria Wegener, *Corpus consuetudinum monasticarum*, 1 (Siegburg, 1963), pp. 157–75. Compare Jean Neufville, 'L'authenticité de l'*Epistula ad regem karolum de monasterio sancti Benedicti directa et a Paulo dictata*', *Studia monastica*, 13 (1971), pp. 295–310, and Josef Semmler, 'Benediktinisches Mönchtum in Bayern im späten 8. und frühen 9. Jahrhundert', in Eberhard Zwink, ed., *Salzburg Diskussionen. Frühes Mönchtum in Salzburg* (Salzburg, 1983), pp. 199–218.

Louis the Pious in 816/817, the subsequent inspections of monasteries by the imperial *missi*, and apparent rewards meted out to those who agreed to live according to the Rule, it is clear that Benedictine monasticism remained simply part of the plethora of responses to the monastic life and was not, at least in the eighth, ninth, and tenth centuries, predominant.[15]

Royal promotion of a particular corrected text of the Gospels was as determined as the promotion of the Rule of Benedict. It has been established that successive attempts were made at the Frankish royal court under Charlemagne, Louis the Pious, Lothar, and Charles the Bald to produce an approved edition of the four Gospels and their accompanying material, with what appear to be successive Frankish adjustments in the originally Roman arrangement of the *Capitulare evangeliorum*.[16] The court edition of the Gospels, moreover, exerted considerable influence, even though it differed from the Tours redaction. The latter formed part of the major revision of the Bible carried out by Alcuin at Tours which in its turn was part of a general effort to produce a correct text of the Bible rather than an official text produced at Charlemagne's command.[17] A rival, and far more scholarly, edition was carried out by Theodulf of Orleans,[18] and Fischer's work has established that other enterprises for the revision of the Bible were undertaken at such centres as Corbie, Lorsch, and

---

[15] For example, Synod of Mainz 813, *MGH Conc*, II. 1, preface, pp. 259–60; Josef Semmler, 'Zur Überlieferung den monastischen Gesetzgebung Ludwigs des Frommen', *Deutsches Archiv für Erforschung des Mittelalters*, 16 (1960), pp. 309–88; 'Studien zum *Supplex Libellus* und zur anianischen Reform in Fulda', *Zeitschrift für Kirchengeschichte*, 69 (1958), pp. 268–98; and 'Corvey und Herford in der benediktinischen Reformbewegung des 9. Jhts', *Frühmittelalterliche Studien*, 4 (1970), pp. 289–319. For grants by Louis the Pious to St Amand and Landevennec on acceptance of the Rule of Benedict, see M. Bouquet, *Recueil des historiens des Gaules et de la France*, 24 vols (Paris, 1869–80), 6, pp. 530–1, 513–14; compare Rosamond McKitterick, *The Frankish Kingdoms under the Carolingians, 751–987* (London, 1983), pp. 109–24.

[16] Wilhelm Koehler, *Karolingische Miniaturen*, II, *Die Hofschule Karls des Grossen* (Berlin, 1958). For a discussion of these attempts in the context of royal patronage see Rosamond McKitterick, 'Royal patronage of culture in the Frankish kingdoms under the Carolingians: motives and consequences', in *Committenti e produzione artistico-letteraria nell'alto medioevo occidentale*, Settimane di Studio del Centro Italiano di studi sull'alto medioevo, 39 (Spoleto, 1992), pp. 93–129, reprinted in McKitterick, *Frankish Kings and Culture in the Early Middle Ages* (Aldershot, 1995), ch. VII.

[17] Bonifatius Fischer, 'Bibeltext und Bibelreform unter Karl dem Grossen' in B. Bischoff, ed., *Karl der Grosse. Lebenswerk und Nachleben II: Das Geistige Leben* (Düsseldorf, 1965), pp. 156–216, and 'Bibelausgaben des frühen Mittelalters', *La Bibbia nell'alto Medioevo*, Settimane di Studio del Centro Italiano di studi sull'alto medioevo, 10 (Spoleto, 1963), pp. 519–600.

[18] E. Dahlhaus-Berg, *Nova antiquitas et antiqua novitas. Typologische Exegese und isidorianisches Geschichtsbild bei Theodulf von Orleans* (Cologne, 1973).

Metz. The Tours Bible has achieved undue prominence in terms of modern historians' perceptions of the influence of its corrected text. In fact, it appears that there were nearly as many versions and amalgamations of Vulgate, *Vetus Latina*, and other old Latin texts, arrangements of the books, and subsidiary matter as there are centres of book production, though the distinctive Tours Bible format had many emulators.[19] Diversity of Bible texts consulted, cited, and produced, with many different responses to the need for a correct Bible text, rather than unity, therefore, was the consequence of the Carolingian stress on correct texts of scripture.[20] It is to be observed throughout the Carolingian period.[21]

Closely related to the question of Bible texts was that of the Homiliaries. Charlemagne in his letter to the Lectors of 786 deplored the variety of Homiliaries then in use. He reported that a recommended version had been compiled, at his behest, by Paul the Deacon:

> We are no less concerned to embellish [all the churches of the Gauls] with a series of readings of great excellence. . . . We long ago accurately corrected, God helping us in all things, all the books of the Old and New Testaments, corrupted by the ignorance of copyists. . . . [We] discovered, that despite correct intentions, the readings compiled for the night office by the fruitless toil of certain men were by no means suitable, inasmuch as they were set out without the names of the authors and abounded with the distortions of innumerable errors, and . . . we charged Paul the Deacon . . . with the completion of this task. He has read through the treatises and sermons of the various catholic fathers, culled all the best things and offered us two volumes of readings suitable for each separate festival throughout the whole course of the year and free from

---

[19] Fischer, 'Bibeltext'.

[20] In, for example, the *De litteris colendis* and the *Admonitio generalis: MGH Cap*, I, no. 29, p. 79 and no. 22, c. 72, p. 60.

[21] Rosamond McKitterick, 'Carolingian Bible production: the Tours anomaly', in R. Gameson, ed., *The Early Medieval Bible. Its Production, Decoration and Use*, Cambridge Studies in Palaeography and Codicology, 2 (Cambridge, 1994), pp. 63–79.

errors. Having examined the text of all these with our perceptive judgement, we confirm the said volumes by our authority and deliver them to your righteousness to be read in Christ's churches.[22]

Certainly thereafter there are copies of the Homiliary of Paul the Deacon to be found all over the Frankish empire, but, as Grégoire has made clear, copies of a great many other homiliaries and collections of homilies by single patristic authors, notably those of Gregory the Great, and many by Carolingian authors, continued to be copied and used during the ninth century.[23] Carolingian sermons and homiliaries in particular also exerted an influence outside the Frankish realms in Anglo-Saxon England.[24] The situation is no less complex as far as penitential practice[25] and canon law is concerned. As early as 774, Charlemagne had received from Pope Hadrian the *Dionysio-Hadriana*, an updated version of the *Dionysiana* collection of the sixth century. A selection of canons from the *Dionysio-Hadriana*, deemed particularly 'necessary', was incorporated into the *Admonitio generalis* of 789,[26] but its subsequent impact on Frankish canon law appears to have been muted and its authority continued to be contested by older collections, such as the *Vetus Gallica, Sanblasiana, Hispana,*

---

[22] *MGH Cap*, I, no. 30, pp. 80–1, trans. King, p. 208.

[23] Reginald Grégoire, *Les Homéliaires du Moyen Age*, Rerum ecclesiasticarum documenta, Series maior, Fontes VI (Rome, 1956) and *Homéliaires liturgiques médiévaux. Analyse des manuscrits*, Biblioteca di studi medievali (Spoleto, 1980); Henri Barré, *Les Homéliaires Carolingiens de l'école d'Auxerre*, Studi e Testi, 225 (Vatican City, 1962); for discussion see McKitterick, *Frankish Church*, pp. 80–114.

[24] Milton McC. .atch, *Preaching and Theology in Anglo-Saxon England: Aelfric and Wulfstan* (Toronto, 1977) and James E. Cross, *Cambridge Pembroke College MS 25*, King's College, London Medieval Studies, 1 (London, 1987).

[25] Raymund Kottje, *Die Bussbücher Halitgars von Cambrai und des Hrabanus Maurus*, Beiträge zur Geschichte und Quellenkunde des Mittelalters, 8 (Berlin, 1980); idem, 'Erfassung und Untersuchung der frühmittelalterlichen kontinentalen Bussbücher. Probleme und Aufgaben einen Forschungsprojektes an der Universität Bonn', *Studi Medievali*, 26 (1985), pp. 941–50; Rob Meens, *Het tripartite boeteboek. Overlevering en betekenis van vroegmiddeleeuwse biechtvoorschriften* (Hilversum, 1994); Ludger Körntgen, *Studien zu den Quellen der frühmittelalterlichen Bußbücher*, Quellen und Forschungen zum Recht im Mittelalter, 7 (Sigmaringen, 1993); Franz Kerff, *Der Quadripartitus. Ein Handbuch der karolingischen Kirchenreform*, Quellen und Forschungen zum Recht im Mittelalter, 1 (Sigmaringen, 1982); Günter Hägele, *Das Paenitentiale Vallicellianum I. Ein oberitalienischer Zweig der frühmittelalterlichen kontinentalen Bußbücher*, Quellen und Forschungen zum Recht im Mittelalter, 3 (Sigmaringen, 1984).

[26] *MGH Cap*, I, no. 22, preface, p.p53; trans. King, p. 210.

*Quesnelliana*, and the original *Dionysiana*, throughout the ninth century.[27]

Like Constantine before him, Charlemagne had urged the observance of Sunday as a day of rest and Christian worship, but he had also urged harmony and concord with the holy apostolic see of St Peter. Although only limited progress was made in establishing one designated text or set of texts for particular aspects of Christian education and worship, the most sustained effort to achieve uniformity was arguably the promotion of what was perceived, by some Franks at least, as the Roman liturgy.

The mass texts and prayers for the other rites of the Church during the liturgical year were gathered together in Sacramentaries, with separate collections, *Ordines*, which contained the descriptions of, and instructions for, the rituals to accompany all the prayers. In the tenth century these two books were combined into one, a Pontifical. Every surviving Sacramentary and volume of *Ordines* was designed for a particular church or group of churches. All vary from each other and thus liturgical uniformity is not in evidence; different rites from various periods and places co-existed in liturgical books everywhere. Even when new collections were formed, as in the tenth century, these were from the older familiar materials. This enables us to see individual response to far greater an extent than in other kinds of evidence; the decisions these individuals have in common, or in which they differ, moreover, tell us much about the communications and differences between different areas, as well as the ideals they held in common. Further work is needed to establish exactly what these were, but some preliminary remarks on the

---

[27] J. Hartzheim, ed. *Collectio-Dionysio-Hadriana*, Concilia Germania, 1 (Cologne, 1759), pp. 131–5; on the seventy-one manuscripts of the *Dionysio-Hadriana* known in 1870, mostly of ninth- and tenth-century date, see Friedrich Maassen, *Geschichte der Quellen und der Literatur des canonischen Rechts im Abendlande bis zum Ausgange des Mittelalters* (Graz, 1980), pp. 441–4; H. Wurm, *Studien und Text zur Dekretalsammlung des Dionysius Exiguus*, Kanonistische Studien und Texte, 16 (Bonn, 1939, reprinted Amsterdam, 1964); P. Fournier and G. Le Bras, *Histoire des collections canoniques en occident. Depuis les Fausses Decretales jusqu'au Decret de Gratien*, 2 vols (Paris, 1931), 1, pp. 36–7; H. Mordek, *Kirchenrecht und Reform im Frankenreich* (Berlin, 1975); Raymund Kottje, 'Einheit und Vielfalt des kirchlichen Lebens in der Karolingerzeit', *Zeitschrift für Kirchengeschichte*, 76 (1965), pp. 323–42; Rosamond McKitterick, 'Knowledge of canon law in the Frankish kingdoms before 789: the manuscript evidence', *JThs*, ns 36 (1985), pp. 97–117, reprinted in Rosamond McKitterick, *Books, Scribes and Learning in the Frankish Kingdoms, 6th–9th Centuries* (Aldershot, 1994), ch. II.

mass books may be made in order to indicate the potential richness of this category of evidence.[28]

The early Frankish books, despite the enormous range of variations, may be divided into four main types. The first among these is the *Old Gelasian*, based probably on a Roman ancestor composed *c*.628–715 but with Gallican and Frankish elements; it separates the 'Temporal', that is, the run of the main liturgical feasts of the year, from the 'Sanctoral', that is, the run of saints' days throughout the year.

The second is the *'eighth-century Gelasian'*, a Romano-Frankish rite current in the Frankish kingdoms and the later eighth century onwards. It incorporates some Gallican (that is Gallo-Roman, pre-Merovingian) saints and many specifically Gallican practices such as the Rogation days, and was designed for use by bishops and abbots. Variation is present even within a type, as is clear from Bernard Moreton's analysis of the extant manuscripts of the eighth-century Gelasian, where very different collections of *missae de devoto* were added to each book, according to what, presumably, were the perceived needs of a specific community.[29]

The third type is the *'Gregorian' sacramentary*, which amalgamates the 'Temporal' and the 'Sanctoral' into a single series of Sundays and Festivals, though sometimes having full sets of prayers for particular festivals. It was put together early in the seventh century and rapidly thereafter diffused north of the Alps in various versions, even as far west as England. Particular local additions and alterations were often made to it.

---

[28] The standard guide to the medieval liturgy, with full bibliographical details, is Cyrille Vogel, *Medieval Liturgy. An Introductcon to the Sources*, translated and revised posthumously by William Storey and Niels Rasmussen (Washington DC, 1986). It is an updated version of Vogel's *Introduction aux sources de l'histoire du culte chrétien au moyen âge* (Spoleto, 1981). For an inventory of the manuscripts see Klaus Gamber, *Codices liturgici latini antiquiores*, 2nd edn (Fribourg, 1968). See also the invaluable exposition by Eric Palazzo, *Le Moyen Age des origines au XIIIe siècle. Histoire des livres liturgiques* (Paris, 1993), which forms an admirable complement to Vogel's handbook, and McKitterick, *Frankish Church*, pp. 113–54. On the *Ordines*, the best edition is M. Andrieu, *Les 'Ordines Romani' du haut moyen âge*, Spicilegium sacrum Lovaniense, 11, 23, 24, 28, 29 (Louvain, 1931–61). See also A.-G. Martimort, *Les 'Ordines', les ordinaires et les cérémoniaux*, Typologie des sources du moyen âge occidental, fasc. 56 (Turnhout, 1991).

[29] Bernard Moreton, *The Eighth-Century Gelasian Sacramentary: a Study in Tradition* (Oxford, 1976); 'The *liber secundus* of the eighth-century Gelasian sacramentaries: a reassessment', in E. A. Livingstone, ed., *Studia Patristica*, XIII, Texte und Untersuchungen zur Geschichte der altchristlichen Literatur, 116 (Berlin, 1975), pp. 382–6. Later examples of the eighth-century Gelasian are Zürich, Zentralbibliothek, MS C43, made 1020–30, and the so-called Missal of Monza, Monza, Biblioteca capitolare, codex F1–101 from Bergamo, s. IX/X.

Finally, there is the most important of these Gregorian sacramentaries, the revised version known as the *Hadrianum*. It is a
late eighth-century version of the Gregorian sacramentary designed for papal use and sent by Pope Hadrian to Charlemagne
as a gift sometime between 784 and 791. In the Frankish kingdoms, Benedict of Aniane corrected and reorganized it and
added a Supplementum containing all the prayers lacking in the
*Hadrianum*, such as those for half the Sundays, a funeral service,
votive masses and extra blessings. Benedict himself worked from
the older Frankish versions of sacramentaries available to him,
'Old Gelasian', 'Frankish-Gelasian', and 'Gregorian'. He did so
with the acknowledgement that 'there were other prayers in use
but which the Holy Father had omitted [from the *Hadrianum*]
because he knew they had already been approved by other
people.' Benedict goes on to stress in his preface to the *Hadrianum*, explaining what he has done:

> Those who find these prayers dear and familiar will be able
> to use them to pay their vows to the Lord and to offer him
> divine worship in a pleasing and worthy manner. Readers
> may be assured that we have inserted nothing in this book
> except the careful compositions of authors of the highest
> reputation for virtue and learning. We have collected many
> items from many authors to serve the needs of all.[30]

Thus the result was an amalgam of current late eighth-century
Roman prayers, older practice understood to be Roman, and
Frankish/Gallican texts.[31] All manuscripts deriving from the
original *Hadrianum* bear the heading: *ex authentico libro bibliothecae
cubiculi scriptum*.[32] The Sacramentary of Bishop Hildoard of Cam-

---

[30] Benedict of Aniane, *Hucusque* preface to his Supplement to the *Hadrianum*, which he regards as
'obviously the work of the blessed pope Gregory' and refers users to the Gregorian sacramentary if
they do not like what he has added in the supplement: R. Amiet, 'Le prologue *Hucusque* et la table
des *Capitula* du Supplément d'Alcuin', *Scriptorium*, 7 (1953), pp. 177–209, but see the revised edition
in Jean Deshusses, *Le sacramentaire grégorien: ses principales formes d'après les plus anciens manuscrits*, 3 vols,
Spicilegium Friburgense, 16, 24, 28 (Fribourg, 1971, 1979, 1982), 1. For the translation, see Vogel,
*Medieval Liturgy*, pp. 87–8.

[31] See Pope Hadrian to Charlemagne, *Codex Carolinus*, Ep. 89, *MGH Epistolae merov. et karol. aevi*, 1
(Hanover, 1892) p. 626; Deshusses, *Le sacramentaire grégorien* and Vogel, *Medieval Liturgy*, pp. 78–92.

[32] On the implications of this and other Roman books brought to Francia see Donald Bullough,
'Roman books and Carolingian renovatio', *SCH*, 14 (1977), pp. 23–50, reprinted in Donald
Bullough, *Carolingian Renewal. Sources and Heritage* (Manchester, 1991), pp. 1–38.

brai, for example (Cambrai, Bibliothèque Muninipale, MS 164 (*olim* 159), fols 35v–203), was wrirten at Cambrai in 811 or 812 and made for that bishop. Lest it should be assumed that Hildoard can be held up as an example of a bishop who promoted the *Hadrianum*, it should be noted that he is thought also to have commissioned the Sacramentary of Gellone (Paris, Bibliothèque Nationale, MS latin 12048), a Sacramentary of the eighth-century Gelasian type. Other surviving manuscripts of the *Hadrianum* add material from the Gelasian Sacramentaries.[33]

The revised *Hadrianum* with Benedict's Supplement did not replace the existing mass books. Choice of which book to adopt in any church clearly rested with the individual. In the Emperor Lothar's palace chapel at Aachen, for example, an earlier stage of Gregorian sacramentary which had been a Roman priest's mass book (as distinct from one for use by a pope like the *Hadrianum*) was used known as the Gregorian Type II (Padua, Biblioteca Capitolare, MS D47).[34] The so-called Sacramentary of Trent was a mass book compiled at Salzburg between 825 and 830, using the seventh century Gregorian, the *Hadrianum* and Supplement, the Frankish Gelasian, and the votive masses composed by Alcuin. At St Amand, successive editions were made of the *Hadrianum* which integrated the Supplement of Benedict of Aniane into the body of the sacramentary and were prepared for different churches – Rheims, Sens, St Denis, Noyon, Chelles – on commission. This adaptation was necessitated in part by one of the most important reasons for liturgical variation in mass books, namely, the accommodation of the local patron saints. These represent the efforts on St Amand's part (at a stage when its abbots were closely dependant on royal patronage) to provide some kind of authoritative text of the liturgy. Certainly there were no complaints about the variations in usage on the part of the recipients, yet there are indications, from the uniform format and the type of 'export-quality' script house style chosen for the texts, that St Amand was indeed promoting a particular set of Mass texts in the latter part of the ninth century, based on the

---

[33] Vogel, *Medieval Liturgy*, p. 82.

[34] Wilhelm Koehler and Florentine Mütherich, *Karolingische Miniaturen IV. Die Hofschule Lothars. Einzelhandschriften aus Lothringen* (Berlin, 1982), and see also Rosamond McKitterick, 'Carolingian uncial: a context for the Lothar Psalter', *The British Library Journal*, 16 (1990), pp. 1–15, reprinted in McKitterick, *Books, Scribes and Learning*, ch. 6.

*Hadrianum* originally recommended by Charlemagne, just as Tours had tried to promote a particular text and arrangement of the Bible.[35] As will be noted below, St Amand had originally preferred the mixed Gelasian type. St Amand's subsequent promotion of the integrated *Hadrianum*, therefore, represents a major alteration of liturgical policy on the part of that centre, and arguably of the centres which commissioned the mass books from St Amand. This is a valuable instance of the Frankish heartlands promoting the officially approved mass book, and spreading its use within the ecclesiastical provinces of Rheims and Sens.[36] The St Amamd mass books also reflect, however, in the limited range of their distribution, the continued diversity of liturgical usage within the Frankish kingdoms and the apparent impossibility of imposing an unchanging standard text.

One further category of evidence, apart from the mass books and *Ordines*, still not fully exploited for what it might reveal of both attitudes to the mass and particular mass texts and the degree of unanimity among the authors, is the plethora of commentaries on the mass produced in the ninth century.[37]

In the later eighth- and early ninth-century redactions of the liturgy, a major concern appears to have been the re-establishment of Roman usage, or, at least, what was understood to be Roman usage. Yet local tastes and affection for particular rites and prayers remained strong. What even this small selection of sacramentaries demonstrates, furthermore, is that there was a variety of sacramentaries sent or acquired from Rome, worked over in the Frankish kingdoms for particular purposes, which subsequently had influence of their own on later redactions.

---

[35] J. Deshusses, 'Chronologie des grands sacramentaires de Saint-Amand', *RB*, 87 (1977), pp. 230–7, and Rosamond McKitterick, 'Carolingian book production: some problems', *The Library*, 12 (1990), pp. 1–33, reprinted in McKitterick, *Books, Scribes and Learning*, ch. XII.

[36] On the earlier St Amand usage exported to Salzburg see below, p. 79. A further factor in the promotion of the Gregorian type of sacramentary represented by the *Hadrianum* may have been its association with a pope, and with not only Gregory but Hadrian as well. As Ann Freeman has demonstrated, Hadrian was held in particular respect by the Carolingians: 'The end of Carolingian orthodoxy', *Viator*, 16 (1985), pp. 65–108.

[37] For example, Florus the Deacon, *De expositione missae*, *PL*, 119, cols 16–72; Ratramnus of Corbie, *De corpore et sanguine domini*, *PL*, 121, cols 103–71, and J. N. Bakhuizen van den Brink, ed., *Ratramnus De corpore et sanguine domini. Texte original et notice bibliographique* (Amsterdam and London, 1974). Amalarius of Metz, ed. J. Hanssens, *Amalarii episcopi opera liturgica omnia*, 3 vols, *Studi e Testi*, 138, 139, 140 (Rome, 1948–50), however, is not representative, and needs to be set against all the other major and minor commentaries from the Carolingian period, many of them scattered throughout the *Patrologia Latina*.

Further, there were the lectionaries or Epistolary and Evangeliary, containing the Epistles and Gospels for the liturgical year, and sometimes a book containing both, known as the Mass Lectionary. (Sometimes the word *pericopes* is used for this book, though strictly speaking this refers to the book, chapter, and verse for each reading, not the text for the reading itself.) Lectionaries demonstrate the greatest local diversity in the arrangement and selection of texts throughout the Middle Ages. These variations and the eventual imposition of stability in 1570 (when the system chosen was in fact a Romano-Frankish one from the Carolingian period) have yet to be charted.[38] The *Antiphonary* was the collection of antiphons or texts based on stichs (a verse selected from scripture and combined with other materials) provided for the psalms and canticles of the daily Office. It was amended and corrected during the reign of Louis the Pious by Amalarius of Metz. Other books were those connected with liturgical chant, such as the Responsaries, Tropers, Sequentiaries, and Hymnaries or Hymnals, and those containing texts used during the mass or in other ceremonies, such as the episcopal Benedictionals[39] and martyrologies.

Liturgical chant further highlights the role of individual bishops (and abbots) and the intensely local adaptation of the texts and the melodies to accord with local cults and local composition. In the late Merovingian and Carolingian periods, just as a hybrid Roman rite had been created by mixing Roman liturgical texts with earlier indigenous Frankish material, so indigenous Gallican musical traditions were also combined with what was understood to be Roman music, in order to create a distinctive liturgical chant commonly known as 'Gregorian'. Crucial contributions to the development of western liturgical music were made in the early Carolingian period, not only with the concerted efforts to promote musical harmony, if not actual uniformity, within the Frankish Church on the part of Charlemagne and Louis the Pious, but also in the all-important

---

[38] Vogel, *Medieval Liturgy*, pp. 291–355; see also Palazzo, *Le Moyen Age*, pp. 163–72, and A.-G. Martimort, *Les Lectures liturgiques et leurs livres*, Typologie des sources du moyen âge occidental, fasc. 64 (Turnhout, 1992).

[39] For example, Robert Amiet, ed., *The Freising Benedictionals, Munich, Bayerische Staatsbibliothek, Cod. lat. 6430*, Henry Bradshaw Society, 88 (London, 1974).

proliferation of musical notations and the expansion of the chant repertoire.[40]

The Carolingian attempts to suppress non-Roman rites in areas they had conquered, such as northern Italy and Septimania, had not met with complete success, most notably in Spain and Italy, where the Old Spanish and the Milanese rites were still current. England was in any case separate in the ninth century, though in the tenth, as a result of the close connections formed within the context of the establishment of Benedictine monasticism in England, there is a clear association between English and Frankish liturgical developments in both the public liturgies of the cathedral and other churches, and the monastic offices. 'Non-Roman' rites such as the 'Celtic rite' in use in Ireland, the Ambrosian or Milanese rite which remained current in parts of northern Italy even into the eleventh century, and the 'Mozarabic' and 'Old Spanish' liturgies, nevertheless played some role in the compilations of the Frankish kingdoms as well, and cannot themselves be said to be completely separate from the Roman-Frankish texts.[41]

Despite efforts to attain liturgical uniformity, indeed, the variety of rite throughout Europe by the end of the ninth century was, if anything, even greater than it had been two centuries earlier, with indigenous traditions heartily preserved. The liturgical evidence from the tenth and early eleventh centuries illustrates how this great local diversity was maintained; what had originally been received from Rome was returned to Rome in the course of the tenth and early eleventh centuries, greatly transformed, with much that was either Gallican or Frankish incorporated.

So far I have written in general terms, with the implication that there is little to distinguish between one area of the Frankish empire and another. It may be helpful to consider one area in detail, and one, moreover, that had an existing ecclesiastical

---

[40] For exposition, interpretation and bibliography see Susan Rankin, 'Carolingian music', in R. McKitterick ed., *Carolingian Culture: Emulation and Innovation* (Cambridge, 1994), pp. 275–316; see also M. Huglo, *Les Livres de chant liturgiques*, Typologie des sources du moyen âge occidental, fasc. 52 (Turnhout, 1988).

[41] This is particularly evident once one explores the musical repertory: see Richard L. Crocker and David Hiley, eds, *The Early Middld Ages to 1300, The New Oxford History of Music*, 1 (Oxford, 1990), especially Kenneth Levy, 'Latin chant outside the Roman tradition', pp. 69–110.

tradition before its incorporation into the Frankish empire. I turn, therefore, to Bavaria. The example of Bavaria may illustrate the extent to which the ecclesiastical organization and liturgical observance of the Frankish heartlands were extended into or emulated within more peripheral areas.[42] Although far from isolated from Frankish developments and influence, it was not until the final humiliation of Duke Tassilo and the formal annexation of the region in 788 by Charlemagne that Bavaria was incorporated into the Frankish empire. It is necessary to determine, therefore, whether there is any evidence to suggest that the Carolingian political takeover also entailed changes in usage and cultural orientation on the part of the Bavarian Church as well as the degree to which that Church had been open to Frankish ecclesiastical influence through non-political channels, long before the formal annexation. Bearing in mind the specific recommendations in the Carolingian capitularies, discussed above, concerning the types of liturgical, biblical, and legal texts to be used in the churches, is there any sign of Bavarian churches producing the required texts and conforming to the stipulations of the ruler and his clerical and lay advisers? Is there, in short, a practical reflection of the promotion of unity?

The Christianization of Bavaria was complete by the beginning of the eighth century, though much still needed to be done in terms of organization and the provision of training for new priests.[43] Although parts of Bavaria, notably the area of the old Roman province of Noricum, show many traces of Christianity, the firm establishment of dioceses and monasteries was primarily due to the work of Frankish and Irish missionaries under Agilolfing ducal patronage in the seventh century. Due to the links with Italy established on the marriage of the Bavarian Catholic princess Theodelinda to the king of the Lombards, there were many

---

[42] Saxony would also serve as a useful area to examine, in that Christianity and ecclesiastical organization were introduced there primarily by the Franks. A study of the ecclesiastical development of Saxony from the later eighth to the tenth centuries is in preparation.

[43] See Gottfried Mayr, 'Frühes Christentum in Baiern', and Wilfried Hartmann and Heinz Dopsch, 'Bistümer, Synoden und Metropolitanverfassung', in Hermann Dannheimer and Heinz Dopsch, eds, *Die Bajuwaren von Severin bis Tassilo 488–788* (Salzburg, 1988), pp. 281–6, 318–26; K. Reindel, 'Die Bistumsorganisation im Alpen-Donau-Raum in der Spätantike und im Frühmittelalter', *Mitteilungen des Instituts für Österreichische Geschichtsforschung*, 72 (1964), pp. 277–310 and F. Prinz, *Frühes Mönchtum im Frankenreich*, 2nd edn (Darmstadt, 1985).

Italian contributions to Bavarian Christian life. In 716 Duke Theodo sent his famous request to the pope for further assistance with the consolidation of ecclesiastical organization in Bavaria.[44] Similarly, thirty years later, Duke Odilo supported a brief period of interference and determined and effective, if partial, reorganization on the part of Archbishop Boniface of Mainz.[45]

If we pursue the notion of unity or diversity in relation to specific Christian texts known or introduced into Bavaria at a particular time, the difficulty of providing exact dating of the palaeographical evidence unfortunately makes it impossible to be precise in more than a few instances. The question of Bavaria's distinctiteness in the Agilolfing or pre-Carolingian period of its history can be explored a little, however, in relation to Freising in the days of Corbinian (a Frankish missionary who died c.730), and the Bavarian Arbeo of Freising (bishop from 764 to 784); that is, in the period shortly before Bavaria's cathedrals and monasteries were apparently overtaken by Carolingian educational principles and norms.[46] Only at Freising is there much by way of manuscript witness from the pre-Carolingian period and thus the means of assessing change. A Gospel Lectionary in seventh-century north Italian cursive, written by the scribe Valerian and customarily associated with Corbinian, may not have had any connection with him (though it appears to have been in Freising from a very early date),[47] but Bishop Erimbert (739–48), who took office at the time of the Bonifacian reorganization, can be associated with a volume of the homilies of Caesarius of Arles.[48]

In the preoccupations of Freising's book production in the first two periods of the scriptorium's activity identified by Bernhard Bischoff, namely under Bishop Arbeo from 764 to 784, and in

---

[44] *Liber Pontificalis*, ed. L. Duchesne (Paris, 1886), section 179, p. 398; see the discussion by T. F. X. Noble, *The Republic of St Peter. The Birth of the Papal State 680–825* (Philadelphia, 1984), pp. 26–7.

[45] Wilhelm Levison, *England and the Continent in the Eighth Century* (Oxford, 1946), pp. 78–80 and Ian Wood, *The Merovingian Kingdoms, 450–751* (London, 1993), pp. 404–9.

[46] G. Baesecke, *Der deutsche Abrogans und die Anfänge des deutschen Schrifttums* (Halle, 1930).

[47] Munich, Bayerische Staatsbibliothek, MS Clm 6224, and E. A. Lowe, *Codices Latini Antiquiores 1–9* + Supplement (Oxford, 1935–1971) [hereafter *CLA*], 9, p. 1249, and see Bernhard Bischoff, *Die südostdeutschen Schreibschulen und Bibliotheken in der Karolingerzeit: 1, Die Bayrischen Diözesen*, 3rd edn (Wiesbaden, 1974), 2, *Die vorwiegend Österreichischen Diözesen* (Wiesbaden, 1980), at 1, pp. 59 and 135.

[48] Munich, Bayerische Staatsbibliothek, MS Clm 6298, *CLA*, 9, p. 1264, and Bischoff, *Die südostdeutschen Schreibschulen*, 1, pp. 59 and 141.

the years of Atto's rule from 784 until 811/12, it can be seen that in general terms there was much in the pre-Carolingian Freising libraries which showed them to be in sympathy with every other pre-Carolingian ecclesiastical establilhment in western Europe at the time; with a greater preponderance of texts by Gregory the Great (the Homilies on Ezekiel and on the Gospels, and the *Moralia in Job*), Jerome, and Isidore of Seville in particular. A striking change thereafter, in periods III and IV under Bishops Hitto (811/12–36), Erchanbert (836–54), Anno (854–75), Arnold (875–83), and Waldo (883–906) is the growing concentration, in Freising at least, not only on contemporary authors, but also on the works of Augustine. In the specific provision of canon law and the Homiliary, moreover, a rapid response to Carolingian recommendations is reflected.[49]

In 789, as mentioned above, the *Dionysio-Hadriana* had been recommended as the authoritative collection of canon law, and from 786 or so Charlemagne encouraged the use of the Homiliary compiled by Paul the Deacon. To the first two periods of Freising's book production period, and in the time of Arbeo or the very early years of Atto's rule, can be set the production of Munich, Bayerische Staatsbibliothek, MS Clm 6243, the so-called *Canones Frisingenses*, long accepted, because of its largely Roman and papal content, as a probably Roman compilation of the late fifth or early sixth century.[50] Even if this be the case, the manuscript compilation as a whole, into which the *Collectio Frisingensis* is incorporated, is to be attributed to the initiative of Arbeo or Atto themselves.[51] The *Collectio Frisingensis* comprises the canons of the eastern councils of the fourth century in the Isidorean version, fragments of papal correspondence from the period between Damasus I and Gelasius I, a series of texts on the Acacian schism, and a collection of the letters of Pope Celestinus primarily concerned with the Council of Ephesus. The inclusion

[49] Bischoff, *Die südostdeutschen Schreibschulen*, 1 and 2.

[50] Maassen, *Geschichte der Quellen und der Literatur*, pp. 476–86.

[51] See A. Schnargel, 'Die kanonistische Sammlung der Handschrift von Freising', in J. Schlecht, ed., *Wissenschaftliche Festgabe zum zwölfhundertjährigen Jubiläum des heiligen Korbinian* (Munich, 1924), pp. 126–46, who noted the separate nature of the so-called Gelasian *Decretum*, but did not comment on the production of the manuscript as a whole. His remarks are confined to the *Collectio Frisingensis*; Fournier and Le Bras, *Histoire des collections canoniques*, 1, p. 25

of the so-called Gelasian decretal (*De libris recipiendis et non recipiendis*) in the manuscript has been thought to confirm the Roman origin of the compilation. If I am right in my argument for the context and origin of this text being *c.*700 in Frankish Burgundy or Picardy,[52] however (quite apart from the fact that other eighth-century Bavarian and Frankish synodal material is included), then the original assumptions about this manuscript reflecting the north Italian and Roman affiliations of Freising are no longer valid. Freising's connections with northern and eastern Francia are suggested not only by the contents of the *Collectio Frisingensis* codex, but also by other books in its early library, notably the copy of Gregory's *Moralia in Job* in Laon a-z script.[53] Even if not actually compiled at Freising itself, the copying of this set of ancient canons, as useful a collection as the original *Dionysiana*, witnesses to an effort on the part of the bishop to equip himself with the canon law he needed for this work. To the next episcopate, however, that of Hitto (811/812–36), is dated the production within the episcopal scriptorium of the recommended Carolingian collection of canon law, the *Dionysio-Hadriana*. It survives in two copies,[54] and would appear to indicate that the diocese of Freising at least toed the line as far as prescriptions from the ruler were concerned.

Further, whereas in periods I and II of the Freising scriptorium the homilies produced were those of Gregory the Great,[55] it is again in period III under Bishop Hitto that no less than three copies of Paul the Deacon's Homiliary were produced,[56] together with two Lectionaries and copies of contemporary texts, episcopal benedictions, and the like. There seems little doubt that the production of the texts, recommended in the *Admonitio generalis* and subsequent capitularies as a means of promoting some degree of uniformity of practice, can be recognized in this pattern of production. It is reinforced by the fact

---

[52] Rosamond McKitterick, *The Carolingians and the Written Word* (Cambridge, 1989), pp. 202–4.

[53] See the discussion by Josef Semmler, 'Zu den bayrisch-westfränkischen Beziehungen', *Zeitschrift für bayerische Landesgeschichte*, 29 (1966), pp. 372–85.

[54] Munich, Bayerische Staatsbibliothek, MSS Clm 6242 and 6355.

[55] At neighbouring Tegernsee the Homiliary attributed to Alanus (Munich, Bayerische Staatsbibliothek, MS Clm 18092) was copied.

[56] Munich, Bayerische Staatsbibliothek, MS Clm 6264a, Bamberg Staatliche Bibliothek, MS B.I.3, and a fragment in Linz, Studienbibliothek, MS 612: Bischoff, *Die südostdeutschen Schreibschulen*, 1, pp. 107–8.

that in the Munich manuscript, Bayerische Staatsbibliothek, MS Clm 6242, which contains the text of the *Admonitio generalis* as well as the *Dionysio-Hadriana*, the clauses enjoining uniformity of practice are particularly noted by an early ninth-century annotator at Freising itself.[7]

At Regensburg, the bishop was also the abbot of the monastery of St Peter and St Emmeram, founded *c*.700. The oldest fragments associated with Regensburg were imports, and even in the last third of the eighth century some of the manuscripts associated with Regensburg indicate connections with not only eastern France but also northern Italy. Soon after the mid-eighth century the earliest Regensburg books were produced with strong signs of insular influence in the script, probably under Bishop Simpert (768–91). Even after the loss of Bavaria's independence, Regensburg remained the administrative centre, and Charlemagne himself made a number of visits there in the 790s, not least for the 792 Assembly and a major discussion of the Adoptionist issue.

It might be thought likely, therefore, that any bishop of Regensburg after 788 would have been particularly concerned to promote Carolingian ecclesiastical policies. The manuscript evidence does not, however, support this. Certainly, Munich, Bayerische Staatsbibliothek, MS Clm 14468, written in 821, is a collection of orthodox manifestoes against Adoptionism, commissioned by Bishop Baturich. Baturich, moreover, presided over the most productive period of the Regensburg scriptorium when it was stocking the library with patristic theology and exegesis, such as we find in most Carolingian libraries of the period in large quantities. The Regensburg library also imported texts from elsewhere. But there is not, in the extant evidence at least, a strong indication of the acquisition of precisely those texts that had been recommended in the Carolingian legislation of Charlemagne. An example is the acquisition of the original *Dionysiana* rather than of the *Dionysio-Hadriana*. One copy of the *Dionysiana* at Regensburg, written *c*.800,[58] came from southwest Germany or Switzerland and the other, dated to the second half

[57] McKitterick, *Frankish Church*, p. 39.
[58] Munich, Bayerische Staatsbibliothek, MS Clm 14517.

of the ninth century,[59] was written in a north Italian style and was possibly also carried into the Moravian mission field at some stage (it has Old Church Slavonic glosses). A further instance of local choice is the Homiliary of Alanus, also copied under Baturich.[60]

If we wish to determine whether the Frankish annexation of 788 made a difference liturgically, we may be on firmer ground. From the Agilolfing period survive not only fragments of an older Gallican Sacramentary written in 'Irish' half uncial of c. 700 but also three bifolia which Gamber suggests are the remains of a Gelasian mass book presented by Boniface to Bishop Gaubald on the occasion of the reorganization of the diocese in 739. The leaves were written in Northumbria but undoubtedly used in Regensburg.[61] In this survival pattern Gamber sees successive changes, with the so-called Irish-Gallican text (the contribution of Emmeram) being replaced by a Gelasian Sacramentary by Boniface in 739.[62] Further, a Gelasian sacramentary, with some distinctive prayers and therefore different from the so-called Boniface Sacramentary, now in Prague (Prague, Knihovna kapituly, MS O LXXXIII, fols 1–120),[63] was also probably used in Regensburg. Gamber even wished to assign it to a ducal scriptorium producing books required in Tassilo's chapel and to see, in effect, both books as instances of Agilolfing liturgical separatism before the introduction of Carolingian norms.[64] What remains in doubt, however, is the degree to which such norms were in fact successively introduced. Work on the Hadrianized Gregorian texts is by no means complete, but it seems so far that Bavaria's

---

[59] Munich, Bayerische Staatsbibliothek, MS Clm 14008.

[60] Munich, Bayerische Staatsbibliothek, MS Clm 14368.

[61] Munich, Bayerische Staatsbibliothek, MS Clm 14429 (palimpsested) (CLA, 9, p. 1298), and Berlin, Deutsche Staatsbibliothek, MS Lat. fol. 877+ Regensburg, Gräflich Walderdorffsche Bibliothek, MS (sn) + Regensberg, Bischöflichen Zentralbibliothek, MS Cim. 1 (CLA, 9, p. 1052). Klaus Gamber, 'Liturgiebücher der Regensburger Kirche aus der Agilolfinger und Karolingerzeit', Scriptorium, 30 (1976), pp. 3–25 and compare Bischoff, Die südostdeutschen Schreibschulen, 1, pp. 183–4, 243 and 2, p. 235.

[62] CLA, VIII, 1052 and Klaus Gamber, ed., Das Bonifatius Sakramentar und weitere frühe Liturgiebücher aus Regensburg mit vollständigen Faksimile des erhaltenen Blätter, Textus patristici et liturgici, 12 (Regensburg, 1975).

[63] A. Dold and L. Eizenhofer, Das Prager Sakramentar, 1 (Beuron, 1944) and 2 (Beuron, 1949) and CLA, X, 1563.

[64] Gamber, 'Liturgiebücher', but compare Bischoff, Die südostdeutschen Schreibschulen, 2, pp. 258–61, who thinks the evidence pointing to both Bavarian and north Italian influence is insufficiently conclusive for a precise location.

reception of the *Hadrianum* was as mixed as elsewhere in the Frankish kingdoms.[65]

If Freising affords us a glimpse of the intellectual, and limited liturgical, reorientation of the Bavarian church in the aftermath of the Carolingian declarations of aims and objectives, Bavarian book production in the scriptoria of the region's cathedrals and monasteries as a whole, so meticulously examined by Bischoff, illustrates how the Frankish renewal of education, morality, and religious education was extended into Bavaria.[66] In this the work of Arno, Archbishop of Salzburg, was crucial.[67] He created a model scholar's library at Salzburg, and was probably the principal means by which Carolingian aims were introduced to the Bavarian church. Previously Abbot of St Amand and a close friend of Alcuin, Arno was in a strong position to act as conduit for Carolingian aims and intellectual preoccupations. The library built up under his aegis, comprising both home-produced and imported volumes, is an impressive array of standard patristic theology, with the major early medieval authors, including Bede and Alcuin himself, though far less comprehensive than that of Freising. As far as liturgical matters were concerned, moreover, it would appear from such manuscripts produced in Arno's time as Paris Bibliothèque Nationale, MS latin 2296 and the Sacramentary now represented by a number of scattered fragments,[68] that the preferred Sacramentary at St Amand in the early ninth century, namely the mixed Gelasian, was the one Arno brought with him to Salzburg.[69] Subsequently in Salzburg, a fresh mass book was compiled from the Gregorian, Gelasian, and *Hadrianum* Sacramentaries.[70] In canon law, similar independence is manifest, for Munich, Bayerische Staatsbibliothek, MS Clm 5508 includes on fols 131–213 a possibly direct copy of the canon law collection in Munich, Bayerische Staatsbibliothek

---

[65] Vogel, *Medieval Liturgy*, pp. 90–1, and notes 221, 232 and 233.

[66] Bischoff, *Die südostdeutschen Schreibschulen* 1 and 2.

[67] On the early development of Salzburg in the Agilolfing and early Carolingian period under Rupert, Virgil and Arno, see Zwink, *Salzburg Diskussionen*.

[68] Sieghild Rehle, *Sacramentarium Gelasianum mixtum von St Amand*, Textus patristici et liturgici, 10 (Regensburg, 1973); idem, *Sacramentum Arnonis, Die Fragmente der Salzburger Exemplars*, Textus patristici et liturgici, 8 (Regensburg, 1970). See also M. B. Parkes, *The Medieval Manuscripts of Keble College, Oxford* (Oxford, 1979), p. 335 and plate 174, and Bischoff, *Die südostdeutschen Schreibschulen*, 2, pp. 101, 127.

[69] On St Amand's later ninth-century liturgical preferences see above, p. 70.

[70] See above, p.69, on the Sacramentary of Trent, and Vogel, *Medieval Liturgy*, pp. 97–102.

Clm 6243, namely the *Collectio Frisingensis*. Other collections of surviving canon law from Salzburg, such as Salzburg, St Peter's Stiftsbibliothek, fragm. a XII 25/22, indicate that the original *Dionysiana* rather than the *Dionysio-Hadriana* was used.

The Carolingian reforms therefore prompted the introduction of many new texts into Bavaria, but in liturgical and legal matters there was no dramatic changeover. Instead old ways, and thus diversity, were maintained, albeit sometimes in new combinations. It is also clear that even before the final annexation of Bavaria, Frankish influence was already reaching Bavaria. This is particularly manifest in the palaeography of the manuscripts, though the major developments in the Bavarian forms of Caroline minuscule and book production were undoubtedly after 788. The Bavarian evidence has shown clearly, moreover, that there might be unity of ritual within a diocese, possibly even a province, but rarely over the whole extent of the Frankish realms. Although it might be argued that the Bavarian experience might have been different from other regions within the Carolingian empire, the evidence of the liturgy, even though far from comprehensively investigated, let alone understood, indicates that liturgical uniformity was not established anywhere. This is the case, as we have seen with the limited adoption of the Rule of Benedict, Homiliary of Paul the Deacon, corrected texts of the Bible emanating from the court, the *Dionysio-Hadrianum*, and the *Hadrianum*, as much in the Frankish heartlands as on the peripheries of the empire.

Individual efforts by bishops in compiling a sacramentary to suit them, from the material available, for the purposes of their own diocesan ministry, were the most important impetus for liturgical production. It was an individual freedom determined by practical necessity, for the required new, authoritative texts could not be produced overnight, nor could exemplars of the correct texts be disseminated so rapidly as to mean instant compliance with wishes expressed in the assemblies and synods of ecclesiastical and lay magnates. New books in any case were expensive to produce.[71] Vogel has suggested that a further consideration was the prestige of older liturgical codices,[72] while

---

[71] On the costs of book production in the ninth century see McKitterick, *Carolingians and the Written Word*, pp. 135–64.

[72] Vogel, *Medieval Liturgy*, p. 92.

attachment to current practice as well as loyalty to local saints and observances undoubtedly played a role.

Diversity in some respects, therefore, was a pragmatic consequence of the particular circumstances and modes of production of the Carolingian world. Such circumstances were recognized even in the recommendation of the *Dionysio-Hadriana* in the *Admonitio generalis* where Charlemagne stated that he had 'seen fit to indicate certain articles that you may apply yourselves to recalling' but also suggested that the bishops could use 'whatever others you know to be necessary'. It is surely this pragmatism that is behind the early Carolingian lack of specific recommendations, other than to '*canones*' or '*regula*'.[73] Yet we should acknowledge the degree to which the Capitularies themselves are setting up a unity of purpose and practice in the kingdom. It is diversity within a certain overall Frankish way of doing things and canon of texts, some of which are perceived as Roman. There was a distinct party within the Church that was anxious to oppose diversity in liturgical observance and introduce a standard text; but it was a party probably originating in Aquitaine in the circle of Louis the Pious with, as we have seen, limited overall influence.[74]

That there were other perceptions of a need for unity, namely those linked with the sense of identity and the sense of a Christian past, is clear from the surviving texts discussed in this paper.[75] In many of the contexts in which we can observe a sense of preoccupation with unity, it is unity with the see of St Peter that is of the greatest importance, even for the Frankish church itself. What brought the Christian churches within the Frankish realms together and what had they in common? The answer might be their ecclesiastical organization into dioceses headed by bishops and served by priests; the institution of monasticism; and, for the laity, the keeping of Sunday as a holy day as well as the major feasts of the Christian year. For those under direct Frankish rule, moreover, it was the use of the Latin language for worship. Yet

---

[73] Compare, for example, the Capitulary of Herstal, *MGH Cap* I, no. 20, cc. 1, 3 and 4, p. 47; the Synod of Frankfurt, c. 53, *MGH Cap* I, no. 28, p. 78; or the General capitulary for the *missi* of 802, cc. 10 and c. 13, *MGH Cap* I, no. 33, p. 93.

[74] McKitterick, *Frankish Church*, pp. 132–3.

[75] Space precludes discussion of these aspects of the topic here but I hope to develop them elsewhere.

within these overarching unities there was, as we have seen, enormous, rich, and continually creative diversity. It is apposite here to recall the passage from the *Admonitio generalis* I citet at the outset of this paper, in which Charlemagne, following his father's lead, expressed the wish that Roman chant in the correct form be learnt for the sake of harmony with the apostolic see and the peaceful concord of God's holy Church.[76] As Karl Morrison has observed in his discussion of Carolingian music, concord, not unity, is the prevailing aesthetic category for Carolingian intellectuals, with 'the polarities of concord and discord normative and pervasive throughout Carolingian literature'.[77] The understanding of music in the Carolingian world was that concord was unison, not unity. Hucbald of St Amand, writing about music at the end of the ninth century, observed that concord could not come from a soloist. It came, rather, from two (or more) entirely different voices singing at the same time and at the mathematical intervals Hucbald defined as 'consonances'.[78] The notes, writes Hucbald, 'will blend with an altogether pleasant and harmonious sweetness, as though the sound were one and single'.[79] It is the musical analogy that best helps us to understand how the diversity within the Carolingian Church was the basis of its strength.

Newnham College, Cambridge

---

[76] *MGH Cap* I, no. 22, c. 80, p. 61.

[77] Karl Morrison, ' "Know thyself ": music in the Carolingian Renaissance', in *Committenti e produzione artistico-letteraria nell'alto medioevo occidentale*, Settimane di Studio del Centro Italiano di studi sull'alto medioevo, 39 (Spoleto, 1992), pp. 369–479, at p. 380.

[78] Hucbald of St Amand, *De harmonica institutione*, ed. Martin Gerbert, *Scriptores ecclesiastici de musica*, 1 (Hildesheim, 1963), pp. 104, 105, 107 and 111, trans. Warren Babb, *Hucbald, Guido and John on Music. Three musical treatises* (New Haven, Conn., and London, 1978). For example: section 107a/3, 'Consonance is the calculated and concordant blending of two sounds, which will come about only when two simultaneous sounds from different sources combine into a single musical whole (*modulatio*), as happens when a man's and a boy's voices sound at once (*pariter*) and indeed in what is usually called making organum (*organizatio*)': trans. Babb, pp. 19 and 25.

[79] Hucbald, *De harmonica institutione*, section 111a/7, trans. Babb, p. 25.

# OTTO III'S PENANCE: A CASE STUDY OF UNITY AND DIVERSITY IN THE ELEVENTH-CENTURY CHURCH

*by* SARAH HAMILTON

In the spring of 999 the Emperor Otto III went on pilgrimage to the shrine of the Archangel Michael at Monte Gargano in southern Italy.[1] His pilgrimage was not widely recorded; it was not referred to in any of the works produced in the Empire in the next half century, and only briefly mentioned in three South Italian works.[2] But Otto's pilgrimage was described more extensively in the eleventh-century *vitae* of two saints: the anonymous Greek *Vita Nili*[3] and Peter Damian's *Vita Beati Romualdi*.[4] This article will make a case-study of the way in which the authors of these *vitae* used Otto's pilgrimage to help construct the sanctity of their own subject, and of how far this reflects the degree of unity, and of diversity, between the Greek and Latin traditions of the Church in southern Italy in the first half of the eleventh century.

Southern Italy in the tenth and early eleventh centuries was well known as an area where Greek-speakers and Latin-speakers could, and sometimes did, mix. Calabria and Longobardia were controlled directly by Byzantium which exercised a considerable, but varying, influence over the three Lombard Latin

---

[1] For the dating of this episode, see Mathilde Uhlirz, *Jahrbücher des deutschen Reiches unter Otto II und Otto III*, II: *Otto III, 983–1002* (Berlin, 1954), pp. 292–3, 534–7. Otto III's surviving charters show him to have been at Capua on 20 Feb. 999 and Benevento on 11 March 999 – *MGH Diplomatum Regum et Imperatorum Germaniae* II, nos. 309–10, pp. 735–7.

[2] The first of the South Italian accounts is eleventh-century: 'In hoc autem venit Otto tertius imperator Capuam, habiit in Gargano ad Sanctum Michaelem et revertit Romam', *Chronicon Comitum Capuae*, ed. N. Cilento in his *Italia meridionale longobarda* (Milan and Naples, 1966), p. 133. The other South Italian sources are twelfth-century: 'Rex Otto venit Beneventum, et fecit praeceptum nostro monasterio de omnibus suis rebus. Postea ivit in monte Gargano', *Annales Beneventani, MGH. SS* III, a. 997, p. 177; 'Imperator Beneventum venit, et causa penitentie quam illi beatus Romualdus iniunxerat abiit ad montem Garganum', *Chronica Monasterii Casinensis*, ed. H. Hoffmann, *MGH. SS* XXXIV, II. 24, p. 208. Hoffmann suggests that the source for this is Peter Damian's *Vita Romualdi*, c. 25, ibid. p. xiii.

[3] βιος και πολιτεια του οσιου πατρος ἡμων Νειλου του Νεου, ed. Giovanni Giovanelli (Grottaferrata, 1972), c. 91, p. 128 [hereafter *VN* ] (the *vita* is more widely available in a less accurate edition in *PG*, 120, cols 9–166; both editions follow the same chapter divisions).

[4] Peter Damian, *Vita Beati Romualdi*, ed. Giovanni Tabacco, *fonti per la Storia d'Italia*, 94 (Rome, 1957), c. 25, p. 53[hereafter *VR*].

principalities of Capua, Benevento, and Salerno, and the duchies of Amalfi and Naples.[5] Nilus was born in Rossano in Calabria in 910; a Greek-speaker, he spent his peripatetic life chiefly within southern Italy, in the Byzantine-dominated areas and also in the Latin principality of Capua.[6] Romuald, in contrast, was born to a noble Latin family in Ravenna in northern Italy in 951. Romuald himself lived a similarly peripatetic life which took him from Ravenna to the Pyrenees, Rome, Capua, and back to Ravenna.[7] Both saints visited the great centre of western monasticism, Montecassino in Capua, although there is no record that they met.[8] But their respective stays at Montecassino exemplify the high degree of contact between Latin and Greek monks in the late tenth century, especially in southern Italy.[9] Certain historians have sought to find in these contacts with the Greeks the source of Romuald's interest in eremitism, and the 'new monasticism' which swept western Europe in the eleventh and twelfth centuries, but we should not place too much reliance on this evidence.[10] Peter Damian did not mention any Greek monks in the *Vita Romualdi*. Nilus' anonymous hagiographer, by contrast, was very conscious of the differences between the Greek and Latin traditions:[11] in an important section of the *Vita Nili*, he described how Nilus and his community, housed for almost fifteen years in a monastery on the lands of Montecassino, visited the Latin community, celebrated the service in Greek in the

[5] J. Gay, *L'Italie méridionale et l'empire byzantin* (Paris, 1904), pp. 289–413; Barbara M. Kreutz, *Before the Normans. Southern Italy in the ninth and tenth centuries* (Philadelphia, 1991), pp. 118–36.

[6] *Vita di S. Nilo, fondatore e patrono di Grottaferrata*, Italian trans. with notes, ed. Giovanni Giovanelli (Grottaferrata, 1966), p. 247.

[7] *VR*, c. 5, pp. 21–5; c. 26, p. 54; c. 27, p. 57.

[8] *VN*, cc. 73–85, pp. 112–23. Bernard Hamilton raises the possibility that Romuald could have met Nilus at the monastery of S. Alessio in Rome in 'S. Pierre Damien et les mouvements monastiques de son temps', *Studi Gregoriani*, 10 (1975), pp. 175–202, reprinted in his *Monastic Reform, Catharism and the Crusades (900–1300)* (London, 1979) [hereafter *Monastic Reform*], ch. 6, p. 184

[9] Patricia M. McNulty and Bernard Hamilton, '*Orientale lumen et magistra latinitas*: Greek influences on western monasticism', *Le Millénaire du Mont Athos, 963–1963. Études et Mélanges*, 1 (Chevetogne, 1963), pp. 181–216 (*Monastic Reform*, ch. 5). Jean-Marie Sansterre, 'Saint Nil de Rossano et le monachisme latin', *Bollettino della Badia Greca di Grottaferrata*, ns 45 (1991), pp. 339–86.

[10] For a review of this historiography, with criticisms, see Marilyn Dunn, 'Eastern influence on western monasticism in the eleventh and twelfth centuries', in J. D. Howard-Johnston, ed., *Byzantium and the West c.850–c.1200. Proceedings of the XVIII Spring Symposium of Byzantine Studies*, Byzantinische Forschungen. Internationale Zeitschrift für Byzantinistik, 13 (Amsterdam, 1988), pp. 245–59.

[11] Nilus, according to his hagiographer, deliberately chose obscurity in Latin-speaking lands when he left Calabria for Capua and Rome, rather than enjoy fame in the Eastern Empire; *VN* c. 72, pp. 112–13.

monastery church, and sang a hymn which Nilus had composed in honour of St Benedict. Afterwards Nilus instructed the Latin monks in the ways of a true monk, and highlighted the differences in practice between Greek monks, followers of St Basil, and Latin monks, followers of St Benedict, on areas such as fasting on Saturday.[12] These neither were nor are important issues of theology, but they show that Nilus and his hagiographer were conscious that the Latin monks were different. Despite the theological and political ecumenism of southern Italy at this time, the differences between the two *vitae* are obvious.[13] They are written in different languages. They are the products of different monastic traditions: the *Vita Nili* makes clear that Nilus was a follower of St Basil,[14] whilst the version of Romuald's monastic rule given by Peter Damian in the *Vita Romualdi* suggests an adherence to the precepts of St Benedict.[15]

But both works were composed soon after the death of their subject as hagiographies of the founder of the community. The *Vita Nili* was probably composed soon after Nilus' death in 1004, by an anonymous member of the community Nilus founded at the end of his life at Grottaferrata, south of Rome.[16] It survives in only one manuscript from the twelfth century, and was intended for use within the community.[17] It was not translated into Latin until the sixteenth century.[18] Peter Damian wrote his life of Romuald, the founder of his order, the Camaldolese, no later than 1042, that is within fifteen years of Romuald's death.[19]

---

[12] *VN*, cc. 73–85, pp. 112–23. Olivier Rousseau, 'La Visite de Nil de Rossano au Mont-Cassin', in *La Chiesa Greca in Italia dall'VIII al XVI secolo. Atti del Convegno Storico Interecclesiale (Bari, 30 Apr.–4 Magg. 1969)*, 3 vols (Padua, 1973), 3, pp. 1111–37.

[13] For theological ecumenism see Bernard Hamilton, 'The monastery of S. Alessio and the religious and intellectual renaissance in tenth-century Rome', *Studies in Medieval and Renaissance History*, 2 (1975), pp. 265–310 (*Monastic Reform*, ch. 2). Hamilton's arguments have now been modified by Sansterre, 'Saint Nil de Rossano et le monachisme latin'. For an example of political ecumenism, see Graham Loud, 'Montecassino and Byzantium in the tenth and eleventh centuries', in Margaret Mullett and Anthony Kirby, eds, *The Theotokos Evergetis and eleventh-century monasticism*, Belfast Byzantine Texts and Translations, 6.1 (Belfast, 1994), pp. 30–55.

[14] Francesco Russo, 'Gli Ascetica di S. Basilio Magno e S. Nilo', *Atti del Congresso Internazionale su S. Nilo di Rossano. 28 settembre–1 ottobre 1986* (Rossano and Grottaferrata, 1989), pp. 307–16.

[15] Hamilton, 'S. Pierre Damien', pp. 184–9.

[16] For consideration of the authorship and dating of the *Vita Nili* see F. Halkin, 'S. Barthélemy de Grottaferrata. Notes critiques', *AnBoll*, 61 (1943), pp. 202–10.

[17] *VN*, editorial preface, pp. 31–45.

[18] *VN*, pp. 35–7.

[19] *VR*, p. liv.

The preface to this work, and its manuscript history – it survives mostly in manuscripts associated with Camaldolese houses – suggests that it was also composed principally for use by members of the monastic order he founded.[20] There is no evidence to suggest that Peter Damian knew the *Vita Nili*.

Having established that these two works are the products of two very different traditions, the Greek and the Latin, I want to examine the accounts given by the authors of each *vita* of Otto III's pilgrimage. Otto's visit to Monte Gargano is not of central importance in either text: the account takes up five out of a total of a hundred chapters in the *Vita Nili* and one out of seventy-two in the *Vita Romualdi*. Both accounts give the same background for Otto's pilgrimage – his involvement in the suppression of the rebellion in Rome in 998. This rebellion was widely reported by at least sixteen contemporary and subsequent eleventh- and even twelfth-century writers.[21] This relatively large volume of references has led several historians to focus on Otto's involvement in the events of 998, but usually as part of a wider study. The only recent exclusive study of the rebellion of 998 is that by Karl Benz, who reviewed all the sources for the rebellion and argued that those which emphasize Otto's guilt in the suppression of the rebellion were the product of a reformed monastic environment rather than an imperial monastic one.[22] He did not, however, distinguish the *vitae* as a separate genre, and this appears to be a

[20] *VR*, pp. iii–xxxiii.

[21] Chronicles: *Annales Quedlinburgenses*, *MGH.SS* III, p. 74; *Thietmari Merseburgensis Episcopi Chronicon*, ed. R. Holtzmann, *MGH.SRG* ns 9, pp. 167–9; *Annales Altahenses Maiores*, ed. E. L. B. ab Oefele, *MGH.SRG* 4, p. 16; *Lamperti Annales*, in *Lamperti Monachi Hersfeldensis Opera*, ed. O. Holder-Egger, *MGH.SRG* 38, p. 48; *Annales Hildesheimenses*, *MGH.SS* III, p. 91; *Brunwilarensis Monasterii Fundatorum Actus*, *MGH.SS* XIV, pp. 131–2; Johannes Diaconus, *Chronica Venetum*, in *Cronache Veneziane Antichissime*, ed. Giovanni Monticolo, *Fonti per la Storia d'Italia*, 9 (Rome, 1890), pp. 154–5; *Arnulfi gesta archiepiscoporum Mediolanensium*, *MGH.SS* VIII, p. 10; *Annales Beneventani*, *MGH.SS* III, p. 177; *Chronica Monasterii Casinensis*, ed. H. Hoffmann, *MGH.SS* XXXIV, p. 208; *Chronicon Romualdi II archiepiscopi Salernitani*, *Rerum Italicarum Scriptores* VII (Milana 1725), col. 165; Rodulfus Glaber, *Historiarum libri quinque*, ed. Neithard Bulst and trans. John France and Paul Reynolds, *OMT*, I.12, pp. 24–7; Adhémar of Chabannes, *Chronique*, ed. Jules Chavanon, *Collection de textes pour servir à l'étude et à l'enseignement de l'histoire*, 20 (Paris, 1897), iii, 31, p. 154. Other works: Peter Damian, *Die Briefe des Petrus Damiana*, ed. K. Reindel, *MGH. Die Briefe des Deutschen Kaiserzeit*, 4 vols (Munich, 1988), 2, no. 89, pp. 539–40; *Benzonis episcopi Albensis ad Heinricum IV imperatorem Libri VII*, *MGH.SS* XI, p. 624; *Bonizonis episcopi Sutrini liber ad amicum*, ed. E. Dümmler, *MGH. Libelli de lite imperatorum et pontificum; saeculis XI et XII conscripti* I (Hanover, 1891), pp. 582–3.

[22] Karl Benz, 'Macht und Gewissen im Hohen Mittelalter. Der Beitrag des Reformmönchtums zur Humaniserung des Herrscherethos unter Otto III', *Studia Anselmiana*, 85 (Rome, 1982), pp. 157–74.

more general omission in the work of other historians who have tended to treat the *vitae* as useful quarries for not wholly accurate information. But *vitae* are not histories, nor even biographies;[23] they are, at their simplest, compositions written with a specific purpose, to demonstrate the sanctity of their subject.[24] Two studies, by Sansterre and Phipps, have considered the problems of genre raised in each *vita* separately, but neither author examined the case of Otto's pilgrimage to Monte Gargano in detail, and no attempt, as far as I know, has been made to compare the two *vitae* and to examine the way in which the two authors portray what was, in effect, the same incident.[25]

In order to understand the account given in the *vitae* it is necessary to give a brief review of the events of the Roman rebellion.[26] In 996 Otto III came to Rome and appointed a German, his cousin Bruno, to the vacant Apostolic See. As Pope Gregory V, Bruno's first act was to crown Otto Emperor. Otto III left Rome that year and returned to Germany. Crescentius, a leading member of the Roman aristocracy, took advantage of Otto's absence to drive Gregory V away from Rome.[27] Crescentius then appointed his own candidate to the Holy See, John Philagathos, Archbishop of Piacenza. John Philagathos seems on the face of it to be an unlikely candidate as an anti-imperial anti-pope. A member of the Greek community in southern Italy, he came to notice at the court of Otto III's father, Otto II, and was appointed Abbot of the important north Italian monastery of Nonantola, Bishop of Piacenza, which was raised to a metropolitan see in his honour, and also Chancellor of Italy, as well as being godfather to Otto III himself. Sent by Otto III in 995 on a diplomatic mission to obtain a Byzantine marriage alliance, on

---

[23] For the view that hagiography should be seen as a form of historical narrative, see Felice Lifshitz, 'Beyond positivism and genre: "Hagiographical" texts as historical narrative', *Viator*, 25 (1994), pp. 95–113.

[24] 'Au moyen âge, écrire la vie d'un saint n'est pas raconter son histoire; c'est faire son éloge, et ce sont là deux tâches différentes', Jean Leclercq, *Saint Pierre Damien, ermite et homme d'église*, Uomini e dottrine, 8 (Rome, 1960), p. 17.

[25] Jean-Marie Sansterre, 'Les Coryphées des apôtres, Rome et la papauté dans les *vies* des Saint Nil et Barthélemy de Grottaferrata', *Byzantion*, 55 (1985), pp. 516–43; Colin R. Phipps, 'Saint Peter Damian's Vita Beati Romualdi: Introduction, Translation and Analysis' (London University Ph.D. thesis, 1988).

[26] This account is based on the version given in the various chronicles referred to at n.21 above.

[27] Teta E. Moehs, *Gregorius V 996–999: A Biographical Study*, Päpste und Papsttum, 2 (Stuttgart, 1972), pp. 42–3.

his return to Rome in 997, he accepted Crescentius' invitation to become Pope John XVI, but his reign was shortlived.[28] Otto III returned in the spring of 998 and within six weeks of his arrival in Rome had restored imperial control: John Philagathos was multilated – his ears, nose, and tongue were cut off, and his eyes put out – and led around Rome sitting backwards on an ass in a parade of humiliation. He was then exiled to Germany where he died in 1013.[29] Crescentius, on the other hand, was executed.

Superficially the accounts given by the two hagiographers of the circumstances behind Otto III's penitential pilgrimage to Monte Gargano could not be more different. The *Vita Nili* was written first and gives an Italo-Greek gloss on events. According to his hagiographer, Nilus, on learning of Philagathos' mutilation, journeyed to Rome to intercede for him. He had an audience with the Emperor and the Pope in which he condemned their behaviour towards their godfather, and asked that he be given custody of Philagathos. Otto III wept on hearing Nilus' condemnation and promised to grant his request, but Gregory V obstructed this plan by leading Philagathos in a parade of humiliation around Rome, removing any possibility of his entering Nilus' custody.[30] Nilus saw Philagathos' treatment as a personal injury to both himself and to God, cursed the Emperor, and left Rome without Philagathos, to pray at his monastery. His prayers were answered. Gregory V died, and Otto III, according to the hagiographer, 'proclaimed that he repented (μετανοια); he went on foot from Rome to the incorporeal commander-in-chief at Gargano'.[31]

This account should be understood within the context of the precepts of St Basil, the guiding father of Greek monasticism. St Basil ordained that tears are one of the 'fruits' necessary for true repentance.[32] Otto, by weeping, demonstrated repentance. But he failed to correct his sin, and compounded it by allowing Gregory to humiliate Philagathos further. St Basil in his 'Shorter Rules' cited Proverbs 26.11, with reference to a man who

---

[28] Ibid., pp. 59–60.

[29] *Annales necrologici Fuldenses*, MGH.SS XIII, p. 210.

[30] *VN*, cc. 89–90, pp. 126–7.

[31] *VN*, c. 91, p. 128.

[32] Basil the Great, *The Morals*, PG, 31, iii, col. 701; idem. *The Shorter Rules*, PG, 31, xiv, col. 1092.

professes that he repents but does not correct himself, likening him to a dog which returns to its vomit.[33] This rule explains why Nilus cursed the Emperor and abandoned Rome, returning to his monastery. Otto was hateful because he had failed truly to repent. Basil's 'Longer Rules' provide a possible further dimension for Nilus' behaviour, for Basil decreed that, if a member of the community is persistently disobedient, he should be cut off.[34] On his return from Gargano Otto visited Nilus at his monastery at Serperi, and offered him a monastic site, which Nilus refused.[35] Otto offered him anything he wanted. Nilus replied that he only wanted the salvation of Otto's soul: 'Even if you happen to be emperor, you have to die as one of mankind and come to judgement, and give an account of the good and evil deeds you have done.'[36] The Emperor was moved to tears by this, and placed his crown in the hands of the saint, and received his blessing.[37] This episode should also be seen in its Basilian context. The hagiographer does not mention that Otto was reconciled or absolved. Instead he was met by Nilus 'with all humility and reverence', his previous curses forgotten, because Otto's act of pilgrimage demonstrated that he had repented, and Basil taught, after Luke 15.6, that he who truly repents should be received with joy.[38] For Basil, forgiveness depends on obedience, and Otto by acknowledging both his sin, through penance, and Nilus' authority, had demonstrated such obedience.[39]

Peter Damian, writing later, provides a different view of these events.[40] He describes the Rome revolt briefly. Crescentius rebelled against the King [i.e. Otto III], and fled to Sant'Angelo, where he was besieged by the King. Tammus, one of the King's men, on the King's orders, promised Crescentius a safe conduct. Crescentius was thus deceived into giving himself up and through pressure from the Pope suffered capital punishment. Afterwards, to compound his sin, Otto accepted Crescentius' wife as a concubine. Tammus confessed his sin to Romuald and

---

[33] Basil the Great. *The Shorter Rules*, PG, 31, vi, col. 1085.
[34] Basil the Great. *The Longer Rules*, PG, 31, xxviii, col. 988.
[35] *VN*, c. 92, p. 128.
[36] *VN*, c. 93, p. 129.
[37] Ibid.
[38] *The Shorter Rules*, viii, col. 1088.
[39] Ibid., xv, col. 1092.
[40] *VR*, c. 25, pp. 52–4.

on his advice became a monk. Otto then followed his example and 'confessed the same sin to the blessed man, (and) for the sake of penance (*paenitentiae causa*) proceeded with bare feet from the city of Rome and continued in that way to St Michael's Church, Monte Gargano'.[41] He then stayed all Lent with Romuald in the monastery of St Apollinaris at Classe, where he undertook various penitential acts. He promised Romuald that he would relinquish the Empire and become a monk.

This much shorter account is, perhaps, easier to follow because it fits into the more familiar patterns of Latin hagiography. The Emperor, like Tammus, confessed his sin, and undertook penance in the form of pilgrimage and penitential acts: he fasted, sang psalms, wore a hair shirt, and slept on rushes which were uncomfortable.[42] This last reference comes from the *Vitae Patrum*; Otto is compared to the rich man who humbled himself, although he failed to reach the extremes of other ascetics in the desert who had less far to travel in abandoning worldly comforts.[43] This reference therefore introduces Otto's promise to become a monk at the end of the chapter by implicitly comparing him to one of the Desert Fathers.

The anonymous author of the *Vita Nili* attributes Otto's penitential act to his guilt at the treatment of Philagathos, and the authority of St Nilus, whilst Peter Damian attributes the same act to Otto's treatment of Crescentius, and the authority of St Romuald. The Greek author sides with the Greek victim, the Latin author with the Latin victim. Despite the factual differences in the accounts by the two authors, their approaches to the subject are very similar. They both view Otto as guilty of the same sin, perjury: he broke his word. This is not explicit in the *Vita Nili*. Nilus is represented there as having told Otto, through his emissary, after he learnt of Philagathos' humiliating parade through Rome, to 'Go away! Know this, just as you did not feel sympathy or show mercy to the man whom God had put into your hands, He who is in heaven will deal similarly with your sins.'[44] Nilus' curse is not surprising in the context of the *vita*. Nilus is

---

[41] Ibid., p. 53.

[42] 'lecto etiam fulgentibus palliis strato, ipse in storia de papiris compacta tenera delicati corporis membra terebat.' Ibid., p. 54.

[43] Pelagius, *Verba Seniorum*, PL, 73, x. 76, cols 925–7.

[44] *VN*, c. 91, pp. 127–8.

not presented as a pleasant, merciful saint but as a powerful, even vengeful, agent of God. The wording of the speech the hagiographer gives to Nilus suggests that the saint is angry because Otto had reneged on a promise, to hand over Philagathos into his care, which the hagiographer shows was given in a public forum. The sin of perjury is made explicit in the *Vita Romualdi*. Peter Damian wrote that Tammus was held 'to be a participant in the fraud (*fraudis conscius*) and guilty of perjury (*periurio . . . obnoxius*)',[45] and was thus told by Romuald to relinquish the world and become a monk, which he did. Although Tammus was held to be specifically guilty of perjury, for he spoke the promise to Crescentius in the knowledge that it would be broken, Otto was implicated in his guilt, for Tammus acted on Otto's orders. Guilt belongs not only to the one who commits the sin but also to the one who orders it to be committed.[46] It is this sin, amongst others, we must presume, which Otto subsequently confessed to Romuald. One of the canon law penalties for perjury at this time is that the sinner should become a monk, as Otto promised to do.[47] Further confirmation of the nature of Otto's sin might be seen to come from the fact that Crescentius was buried in the church of S. Pancrazio, outside the walls of Rome; as Gregorovius noted, St Pancras is the patron saint against oath breakers.[48]

The language used by both authors to refer to Otto suggests that each deliberately included the incident to promote the sanctity of his respective saint. The *Vita Nili* describes Otto as βασιλευς throughout its account; he is not referred to by name. βασιλευς can mean king, but it is usually used to mean emperor. It would therefore appear that Nilus' hagiographer recognized Otto's imperial title, unlike members of the Byzantine court: Leo, the Metropolitan of Synades and Syncellos, the Byzantine ambassador in Rome at the time of Crescentius' rebellion and its suppression, in his letters back to Byzantium reserved the title of βασιλευς for the Byzantine emperor, and

---

[45] *VR*, c. 25, p. 53.

[46] The most popular canon law collection of the eleventh century, *c*.1020, Burchard of Worms' *Decretum*, contains several canons to this effect, e.g. *PL*, 140, xix, c. 5, cols 954–5.

[47] Ibid., col. 956.

[48] Ferdinand Gregorovius, *History of the City of Rome in the Middle Ages*, trans. Mrs G. W. Hamilton, 2nd edn, 8 vols (London, 1900–9), 3, p. 433.

merely referred to Otto by name.[49] But Nilus' hagiographer had cogent reasons for recognizing Otto's imperial title. One theme of the *Vita Nili* is the superiority of spiritual over secular authority. His hagiographer wrote that Nilus was viewed with honour and glory not only by Christian kings, *principes*, patriarchs, and pontiffs from within and outside Byzantium, but also by infidel tyrants.[50] Nilus' encounter with Otto III comes as the culmination of a series of victorious encounters with secular authority; Eupraxius, prefect of Calabria, for example, became a monk on his deathbed at Nilus' instigation.[51] Abara, widow of Pandulf, Prince of Capua, sought his advice for her involvement in murder; she rejected the advice, but the outcome which the saint had ordained came to pass.[52] There are several other instances of Nilus' powers of prophecy,[53] a sign of sanctity taken from the early monasticism of the Desert Fathers.[54] The account of Otto's encounter with Nilus therefore embodies two major themes of the *vita*, the superiority of the spiritual to the secular life, and the saint's powers of prediction, as God's agent. The account demonstrates the saint's importance, by showing his superiority over not only local princes, but also the Emperor. Whilst the account comes at the end of the life, fitting into the chronology of Nilus' own life, it also fits the structure of the *vita*, by culminating in a demonstration of the saint's superiority over the man who was the highest secular authority in the region.

Peter Damian used Otto's penitential encounter with Romuald in a similar way. He too did not refer to Otto by name, but as *rex*, in the first half of the account, in which he dealt with Tammus' relations with Otto – how Tammus, as an intimate of Otto, conducted the siege, including perjury, on Otto's orders, and finally was released by him to become a monk. As soon as Peter Damian began to describe Otto's relations with Romuald,

---

[49] J. Darrouzès, *Épistoliers Byzantins du X<sup>e</sup> siècle*, Archives de l'orient Chrétien, 6 (Paris, 1960), no. 12, p. 175.

[50] *VN*, c. 14, p. 62.

[51] *VN*, c. 53, pp. 95–6.

[52] *VN*, c. 79, pp. 117–18.

[53] *VN*, c. 9, pp. 54–8; c. 52, pp. 54–5; c. 72, pp. 111–12; c. 85, p. 123.

[54] Rita Masullo, 'La *Vita de San Nilo* come testo biografico e narrativo', in *Atti del Congresso Internazionale su S. Nilo di Rossano. 28 settembre – 1 ottobre 1986* (Rossano and Grottaferrata, 1989), pp. 463–75.

he identified Otto as *imperator*.[55] One should not make too much of this; for elsewhere he referred to Otto as *rex* when describing his relations with Romuald.[56] By referring to Romuald's authority over the man with the highest secular authority, Peter Damian, like Nilus' hagiographer, sought to demonstrate the superior spiritual power of his saint. Otto's promise of monastic conversion is merely one of Romuald's conversion-encounters with lay noblemen. The Emperor represented Romuald's biggest 'catch' amidst other laymen of position and power, including Peter Orseolo, ex-Doge of Venice, Count Oliba of Gaul, Tammus, and the son of the duke of the Poles.[57] Romuald's hagiographer was also, as we have seen, influenced by the *Vitae Patrum*. Like Nilus, his saint had powers of prophecy: Romuald predicted Otto's death.[58] Peter Damian drew attention to this influence not only with verbal reminiscences, but also by duplicating actual incidents: for example, Romuald chased a demon from his cell as Anthony did in the *Life of Anthony*.[59]

It has long been recognized that both works are historically inaccurate. Peter Damian appears to have fused Tammus' involvement in the siege of Tivoli in 1001 with Crescentius' Roman rebellion of 997–8.[60] He also omitted John Philagathos from his account of the rebellion, but this was not through ignorance; in a letter of 1062 he mentioned John of Piacenza who invaded the apostolic see and was mutilated by the crowd.[61] Philagathos' omission was deliberate; it was not necessary to Peter Damian's argument. The *Vita Nili*'s claims to historical accuracy are more sound; for example, its account of the humiliation parade of Philagathos through Rome is described in much greater detail in a contemporary letter by the Byzantine envoy Leo.[62] But Mathilde Uhlirz has demonstrated that Otto must have visited Serperi before he went on to Gargano.[63] These inconsistencies, amongst

---

[55] *VR*, c. 25, p. 53.

[56] For example, *VR*, c. 23, p. 49; c. 27, p. 56; c. 30, p. 66. He also described Otto as *imperator* when mentioning his relations with Crescentius' wife, p. 53.

[57] *VR*, c. 5, pp. 21–5; c. 11, pp. 32–3; c. 26, pp. 54–6.

[58] *VR*, c. 30, p. 66.

[59] *VR*, c. 7, pp. 26–7.

[60] Phipps, 'Saint Peter Damian's Vita Beati Romualdi', pp. 200–3.

[61] Reindel, *Die Briefe des Petrus Damiana*, no. 89, pp. 539–40.

[62] Darrouzès, *Épistoliers Byzantins du X^e siècle*, no. 1. pp. 165–6.

[63] Uhlirz, *Jahrbücher des deutschen Reiches*, pp. 291–2, 534–7.

others, confirm the idea that the *vitae* are artificial compositions, constructed for a purpose, rather than conceived as historiography.

Both these Latin and Greek hagiographers share a common approach to Otto's pilgrimage to Gargano. They also share a common structure. The Emperor committed perjury, he was called to account by the saint, repented, went on pilgrimage to Monte Gargano, and then returned to visit the saint at his monastery, where he acknowledged the saint's superiority – in the case of the *Vita Nili* by placing his crown in the hands of the saint, in the case of the *Vita Romualdi* by promising to become a monk. In showing the similarity between the two *vitae* I do not mean to imply that they influenced each other. Any such influence is unlikely. There is little evidence that Greek monasticism in southern Italy had any direct influence on Romuald or his order.[64] Instead, their similarities should be traced back to the Desert Fathers, the founders of medieval monasticism and eremitism. The hagiographers of both saints stress the influence of the *Vitae Patrum* on their respective saints and both saints are reported to have read these lives.[65] The apparent unity in the way both the Greek and Latin authors approached and used Otto's pilgrimage to Monte Gargano as part of their portrayal of the sanctity of their subjects was derived from their common origins in the monastic traditions of the fifth century. But, despite the many contacts between Latins and Greeks in southern Italy, the *Vita Nili* and the *Vita Romualdi* demonstrate the very real diversity which existed between the Latin and Greek traditions of the Church by the mid-eleventh century.

King's College, London

[64] Hamilton 'S. Pierre Damien'.
[65] *VN*, c. 2, p. 48; *VR*, c. 8, p. 28.

# SANCHO RAMÍREZ AND THE ROMAN RITE

by DAMIAN J. SMITH

The problem could scarcely have been resolved more precisely. 'Et tunc intravit lex romana in Sanctum Iohannem de la Penia XI° kalendas aprilis, secunda septimana quadragessimae, feria III<sup>a</sup>, hora prima et tertia fuit Tholetana, ora sexta fuit romana, anno Domini millesimo LXXI° et inde fuit servata lex romana.'[1]

So the *Crónica de San Juan de la Peña* – the late fourteenth-century official guide to the Aragonese past – briefly explained what it saw as an effortless transition from the old Hispanic to the Roman rite. The diversity of liturgical practice had seemingly been easily quashed as the reform papacy successfully suppressed the autonomy of the Aragonese Church and brought this Spanish kingdom under Roman control. Yet how accurate was the Chronicle here? In Castile, the Chroniclers insisted on champions jousting in the cause of the two rites,[2] on an ordeal by fire to prove the utter incorruptibility of the Toledan books,[3] and on heroic monks striving for the good old days.[4] After a protracted struggle, the Castilians, in their own eyes sportingly, accepted the liturgical change, though always remaining convinced of their own rectitude and Rome's folly.[5] Was unity of practice more easily achieved in Aragon than in Castile?

King Sancho Ramírez (1064–94) would not have thought so. The little kingdom of Aragon, the least of all the lands of Spain,

---

[1] *Historia de la Corona de Aragón, conocida generalmente con el nombre de Crónica de San Juan de la Peña*, ed. T. Ximénez de Embún (Zaragoza, 1876), p. 51.

[2] *Chronicon Burgense* in *España sagrada*, ed. E. Flórez and M. Risco, 2nd edn, 51 vols (Madrid, 1754–1879) [hereafter *ES* ], 23, p. 309; *Annales Compostellani*, *ES*, 23, p. 320; *Crónica Najerense*, ed. A. Ubieto Arteta (Valencia, 1966), c. 3, p. 49; Lucas de Tuy, *Chronicon mundi*, ed. A. Schottus, *Hispania illustrata*, 4 (Frankfurt, 1608), p. 100; Rodrigo Ximénez de Rada, *Historia de rebvs Hispanie sive Historia Gothica*, ed. J. Fernández Valverde, CChr. *CM*, 72 (1987), pp. 207–8.

[3] *Crónica Najerense*, c. 3, p. 49; *Chronicon mundi*, p. 100; *Historia de rebvs Hispanie*, p. 208.

[4] On the rebellion of the monk Roberto, see Gregory VII, *Das Register*, ed. E. Caspar, 2nd edn, 1 vol. in 2, MGH Epistolae Selectae, 4–5 (Berlin, 1955) [hereafter *Registrum*], viii, 2–4, pp. 517–21; *La documentación pontificia hasta Inocencio III (965–1216)*, ed. D. Mansilla (Rome, 1955) [hereafter *MDhI* ], nos 19–21, pp. 32–6; *Regesta pontificum romanorum*, ed. P. Jaffé, rev. S. Loewenfeld (Leipzig, 1885) [hereafter *JL*], 5173–5.

[5] See Luciano de la Calzada, 'La proyección del pensamiento de Gregorio VII en los reinos de Castilla y León', *Studi Gregoriani*, 3 (1948), p. 65; Peter Linehan, *History and the Historians of Medieval Spain* (Oxford, 1993), pp. 188–9.

had been no more than the afterthought of Sancho the Great of Navarre. The royal house lacked any recognizable prestige or sound claim to existence. Continuity or survival was endangered by the enclosing threats from the Moors, Castile, Navarre, and the Counts of Pallars and Urgel. Aragonese society was divided by poverty and ideological differences. The King had had little choice but to look for outside support, to Rome and to Cluny, so that they might bestow upon it legitimacy and lend it opportunity for expansion.[6] Thus Sancho Ramírez sought a change that was to overturn the ecclesiastical order, further split Aragonese society into two camps, and crucially raise the question of the identity of the kingdom as a Pyrenean or a Mozarabic land.

The rite in Spain had always been in some measure at variance with the rest of the West. The prolix multiplication of the hours of the monastic office, the dogmatic preoccupation of a mass forged in the heat of the Arian conflict, the enthusiastic cries of 'Amen' through the paternoster, the division of the Sacred Host into nine portions, may have been peculiarities in the past but they hardly seemed to stretch to errors of faith.[7] Pope John X (914–28) had seemingly received the Spanish liturgical books, examined and approved them, though recommending that they should at least adopt the Roman formula for the consecration.[8] Abbot Odilo (994–1049) had allowed Spanish monks visiting Cluny to celebrate the Annunciation on 8 December, according to their own custom.[9]

[6] On the Kingdom and Church of Aragon in this period, see Antonio Durán Gudiol, *Ramiro I de Aragón* (Zaragoza, 1978); D. J. Buesa Conde, *El rey Sancho Ramírez* (Zaragoza, 1978); J. M. Ramos Loscertales, *El reino de Aragón bajo la dinastía pamplonesa* (Salamanca, 1961); Antonio Ubieto Arteta, 'Ramiro I de Aragón y su concepto de la realeza', *Cuadernos de Historia de España*, 20 (1953), pp. 45–62; Antonio Durán Gudiol, 'La iglesia de Aragón durante el siglo XI', *Estudios de la Edad Media de la Corona de Aragón* [hereafter *EEMCA*], 4 (1951), pp. 7–68, idem, 'La iglesia de Aragón durante los reinados de Sancho Ramírez y Pedro I (¿1062?–1104)', *Anthologica Annua*, 9 (1961), pp. 85–277; Paul Kehr, 'Cómo y cuándo se hizo Aragón feudatorio de la Santa Sede', *EEMCA*, 1 (1945), pp. 285–326; idem, 'El papado y los reinos de Navarra y Aragón hasta mediados del siglo XII', *EEMCA*, 2 (1946), pp. 74–186.

[7] See Marius Férotin, *Le Liber Ordinum en usage dans l'église Wisigothique* (Paris, 1907); Manuel Germán Prado, *Historia del rito mozárabe y toledano* (Madrid, 1928); Pierre David, *Études historiques sur la Galice et le Portugal du VIᵉ au XIIᵉ siècle* (Lisbon, 1947); W. C. Bishop, *The Mozarabic and Ambrosian Rites* (London, 1924); Louis Brou, 'Bulletin de liturgie mozarabe, 1936–1948', *Hispania sacra* [hereafter *HS*], 2 (1949), pp. 459–84, idem, ' "Liturgie mozarabe" ou "liturgie hispanique" ', *Ephemerides liturgicae*, 63 (1949), pp. 66–70; J. M. Pinell, 'Liturgia Hispánica', *Diccionario de Historia Eclesiástica de España*, 2 (Madrid, 1972), pp. 1303–20.

[8] *ES*, 3, p. 84.

[9] Ralph Glaber, *Historiarum libri quinque*, ed. and trans. J. France, in *Rodulfus Glaber Opera*, ed. J. France, N. Bulst and P. Reynolds (Oxford, 1989), bk 3, iii, pp. 114–15. The older monks of Cluny had great misgivings about the whole thing.

Yet in the eleventh century the Hispanic rite became the crucial symbol of the insular past. The reformers at Rome began to perceive that Spain was, very noticeably, different. Outside Catalonia, contact was disturbingly negligible.[10] Each side had previously been too much preoccupied with internal affairs to give much notice to the other. Now arrived the occasion for exchange.

Thus Alexander II (1061–73) sent Cardinal Hugh Candidus on two separate legations between 1065 and 1071 to pull the Spanish kingdoms into the Roman orbit, through the protection of monasteries, the organization of the wars against the Moors, and, of course, the change of rite.[11] The success of the legate in this last matter, though limited to San Salvador de Leire in Navarre,[12] sparked fierce peninsular reaction. In 1067, an embassy, led by Bishops Nuño of Calahorra, Jimeno of Burgos, and Fortún of Álava, marched on Rome to secure the approval of the missals, breviaries, and ritual of the Hispanic rite, and it would seem that Alexander II tentatively accepted the orthodoxy of the Spanish liturgy or, at least, allowed it a reprieve.[13]

Hugh, however, earned an unexpected success in another matter. Sancho Ramírez, out of devotion to the Apostolic See, and, some might say, out of desperation at Castilian domination, decided to make a pilgrimage to Rome, and there in early 1068

---

[10] The Roman rite, as one would expect, was introduced into Catalonia in the ninth century. The two liturgies must have co-existed for some time, though, as the reformers were utterly silent on the question, it would seem the process of change was already complete. On this problem, see J. F. Rivera, 'Gregorio VII y la liturgia mozárabe', *Revista Española de teología*, 2 (Madrid, 1942), pp. 13–14; Antonio García y García, 'Reforma Gregoriana e idea de la "militia Sancti Petri" en los reinos Ibericos', *Studi Gregoriani*, 13 (1989), p. 257.

[11] On Hugh Candidus and subsequent reforming legates in Spain, see G. Säbekow, *Die päpstlichen Legationen nach Spanien und Portugal bis zum Ausgang des 12. Jahrhunderts* (Berlin, 1931), pp. 12–34, 62–9.

[12] *Papsturkunden in Spanien, 2: Navarra und Aragon*, ed. Paul Kehr (Berlin, 1928), pp. 257–60. The document is a forgery, but the false privileges are wrapped up in real events. See Antonio Ubieto Arteta, 'La introducción del rito romano en Aragón y Navarra', *HS*, 1 (1948), p. 306; Rivera, 'Gregorio VII y la liturgia mozárabe', p. 11; Kehr, 'El papado y los reinos de Navarra y Aragón', p. 93.

[13] David, *Études historiques*, pp. 394–5, raised serious doubts about the authenticity of Alexander's letter as it appears in the *Codex Aemilianensis* (*ES*, 3, p. 273). That the traditionalists were using forged pontifical letters to defend themselves is probable from Gregory VII's letter of May 1076 to Bishop Jimeno of Burgos (*Registrum*, iii, pp. 283–4; *MDhI*, no. 12, pp. 20–1; *JL*, 4993): 'Quod autem filii mortis dicunt se a nobis litteras accepisse, sciatis per omnia falsum esse. Procura ergo, ut Romanus ordo per totam Hyspaniam et Gallitiam et ubicumque potueris in omnibus rectius tueatur.' It is very possible that Alexander tried to sit on the fence in 1067 and this was interpreted as approval of their rite by the Spanish embassy. See Ubieto Arteta, 'La introducción del rito romano', p. 308; Kehr, 'El papado', p. 93; Rivera, 'Gregorio VII y la liturgia mozárabe', p. 8; Durán Gudiol, 'La iglesia durante el siglo XI', p. 44.

placed his person and his kingdom in the hands of God and St Peter.[14] As Johannes Fried has explained, this did not leave the Aragonese king in a status of feudal subjection but rather gained for him pontifical protection.[15] No doubt the legate had pointed out the benefits that would be conferred upon the kingdom and, furthermore, a French military expedition was arranged a little time after which would give all three parties opportunity for both economic and ideological exploitation of the lands gained from the Moors.[16] Most probably as part of this agreement, Sancho Ramírez was married to Felicia, the sister of the Count of Roucy who was to lead the expedition.[17] Thus the question of the rite and the military expeditions now became crucially linked as the twin towers of the pontifical pretensions in Spain, the one the spiritual, the other the material expression of Rome's right to the peninsula.

Sancho Ramírez knew that the only way to change the liturgy was through weakening an Aragonese episcopate and traditional monasticism hostile to the move, and the only way to do this was by strengthening the reform monasticism of Cluny, up to then of little power in the kingdom.[18] The Cluniacs, though they had not suggested any strong abolitionist tendencies, were keen on the new territory and appreciated the advantages of liturgical unity in the West. The reform was accepted at San Juan de la Peña and San Victorián de Asán in March 1071, and also at the Augustinian Canonry of San Pedro de Loarre, newly instituted

---

[14] *Documentos correspondientes al reinado de Sancho Ramírez*, ed. J. Salarrullana de Dios and E. Ibarra y Rodríguez, 2 vols (Zaragoza, 1907–13) [hereafter *DSR*], 1, no. 3, pp. 7–8; *JL*, 5398; Johannes Fried, *Der päpstliche Schutz für Laienfürsten: Die politische Geschichte des päpstlichen Schutzprivilegs für Laien (11.–13. Jahrhundert)* (Heidelberg, 1980), pp. 52–9, 63–70; Kehr, 'Cómo y cuándo', p. 302; García y García, 'Reforma Gregoriana', p. 253; Kehr, 'El papado', p. 94; Buesa Conde, *El rey Sancho Ramírez*, pp. 16–17, 43; Durán Gudiol, 'La iglesia durante los reinados', p. 101.

[15] Fried, *Der päpstliche Schutz*, pp. 53–6; *JL*, 5398 (1 July 1089), for Urban II's subsequent protection of Sancho Ramírez, his sons and his kingdom, in return for an annual tribute.

[16] On this seemingly abortive enterprise, see J. Goñi Gaztambide, *Historia de la Bula de la Cruzada en España* (Vitoria, 1958), pp. 52–5; Marcus Bull, *Knightly Piety and the Lay Response to the First Crusade: The Limousin and Gascony, c.970–c.1130* (Oxford, 1993), pp. 81–2; Kehr, 'El papado', p. 102.

[17] David, *Études historiques*, pp. 376–7; Durán Gudiol, 'La iglesia durante los reinados', pp. 100, 120; Buesa Conde, *El rey Sancho Ramírez*, p. 25; Bull, *Knightly Piety*, p. 86, has very reasonable doubts about the marriage actually being dated to 1068 and a date after 1069 would seem more reasonable as Peter I was apparently born then; Felicia was the mother of kings Alfonso I and Ramiro the Monk.

[18] Durán Gudiol, 'La iglesia durante el siglo XI', p. 38; Ubieto Arteta, 'La introducción del rito romano', p. 301; M. Defourneaux, *Les Français en Espagne aux XIe et XIIe siècles* (Paris, 1949), would seem to have overestimated Cluniac influence.

by Sancho Ramírez.[19] Abbot Aquilino of San Juan and Hugh Candidus then left for Rome and Alexander II conferred upon the three foundations pontifical protection, in much the same manner as the King had received three years before, and left them exempt from episcopal control in return for an annual payment of a half an ounce of gold each. After a poignant lament on the state of the Aragonese Church, Alexander praised his legate for having destroyed the errors of Toledo.[20] The reformed monasteries were now free to institute the new liturgy in those houses subject to their control. Sancho Ramírez most probably made generous donations to these houses as a reward, although the immense enthusiasm of the monks of San Juan for forging even the actual truth, leaves the matter somewhat vague.[21]

Alexander II's projected attack on the Moors was eagerly taken up by Gregory VII. On 30 April 1073, just eight days after his election, Gregory gave the go-ahead to the Count of Roucy's expedition and generously shared with the French knights his notion, based certainly upon the Donation of Constantine, that the land of Spain anciently pertained to St Peter and, however long it may have been occupied by invaders, it could not pertain to any but the Apostolic See. Any lands the Count of Roucy and his men took were to be possessed as a fief from the Holy See.[22]

While this pseudo-crusade, like so many other French adventures in Spain, busied its way into historical obscurity, Gregory's tactic on the liturgical front seemed to be working. Spanish resistance would be diminished through the exploitation of the

---

[19] *Crónica de San Juan de la Peña*, p. 51; *JL*, 4691; *MDhI*, no. 4, pp. 7–9; Kehr, *Papsturkunden*, 2, nos 3–4, pp. 260–5.

[20] '. . . Christiane fidei robur et integritatem ibi restauravit, simonyace heresis inquinamenta mundavit, et confusos ritus divinorum obsequiorum ad regulam et canonicum ordinem reformavit': *JL*, 4691; *MDhI*, no. 4, p. 8. The letters to San Victorián and San Pedro de Loarre are printed in Kehr, *Papsturkunden*, 2, nos. 3–4, pp. 260–5.

[21] *DSR*, 2, pp. 85–7.

[22] *Registrum*, i, 7, pp. 11–12; *MDhI*, no. 6, pp. 12–13; *JL*, 4778; Kehr, 'El papado', p. 104: 'Non latere vos credimus regnum Hyspanie ab antiquo proprii iuris s. Petri fuisse, et adhuc licet diu a paganis sit occupatum, lege tamen iustitie non evacuata, nulli mortalium sed soli apostolice sedi ex equo pertinere. Quod enim auctore Deo semel in proprietate ecclesiarum iuste pervenerit, manent eo, ab usu quidem, sed ab earum iure, occasione transeuntis temporis, sine legitima concessione divelli non poterit. Itaque comes Evulus de Roceio, cuius famam apud vos haud obscuram esse putamus, terram illam ad honorem s. Petri ingredi et paganorum manibus eripere cupiens hanc concessionem ab apostolica sede obtinuit, ut partem illam, unde paganos suo studio et adiuncto sibi aliorum auxilio expellere posset, sub conditione inter nos facte pactionis ex parte s. Petri possideret.'

weak link in Aragon, where Gregory would establish a temporal pontifical kingdom, presided over by Sancho Ramírez.[23]

At the Rome Lenten Council of 1074 (9–15 March), the Spanish bishops in attendance accepted that the Roman rite must depose the Toledan.[24] On 19 March, the liturgical error acting as a very thin cloak, Gregory was sufficiently encouraged to write to Alfonso VI of Castile and Sancho IV of Navarre, in order that he might interpret Spain's lamentable waywardness from its righteous place under Roman control. Evangelized by St Paul and afterwards instructed by the seven bishops sent from Rome, the people of Spain had been united to Rome in origin both in religion and in the divine office. Yet afterwards the poison of Priscillianism had polluted, and the treachery of the Arians depraved, and Spain became separated from the Roman rite. If this had not been enough, the onrush of the Goths and the invasion of the Saracens had further weakened both religion and the temporal Christian domain. Therefore the two Kings were ordered to accept the order and office of the Roman Church, which was founded by Peter and Paul through Christ on a firm rock, and consecrated by blood, so that the gates of hell, that is, the tongues of heretics, should never be able to prevail against it. They should accept the rite as the rest of the West accepted it, and as had been directed over the centuries by many popes in many letters to Spain and by many Spanish Councils.[25]

While these rulers of Castile and Navarre were admonished, Sancho Ramírez, very much the lone white sheep in Gregory's Spanish flock, was gaining favour. Sancho had dispatched some letters that the Pope had found 'full of sweetness', in which his devotion to the Apostles Peter and Paul and to the Roman Church was manifest. Moreover, the Apostolic legates had sent good reports of Sancho back to Rome. Sancho, entitled *rex Aragonum*, was showing, in Gregory's opinion, the friendship to the Roman pontiffs that had been given by the Spanish kings of

---

[23] Durán Gudiol, 'La iglesia durante el siglo XI', p. 49.

[24] For the letter of Gregory recommending to Alfonso VI Bishop Pablo Muñoz of Burgos, see *Registrum*, i, 83, pp. 118–19; *MDhI*, no. 10, pp. 17–18; *JL*, 4871: 'Romanum ordinem in divinis officiis, sicut ceteri Hyspani episcopi, qui synodo interfuerunt, se celebraturum, et ut melius poterit observaturum promisit.'

[25] *Registrum*, i, 64, pp. 92–4; *MDhI*, no. 8, pp. 15–16; *JL*, 4840.

old. What was more, under Sancho's own guidance, the Roman rite had been accepted into his kingdom.[26]

Or so, at least, Gregory thought. Sancho, however, was having problems he would not wish the Pope to know about. It is hardly surprising that the Aragonese monastic world en masse did not immediately accept the loss of their age-old office and the covert insult to the saints of Spain. The liturgy that had withstood so many invasions was now subject to a new more sinister Arianism, as the reformers, despite accepting the orthodoxy of the liturgical books in the past, now burnt them and, hence, attacked the Holy Trinity.[27]

Opposition was led by Banzo, the most powerful prelate in the kingdom, for thirty-five years abbot of San Andrés de Fanlo, the centre of Mozarabic Serrablo.[28] His rebellion against the progresives seems to have been shared by the community of Fanlo and such immediate opposition was unwelcome for Sancho. His solution, apparently, was a very simple one. Abbot Banzo was forced to flee the monastery and found exile in the old church of San Martín de Cercito, which the monks of San Juan offered him as a quiet refuge where he might cease to be a nuisance. The community of Fanlo was broken up and Sancho Ramírez transferred the monastery's property to the Augustinian canons of San Pedro de Loarre.[29]

Worse problems were to come for the King. Bishop Sancho of Jaca was likewise unable to accept the change. The support of this notable administrator, most probably once the guardian of Sancho Ramírez,[30] and now his trusted advisor, was absolutely

---

[26] *Registrum*, i, 63, pp. 91–2; *MDhI*, no. 9, pp. 16–17; *JL*, 4841: 'Litteras nobilitatis tue suavitate plenas leti suscepimus, in quibus quanta fidelitate erga principes apostolorum Petrum et Paulum ac Romanum ecclesiam ferveas satis perspeximus; quam tamen, si litteras tuas nullas videremus, per legatos apostolice sedis evidenter compertam habebamus. In hoc autem quod sub ditione tua Romani ordinis officium fieri studio et iussionibus tuis asseris, Romane ecclesie te filium, ac eam concordiam et eamdem amicitiam te nobiscum habere, quam olim reges Hyspanie cum Romanis pontificibus habebant, cognosceris.'

[27] See Fray Justo Pérez de Urbel, 'El último defensor de la liturgia mozárabe', in *Miscellanea liturgica in honorem L. Cuniberti Mohlberg*, 2 vols (Rome, 1949), 2, pp. 189–97; R. Menéndez Pidal, *La España del Cid* (Buenos Aires, 1939), p. 163; David, *Études historiques*, p. 399.

[28] See Antonio Baso Andreu, 'La iglesia aragonesa y el rito romano', *Argensola*, 7 (1956), p. 163; Buesa Conde, *El rey Sancho Ramírez*, pp. 44–7; Buesa Conde, 'El abad Banzo y el cambio de rito en el Serrablo (1071)', *Amigos del Serrablo*, 4 (1972), pp. 9–10.

[29] *DSR*, i, pp. 22–4; Federico Balaguer, 'Los límites del obispado de Aragón y el concilio de Jaca de 1063', *EEMCA*, 4 (1951), p. 119.

[30] Buesa Conde, *El Rey Sancho Ramírez*, p. 20; also Balaguer, 'Los límites del obispado de Aragón', pp. 116–20; J. Gavira Martín, *Estudios sobre la iglesia española medieval: Episcopologios de sedes navarro-aragonesas durante los siglos XI y XII* (Madrid, 1929), pp. 39–44.

crucial to the stability of the kingdom. Jaca was the capital for the King's court, a mercantile city, the political and economic centre of the land, ideally situated on the pilgrim road to Santiago and on the ancient road from Béarn to Zaragoza, its tolls the crucial source of revenue for the Crown and the Church. Jaca was also the symbol of the ultra-pyrenean orientation of Aragon, holding as it did a large number of settlers from Toulouse and Gascony.[31] The support of the Bishop in the development of Jaca was essential to Sancho Ramírez.

Yet Bishop Sancho, rather than resign himself to the new rite, decided to resign altogether. This Hannibalic hero, whom, indeed, neither the Pyrenees nor the wintry Alps could hold, took the long and arduous journey to Rome to inform the Pope that he was far too old and unwell to continue in his office. Sancho Ramírez had been informed of the prelate's intentions but seemingly did not approve of them. Nor did Gregory VII, who, above no doubt marvelling at the athletic energy with which the Bishop sought to fail his medical, was unhappy with the suggested replacements (both of whom were the sons of concubines). Gregory, one expects, was also disconcerted by the realization that his attempts at domination in Spain were weakening the episcopate far more than the secular power. Gregory urged Sancho to continue with the help of an auxiliary in the hope his health would recover.[32]

That, however, is the last we ever hear of Bishop Sancho. The infante García, Sancho Ramírez's brother, replaced him in the see of Jaca and immediately introduced the Augustinian rule among the canons of the cathedral church of Jaca and with that brought about the change from the Hispanic to the Roman rite.[33] Then García, in combination with Sancho Ramírez, gave a series of privileges to the Jacan church that offset the loss of

---

[31] See J. M. Lacarra, 'Desarrollo urbano de Jaca en la Edad Media', *EEMCA*, 4 (1951), pp. 139–55; Buesa Conde, *Sancho Ramírez*, pp. 50–4; J. M. Lacarra, 'Les villes-frontière dans l'Espagne des XI⁰ et XII⁰ siècles', *Le Moyen Âge*, 69 (1963), pp. 205–22; Thomas N. Bisson, *The Medieval Crown of Aragon* (Oxford, 1986), pp. 13–14.

[32] *Registrum*, ii, 50, pp. 190–2; *MDhI*, no. 11, pp. 18–20; *JL*, 4927; Gavira Martín, *Episcopologios*, pp. 44, 104; Durán Gudiol, 'La iglesia durante los reinados', p. 108 (on the King's disapproval of the Bishop's actions).

[33] *Colleción diplomática de la catedral de Huesca*, ed. A. Durán Gudiol, 2 vols (Zaragoza, 1965–9), 1, no. 39, pp. 54–6; *El libro de la cadena del Concejo de Jaca*, ed. Dámaso Sangorrín (Zaragoza, 1921), no. 6, pp. 87–97, no. 7, pp. 99–108, is a letter of Gregory VII, confirming the privileges of the Jacan see.

revenue suffered through the freedom of San Juan de la Peña.[34] The crucial change had taken place. Yet the see of Roda accepted the substitution no more gracefully. Although the church of Roda was fragile and very poor compared with that of Jaca, Roda was at the centre of the frequent battles between Aragon and the Counts of Pallars and Urgel.[35] The Bishop of Roda, Salomón, a Catalan from the monastery of Santa María de Ripoll, who maintained the unfortunate Catalan habit of dating his documents from the year of the French king's reign and who had perhaps been imposed on the see against Sancho Ramírez's wishes, was suspected of at least not having the interests of Aragonese expansion entirely in his mind and at most of supporting Pallars and Urgel against the King.[36] The resistance of Salomón to liturgical reform gave Sancho Ramírez the further opportunity to demonstrate his unfailing loyalty to the Holy See, and to oust the unwanted prelate who stood in opposition to Aragon's formation into a single political unity. While the exact nature of Sancho's complaints to Gregory concerning Salomón are lost, the question of the rite was most probably to the fore; and although Gregory felt himself unable to judge the issue at such a distance, this mattered very little, since Salomón was forced to abandon his see and return to Ripoll.[37]

Feelings in Roda, however, ran high. The expulsion of Bishop Salomón was not appreciated by the men of the town. Cardinal Walter of Albano, approving the privileges of the church of Roda, spoke of some trouble in the kingdom at this time.[38]

[34] Sangorrín, *El libro de la cadena*, no. 6, pp. 87–97.

[35] See Ramon de Abadal, 'Origen y proceso de consolidación de la sede ribagorzana de Roda', *EEMCA*, 5 (1952), pp. 7–82; F. Arroyo Ilera, 'El dominio territorial del obispado de Roda (siglos XI y XII)', *HS*, 22 (1969), pp. 69–128; E. Gros Bítria, *Los límites diocesanos en el Aragón Oriental* (Zaragoza, 1980), esp. pp. 45–84.

[36] M. Serrano y Sanz, *Noticias y documentos históricos del condado de Ribagorza hasta la muerte de Sancho Garcés III* (Madrid, 1912), p. 59; Gavira Martín, *Episcopologios*, pp. 103–4; Durán Gudiol, 'La iglesia durante el siglo XI', pp. 41–2, 51.

[37] *Registrum*, i, 63, pp. 91–2; *MDhI*, no. 9, pp. 16–17; *JL*, 4841; Salomón lived on until 1097, and the measure of respect in which he was held can be discerned from the *Necrologio de Roda*, ed. J. Villanueva, *Viage literario a las iglesias de España*, 22 vols (Madrid, 1803–52) [hereafter *VL*], 15, p. 334: 'Anno MXC. VII obiit Salomon Episcopus Rotae. Capta est civitas Oscha et civitas Jherusalem'; Salomón is also described as bishop in the *Chronicon alterum Rivipullense*, *VL*, 5, p. 246: '1097 ob. Salomon monachus et episcopus; a letter of Salomón in 1095 to Peter I (*VL*, 15, pp. 355–6), in which he laments that when he had been bishop all monasteries had been under episcopal control, is testimony to the success of Sancho Ramírez.

[38] *El Cartulario de Roda*, ed. Juan. F. Yela Utrilla (Lérida, 1932) [hereafter *CR*], p. 20; Ubieto Arteta, 'La introducción del rito romano', p. 313; Kehr, 'El papado', p. 127.

Sancho Ramírez and his eldest son Peter came to Roda and swore that the election of the next bishop would take place according to the wishes of the people and the canons of the church of San Vincente de Roda.[39] The new Bishop, Raymond, elected by a council, accepted by the people and canons, and recommended to Sancho Ramírez by Gregory VII,[40] turned out to be a fortunate choice, showing unflagging loyalty to the Crown, reforming the monastery of Santa María de Alaón in 1078,[41] implanting the Roman liturgy there, and ultimately completing the process of reform when restoring the canonical life of San Vicente de Roda in 1091.[42]

The rapidity of reform in Aragon could not be expected in Navarre. Although San Salvador de Leire had accepted the change, it had been the Navarrese prelates who had led the embassy to Rome and a then Navarrese monastery, San Millán de la Cogolla, has left the fullest exposition of the opposition to the Romano-Frankish influence.[43] Gregory VII had had to reprimand Sancho IV for his spiritual laxity, and when this ruler was assassinated on 4 June 1076 it was to be one of the most significant events in eleventh-century Spanish history. While the lands of Álava fell to Alfonso VI of Castile, Sancho Ramírez annexed the rest of the kingdom which thus came under papal guardianship and thus acquired the Roman rite.[44] When Blas, Bishop of Pamplona, died in 1078, Sancho Ramírez, never strong on the finer points of canon law, imposed his brother García on the see, although he was still Bishop of Jaca.[45] When García fell out of

---

[39] *CR*, p. 19; Sancho Ramírez gave a series of donations to the Rodan see (*CR*, pp. 24–5, 58, 61–2, 329–30); Arroyo Ilera, 'El dominio territorial', p. 79.

[40] *CR*, p. 87; *VL*, 15, p. 192; Gavira Martín *Episcopologios*, pp. 104–7, 150; Kehr, *Papsturkunden*, 2, pp. 36, 43; idem, 'El papado', p. 117.

[41] *Cartulario de Alaón*, ed. José Luis Corral Lafuente (Zaragoza, 1984), no. 268, pp. 252–3.

[42] *VL*, 15, p. 301.

[43] Pérez du Urbel, 'El último defensor', pp. 196–7.

[44] J. M. Lacarra, ' "Honores" et "Tenencias" en Aragon (XIᵉ siècle)', *Annales du Midi*, 80 (1968), p. 485; Durán Gudiol, 'La iglesia durante el siglo XI', pp. 53, 56.

[45] Gavira Martín, *Episcopologios*, pp. 44, 84; Kehr, 'El papado' p. 116; Gros Bítria, *Los límites diocesanos*, p. 75. The letter obtained by García from Gregory VII in 1084/5, in which the Pope attributes to this Bishop and his father Ramiro I the introduction of the Roman rite (in Kehr, 'Cómo y cuándo', pp. 314–17), is authentic. Yet, as Kehr has shown, the Bishop had the interests of his Jacan see at heart and the situation of the Pope in these years was an ideal opportunity for pulling the pallium over his eyes ('Cómo y cuándo', pp. 289–313); Ramiro I, nevertheless, did make generous donations to St Peter's in his will of 1061; see *Cartulario de San Juan de la Peña*, ed. A. Ubieto Arteta, 2 vols (Valencia, 1962–3), 2, no. 159, p. 199.

favour after 1083, another amenable candidate, Peter of Roda, was chosen to install the rite in the Navarrese monasteries.[46]

Thus Castile stood alone in the West against the Roman rite. Alfonso VI was keen to accept the abolition of the Hispanic rite and bring about absolute liturgical and disciplinary unity, much less because he needed any papal support or would make himself receptive to Gregory's interpretation of the past, than because ultra-pyrenean influences, and most of all the support of Cluny, were beneficial to the kingdom.[47] In 1080 the reform was sanctioned by the Council of Burgos and the following year Gregory VII registered his great joy that the rite that really was full of errors had been exchanged for the Roman rite, which was the primitive liturgy of Spain.[48]

On 25 May 1085, Gregory VII died, and, on that same day, Alfonso VI made his triumphal entry into Toledo. Thereby the Roman rite was opened to a whole new sphere. Yet if Gregory had won this battle he had most definitely lost the war at the same instant. For the rapidity of liturgical change had been brought about by the annexation of Navarre by Sancho Ramírez, and the strong kingdoms of Castile and Aragon were unwilling to accept Gregory's unique historical perspective. After a brief sortie in 1077,[49] the claim to Spain was dropped. From now on Sancho Ramírez would pick and choose the French adventurers he allowed into his kingdom and his successors would very much select the moment when they responded 'Amen' to a papal petition.[50]

University of Birmingham

---

[46] Ubieto Arteta, 'La introducción del rito romano', p. 321.

[47] De la Calzada, 'La proyección del pensamiento de Gregorio VII', p. 63.

[48] *Registrum*, ix, 2, pp. 569–72; *MDhI*, no. 22. pp. 36–9; *JL*, 5205. For the difficulties in Castile after 1080, see Ramón Gonzálvez, 'The Persistence of the Mozarabic Liturgy in Toledo after A.D. 1080', in *Santiago, Saint-Denis, and Saint Peter: the reception of the Roman Liturgy in León-Castile in 1080*, ed. B. F. Reilly (New York, 1985), pp. 157–85.

[49] *Registrum*, iv. 28, pp. 343–7; *MDhI*, no. 13, pp. 21–5; *JL*, 4993: 'Preterea notum vobis fieri volumus quod nobis quidem facere non est liberum, vobis autem non solum ad futuram sed etiam ad presentem gloriam valde necessarium, videlicet, regnum Hyspanie ex antiquis constitutionibus beato Petro et sancte Romane ecclesie in ius et proprietatem esse traditum.'

[50] See the will of Lopé Garcés in c.1080: 'Eo anno venit comes Pictavensis in Ispania et gloriosus rex Sancius fecit illum reverti in patria sua': *DSR*, 2, p. 134; for the interpretation of Sancho's devotion by his successors, see B. Palacios Martín, *La coronación de los reyes de Aragón* (Valencia, 1975).

# WAS THERE A 'THE CHURCH' IN THE MIDDLE AGES?

*by* GARY MACY

Scholarly works on the Middle Ages frequently enough mention 'the Church in the Middle Ages', or 'the teaching of the Church in the Middle Ages' without further specification, as if the reader could immediately identify the institution to which the author is referring. The authors of such works assume both that the reader readily recognizes what the author means by the phrase, but also, and perhaps more troubling, assume that there *was* an easily identifiable group in the Middle Ages that was 'the Church'. Yet, when one tries actually to establish some agreement among medieval sources as to what constituted 'the Church' or even some agreement as to the criteria by which one could recognize a 'the Church', the 'the Church' which ought to be so solid seems to disappear into a thousand disparate factions. If, in fact, 'the Church' is really better described as a set of common traditions rather than as an institutional monolith, then the question of unity within 'the Church' would centre more on the commonality of this tradition than on the structural integrity and uniformity of belief within the institution. In short, how one understands and defines 'the Church' will determine the criteria by which one affirms or denies the unity of that Church. A discussion of what 'the Church of the Middle Ages' might be seems to be methodologically prior to any determination of the unity or disunity of Christianity in the Middle Ages. This contribution will limit itself to an exploration of some of the problems inherent in assuming that there was a 'the Church in the Middle Ages' and, further, that this 'Church of the Middle Ages' can be easily identified and defined.

The first and most pestering of these problems would, of course, entail what exactly 'the Middle Ages' might be. The designation is a highly politically charged appellation invented in the nineteenth century and usually carrying a derogatory implication, especially in the United States.[1] As important as an

[1] For an interesting discussion of how the United States views the Middle Ages, see Matteo Sanfilippo, *Il medioevo secondo Walt Disney: come l'America ha reinventato l'età di mezzo* (Rome, 1993).

exploration of this construct might be, let it suffice to mention that such a consideration of the Middle Ages as somehow a unity reinforces the odd notion that the Irish Church in, say, the seventh century was the same institution as that of the Roman Church of the fourteenth century.

Although other sources could also be cited, I will give only two examples of scholars who assume in their work that a fairly clearly defined 'the Church' existed in the Middle Ages. Both examples are taken from my own particular field of study, the history of the theology of the eucharist. The first author, Pietro Redondi, explains in his study, *Galileo Heretic*, that

> With the Thomistic theory of 'accidents without subjects', the doctrine of transubstantiation had been given a rational shelter against the risk that a philosopher in the mood for dialectical discussion would appeal to the problems surrounding the sensible experiences of heat, taste and smell. . . . Aware of the inestimable apologetic value [of this argument], the Church officially appropriated the idea of 'accidents without a subject'.[2]

At this point, Redondi does not identify the particular group of theologians or canonists or official statements which appropriated the idea. On the basis of this assumption, Redondi goes on to argue that the Council of Constance missed an opportunity to reassert this doctrine in its condemnation of Ockham's teaching on the eucharist. 'By not intervening radically right away', Redondi continues, 'the Church condemned itself to prosecuting repeatedly every single philosophical and scientific thesis that would inevitably conflict with doctrinal dogma.'[3]

While it is true that Lollards could be, and were, tested for their belief on this point, and that during the Reformation the Roman Church adopted Thomistic teaching on the eucharist as the most acceptable, it is not at all clear that the decision to accept 'the Thomistic theory of "accidents without subjects" ' was made by any particular 'official group' before the Council of Trent.

---

[2] Pietro Redondi, *Galileo Heretic* (Princeton, NJ, 1987), p. 213.
[3] Ibid., p. 218.

Redondi's argument depends on 'the Church' having made an unequivocal decision to accept a particular explanation concerning the mode of presence of Christ in eucharist, of which Trent was merely the final formal assertion of 'what the Church had always taught'. But the difficulty of this approach lies in the rejection by at least part of 'the Church' of Thomas's teaching. The perfectly orthodox Franciscan theologians Bonaventure and Duns Scotus both rejected the Thomistic approach and at least part of Thomas's teaching was condemned itself in 1277.[4] Thus it would appear that 'the Church' had not yet adopted the Thomistic approach as doctrine, as Redondi's argument assumes, or that those who did not accept Thomas's explanation were not part of 'the Church'. The endorsement of Aquinas at the Council of Trent as a spokesman for a particular form of Roman Catholicism hardly solves the problem, since this would imply a strange form of anachronism in which the Reformation claims determined the identity of the late medieval Church.

Gavin Langmuir suggests a second source as 'the Church', or to use his phrase, 'the authorities of the Catholic religion', in his recent study, *History, Religion, and Antisemitism*. 'By the end of the twelfth century, theologians had developed the doctrines of concomitance and transubstantiation in order to reconcile their faith and their reason, and in 1215 the pope made the doctrine of transubstantiation dogma.'[5]

Based on this assumption, Langmuir continues,

> As we saw earlier, the belief that Jesus Christ was physically present in the consecrated bread and wine of the Eucharist had become the object of widespread doubt by the middle of the eleventh century, and the authorities of the Catholic religion responded by modifying the formulation of the belief, but they also prescribed in 1215 that Catholics had to believe it. Since the religious authorities had developed formidable means to repress open dissent by 1215, and since these were strengthened by the organization of the Inquisition starting in 1231, it became very dangerous to express

---

[4] Cf. Gary Macy, 'Reception of the eucharist according to the theologians: a case of diversity in the 13th and 14th centuries', in John Apczynski, ed., *Theology and the University*, Proceedings of the Annual Convention of the College Theology Society, 1987 (Lanham, Maryland, 1990), pp. 15–36.

[5] Gavin Langmuir, *History, Religion, and Antisemitism* (Berkeley, Cal., 1990), pp. 250–1.

doubts openly. Heretics such as the Cathars continued to do so amongst themselves, but most kept quiet.[6]

There are several interesting problems with this argument, including a misunderstanding of transubstantiation, which specifically rejects a physical presence in the eucharist, as well as a confusion of transubstantiation with belief in the real presence.[7] The relevant point of this discussion, however, is that Langmuir assumes that Lateran IV was understood in an unequivocal manner by theologians, canonists, and inquisitors alike. Langmuir refers to only one medieval theologian in the development of this argument, the omnipresent Thomas Aquinas, and offers no analysis of how Lateran IV was received by the diverse groups of 'religious authorities' in later centuries.

For both Redondi and Langmuir, 'the Church' seems to be a group of theologians and members of the hierarchy, difficult to identify, but certainly including Thomas Aquinas and Innocent III, who had a clear idea of what authorities constituted the teaching of 'the Church', and who were single-minded in their enforcement of belief in that teaching. The real difficulty comes in trying actually to pin down this elusive Church as an historical entity.[8]

Even the theologian most often referenced as a stalwart supporter of 'the Church', the Angelic Doctor himself, described the Church quite differently in his discussion of the eucharist in his final work, the *Summa theologiae*. When asking the question of whether the eucharist was necessary for salvation, Thomas responded that since the eucharist was the sign of the unity of the

[6] Ibid., p. 259.

[7] As one of several possible explanations for the real presence of Christ in the eucharist, transubstantiation argues that the substance (the unsensed essence) of the bread and wine change into the substance of the body and blood of Christ. The accidents (that which is sensed) remain unchanged. Thus transubstantiation was put forward as a way of explaining how a real change could take place without any sensed change occurring. This would make the change a metaphysical rather than a physical one. More precisely, it would be an intellectual change, since substance can only be grasped by the intellect. The belief that a true physical change took place in the eucharist was actually a heresy, that of Capharnaism. For a brief explanation of this aspect of transubstantiation, see Gary Macy, *The Banquet's Wisdom: a Short History of the Theologies of the Lord's Supper* (Mahwah, NJ, 1992), pp. 104–9.

[8] Professor Langmuir, of course, describes in detail what he means by 'religion' and 'religiosity', and it is not to these precise definitions that I refer. What he fails to do is offer a convincing argument for the existence of a distinctly separate 'papal' or 'Roman Catholic' religion in the late Middle Ages. See, for instance, *History, Religion, and Antisemitism*, pp. 137–40, 181–2, 188–91.

Church, and there was no salvation outside the Church, then, of course, one had to partake of the eucharist in order to be saved. A straightforward defence of ecclesial authority, it would seem, until Thomas added that one could also receive the eucharist by desire, just as one could be baptized by desire. By simply desiring to know and trying to do God's will, one was part of the unity of the mystical body, that is, the Church, and therefore the effect of the sacrament could be attained before the actual ritual was ever undergone.[9]

In this passage at least, 'the Church' for Thomas was the community of all just people. This particular 'the Church' would not at all fit the assumptions of Redondi and Langmuir, but was a perfectly acceptable way of speaking of the Church in the Middle Ages. I am not suggesting that this is Aquinas's most sophisticated discussion of the Church, which of course it is not; but rather, that his understanding of the Church was quite complex, particularly when speaking of exactly that issue for which Redondi and Langmuir claim his support, that is, his teaching on the eucharist.

Then there is the equally knotty problem of the reception of Innocent III's claims of authority made at the Fourth Lateran Council. According to a recent article by G. R. Evans, the authority claimed by Innocent III at Lateran IV for the Roman Church was 'variously seen by different schools and factions as speaking through the pope alone, through councils alone, through the *consensus fidelium*, as the voice of the Roman Church, as the voice of one of the churches speaking through Rome'. In fact, again according to Evans, 'the key question of the last medieval centuries was whether a "universal" authority residing in the Roman Church was vested in the community as a whole, in councils, or in the person of the pope.'[10] I have argued elsewhere that few theologians or canonists understood the Fourth Lateran Council to have even intended to define transubstantiation before Duns Scotus in the fourteenth century.[11]

---

[9] Pars iii, q. 73, art. 3. *Summa theologiae . . . cum textu ex recensione Leonina* (Rome, 1953), pp. 482–3.

[10] G. R. Evans, 'Exegesis and authority in the thirteenth century', in Mark D. Jordan and Kent Emery, Jr., eds, *Ad litteram: Authoritative Texts and their Medieval Readers* (Notre Dame, Ind., 1992), pp. 96–7.

[11] G. Macy, 'The dogma of transubstantiation in the Middle Ages', *JEH*, 45 (1994), pp. 11–41.

From where then does the 'the Church' of Langmuir and Redondi come? I would suggest that this 'the Church' is a construct of the Reformation debates which continued well into the Enlightenment period and beyond. Langmuir's description of events parallels almost exactly that of John Cosin, the seventeenth-century Bishop of Durham:

> That same pope [Innocent III], after having declared to be heretics those who from then on would deny 'the body of Christ and the blood to be truly contained in the sacrament of the altar, under the species of bread and wine, the bread having been transubstantiated into the body and the wine into the blood'; handed over all of them, of whatever rank or office they might be, to be punished by the secular powers, once their crime had been brought to their attention; that is, he handed them over to be burned.[12]

Redondi and Langmuir, I would suggest, have simply accepted uncritically the Reformation construct which defined the medieval Church as 'the Roman Church' a sort of proto-Tridentine Church, to be praised or despised depending on how you feel about Trent. What I am particularly concerned about is not that these otherwise fine scholars should adopt such a stance, but that they should do so uncritically. Neither makes any attempt to prove that this particular representation of the Church in the Middle Ages has grounding in medieval sources, and both assume that the reader will instantly identify with this picture of 'the Church'.

An argument might be made that the Roman hierarchy, or a majority of the bishops, or the majority of the canonists, or the majority of the theologians, or any group of them, should be seen as embodying 'the Church' at any particular point in the Middle Ages, but those arguments must be made. At the very least, when a scholar argues that the Church taught or believed a particular teaching, the source for that teaching should not only be identified, but then that choice also justified. Why should Thomas Aquinas, to use the most commonly abused source, be

---

12 *Historia transubstantiationis papalis* (London, 1675), p. 150.

accepted as a spokesperson for the Church in the thirteenth century? His teaching had no official standing in the Middle Ages, was frequently controversial, and went out of vogue for much of the fourteenth century. Yet his works are those most frequently found in footnotes to sentences that end, 'as the Church in the Middle Ages taught'. The same can be said for the Fourth Lateran Council. However widely and rapidly the pastoral decrees of the Council were disseminated and accepted by most of Europe, the discussion of the authority claimed by the Council continued up until the time of Trent and beyond. Historians who wish to state the teaching of the Church on a particular issue have, alas, the additional burden of explaining why the particular source upon which they base that decision should be taken seriously as a representative voice of the Church.

As must be coming clear, the problem is not so much whether there was a 'the Church in the Middle Ages'; after all there was a separate institution of clerics, at least in the late medieval centuries, with a clearly separate code of law and way of life which constituted a separate institution to be studied like any other. The important question becomes, rather, which was the *real* Church in the Middle Ages, which was the Church which spoke with authority; and herein lies the rub. This was the very question at the heart of many of the great medieval debates. Was the real Church visible or invisible; was the real Church governed by king, pope, or bishops in council; was the real Church determined by moral or by legal criteria? This was not a question settled in the Middle Ages, or indeed within the wider body of Christianity today, and it seems presumptuous for historians to settle it by fiat.

To settle on the teaching of Thomas Aquinas or the Fourth Lateran Council, or indeed that of the Waldensians or the Cathars, as representing the real Church, can mislead in several important ways. First of all, it gives the false impression that issues hotly debated at the time were in fact already solved, usually in light of the outcome of those debates during the Reformation. This is particularly egregious when one presents the late medieval Church as if it were simply an early version of the post-Tridentine Roman Catholic Church. Secondly, the tension of the period itself is lost. Contemporaries were not always so certain that papal or royal or episcopal or conciliarist views would win the day, and to write assuming that they did reads a direction and purpose back into history that contemporaries themselves would not have experienced. Most of their responses were, probably, more reactions to particular situations than the sustained policies of centuries leading consciously and inevitably towards Trent.

Again, to quote Dr Evans:

> If we were to bring together the experience of the scholars who were weighing authorities in detail in their works as theologians and that of the Church as a whole facing the need to decide what had to be defined as a matter of faith among the proliferating mass of theological topics under consideration in the schools, we shall find no statements of policy about authority and exegesis in the thirteenth century that recognize the new difficulties clearly. The academic world was doing its job, and in part that was creating the problem. The *ecclesia Romana* made a magisterial pronouncement from time to time in a general council, as at Lateran IV and at Lyons in 1274, but it did not yet spell out a theology of decision making in matters of faith, still less of reception. Nor did it prove necessary, as it would be at Trent, to marshal a defense on the subject of the supremacy of the Church over Scripture and other authorities. The developments we see in the thirteenth century have a natural, an organic quality; they were responses to need. They do not represent a deliberate change of direction on the part of the medieval Church.[13]

What I am suggesting, in brief, is that the Church in the Middle Ages, like that other etheral Platonic entity, the State, was more often a muddle than a monolith. To put it in the terms of the theme of this volume, it was more a diversity within broad outlines than a true unity. A different and perhaps truer history of this Church would be rather less romantic, more tedious, and more amorphous than some recent studies would have the reader believe. Again, there was certainly 'a Church in the Middle

---

[13] 'Exegesis and authority', pp. 107–8.

Ages', in the sense that there existed, in the late Middle Ages at least, a clear separation between clergy and laity; but to say more than that becomes precarious. Few contemporaries identified the institutional church with 'the Church', the real Church, the Church of the saved, and this distinction deserves respect from historians. Many contemporaries did make claims for particular groups as best representing the true Church, but these claims were often in conflict with one another.

Historical sources, with all their ambiguities and tensions and hesitations, have as much right to be taken seriously, I would propose, as we do. What they thought the Church ought to be should carry some weight in our determining what we are going to call the Church, because this tells us what that society *said* it wanted to be, and the dreams to which people aspire are not to be lightly dismissed.

Take, for a moment, one group of distant descendants of the medieval *magistri*. One could analyse the economic structures of academics in the Unites States (or Europe) and conclude that the entire enterprise is driven by greed and pride. Scholarly publication only takes place to advance one's standing in the academic community, and one's salary. Those who do so advance protect their positions by attacking all challengers and by producing loyal graduate students who will advance their positions. Further, those positions are rather narrowly focused, so that only certain approaches are rewarded. Deviance is punished by the inability to get published, resulting in obscurity, reduced income, and eventual expulsion from the profession.

Now as true as this picture might be, it is not the whole picture, nor is it what scholars say, and often believe, they are doing. They will say that they are interested in uncovering the truth; they will say that they are trying to correct errors in understanding the past; they will say they believe that education will advance humankind; they might even say that they are simply insatiably curious and this is all great fun. At least in their better moments, they will not be lying. Greed, pride, and elitism may play a major role in modern academia, but these are not the ideals of academics, and the actual lives of academics are torn between ideals and temptations. It would be very unfair, not to mention infuriating, to be told that one's ideals are merely clever subterfuges for one's vices. Some best-selling books really were

115

written to inform, some technical language really is needed to clarify issues; many scholars would really rather be found out to be wrong if they *are* wrong.

I feel it is worth extending the same courtesy to the medievals that we would wish extended to ourselves as scholars. Of course we should be suspicious of the medieval ideals of Christianity contained in the special pleading of the many groups claiming to be the legitimate Church, just as we should be suspicious of our own motives. But not to know what a group's motives are (or at least, what they purport to be), and to dismiss or misunderstand the goals and ideals of a society, will produce a grossly distorted picture of that society. And if, as in the case of the Church, the society was often torn by conflicting views of what those ideals were and how they should be carried out, then that dichotomy, that diversity, that tension, deserves proper representation.

University of San Diego

# THE CARMELITE ORDER AND GREEK ORTHODOX MONASTICISM: A STUDY IN RETROSPECTIVE UNITY

## by ANDREW JOTISCHKY

On his embassy from Constantinople to the papal curia in 1339, the Greek Orthodox envoy Barlaam confided to Benedict XII his pessimistic belief that genuine union between the Churches was rendered impossible less by theological difference than by the shared history of relations between eastern and western Christendom:

> It is not so much the difference in doctrine that alienates the hearts of the Greeks from you as the hatred against the Latins that has entered their souls because of the great number of evils they have suffered at the hands of the Latins at different times, and which they still suffer every day. Unless this hatred is dispelled, union can never be achieved.[1]

Barlaam's appraisal of the underlying causes of disunity between the Churches finds echoes in the prevalent attitudes of distrust and resentment shown by Byzantine and Latin clergy toward one another throughout the thirteenth and fourteenth centuries. The conversion of John V Palaeologus and a few of his intimates caused expectations of reunion in the West that were unrealistic and unfulfilled.[2] Even a tolerant pro-unionist like the Calabrian Barlaam found that history was less yielding than theology. The Greeks could not forgive Latin wrongs, Barlaam surmised, because they could not forget the past. But how fully was the bitter history of Orthodox-Latin relations remembered and understood in the West? Below the level of theological debate and diplomacy, did the Church in the West have a consistent 'official' memory of the shared history of Latins and

---

[1] *Acta Benedicti XII (1334–1342)*, ed. A. L. Tautu (Vatican City, 1958), no. 43.

[2] J. Gill, *Byzantium and the Papacy 1198–1400* (New Brunswick, 1979); O. Halecki, *Un empereur de Byzance à Rome*, new edn (London, 1972); D. M. Nicol, 'Byzantine requests for an oecumenical council in the fourteenth century', *Annuarium Historiae Conciliorum*, 1 (1969), pp. 69–95; J. Meyendorff, 'Projets de concile oecuménique en 1367: un dialogue inédit entre Jean Cantacuzène et le légat Paul', *Dumbarton Oaks Papers*, 14 (1960), pp. 147–77. On Barlaam's embassy, see Gill, *Byzantium and the Papacy*, pp. 196–9, and Nicol, 'Byzantine requests', p. 76.

Greeks in the parts of the Mediterranean where they came into contact? This paper explores some fourteenth-century conceptions of Latin/Orthodox relations through the medium of the Carmelite Order's accounts of its origins and early history in the Holy Land. The attempt to develop a coherent tradition of their origins led the Carmelites to emphasize both unity and diversity in their perception of the order's role in the Church. Carmelite apologists wanted to show the quality of their difference from other mendicant and monastic orders. Although this could best be accomplished by recounting the long history of the order in the Holy Land before the migration to the West, such a strategy also forced Carmelite historians to accept a degree of unity with the indigenous Greek Orthodox Church of the crusader states.

The religious orders became increasingly concerned in the fourteenth century with the connection between antiquity and authenticity; with defining the monastic profession and determining their own claim to be recognized as older, and thus more genuine, than their rivals.[3] This debate over historical priority naturally entailed an examination of the history of monasticism, and, inevitably, a consideration of the Greek Orthodox monastic tradition. Because the geographical origins of monasticism lay in the eastern Mediterranean, the religious orders confronted a past that was as much Greek as Latin, but at a time when, in the West, Greek Orthodoxy was commonly viewed as schismatic or even heretical. For most orders, this caused no problem. Eastern Desert Fathers could safely be recognized as precursors of Benedictine monasticism,[4] because they predated any parting of the ways between East and West. But the Carmelites, who had arrived in the West from the Crusader states in the mid-thirteenth century, could not claim an antiquity stretching back beyond the foundation of the Kingdom of Jerusalem in 1099 without embracing the indigenous Greek Orthodox monasticism of the eastern Mediterranean. In establishing their historical

---

[3] W. A. Pantin, 'Some medieval English treatises on the origins of monasticism', in V. Ruffer and A. J. Taylor, eds, *Medieval Studies Presented to Rose Graham* (Oxford, 1950), pp. 189–215. For mendicant interests in monastic origins, see K. Elm, 'Elias, Paulus von Theben und Augustinus als Ordensgründer', in H. Patze, ed., *Geschichtsschreibung und Geschichtsbewusstein im später Mittelalter*, Vortrage und Forschungen, 31 (Sigmaringen, 1987), pp. 371–97; for pagan antiquity, Beryl Smalley, *English Friars and Antiquity in the Early Fourteenth Century* (Oxford, 1960).

[4] E.g., *The Letters of Peter the Venerable*, ed. G. Constable, 2 vols (Cambridge, Mass., 1967), 1, p. 29 and *De prima institutione monachorum* in Pantin, 'Some medieval English treatises', p. 199.

pedigree, the Carmelites of the late thirteenth and fourteenth centuries developed foundation legends that implied ignorance of the historical foundations of the schism between Orthodox and Latin Churches, and proposed an apparently simplistic harmony between Orthodox and Latin monks in the Holy Land.

Before discussing Carmelites' accounts of their history, it is advisable first to examine the early history of the Order from independent evidence. Twelfth-century pilgrims to the Holy Land knew that Mount Carmel, the high ground rising to a peak overlooking the town of Haifa, was associated with the activities of Elijah in the Old Testament.[5] A monastic presence on Mount Carmel is attested by the Jewish traveller Benjamin of Tudela in the late 1160s, who reported that a church dedicated to Elijah had been built by the 'cave of Elijah', just below the promontory of the mountain.[6] About fifteen years later the Greek pilgrim John Phocas described an eremitical community founded by a Calabrian (and presumably Orthodox) priest on another part of Mount Carmel, at the ruins of the early Christian monastery of St Elisha, by the 'spring of Elijah' (*wadi 'ain as-siah*).[7] The sources are then silent until the appearance of the Rule of Albert, Patriarch of Jerusalem (1205–14), the preface of which explains that it was written at the request of a community of hermits who lived at the 'spring of Elijah'.[8] The hermits were recognized as an order by Honorius III in 1226, and their Rule was modified to bring it in line with mendicant, rather than monastic, practice by Innocent IV in 1247.[9] By this time they had already begun to spread to Western Europe, a process initiated in 1238 when Muslim attacks forced them to move temporarily to Cyprus and Sicily.[10] From 1247 onward, although the original foundation on Mount Carmel was retained until 1291, the Carmelites lived in

[5] *The Life and Journey of Daniel, Abbot of the Russian Land*, trans. W. F. Ryan, in J. Wilkinson, *Jerusalem Pilgrimage 1099–1185* (London, 1988), p. 152.

[6] *The Itinerary of Benjamin of Tudela*, ed. and trans. M. N. Adler (London, 1907), p. 19.

[7] John Phocas, *Descriptio Terrae Sanctae*, PG, 133, cols 961–2. The translation by Aubrey Stewart reproduced in Wilkinson, *Jerusalem Pilgrimage*, pp. 335–6, is inexact. For the topography of early foundations on Mt Carmel, see Elias Friedman, *The Latin Hermits of Mount Carmel* (Rome, 1979).

[8] *La règle de l'Ordre de la Bienheureuse Vierge Marie du Mont Carmel*, ed. and trans. M. Battman (Paris, 1982), p. 16.

[9] *Bullarium carmelitanum*, ed. E. Monsignani and J. A. Ximinez, 4 vols (Rome, 1715–68), 1, p. 1; A. Staring, 'Four bulls of Innocent IV. A critical edition', *Carmelus*, 27 (1980), pp. 273–85. For general discussion of Carmelite legislation, see C. Cicconetti, *La Regola del Carmelo: origine, natura, significato* (Rome, 1973).

[10] Vincent of Beauvais, *Speculum Historiale*, ed. B. Beller (repr. Graz, 1965), XXX, 123, pp. 1274–5.

convents like those of the other mendicant orders, established provinces with *studia*, and went to university. The polemical literature on the origins of the order written in the late thirteenth and fourteenth centuries was largely the product of university-trained friars.

The period of darkness between the Calabrian foundation and Albert's Rule is crucial for an understanding of the Carmelite perception of the order's origins. Albert did not found a community, but legislated for an existing one which had reached the point of maturity of needing a written rule. Did this community comprise elements of the original Calabrian Orthodox foundation on the same site? If so, then the earliest Carmelites must have been a mixed Orthodox/Latin community unique in the Crusader States.[11] It is quite possible that in the period before a rule, Frankish hermits and monks who had been forced to flee from their habitats by Saladin's invasion in 1187 took refuge with, or near, the Orthodox community on Mount Carmel. But in this case, and assuming that the Orthodox component continued over the next twenty years, did Orthodox monks accept the Rule of Albert and become part of a Latin order? It is this question that lies at the heart of the Carmelites' investigation of their origins.

The common association of Elijah with Mount Carmel enabled the Carmelites to claim, in a rubric to the order's first surviving set of constitutions in 1281, that the prophet had been their founder: 'We assert that, according to true testimony, from the time of the prophets Elijah and Elisha, inhabitants of Mount Carmel, the holy fathers of the New and Old Testaments, . . . lived . . . next to the spring of Elijah there in holy penance and were followed without a break by their holy successors.'[12]

The *rubrica prima* had nothing to say about the eremitical tradition on Mount Carmel between Elijah and Patriarch Albert. Then, in the pontificate of Innocent III, Patriarch Albert appar-

[11] Such mixed communities had, however, been known in tenth-century Rome; Bernard Hamilton, 'The monastery of S. Alessio and the religious and intellectual renaissance in tenth-century Rome', *Studies in Medieval and Renaissance History*, 2 (1965), pp. 265–310.

[12] *Rubrica prima* of 1281 in A. Staring, *Medieval Carmelite Heritage. Early Reflections on the Nature of the Order*, Textus et studia Carmelitana, 16 (Rome, 1989) [hereafter *MCH*], pp. 40–1. This welcome edition of texts produced within the order from the 1280s to the 1370s now makes a detailed study of medieval Carmelite historiography possible.

ently collected together a disparate group of hermits into a *collegium* and gave them a Rule. The rubric, which was repeated with variations in subsequent constitutions, was specifically designed to answer queries made to Carmelite friars by a younger generation of recruits to the order at a time when it had been established in the West for a generation, but when memories of its eastern origins had grown dim. The rubric served equally well to defuse more aggressive criticism from other orders. It first appeared only seven years after the Second Council of Lyons (1274) had decreed that any order founded since 1215 be suppressed. The Carmelites, like the Augustinian friars, were permitted a stay of execution, and their status had not yet been confirmed in 1281;[13] it was a crucial time for the Carmelites to establish the credibility of their claim to antiquity.

During the next hundred years, a number of Carmelite texts filled the gap between Elijah and Albert by an assiduous combination of speculation and an optimistic reading of sources. These texts form a chain, in which the later are heavily dependent on the *rubrica prima* and its subsequent variations. A short chronicle from the end of the thirteenth century, known from its opening words as *Universis christifidelibus*, tackled the problem of the pre-Albertian period by introducing a previous Patriarch of Jerusalem, John, as the first regulator of the hermits. John is not given a date, but the rule he supplied is said to have been that of Basil and Paulinus, and he is described as ruling the church in Jerusalem not long after Peter was Bishop in Antioch.[14] Patriarch John must refer to the John who was Bishop of Jerusalem from 387 to 417. Although he was a monk, no rule has been attributed to him.[15] The figure of Paulinus presents a further problem, for the obvious candidate, Paulinus of Nola, wrote no rule. Staring has pointed out that the *Codex regularem* of Benedict of Aniane (750–821) ascribes a Latin rule to Basil which is similar to the *Liber exhortationis* of Paulinus of Aquileia (787–802), and that the author of the *Universis christifidelibus* must have known the *Codex* or a dependent source.[16]

---

[13] Mansi, 24, cols 96–7. As Staring, *MCH*, p. 34 and Cicconetti, *La regola*, pp. 89–90, argue, the rubric was probably composed as early as 1238–47.

[14] *MCH*, pp. 83–4. The *Universis christifidelibus* is an extended form of the *rubrica prima*.

[15] G. Graf, *Geschichte der christlichen arabischen Literatur*, 1, *Studi e Testi*, 118 (Vatican, 1944), p. 337.

[16] *MCH*, p. 75.

Between Patriarch John and Albert's foundation of a *collegium*, the chronicle supplies no further details. The obvious question remains of the status of the succession of hermits who supposedly lived *incessanter* on Mount Carmel during this long period. The indigenous Christians of Palestine were largely (and still remain) Arabic-speaking Greek Orthodox, to whom the Basilian Rule would have been familiar. The problem posed to the Carmelites was how to reconcile the Greek origins of any order that might have existed on Mount Carmel before the crusader period with the firmly Latin character of the order since Albert's re-foundation; in other words, how to emphasize both unity and diversity. But no Carmelite source says that Albert refounded a Greek community as a Latin; Albert's activity of collecting disparate hermits into a *collegium* is presented, rather, as the natural and organic development of an order.

A slightly later anonymous chronicle, *De inceptione ordinis*, takes the story further.[17] Patriarch John makes no appearance here, but a new attempt is made to flesh out the twelfth-century period of the order by using a non-Carmelite source, the Dominican Stephen of Salagnac. Stephen, writing before 1277/8, described the dispersal of the Carmelites to Europe in 1238, but went on to attribute the earlier regulation of the hermits not to Albert but to Aimery, Patriarch of Antioch (1140–93).[18] At first sight there is no rationale for this other than simple error. Stephen, however, was interested in Aimery because they were both natives of the Limousin.[19] The slip into which his patriotism led Stephen was a boon for a Carmelite author looking for ways of developing knowledge of his order's origins, and, especially, of extending the evidence for those origins back before 1215. The *De inceptione* took over Aimery from Stephen, but also retained Albert. Aimery, having read of the way of life led by the hermits who lived in individual cells on Mount Carmel, brought them together *sub cura unius*, and bound them to follow a more

---

[17] *MCH*, pp. 91–106; Staring dates the text to *c.* 1324.

[18] Stephen of Salagnac and Bernard Gui, *De quatuor in quibus Deus praedicatorum ordinem insignavit*, ed. T. Kaeppeli, *Monumenta ordinis praedicatorum historica*, 12 (Rome, 1949), pp. 179–81. Bernard Gui edited Stephen's work. Two other works of Bernard's are cited in the *De inceptione ordinis*.

[19] Hamilton, *The Latin Church in the Crusader States* (London, 1980), p. 38. Stephen, *De quatuor*, p. 181, makes a point of saying that Aimery was a native of his own town, Salagnac.

regulated profession, with a collective name but as yet no written rule.[20]

The actions of Albert in forming a *collegium* and supplying a rule were thus shared out, in Carmelite tradition, between two figures: Aimery was given the role of founding a *collegium* and Albert of writing the rule.[21] By emphasizing the eremitical character of these putative twelfth-century Carmelites, the author of the *De inceptione* may have thought to avoid the issue of whether they were native Orthodox or Franks. But the passage makes it clear that the hermits whom Aimery collected together were to be identified with the successors of Elijah in the early Christian period.[22] Moreover, the description of the hermits as living in individual cells (*ipsos separatim in cellulis per totum montem Carmeli habitantes . . . colligavit*)[23] recalls the structure of a typical Byzantine laura rather than of a western eremitical community.[24]

Another fourteenth-century Carmelite, John de Cheminot, reconciled the two traditions of Patriarchs John and Aimery by merging the relevant passages from the *Universis christifidelibus* and the *De inceptione*. This change, of course, meant that Aimery was reforming an existing order. John himself is described as being *de religione praedicta quidam frater*, leaving no doubt that the Carmelites were to be considered a single order with a continuous existence, but also implying that they were, at the time when Aimery re-organized them, Orthodox.[25] This tradition reached its fullest development in the complex edifice of the Carmelite prior-provincial of Catalonia in the 1370s, Philip Ribot.

---

[20] *MCH*, p. 99.

[21] Stephen of Salagnac's use of Aimery was not implausible. Aimery's own suffragan Bishop of Laodicea, Gerard of Nazareth (1140–61), reported Aimery's regulation for supervised eremitical communities on the Black Mountain, outside Antioch, B. Z. Kedar, 'Gerard of Nazareth, a neglected twelfth-century writer of the Latin east', *Dumbarton Oaks Papers*, 37 (1983), p. 74. As Patriarch of Antioch, however, Aimery had no ecclesiastical jurisdiction over Mt Carmel, which was in the diocese of Acre.

[22] *MCH*, p. 99. The passage following a reference to hermits building a church on Mt Carmel after the incarnation of Christ begins 'Quos . . . Aymericus Malafayda . . . ipsorum laudabilem conversationem attendens . . .'.

[23] *MCH*, p. 99.

[24] For a description of a twelfth-century laura in Palestine see *Work on Geography* in Wilkinson, *Jerusalem Pilgrimage*, p. 35: '[The monks and hermits] live alone in individual cells, not together, yet sharing a communal life.'

[25] John de Cheminot, *Speculum fratrum ordinis beatae Mariae de Monte Carmeli*, in *MCH*, pp. 130–1. Jean was active in Paris 1336–9.

Ribot's *De institutione et peculiaribus gestis Carmelitarum* is an imaginative synthesis drawn from existing traditions and presented as a compilation of historical texts.[26] The section of the book dealing with the origins of the order purports to be Ribot's edition of the *Liber de institutione primorum monachorum* written by Patriarch John himself in 412. Not content with simply citing or discussing John's role, Ribot offers a text heavily reliant on the *rubrica prima* and the *Universis christifidelibus* as John's own work, and supplements this with a section describing the activities of Aimery and Albert, presented as the work of a thirteenth-century prior-general of the order, Cyril. Ribot's main concern was to establish the continuity of monasticism on Mount Carmel. As he realized, this meant recognition that an order established by a Greek-speaking prelate, John, with a Greek rule, remained Greek, and thus Orthodox, throughout the period of the Byzantine and Arab occupation of Palestine. Not until the arrival of the Franks in 1099 did the monks of Mount Carmel have the opportunity to be reformed. The need for such reform gave Aimery a more prominent role in Ribot's vision of the past. After 1099, according to Ribot, so many Franks joined the hermits on Mount Carmel that the original purity of the order was threatened. The Franks, who could not understand Greek, did not follow John's rule. Aimery's solution was to have the rule of Patriarch John translated into Latin, and to gather the hermits together into a *collegium*: 'In order to restrain the temerity of those inadequate [recruits] and preserve the innocence of the old hermits of the mountain, he bound them all with the bond of obedience.'[27] Ribot, disingenuously, omits to mention what provision was made for the original Greek-speaking hermits. The assumption is that they were forced to join the new community administered by a Latin prior, Berthold.[28] As we have seen, this may indeed have been the situation at the 'spring of

---

[26] The most accessible edition is in Daniel a Virgine Maria, *Speculum Carmelitanum*, 2 vols in 4 (Antwerp, 1680), 1, pp. 1–128 (separate pagination). A critical edition by Paul Chandler is currently in preparation. Ribot wrote after 1374 (and probably after 1379), and died in 1391. L. Saggi, *S. Angelo di Sicilia*, Textus et studia historica Carmelitana, 6 (Rome, 1962), p. 31, argues that his work was not widely known even within the order until *c*.1413.

[27] Ribot, *De institutione*, VIII, 2, p. 75. Ribot's wording, although his own, ultimately derives from John de Cheminot, the *De inceptione* and Stephen de Salagnac.

[28] Ribot, *De institutione*, VIII, 2, p. 75. Ribot, who seems to be the first to mention Berthold, says that he began his rule as prior in 1121, and started on the construction of a monastery, but that is 19 years before Aimery began his pontificate in Antioch.

Elijah' when Albert wrote his rule for a group of hermits who desired a greater degree of coherence.[29]

Ribot's reconstruction reveals the boldness, but also the limitations of Carmelite historical perception in the fourteenth century. Neither Ribot nor any of the Carmelite sources on which he relied raised the issue of doctrine. It seemed natural to them that hermits living in individual cells should be brought into a *collegium* under the rule of a prior: effectively exchanging Orthodox practice for Latin. But the questions of theology and ecclesiastical custom that aroused such great hostilities between Latins and Orthodox, and that might be expected to have caused problems in such a mixed foundation, were considered, by the Carmelite authors, irrelevant to the question of the order's composition and development. The organizational structure was more important than the theological allegiance of the hermits. Language Ribot recognized as a problem, but not doctrine.

It is easy to see the reason for these priorities. At the time he was writing, the integrity of the Carmelite order was being challenged by the Dominicans. It was not doctrinal orthodoxy that concerned the challengers but the order's status in canon law and the legality of its claims to antiquity.[30] In this sense the demands of Carmelite historical literature of the fourteenth century had not moved far from the perilous situation of 1274. Ribot was anxious to prove that the order was indeed as old as the *rubrica prima* claimed, and to clarify its status as an order within the Church. If this meant absorbing Greek Orthodox laura-hermits, it was a price worth paying. Nevertheless, it is difficult to believe so absolutely in the compliance of Greek Orthodox monks as Ribot's historical model demands. The manuscripts produced by the monks of St Sabas and by the Orthodox community at the Holy Sepulchre in the twelfth and thirteenth centuries show a continuing interest in Orthodox doctrine and in anti-Latin polemic.[31] A twelfth-century

---

[29] But for the continued independence of Greek Orthodox monastic life in the Kingdom of Jerusalem in this period, see Andrew Jotischky, *The Perfection of Solitude: Hermits and Monks in the Crusader States*, (University Park, Penn., 1995), ch. 3.

[30] J. P. H. Clark, 'A defence of the Carmelite Order by John Hornby, O. Carm., A.D. 1374', *Carmelus*, 32 (1985), pp. 73–106. See also the treatises of Bernard Oller and Robert of Ormeskirk in *MCH*, pp. 395–421.

[31] A. Papadopoulos-Kerameos, Ἱεροσολομιτικη βιβλιοθηκη new edn, 5 vols (Brussels, 1963), 1, pp. 115–20, 186–92; 2, p. 485.

Orthodox monk and lauriote who had lived among hermits in the Holy Land, Neophytus of Cyprus, was vehemently anti-Latin, especially after the Latin conquest of Cyprus in 1191.[32] Although little is known about the level of Latin/Orthodox doctrinal controversy in the Kingdom of Jerusalem, the Carmelites' vision of harmony on Mount Carmel stretches credulity. The omission of any notion of doctrinal difference in Ribot's work suggests a startling naiveté in the fourteenth century in the general level of understanding of the history of Orthodox/Latin relations. Perhaps even more telling than Ribot's omission is the failure of the Carmelites' opponents to make a case against them on the basis of their Orthodox origins.

Ribot's work, dependent as it was on the official line taken in the *rubrica prima*, represents the mainstream Carmelite tradition. A contemporary English Carmelite, however, represents a separate tradition about the Carmelite past that was less sanguine about Orthodox involvement. William of Coventry's *De duplici fuga fratrum de Carmelo*, written in 1360, introduces an earlier date for the dispersal of the hermits from Mount Carmel than the 1238 provided by Vincent of Beauvais and used by other Carmelites.[33] William surmised that in the Muslim invasion of 1187 many Carmelites were martyred, and that 'the vine of the Carmelites planted by the mother of Christ would have been uprooted had the Lord not left that seed already planted in Cyprus and Sicily.'[34] This enabled William to weave into Carmelite history Richard I's conquest of Cyprus from the Byzantines in 1191, for which his source was Roger de Hoveden. According to William, two English clergymen convinced Richard to found Carmelite convents in Limassol and Fortamia to the memory of the Carmelites martyred in the Holy Land. This was not the first Carmelite presence in Cyprus, for the seed had already been planted ( *per antea radicatum*) at the time. But the new foundations

---

[32] Catia Galatariotou, *The Making of a Saint. The Life, Times and Sanctification of Neophytus the Recluse* (Cambridge, 1991), pp. 230–43.

[33] William of Coventry, *De duplici fuga fratrum de Carmelo*, in *MCH*, p. 279. John Bale gave the date of William's work as 1340 in a notebook of transcriptions compiled *c.* 1527–33, Oxford, Bodleian Library, MS Selden Supra 41, fol. 107r, but in his *Scriptorum illustrium Maioris Britanniae . . . Catalogus*, 2 vols (Basel, 1557–59), 1, 461–2, he changed this to 1360.

[34] *MCH*, p. 280.

would serve the further purpose of strengthening the Catholic Church at the expense of the native Orthodox:

> There were no Catholics in Cyprus except for those Carmelite brothers already established there; for all the others were Greeks who neither believed in nor celebrated according to the Roman Church. But the Carmelites had taken their faith, their rule and ordinal from Christ and the church of Jerusalem, which always believed and celebrated according to the Latin Catholic Church.[35]

Inserted into the narrative is thus a polemic, the purpose of which is the appropriation of the Church in the Holy Land for the Carmelite Order. The Carmelites are presented as the followers of an original Latin Catholicism handed down by the apostolic Church in Jerusalem who maintained 'true' doctrine in the teeth of the Greek schismatics. In the *De duplici fuga* there is no mention of Patriarch John's rule, or of Basil. In his *Chronica brevis*, which is a simple chronology derived from John de Cheminot, William's only entry for the period between the incarnation and 1099 is the claim that the Carmelites had built a chapel dedicated to the Blessed Virgin on Mount Carmel in AD 83.[36] Whereas John de Cheminot and Ribot saw the putative Orthodox origins as necessary for placing the order within a recognizable context of early Christian monasticism, William saw the danger in such a strategy. He was determined that no taint of Greek Orthodoxy be found even in the primitive order. For William, Latinity, and thus diversity, had greater priority than antiquity; the past could not wholly be trusted.

To understand why William took such a radically different view of his order's past we must turn back to Orthodox/Latin relations in his own day. In 1357 the Carmelite bishop Peter Thomas, the papal legate sent to Constantinople to receive the submission of John V Palaeologus, retired to Cyprus, and used the island as his base from 1359, when he was appointed papal

---

[35] *MCH*, p. 281. Limassol and Fortamia appear in a list of Carmelite houses in the East; *MCH*, pp. 265–6.
[36] *MCH*, p. 273. This detail first appeared in the *De inceptione ordinis*, *MCH*, p. 42.

127

legate in the East, until his death in 1366.[37] Peter used his legatine powers to enforce the submission of Orthodox clergy in Cyprus to the Roman Church. In 1360 he was almost lynched by a Greek mob when he tried to preach to the Orthodox clergy on their doctrinal errors and to enforce their obedience to him.[38] Peter was simply following the traditional papal policy since the 1220s of subordinating the Greek clergy to the Latin episcopal hierarchy.[39] But he was dealing not only with Greek intransigence but the disinterest in doctrinal polemic of the Latin population. According to Philip de Mézières, he came to despair of the Latin Church in Cyprus; not without cause, for in 1368 Urban V had to complain to the king of the number of Latin women who were attending Greek churches.[40]

William of Coventry was writing at a time when a prominent Carmelite prelate was actively persecuting Orthodoxy in Cyprus. Although there is no evidence that William knew of Peter's activities, the legate's insistence on Orthodox obedience to the papacy is thrown into high relief by this contemporary Carmelite tradition of a pristine Catholic observance maintained by the Carmelites since the apostolic Church. Given his general dependence on existing sources, William's account of the Cypriot Carmelite foundation probably represented a current English tradition that Peter Thomas, a Gascon who had entered the Carmelite order at Bergerac, on English sovereign territory, might have known.[41] Even if no connection can be made be-

---

[37] Peter's contemporary biographer Philippe de Mézières treated John V's conversion in 1357 as definitive: *The Life of Saint Peter Thomas by Philippe de Mézières*, ed. J. Smet, Textus et studia historica Carmelitana, 2 (Rome, 1954), pp. 75–9; Philippe is followed uncritically by F. J. Boehlke, *Pierre de Thomas. Scholar, Diplomat and Crusader* (Philadelphia, 1966), pp. 147–70. Halecki, *Un Empereur de Byzance*, p. 62, and Nicol, 'Byzantine requests', p. 87, are more sceptical about the success of his mission.

[38] *The Life of Saint Peter Thomas*, pp. 92–3; Macheras, *Recital Concerning the Sweet Land of Cyprus*, ed. and trans. R. M. Dawkins, 2 vols (Oxford, 1932), 1, pp. 90–1.

[39] Mansi, 22, cols 1037–46; G. Hill, *A History of Cyprus*, 4 vols (Cambridge, 1940–52), 3, pp. 1042–84. Boehlke, *Pierre de Thomas*, pp. 168–9, defends Peter against Halecki's assertion, *Un Empereur de Byzance*, pp. 60, 70–1, that the legate resorted after 1357 to a general policy of forceful repression against the Orthodox after persuasion had failed. But as Boehlke, *Pierre de Thomas*, p. 193, admits, Peter became a 'target for hatred' among Orthodox intellectuals.

[40] *The Life of Saint Peter Thomas*, p. 92; Hill, *History of Cyprus*, 3, pp. 1082–3.

[41] *The Life of Saint Peter Thomas*, p. 53. Peter was born c.1305 in the county of Perigord. William was dependent on John de Cheminot, but introduced a variant tradition of the Carmelite settlement in the West, making England rather than France the site of the first western foundations: *De adventu Carmelitarum ad Angliam*, in *MCH*, pp. 282–6.

tween Peter Thomas's activities as legate and William's work, the *De duplici fuga* acts as a reminder of the prevalent clerical attitudes toward the Orthodox at the time of the negotiations for the union of the Churches between the 1350s and 1380s. If William's approach represents typical attitudes, this only reveals the mainstream Carmelite tradition as more remarkable in its breadth of vision. But the lack of hostility toward the Orthodox that Peter Thomas found among the Latins of Cyprus shows perhaps that the ingenuous vision of Latin/Orthodox co-operation in the wadis of Mount Carmel gives a truer picture of actual relations than the diplomatic exchanges between Constantinople and the papal curia.

Carmelite historical writing in the later Middle Ages may itself be said to be an example of diversity within unity. There was no single coherent account of Carmelite origins. The manifest need to establish a credible antiquity led Carmelites into appropriating early Church history and geography. This interest in the antiquity of monasticism in Palestine is common to all medieval Carmelite writing. Within this assumed framework, however, there was room for divergence. Most apologists stressed the antiquity of the order above all, and in doing so proposed unity with Greek Orthodox monks as a fundamental element in the composition of the order. How Carmelites dealt with the legacy of Greek Orthodoxy in the Holy Land illuminates not only the intellectual concerns of religious orders in the later Middle Ages but, more specifically, the sense of the past that informed western attitudes to the Orthodox during the negotiations for the union of the Churches.

University of Lancaster

# RITES AND WRONGS: THE LATIN MISSION TO NICAEA, 1234*

by JOHN DORAN

In 1232 Germanus II (1223–40), the Nicaean Patriarch of Constantinople, wrote to Pope Gregory IX and to the cardinals of the Roman Church requesting discussions on the reformation of peace between the Greek and Roman Churches.[1] In response to this request the Pope sent two English Franciscans and two French Dominicans, at least one of them proficient in Greek, as his representatives to Nicaea.[2] After their return the friars presented a detailed account of the mission to the Pope, which was copied into the *Liber Censuum*.[3] The extant documentation of the mission allows us to examine the ideas of the Greeks and Latins about unity and schism in the Church.[4] And it shows us that there was no prospect of a union of the Churches because each had a fundamentally different conception of the nature of ecclesiastical authority.

---

*I should like to thank Dr Margaret Harvey and Professor Bernard Hamilton for their helpful comments upon earlier versions of this paper.

[1] A. L. Tautu, *Acta Honorii III et Gregorii IX*, Pontificia commissio ad redigendum codicem iuris canonici orientalis, Fontes ser. III, 3 (Vatican City, 1950), no. 179a, pp. 240–9 (Germanus' letter to Gregory IX), no. 179b, pp. 249–52 (Germanus' letter to the cardinals). The texts of the letter to Gregory, together with his replies, are also in Mansi, 23, cols 279–319.

[2] For brief descriptions of the mission see: J. Gill, *Byzantium and the Papacy 1198–1400* (Brunswick, NJ, 1979), pp. 63–72; M. Angold, *A Byzantine Government in Exile: Government and Society under the Laskarids of Nicaea (1204–1261)* (Oxford, 1975), p. 14: idem, 'Greeks and Latins after 1204: the perspective of exile', in B. Arbel, B. Hamilton and D. Jacoby, eds, *Latins and Greeks in the Eastern Mediterranean after 1204* (London, 1989), pp. 78–9; R. L. Wolff, 'The Latin Empire of Constantinople and the Franciscans', *Traditio*, 2 (1944), pp. 229–30; C. J. Hefèle and H. Leclercq, *Histoire des Conciles*, 5, pt 2 (Paris, 1913), cols 1565–72. For a useful introduction to the series of unity negotiations see M. Jugie, *Le Schisme Byzantin* (Paris, 1941), pp. 247–58. One of the Franciscans, Haymo of Faversham, was later a General of the order; see G. Golubovich, *Biblioteca Bio-bibliografica della Terra Santa e dell' Oriente Francescana*, 5 vols (Florence, 1906–23), 1, pp. 163–9.

[3] H. Golubovich, 'Disputatio Latinorum et Graecorum seu Relatio Apocrisariorum Gregorii IX de gestis Nicaeae in Bithynia et Nymphaeae in Lydia', *Archivum Franciscanum Historicum*, 12 (1919), pp. 418–70, at p. 426.

[4] Golubovich, 'Disputatio', pp. 421–4, provides a list of the documentation of the mission. But see note 1 above for more recent editions of the initial correspondence. For a Greek description of the mission of 1234, confirming the accuracy of the friars' report, see A. Heisenberg, ed., *Nicephori Blemmydae Curriculum Vitae et Carmina* (Leipzig, 1896), pp. 63–7, XV–XVI, XLI–XLIII. For a full account of the Greek documentation of the mission see V. Laurent, *Les Regestes des Actes du Patriarcat de Constantinople*, 1, fasc. 4, 'Les Regestes de 1208 à 1309' (Paris, 1971), pp. 62–8; 76–85.

The sending of a mission to Nicaea was a recognition that the fall of Constantinople in 1204 had not heralded the disappearance of the Greek Church. Once political dominion had passed to the Latins, Innocent III had believed that the rites of the Greek Church would be subsumed into those of the Church of Rome.[5] As in southern Italy the Greek rites would be tolerated in the private context of monastic communities, but the public worship of the Church would be conducted in the Roman rite.[6] However, this train of thought assumed the permanence of Latin rule in the former Greek lands and Innocent III effectively put off Latinization *sine die*.[7]

The Greek Church had survived under Greek political rule in various areas of the former Empire. The most important of these states was the Empire of Nicaea. After the death of the Patriarch of Constantinople, John X Camaterus (1198–1206), who had refused an invitation to reside at Nicaea, the Greeks of Constantinople requested permission to elect a Greek patriarch from Innocent III.[8] We do not know the response of the Pope, but in March 1208 Theodore I Laskaris (*c*.1206–22), the Nicaean ruler, gathered the exiled Greek hierarchy in Nicaea to elect an orthodox patriarch and to witness his first public act, the crowning of Theodore as Emperor.[9]

The presence of the Patriarch and the Emperor in Nicaea was effectively a re-establishment of the Empire in exile, but the contradictions of the new state made any reunion of the Greek and Latin Churches unlikely. Indeed, the weakness of the patriarch led to the break up of the patriarchate of Constantinople itself, with many churches becoming de facto autocephalous and some seeking an accommodation with the papacy, while the heightened sense of Greek nationalism engendered by the court of Nicaea alienated some branches of the Orthodox Church.[10] The Emperor needed to seek an accommodation with the

---

[5] M. Jugie, *Le Schisme Byzantin*, pp. 252–4; J. Gill, 'Innocent III and the Greeks: aggressor or apostle?', in D. Baker, ed., *Relations between East and West in the Middle Ages* (Edinburgh, 1973), pp. 95–108.

[6] Angold, 'Greeks and Latins', p. 64; B. Hamilton, *The Latin Church in the Crusader States: The Secular Church* (London, 1980), pp. 159–87.

[7] M. Jugie, *Le Schisme Byzantin*, pp. 253–4.

[8] *PG*, 140, cols 293–8; Gill, *Byzantium and the Papacy*, pp. 34–5.

[9] Angold, *Byzantine Government*, p. 13, idem, 'Greeks and Latins', p. 67.

[10] Angold, *Byzantine Government*, pp. 21–4, 28–32; J. Spiteris, *La Critica Bizantina del Primato Romano nel secolo XII*, Orientalia Periodica Analecta, 208 (Rome, 1979), p. 321.

papacy in order to protect his own borders immediately and to regain Constantinople in the long term. At the same time, however, the Greek clergy, led by the Patriarch, encouraged the growth of anti-Latin sentiment precisely because it was a unifying factor within the Greek Church. The fact that papal representatives were requested by the anti-Latin Germanus is an indication that the Emperor John III Doukas Vatatzes (1222–54) had brought some pressure to bear on him for the political good of the state, but this in itself did not bode well for the success of the mission.

The initial letter of Germanus to Gregory IX opened with an affirmation of the primacy of Christ over the Church.[11] He had decided to write to the Pope because of a chance encounter with five Franciscans who had sought the protection of the Emperor while returning from a pilgrimage to Jerusalem. Germanus was obviously impressed by the simple holiness of the Franciscans, but he gave no indication of the precise nature of their encounter or why it had led him to write.[12] The Franciscans reminded him not only of the five wise virgins of the Gospel but also of the five patriarchates among which he hoped to restore peace.[13] They must appeal to Christ together to restore unity.[14] Germanus asked Gregory to heal the wound of schism if it had been inflicted by the Greeks, but he made it clear that it was rather the Latins who were at fault.[15] The Pope was exhorted to put a stop to those things which caused discord among the churches, or which were contrary to dogma, or tended towards the destruction of the canons or rites passed down by the Fathers of the Church.[16] Basically the Pope was to conform the customs and usages of the Roman Church to those of the other four patriarchates, which, of course, were Orthodox. Germanus was also prompted to write to the cardinals of the Roman Church and noted that the Franciscans had told him what an august body their college was. As well as repeating the main points of his letter to the Pope, Germanus made the observation that human affairs were better conducted with the advice of a college of

[11] Tautu, *Acta Honorii*, pp. 240–1.
[12] Golubovich, *Biblioteca Bio-bibliografica*, pp. 161–2.
[13] Tautu, *Acta Honorii*, p. 242.
[14] Ibid., p. 243.
[15] Ibid., pp. 244–5.
[16] Ibid., p. 245.

prudent and learned men.[17] The Patriarch clearly had the college of the five patriarchs in mind as well as the college of cardinals.

The letters of Germanus reveal that he was imbued with the idea of ecclesiastical authority which had been developed in the Byzantine Church in the period after the Photian Schism.[18] The chief characteristic of this development was the denial of papal primacy.[19] On his own, the pope had no authority to act for the Universal Church, but only for his patriarchate. The only authority for the Universal Church was the college of the five patriarchs acting in unison,[20] and the forum for such action was the general council. As in Byzantine polemical works against the papacy, Germanus used Peter as a reproach to the pope: was it the successor of the meek and humble Peter who had ordered the martyrdom of Greeks in Cyprus?[21]

Germanus ended his letter by admonishing the Pope to admit that the Roman Church had erred.[22] In order to rejoin the collegial pentarchy the Roman Church must look at her face in the mirror and see her blemishes. This mirror was the Gospels, the writings of the apostles and the theological works of the Fathers. These were the ultimate repository of the faith for the Church. The fact that Rome had fallen away from the faith was obvious to all except the Romans, because they had never looked. Germanus urged Gregory to look in the mirror, 'For whoever is invited to look into a mirror for the first time, on his return, however unwilling, will admit that his face is ugly.'[23]

Gregory IX sent two letters to Germanus in reply. The first was an enthusiastic agreement to send a mission.[24] However, the letter clearly showed that Gregory's idea of the exercise was not at all the same as Germanus'. He promised to send learned and

---

[17] Ibid., p. 250.

[18] For a discussion of Byzantine ideas of authority in the Church see J. Meyendorff, *Byzantine Theology: Historical Trends and Doctrinal Themes* (London and Oxford, 1974), pp. 97–102.

[19] F. Dvornik, *Byzantium and the Roman Primacy* (New York, 1966), pp. 124–70, idem, *The Photian Schism* (Cambridge, 1948), pp. 383–402; J. Spiteris, *Critica Bizantina*, pp. 1–24, 300–22; M. Jugie, 'La primauté romaine dans l'église byzantine à partir du IX<sup>e</sup> siècle jusqu'à la dernière tentative d'union avec Rome, au concile de Florence', in A. Vacant, E. Mangenot, and E. Amann, eds, *Dictionnaire de théologie catholique* 13/i (Paris, 1936) [hereafter *DTC*], cols 357–77.

[20] Jugie, *DTC*, col. 639.

[21] Tautu, *Acta Honorii*, p. 246.

[22] Ibid., pp. 247–8.

[23] Ibid., p. 248: 'Qui autem ad speculum fuerit invitatus causa experientiae, cum recesserit, confitebitur, etiam invitus, suum vultum esse deformem.'

[24] Ibid., no. 179, pp. 235–9. Gregory's second letter: ibid., no. 193, pp. 266–8.

honest men to the Patriarch, 'For hearing the wise he will become wiser, and understanding he will find direction.'[25] Gregory agreed that Christ was the foundation of the Church, but the apostles were the foundation that Christ himself had put in place, and the chief of the apostles was Peter, not by accident, but at the express command of Christ. Gregory then set out what was to be the theme of the mission. The primacy over the apostles was given to Peter for the specific purpose of confirming his brothers in the faith. As the successor of Peter, Gregory was to remove scrupulous doubts from the minds of all, not opposing them with pride or contention, but with all patience and instruction.[26] The insistence that the popes were the successors of Peter was a deliberate rebuttal of the Greek claim that the primacy of Peter had been a personal honour and had died with him. The ultimate authority in the Church was the pope. As Gregory pointed out, a body with many heads is monstrous, while with no head it is headless.[27] For Gregory authority in the Church was certainly not collegial.

Gregory urged Germanus to put aside his superstitions and look into the mirror he himself proposed. He would see that there was nothing professed by the Roman Church which did not comply with the unity of the faith.[28] If they would repent of their errors the Greeks would be welcomed back by the Roman Church, the Mother and Mistress of all churches. If not, they would suffer the destruction of their rites and liberty. Given the events of 1204 this was no idle threat.

On their arrival in Nicaea the four friars were asked whether they wanted to be received as legates of the Pope, but they insisted that they were merely messengers.[29] The friars repeated this description of themselves before the Emperor John III on the following day. The reason for this insistence was the suspicion that the Greeks might in future claim to have convened a general council in order to judge the errors of the Roman Church. There immediately arose the problem which was to recur almost daily during the mission, that of who should speak

---

[25] Ibid., pp. 235–6.

[26] Ibid., p. 236.

[27] Ibid., p. 237: 'et corpus cum multis capitibus monstruosum, et sine capite acephalum censeatur'.

[28] Ibid., p. 238.

[29] Golubovich, 'Disputatio', p. 428.

first. The friars refused to begin the discussion, declaring that, 'We were not sent to dispute some article of faith with you over which we or the Roman Church have doubts, but to discuss your doubts amicably. Thus it is for you to show these things and for us, by the grace of God, to enlighten you.'[30] This response reflected the letter of Gregory IX. The friars, on behalf of the Pope, were to remove the scrupulous doubts of the Greeks and bring them back into the unity of the Church. The Greeks, however, were unwilling to admit to any doubts, but after some discussion they decided that the issues they wanted to discuss were the procession of the Holy Spirit and the sacrament of the altar. The friars then announced that the object of the mission would be to discover whether these matters constituted sufficient cause for the Greeks to have subtracted their obedience from the see of Rome.[31]

On the first day of real debate, the friars wanted to discuss the sacrament of the altar, but the Greeks insisted that the discussion should be on the procession of the Holy Spirit. The controversy over the addition of the *filioque* had been the most consistently used argument against the claims of papal primacy since the Photian Schism of the ninth century.[32] The question which interested the Greeks was whether the Roman Church had added anything to the creed of the First Council of Nicaea (325). In 1054 Cardinal Humbert of Silva-Candida had excommunicated the officials of Michael Keroullarios, claiming that the Greeks had omitted the *filioque* from the creed.[33] However, in 1234 the friars accepted that the words 'and from the son' had indeed been added to the Nicene Creed, but they insisted that the Roman Church had not added them illicitly. For the friars the question was not one of theology but of authority.

The friars had found a convincing argument on the addition to the creed. The Greek charge against the Roman Church was that it had no authority to add to the creed because the fathers of Nicaea had strictly forbidden additions under pain of anathema.[34] However, the friars pointed out that the Nicene Creed had

[30] Ibid., p. 429.
[31] Ibid., pp. 429–30.
[32] Jugie, *DTC*, col. 367; Meyendorff, *Byzantine Theology*, pp. 90–4.
[33] Dvornik, *Roman Primacy*, p. 134.
[34] Golubovich, 'Disputatio', pp. 431–2; Mansi, 2, col. 666.

indeed been added to, since the Symbol of the Council of Constantinople[35] (381) was not the same as that of the Council of Nicaea. The friars asked who had dared to alter the creed and reported that the Greeks had attempted to evade the question,[36] eventually replying that it was not an addition, but merely an expression of the truth.[37] The friars then insisted that the *filioque* was not an addition to or mutation of the creed, but also an expression of the truth. Since it was not against the faith, it was not forbidden to say it, write it, or chant it liturgically. The Greeks then demanded that the friars prove the orthodoxy of the *filioque*.

In this initial encounter the friars had been successful in countering the first of the Greek arguments. It has often been stated that the basis of all of the arguments between the eastern and western Churches throughout the thirteenth century and beyond was the primacy of the pope.[38] Yet the discussions aimed at restoring unity in the thirteenth century never mentioned papal primacy explicitly.[39] The opening salvo of the 1234 negotiations shows that the real issue was not the orthodoxy of the *filioque* but whether or not the pope inherited the primacy of Peter and whether that primacy gave him the authority to add to the dogmatic formulations of the ecumenical councils. Dvornik has shown that there was a profound difference between East and West in the conception of authority from the sixth century onwards.[40] The popes had a conception of their own office which allowed them to abrogate and promulgate canons without reference to any other authority, be it the emperor or the other patriarchs.[41] The developing theory of papal primacy gave the West a dynamic authority which was able to cope with change by legitimizing it. In the East, however, the unresolved question of

[35] Mansi, 3, col. 565.

[36] Golubovich, 'Disputatio', p. 432.

[37] Ibid., p. 433.

[38] Jugie, *DTC*, cols 369–77; D. M. Nicol, 'The papal scandal', *SCH*, 13 (1976), pp. 141–68; Spiteris, *Critica Bizantina*, pp. 300–21; Dvornik, *Roman Primacy*, pp. 155–67.

[39] Jugie, *DTC*, col. 373.

[40] Dvornik, *Roman Primacy*, pp. 124–5; see also Meyendorff, *Byzantine Theology*, pp. 97–9; D. J. Geanakoplos, *Byzantine East and Latin West: Two Worlds of Christendom in the Middle Ages and Renaissance* (Oxford, 1966), ch. 2, 'Church and State in the Byzantine Empire: a reconsideration of the problem of Caesaropapism', pp. 55–83.

[41] W. Ullmann, *The Growth of Papal Government in the Middle Ages* (London, 1955), pp. 289–99; J. Gaudemet, 'Aspects de la primauté romaine du Vᵉ au XVᵉ siècle', *Ius Canonicum*, 11/22 (1971), pp. 106–16.

the authority of the emperor meant that in order to be binding, canons, even those of a general council, had to be promulgated as imperial law.[42] Moreover, once canons were promulgated there was no authority on earth which might abrogate them.

The Greek Church maintained that the ultimate authority in the Universal Church was a general council, yet the era in which general councils had been held more or less coincided with the period of Byzantine rule or influence in Italy. In the centuries after the Photian Schism the Greeks maintained that the popes had fallen into heresy and that the primacy had thus passed to Constantinople, or to the college of the four orthodox patriarchs, all of them under Greek control.[43] The friars had thus set out to demonstrate that the Roman Church did not profess anything which was heretical. For them the issue was primarily one of obedience. If the Greeks could be convinced that the Roman Church professed no heresy they could have no objection to returning to the fold of unity. In practice, however, the Patriarch of Constantinople had become, since the eleventh century, a veritable eastern pope, and this was reflected in the disappearance in Greek theology of the notion of papal primacy and the affirmation that the *dignitas imperii* rather than apostolicity conferred primacy.[44] Thus, while the friars tried to convince the Greeks that the pope was not a heretic, the Greeks had already developed an ecclesiology in which the opinion of the pope, whether heretical or not, had no validity for the Universal Church.

After having spent days producing lengthy arguments drawn from Greek and Latin sources in order to prove that the *filioque* was not a heresy, the friars refused to discuss the matter any further. If the Greeks would not believe their own Fathers, whom would they believe?[45] Moreover, they would not state that the Holy Spirit did *not* proceed from the Son, prompting the accusation from the friars that they were afraid to profess what they believed.[46] The Greeks eventually agreed to discuss the eucharist, but the Patriarch announced that because the subject

---

[42] Geanakoplos, *Byzantine East*, pp. 68–9.

[43] Dvornik, *Roman Primacy*, pp. 140–2; Jugie, *DTC*, col. 327; Spiteris, *Critica Bizantina*, pp. 306–11.

[44] Jugie, *DTC*, col. 367; Dvornik, *Roman Primacy*, p. 147; Spiteris, *Critica Bizantina*, pp. 301–2, 314.

[45] Golubovich, 'Disputatio', p. 444.

[46] Ibid., p. 434.

was so arduous he would have to convene a council, since he could not discuss it without his brother patriarchs. The friars again insisted that they had not been sent to a council. Germanus should hold his council and send its decisions to them at Constantinople so that they could carry them to the Pope.[47]

When the friars went to ask for permission to leave from John III they found him with Germanus.[48] In a private interview, in contrast to the public debates held in the previous days, the Emperor asked what the Patriarch and the Greek Church had to do in order to be reconciled to Rome. The friars replied that the Patriarch must believe what the Roman Church believed, and preach it, and that he must obey her in the same way and in the same things as before the schism. The Emperor then put the obvious question. If Germanus were to do these things, would the Pope restore his rights to him? Since Gregory IX was really not in a position to restore Constantinople to Germanus the friars answered ambiguously that if he would obey his mother the Patriarch would find more mercy than he believed possible from the Pope and the whole Roman Church. John III then gave them licence to leave, but the interview had made clear that whatever the Emperor might gain politically from a rapprochement with the papacy there was very little to encourage the Patriarch.

The friars were in fact persuaded eventually to attend Germanus' council, necessitating the arduous and dangerous journey to Nymphaion, an imperial residence 28 kilometres east of Smyrna and, as the friars complained, six days' travel from the sea of Constantinople.[49] After further delays lasting a whole week the Greeks agreed to discuss the eucharist. However, it became apparent at once that Gregory IX's neat formula to explain differences of rites was unacceptable to the Greeks. Gregory, following Innocent III, had stated that the Greek Church was founded by the apostle John, who had run to the tomb before Peter, but who had not gone in.[50] The Greeks, in consequence, had a more physical conception of Christ in contrast to the more

---

[47] Ibid., p. 444.

[48] Ibid., p. 445.

[49] Ibid., p. 465.

[50] Tautu, *Acta Honorii*, no. 193, pp. 266–8, at pp. 267–8. For Innocent III's letter making the same point see: J. Haluscynskyj, *Acta Innocentii III*, Pontificia commissio ad redigendum codicem iuris canonici orientalis, Fontes ser. III, 2 (Vatican City, 1944), no. 65, pp. 277–83.

spiritual appreciation of the Latins, and celebrated the eucharist in leavened bread. The idea that there had been more than one tradition was anathema to the Greeks. They maintained that the Roman Church had received the tradition of the use of leavened bread from the apostles and would hold it again.[51] The friars were somewhat flustered by this reaction and insisted that if the Greeks wanted an explanation of the Pope's letter they should ask Gregory IX himself. This bad-tempered altercation ended with the friars denouncing the Greeks for their hatred of the Latin eucharist.[52] As evidence, the friars stated that the writings of the Greeks were full of this heresy; that they had not dared to reply to the question lest their heresies be exposed; that they proved it by washing their altars after Latins had celebrated and forcing Latins to abjure the Latin faith before allowing them to communicate; that they had excluded the pope from their diptychs and that they excommunicated him annually.

The *chartophylax*, the treasurer of the patriarchal cathedral, denied that the pope was excommunicated by the Greeks, but he used the atrocities committed by the crusaders in Constantinople to show that it was rather the Latins who hated the Greek faith.[53] The friars demanded to know why the Greeks had removed the pope from their diptychs. Germanus countered by asking why the Pope had removed him from Latin diptychs, to which the friars replied that the Pope had never removed *him* because *he* had never been there. As for his predecessors, they were removed only after they had removed the pope.[54] The friars noted that the exclusion of the pope was an affirmation that he was either excommunicate or a heretic.[55] After the conquest of Constantinople Innocent III had been unable to force the Greeks to include his name in the liturgy, perhaps because he equated this with a public act of submission to the Roman Church. He had to content himself with an extra-liturgical acclamation by the people, such as the emperor had formerly enjoyed, rather

[51] Golubovich, 'Disputatio', pp. 454–5; 'estimamus autem quod et diocesis antiquioris Rome sic et accepit et tenebit'.
[52] Ibid., p. 451.
[53] Ibid., p. 451.
[54] Ibid., p. 451. On the development of the diptychs see F. Cabrol, 'Diptyques (Liturgie)', in F. Cabrol, ed., *Dictionnaire d'archéologie chrétienne et de liturgie*, 4/i (Paris, 1920) [hereafter *DCL*], cols 1045–94.
[55] Golubovich, 'Disputatio', p. 451.

than inclusion on the diptychs.[56] We should note that the reading of the diptychs was a much more public affair in the Greek liturgy than it was in the Latin,[57] and that Germanus himself was jealous of his own first place on the diptychs of the autocephalous Orthodox churches.[58]

The eagerness of the friars to discuss the eucharist and the equal unwillingness of the Greeks is the clearest sign in the whole mission that the Greeks were in fact intolerant of diversity. The Council of Union (879–80) had proclaimed that differences in 'ancient traditional practices' were not to be discussed or quarrelled over. All of the churches were to preserve those customs passed on to them from the past.[59] However, both churches had used the difference in rites for polemical purposes.[60] Greeks and Latins abused one another with the names 'azymites' and 'fermentaries'.[61] Innocent III noted in his treatise *On the Mysteries of the Mass* that through their use of yeast the Greeks had risen from being mere heretics to become heresiarchs.[62] But the Roman Church was generally tolerant of the rites of other churches. Only minor changes were requested of the Bulgarians on their rapprochement with Rome in 1203 to bring them into conformity with the Latin practice of anointing at priestly ordination and episcopal consecration.[63] It is easy to confuse the polemical insistence of some Latins in the eleventh and twelfth centuries that the Greeks should adopt the Roman rite with the official preference of Innocent III for a gradual adoption of the rite in Greek lands which had fallen under Latin rule.[64] The mission to Nicaea was recognized as an attempt at restoring unity with a Greek church under Greek political control. In such cases there could be no question of the Roman Church demanding the abandonment of traditional rites. In 1234 it was the Greeks who were insistent that the Roman Church had strayed from tradition and must re-adopt the traditional rites

---

[56] Gill, *Byzantium and the Papacy*, p. 39; Jugie, *Le Schisme Byzantin*, p. 253.

[57] Cabrol, *DCL*, col. 1050.

[58] Angold, *Byzantine Government*, p. 21.

[59] Mansi, 17, cols 497, 489; Dvornik, *Roman Primacy*, pp. 124–5.

[60] J. Parisot, 'Azymes', *DTC*, 1/ii (Paris, 1903) cols 2653–64.

[61] Ibid., col. 2653.

[62] *PL*, 217, cols 857–8.

[63] Haluscynskyj, *Acta Innocentii*, no. 52, pp. 258–60; Gill, *Byzantium and the Papacy*, pp. 21–2.

[64] Jugie, *Le Schisme Byzantin*, pp. 253–4; Dvornik, *Roman Primacy*, p. 147; Gill, 'Innocent III and the Greeks', pp. 98–101.

as practised by the Greek Church. To the Greeks the Roman rite was one of those things which caused great discord in the Church. Consequently they wanted the Pope to suppress it.

Gregory IX had written in his letter that after the consecration whatever bread had been used ceased to be bread anyway.[65] Greek theologians of the twelfth century had admitted that the type of bread used by Christ at the last supper could not be discerned accurately from the Gospels and that it was thus useless to pursue controversies on the matter.[66] Yet the Archbishop of Samastria stated at Nymphaion that the eucharist could not be confected with unleavened bread.[67] The friars asked him whether he meant the thing was physically impossible or whether it was impossible *de iure*. He replied that it was physically impossible. The question which the friars had asked, of course, was whether the issue was theological or juridical. The Archbishop insisted that Christ had instituted the sacrament in leavened bread and this practice had been kept by Christian tradition. The friars publicly announced that this opinion was a heresy, held out of malice or ignorance.[68] and proceeded to prove the Roman tradition from the Gospels, noting that remarkable though it was among such a multitude at the gathering not one Old or New Testament could be found.[69] The friars tried to prove their point further from the Greek Fathers, but complained that the Greeks would not listen. This was effectively the end of the negotiations.

When the friars went to take their leave of the Emperor he proposed to them the sort of trade-off agreement he was accustomed to use in secular affairs.[70] If the Roman Church would abandon the *filioque* the Greeks would drop their objection to the use of unleavened bread in the eucharist. The friars announced that the Roman Church would not abandon one iota of its faith. The Greeks must accept and preach the validity of the Latin as well as the Greek eucharist and that the Holy Spirit proceeds from the Father and from the Son, although the Pope would not force them to chant this in the liturgy. This response angered the Emperor and the friars began to fear for their safety.

[65] Tautu, *Acta Honorii*, no. 193, p. 267.
[66] Parisot, *DTC*, col. 2663; Dvornik, *Roman Primacy*, p. 140.
[67] Golubovich, 'Disputatio', pp. 453–4.
[68] Ibid., p. 458.
[69] Ibid., p. 459.
[70] Ibid., p. 462.

The account of the mission of 1234 shows us that the friars and the Pope believed that the Emperor could impose a union on the Greek Church. The account stressed that it was only when John III was absent that the Greek prelates showed their true hostility to the Roman Church. On one occasion, according to the friars, the Greeks read out before the Emperor a blatantly falsified account of what had happened in his absence.[71] When the friars complained to the Emperor of the hostility which they had encountered he assured them that it would not have happened in his presence.[72] His exasperation with his own clergy was shown when he complained that the schism had lasted for over 300 years and that the popes had nevertheless been on friendly relations with his predecessors.[73] By this point he had given up on the council. The scars of 1234 were perhaps shown on the death of Germanus II when John III refused to appoint Nicephorous Blemmydes in his stead 'because he feared the man's zeal'.[74] Blemmydes refused the patriarchate on the death of John III because he did not want to be the minister of religion of his former pupil, Theodore II Laskaris.[75] In order to counter what was effectively a vacuum at the heart of the Greek Church, Theodore II claimed that the Emperor had the right to decide matters unresolved by a general council, but this was more than any emperor had ever been able to achieve.[76] There was no guarantee anyway that the people, the 'conscience of the Church', would accept such a council.[77]

John III asked the friars to present themselves to the council as a sign of respect before they left. However, when they arrived at the Patriarch's house they found a large crowd gathered and the council assembled in its midst.[78] They were then asked to declare publicly the faith of the Roman Church on the procession of the Holy Spirit. In spite of, or perhaps because of, their fear, the friars interrupted Germanus as he was about to speak and declared that he was a heretic. As the crowd became more agitated

---

[71] Ibid., p. 437.
[72] Ibid., pp. 452–3.
[73] Ibid., p. 453.
[74] Angold, *Byzantine Government*, p. 50.
[75] Ibid., p. 51.
[76] Ibid., p. 57.
[77] Geanakoplos, *Byzantine East*, pp. 73–80.
[78] Golubovich, 'Disputatio', pp. 462–4.

the friars left, noting only that the Emperor looked troubled because they were leaving in discord.

It appears that the final act of the mission of 1234 had been a show of strength engineered by the Patriarch to warn the Emperor that there were limits on his authority. Yet in the absence of that authority there could be no union with the Church of Rome. The fact was that for as long as the Greeks claimed that the only authority in the Universal Church was a general council there could be no movement at all. General councils did not happen any more as far as the Greeks were concerned. When they were to happen in the future, as at Lyons or Florence, the response of the majority of the Greek clergy and people was to repudiate the councils on the grounds that they were illegitimate.[79] While the West had developed an ecclesiastical government which claimed to have the authority to interpret tradition and thus to accommodate change, the Greeks had to look back to a tradition which had ossified. The Roman Church was able to pursue its claim to catholicity by embracing and accommodating diversity, while the Greeks, claiming to defend the apostolic tradition, were left to attack anything which their own Church did not profess. This stance managed to alienate many of the Orthodox Churches which were not politically Greek as well as the Roman Church.

The inability of the Greek Church to accept innovation is another factor to add to the list drawn up by Professor Frend when he wrote, 'Whether one turns to the art of war, to political thought or to historical writing the evidence for the backward-looking tendency in Byzantium is clear. It must be accepted as one of the factors that led to the extinction of its empire and of itself.'[80] Given this tendency the mission of 1234 was bound to be a failure, and it was to be one of many.

Royal Holloway and Bedford New College,
University of London

---

[79] D. M. Nicol, 'The Byzantine reaction to the Second Council of Lyons, 1274', *SCH*, 7 (1984), pp. 113–46.

[80] W. H. C. Frend, 'Old and New Rome in the age of Justinian', in D. Baker, ed. *Relations between East and West in the Middle Ages* (Edinburgh, 1973), p. 11.

# UNITY AND DIVERSITY: PERCEPTIONS OF THE PAPACY IN THE LATER MIDDLE AGES*

by MARGARET HARVEY

One feature of late medieval life always strikes the modern student as most strange: the Roman Church was an institution which you could, if you had the courage, opt *out* of, but you did not opt in, or rather, it was assumed that you were in unless you took steps to make dissent clear. Here I would want to add that being 'in' included accepting the papacy. My object in this paper is to discuss aspects of this situation, to ask how the papacy was perceived before opinions were distorted by the need to accommodate the impact of Luther. There are few areas where it is more important not to write history from the Reformation backwards; between Protestant polemic and Catholic apologetic the late medieval papacy remains in need of an impartial historian. Textbooks are few and detailed studies of many aspects non-existent.[1] In this paper I will merely try to illuminate a few questions which arise when one begins to consider what it meant to say that in the late Middle Ages all orthodox Latin Christians accepted the papacy.

One may begin with my last assertion. Did all orthodox Latin Christians accept the papacy, considering that there had been the Great Western Schism, with its three popes? I would argue that they did, though not that this acceptance meant either uniformity of belief about the papal office or obedience to it in all matters. Before the Reformation, belief in the papal office was compatible with serious disagreement with the pope. There is no evidence that faith in the papacy as an institution was lastingly undermined by the schism. The genius of the Council of Constance was that it settled the matter and quieted consciences, without having to decide which was the 'true' pope.[2] During the schism some had indeed had doubts; in 1398, at the gathering of

---

* I would like to thank Dr R. Britnell and Dr J. Britnell for helpful discussions of many matters in this paper.

[1] An exception is J.A.F. Thomson, *Popes and Princes, 1417–1517. Politics and Piety in the Late Medieval Church* (London, 1980).

[2] See comment by C. M. D. Crowder, *Unity, Heresy and Reform, 1378–1460. The Conciliar Response to the Great Schism*, Documents of Medieval History, 3 (London, 1977), pp. 11–14.

French clergy to decide whether to withdraw obedience from Benedict XIII, the Archbishop of Rouen, Guillaume de Vienne, referred to 'the doubts and peril of souls and the shadows we are in concerning both the sacraments of holy Church and the execution of the sacraments, as well as other damnable inconveniences and perilous cases which may daily arise and affect the consciences of good Christians.'[3] But Martin V was accepted as pope and employed *curiales*, papal officials, from all his predecessors, including all the cardinals and many former supporters of the deposed popes.[4] It was expensive for Martin but there was no purge of 'schismatics'. The approval of the General Council covered most cases. An outstanding English example is William Swan, a papal secretary, who had refused to desert Gregory XII when the latter was deposed at Pisa in 1409 but who finally joined the Council of Constance and was then employed in the Curia until 1442.[5] Juan de Torquemada, the archetypal papal supporter, in his 1439 disputation with Juliano Cesarini, pointed out that the famous decree of Constance, *Haec Sancta*, which declared that councils were superior to popes for certain purposes, had been passed when the assembly represented only John XXIII's obedience, and that there was then doubt where the 'true' Church was.[6] He professed unwillingness to accept *Haec Sancta* as a pronouncement of the Universal Church, since this would have been an affront to the consciences of the other obediences. But nevertheless for him Constance's other achievement, the election of Martin V, was the election of an undoubted pope.

Constance succeeded because the vast majority of Western Christians, both lay and ecclesiastical, assumed the necessity of a Christendom not just united, but united under one pope. To persist in schism was to risk heresy. Support for attempts of the French government to end the schism by forcing the resignation of the popes was driven by considerations of this kind. In 1398

---

[3] *Le Vote de la soustraction d'obedience en 1398*, ed. H. Millet and E. Poulle, 1 (Paris, 1988), no. 14, p. 59.

[4] P. Partner, *The Pope's Men: The Papal Civil Service in the Renaissance* (Oxford, 1990), pp. 8–10; C. Schuchard, *Die Deutschen an der papstlichen Kurie im späten Mittelalter (1378–1447)* (Tubingen, 1987), p. 46.

[5] M. Harvey, *England, Rome and the Papacy, 1417–1464 The Study of a Relationship* (Manchester, 1993), pp. 26, 30.

[6] J. de Torquemada, *A Disputation on the Authority of Pope and Council*, ed. and trans. T. M. Izbicki, Dominican Sources, 4 (Oxford, 1988), p. 3. For the man see T. M. Izbicki, *Protector of the Faith* (Washington DC, 1981).

the clergy of France had discussed the legitimacy of withdrawing obedience from Benedict XIII, whom for many years the French had acknowledged as the true pope. A large assembly of archbishops, bishops, and representatives of chapters and universities debated at length. Out of an assembly of 309 voters the government claimed 247 votes in favour of withdrawal.[7] Though the numbers have been disputed, the great majority did agree not to obey Benedict. This was not a vote to abolish the papacy; far otherwise. It was a serious attempt to force an undoubtedly legitimate pope (in the eyes of the voters) to do his duty, which was to ensure the unity of the Church. The Archbishop of Rouen expressed his feelings thus:

> I consider in my conscience that total withdrawal of obedience ought to be made from him by all Christian kings and others who hold the faith of that King of whom he calls himself vicar and from whom he holds his kingdom to perpetual damnation if he does not provide a remedy. I consider that every good Christian is bound by the needs of his soul to try to provide a prompt and speedy remedy and especially kings who are established for that. . . .[8]

Schism is a perilous state, which must be brought to an end. The Pope is prolonging it; the duty of all Christians, but particularly kings 'qui ad ceci sont ordonnez', is to end it. Withdrawal was a means to that end. The goal was a united Church with at its head a pope whom all could accept. The problem in 1398 was to achieve this when neither Benedict XIII nor Boniface IX showed any real determination to end the impasse. Constance finally did so.

Constance also set itself to remedy the abuses resulting from the schism, particularly by passing the decree *Frequens*, insisting that regular general councils would in future be held for reform. *Haec Sancta* and *Frequens*, however, were not envisaged at the time as hostile to the papacy.[9] *Haec Sancta*, declaring the Council

---

[7] Millet and Poulle, *Le Vote*, pp. 27, 37.

[8] Ibid., p. 59.

[9] See most recently, P. H. Stump, *The Reforms of the Council of Constance (1414–1418)*, Studies in the History of Christian Thought, 53 (Leiden, 1994), pp. 14–16, and W. Brandmüller, *Das Konzil von Konstanz 1414–1418*, 1, *Bis zur Abreise Sigismunds nach Narbonne* (Paderborn, 1991), pp. 239–61. Also important: T. H. Morrissey, 'The decree *Haec Sancta* and Cardinal Zabarella', *Annuarium Historiae Conciliorum*, 10 (1978), pp. 145–76.

superior to the pope for certain purposes, was thought necessary in the particular circumstances of 1415 and presumably in any case when they recurred. It was only later, at Basel, that it became a weapon in the hands of those determined to attack the pope; after that it was targeted by pro-papalists like Torquemada, who spent a great deal of effort proving that it was not a decree of a valid council. But Torquemada's view was by no means universally accepted. *Frequens* similarly was intended to ensure that the delegates of Constance could elect a pope confident that he or his successors would undertake the reforms which the Council had begun. It was not aimed against the papacy, but to ensure that pope and council would reform together.[10] In practice already in 1424–5 the English government, for its own ends, was threatening the 'acceleration' of a council to force the pope to grant local privileges, so that perhaps Eugenius IV was right to find councils frightening; but Constance had not intended this.[11]

None the less, although the latest research on Constance is very favourable to its reforms, a great deal was left undone. In effect Constance shows that there was general agreement that there should be one pope and that all must be in communion with him. This certainly did not imply agreement about the limits of his power nor about the implications of obedience (not identical with communion), nor the possibility of the Church modifying the office. At Constance there was remarkable agreement about many practical reforms but almost certainly a great deal of disagreement about theory.[12] If anyone had asked 'why have a pope?' probably only Lollards and Czech Taborites would have questioned the need. Even the Greeks thought a Western Patriarch necessary for a valid General Council.[13] Eugenius IV was able to capitalize on this for his Council of Florence, and the Greeks there accepted a very papal definition of papal primacy, softened for them by a phrase about the hierarchy of other patriarchates 'saving all their privileges and rights'. It is certain, however, that each side understood this phrase differently and

---

[10] Stump, *Constance*, pp. 104–8, 244–5, 272.

[11] Harvey, *England, Rome*, pp. 140–3.

[12] Stump, *Constance*, pp. 22–48, for overview.

[13] M. A. Schmidt, 'The problem of papal primacy at the Council of Florence', *ChH* 30 (1961), pp. 35–49; J. Helmrath, *Das Basler Konzil, 1431–1449 Forschungstand und Probleme*, Kölner Historische Abhandlungen, 32 (Cologne, 1987), pp. 377–82; J. Gill, *The Council of Florence* (Cambridge, 1959), pp. 56, 65n., 66, 69, 81, 84; idem, *Personalities of the Council of Florence* (Oxford, 1964), pp. 264–86.

equally certain that not all Latins understood papal primacy in the papal way.[14]

At the highest level of abstraction we get accounts of idealized popes. In 1408, preparing for the Council of Pisa, Richard Ullerston provided the English with a portrait of the ideal pope.[15] He must be, as far as it was possible to ascertain, chosen by God, skilled in the law of God, of upright life. Ambition was a disqualification. His task was to guide the people of God according to the law of God, with responsibility before God for all humans. The task thus included evangelization of infidels and Christians. The latter must be confirmed in their faith. As chief hierarch on earth he must channel to the rest of the Church the divine illumination. The exemplar, after Christ himself doing the will of the Father, was Peter who had been elected by Christ to complete the work Christ had begun.

According to Ullerston the pope could wholly fail to fulfil the duties of the office; certainly his words were not law; he spoke with the power of the Spirit only if he lived up to the task enjoined.[16] In the rest of the work Ullerston pointed out actions of the pope which were ultra vires: *motu proprio* appropriations, and certain dispensations for instance. These were so contrary to the natural organization of the Church that the pope had no right to make them and ought not to be obeyed when doing so. Here is the paradox of talking of the office in the loftiest (pseudo-)Dionysian terms, whilst restricting possible actions because, on grounds equally Dionysian, other hierarchs, notably bishops, must not be prevented from using their power.

Arguments of this kind were behind some of the most trenchant criticisms at Constance[17] and throughout the period a constant theme, even in the Curia itself, was that the pope must be a reformer and must start work at the centre.[18] The pope prophecies, immensely popular, with an angelic pope as a radical

---

[14] The decree: *DEC*, 2, p. 528. For discussion: H. Chadwick, 'The theological ethos of the Council of Florence', in G. Alberigo, ed., *Christian Unity* (Louvain, 1991), pp. 229–39; Gill, *Personalities*; Schmidt, 'Papal primacy'.

[15] Harvey, *England, Rome*, p. 215.

[16] Ibid., p. 229.

[17] Stump, *Constance*, pp. 132–4, 211–13, 248–9.

[18] J. M. McManamon, 'The ideal Renaissance Pope: funeral oratory from the papal court', *AHP*, 14 (1976), pp. 5–70, esp. pp. 46–8.

reforming figure, were as ambiguous as Ullerston's ideas. In the early sixteenth-century *Apocalypsis nova*, the pope is a spiritual leader, leaving temporal affairs to others.[19] Erasmus's *Julius exclusus* fits into this tradition, with his St Peter who is a simple fisherman, pacifist and poor, winning by example, holiness, and miracles, who does not understand what 'the Patrimony of St Peter' means.[20] Pierre Gringore's *Le Prince des Sotz et Mere Sotte*, staged at Les Halles on Shrove Tuesday 1512, at the height of the French polemic against Julius II, presents Julius as *homme obstiné* who is all that a pope should not be: a liar, treacherous, punishing the innocent, he refuses to listen to Divine Retribution and with his courtiers Simony and Hypocrisy wants to rule the world in a thoroughly secular kingdom.[21] Evidently a true pope would be quite different from this.

Matching these ideals to fifteenth-century reality was not easy. The papacy was not wanted as a mere figurehead. Ullerston's account is typical. His pope would still have been the last resort for appeals; major cases remained with the Curia. His papacy was also a centre for missionary activity to non-Christians; and would have been working for reunion of Christendom and peace between Christians. The pope would have had minimum powers in appropriations, with the main decision resting with the diocesan. Privileges would have remained possible but very restricted, with the power of the bishop to scrutinize much enhanced. Dispensations would have been allowed, for example for plurality where benefices were very poor, but again the main power to decide rested with the local bishop *ex officio*. Other writers would certainly have added crusade to the tasks which the pope must undertake.

One of the main defects of all this idealism was that it did not discuss central finance seriously enough. If Ullerston had had his

---

[19] M. Reeves, 'The medieval heritage', and A. Morisi-Guerra, 'The *Apocalypsis Nova*: a plan for reform', in M. Reeves ed., *Prophetic Rome in the High Renaissance Period* (Oxford, 1992), pp. 7–13, 35–6; B. McGinn, 'Angel pope and papal Antichrist', *ChH*, 47 (1978), pp. 155–73.

[20] D. Erasmus, *The 'Julius Exclusus'*, trans. P. Pascal, ed. J. K. Soward (Bloomington, Ind., 1968). H. J. M. McSorley, 'Erasmus and the primacy of the Roman pontiff', *Archiv für Reformationsgeschichte*, 65 (1974), pp. 37–54, esp. p. 43 note 34. MacManamon, 'The ideal Renaissance Pope', pp. 5–70.

[21] P. Gringore, *Oeuvres Complètes*, ed. C. D'Héricault and A. de Montaiglon, 2 vols (Paris, 1858), 1, pp. 199–269; P. A. Jannini, ed., *La Sottie du Prince des Sotz* (Milan, 1957); C. Oulmont, *Pierre Gringore* (Paris, 1911), pp. 39–40, 271–93; A. Renaudet, *Préréforme et humanisme à Paris pendant les premières guerres d'Italie (1494–1517)*, 2nd edn (Paris, 1953), p. 546.

way the papacy would still have had to maintain a large bureaucracy; who was to fund it and how? Constance equally did not consider who was to foot the bill for the regular councils.[22] Basel had to raise (of all things) an indulgence and one of the reasons why a council for reunion was held in Florence was that the Medici, for their own political ends, would lend money for the huge Greek delegation which was too poor to finance itself. Even then the Greeks complained bitterly that they had been kept short of cash.[23]

Constance did not attempt to define limits to papal power; it settled for papal agreements with individual countries, tailored to suit the needs of each, with *Frequens* in reserve.[24] This suited the post-schism situation, since different areas had suffered differently. But it also concealed problems. At the Council the deepest, insoluble disagreement concerned the nature of the benefice and of the papal system of provisions, particularly the raising of money from appointments.[25] The problem was to separate benefice (the revenue) from office (the duties). No-one could decide whether annates were simoniacal. If they were, what should replace them? They had been a major source of revenue for the Avignonese papacy; by 1429 'spiritual' revenue (much probably from annates) had fallen by one third.[26] Philip Stump has concluded that the reforms of Constance did in fact improve the benefice regime which had grown up during the schism, but he acknowledges that the benefice remained the most intractable problem.[27] This continued to be the case even after Trent and even in some countries, like England, which had a Reformation. When Stump asserts that the reforms of Constance were remarkably successful, he is also implying that a poorer papacy had been restored to a Church which had yet to decide how to fund it if

[22] Stump, *Constance*, pp. 317–18.

[23] Basel: Crowder, *Unity, Heresy*, p. 23; Helmrath, *Das Basler Konzil*, pp. 52–3; Stump, *Constance*, pp. 71–2. Florence: Gill, *Florence*, pp. 177–9, 290–1; A. Mohlo, 'Fisco ed economia a Firenze alla vigilia del concilio', in P. Viti, ed., *Firenze e il concilio del 1439*, 2 vols (Florence, 1994), 2, pp. 59–94, esp. pp. 88–92.

[24] Stump, *Constance*, pp. 44–8, 167–9.

[25] Ibid., pp. 72–103.

[26] P. Partner, 'Papal financial policy in the Renaissance and Counter-Reformation', *PaP*, 88 (1980), pp. 17–62, esp. pp. 17–21: idem, 'The budget of the Roman Church in the Renaissance period', in E.F. Jacob, ed., *Italian Renaissance Studies. A Tribute to the Late Cecilia M. Ady* (London, 1960), pp. 256–78, esp. pp. 259, 262.

[27] Stump, *Constance*, pp. 100–3, 270.

remaining revenue proved inadequate, as it did. Sections of the Church were increasingly unwilling to provide the money.

It might seem banal to assert that if the European Church wanted a papacy, it should have been prepared to pay. There is nothing intrinsically wicked about a centralized appointment system nor about a pope who asks regularly for a clergy tax. Immediately after Constance the papacy defined willingness to accept its benefice regime as indicative of obedience. Not surprisingly, Martin V tried hard to reestablish a system of appointments and of taxation which would allow him to tap revenue from European benefices. The Concordats with all countries except England allowed pope and local church to share appointments, the assumption being that benefices were mainly a source of patronage and/or revenue.[28] The English Concordat contained no arrangement about benefices, because the Statutes against Provisors kept out papal interference.[29] In his part of France likewise the Dauphin (later Charles VII) introduced a regime intended to keep the Pope out, protecting 'the liberties of the Gallican Church'.[30] Martin refused to accept either arrangement, regarding both as disobedient. In England no papal provision to a lesser benefice could succeed unless the king agreed. Very few were attempted after 1406. Major benefices continued to be appointed in consistory after 1418 and to pay services (very lucrative from England) but in practice the king's will prevailed. In France the logic of complaint produced in 1438 the Pragmatic Sanction of Bourges, which embodied a local appointment system, with adoption of some major reforms from the Council of Basel.[31] It did not wholly abolish payments but in practice the king gained control over benefices.[32]

Local bishops must have acquiesced in this 'disobedience' on some definition of the office of bishop which made papal claims to benefices and to local revenues ultra vires. Acceptance of a

---

[28] For the Concordats: A. Mercati, ed., *Raccolta di concordati su materie ecclesiastche tra la Santa Sede e le autorita civili* (Vatican City, 1954); Stump, *Constance*, pp. 99–103.

[29] Harvey, *England, Rome*, p. 75.

[30] Ibid., chs 7 and 8, with further bibliography there.

[31] Bourges: N. Valois, *Histoire de la Pragmatique Sanction de Bourges sous Charles VII* (Paris, 1906), pp. lii–xcii; V. Martin, *Les Origines du Gallicanisme*, 2 vols (Paris, 1939), 2, pp. 293–315; H. Müller, *Die Französen, Frankreich und das Basler Konzil (1431–1449)*, 2 vols, Konziliengeschichte: Reihe B, Untersuchungen (Paderborn, 1990), 2, pp. 826–8.

[32] Martin, *Les Origines*, 2, p. 308.

pope without accepting all his demands is labelled Gallicanism in France, but there are no complaints about the Statutes from English bishops either, though Martin V called on Beaufort to be another Becket![33] Ullerston's work helps to explain how English bishops were able to justify 'disobedience'; so does the work of Thomas Gascoigne in mid-century. In Gascoigne's theological dictionary, *Liber veritatum*, by far the longest section, 143 pages, is devoted to *Episcopus*.[34] He made many of the same points as Ullerston about papal undermining of bishops, yet desired a united Christendom under one pope (the Council of Florence was an occasion of rejoicing). The pope was necessary but not absolute; his power should build up, not undermine.

The system of provisions was indeed ramshackle by the fifteenth century but its virtual absence from England did not make the appointment system in that country any fairer nor more productive of good parish clergy.[35] English bishoprics were much richer than most and their payments of services seem scarcely to have injured them.[36] The regime in France whether under the Pragmatic Sanction of Bourges or later Concordats was just as corrupt as, and in some ways less fair to some groups than, the papal system.[37] But if these methods were not acceptable, others should have been suggested. Of course they were not.

Annates, lengthily discussed at Constance, were finally abolished by Basel in June 1435 in one of its most controversial reforms.[38] This left the Pope with no revenue in their place. The decree convinced some delegates of the unacceptable extremism of the Council; part of the point certainly was to intimidate Eugenius IV. In France in the Pragmatic Sanction this part of the Basel decrees was modified.[39] Abolition was accepted in Germany by all who received the Acceptation of Mainz, by

---

[33] Archivio Segreto Vaticano, *Armarium*, 39, vol. 6, fol. 153r, *Ex fide relatione*.

[34] Oxford, Lincoln College MS 117, pp. 298–441. Discussion in Harvey, *England, Rome*, pp. 230, 234–5.

[35] R. N. Swanson, *Church and Society in Late Medieval England* (paperback ed. Oxford, 1993), ch. 2.

[36] See comparisons with Italy in D. Hay, *The Church in Italy in the Fifteenth Century* (Cambridge, 1977), pp. 10–11.

[37] Valois, *Pragmatique*, pp. xcix–cxv; P. Ourliac, 'The Concordat of 1472: an essay on the relations between Louis XI and Sixtus IV', in P. S. Lewis, ed., *The Recovery of France in the Fifteenth Century* (London, 1971), pp. 102–84; R. J. Knecht, 'The Concordat of 1516', *University of Birmingham Historical Journal*, 9 (1963), pp. 16–32; R. J. Knecht, *Francis I* (Cambridge, 1982), ch. 4.

[38] Crowder, *Unity, Heresy*, p. 23.

[39] Above, note 32.

which the German princes remained neutral between the pope and Basel but accepted some of the Basel reforms.[40] In many princedoms, however, the bishop put into effect not those Basel decrees demanding regular synods, but only those concerning payments.[41] Refusal to pay the pope, not reform, was the result. Dr Helmrath considers that the Concordat of Vienna (1448) and its equivalents were probably more beneficial to the German localities than the considerable uncertainties of the preceding neutrality between Basel and the pope, but under either the emphasis was still on the benefice as revenue and patronage, and not on reform of pastoral care.[42] And the blame here lies with the localities as much as with the papacy.

Basel was a failure. A vast recent investigation shows that many aspects still need to be explored but it seems clear that the Council failed largely because of its own defects.[43] It adopted a new, non-traditional voting method, giving a voice to lower clergy.[44] This pleased some theologians, but made the Council suspect not only to the pope but also to some secular rulers.[45] Determination to deprive the pope of revenue came to look like sheer vindictiveness; less extreme reformers realized that some respectable method of finance must replace annates but no-one could think what this should be. Finally, perhaps most importantly, delegates refused to leave Basel to join Eugenius' Council of union with the Greeks.[46] This looked merely obstinate, putting victory over the pope above the chance of the union of Christendom. After the shambles of the vote about the Greeks, leading members began to trickle sadly back to the pope.[47]

[40] J. W. Stieber, *Pope Eugenius IV, the Council of Basel and the Secular and Ecclesiastical Authorities of the Empire. The Conflict over Supreme Authority and Power in the Church*, Studies in the History of Christian Thought, 13 (Leiden, 1978), pp. 164–6; Helmrath, *Das Basler Konzil*, pp. 345–7.

[41] Stieber, *Pope Eugenius IV*, pp. 170–3; Helmrath, *Das Basler Konzil*, pp. 346–7.

[42] Helmrath, *Das Basler Konzil*, pp. 320–1.

[43] Ibid., pp. 498–9.

[44] Crowder, *Unity, Heresy*, pp. 29–31. Several works by A. Black are pertinent, most recently, 'The conciliar movement', in J. H. Burns, ed., *The Cambridge History of Medieval Political Thought* (Cambridge, 1988), pp. 573–87.

[45] Interesting discussion in A. Black, *Council and Commune. The Conciliar Movement and the Fifteenth Century Heritage* (London, 1979), pp. 215–22.

[46] *Monumenta Conciliorum Generalium Sec. XV*, 4 vols (Vienna and Basel, 1857–1935), 2, pp. 965–6; Gill, *Florence*, p. 73.

[47] Caesarini: G. Christianson, *Cesarini: The Conciliar Cardinal*, Kirchengeschichtliche Quellen und Studien, 10 (St Ottilien, 1979), pp. 169–80. Nicholas of Cusa: J. Biechler, 'Nicholas of Cusa and the end of the Conciliar Movement', *ChH*, 44 (1975), pp. 5–21, esp. pp. 6–7, 8.

The Councils of Constance and Basel thus failed to grasp the nettle of papal finance, criticizing existing methods, and in Basel's case abolishing some, but agreeing nothing satisfactory in their place. Basel also revealed wide disagreements about the proper role of the papacy itself. One may lay all the blame on Eugenius IV; he should perhaps have accepted the spirit of *Frequens* and co-operated from the start. Perhaps he drove the Council into radicalism, though that is by no means clear. It is evident, however, that while the majority of western bishops seem to have been deeply reluctant to follow Basel into accepting an antipope, large numbers of Christians, episcopal and otherwise, hankered after the Basel reforms. Refusal to accept the antipope Felix V by no means revealed enthusiasm for Eugenius IV. Henry VI's royal council tried to keep some communication with the Council, but was reluctant to accept it and its antipope 'lest the King fall into schism'.[48] The Pragmatic Sanction was an attempt to accept some of Basel's results whilst also acknowledging Eugenius. Neutrality between Council and pope was the best answer from much of Germany.

In the aftermath many well-known thinkers who began as supporters of Basel ended as papalists, but seldom totally denied the authority of councils under some circumstances. The preferred 'papal' viewpoint came to be epitomized by Juan de Torquemada, in, for instance, his reply of 1439 to Juliano Cesarini, where Basel is the background.[49] This was a high doctrine of papacy, utterly denying that *Haec Sancta* was the decree of a properly constituted General Council, which had established the supremacy of councils over popes as a doctrine of the Church.[50] This had been the interpretation of supporters of Basel. Torquemada asserted that all jurisdiction came from the pope to other prelates. Yet even he continued to maintain that the pope must act for the good of the Church, must remain orthodox and uphold right order. The pope could define nothing against the law of God. This was totally traditional. Nicholas of Cusa similarly came to accept that jurisdiction flowed from the pope. He moved from a position like Ullerston's, asserting

---

[48] H. Nicolas, ed., *Proceedings and Ordinances of the Privy Council of England*, 7 vols (London, 1835), 5, p. 98.

[49] Torquemada, *Disputation*, pp. xx–xxi and references there.

[50] Ibid., pp. xviii, 45–8, 50–1.

that Christ had given power to both bishops and pope, to one where bishops received their power via the pope.[51] Yet he also retained the old notion that the pope must use his power for the good of the Church, not interfering in the lower offices except for their good. He continued to acknowledge that heretical popes could be deposed, though he altered his views about the extent to which their formal doctrinal pronouncements were protected from error. But Nicholas's pope, even in the later treatises, is not absolute, though Nicholas was in two minds about what to do if the pope were incorrigible, heresy apart.[52] At most he allowed that correction of the pope must be by a unanimous council. The shift in thinking had been caused by the spectre of schism raised by Basel: 'rather a bad pope should be tolerated than occasion be given . . . of dividing the Church'.[53]

Nicholas cannot be considered an enthusiastic papalist in the sense which a modern pope would understand. Pius II recorded that when in 1461 he told Cusa that he would make new cardinals, the reaction was:

> You ignore the ordinance of the synod [Constance] and do not ask the consent of the college . . . if you can hear the truth, nothing that is done in this curia pleases me. Everything is corrupt, no-one fulfils his office satisfactorily. Neither you nor the cardinals care for the Church . . . all are full of ambition and avarice. I am laughed at if I mention reform in consistory. It is pointless for me to be here. Give me permission to go. I cannot bear these practices.

And saying this he burst into tears.[54] One easily forgets that belief in the divine foundation of an institution does not make one love

---

[51] The literature on Cusa is vast. See most recently Nicholas of Cusa, *The Catholic Concordance*, ed. and trans. P. E. Sigmund (Cambridge, 1991). Also Stieber, *Pope Eugenius IV*, pp. 401–2; P. E. Sigmund, *Nicholas of Cusa and Medieval Political Thought* (Cambridge, Mass., 1963), esp. ch. 11; M. Watanabe, *The Political Ideas of Nicholas of Cusa, with Special Reference to his De Concordantia Catholica* (Geneva, 1963), esp. pp. 101–14.

[52] Sigmund, *Cusa*, pp. 271–2; Cusa, *Concordance*, p. xxxiii.

[53] Stieber, *Pope Eugenius IV*, p. 402, accuses him of opportunism. The quotation is from Sigmund, *Cusa*, p. 275, from *Deutsche Reichstagsakten unter Kaiser Friedrich III*, 15, ed. H. Herre (Gotha, 1914), p. 772. See also E. Meuthen, *Die letzen Jahre des Nikolaus von Kues* (Cologne and Opladen, 1958), pp. 78–81.

[54] Pius II, *Commentarii rerum memorabilium que temporibus suis contigerunt*, ed. A. van Heck, *Studi e Testi*, 312, 313 (2 vols, Vatican City, 1984), 2, bk 7, ch. 9, p. 446.

it in practice. Not surprisingly this passage was omitted from the first printed edition of Pius' *Memoirs.*

Alister McGrath asserts that the late Middle Ages was a time of great theological diversity; there was real difficulty in discerning 'the locus of authority in the Church'; 'confusion concerning the precise status of [conflicting] opinions'.[55] By mid-century the General Council, far from uniting, divided. It became a useful weapon to frighten the pope. This clearly threw some thinkers back to a more absolute and infallibilist view of papal power, but not only were there almost no total absolutists or infallibilists, there remained many other viewpoints, most of which were not heretical.

In England, for example, Ullerston's type of view seems to have remained acceptable. Thomas Gascoigne certainly shared it and quotes at least one bishop prepared to disobey the pope because a particular grant undermined 'all power granted by God to bishops'.[56] This suggests a view that episcopal power came *iure divino*, not flowing via the pope. In about 1440 John Whethamstede outlined six possible views of the papacy, several of which he had read for himself.[57] They ranged from an extreme papalist view, giving the pope the role of God in the celestial hierarchy, locating all power both secular and ecclesiastical in him, and maintaining that the pope could do no wrong either in temporal or spiritual matters. One is reminded of the *Consilium de emendenda ecclesia*, drawn up by a reform commission of cardinals in 1537, which said that the main cause of all problems was that: 'Flatterers have led some popes to imagine that their will is law . . .'[58] At the other extreme was a pope with no temporal role nor possessions. This Whethamstede was prepared to label Waldensian, that is, heretical. A further view, called Greek by Whethamstede, made Peter *primus inter pares* and removed the notion of papal jurisdiction as understood in the West. Whethamstede seemed to sympathize; he had studied that position. He also seemed sym-

---

[55] A. McGrath, *The Intellectual Origins of the European Reformation* (Oxford, 1987), ch. 1, esp. pp. 24–5, 28.

[56] Harvey, *England, Rome*, p. 235.

[57] M. Harvey, 'John Whethamstede, the Pope and the General Council', in C. M. Barron and C. Harper-Bill, eds, *The Church in Pre-Reformation Society. Essays in Honour of F. R. H. Du Boulay* (Woodbridge, 1985), pp. 108–22, esp. 115–22.

[58] *Concilium Tridentinum diariorum, actorum, epistularum, tractatuum nova collectio* 12 (Freiburg in Br., 1930), pp. 131–45, esp. p. 135. See also H. Jedin, *A History of the Council of Trent*, trans. E. Graf from ed. of 1949 (London, 1957), 1, p. 424.

pathetic to conciliarism, where the council could correct and even depose the pope in case of heresy or notorious, pertinacious crime. He accepted *Haec Sancta* and *Frequens* as valid. England was not a particularly lively centre for thought about the papacy when Whethamstede was noting these opinions, but the Council of Basel had concentrated minds.

Variety extended even to disagreement about the exegesis of scriptural passages commonly used to defend the institution. The best example is Matthew 16.13–19, Christ's words to Peter, 'Thou art Peter . . .'. The papal view, represented by Torquemada, arguing with Cesarini, interpreted this passage to mean that Christ gave the keys to Peter, rather than to 'the Church' in the person of Peter, as if Peter had been merely a representative of the Church.[59] Torquemada considered that Peter received this power for the Church, but not in his person alone; rather he could pass it on to his successors. As Peter had primacy so had his successors. All prelates had indeed power to bind and loose, but Peter had it in a particular way: 'Peter received the power of the keys more particularly than the Church as a whole and, secondly, . . . everyone depends on Peter in such a way that those who separate themselves from fellowship with him and from the unity of the faith cannot be released from their bonds or enter heaven.'[60] Caesarini, a conciliarist, had also argued that 'upon this rock' referred to Christ. Torquemada insisted that Peter was the foundation of foundations after Christ.[61] He denied too that the other apostles had equal power with Peter. He quoted Clement: 'There was no parity of appointment among the Apostles, but one was superior to the others.'[62]

Though Caesarini's work is now lost, one can see clearly what arguments he had adduced to support the superiority of a council over the pope. He could quote Augustine to prove that plenitude of power went to the Church, not to Peter; Jerome, that the rock on which the Church was founded was not Peter but Christ; and Cyprian, from the *Decretum*, to suggest that all the apostles were equal.[63]

[59] Torquemada, *Disputation*, pp. 35–7.
[60] Ibid., pp. 39–40.
[61] Ibid., pp. 40–1.
[62] Ibid., p. 41.
[63] Ibid., Augustine: pp. 32, 34, 35; Jerome: p. 40; Cyprian: p. 41.

These were all familiar points from late medieval polemic. Reginald Pecock in the 1440s and 1450s is witness to this diversity of interpretation in his writing against the Lollards.[64] If his opponents wished to know when Christ made Peter head of the Church, he cited Peter being called Cephas, which he interpreted as head. He then argued that Christ had made Peter head either while he lived or after the Ascension 'by the eleccion and ordinaunce of the Apostolis and of the clergie; or ellis that al the while Petir him silf was Bishop of Rome, he was not thus heed over al the Church of God, but that the successoris of Petir in the Chirche of Rome weren heedis to al the Chirche of God, and that bi eleccioun and ordinaunce of men'.[65] The possibility that only Peter's successors became heads of the Church did not trouble Pecock because he believed that the guidance of God was in the development of the institution: 'зit certis thou maist not seie nayh but this was doon bi Goddis puruyaunce and prouydence, and bi Goddis welwilling that it schulde be doon.'[66] He also pointed out that 'some men' understood the rock to refer to Christ, others to Peter's faith, whereas he thought it more likely to refer to Peter's person.[67] The range represents mid-fifteenth-century orthodox opinion.

It is thus wholly to be expected that there would be disagreement about the foundation and the scope of papal power in the later fifteenth century. Thomas More is a famous witness to this. In his well-known letter to Cromwell of 1534 he traced the evolution of his own thought.[68] He had begun by thinking that the primacy of the pope was not of divine institution. Since reading the king's book (on the seven sacraments) and many other works (from about 1523), he had concluded that the primacy was agreed by the ancient authorities and councils and was provided by God. At the least he thought it had been provided by 'the common corps of Christendom' to avoid schism. This is an approach very like Pecock's. More saw no point in debating whether God directly or the Church indirectly

---

[64] Harvey, *England, Rome*, pp. 220, 232–3.

[65] R. Pecock, *The Repressor of Over Much Blaming of the Clergy*, ed. C. Babington, 2 vols (London, 1860), 2, p. 439.

[66] Ibid., p. 439.

[67] Ibid., p. 441–2.

[68] T. More, *The Correspondence of Sir Thomas More*, ed. E. F. Rogers (Princeton, 1947), pp. 498–501.

had ordained the papacy; in either case only the whole Church could decide what to do about it. In such matters a General Council was to be believed, otherwise there was no certainty. He clearly thought that councils had ultimate authority in the Church, and did not believe that popes were above councils. He was well aware that Peter's position did not necessarily provide arguments for the position of the present pope.[69] In the aftermath of the Council of Basel, without considering the effects of humanism and Luther, many supporters of the papacy must have shared some of these views. Almost certainly More considered that the question of the divine origins of the papacy remained open.[70]

The correct relation between pope and bishops remained equally unresolved. A bitter quarrel on the subject nearly ended the Council of Trent.[71] When in September 1562 the Council debated the sacrament of orders, the drafters of the proposed decree included an article declaring that episcopacy differed from priesthood 'by virtue of divine law'. The legates representing the pope struck the clause out. In October fifty-five out of 130 prelates voted to restore it. They included Spanish, French, and Imperial representatives, but also some Italians. To most ardent papalists this phrase suggested that episcopal authority flowed directly from God, which smacked of conciliarism. The French thought the phrase vital as a bulwark against papal abuse of authority. Ullerston would have understood; so would Gascoigne. In the end the Council fudged the issue rather than risk a split, leaving the Second Vatican Council to attempt to sort the matter out. The status of episcopacy remains a source of tension and not just in Roman Catholic theology.

The evolution of the papacy after Basel did not help. Finance remained its Achilles heel.[72] Constance had assumed that, once recovered, the Papal States would constitute a main source of papal finance; they must not be alienated. This was the ecclesias-

---

[69] B. Gogan, *The Common Corps of Christendom. Ecclesiological Themes in the Writings of Sir Thomas More*, Studies in the History of Christian Thought, 26 (Leiden, 1982), pp. 247–66, and his bibliography.

[70] Ibid., pp. 257–8.

[71] For what follows: H. Jedin, *Crisis and Closure of the Council of Trent. A Retrospective View from the Second Vatican Council*, trans. N. D. Smith (London, 1967), chs 5 and 6, esp. pp. 114–15. Decrees of Trent and Vatican II, see *DEC*, 2, pp. 743, 921–4.

[72] In general Thomson, *Popes and Princes*, ch. 4, and articles by Partner cited in note 26 above.

tical equivalent of 'the King shall live of his own'.[73] It is not clear how realistic it would ever have been, and in fact other methods of raising money were increasingly tried, including sale of office in the bureaucracy as a major source of revenue, resulting in multiplication of *curiales*, with a consequent rise of prices for the services they gave.[74] This fuelled complaints from the likes of Luther about papal greed. Criticisms may have worsened in mid-century because of the European-wide bullion shortage.[75]

As the century progressed, however, the papacy did rely more and more on the Patrimony, but the consequence was not necessarily beneficial to the Universal Church.[76] The expense of defending territory was very great, and its strategic position dragged the papacy willy-nilly into Italian politics. The cardinals and the bureaucracy became more and more Italianized.[77] In the late fifteenth century, when the French were frequently tempted to interfere in the Italian balance of power, the papacy found itself trapped between French and Spanish interests.

It is thus hardly sensible to accuse late fifteenth-century popes of becoming Italian princes. They had been Italian princes since the Papal States began; dependence on the patrimony for major revenue forced them to become ever more conscious of this. The question was rather what kind of secular prince to be. The secular model in this period was the prince whose authority was symbolized by the great state he maintained, by his outward grandeur and generosity.[78] Henry VII's first Parliament, for instance, reminded him of the need to keep an 'honourable household . . . kept and borne worshipfully and honourably, as it accordeth to the honour of your estate and your said realm'.[79]

---

[73] P. Partner, *The Lands of St Peter. The Papal State in the Middle Ages and the Early Renaissance* (London, 1972), pp. 394–5, 446; Stump, *Constance*, pp. 113–17, 127, 129–31.

[74] Thomson, *Popes and Princes*, pp. 89–90; J. F. D'Amico, *Renaissance Humanism in Papal Rome. Humanists and Churchmen on the Eve of the Reformation* (Baltimore and London, 1983), pp. 27–8.

[75] H. A. Miskimin, *The Economy of Early Renaissance Europe, 1300–1460* (Englewood Cliffs, 1969), pp. 144–7; P. Spufford, *Money and its Use in Medieval Europe* (Cambridge, 1988), ch. 15, esp. pp. 356–9; J. Day, *The Medieval Market Economy* (Oxford, 1987), ch. 1, esp. pp. 40–5.

[76] Thomson, *Popes and Princes*, p. 81.

[77] Hay, *Church in Italy*, pp. 38–45.

[78] D. Thomson, *Renaissance Architecture. Critics. Patrons. Luxury* (Manchester, 1993), for the whole subject, esp. ch. 1; Aristotle, *The Ethics of Aristotle*, trans. J. A. K. Thomson (Harmondsworth, 1953), pp. 109–15 for the theory; McManamon, 'The ideal Renaissance Pope', pp. 34–5, 39–40.

[79] *Rotuli Parliamentorum*, 6 vols (London, 1767–77), 6, p. 336, quoted by B. Wolffe, *Henry VI* (London, 1981), p. 95.

The fact that this usually involved living beyond one's means was not important. Magnificence in the surrounding courtiers reflected the honour of the ruler. So, even had the cardinals not been for the most part of princely and aristocratic background, they would almost certainly have kept up a princely style of life. In 1508 Julius II rebuked the austere Cardinal Ximenes de Cisneros (resident in Spain) for living too modestly; that was acceptable *in interiori conscientia* but not *extrinsecus*.[80] Anything shabby and mean reflected on the central authority. It is sometimes argued that Wolsey's grandeur and position as cardinal fuelled anti-papal sentiment in England. Clearly after his fall this was used as a stick with which to beat the papacy, but it is hard to produce evidence from beforehand. Wolsey's style reflected his two masters: the Pope and Henry VIII. Of these Henry VIII was just as lavish as Leo X and of course much nearer at hand.

Secondly, pomp and beauty in the setting of liturgy and ceremony were considered necessary.[81] After Basel Nicholas V made explicit what had been implicit earlier: the papacy must make Rome a living symbol of papal authority, where pilgrims would be impressed by the outward signs of authority; the beauty of the setting would reflect the majesty of the God whose authority was being mediated.[82] The symbolism matched the ideology expressed by Torquemada. The pope was represented, for instance, by Moses the lawgiver leading his people.[83] Papal Rome was to be the fitting Christian heir to its glorious imperial predecessor.[84] Every type of Renaissance art and rhetoric was employed to emphasize power and authority.

There were thus many reasons why Rome became the expensive centre for an expensive court. It is also evident why popes were tempted to use any means at hand to raise money.

---

[80] D'Amico, *Renaissance Humanism*, p. 48. In general: D. S. Chambers, *A Renaissance Cardinal and His Worldly Goods: The Will and Inventory of Francesco Gonzaga (1444–1483)*, Warburg Institute Surveys and Texts, 20 (London, 1992), esp. ch. 2; K. J. P. Lowe, *Church and Politics in Renaissance Italy. The Life and Career of Cardinal Francesco Soderini (1453–1524)* (Cambridge, 1993), esp. chs. 15, 16, 17, 18, 19.

[81] Good account in Lowe, *Soderini*, pp. 165–9.

[82] C. W. Westfall, *In this most perfect Paradise; Alberti, Nicholas V and the Invention of Conscious Urban Planning in Rome, 1447–55* (University Park, Penn., and London, 1974), esp. ch. 2, p. 33; D'Amico, *Renaissance Humanism*, pp. 120–2; C. L. Stinger, *The Renaissance in Rome* (Bloomington, Ind., 1985), pp. 156–8; McManamon, 'The ideal Renaissance Pope', p. 49.

[83] Stinger, *Renaissance in Rome*, pp. 201–21.

[84] Ibid., ch. 5.

Throughout the early modern period the cardinals and *curiales* continued to be financed partly by plurality of benefices, from all over Europe.[85] The Council of Trent did not solve the problem of the benefice. Much has been said, rightly, about the scandalous misuse of indulgences, for instance to build St Peter's.[86] It is not often pointed out that asking for alms without offering something was thought unlikely to raise much money. The English group in Rome, trying to build a new hospice church in the 1450s, was advised by its collector in England to obtain greater papal privileges for subscribers.[87] Martin Luther, visiting Rome in 1511, praised Italian hospitals, probably including the German hospice in Rome, for their charity, perhaps not realizing that most, and certainly the German, were partly financed from indulgences.[88] Perhaps the answer should have been to do without new buildings, but that would have meant doing without the Sistine Chapel and St Peter's itself.

There evidently were local critics of all this lavishness, both secular and ecclesiastical.[89] One of the few critics known in Rome was Raffaele Maffei, who condemned Julius II's building programme, including the new St Peter's.[90] But he was an exception; we do not hear much criticism from the papal entourage. Short of total condemnation, however, there remained genuine puzzles about where to draw lines. Clearly, as Macchiavelli pointed out, Alexander VI seriously overstepped the bounds by using the Papal States for his own children.[91] Not only should he not have had any, but the Patrimony was his only on trust.[92] But the career of Julius II shows the real problems about acceptable ways of defending that trust. Julius owed his papacy to

---

[85] B. M. Hallman, *Italian Cardinals, Reform and the Church as Property, 1492–1563* (Los Angeles, 1985), esp. ch. 2.

[86] Thomson, *Popes and Princes*, pp. 87–9; Stump, *Constance*, pp. 67–72.

[87] Harvey, *England, Rome*, p. 66.

[88] M. Luther, *Table Talk* in *Works*, 54, ed. and trans. T. G. Tappert (Philadelphia, 1967), p. 296; C. W. Maas, *The German Community in Renaissance Rome, 1378–1523*, Römische Quartalschrift für christliche Altertumskunde und Kirchengeschichte, Supplementheft 39 (Rome, 1981), p. 99.

[89] Thomson, *Architecture*, p. 18; D'Amico, *Renaissance Humanism*, pp. 220–6.

[90] D'Amico, *Renaissance Humanism*, p. 222.

[91] N. Machiavelli, *The Prince*, trans. P. Bondanella and M. Musa (Oxford, 1984), ch. 11, p. 40.

[92] Interesting comment in Partner, *Lands of St Peter*, pp. 443–6; see B. Tierney, *Foundations of the Conciliar Theory. The Contribution of the Medieval Canonists from Gratian to the Great Schism* (Cambridge, 1955), pp. 118–27.

nepotism; he would have been better as a warrior.[93] Faced with
the ruinous situation left by Alexander VI he strengthened, and
tried to secure the independence of, the Papal States, often, since
he could find no trustworthy generals, leading his armies himself.
His latest biographer argues that he genuinely believed that his
actions were for the good of the Church and the increased
authority of the papacy.[94] Some contemporaries hailed him as a
temporal saviour.[95] Erasmus, on the contrary, thought that such
use of force and spilling of Christian blood would earn him
eternity in hell.[96] It is difficult to see how the idealized St Peter
of *Julius exclusus* could have survived in Rome in 1513.

Nepotism was equally ambiguous.[97] If the Papal States were
held on trust it remained unclear what part of the revenue of the
papacy or a cardinalate was a personal stipend. The boundary
between generosity and extravagance, necessary care of depend-
ants and nepotism, was shadowy. The problem is epitomized by
the Fifth Lateran Council, summoned, we may recall, by Julius
II to counter a French-summoned rival Council at Pisa.[98] In
1516 it said of cardinals financing their relatives:

> It is entirely unfitting to pass over persons related to them
> by blood or marriage, especially if they are deserving and
> need help. To come to their assistance is just and praise-
> worthy. But we do not consider it appropriate to heap on
> them a great number of benefices or church revenues, with
> the result that uncontrolled generosity in these matters may
> bring wrong to others and cause scandal.[99]

Cardinals (and more so popes) were supposed to know the
difference between reasonable generosity and abuse, just as kings
were expected to reward service without favouring a clique.

Pilgrims contemplating all this splendour were often impressed, as they were meant to be. But ordinary lay people would
most usually encounter the papacy not on pilgrimage but as a

---

[93] C. Shaw, *Julius II. The Warrior Pope* (Oxford, 1993), for modern account.
[94] Ibid., p. 314.
[95] Ibid., p. 313.
[96] Above, n. 20.
[97] Trenchant comment in Shaw, *Julius II*, pp. 7–8.
[98] Background: Shaw, *Julius II*, pp. 281–6, 291–2, 298–9; N. M. Minnich, *The Fifth Lateran Council 1512–17* (Aldershot, 1993); idem, *The Catholic Reformation* (Aldershot, 1993), chs II, III and IV.
[99] *DEC*, 1, p. 618.

source of judicial authority or spiritual power.[100] As judicial authority the pope impinged on lay people through 'reserved' sins: those serious sins for which the papal penitentiary had to be approached before one could be absolved, freed from canonical penalties. Bishops found this jurisdiction helpful to support their own authority. The bishop of St David's reserved cattle rustling; his subjects appear in the penitentiary registers, seeking pardon.[101] But the registers show some Christians simply coming to the penitentiary because they needed to feel that the highest Church authority had absolved them, using the papacy as 'the well of grace', in the phrase from the Paston letters. This felt need is reflected in vernacular literature, where we find really great sinners coming to the pope for absolution.[102] Sometimes in real life also they came in person, especially when 'for fear of a person' the matter was too difficult to sort out locally. Matrimonial entanglements, particularly among the great, might best be unravelled in Rome; even if the Curia was not free of political considerations, one was more likely to obtain some kind of reasonable hearing away from the countries of origin of the parties. And all sides were more likely to accept offspring as legitimate if the pope pronounced the marriage valid.[103]

That the pope could appear as the fount of justice even to an illiterate lay person is exemplified by the trial of Joan of Arc. She believed that pope and bishops existed to defend the faith and to ensure that deviations from it were punished.[104] The pope must have seemed an ultimate earthly court of appeal. Asked if she would submit to him she replied with great spirit: 'Lead me to him and I will reply to him.'[105] She professed willingness to submit everything she had said and done to him, clearly feeling

---

[100] For all that follows: J. A. F. Thomson, 'The "well of grace": Englishmen and Rome in the fifteenth century', in R. B. Dobson, ed., *The Church, Politics and Patronage in the Fifteenth Century* (Gloucester, 1984), pp. 99–114; Harvey, *England, Rome*, ch. 6, pp. 101–14.

[101] Harvey, *England, Rome*, p. 111.

[102] A. de la Sale, *La Salade*, in *Oeuvres Complètes*, ed., F. Desonay, Bibliothèque de la Faculté de Philosophie et Lettres de L'Université de Liège, 68 (Liège, 1935), 1, p. 105.

[103] See for example the marriage dispensations for kings of England: Henry VII: S. B. Chrimes, *Henry VII* (London, 1972), p. 66 and Appendix D; Henry VIII: J. J. Scarisbrick, *Henry VIII* (London, 1968), pp. 23–4, and ch. 7.

[104] *Procès de Condamnation de Jeanne D'Arc*, ed. P. Tisset, 3 vols (Paris, 1960–71), 1, p. 193; 3, pp. 108–13.

[105] Ibid., 1, pp. 176, 343.

that she might then get the justice not coming from the tribunal: 'I refer to God and to our Lord the Pope.'[106] It might seem that she was hauling him in as a last resort, to play off against the local ecclesiastical authority. That is probably the case. It could be one of the useful papal functions to provide an antidote to an otherwise excessively political local court.

But for most lay people the pope would have been primarily a source of great spiritual power, revealed particularly in indulgences. In the late Middle Ages any indulgence of more than forty days had to be authorized by the pope; they were valued and used by many with great devotion. There was also great misunderstanding. Despite evidence throughout the period for preaching on the need for repentance and confession of sin as part of an indulgence, the laity persisted in believing that indulgences forgave sins; the emphasis to the contrary in many a sermon underlines this.[107] Equally, the fact that important indulgences had to come from the pope emphasized the power of the grantor, as it was meant to do. The penumbra of popular belief reveals much about attitudes to the papacy. Prayers appear saying that the indulgence attached to saying them is written in St Peter's in Rome, authenticated by a papal bull.[108] The mass to avoid being visited by sudden death was authorised by Pope Clement VI, with spectacular claims for the consequences of devout attendance. The Mass of the Five Wounds was said to have been revealed by the Archangel Raphael to 'Pope Boniface', again with extravagant claims about its power. Dr Duffy cites the Trental of Pope Gregory as another example of a popular devotion with a 'papal' authentication. This is the world in which there flourished prophecies about angelic popes who would bring the New Jerusalem and antichrist popes who would herald the end.[109]

None of this would make sense unless the pope was popularly supposed to have mighty spiritual power; in some sense he interpreted God to man. Thomas Gascoigne thought the untu-

---

[106] Ibid., 1, p. 387.

[107] Harvey, England, Rome, pp. 236–7; E. Duffy, The Stripping of the Altars. Traditional Religion in England c.1400–c.1580 (New Haven, Conn., and London, 1992), pp. 287–98; Swanson, Church and Society, pp. 227–8 and 292–4.

[108] See Duffy, Stripping of the Altars, pp. 287–98, for English examples in rest of paragraph.

[109] Reeves, 'The medieval heritage', in Reeves, Prophetic Rome, pp. 32–6; McGinn, 'Angel pope', passim.

tored masses believed that the pope spoke regularly with God, to know what to bind and loose.[110] He occupied a necessary place at the summit of earthly religious power. In 1402 the wife of a tailor of Baldock was said to have been spreading information heard from some friars to the effect that the pope had issued an indulgence against Henry IV, in favour of those who supported the Earl of March and Owen Glyn Dwr. 'And in as much as the King [Henry IV] did not wish to obey the Pope of Rome, for that reason all the bad weather had happened for many days past.'[111] I take it that this implies that the right hierarchy must be maintained or no good can come of it. Such views were both dangerous and ambiguous. For spreading them in 1402 John Sparrowhawk was sentenced to be hanged, drawn, and quartered. This small glimpse of popular belief explains why fifteenth-century English monarchs were so anxious to have their titles accepted by the pope.[112] It also explains why in 1533, when the royal council ordered sermons against the pope, it also issued a pamphlet defending Henry's divorce, saying that God's favour to the royal religious policy was revealed by the birth of a healthy child to Anne Boleyn and by the good weather.[113]

When judging the strength of adherence to the papacy in late medieval England one must not neglect this largely uncharted area of popular belief. Nor should one underestimate the importance, after Basel, to those who thought about it, of the unity of the Church. It has become almost a commonplace to dismiss loyalty to the papacy as a religious factor in England, but this has largely been done by scholars equating loyalty with willingness to pay. One would expect Professor Dickens to play down the papacy, but one cannot accuse Dr Haigh of being a Dickensian. He judges that for the English the papacy was 'not much more than a symbol of the unity of Christendom. Papal authority was neither loved nor hated: it was not important enough' for that.[114]

---

[110] Harvey, *England, Rome*, p. 234.

[111] *Select Cases in the Court of King's Bench under Richard II, Henry IV, and Henry VII*, 7, Selden Society, 88 (1971), no. 13, pp. 123–4. For background: P. McNiven, 'Rebellion, sedition and the legend of Richard II's survival in the reigns of Henry IV and V', *BJRL*, 76 (1994), pp. 93–117, esp. pp. 100–3.

[112] E.g. Henry V and France: Harvey, *England, Rome*, ch. 7.

[113] G. R. Elton, *Policy and Police. The Enforcement of the Reformation in the Age of Thomas Cromwell* (Cambridge, 1972), p. 181; N. Pocock, *Records of the Reformation: the Divorce 1527–1533*, 2 vols (Oxford, 1870), 2, p. 530.

[114] C. Haigh, *English Reformations: Religion, Politics and Society under the Tudors* (Oxford, 1993), p. 8.

Nicholas of Cusa's attitude suggests that this dichotomy may be misplaced. But why a symbol of the unity of Christendom should be unimportant is likewise unexplained. Thomas Cromwell thought otherwise. The clergy could not forget the pope; daily in the canon they offered the mass for the whole Church, praying that God would guide it in peace and unity throughout the world, 'together with N. our Pope and N. our Bishop'. In the Sarum rite the king is also mentioned, but last in the hierarchy. The laity also prayed for the pope in English every week at Sunday mass in the bedes or bidding prayers.[115] In 1533 Cromwell ordered all references to the pope to be erased from all service books.[116] We do not know how many priests continued to include the pope in the canon, but that was by far the most telling place where he was mentioned. In a world where the mass was said daily, the papacy was most noticeable not as a centre of jurisdiction, nor as an exactor of obedience, nor as a collector of money, but as the focus of Catholic communion. To repudiate that was a serious matter.

Thus just before the Reformation communion with the papacy was considered essential in the Western Church, but almost nothing else was agreed. Local churches refused to fund it properly, accusing it of greed but demanding service. Majesty was expected by most people, but funding for majesty came from benefices, indulgences, and a secular state which forced popes to be princes. Papal ideology, epitomized by Torquemada, was clear, but not all shared it and the papacy had no means to insist on it; Pius II's *Execrabilis* of 1460,[117] condemning appeal to a General Council, had not killed conciliarism. In popular imagination the papacy wielded mighty power for both good and evil; angel and antichrist were very close. The boundaries between episcopal and papal power were shadowy, allowing resistance and argument; the *de facto* power of the crown was nearly always greater than either. Even the Council of Trent did not attempt to define the exact relation between pope and council, nor the

---

[115] Clergy: F. H. Dickinson, *Missale ad usum Sarum* (Burntisland, 1861–83), col. 613. Laity: Duffy, *Stripping of the Altars*, p. 124; *The Lay Folks' Mass Book or The Manner of Hearing Mass*, ed. T. F. Simmons, *EETS*, Original Series, 71 (London, 1879), pp. 64, 68, 74–5.

[116] Haigh, *English Reformations*, pp. 123–4; Elton, *Policy and Police*, pp. 232–40.

[117] H. J. Becker, *Die Appellation vom Papst an ein allgemeines Konzil* (Cologne and Vienna, 1988), esp. pp. 162–202.

limits of papal power. If it had tried there would have been instant disagreement, though all present accepted the necessity for a papacy. At the centre Basel left a legacy of fear, with secular rulers (as the French in 1511) using councils as political weapons. Papal weakness rather than papal power strikes one; confusion rather than certainty, diversity rather than uniformity. This was the background to Luther's protest.

University of Durham

# CONTINUITY AND DIVERGENCE IN TUDOR RELIGION

## by EAMON DUFFY

On a mild spring evening in late April 1537 a group of men from the Wiltshire villages of Mere and Bledney sat drinking 'without the door' of a neighbour, William Brownyng. It was St Mark's Day, traditionally a holy-day on which labour was forbidden, but recently demoted by royal command. Thomas Poole had accordingly gone about his normal work that day, but was denounced by John Tutton as a heretic 'because he wrought on St Mark's day'. Poole defended himself by invoking the new law, tempers flared, and Tutton imprudently aired his opinion that the moving spirit behind the new reforms, Thomas Cromwell, was, like all his 'witholders' a 'stark heretic'; 'Shall I obey the King's commandment and it be naught?' he asked. 'Marry I will not.'[1]

We happen to know about this unimportant incident because, like so many others, a report of it found its way on to Cromwell's desk. It was a scene duplicated the length and breadth of England, from the 1530s to the death of Elizabeth and beyond. The Henrician authorities themselves, who had set in motion the process of reformation, above all by the encouragement of lay Bible-reading, were periodically panic-stricken by the 'contention, division and contrariety of opinion in the unlearned multitude' to which the religious changes gave rise, especially 'in open places, taverns and alehouses'.[2] Such fears contributed in 1543 to a conservative coup at Henry's court, and the passing in May of that year of the notorious and provocatively named act 'for the advancement of true religion' which sought to curb the flood of 'gnorances, fond opinions, errors and blindnesses' now possessing the people, by cracking down on freedom of the press and banning Bible-reading by women, apprentices, and the entire labouring classes under the rank of yeoman.[3] Henry VIII

[1] J. S. Brewer, J. Gairdner and R. H. Brodie, eds, *Letters and Papers, Foreign and Domestic, of the Reign of Henry VIII* (London, 1862–1910), 12/i, no.567 (p. 264).

[2] R. B. Merriman, *The Life and Letters of Thomas Cromwell*, 2 vols (London, 1902), 2, pp. 111–12: Paul L. Hughes and James F. Larkin, eds, *Tudor Royal Proclamations*, 3 vols (New Haven, Conn., and London, 1964–9), 1, p. 271.

[3] E. Duffy, *The Stripping of the Altars* (London and New Haven, Conn., 1992), pp. 432–3.

himself harangued his last Parliament in 1545 on the divisions and name-callings which religious controversy had brought,[4] and that theme was enshrined two years later in the Edwardine *Homelie agaynst Contencion and Braulyng:*

> For to(o) many there be which upon the alebenches or other places delight to propounde certayne questions . . . and so unsoberly to reason and dispute that neyther party will give place to other, they fall to chydyng and contencion, and sometyme from hote wordes to further inconvenience. Sainct Paul could not abyde to heare emong the Corinthians these wordes of discorde or dissencion: I holde of Paule, I of Cephas, and I of Apollo. What would he then say, if he hearde these wordes of contencion, whiche be now almoste in every mans mouth: he is a Pharise, he is a gospeler, he is of the new sorte, he is of the old faythe, he is a new broched brother, he is a good catholique father, he is a papist, he is an heretique? Oh how the churche is divided! Oh how the cyties be cutte and mangled! Oh how the coote of Christ, that was without seame, is all to-rent and torne! Oh body misticall of Christe: where is that holy and happy unitie, out of which whosoever is, he is not in Christ?[5]

Religious diversity was, therefore, not a notion to conjure with in Tudor England. Both Catholic and Protestant were agreed that religious unity involved not merely a common faith, but a single discipline and a single form of common prayer – the phrase 'common prayer' itself would assume great importance in the liturgical changes of Edward's reign. Ritual and doctrinal diversity were evils, aspects of social and religious disunity.

This, to begin with, had of course been a distinctively Catholic theme, with Protestantism seen as bringing not merely diversity but dissension and the breakdown of unity. That notion had been given decisive formulation in the polemic of Thomas More during the late 1520s and early 1530s, in which the chaos and religious strife of Germany was presented as an object lesson in

---

[4] Printed in J. Townsend and S. R. Cattley, eds, *The Acts and Monuments of John Foxe*, 8 vols (London, 1837–41), 5, pp. 534–6.

[5] R. B. Bond, ed., *Certain Sermons or Homilies 1547: A Critical Edition* (Toronto, 1987), p. 191.

the evil effects of reformation. – 'For in Saxony fyrst and among all the Lutheranes there be as many heddes as many wyttes. And all as wyse as wylde gees . . . .One fayth in the towne/another in the felde. One in (P)rage/another in the next towne. And yet in (P)rage it selfe one fayth in one strete/an other in the nexte . . .'[6] But these foreign dissensions were quickly naturalized in England, as Protestant groups established themselves in many towns, and a struggle for the soul of the community began. Preaching in Bristol in the 1540s, the conservative Roger Edgworth drew directly on that passage from More to evoke the evils of dissension, and to plead for mutual forbearance and unity:

> For where is concord and vnitie, there the holye gost spreadeth his grace aboundantly, and contrarye where be scismes and diversitie of errours and opinions, God withdraweth grace, and then men rune wythout brydell from one opinion to another, from one heresie to an other, tyll men be set all on a rore and out of quietnes, as it appeareth evidently in Germany, where be almost as manie heresies and divers waies in theyr fayth, as be cities or townes.

That corrosive diversity was now established among his hearers, threatening Bristol's very survival:

> Here among you in this citie some wil heare masse, some will heare none by theyr good wils, som wil be shriuen, some wil not . . . . Some wil pray for the dead, som wil not . . . . I pray you accord you (good maisters & frends) for feare least the anger of God fall vpon this citye, which God forbidde it should.[7]

This gloom about the likely effect of religious difference within the community was not born of a failure of imagination. Tudor men and women were perfectly well able to conceive of religious diversity as a tolerable possibility: it was the practical

---

[6] Thomas More, *A Dialogue Concerning Heresies*, in T. M. C. Lawlor, G. Marc'Hadour and R. C. Marius, eds, *The Complete Works of St Thomas More*, 6/i (New Haven, Conn., and London, 1981), p. 192.

[7] Janet Wilson, ed., *Sermons Very Fruitfull, Godly and Learned by Roger Edgeworth* (Cambridge, 1993), pp. 280–1.

reality of it in the conditions of sixteenth-century Europe which shaped the universal agreement that diversity was not to be borne. In 1516, on the very eve of the Reformation, Thomas More himself had presented a much more favourable vision of religious diversity within a single community, in the famous account of the religions of Utopia in the second book of his great fable. The opening sentence of that section, 'There be divers kindes of religion not onlie in sondrie partes of the Ilande, but also in divers places of every citie', uncannily prefigures the very phrasing of his later denunciations of Protestant divisiveness within the cities of Germany, but the tone of the passage as a whole is quite different.[8] There is, it is true, the same conviction that 'continuall dissension and strife among themselves for their religion' fatally weakened a nation, for it was their internecine religious feuds which had enabled King Utopus to conquer the Utopians in the first place. Yet the Utopians permit every man to follow his own religion, and to try to persuade others to the same opinion, provided all is done 'peacablie, gentelie, quietly, and soberlie, without hastie and contentious rebuking and invehing against other'. King Utopus himself even wondered whether God did not actually desire 'manifolde and diverse sortes of honour' and had therefore inspired 'sondry men with sondrie kindes of religion'.

Utopus had indeed believed that if only all would attend to true reason in their religious discussions, the one true religion would triumph, and this was a view which, at this stage of his life at least, More seems to have shared: hence the enthusiasm and readiness which he attributes to the better sort of Utopians in response to the preaching of the Christian gospel. Yet Utopus, like More, understood that 'if contention and debate in that behalf should continually be used', the worst, not the best, in human nature would triumph. As the 'woorste men' are the most obstinate and vocal in defence of their 'evyll opinion', so Utopus perceived 'that then the beste and holyest religion would be trodden underfote and destroyed by most vaine supersticions, even as goode corne is by thornes and weedes overgrowen and

---

[8] I have preferred to quote from the Tudor translation printed in the old Everyman Library edition, *Utopia with the dialogue of Comfort, by Sir Thomas More* (London, 1910), quotation at p. 100. For the Latin text with a modern translation, E. Surtz and J. H. Hexter, eds, *Utopia*, in *The Complete Works of St Thomas More*, 4 (New Haven, Conn., and Toronto, 1965).

chooked'. Alehouse disputation was, therefore, definitely ruled out, in favour of earnest debate, conducted with 'reason and sober modestie'. More even seems to blame the zealotry of the Utopian convert to Christianity who, against the advice of Hythlodaeus and the other Christian travellers to Utopia, had violently denounced the superstitions of his pagan fellow-countrymen. And the Utopians themselves drew the line at allowing any public expression before the common people of atheism or any denial of the immortality of the soul, free will, and moral answerability in heaven or hell.[9]

Despite its apparent indulgence towards the religious liberalism of the Utopians, therefore, many of the fundamental themes of later Tudor hostility towards religious diversity are implicit in book two of *Utopia*: the emphasis on the necessity of sober, measured discussion, best confined to the wise, the horror of loud-mouthed rancour, the conviction that in alehouse debate the best lack all conviction while the worst are full of passionate intensity, the assumption that religious dissension fatally undermines the stability and security of the state. Even More's own later persecuting zeal against Protestants as Lord Chancellor is adumbrated there, for Lutheranism's worst sins in his eyes included the doctrines of *sola fide* and predestination, which seemed to him to repudiate precisely that moral answerability which even the Utopians insisted upon and enforced. In the wake of the Peasants' Revolt and the outbreak of religious war and religious atrocity in Germany, More perceived Protestantism as the triumph of irrationality, immorality, and the mob, over against the reason of ages, legitimate authority, and sober wisdom. And he rapidly came to see that all this was a possibility for England also. As native Protestant opinion began to make itself felt he came to long and pray for the country to be 'settled in a perfect uniformity of religion', but to fear that one day Catholics would have to come to a 'league and composition' with Protestants, 'to let them have their churches quietly to themselves, so that they would be content to let us have ours quietly to ourselves'.[10]

---

[9] More, *Utopia*, pp. 101–3; Latin text, *Complete Works*, 4, pp. 216–22.
[10] William Roper, *The Life of Sir Thomas More, Knight* (London, 1963), pp. 14, 18–19.

It is no great surprise that Catholics like More should fear religious disunity, or condemn what Mary's government would describe as 'diverse and strange opinions and diversities of sects'. But this was by no means a Catholic peculiarity. In due course the ascendant Protestant party would long in just the same way for a 'perfect uniformity of religion'. The fundamental piece of Edwardine religious legislation was indeed the Act of Uniformity of 1549, and it was saturated with precisely the same rhetoric, of a country torn by 'divers forms . . . and sundry rites', of division, offence, and discontent, partly inherited from the past, partly the product of innovation and excess of zeal, now at last to be quieted by 'a uniform quiet and godly order' of common prayer, compiled by the most learned and discreet, and concluded 'by the aid of the Holy Ghost, with one uniform agreement' with a resulting 'great comfort and quietness of mind.'[11]

There were of course problems for Protestants seeking to appropriate such a rhetoric of godly uniformity over against destructive diversity, for in the nature of things it was they who were perceived as seeking change in an established order, and as those who had introduced diversity by challenging the Catholic order in the first place. The Edwardine regime tackled this difficulty by the bold expedient of identifying the Catholic past, not the Protestant present, with chaos and diversity, presenting the new Protestant dispensation as bringing harmony and light out of chaos, and 'such an order wherby the same shall be redressed'.[12] According to the preface to the first Edwardine *Book of Common Prayer*, the medieval Church had involved its priests and people in endless liturgical confusion and complication, its worship a bewildering and degenerate hotch-potch, the 'Godly and decent ordre of the auncient fathers . . . altered, broken and neglected'. There had been, moreover 'great diversitie in sayinge and synging in churches within this realme' not because of Reformation innovations, but because of the liturgical diversity of the medieval rites, 'some following Salsbury use, some Hereford use, some the use of Bangor, some of Yorke, and some of Lincolne'. Into this chaos and division the Reformation would

---

[11] 2 & 3 Edward VI, Cap I, cited from the text in H. Gee and W. J. Hardy, *Documents Illustrative of English Church History* (London, 1896), pp. 358–66; the Marian phrases taken from I Mary, Statute 2, Cap 2, ibid., p. 377.
[12] *The First and Second Prayer Books of King Edward the Sixth* (London, 1910), p. 4.

at last bright light, rationality, and unity: 'Now, from hence-furth, all the whole realme shal have but one use.'[13]

That same assertion of popish division was transferred from an assessment of the historic past to a picture of the present by controversialists like John Jewel, who claimed that it was the Catholics, not the Protestants, who were unable to agree among each other: 'Good God! what manner of fellows be these, which blame us for disagreeing? And do all they themselves, ween you, agree well together?' Thomists fought against Scotists, nominal-ists against realists, while the contentions of 'so many diversities of friars and monks' were too numerous to be detailed. In short, 'hardly at any time do they agree among themselves'. By com-parison, Protestant divisions, even those between Zwinglians and Lutherans, were unimportant, for 'they of both sides be Chris-tians, good friends and brethren', differing only on a single minor point 'which is neither weighty nor great: neither mistrust we, or make doubt at all, but they will shortly be agreed'.[14]

But there were limits to how far uniformity or even unity could be adopted as an absolute ideal by consistent Protestants. Truth was more important than harmony, and unity was bought at too high a price if it involved the toleration of damnable error. 'Of a truth', wrote Jewel, 'unity and concord doth best become reli-gion; yet is not unity the sure and certain mark whereby to know the Church of God. For there was great consent that might be amongst them that worshipped the golden calf, and among them which with one voice jointly cried against our Saviour Jesus Christ, "Crucify him".'[15] John Foxe, reflecting on Henry VIII's 1545 speech to Parliament, with its denunciation of religious division and name-calling, was unconvinced. Nicknames like papist and Protestant, heretic and pharisee, 'the old mumpsimus and the new sumpsimus', might indeed be '*symptomata* of a sore wound in the commonwealth'. But 'he that will amend this wound must first begin to search out the causes', and in this case, the cause was the inescapable conflict of truth and error, as two 'mighty flints thus smiting together, cometh out the sparkle of

[13] Ibid., pp. 3–5, 286–8.

[14] John Jewel, *An Apology of the Church of England*, in *The Works of John Jewel*, ed. J. Ayre, 4 vols, PS (Cambridge, 1845–50), 3, pp. 68–70.

[15] Ibid., p. 69.

this division, which can in no wise be quenched, but that one part must needs yield and give over'. There could be 'no neutrality, nor mediation of peace, nor exhortation to agreement, that will serve between these two contrary doctrines'.[16]

The notion that the gospel almost inevitably provoked dissension and hatred, because of the furious opposition of the ungodly and the incompatibility of truth and error, became something of a *topos* in Protestant thought about unity. In the early 1530s More noted the appearance of this conviction, reporting the reply of 'one of this sorte of this new kynde of prechers' who, when asked why he thought that nowadays the gospel was not well preached, answered that 'he thought so bycause he saw not the prechers persecutyd / nor no stryfe nor business aryse vpon theyr prechyng'.[17] If More intended this as satire, he certainly hit the mark, for it became a commonly held position among zealous Protestants in the second half of the century. In 1581 George Gifford's ardent preacher, Zelotes, denounced the notion that its divisiveness was a sign of the falsity of Protestantism: 'I pray you tell me, can ye put fire and water together but they will rumble? Will ye have light and darknesse for to agree as companions together? . . . Will ye charge Christ and his Gospell, because as he saith, he came not to send peace, but a sword, to set the father against the son?'[18]

Nevertheless, however defiantly defended by the godly, precisely this propensity of Protestantism to set the father against the son, its decisive break with and difference from the Catholic past, was a liability in a society which, with the establishment of the Settlement of 1559, had become nominally Protestant, but in which huge numbers of the clergy and laity clung or looked back to the old ways. If unity was a fraught issue in accounting for the diversities of Protestants, *continuity* with the religion of the past was even more so. Indeed, continuity and unity were conventionally associated in the popular mind. Gifford's Essex countryman declared that he would 'follow our forefathers, and do no worse than they did: what should we seek to be wiser or better than they? . . . Now there is no love: then they lived in friend-

[16] Foxe, *Acts and Monuments*, 5, pp. 536–7.

[17] More, *Dialogue Concerning Heresies*, p. 124.

[18] George Gifford, *A Briefe discourse of certaine points of the religion, which is among the common sort of Christians, which may be termed the Countrey Divinitie* (London, 1612 [first published 1581]), pp. 85–7.

ship, and made merry together.'[19] This perennial and widely shared conviction that the divisions of the contemporary community were the direct result of a violent break with the past was erected into a controversial principle by the defenders of the old religion. In the debates over the Elizabethan Settlement in the Lords in April 1559, Cuthbert Scot, Marian bishop of Chester, denounced the Protestant attack on the religion in which 'our forefathers were born, brought uppe, and lived in, and have professed here in this realme, without any alteration or chaunge, by the space of nine hundred yeres and more; and hathe also ben professed and practised in the universall churche of Christe synce the apostells tyme'. He deplored a speech made the day before by one of the lay lords, which had urged the acceptance of the Reformation because 'our fathers lived in blindness'. Scot reminded the House of the injunction of Scripture, 'Aske of thy father, and he shall declare the truthe unto thee, and of thyne auncestors, and they will tell thee.'[20]

Protestant apologists were therefore left with the problem of squaring the circle, of explaining how it was that the new faith, so evidently and deliberately different from the old, was nevertheless not 'yesterday's work', no 'new comen up matter', no novelty. Underneath the changed externals, the Protestant faith was the one true faith inherited from the apostles. John Jewel solved this dilemma by appealing from the proximate to the remote past. Turning his back on the medieval inheritance of the reformed Church of England, he affirmed instead its continuity 'from the primitive church, from the apostles, and from Christ'. This was true antiquity, whereas what the papists claimed as the immemorial customs and traditions of the Church, the medieval and early Tudor face of Christianity as most of his adult readers had known it had been in fact 'but new, and devised of very late'.[21] This, under the rubric of asserting continuity with the primitive church, in fact abandoned any real claim to organic continuity, for it simply wrote off the centuries between the

---

[19] Ibid., pp. 6–7.
[20] The speech is printed in J. Strype, *Annals of the Reformation*, 4 vols in 7 (Oxford, 1824), 2/ii, pp. 438–50, quotation at p. 442, and also (modernized) in H. Gee, *The Elizabethan Prayer-Book and Ornaments* (London, 1902), pp. 236–52, quotation at pp. 241–2. The scriptural citation is from Deut. 32.7.
[21] Jewel, *Apology*, p. 85.

remote past of the primitive Church and the Protestant present. In a society which valued tangible signs of continuity, this was a dangerous procedure.

John Foxe, every bit as hostile to the medieval inheritance of the reformed Church, nevertheless pursued a different strategy. His *Acts and Monuments* self-consciously set out to establish the 'continual descent of the church till this present time' not through institutional continuity or episcopally handed-on Apostolic Succession, but via the martyrs and heretics of the Middle Ages, through whose pedigree it could be shown that the reformed Church of the present was no 'new begun matter, but even the old continued church'.[22]

These were theoretical, theological resolutions of a problem which was absolutely fundamental to the practical question of the unity and identity of the Elizabethan Church of England. Was Elizabeth's Church the same Church as Mary's Church, and Henry's Church, or another and different one? Radical Protestants, inheriting the polarized apocalyptic mentality of Bale's *Image of Both Churches*, were certain, indeed determined, that the cleansed Church of the present was not the same as the filthy sty of the past, and sought means of distancing the new Church from the synagogue of Satan which had been the old: as is well known, that polarity is fundamental to the most important of all Elizabethan Protestant books, Foxe's *Acts and Monuments*.[23] But for most of the population at large it was just as important to assert the opposite, to affirm that Elizabeth's Church was indeed Mary's Church, the faith of our fathers reformed but preserved essentially intact under changed but substantially identical forms of worship and belief.

In this assertion of the continuing identity of the Church of the present with the Church of the pre-Reformation generations, continuity of clerical personnel, organization, and ritual observance were crucial. The continuing presence in the parishes during the first decade or so of the new regime of a majority of the Catholic clergy, administering the traditional rites of passage

---

[22] Foxe, *Acts and Monuments*, 1, 'To the True and Faithful Congregation of Christ's Universal Church', pp. 512–20, quotation at pp. 519–20.

[23] V. N. Olsen, *John Foxe and the Elizabethan Church* (Berkeley and London, 1973), pp. 51–100; P. Christianson, *Reformers and Babylon* (Toronto and London, 1978), pp. 13–46; K. R. Firth, *The Apocalyptic Tradition in Reformation Britain, 1530–1645* (Oxford, 1979), pp. 1–110.

in something approximating to the traditional way, was undoubtedly one of the decisive factors in carrying the population at large along with the changes. The ambiguities of the reformed Church of England's forms of worship were probably at least as important. The Elizabethan Church in the 1560s looked to the Churches of Switzerland for inspiration and support, and the Elizabethan Church was, fundamentally, a Reformed or as we should say Calvinist church. But uniquely among Calvinist churches, it retained totally unchanged the full medieval framework of episcopal church government. In Cranmer's Prayer Book it also had a form of worship saturated with echoes of medieval Catholicism, or, as its Puritan critics put it, 'culled and picked out of that popishe dunghil, the Masse booke full of all abominations'.[24] Its eucharistic lectionary preserved not only the Sarum mass-readings, but with them the fundamental framework of the medieval liturgical year. Its collects were for the most part translated direct from the Missal. And at precisely those points where the medieval Church had sought to sacralize the day-to-day life of the people, the Church of England retained remarkably conservative religious forms for the main rites of passage such as marriage, the churching of women, and the burial of the dead, appearing in the process to radical Protestant eyes to retain much of what was worst in medieval Catholic teaching. The theological paradoxes and indeed incoherence implicit in the retention of such rites can best be gauged from the survival of an unmistakeably Catholic 'juridical' form of absolution, directly translated from the medieval Sarum original in the office for the Visitation of the Sick, though Cranmer had certainly repudiated the understanding of priesthood and of confession implicit in the retention of the old form.[25]

---

[24] The phrase is from the 'Admonition to Parliament', note 25 below, p. 21.

[25] Radical objections to these conservative elements in the Prayer Book are summarized in the 'View of Popishe abuses yet remaining in the Englishe Church' appended to the 'Admonition to Parliament', in W. H. Frere and C. E. Douglas, eds, *Puritan Manifestoes* (London, 1954), pp. 20–37, and explored at greater length in *A Survey of the Booke of Common Prayer* (Middelburg, 1610 [first published 1606]). This is number 16451 in W. A. Jackson, F. S. Ferguson, and K. F. Panzer's revised second edition of A. W. Pollard and G. R. Redgrave, eds, *A Short Title Catalogue of Books Printed in England, Scotland and Ireland, and of English Books Printed Abroad, 1475–1640*, 3 vols (London, 1976–91) [hereafter RSTC]. Famously, the Fifth Book of Hooker's *Laws of Ecclesiastical Polity* is devoted to refuting such criticisms.

Accordingly, throughout the 1560s and 1570s priests and congregations all over the country practised forms of religion which deliberately sought and easily found continuities with the past. Clergy 'counterfeited the Mass' at the new communion service, to the rage not only of Puritans, but of the Elizabethan episcopate. Ministers stood at the communion table as they had at the altar, held up the eucharistic bread to be venerated, blessed candles at Candlemas, wore surplices and followed crosses, banners, handbells, and streamers at the Rogation processions, and recited the *De profundis* at funerals for the repose of the souls of the dead. Three generations on, Richard Baxter would complain of the 'profane, ungodly, presumptuous multitude . . . as zealous for crosses and surplices, processions and perambulations . . . with a multitude of things which are only the traditions of their fathers'.[26] A good many of this 'multitude of things' were of course ritual survivals not prescribed in the Prayer Book nor in any official documents of the Church, but continuing nevertheless in popular practice.[27] But the nature of the English religious settlement itself ensured the presence of elements of Catholic practice which guaranteed a certain continuity of religious experience between the medieval and reformed churches, of which perhaps the most striking is the practice of confirmation.

The medieval church required the laity to have their children confirmed by a bishop before admission to communion. Bishops were few and far between, so the laity sought confirmation when and where they could. Representations of the rite of confirmation on late medieval seven-sacrament fonts reflect this difficulty of access – the confirming bishop is often portrayed not in pontificals but in his travelling clothes, and it has been suggested by the leading authority on these fonts that bishops sometimes confirmed the children presented to them by flocking parents without any chrismation, by the simple imposition of hands. Some medieval pontificals appear to have provided a specially shortened two-sentence rite for just such wayside celebrations of the sacrament, and it was a routine commendation of saintly bishops that they actually took the trouble to descend from their

---

[26] There is a convenient summary of episcopal concern about such practices in W. P. M. Kennedy, *Elizabethan Episcopal Administration*, 3 vols., Alcuin Club Collections, 25–7 (1924), 1, pp. lxii–lxxv; for the Baxter quotation, Duffy, *Stripping of the Altars*, p. 578.

[27] As the godly themselves admitted – Frere and Douglas, *Puritan Manifestoes*, p. 28.

horses when confirming![28] Despite increased difficulty of access to this episcopal sacrament as a result of the abolition of suffragan bishops, the laity of the reformed Church of England remained eager to secure the benefits of 'bishoping' for their children. Richard Baxter recalled his own confirmation in rural Shropshire in the early 1630s when 'the bishop coming into the Country' many flocked to him to be confirmed. Baxter, understanding nothing of the meaning of the rite, went with about 30 or 40 other boys to a church-yard, 'of our owne accord to see the bishop only', where they were lined up to be confirmed, the bishop passing along the line 'laying his hands on our head, and saying a few words'. Medieval children would have been presented for this rite at a younger age, but in all its essentials this was a medieval scene, representing a continuity of religious culture which Puritans found profoundly shocking.[29]

The early Elizabethan religious authorities, every bit as Protestant as their Puritan critics, were often shocked too, but were also well aware of the importance of such ritual gestures in retaining the loyalty of the laity. They were thus caught on the horns of a dilemma: understanding the attraction of such signs of continuity with the past, they were nevertheless theologically committed to extirpating them, at whatever cost in terms of the alienation of the unlearned. The Elizabethan Homily 'Of the Place and Time of Prayer' complained that for many the scouring of the Church of 'such gay gazing sights, as their gross fantasy was greatly delighted with', and the abandonment of false religion in favour of 'the true restored' was 'an unsavoury thing to their unsavoury taste': such relics of popery were rightly 'utterly abolished', but the author neverthless realistically imagined the consequent parish lamentation – 'Alas, Gossip, what shall wee now do at Church, since all the saints are taken away, since all the goodly sights wee were wont to have, are gone?' The Homily softens this condemnation by pointing out, in an echo of

---

[28] A. E. Nichols, *Seeable Signs: the Iconography of the Seven Sacraments, 1350–1544* (Woodbridge, 1994), pp. 207–21; I am not entirely persuaded, however, that the absence of a chrismatory in the font representations reliably indicates that confirmation without the use of chrism was actually practised, given that by the later fifteenth century St Thomas's view that anointing rather than laying on of hands constituted the matter of the sacrament was universally accepted.

[29] Richard Baxter, *Confirmation and Restauration, the necessary means of Reformation and Reconciliation* (London, 1658), pp. 154–5.

the Prayer Book's note 'Of Ceremonies', that though all such superstitions are deservedly abolished, yet 'those things that either God was honoured with, or his people edified, are decently retained, and in our churches commonly practised', a tentative gesture towards the *via media* and an affirmation of continuity forced on the authors, one suspects, by circumstance rather than conviction.[30]

For there can be little doubt that the majority of reformers of the generation responsible for the Elizabethan Homilies, bishops included, would have preferred a clean sweep of all such links with the Catholic past, to make clear their decisive separation from the medieval church. Archbishop Parker might talk to foreign Catholic observers of the 'reverend mediocrity' of the English Church's attitude to ceremonies, but that was a phrase and an attitude few of his colleagues cared to endorse. John Jewel mocked precisely those who, in ceremonial matters, sought 'a golden, or as it seems to me, a leaden mediocrity': they were, he thought, men crying out that 'half is better than the whole', and he longed for the total abolition of such 'tawdry fooleries'.[31] Peter Martyr thought it imperative that the Church of England signal its separation from the Church of Rome by departing 'as far as possible from their pernicious institutions',[32] a view echoed by Myles Coverdale in the heat of the Vestiarian troubles of 1566, insisting that the Church should 'not be connected by any similarity of rites with those from whose religion we are utterly abhorent'.[33] For in similarity of custom and habit lay at least the appearance of unity of substance, so that, as Thomas Lever told Bullinger, the retention of popish ceremonies and garb 'so fascinate the ears and eyes of the multitude, that they are unable to believe, but that either the popish doctrine is retained, or at least that it will shortly be restored'.[34] And since similarity of ceremonies betokened unity of doctrine, the Church of England had an obligation to conform itself to the pattern of other reformed

---

[30] *Sermons or Homilies Appointed to be Read in Churches in the Time of Queen Elizabeth* (London, 1833), p. 381.

[31] J. Bruce and T.T. Perowne, eds, *Correspondence of Matthew Parker*, PS (Cambridge, 1853), p. 215; H. Robinson, ed., *The Zurich Letters*, 2 vols, PS (Cambridge, 1842–5), 1, p. 23.

[32] Robinson, *Zurich Letters*, 2, p. 26.

[33] Ibid., p. 122.

[34] Robinson, *Zurich Letters*, 1, p. 85.

Churches. 'Why should we receive Christ rather maimed than entire, and pure, and perfect', Laurence Humphrey and Thomas Sampson asked Bullinger in 1566,

> Why should we look for precedents from our enemies, the papists, and not from you, our brethren of the reformation? We have the same confession in our churches, the same rule of doctrine and faith; why should there be so great a dissimilarity and discrepancy in rites and ceremonies? The thing signified is the same; why do the signs so differ as to be unlike yours, and to resemble those of the papists?[35]

There were many in high places in the Elizabethan Church who felt just as acutely the tension of functioning within a reformed church which looked more like Rome than Geneva. That tension surfaced in a pointed and acrimonious way in October 1578, in the conflict between William Whittingham, Dean of Durham, and Archbishop Sandys of York. Whittingham had been ordained at Geneva, but was accused by Sandys of irregularity because he had no episcopal orders. Matthew Hutton, the Dean of York, himself a future Archbishop, sprang to Whittingham's defence, saying that Genevan ordination, far from being defective, was better than popish ordination, and when angrily rebuked by the Archbishop, Hutton retorted that for that matter his own orders were better than Sandys's orders, for, declared Hutton, he himself 'was made a minister by order of the Queenes maiestie and Lawes now established, and your grace a priest after thorder of Poperie, which order of this realme is better then your graces order, or anie popishe orders. What said tharchbushop dost thow call me a papist?'[36] It was a good question, which might well occur to anyone who comes across Sandys's splendid tomb in Southwell minister, where he lies, uniquely among Elizabethan ecclesiastics, vested in a richly embroidered chasuble. But it was also a question which many zealous Protestants were to answer in the affirmative after 1565, when the Queen increasingly insisted on the enforcement by the

---

[35] Ibid., p. 162.
[36] R. A. Marchant, *The Puritans and the Church Courts in the Diocese of York, 1560–1642* (London, 1960), p. 19.

bishops of the wearing of pre-Reformation clerical garb, and the conservative ritual requirements of the Settlement of 1559, which seemed to them to subvert what Protestant integrity the Prayer Book had. The enforcers of the Settlement, many of them as reluctant as Edmund Grindal, Bishop of London, might claim that the ceremonies of the Prayer Book and the prescribed clerical garb were the badges of solidarity not with popery, but with the Marian martyrs who had died for the Prayer Book reforms: in using them, it was claimed, 'we hold the reformation that was in King Edward's day'.[37] But it was a claim made uneasily, not least because some of the requirements of the ritual enforcement of the mid-1560s, like the use of wafer bread commanded in the Injunctions rather than loaf bread required by the Prayer Book, clearly subverted the more militantly Protestant dimensions of the Prayer Book itself.[38] On the ambiguities and tensions of the Settlement elicited by the Vestiarian disputes of the mid-1560s would be founded much of the later Anglo-Catholic interpretation of the origins of the Church of England, read as a reform preserving continuity and identity with, rather than a decisively Protestant break from, the medieval Catholic *Ecclesia Anglicana*. That selective reading of the history of the English Reformation was, of course, precisely such an outcome as the Elizabethan episcopate, had they been granted prevision, would for the most part have deplored; but equally, it was the one which their Puritan opponents had grimly predicted.

We have been dealing so far with the tensions and difficulties which arose out of Tudor concern with questions of unity and

---

[37] W. Nicholson, ed., *Remains of Edmund Grindal, PS* (Cambridge, 1843), pp. 211–13. Grindal was consistent here, for he had intervened in the dispute over the Prayer Book at Frankfurt in Mary's reign, urging conformity to the book for the sake of solidarity with those who were suffering for it in England; P. Collinson, *Archbishop Grindal* (London, 1979), pp. 73–9.

[38] The sixth rubric after the Communion service required the use of ordinary wheaten bread, though of the best quality, and directed that any remaining after the service should be taken home by the curate for his lunch, a directive which radical Protestants did not hesitate to apply to the consecrated species, to the discomforture of later generations of Anglo-Catholics: F. Proctor and W. H. Frere, *A New History of the Book of Common Prayer* (London, 1925), p. 501. Significantly, Anglo-Catholic commentaries on the Prayer Book and the history of Anglican liturgical practice were sometimes unable even to contemplate the enormity of the practice prescribed in this rubric. It is never discussed, for instance, in Vernon Staley's *Hierurgia Anglicana*, 3 vols (London, 1902–4), and in citing the sixth rubric Staley actually suppressed the crucial sentence directing the profane consumption of the remaining bread: ibid., 2, p. 129.

diversity, continuity and divergence – in particular with the ideological content of difference or similarity of forms – the politics of gesture. I want now to turn to a rather different dimension of the issue, and to consider an aspect of Tudor religious experience in which the polarities of the debate we have been considering were, though not entirely banished, at least to some extent subverted. I want now to consider the much neglected phenomenon of the common rhetoric of devotion which united men and women of quite opposite religious views, and which provided a source of continuity and of unity in the flux of Reformation – a fact which successive regimes noted and sought to exploit. A full consideration of this subject would start with the remarkable devotional writing of the group of early Tudor writers associated with Syon Abbey, and in particular with Richard Whytford, whose *Werke for Householders* has a strong claim to have created much that was to be most characteristic in Tudor devotional writing. I shall focus in this paper, however, on another and later issue – the devotional material which was added to the mid-century English primers.[39]

For the majority of Tudor people the stark and mutually exclusive alternatives of the ideologues were less in evidence than muddle and uncertainty, compromise and accommodation. There were of course issues and institutions which came to function as flags, signalling alternate or rival allegiances, religious difference – the reception of reformed communion, sermon-going, the use of English Bibles as opposed to rosaries or Latin primers. But most people lived a religious life which avoided declaratory gestures that might set them apart from their neighbours. As one country aphorism had it, it was 'safest to doe in religion as most doe'.[40] And so they made do with the religious forms and resources available to them: whatever their inner convictions, they prayed on the books provided or approved by

[39] For Whytford and his associates, see G. Williams, 'Two neglected London-Welsh clerics', *Transactions of the Honourable Society of Cymmrodorion*, 1961/i (1961), pp. 23–44; P. Caraman, 'An English monastic reformer of the sixteenth century', *Clergy Review*, ns 28 (1947), pp. 1–16; J. T. Rhodes, 'Syon Abbey and its religious publications in the sixteenth century', *JEH*, 44 (1993), pp. 11–25; *Werke for Householders* has been edited with an introduction in J. Hogg, *Richard Whytford's 'The Pype or Tonne of the Lyfe of Perfection'*, 5 vols, Salzburg Studies in English Literature: Elizabethan and Renaissance Studies, 89 (Salzburg, 1979–89), 5, pp. 1–62.

[40] Quoted by William Perkins in 'The Foundations of Christian Religion', in *The Workes of that Famous and Worthy Minister of Christ . . . Mr William Perkins*, 3 vols (London, 1612–13), 1, sig. A2.

authority, they attended their parish churches. As a result, even men and women of strong conviction absorbed the influence of points of view often opposite to their own: in the fabric of Tudor religious experience, so often officially polarized, were many harmonizing, even homogenizing factors.

We can catch these harmonizing factors at work in the will of George Lowes, former mayor and sometime MP for Winchelsea, made in September 1553.[41] Lowes was a well-known religious conservative, who no doubt rejoiced to see the restoration of Catholicism which was just beginning under Mary. His will, however, is an extraordinary document, whose language testifies to the complexities of Tudor religious awareness. Deploring the decay of auricular confession, Lowes included an elaborate confession of sins in his will, which seems to be fairly closely modelled on the 'Form of Confession' commonly found in the printed primers of the 1520s and 1530s, and shortly to be revived in the official primers of Mary's reign.[42] He went on to elaborate protestations of Catholic orthodoxy, and to request the prayers of all who heard or read his will 'that I may . . . be one of them that shall be called to be saved at his right hand'. The historian of Reformation Sussex who first published this will saw in it evidence that even at the end of Edward's reign, and in so Protestant a town as Winchelsea, 'there were . . . powerful local figures who were *quite unmoved* by the religious changes that had taken place', and who would be ready to 'welcome the Catholic reaction when it came'.[43] What Lowes's will actually shows, it seems to me, is the extent to which a committed Catholic, who certainly was eager to welcome the Marian restoration, might nevertheless absorb and employ religious language which unmistakably echoes the English Bible, the Edwardine Prayer Books and other Protestant formularies. Lowes, in affirming his belief in the Apostles', Athanasian, and Nicene creeds, for example, remarks of the latter that it 'is said in the Holy Communion': he places great emphasis on the Scriptures, received by 'the whole congregation of Christ's whole Church . . . and set forth to be

[41] G. J. Mayhew, 'The progress of the Reformation in East Sussex: the evidence from wills', *Southern History*, 5 (1983), pp. 44–5.

[42] Duffy, *Stripping of the Altars*, pp. 61, 80–1, 541; the 'Form of Confession' is printed in full in W. Maskell, *Monumenta ritualia ecclesiae Anglicanae*, 3 vols (London, 1846–7), 2, pp. 271–83.

[43] Mayhew, 'Progress of the Reformation', p. 45.

the true prophet and lively word of God', and the rest of his will abounds in phrases which have the idiom of Cranmer and the English Bible stamped all over them – 'my bounden duty', 'breaking and transgressing his ten commandments, wherein hangs the whole law and the prophets'. Here, surely, is a Catholic who, if his devotional language is anything to go by, was anything but 'unmoved' by the changes of the previous twenty years. The existence of men like Lowes should alert us to the existence of a Tudor devotional idiom which was shared by Protestants and Catholics. Consider Lowes's penitential affirmation that

> with a contrite heart, I bewail, sorrow and lament my sins, and with that heart, I most humbly and meekly pray, require and desire of Almighty God that he would of his clemency, pity and mercy, forgive me, being a wretched sinner, but yet his creature, my sins and trespasses . . . that it would please his majesty not to enter into judgement with me his poor creature, for in righteousness, neither I, nor no man living, is nothing worth in the sight of him.

Such a declaration would be difficult to categorize as either Protestant or Catholic: that he could write or have written for him such a prayer was the outcome of an extraordinary evolutionary process in English devotional writing in which both Catholics and Protestants had played a part over the previous generation.

To trace the emergence of that idiom we need to turn to the flood of devotional material produced or approved by successive Tudor regimes. I have written elsewhere of the central role which officially produced devotional books such as the primer played in the successful engineering of religious change and restoration in Tudor England.[44] From the mid-1530s the presses poured out a series of these increasingly 'official' prayer books for the devotional use of the laity at home and in church. Some

---

[44] Duffy, *Stripping of the Altars* pp. 382–3, 402, 444–7, 537–43, 567. And on this whole area, see the pioneering and still indispensable work by H. C. White, *The Tudor Books of Private Devotion* (Wisconsin, 1951), and the more specialized work (concentrating on the question of versions of scripture in the primers) by C. Butterworth, *The English Primers 1529–1549* (Philadelphia, 1954).

of these books were agressively iconoclastic, like William Marshall's *Prymer in Englysche* of 1535, with its excoriating attack on Catholic prayer books – those 'innumerable pestilent and infectious bokes and lernynges, with the whiche the christen people have ben pituously sedused and deceyved, broughte up in diverse kyndes of diffidence and false hopes'.[45] Marshall's primers had Cromwell's backing and a crown patent, but they were not official acts of state. The official Tudor primers *were* acts of state, however, and they were intended to quiet disputes, rather than to invite them. Henry VIII characteristically prefaced his Primer of 1545 with an 'Injunction' banning and calling in all others, 'for the avoyding of the diversite of primer bokes, that are now abroade, wherof are almooste innumerable sortes which minister occasion of contencions and vain disputations, rather than to edifie': he therefore intended the new book to provide 'one uniforme ordre of all suche bokes throughout our dominions.'[46] Though it was in many respects a Protestant book, drastically whittling down the calendar of saints' days, transforming the Office for the Dead by omitting many of the traditional psalms and prayers of intercession, and bowdlerizing almost all the Marian material, Henry's Primer was a conscious attempt to use a traditional devotional format to move the population at large in a reformed direction. It included, as primers since the 1520s had increasingly done, an extensive selection of prayers for many occasions – for morning and night, against adversity, for protection in time of temptation, and so on. This was a very eclectic selection, drawing on traditional materials like the so-called prayer of St Bernardino, 'O Bone Jesu', on the biblical prayers and paraphrases of reformers like Richard Taverner, but above all on the Latin prayers of Catholic humanists like Erasmus and, especially, Ludovicus Vives.[47] The resulting tone of the collection is sober, discursive, full of scriptural reference, but full also of a warmth and affectivity reminiscent of much late medieval

---

[45] White, *Tudor Books*, pp. 91–100.

[46] *The Primer, in Englishe and Latyn, set foorth by the Kynges maiestie and his Clergie* (London, Richard Grafton, 1545). The 'Injunction' is also printed in Hughes and Larkin, *Tudor Royal Proclamations*, I, pp. 349–50, and in E. Hoskins, *Horae Beatae Mariae Virginis or Sarum and York Primers with Kindred Books* (London, 1901), pp. 237–8.

[47] Sources identified in the collation by Hoskins, *Horae*, pp. 237–44.

devotional writing. Its eclecticism gives us entry into a little noted Tudor devotional world which, under all the religious transformations of the century, and despite the deliberate harnessing of such prayer books by successive regimes to promote change, united Catholics and Protestants in a single language of piety, a single devotional tone of voice, different from pre-Reformation piety but in clear continuity with it.

The Henrician Primer was the fundamental Protestant primer, serving, with only trivial variations, as the basis of all the official primers of Edward's reign, till the radical but short-lived revision of 1553, itself based on the Second Prayer Book. It was, however, the 1545 book, rather than that dramatically more Protestant Edwardian revision, which was adopted as the basis of the Elizabethan Primer of 1559.[48] Much more remarkably, its collection of English prayers also formed the basis for the additional material in the officially restored Sarum *Horae* of Mary's reign, the series of Catholic primers issued under the supervision of theologians in Cardinal Pole's entourage from 1555, and printed by the Crown publisher John Wayland. These books restored to their medieval form the liturgical sections of the primer which Henry had emasculated (though in translation), but the additional vernacular devotional material provided in these official Catholic publications was essentially identical with that provided in the primers of the two previous Protestant regimes. The Marian editors slightly rearranged the material, omitting one or two doctrinally unacceptable prayers, and adding a handful of others, mostly from the traditional medieval primer repertoire. The clear evidence of discriminating selection, however, makes all the more startling the willingness of the Marian editors to include material of quite definitely Protestant provenance.[49] When in 1553 the Edwardian authorities finally abandoned the Henrician Primer in favour of a book modelled on the daily offices in the Second Prayer Book, they had replaced the supplementary Henrician devotional material with a series of prayers drawn largely from publications by Cranmer's chaplain, Thomas Becon, in particular the *Flower of Godly Prayers*[50] and the *Pomander of*

---

[48] Ibid., nos 174–96 and 239–40.

[49] I have discussed these issues in *Stripping of the Altars*, pp. 537–43.

[50] *The Flower of Godly Prayers* ([London], *c.*1550), RSTC, 1719.5–1720.7; modernized text in J. Ayre, ed., *Prayers and Other Pieces of Thomas Becon*, PS (Cambridge, 1844), pp. 1–72.

*Prayer*.[51] The first surviving edition of the *Pomander* dates from 1558, but it is dedicated to Anne of Cleves, who died in 1557, so there was almost certainly an earlier edition: at any rate, its contents were sufficiently innocuous to pass muster as a Catholic book in Mary's reign. But the *Flower of Godly Prayers* was a militantly reforming book, with a preface praising the Protestant martyrs of Henry's reign. It included a number of items which were in fact bare-faced polemics for Protestantism – attacks on the 'shaveling' Catholic clergy, and a prayer for recitation before communion which strongly emphasized the doctrine of the real absence.[52] It is all the more remarkable, therefore, that the Catholic editors of the official Marian Primer were willing to draw material even from this rabidly reformed collection. So Becon's first prayer 'for the morning', with its characteristically 'Protestant' emphasis on the devotee's vocation and duty to his neighbour, was added by the Marian editor to the Henrician material in the prayers provided for each morning of the week.[53]

The Primer produced as part of the religious settlement of 1559 consolidated this policy of devotional continuity. It returned to the arrangement of the material first included in the Henrician Primer of 1545, but this was substantially the same as that of Mary's Primers: however different the official liturgy might be from the mass, the pattern of private prayer offered by the new regime was therefore continuous with that current since the last years of Henry's reign. This could hardly last: the primers, with their essentially monastic format and their prayers for the dead, could not long survive in the increasingly Protestant milieu of Elizabeth's reign. There were two English editions of the Primer and a Latin translation in 1560, another reprint in 1565, and a final one in 1575, and then silence, till John Cosin produced his notorious 'Devotions', based on the Elizabethan book, in 1627.[54]

The distinctive mid-Tudor primer, based on the Little Hours of the Virgin and the Office for the Dead, was, then, doomed to

[51] *The Pomander of Prayer* ([London], 1558), RSTC, 1744–8, modernized text in Ayre, *Prayers and Other Pieces*, pp. 73–85; the revised Edwardian Primer of 1553 is reprinted in modernized spelling in J. Ketley, ed., *The Two Liturgies . . . set forth by Authority in the Reign of King Edward VI*, PS, (Cambridge, 1844), pp. 357–484.

[52] Ayre, *Prayers and Other Pieces*, pp. 3–13, 21–4, 53–5.

[53] Discussed more fully in White, *Tudor Books*, pp. 129–30.

[54] RSTC, 16087–92: J. Cosin, *A Collection of Private Devotions . . . as they were after this maner published by Authoritie of Q Eliz 1560* ([London], 1627), RSTC, 5815.5–5919.

disappearance. The devotional style it represented, however, was not. It survived in a number of alternative collections. The martyr John Bradford had produced a series of prayers and meditations drawn from the writings of Vives, which duplicated much of the additional devotional material in the Henrician, Edwardian, and Marian Primers: from 1559 onwards his 'godly medytacyons' became devotional classics, which helped shape the prayer-life of generations of zealously Protestant Christians – Bradford's prayers were a staple of family devotion in Richard Baxter's childhood in early Stuart rural Shropshire.[55] A series of other publications throughout the 1560s, 1570s, and 1580s likewise ensured that the range of medieval and humanist devotional material included in the primers of the mid-century continued to influence devotional styles to the end of the century. Of these easily the most remarkable was the so-called 'Queen's Prayerbook', first produced by John Daye in 1569 and then in a much revised and expanded edition in 1578 under the title *A Booke of Christian Prayers collected out of the auncient writers, and best learned in our tyme*, which was reprinted several times into the seventeenth century: it is the 1578 edition I shall concentrate on here.[56] Daye was John Foxe's printer, and there is no doubting the firm Protestantism of these collections of prayers, which were themselves based on an earlier compilation by the Protestant devotional writer Henry Bull. The book includes material by Bradford, and from the liturgical writings of Calvin and Knox. It has prayers for distinctively godly activities, like the 'Prayer at our going to a Sermon', with its lamentation over the state of the clergy 'for the most part they be all ignorant . . . and as for true preachers . . . the number of them is very small'.[57] In a similar militantly Protestant vein is the extended prayer for the Church by John Foxe, which is in effect a prayer against the pope and especially against the English Catholics, who, as Foxe informs the Almighty, 'although they eat the fat of the land, and have the best preferments and offices, and live most at ease, and ail nothing, yet are they not therewith content. They grudge,

[55] *A Godlye Medytacyon composed by JB, latlye burnte at Smytfelde* (London, 1559), RSTC, 3483–3493.5; M. Sylvester, ed., *Reliquiae Baxterianae* (London, 1696), p. 4.

[56] Modernized edition in W. K. Clay, ed., *Private Prayers put forth by Authority During the Reign of Queen Elizabeth PS*, (Cambridge, 1851), pp. 429–561; discussion of the book and its contents: White, *Tudor Books*, pp. 188–96.

[57] Clay, *Private Prayers*, p. 515.

they mutter and murmur, they conspire and take on against us'.[58] Yet balancing these aggresively Protestant elements is a wealth of medieval Catholic material, derived from 'auntient writers' like Augustine and Bernard, and from the medieval and early Tudor primers. Ten of the famous medieval sequence of fifteen prayers on the seven last words of Christ, known as the 'Oes of St Brigid', are included, as well as a version of the prayer of St Bernardino, 'O Bone Jesu' – both of these were regular favourites in English Catholic primers and prayer books. Erasmus is strongly represented, but once again the largest single contributor from among the 'godly learned' of modern times, as in the King's Primer of 1545 and its derivatives, was Ludovicus Vives.[59] All this material combines to produce a tone which traditionally-minded readers would have found entirely familiar, and comfortingly Catholic. Even the communion devotions provided in the book, for example, though capable of a reformed reading, nevertheless offered a high doctrine of the real presence, saturated in the phraseology of medieval eucharistic devotion: 'Hail, O Bread of Life, which camest down from heaven, and which givest life to as many as receive thee worthily . . . He that eateth thee is turned into thee . . . O sacred pittance of our pilgrimage . . . Man fell from God by eating the food of the forbidden tree, but by this food he is releved again to endless glory.'[60]

But it is the highly decorated physical format of the 'Queen's Prayers', illustrated throughout like a pre-Reformation Book of Hours, that is most startling. Early Tudor printed primers had often been elaborately decorated, with marginal, initial, and full-page illustrations to amplify and complement the text. These marginal motifs included scenes from the lives of Mary and Jesus, usually flanked by Old Testament types derived from works such as the *Biblia pauperum*: it can be seen in use in a typical primer printed for the English market in 1497 by Thielman Kerver (Plate. 1).[61]

---

[58] Ibid., p. 464.

[59] This discussion is based on Clay's edition, which provides attributions and sources for most of the prayers. For a discussion of the Fifteen Oes and related Primer material, Duffy, *Stripping of the Altars*, pp. 248–54.

[60] Clay, *Private Prayers*, pp. 519–20.

[61] The windows of King's College Chapel, Cambridge, are the best-known English examples of this method of biblical illustration; it was extremely popular in late medieval and Renaissance religious illustration in all media; Emile Mâle, *Religious Art in France, the Late Middle Ages* (Princeton, 1986), pp. 219–30.

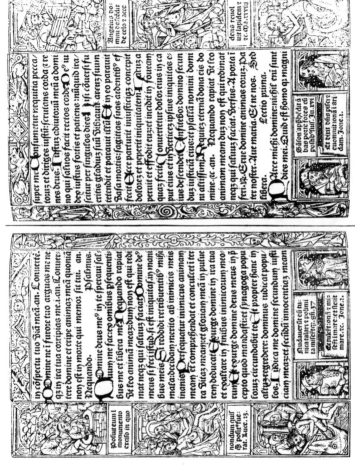

*Plate 1* 'Biblia pauperum' illustrations from a Sarum Primer by Thielman Kerver, 1497, RSTC 15885: reproduced by kind permission of the Syndics of Cambridge University Library.

*Plate 2a* Virtues, the Mass of St Gregory and the sacraments of penance and matrimony from a sarum Primer of 1512 by Simon Vostre, RSTC 15913. Note the figure of charity trampling heresy, top right.: Reproduced from Oxford, Bodleian Library, Gough Missals 87, by kind permission of the Keeper of Private Books and the trustees of the Bodleian Library.

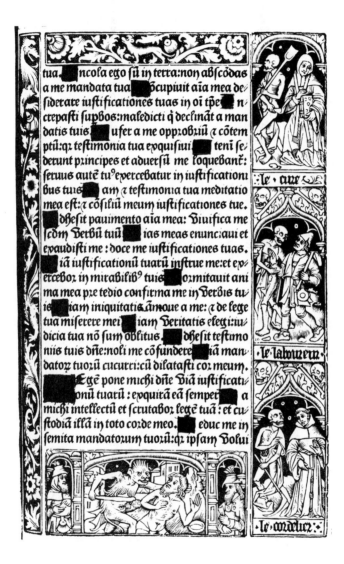

*Plate 2b* The Danse Macabre from RSTC 15913. Reproduced from Oxford, Bodleian Library, Gough Missals 87, by kind permission of the keeper of Private Books and the trustees of Bodleian Library.

*Plate 3* 'Biblia pauperum' illustrations from the 1578 edition of Daye's *A Booke of Christian Prayers*, RSTC 6429: reproduced by kind permission of the Syndics of Cambridge University Library.

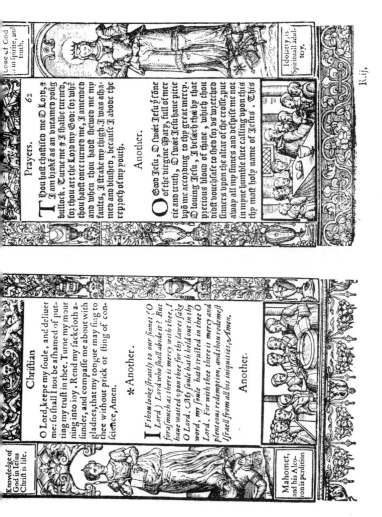

*Plate 4* Virtues and the sacraments of baptism and Holy Communion from RSTC 6429; note the figure of charity trampling popish idolatry, right.

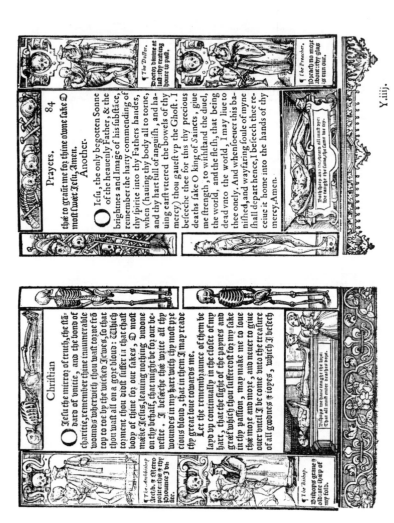

*Plate 5* The Danse Macabre figures of the clergy from RSTC 6429.

These early Tudor Primers often also included versions of the *danse macabre* and other catechetical illustrations such as representations of the sacraments, or the Sybils and the cardinal virtues (Plates 2a & 2b). By the 1560s such heavily ornamented books must have been becoming rare. The production of illustrated primers for the English market ceased in the mid-1530s, and the publisher who had cornered the English market by then, Philip Regnault, went bankrupt as a result.[62] Unsurprisingly the reformed primers of Henry and Edward's reign had no illustrations, but, less predictably, neither did the revived Marian primers of the 1550s. Of course illustrated primers survived in significant numbers, and many continued in use: Elizabethan bishops were struggling to ban the use of 'superstitious popish primers or other like books' by the laity in church and home into the 1570s.[63] Nevertheless the remarkable revival in these Protestant prayer books of the early Tudor Catholic iconographic programme presumably represents a conscious attempt to appeal to a constituency which valued and was still using that older devotional tradition, and seems to have been designed to wean such traditionalists to a more wholesome Protestant devotional diet. It includes many of the constitutive elements of the old scheme – the life of Christ with its *Biblia pauperum* types, the *danse macabre*, the Sybils, and a sequence illustrating the Last Judgement.

The decoration, however, is by no means slavishly derivative. The virtue of Charity, portrayed as is usual treading down Idolatry, has been made politically correct by having a chalice and host, a crosier and mitre, a set of rosary beads, and a penitential scourge added to the instruments of idolatry at her feet (Plate 4, cf 2a). Between the 1569 and 1578 editions the scheme was further Protestantized. Illustrations of the Pieta in the Passion sequence in the margins were physically cut out and replaced by less papistical representations of the burial and the

[62] For a discussion of the illustrations of Tudor primers, see Duffy, *Stripping of the Altars*, pp. 225–32; Regnault's primers abandoned the convention of framing each page of text in an ornamented surround, based on medieval manuscript book-production, in favour of a more modern page layout in which occasional whole-page pictures and inset vignettes were used instead: M. C. Erler, ' "The Maner to lyve well" and the coming of English in Francois Regnault's Primers of the 1520s and 1530s', *The Library*, 6th ser., 6 (1984), pp. 229–43.

[63] W. H. Frere, ed., *Visitation Articles and Injunctions of the Period of the Reformation, III, 1559–75*, Alcuin Club Collections, 16 (1910), pp. 157 and 289; J. S. Purvis, *Tudor Parish Documents of the Diocese of York* (Cambridge, 1948), p. 31.

holy women at the tomb, and illustrations of the two 'gospel' sacraments were included in a definitely Protestant form. In baptism the godmother holds the swaddled infant over the font while the surpliced minister sprinkles water, a decisive abandonment of the Sarum triune immersion of the naked baby. In Communion, the minister, again in a surplice, dispenses chunks of wheaten loaf to a congregation kneeling on all sides of a table in the body of the church (Plate 4). A page with four clerics has been added to the *danse macabre* – archbishop, bishop, doctor, and preacher, all dressed correctly in canonicals, as required by the Advertisments of 1566 (Plate 5). All these elements are the pictorial equivalent of Foxe's prayer against the pope or the prayer before attending a sermon. They register the firmly reformed context of the book, and the deliberation with which it was edited, but if anything serve to heighten the remarkable impact of this exercise in critical continuity with – or perhaps even deliberate recovery of – an earlier, Catholic, tradition, for we need to remind ourselves that devotional books as elaborately decorated as these had not been produced for the English religious market since the early years of Henry VIII's reign.[64] It is especially remarkable that this illustrated prayer book should have run through at least three further editions in the very depths of the period characterized by Patrick Collinson as one of Protestant 'Iconophobia'.[65]

The Daye prayer books are the most striking example of the conscious cultivation of a devotional idiom which synthesized Protestant conviction with Catholic piety, but they were by no means isolated. A little devotional treatise produced at the end of the reign, and now surviving in a single copy in the Folger library, provides my final example of the employment of this common idiom. *A Right Godly Rule, how all faithful Christians ought to occupie and exercise themselves in their dayly prayers*, published in 1602, is a representative example of a type of book with which we are by now familiar, providing occasional devotions

---

[64] The programme of the illustrations to the Daye prayer-books, and the changes between editions, are discussed more fully in S. C. Chew, 'The iconography of *A Book of Christian Prayers* (1578) illustrated', *Huntington Library Quarterly*, 8 (1944–5), pp. 293–305.

[65] Patrick Collinson, *From Iconoclasm to Iconophobia* (Reading, 1986), and *The Birthpangs of Protestant England* (London, 1988), ch. 4; but see the caveat by Tessa Watts, *Cheap Print and Popular Piety, 1550–1640* (Cambridge, 1991), pp. 134–9.

for morning and night, for attendance at communion, for temptation, trouble, in the face of death, and so on.[66] A glance through it reveals that it contains the selection of prayers which we encounter again and again from the King's Primer of 1545 onwards, through the Marian and Elizabethan primers of the 1550s and 1560s, and, to a lesser extent, in collections like the Daye prayer books. But closer examination reveals the remarkable fact that the copy-text from which the editor worked was not any of the Protestant primers of Henry, Edward or Elizabeth's reign, but the Catholic version of Mary's reign. While the content is substantially the same in all these primers, the *Right Godly Rule* follows the distinctive arrangement of the Marian books, and includes a number of prayers found only in them, in precisely the same order.[67] There can be no doubt of the intended Protestant audience for the book, for certain Catholic features have been altered or removed. The Marian primers provided a prayer for Sunday mornings which was in fact a direct translation of a quasi-exorcistic invocation of the Trinity and the Cross found in Latin in most early Tudor primers: this is replaced by a prayer on the keeping of the Sabbath. A prayer against the devil which in the Marian primers contained the sentence 'we beare before us, and show furth in our syghte the cross thy banner' is altered to 'we beare before us the sword of the spirit in our sight', which makes less sense but avoided 'idolatrous' overtones. A prayer before communion which in the primer version read 'I come to receave thy blessed bodie as a sick creature to thou that art the health of life' becomes 'I come to receive they blessed body, not grossely and carnally as the blinde suppose, but spiritually and by faith, together with all the fruits and effects of thy sufferings'.

Nevertheless, the essential character and most of the actual wording of the additional devotions in the Marian primers is preserved in this Protestant prayer book, including medieval liturgical material such as a translation of the hymn *Conditor Coeli*, and classical affective devotions such as the 'O Bone Jesu', though the Catholic overfamiliarity of such phrases as 'O good

---

[66] RSTC, 21446.7. I have worked from the University Microfilm copy, reel 717, where the book is misnumbered as 21056b. It is unpaginated, so no page references are given in the following discussion.
[67] I have collated the *Right Godly Rule* with CUL Young 263, *The Primer in Latin and Englishe (after the Use of Sarum) with many godlye and devoute prayers* (London, 1555), RSTC, 16065.

Jesu' and 'O sweet Jesu' in that prayer is characteristically altered to the more distant and deferential 'Lord Jesu'. Nevertheless, pious Elizabethans using this impeccably correct Protestant prayer book would have been using much of the devotional repertoire familiar to their Catholic parents and grandparents. They would also have been using the same prayers as many of their traditionalist or Catholic neighbours, plying their antiquated and 'superstitious' primers in defiance of Protestant ecclesiastical authority.

But by 1602 the days of that particular coincidence in devotion were numbered.[68] For much of the Elizabethan period, Catholics wanting to use a primer in English had no choice but to use a second-hand book from the reign of Mary or earlier: English versions of the Sarum Primer, supplemented with the type of devotions we have been discussing, were not produced for Catholics in Elizabeth's reign. In the late 1560s the papacy ordered a reform of the primer, to bring it into line with the Tridentine reform of the Missal and Breviary: all versions of the primer not in continuous use for at least 200 years were banned, and the *editio typica* of the revised Roman Primer, published in 1571, did not of course include the prayers by Erasmus, Vives, and others which had characterized the Tudor English primers, and which, as we have seen, survived the decay of the primer form itself. The first English translation of the new post-Tridentine Primer did not appear until 1599. In the meantime the vernacular devotional book which had taken the place of the primer for Catholic readers was the *Manual of Devout Prayers*, and it in fact contained relatively little material overlapping with the additional devotional content of the Catholic and Protestant mid-Tudor primers.[69] Some recusants went on using the older

---

[68] There were others, which I cannot discuss here: the best known of them was the 'borrowing' of Robert Parson's stupendously popular and influential *Christian Directorie* by the Protestant Edmund Bunny; 'Bunny's Resolution' itself became a key converting work in the early seventeenth century. An old copy given by a pedlar to Richard Baxter's father was a key text in Baxter's spiritual development. For Parson's outrage, see R. Parsons, *A Christian Directorie Guiding Men to their salvation . . . set forth now again with many corrections . . . with reprofe . . . by E. Bunny* (Louvain, 1598); RSTC, 19353–19354.9 (Catholic versions) and 4088, 19355–19389 (Protestant versions); A. C. Southern, *Elizabethan Recusant Prose 1559–1582* (London, 1950), pp. 181–93: Brad S. Gregory, 'The "True and Zealouse Service of God": Robert Parsons, Edmund Bunny, and *The First Booke of the Christian Exercise*', *JEH*, 45 (1994), pp. 238–68.

[69] This whole development is discussed in J. M. Blom, *The Post Tridentine English Primer*, Catholic Record Society Publications (Monograph Series) 3 (1982).

books, of course, and the seminary priests were explicitly instructed that their penitents might continue to make use of these early and mid-Tudor survivals, just as they themselves were permitted the continued use of the Sarum Missal, Manual, and Breviary. But the older primers suffered from a grave disadvantage in Counter-Reformation eyes. From the 1530s onwards, all primers for the English market had necessarily excluded any mention of indulgences, and the editors of the Marian primers had prudently not restored the controversial indulgence rubrics which had been so notable a feature of such books till the 1520s. Recusant casuists therefore took the view that although these older books were licit, 'it is stupid to want to read those editions which carry no indulgences, and to refuse to read those books which have indulgences'.[70] With their abandonment came a parting of the ways, as both Catholics and Protestants turned to divergent forms of piety. For Protestants the devotional future lay with texts like Lewis Bailey's *The Practice of Piety*. For the recusant community, new and more ardent currents of Counter-Reformation devotion, especially the writings of Francis de Sales, would mean the final abandonment of the more sober and humanist mid-Tudor material.[71] For their different reasons, both communities moved away from that common devotional idiom which had survived the traumas of Reformation in mid-century, and which, even in books which self-consciously and polemically sought to proclaim religious difference, had provided a unifying discourse at prayer.

Magdalene College, Cambridge

[70] P. J. Holmes, *Elizabethan Casuistry*, Catholic Record Society Publications (Records Series) 67, (1981), p. 24.
[71] E. Duffy, 'The English secular clergy and the Counter-Reformation', *JEH*, 34 (1983), pp. 214–30.

# DIVERSITY OR DISUNITY? A REFORMATION CONTROVERSY OVER COMMUNION IN BOTH KINDS

## by DAVID BAGCHI

In principle, a distinction has often been made between the Church's faith and its order, between what is essential to Christianity and the structure required to preserve that essence. In practice, this distinction has never been a clear-cut one, and the ideal of a unity of faith which can tolerate a diversity of rite has rarely been achieved. On the one hand, as Flacius Illyricus reminded Melanchthon in the Adiaphoristic controversy, the external organization, rites, and customs of a church are an organic expression of its beliefs: *lex credendi* becomes *lex orandi*. On the other, as Geoffrey Wainwright amongst others has noted, doctrines have frequently been formulated to reflect or to justify existing liturgical practices: *lex orandi* becomes *lex credendi*.[1] A matter of order can become a matter of faith, and in the process what was once regarded as legitimate diversity can come to be seen as illegitimate disunity.

A good illustration of this process from the Reformation period is the debate over communion in both kinds. Admittedly, other examples from the period would be just as pertinent to the theme of this volume. The marriage of clergy, for example, was frequently twinned with the question of the lay chalice as another inessential matter which might legitimately be conceded in the cause of unity. But because the lay chalice affected the *laity* so directly, it was a practical and immediate issue for potentially the greater part of the population of western and central Europe: the battle for the chalice became, for many, the outward and visible sign of the inward and spiritual struggle of the Reformation. And because the eucharist was acknowledged by all sides as the sacrament of unity, the question of unity was much more explicit in this debate than in other debates involving 'inessentials'. In this paper, I want to look first at the Protestant side of the case as expounded by Luther, then at the Catholic side as it

---

[1] G. Wainwright, *Doxology: The Praise of God in Worship, Doctrine and Life. A Systematic Theology* (London, 1980), esp. pp. 218–83.

emerges from the writings of some pre-Tridentine Catholic theologians.

Communion in both kinds became a Reformation issue almost by accident. Late in 1519, Luther wrote a series of three devotional tracts on the sacraments for Duchess Margaret of Brunswick. The last of these was an extended meditation on the eucharist as the sacrament of unity.[2] The signs of this sacrament, Luther explains, are bread and wine; but it is not necessary for the laity to receive both kinds because the priest does that on their behalf. Then he adds an aside that in his view it would be fitting for a general council to restore both kinds to the people; not because both kinds are necessary, but because this sacrament, which signifies the full and undivided communion of saints, is more fittingly represented by its full and undivided sign.[3]

This brief aside was enough to have the tract banned in the diocese of Meissen (the first of three occasions on which Meissen would play a decisive part in the controversy), and Luther was obliged to defend his views more fully in a succession of writings in mid-1520, most notably in the famous treatises *An den christlichen Adel* and *De captivitate Babylonica*. He continued to address the question up to 1523.[4] Luther's position on the lay chalice in these early writings is rather puzzling, because against his opponents he asserted its legitimacy with growing vehemence, while persuading his own side to desist from it for the sake of weaker brethren.[5] It is little wonder that at least one of Luther's opponents thought it sufficient refutation of his views simply to juxtapose some of his more blatantly contradictory statements, especially on the role of a general council in resolving the

---

[2] *Ein Sermon von dem hochwürdigen Sakrament des heiligen wahren Leichnams Christi*, in *D. Martin Luthers Werke. Kritische Gesamtausgabe*, ed. J.C.F. Knaake et al., 65 vols (Weimar, 1883–) [*Weimarer Ausgabe* –hereafter *WA*], 2, pp. 742–58. Eng. tr. in *Luther's Works*, ed. J. Pelikan and H.T. Lehmann, 56 vols (Philadelphia and St Louis, 1955–86) [hereafter *LW*], 35, pp. 49–73.

[3] *WA*, 2, pp. 742–3 = *LW*, 35, p. 50.

[4] Apart from the 1520 treatises, Luther's most important discussions were in: *Assertio omnium articulorum per bullam Leonis X novissimam damnatorum*, article 16, *WA*, 7, pp. 122–4; *Grund und Ursach aller Artikel D. M. Luthers, so durch römische Bulle unrechtlich verdammt sind*, article 16, *WA*, 7, pp. 389–400 = *LW*, 32, pp. 55–62; *Formula missae et communionis* (1523), *WA*, 12, pp. 217–18 = *LW*, 53, pp. 34–6. A valuable account may be found in Hans-Bernhard Meyer, *Luther und die Messe* (Paderborn, 1965), pp. 334–8.

[5] See esp. the sermon for the Thursday after Invocavit, 13 March 1522, *WA*, 10.III, pp. 45–7 = *LW*, 51, pp. 90–1, and *Von beider Gestalt des Sakraments zu nehmen* (1522), *WA*, 10.III, pp. 11–41 = *LW*, 36, pp. 237–67.

question.[6] Nonetheless, it seems to me that three elements can be identified in Luther's call for the restoration of the chalice. First is the importance of unity, both the symbolic unity of the sacrament and the unity of the Church. He insisted that the Bohemian, Greek, and Russian Churches were not to be considered un-Christian simply because they differed in matters of ritual.[7] If the Roman Church can tolerate such diversity of rite as exists between one collegiate church or one religious order and another, it can surely tolerate other differences, provided that the same faith is professed.[8] The priority must be to maintain 'that unity of the Spirit in the bond of peace which is especially signified by this sacrament'.[9]

The second element in Luther's thinking on the chalice is the primacy of faith. It should not matter to Christians whether they receive one kind, or both kinds, or neither kind. Much more important is the 'desire of faith'. Luther puts St Augustine's question more than once: 'Why do you make ready your teeth and your stomach? Only believe, and you have eaten already.'[10] This emphasis on faith distinguished Luther from the Bohemian Utraquists who, citing John 6.53 ('Unless you eat the flesh of the Son of Man and drink his blood, you have no life in you'), held that communion in both kinds was a prerequisite for salvation. Such a distinction was, however, lost on many of Luther's Catholic opponents, who deployed the stock anti-Hussite arguments against him indiscriminately.

The third element concerns the danger of coercion. Luther took Christ's command, 'Do this, as often as you drink it, in remembrance of me' (I Cor. 11. 25), to mean that Christ had left both the frequency and the mode of reception to the individual

---

[6] See esp. Johann Cochlaeus, *Sieben köpffe Martini Luthers vom hochwirdigen Sacrament des Altars* (Leipzig, 1529), a translation of chapters 19–24 of the same author's more famous *Septiceps Lutherus*.

[7] *Sermon von dem Neuen Testament, WA,* 6, p. 355 = *LW,* 35, p. 81.

[8] *Verklärung D. Martin Luthers etlicher Artikel in seinem Sermon von dem heiligen Sakrament* (1520), *WA,* 6, p. 80.

[9] Ibid., 6, p. 80. For a similar expression in a related tract of the following month, see *Ad schedulam inhibitionis sub nomine Episcopi Misnensis editam super sermone de sacramento Eucharistiae responsio, WA,* 6, pp. 144–53, at p. 145, lines 10–11.

[10] Augustine, *Tractatus in evangelium Ioannis* 25.12 (*PL,* 35, col. 1602). See Luther, *Sermon von dem hochwürdigen Sakrament, WA,* 2, p. 742, lines 27–9 = *LW,* 35, p. 50; *De festo Corporis Christi sermo* (1519/20), *WA,* 4, p. 701, lines 33–4; *Sermon von den Neuen Testament, WA,* 6, p. 372, lines 20–1 = *LW,* 35, p. 104; *De captivitate Babylonica, WA,* 6, p. 502, line 14 and p. 518, line 19 = *LW,* 36, pp. 19 and 44; *Festpostille* (1527), *WA,* 17.II, p. 434, lines 18–19; *Daβ diese Wort Christi, 'Daβ ist mein leib', noch fest stehen* (1527), *WA,* 23, p. 243, lines 5–6 = *LW,* 37, p. 124.

believer. Thus the Desert Fathers quite legitimately abstained from communion altogether for years at a time.[11] The Roman Church was therefore wrong to enforce communion in one kind;[12] but the Bohemian Utraquists were equally wrong to enforce communion in both kinds. This fear of coercion explains why Luther's major treatise *Von beider Gestalt zu nehmen* was a dissuasive against over-hasty innovation in Wittenberg, why the chalice was not introduced there on a regular basis until 1523, and why, as late as 1528, Luther was still careful to instruct the Saxon visitation teams that no-one who did not yet receive in both kinds should be forced to do so.

While these three elements were kept in balance, Luther could not regard the lay chalice as an essential issue and was prepared to tolerate a range of practices: diversity did not necessarily lead to disunity, but a headlong dash towards uniformity might. Any shift of this balance would, however, entail a change in Luther's position. This is what finally happened in the late 1520s, when one evangelical after another was killed for administering or receiving communion in both kinds. In a letter written to one of the bereaved congregations, Luther advises that the best way to honour one who died for the chalice is to continue to receive it, in the face of persecution.[13] If more deaths should follow as a result, happy are they who die in the Lord, for the Devil is bringing great misery on the world, in which disunity and warfare will reign. The wording of this prediction is significant. For Luther, the martyrdoms represent such an increase in coercion that the need to preserve unity is no longer a factor; in fact, unity itself is passing away in these last days. The lay chalice ceases to be an indifferent matter to the Christian, and has become to all intents a *status confessionis*.

---

[11] *Verklärung*, WA, 6, p. 79, line 34; *De captivitate Babylonica*, WA, 6, p. 507, lines 18–20 = *LW*, 36, pp. 27–8.

[12] This judgement was, however, qualified immediately by the injunction to endure tyranny until such time as a general council should cede the chalice. See *De captivitate Babylonica*, WA, 6, p. 507, lines 27–33 = *LW*, 36, p. 28.

[13] *Tröstung an die Christen zu Halle über Herrn Georgen [Winkler], ihres Predigers Tod* (1527), WA, 23, pp. 402–31 = *LW*, p. 43, lines 145–65. For the other murders (and one suicide) connected with use of the chalice from this time, see esp. Luther's letter to Gabriel Zwilling of 7 March 1528, *D. Martin Luthers Werke, Kritische Gesamtausgabe: Briefwechsel*, 18 vols (Weimar, 1930–85) [hereafter *WABr*], 4, p. 404, no. 1236.

The martyrdoms had taken place in and around the diocese of Meissen; and when the Bishop of Meissen issued another mandate against both kinds in 1528, Luther replied with an important but little known treatise, *Ein Bericht an einem guten Freund*.[14] Although it is directed against the Bishop's mandate, only a comparatively small proportion is given over to discussing the reservation of the chalice. The rest is taken up with proving that the Bishop's church cannot be Christ's church, because it alters his commands so readily, and since it is not Christ's church, it is no sin to be separated from it. He dismisses all the sophistical arguments against the chalice as fundamentally insincere, and opposes them either with the stubborn fact of Christ's words, 'Drink this, all of you', or by reducing them to absurdity. The doctrine of concomitance seemed to him particularly laughable. If Christ's body and blood are present under each kind, a celebrant who consumes both kinds receives Christ twice over: mass-priests should immediately claim double pay! Luther then uses a series of mock-syllogisms to 'prove' that nothing, strictly speaking, could be excluded from the concomitances: the Son's divinity cannot be separated from the Trinity as a whole, nor the Trinity from its work of creation, nor the creation from individual creatures. 'It follows, therefore, that a priest of the Meissen diocese must eat and drink his own Bishop twice every mass.' Knockabout stuff it may have been, but Luther's purpose was serious enough. The doctrine of concomitance must be Satan's work, to tear us from the plain words of Christ and from our salvation.[15] (The parallels with Luther's exactly contemporary position over against the sacramentarians, who wished to circumvent those other plain words, 'This is my body', are self-evident.)[16]

In the *Bericht*, the basic elements behind Luther's original appeal are all still present: the importance of unity, the primacy of faith, and opposition to tyranny. But the martyrdoms for the sake of the chalice in the late 1520s had for Luther fundamentally

---

[14] *Ein Bericht an einem guten Freund von beider Gestalt des Sakraments aufs Bischofs zu Meißen Mandat*, WA, 26, pp. 560–618.

[15] *WA*, 26, p. 605, line 27, to p. 606, line 29.

[16] In March 1528 (at the time he was writing the *Bericht*), Luther published *Vom Abendmahl Christi. Bekenntnis* (WA, 26, pp. 240–509 = LW, 37, pp. 151–372) against the sacramentarians. Not surprisingly, the semi-scholastic doctrine of ubiquity propounded there was to be treated by Zwingli and Oecolampadius with precisely the same contempt Luther showed the doctrine of concomitance in the *Bericht*!

shifted the balance of the three, so that the imperative to unity no longer applied and tyranny had now to be opposed at all costs. It was with this 'fortress mentality' that, two years later, he set off for the Coburg fortress to advise the Protestant princes and theologians at Augsburg on the disputed questions – not least the question of communion in both kinds.

In the case of Luther's attitude to the lay chalice we see how, over a period of ten years or so, a matter of order could become a matter of faith, and a sign of diversity a sign of disunity. It is more difficult to see such a clear progression on the part of Catholic theologians over the same period, for two reasons. On one hand, more than a dozen major Catholic authors wrote on this subject in the 1520s and early 1530s (even restricting ourselves to the controversy with Luther, and saying nothing of other debates such as Bucer's passage of arms with Cenalis and Bartholomew Latomus), and their response was inevitably a diverse and complex one. But equally, the Catholic theologians could draw upon a tradition of anti-Hussite and anti-Wycliffite literature more than a century old, which already depicted the desire for the chalice as un-Christian and destructive of unity,[17] so that the process which Luther took ten years to complete was fulfilled on the Catholic side before anyone put pen to paper.[18]

---

[17] The tradition on which our controversialists drew included Thomas Netter, *Doctrinalis antiquitatum ecclesiae Jesu Christi liber quintus, ac tomus secundus de sacramentis editus in Witcleffistas et eorum asseclas* (Paris, 1521; written *c*.1425); John of Ragusa's 'Oratio de communione sub utraque specie' (1433), in Mansi, 29, pp. 699–868; Juan de Torquemada's *Commentaria super toto Decreto*, 6 vols (Lyons, 1519–20); and lectio 84 of Biel's *Expositio* (see *Gabrielis Biel Canonis missae expositio*, ed. H. A. Oberman and W. J. Courtenay, 4 vols, Veröffentlichungen des Instituts für Europäische Geschichte, Mainz, 31–4 [Wiesbaden, 1963–7], 4, pp. 85–95). For a fuller account of earlier anti-Hussite writings, see H. Kaminsky, *A History of the Hussite Revolution* (Berkeley, Cal., 1967), esp. pp. 108–40. For the use of Netter by John of Ragusa and by the sixteenth-century controversialists, see Margaret Harvey, 'The diffusion of the *Doctrinale* of Thomas Netter in the fifteenth and sixteenth centuries', in Lesley Smith and Benedicta Ward, eds, *Intellectual Life in the Middle Ages. Essays Presented to Margaret Gibson* (London and Rio Grande, 1992), pp. 281–94. I am indebted to Dr Swanson for drawing my attention to this important work.

[18] The Franciscan provincial, Caspar Schatzgeyer, was the only Catholic writer to undergo a hardening of attitudes over time similar to Luther's. His first work, the *Scrutinium* of 1522, was an attempt to find convergence between Luther and the Catholic position on the basis of Scripture alone. His treatment of both kinds here is quite different from that of his colleagues. It is a positive, at times rhapsodic, meditation on the benefits of communion, by which Christ dwells in us and we in Christ, which in many ways comes close to Luther's own position. Schatzgeyer concludes that communion in both kinds is not illicit, because Christ himself commanded it. But to reinstate it without the express agreement of a general council would be to scandalize the weak and to act impiously towards our mother the Church. The lay chalice is pleasing to God, but unity is more pleasing (Conatus VIII, 'De communione sub utraque specie', in *Kaspar Schatzgeyer, O.F.M., Scrutinium divinae Scripturae pro conciliatione dissidentium dogmatum 1522*, ed. Ulrich Schmidt, Corpus Catholicorum [hereafter CCath],

An author who typifies this approach is Johann Cochlaeus.[19] Between 1528 and 1533, when he was court chaplain to Duke George of Saxony, Cochlaeus produced a large number of pamphlets in defence of George's policy of persecuting those associated with the lay chalice in the two Saxon dioceses of Merseburg and Meissen.[20] He draws heavily on the existing arsenal of anti-Hussite arguments, listing the practical difficulties that attend the administration of the chalice, especially the risk that Christ's blood might be knocked from the priest's hands, or deposited on a communicant's beard, or vomited up by women and children, or dropped by the priest himself on his way to the sick.[21] Communion in both

5 [Münster, 1922], pp. 106–15). *Mutatis mutandis*, these words could have come from Luther's exactly contemporary *Invocavit* sermons. But when Schatzgeyer came to deal with the question again in 1525, he declared outright that a lay person who communicates in both kinds sins (*Vom hochwirdigsten sacrament des zartten Fronleichnams Christi*, in Kaspar Schatzgeyer, *O.F.M., Schriften zur Verteidigung der Messe*, ed. Erwin Iserloh and Peter Fabisch, CCath, 37 [Münster, 1984], p. 485), a judgement repeated in his *Ein gietliche und freuntliche Anntwort* of 1526 (CCath, 37, p. 608). It is interesting that Schatzgeyer's most recent editors notice a similar hardening of his attitude towards the licitness of vernacular liturgies (CCath, 37, p. 137).

[19] The most recent biography of Cochlaeus is Remigius Bäumer's *Johannes Cochlaeus (1479–1552). Leben und Werk im Dienst der katholischen Reform*, Katholisches Leben und Kirchenreform, 40 (Münster, 1980), soon to be joined by a forthcoming study by Monique Samuel-Scheyder. For now the definitive life is still Martin Spahn, *Johannes Cochläus: ein Lebensbild aus der Zeit der Kirchenspaltung* (Berlin, 1898; repr. Nieuwkoop, 1964). Appended to Spahn's work is the standard bibliography of Cochlaeus's works published between 1522 and 1550, hereafter cited as 'SV'.

[20] The works are: *Auff Martin Luthers Schandbüchlin an die Christen von Halle geschriben, Antwort. Ein kurtzer Ausszug von beyder gestalt des hochwirdigen Sacraments* ([Cologne], 1528), SV, 51; *Sieben köpffe Martini Luthers vom hochwirdigen Sacrament des Altars* (Leipzig, 1529), SV, 57a; *XXV Ursachen, unter eyner Gstalt [sic] des Sakrament den leyen zu reichen* (Leipzig, 1529), SV, 58a; *Vorteidigung Bischofflichs Mandats zu Meissen, wider Martin Luthers Scheltworte 'Bericht an einen guten Freund,' etc.* (Leipzig, 1529), SV, 59; *Fasciculus calumniarum, sannarum et illusionum Martini Lutheri, in episcopos & clericos, ex uno eius libello Teuthonico, contra episcopi Misnensis mandatum ædito collectarum* (Leipzig, 1529), SV, 68; *Ernstliche disputation vom heyligen sakrament des altars. Von der mess. Von beyder gstalt [sic]* (Dresden, 1530), SV, 71; *Auff Luthers Trostbrieff an ettliche zu Leyptzigk, Antwort und grundtliche unterricht, was mit denselbigen gehandelt. Und von beider Gstalt [sic] des Sacraments – Mit einer Vorrede von grossem Schaden des Teutschen lands, aus Luthers Schrifften* (Dresden, 1533), SV, 87.

[21] See Johann Cochlaeus, *Glos und Comment uff CLIIII Artikeln gezogen uss einem Sermon Doc. Mar. Luters von der heiligen mess und nüem Testament* (Strasbourg, 1523), sig. 2Lii$^r$; idem, *Auff Luthers Schandbüchlin Antwort*, sigs Div$^v$–Ei$^r$; idem, *Epistola ad quendam amicum*, in *Fasciculus*, fols 96$^v$, 98$^v$–99$^r$, 105$^v$–106$^r$; idem, 'Responsio' (1530), in *Historia comitiorum anno MDXXX Augustae celebratorum*, ed. G. Coelestinus, 4 vols (Frankfurt a. d. Oder, 1597), 1, fol. 20$^v$. See also the *Confutatio confessionis Augustanae* [hereafter *Confutatio CA*], in *Die Confutatio der Confessio Augustana vom 3. August 1530*, ed. H. Immenkötter, CCath, 33 (Münster, 1979), pp. 137–8; Johann Eck, *Enchiridion locorum communium adversus Lutherum et alios hostes ecclesiae*, ed. P. Fraenkel, CCath, 34 (Münster, 1979), pp. 137–8; idem, *Homiliarum adversus Lutherum et caeteros haereticos de septem ecclesiae sacramentis tomus quartus* [hereafter *Homiliae*] (Paris, 1575), fols 98$^r$–98$^v$; John Fisher, *Assertionis Lutheranae Confutatio* (1523), in *Opera omnia* (Würzburg, 1597; repr. Farnborough, 1967), cols 132–5, 145; idem, *Assertionum Regis Angliae de fide Catholica adversus Lutheri Babylonicam captivitatem defensio* (1525), in *Opera omnia*, col. 477.

kinds was not only impractical, it was also conducive to heresy, as the examples of the Bohemians and the Greek Orthodox show: 'Wherever heresy marches, this article takes the lead. As soon as it has established itself, revolution and heresies follow.'[22] Cochlaeus adds that its continued use among Protestants has finally led to the denial of Christ's presence in the eucharist by such as Zwingli.[23] Indeed, the demand for the chalice is not only associated with heresy but is itself heretical, condemned by the Council of Constance.[24] The greatest danger of all was the belief that more grace was conveyed by two kinds than by one, which contradicted the principle of concomitance,[25] the nice, knock-down Thomist doctrine cited by all the controversialists.[26] To

---

[22] *Auff Luthers Trostbrieff Antwort*, sig. bii$^r$

[23] Ibid. See also Cochlaeus, *Vorteidung*, sig. Eiii$^v$; Augustinus von Alveld, *Tractatus de communione sub utraque specie quantum ad laicos: An ex sacris litteris elici possit, Christum hanc, vel praecepisse; vel praecipere debuisse, et quod in re hac sentendium pie sane, catholice sit, iuxta veritatem evangelicam* ([Leipzig], 1520), sig. Ciii$^r$; Eck, *Homiliae*, fols 95$^r$–95, 98$^v$–99$^r$. A persistent notion was that the arch-heretics Pelagius and Nestorius had especially championed the chalice. In fact, the opposite was the case: reception in one kind was considered a sign of heresy by Pope Leo I (*Sermo* 42.4, *PL*, 54, cols 278–80), and Pope Gelasius commanded that communion should be in both kinds or not at all (D.2 de cons. c.12, in *Corpus Iuris Canonici*, 1, ed. A. Friedberg [Leipzig, 1879], col. 1318). The Gelasius text is glossed by Gratian as referring only to priests, and the Catholic controversialists understood it accordingly.

[24] Cochlaeus, *Epistola*, fol. 105$^v$. See also Alveld, *Tractatus*, sig. Eiii$^v$; Eck, *Catholica et quasi extemporalis responsio*, in J. Ficker, *Die Konfutation des Augsburgischen Bekenntnisses. Ihre erste Gestalt und ihre Geschichte* (Leipzig, 1891), pp. 78–9; idem, *Homiliae*, fols 100$^r$–100$^v$; Fisher, *Confutatio*, cols 476–7, 480.

[25] The doctrine taught that, in the same way as in a natural, living body, flesh and blood are not separated, so Christ's flesh under the form of bread is never without its concomitant blood, nor without the grace which divine blood conveys. (See J. J. Megivern, *Concomitance and Communion. A Study in Eucharistic Doctrine and Practice*, Studia Friburgensia, ns 33 [Fribourg, 1963].) This doctrine, which had been confirmed by the Council of Constance, no doubt contributed to the growth in popularity of stories of bleeding hosts in the twelfth and thirteenth centuries. Eck employs such a story, taken from Alexander of Hales, explicitly to support the concomitance doctrine in his sermons and in the popular *Enchiridion* (*Homiliae*, fol. 98$^v$, *Enchiridion*, p. 138). For the doctrine's official reception at the thirteenth session of the Council of Constance, 15 June 1415, see *DEC*, 1, p. 419.

[26] Cochlaeus, *Epistola*, fol. 99$^r$; idem, *Vorteidung*, sig. Eiii$^v$. See also *Confutatio CA*, pp. 141–2; Contarini, *Confutatio articulorum seu quaestionum Lutheranorum* (*c*.1531), in *Gasparo Contarini, Gegenreformatorische Schriften (1530c.–1542)*, ed. F. Hünermann, CCath, 7 (Münster, 1923), p. 20; Eck, *Enchiridion*, pp. 138–9; idem, *Homiliae*, fols. 93$^r$–94$^v$; Fisher, *Confutatio*, cols 478, 481; Johann Mensing, *Von den Concomitantien, unnd ob Hiesus Christus unßer Herre ym Sacrament seyns waren heyligen leibs und bluts volkommen sey: widder M. Luthers Schmehungen yn einen bericht widder des Bischoffs von Meissen Mandat geschriben* (Frankfurt a. d. Oder, 1529), esp. fols xx$^v$–xlviii$^r$; Schatzgeyer, *Scrutinium*, pp. 107, 110; idem, *Examen novarum doctrinarum pro elucidatione veritatis evangelicae et catholicae omnibus studiosis divinorum voluminum scrutatoribus pro salubri exercitio evulgatam* (1523), CCath, 37, pp. 108–9; idem, *Tractatus de missa* (1525), CCath, 37, p. 361. Henry VIII also appealed to the doctrine indirectly: see *Assertio septem sacramentorum adversus Martinum Lutherum* (1521), ed. P. Fraenkel, CCath, 43 (Münster, 1992), pp. 133–4.

A subsidiary argument was that, although Christ explicitly spoke of his blood in connection with the remission of sins, the administration of the chalice is not thereby made more necessary: the remission of sins was achieved by the Passion, which is represented by the mass, not by (lay)

the objection that concomitance does away with the need for priests to communicate in two kinds, Cochlaeus explained that the priest's communion is closely related to the sacrifice of the mass, in which the signification of the separated body and blood is especially appropriate.[27] He could support this argument by pointing to the fact that not just laity but also non-celebrant priests communicated in one kind only, so the practice could hardly be decried as the unjust tyranny of priests over lay people.[28]

The anti-Hussite literature also provided Cochlaeus and his fellow-controversialists with guidelines for dealing with the biblical and historical evidence. 'Drink this, all of you' was addressed not to lay people but to the apostles,[29] who had been given the priestly power of offering the sacrifice of the mass by the preceding command, 'Do this in remembrance of me.'[30] Christ had taught his disciples through the Lord's Prayer to pray for supersubstantial bread, not wine.[31] At Emmaus he had broken bread, but there is no mention of wine.[32] In the same way, Acts speaks only of the early Christians breaking bread.[33] John Fisher

communion. See Fisher, *Adversus Babylonicam captivitatem*, cols. 145, 148; Schatzgeyer, *Scrutinium*, p. 108; idem *Vom hochwirdigsten sacrament des zartten Fronleichnams Christi* (1525), CCath, 37, p. 484.

[27] 'In passione autem et morte eius separatus erat a corpore sanguinis, ideo separatim utranque speciem consecrat ac sumit sacerdos, et in persona omnium offert' (Cochlaeus, *Epistola*, fol. 99ʳ). See also Alveld, *Tractatus*, sig. Eivᵛ, Eck, *Homiliae*, fol. 105ʳ; idem. *Enchiridion*, p. 139; Fisher, *Confutatio*, cols 478, 482; Schatzgeyer, *Anntwort*, p. 608.

[28] 'Unde adhuc hodie sacerdotibus quoque extra sacrificium una tantum species porrigitur, aeque ac laicis, ut nemo iure conqueri possit, laicis per iniuriam aliquam subtraxisse clericos alteram speciem' (Cochlaeus, *Epistola*, fol. 95ᵛ). See also *Confutatio CA*, p. 137; Fisher, *Confutatio*, cols 475, 482. Cf. Eck, *Homiliae*, fol. 101ʳ.

[29] Cochlaeus, *XXV rationes quo Ecclesia possit in Laicis venerabile Sacramentum sub una tantum specie dare*, in *Fasciculus*, fol. 82ʳ; idem, *Epistola*, fol. 94ʳ. See also Alveld, *Tractatus*, sig. Ciʳ; *Confutatio CA*, p. 141; Eck, *Enchiridion*, p. 137; idem, *Homiliae*, fols 99ᵛ–100ʳ; Fisher, *Confutatio*, col. 477; idem, *Adversus Babylonicam captivitatem*, col. 144; Schatzgeyer, *Scrutinium*, p. 107; idem, *Examen*, p. 108; idem, *Tractatus*, pp. 355, 359; idem, *Vom hochwirdigsten sacrament*, p. 465.

[30] Cochlaeus, *Epistola*, fol. 95ʳ; idem, *Vorteidung*, sig. Biᵛ. See also Alveld, *Tractatus*, sig. Ciʳ; Thomas de Vio (Cajetan), De communione sub utraque specie (Rome, 1531), p. 44; Eck, *Enchiridion*, p. 137; idem, *Catholica responsio*, p. 79; idem, *Homiliae*, fol. 104ʳ; Fisher, *Confutatio*, col. 481. Schatzgeyer follows an independent line, taking 'Hoc facite' to refer to the sacrament as a whole, not to any one part of it, such as the administration of the chalice (see *Tractatus*, p. 357, and *Anntwort*, p. 606).

[31] Cochlaeus, *Epistola*, fol. 97ᵛ. See also Eck, *Enchiridion*, p. 134; Fisher, *Confutatio*, col. 482.

[32] Cochlaeus, *Epistola*, fols 95ᵛ, 98ʳ; idem, *XXV rationes*, fol. 77ᵛ. See also Alveld, *Tractatus*, sig. Divʳ; Eck, *Enchiridion*, p. 134; idem, *Homiliae*, fol. 96ᵛ; Fisher, *Confutatio*, col. 472.

[33] Cochlaeus, *XXV rationes*, fols 77ᵛ–78ʳ. See also Alveld, *Tractatus*, sig. Divr; *Confutatio CA*, p. 133; Eck, *Enchiridion*, p. 134; idem, *Homiliae*, fols 96ᵛ–97ᵛ; Contarini, *Confutatio*, p. 20; Fisher, *Confutatio*, col. 474; Schatzgeyer, *Vom hochwirdigsten sacrament*, p. 485. The wording of the Fisher and Schatzgeyer passages is close enough to suggest dependence.

even cited the miraculous feeding of the five thousand as evidence for the reservation of the chalice, again because bread is mentioned but not wine. He quickly realized that, on this argument, Christ had instituted holy communion under two kinds after all (bread and fish), and hurriedly recovered himself by reminding his readers twice in five lines that the miracle is only 'an adumbration, as it were' of the eucharist.[34] Cochlaeus could also concede that the lay chalice was an ancient practice which dated to the infancy of the Church;[35] but, under the guidance of the Holy Spirit, the Church is able to make new laws and change old ones,[36] even those instituted by Christ himself. Christ had commanded his disciples to baptize in the threefold name (Matthew 29. 19); but in Acts we find the apostles baptizing in Jesus' name alone. The change must have been made on the apostles' own authority, just as they made new regulations at the Council of Jerusalem.[37]

It may seem at first sight that Cochlaeus has simply thrown down indiscriminately all the arguments he could think of in favour of communion in one kind and against communion in both. Pragmatic and prescriptive arguments jostle each other for attention rather incongruously, and Cochlaeus is never entirely clear whether lay communion in one kind was instituted by Christ during his earthly ministry or by the Church under the guidance of the Spirit. But that was hardly the point. For Cochlaeus and his colleagues, arguments about the lay chalice were irrelevant, as was the lay chalice itself:[38] it did not matter whether or not it had been the majority tradition in the West until the

---

[34] Fisher, *Confutatio*, col. 482.

[35] Cochlaeus, *Epistola*, fol. 99[v]. See also *Confutatio CA*, pp. 139–40; Eck, *Enchiridion*, p. 137; idem, *Homiliae*, fols 95[v]–96[r]; Fisher, *Confutatio*, col. 477; idem, *Adversus Babylonicam captivitatem*, col. 146; Schatzgeyer, *Examen*, p. 108; idem, *Tractatus*, pp. 353–5. Contarini went so far as to concede that Christ had instituted the lay chalice, or at least had not excluded it, at the Last Supper (*Confutatio*, p. 18).

[36] Cochlaeus, *XXV rationes*, fols 78[r]–78[v] and *passim*; idem, *Responsio*, fol. 20[r] See also *Confutatio CA*, p. 139; Eck, *Catholica responsio*, p. 80; idem, *Homiliae*, fol. 103[r]; Fisher, *Confutatio*, cols 475–6; idem, *Adversus Babylonicam captivitatem*, cols 139–43, 147, 150; Henry VIII, *Assertio*, p. 136; Schatzgeyer, *Tractatus*, p. 361; idem, *Vom hochwirdigsten sacrament*, pp. 483, 485; idem, *Anntwort*, pp. 606–7.

[37] Cochlaeus, *XXV rationes*, fol. 79[r]. See also Eck, *Homiliae*, fol. 107[r]; Fisher, *Confutatio*, cols 471–2, 479–80, 483; idem, *Adversus Babylonicam captivitatem*, cols 150–3; Schatzgeyer, *Scrutinium*, pp. 107–8.

[38] For assertions that the lay chalice was in itself neither good nor bad, see Cochlaeus, *Auff Luthers Trostbrieff Antwort*, sig. bi[r]; Schatzgeyer, *Scrutinium*, p. 115; Eck, *Homiliae*, fol. 110[r] (i.e. 100[r]).

twelfth century, or why exactly it had been withdrawn.[39] What mattered was that the Church has decided that it should be withdrawn, and that to deny communion in one kind was to deny the Church its legislative authority.[40] Johann Eck pointed out that the Church has sometimes abolished things quite harmless in themselves because heretics have abused them. Thus the use of unleavened bread was once outlawed because of Judaizers, and the title 'Christotokos' for the Virgin Mary condemned because of its association with Nestorius.[41] But it would make no difference if there were no particular reason for reserving the chalice, or if that reason were now lost in the mists of time. That is why Henry VIII and the Dutch controversialist Eustachius van Sichem did not bother to provide theological reasons when they came to this topic: all that was required was faith in the Church's decisions.[42]

For both Luther and his Catholic opponents, the debate over communion in both kinds led to a polarization of attitudes, whereby a matter of the utmost indifference became a *status confessionis*, and a matter of order one of faith. For both sides, the all-pervading question of authority came to dominate.[43] But this process makes problematic the very course of the literary debate. It was understandable that Luther should have thrown more and more ink at the issue as it grew in importance for him. But why

---

[39] For the history of the withdrawal of the lay chalice, see Dieter Girgensohn, *Peter von Pulkau und die Wiedereinführung des Laienkelchs. Leben und Wirken eines Wiener Theologen in der Zeit des grossen Schismas*, Veröffentlichungen des Max-Planck Instituts für Geschichte, 12 (Göttingen, 1964), esp. pp. 82–120, and G. Constant, *Concession à l'Allemagne de la communion sous les deux espèces. Etude sur les débuts de la réforme catholique en Allemagne, 1548–1621*, 2 vols, Bibliothèque des écoles françaises d'Athènes et de Rome, 128 (1923), 1, ch. 1. Useful material can also be found in E. Dublanchy, 'Communion sous les deux espèces', *Dictionnaire de théologie catholique*, ed. A. Vacant, E. Mangenot and E. Amann, 15 vols (1903–50), 3/1 (1923), pp. 552–72.

[40] Cochlaeus made precisely this point in 1529 when he wrote his *XXV Ursachen, unter eyner Gstalt [sic] des Sakrament den leyen zu reichen*. The title in German is rather misleading, but the title of the Latin translation makes Cochlaeus' intention explicit: *XXV rationes quo Ecclesia possit laicis venerabile Sacramentum sub una tantum specie dare*. Significantly, more than half the *rationes* here listed (nos 3–6, 9, 10, and 17–23) do not even mention the lay chalice, because the emphasis is laid so heavily on the authority of the Church.

[41] Eck, *Homiliae*, fols 103ʳ–103ᵛ, 107ʳ.

[42] Henry, *Assertio*, p. 133; Sichem, *Sacramentorum brevis elucidatio simulque nonnulla perversa Martini Luther dogmata excludens, quibus et sacramenta temerare ausus est, tum ecclesiasticam ierarchiam prorsum abolere* (Antwerp, 1523), sig. Hiiᵛ.

[43] For the Catholic polemicists' preoccupation with authority, see David V. N. Bagchi, *Luther's Earliest Opponents. Catholic Controversialists, 1518–1525* (Minneapolis, 1991). For a much more wide-ranging treatment of the topic, see G. R. Evans, *Problems of Authority in the Reformation Debates* (Cambridge, 1992).

did the Catholics take such pains to catalogue their *rationes* against the lay chalice when the fundamental issue for them was one of *auctoritas*? Was it simply literary ballast, simply a fifteenth-century controversy being re-run in the sixteenth, or was it to have some more lasting effect? I end with two postscripts, from some years after the period we have been considering, which support each view in turn.

In 1539, Duke George of Saxony died. The Bishop of Meissen (by now a new one) sought ways of avoiding the expected wholesale defection of the diocese, and decided to petition Rome to allow his priests to marry, and his laity to receive the chalice, for fear of their turning Protestant. The theologians he entrusted with this mission were Julius Pflug and Johann Cochlaeus.[44] That Cochlaeus was happy to join the mission was not evidence of late repentence: he merely believed that the Church which had the power to withdraw the chalice had also the power to restore it. Clearly, not one of the biblical, historical, theological, or pragmatic arguments against the chalice, which Cochlaeus had spent six years cataloguing, had had the slightest effect on the author himself. Here episcopal *auctoritas* outweighed *rationes*.

For the second postscript we run forward to 1562 and the twenty-first session of the Council of Trent, which was debating the legitimacy of conceding the chalice to laypeople. The general of the Jesuits, Diego Lainez, made a three-hour speech against the chalice, in which he argued, amongst other things, that if the pope and the Council permitted concessions, then the pope and the Council would be wrong![45] The Jesuits, acting in concert, not only wrecked this initiative at Trent but when, two years later, Pius IV finally conceded the chalice to Germany, they wrecked it on the ground as well.[46] Clearly, this was a case in which *rationes* outweighed even papal *auctoritas*.[47] It may be that the arguments of the pre-Tridentine controversialists made a deeper impression than their authors either imagined or in-

---

[44] See Spahn, *Cochläus*, pp. 271–5.

[45] Constant, *Concession à l'Allemagne*, 1, pp. 166, 234, 306.

[46] Ibid., pp. 687–768.

[47] It could be argued, however, that, as the Jesuits were acting at Trent under the orders of Philip of Spain and in Bavaria under those of Duke Albert, even they were subject to *auctoritas* – though of a secular rather than an ecclesiastical kind. I am indebted to Dr A. D. Wright for this observation.

tended, and that what had begun as a united front against Luther had ended as diversity and even disunity within the Catholic camp.

University of Hull

# UNITY AND DIVERSITY AS A THEME IN EARLY MODERN DUTCH RELIGIOUS HISTORY: AN INTERPRETATION

by JOKE SPAANS

The Reformation in the Low Countries fascinates both church historians and general historians. Religious change and political revolution went hand in hand. The history of the Reformation is an integral part of the history of the birth of the Dutch nation. Although well-researched, its attraction is renewed with each successive historiographical fashion.

Far less well-known is the history of Dutch religious life after the Reformation. Although a lot of detailed research has been done in this field, it is very difficult to give a synthesis of Dutch church history during the early modern period. The main problem is the apparent impossibility of integrating church history into the general history of the Dutch Republic.[1] In modern works on Dutch history religion simply fades away somewhere around the middle of the seventeenth century, only to reappear around the middle of the nineteenth century.[2] No conceptual tools have been devised to come to grips with all that lies in between.

Church historians have mainly focused their attention on biographies of ministers and academic theologians and on the history of ideas. General historians have lost interest. I would argue that the root of the problem is twofold. Firstly: church historians only rarely overstep the boundaries set by the tradition of their own Church. Thus they fail to see the overwhelming influence of the confessionally diverse surrounding culture on each Church. Secondly: historians have undervalued the religious policy of public authorities. It is generally assumed that there was no such policy. The role of magistrates has been

---

[1] Cf. the standard overview of Dutch church history: Otto J. de Jong, *Nederlandse kerkgeschiedenis* (Nijkerk, 1972). Attempts at synopsis: J. van den Berg, 'Die plurailistische Gestalt des kirchlichen Lebens in den Nederländen, 1574–1974', in J. van den Berg and J. P. van Dooren, eds, *Pietismus und Reveil. Referate der internationalen Tagung, Der Pietismus in den Niederländen und seine internationalen Beziehungen, Zeist, 18.–22 Juni 1974*, Kerkhistorische Bijdragen, 7 (Leiden, 1978), pp. 1–21; C. Augustijn, 'Niederlände', *Theologische Realenzyklopädie* (in press).
[2] Cf. the new *Algemene geschiedenis der Nederlanden*, 15 vols (Haarlem, 1978–83).

221

depicted as one of both neglect towards the legitimate demands of the Reformed Church to maintain its rights, and of an often grudging and erratic toleration of other faiths. An approach to Dutch ecclesiastical history in terms of unity and diversity is highly suggestive of the way in which the gap can be filled.

The Reformation in the Netherlands had only a partial success. Calvinist opposition to Habsburg rule had been the mainstay of the Revolt. Once the rebel provinces declared their independence, the Reformed Church was given the position of public Church. Officially the Dutch Republic was a Protestant state. The public Church was, however, no state church. Membership was voluntary, not least because its theologians wanted a pure rather than a broad Church. Consequently the Reformed Church counted only a minority of the population as its members. This minority is estimated as about twenty per cent in the first half of the seventeenth century. Those of other faiths were denied public worship and public office. According to the Union of Utrecht (1579), a treaty which functioned as the constitution of the Republic, religious persecution was prohibited. The state protected the public Church, and though it restricted non-Reformed worship to the private sphere, it did not persecute heresy. It did however maintain general Christian norms and values in public life: un-Christian behaviour, such as blasphemy, was considered a criminal offence.

Under this constitution a number of tolerated religious communities flourished. There were large minorities of Mennonites and Roman Catholics, smaller groups of Lutherans, Jews, and, from the 1620s, Arminians. Recently a number of local studies have shown that as late as the first half of the seventeenth century, two generations after the introduction of the Reformation, a large minority, sometimes half of the population, did not belong to any of the organized Churches.[3] It is highly unlikely that such people were conscious atheists. Some may have been unable to choose. Some may have been afraid to commit themselves to one or another Church as long as the war with Spain was not officially ended. More important may have been a

---

[3] J. J. Woltjer, 'De plaats van de calvinisten in de Nederlandse samenleving', *De zeventiende eeuw*, 10 (1994), pp. 3–23.

widespread dislike of the ways in which all Churches set themselves apart from Christian society as a whole. They all had to forge a new organization after the upheavals that went with the prohibition of the traditional Catholic Church and the installation of a new public Church. All of them comprised only a part of what traditionally had been an undivided Christian society. They had to knit their members together into communities with distinct religious identities. Confessional polemics were an important part of the craft of ministers of every persuasion. This culture of mutual exclusion was seen by many among the laity as incompatible with the Christian command of brotherly love.

The religious landscape of the Dutch Republic was thus characterised by diversity. As all Churches developed their own confessional identity, they tended towards doctrinal orthodoxy. This was a common European phenomenon. The sixteenth and seventeenth centuries saw the development of orthodoxy in all mainline Churches. The Dutch Reformed Church, which emerged from the Revolt with considerable variety of opinion upon points of doctrine, established its orthodoxy in the violent political and confessional clashes during the Twelve Years' Truce (1609–21), culminating in the condemnation of Arminianism at the Synod of Dort. From that moment on, the Reformed Church would follow the model set by the Genevan Reformation, as realized in the French Calvinist Churches. Other Reformed ecclesiological projects were excluded, such as those of Zwingli or Bullinger, which had formerly exercised influence together with that of Calvin. Catholics and Lutherans in the Netherlands derived their orthodoxy from co-religionists elsewhere. Only among the Mennonites was confessional identity not so much vested in purity of doctrine, but rather in the purity of their communal life.[4]

Such orthodoxies constituted the core of the religious identities of the majority of Christian groups. They became fixed in the first half of the seventeenth century. Most Churches had internal quarrels and some even experienced schism in the later seventeenth and eighteenth centuries, but doctrine usually was not the main issue. In all Churches a core of essential teaching and church ordinance was never called into question.

[4] C. Augustijn, 'Niederlände'.

All Churches enjoined a distinctive religious practice upon their members. The religious sincerity of individuals was judged by the measure in which they lived up to the precepts of their Church. The standing of the various congregations was judged by the measure in which the conduct of their members bore out their claims to possess the sole truth. The social obligation to live up to one's religious convictions in a confessionally diverse society strongly promoted unity within the Churches.[5] This internal unity was underpinned by church discipline.

However, opinions differed on the extent to which confessional identity should be borne out in the life of the community and the lives of its members. In social life people of diverse religious convictions mixed freely. How exactly was the relation between the community of the believers and Christian society as a whole to be imagined? And how was this imagined relation to be expressed in daily life?

In the public Church a pietistic tendency was present from very early on. It became important around the middle of the seventeenth century, when it became intermingled in the divergence of the theological schools of the Utrecht professor Voetius and his Leyden colleague Cocceius. Voetians tended to combine a Reformed scholasticism with the propagation of a Puritan-inspired piety, focusing on the sanctification of Sunday. They sought further edification in conventicles for the study of the Bible and the catechism, complementary to the church services. Members of these circles distinguished themselves from the commoner sort of church members by ostentatious godliness.

In the later decades of the seventeenth century the so-called Labadistic crisis threw suspicion on the activities of the conventicles, which initially had convened with the blessings of Voetian-inspired local ministers. Jean de Labadie, a deposed minister of the public Church, openly preached separatism. The consequent withdrawal of official support for the conventicles made some of their remaining defenders overtly criticize the Church and its ministry for the neglect of its prophetic mission. Some conventicles took a radical turn. The demands they laid on

---

[5] Examples in Joke Spaans, *Haarlem na de Reformatie. Stedelijke cultuur en kerkelijk leven 1577–1620* (The Hague, 1989), pp. 195–7.

their members bordered on asceticism and only very narrowly stopped short of preaching abstention from the ministrations of the corrupted public Church. Governing bodies of the Church and secular magistrates worked together in bridling this radicalism. Courses on the Bible and the catechism were brought under the exclusive control of the local consistory and any danger of pietistic competition with the regular church order was effectively stopped by the second half of the eighteenth century.[6]

The Cocceians underwrote the Confession of the Dutch Reformed Church, the Heidelberg Catechism and the Canons of the Synod of Dordt (the so-called Three Forms of Unity) and as such were orthodox Calvinists. They rejected the Aristotelian metaphysics and Reformed scholasticism of the Voetians. They took biblical exegesis as the basis for their theology. This made them more open to the newer developments of philosophy and biblical scholarship. They rejected the Sabbatarianism of the Voetians by declaring that this biblical precept was meant for biblical times only.

Theological discussion on the differences accruing from the diverging theological methods followed by the schools was forbidden by the Estates, thus avoiding another schism like that of the secession of the Arminians in the early seventeenth century. In the local churches it was effectively stopped by the widespread practice of calling ministers from both schools in equal numbers.[7] As ministers, together with the usually patrician elders, were responsible for maintaining harmony within their church, dogmatic controversies were evaded. Thus the State enforced unity on the basis of the confessional documents of the public Church. What remained was difference of opinion about the Christian life. Voetians attached great value to distinguishing themselves by godly conduct, whereas Cocceians considered this unimportant: the Reformed community needed not to be set apart from Christian society.

---

[6] F. A. van Lieburg, 'Het gereformeerde conventikelwezen in de classis Dordrecht in de zeventiende en achttiende eeuw', *Holland*, 23 (1991), pp. 2–21.

[7] J. Reitsma and J. Lindeboom, *Geschiedenis van den hervorming en de hervormde kerk der Nederlanden* (The Hague, 1949), pp. 324–37. Examples of calling exponents of different schools in equal numbers in: *Contracten van correspondentie en andere bijdragen tot de geschiedenis van het ambtsbejag in de Republiek der Verenigde Nederlanden*, ed. with an introduction by J. de Witte van Citters (The Hague, 1873), pp. 310–26.

Among Roman Catholics, Mennonites, and Lutherans similar divergencies resulting from varying confessional self-conceptions and ideas about the Christian life can be detected. The Catholics had had rigorously to reorganize their religious life. Their Church was denied any public role, their bishops had fled the country, monasteries were dissolved, and most of the priests had either left for Catholic countries or laid down their ministry. With only a handful of priests and the remnants of the cathedral chapters of the vacant sees of Utrecht and Haarlem, a new church organization, adapted to the officially Protestant environment, was created. It heavily depended on lay assistance, but it managed to rally a sizeable minority of the Dutch population to the restyled organization, especially in the provinces of Holland and Utrecht. The sometimes makeshift arrangements that made this remarkable feat possible were eyed with suspicion by Rome. The hierarchy preferred to treat the Republic as mission territory, thus denying that the efforts of the remaining canons, priests, and laypersons amounted to a legitimate continuation of the medieval Church.

In the second half of the seventeenth century, some of the indigenous clergy, notably secular priests of patrician stock, fiercely defended the continuity of the Dutch Catholic Church against the Roman view of its total ruin. They formed into a party under the name of Old Episcopal Cleresy, thereby stating their claim to continuity, and embraced a somewhat rigorous and ascetic devotion. They thus distinguished themselves from the missionaries sent by Rome, often regulars, whom they accused of moral laxity. At the same time they bent the prescriptions of Catholic canon law in order to allow Dutch Catholics to take part in the social life of their religiously diverse environment. The indigenous clergy thus converged towards the religious mentality of the surrounding Protestants. This was taken by Rome as a sign of contamination with Jansenist errors, but earned them the sympathy of the ruling elites, who distrusted the foreign missionaries as possible agents of the Catholic enemies of the Republic.

At the beginning of the eighteenth century these existing differences flared into open schism. The Vicar Apostolic of the Seven Provinces, one of the heads of the Cleresy, was called to Rome to face charges of Jansenism. The Estates of Holland demanded and obtained his return to the Republic on the grounds that one of their citizens could not be cited before a foreign court of justice. The man died before the allegations of heresy had been either proved or disproved. Given the rejection of its claims by the hierarchy and the sympathy of the Dutch government, the Cleresy elected a bishop of its own and had him ordained by a sympathetic French bishop of Jansenist convictions, who happened to be passing through Amsterdam. However, the majority of both priests and laity did not recognize his authority.[8]

The existence of two competing Catholic Churches offered Estates and local magistrates the opportunity to strengthen their control over the Catholic community. Locally magistrates could arbitrate in conflicts between the two parties. On the level of the sovereign provinces the Estates could command the loyalty of both Catholic clergies by playing one against the other. This game had not been concluded when the Batavian Revolution of 1787 and the French invasion of 1795 decisively changed the rules.[9]

The Mennonites recognized very little in the way of confessions or church ordinances outside the Bible. They distinguished themselves from the bulk of Christianity by their rejection of infant baptism, and their refusal to take oaths and bear arms – measures to ensure that they would remain unpolluted by the wickedness of the world. From the beginning they were organized along more or less 'national' lines, according to their places of origin. The largest of these 'nations' were the Flemish, the Frisians, the Germans, and those from the Waterland north of Amsterdam. Already at the end of the sixteenth century these names came to designate parties rather than 'nations'. As the Golden Age brought wealth to the Dutch, and perhaps even especially to the sober and thrifty Mennonites, their communities were riddled with conflicts about the extent to which the rather attractive world of Dutch society should be shunned.

---

[8] Standard overviews: L. J. Rogier, *Geschiedenis van het katholicisme in Noord-Nederland in de 16e en 17e eeuw*, 3 vols (Amsterdam, 1945–7); P. Polman, *Katholiek Nederland in de achttiende eeuw*, 3 vols, (Hilversum, 1968).

[9] Joke Spaans, 'Katholieken onder curatele. Katholieke armenzorg als ingang voor overheidsbemoeienis in Haarlem in de achttiende eeuw', *Trajecta*, 3 (1994), pp. 110–30.

As the Mennonites recognized no central authority among themselves, this resulted in an endless series of splits and partial reunions. Those who clung to the old ways of radical rejection of the world rapidly dwindled into insignificance. Roughly speaking, two large groups remained, allowing for considerable local variation. There are no useful general terms to designate them. It is best to call them by their contemporary names, derived from the names of two Mennonite church buildings in Amsterdam: 'those of the Sun' and 'those of the Lamb'. The rivalry between them is known as The War of the Lambs. 'Those of the Sun' wanted the disparate Mennonite community consolidated and united by binding it to a number of so-called confessions. These were originally peace treaties, drafted on the occasion of the reunion of parties. One of them was actually called the Olive Branch. 'Those of the Sun' wanted to accord these documents the authority of confessions of faith, whereas 'those of the Lamb' held that such authority as they might have had at first automatically lapsed once they had served their purpose.[10] For them Mennonite identity centred on sole reliance on the Bible and freedom from all binding confessions. They recognized true Christianity also outside their own community.

As with the Cleresy among the Catholics, 'those of the Sun', assimilating more closely to the model of the public Church, seem to have enjoyed the sympathy of governing bodies. However, as the Mennonites lost their typical character, their membership declined dramatically. Consequently it was hardly worth a magistrate's while to capitalize on the Mennonite division, as it was in the case of the Catholic community.

The Lutherans were centred on Amsterdam. Compared with the large congregation there the other Lutheran communities, spread over the country, were small and poor. For most of the period of the Republic the Dutch Lutherans were effectively ruled from Amsterdam. As no recognized Lutheran Church order warranted such a domination of one church over all others, this resulted in a number of conflicts. Apart from some radical pietistic influence, which may have been rather incidental, there was virtually no dogmatic controversy. This may be related to the absence of professional Lutheran theologians within the

---

[10] N. van der Zijpp, *Geschiedenis der doopsgezinden in Nederland* (Arnhem, 1952).

Republic. Whenever a problem arose, advice was sought from orthodox Lutheran theological faculties in the Holy Roman Empire. The Dutch Lutherans depended on these German theological faculties also for the education of ministers. This may have seemed only natural, as a large proportion of the Lutheran communities was of German extraction. Hence the bulk and powerful position of the Amsterdam community, peopled by immigrants attracted by the commercial metropolis. Garrison towns also had Lutheran churches for the many German officers of the Republican army and their German troops. In the second half of the seventeenth century Dutch Lutherans developed two wings, taking their inspiration respectively from the strictly orthodox German university of Wittenberg and the more latitudinarian Helmstedt. Those following the direction of Helmstedt were called the Dutch wing, presumably because its followers were mainly Dutch born, whereas the Wittenbergers were made up of more recent immigrants. The Dutch wing was supported by the city magistrates. It was only after the suppression of the Batavian Revolution that the orthodox party, who then enjoyed government support, found the opportunity to secede.[11]

In this way, there arose in all Churches a division, not on points of doctrine, but on differences of opinion on whether and how the confessional heritage (of which the dogmatic core was acknowledged by all) ought to be expressed in the daily life of their members. Where originally all had developed characteristic forms of religious behaviour to uphold their claims to true Christianity in a multi-confessional society, the latter half of the seventeenth century showed everywhere a marked divergence between those who wanted to stress the distinction from the common culture and those who did not. The latter were content to live according to the common Christian morality upheld by public authority. In the Reformed Church the state did not take sides. By prohibiting further discussions it forced both parties to remain united. In the tolerated Churches however, the state did show partiality. It played upon the differences in order to further its own religious policies.

---

[11] J. Loosjes, *Geschiedenis der Luthersche kerk in de Nederlanden* (The Hague, 1921).

Two exceptions prove this rule in very different ways: the Sephardic Jews and the Arminians. Both refrained from building a separate moral community apart from society as a whole. Instead they chose forms that allowed them maximal adaptation to Dutch society. From the beginning the Sephardic Jews seem to have been highly assimilated to the style of religious life they found in the Republic. Of course their own sense of religious identity was assured. But they went very far in their assimilation: the organization of synagogue services, and the intellectual formation and social standing of rabbis, formed close parallels to what was common practice in the Dutch Reformed Church.[12]

The Arminians, from the moment they appeared as a separate religious community, advocated a broad church model, in line with the Anglican Church, more fitting to a state church than to the Brotherhood they actually were. But although they were small, they always considered themselves an alternative public Church. After initial fierce persecution by the government, they eventually gained toleration around the middle of the seventeenth century. Both the Sephardim and the Arminians had good cause to reject distinctive religious behaviour: the first because they were not Christians, the second because they were by their very nature in opposition to the public Church.

Any sovereign in the early modern period knew that religion was to be taken seriously. It could be extremely divisive both politically and socially. All Protestant Churches were held under the the firm control of their princes, and Catholic rulers showed the same ambition. At first sight the Dutch Republic seems to be an exception. At the Synod of Dordt the Reformed Church had gained sole authority in doctrinal matters. With the condemnation of the Arminians it had narrowed down its originally much broader Reformed character to a Genevan-style Calvinism. On this same occasion it had, however, decisively lost its claim to determine its own church order. This now belonged to the secular power: local congregations had to defer to their magistrates, provincial synods to the provincial Estates, who were

---

[12] R. G. Fuks-Mansfeld, *De Sefardim in Amsterdam tot 1795. Aspecten van een joodse minderheid in een Hollandse stad* (Hilversum, 1989), pp. 132–8. Ms. Fuks explains this from the strong Iberian cultural identity of the Sephardic Jews. The wishes of the Amsterdam magistrate may have had some influence too.

sovereign in matters of religion. No ecclesiastical authority higher than a provincial synod was recognized. The same practical Erastianism took place with regard to the other Churches. The much-praised toleration enjoyed by other faiths did not mean that governing bodies left them to themselves.

The public authorities exercised considerable control over all Churches, most markedly in Holland, which was confessionally most diverse. They could not interfere openly in the affairs of religious bodies they did not officially recognize. Off the record, however, from the late sixteenth century they kept a close watch over the non-Reformed clergy to ensure their loyalty to the Republic. They allowed them to organize congregations and exercise church discipline over their members, but banned those who preached against the existing political and religious constellation.

Around the middle of the seventeenth century, the division of the great majority of Churches into two wings, as described above, allowed public authority a far stronger grip on the various religious communities. This division enabled it to favour in each Church the variety that was closest to its own ideal of the place of religious communities within society as a whole. It wanted Churches first of all to behave wholeheartedly as parts of Dutch society. Further it preferred Churches that had an organization more or less parallel to the decentralized Dutch structure of government, to ensure effective control. A Catholic Church with a national hierarchy was to be preferred over one that had to be approached via foreign prelates through the offices of residing diplomats of Catholic countries. Lutherans with a Dutch national identity were to be preferred over Lutherans with stronger ties to the Empire, who could always invoke the support of German princes. Mennonites who adhered to written confessions could be treated as a Church, whereas Mennonites who allowed each local community to work out its own principles were hard to grasp. In this way public authority in fact defined the relation between religious communities and society as a whole.

Religious policy, however, did not stop at this. The fact that Churches now contained a wing that rejected distinctive piety, made them less exclusive than they had been originally. Church discipline flagged. Becoming a full member seems to have become a sign of respectability.[13] As the eighteenth century progressed public authority sought, with success, neatly to divide the entire population among the various Churches. Under the Dutch constitution there was no way to force people into any Church. But it is apparent from the facts that, gradually, the large category of people not belonging to any Church disappeared. A powerful tool in achieving this seems to have been the Dutch system of poor relief. Each locality had general welfare officers for the local poor, in addition to which all Churches had some funds for their needy members, although these were not always adequate for all. In the late seventeenth and eighteenth centuries Mennonites and Lutherans gained some form of recognition. From that moment on they had to care for all their own poor. Even Catholic poor were rejected by the public welfare officers and directed to their parishes. Very detailed rules were devised to determine who belonged to which Church, and so the boundaries of religious communities were defined. All those not attached to any other Church were assumed to be Reformed.[14] Religion thus had become an organizing principle for the ordering of society.[15] And as the Churches were expected to instill at least into the recipients of their charity the fear of God and of the powers that be, this was a tool in the hands of the authorities to maintain public order.

There was an inherent contradiction in this religious policy. By favouring the more adaptive, more indigenous wings of the various Churches, over those attached to a distinguishing orthodoxy, the actual differences between them became more fluid. From the very beginning of the Republic scattered instances can be found of proposals to set aside doctrinal differences and to form a further union of all Protestant Churches. In the first half of the seventeenth century these had foundered on the high value set on orthodoxy. From the middle of the century they gained new force among those who rejected distinctive forms of

---

[13] Herman Roodenburg, *Onder censuur. De kerkelijk tucht in de gereformeerde gemeente van Amsterdam, 1578–1700* (Hilversum, 1990), pp. 135–41.

[14] Spaans, 'Katholieken onder curatele'.

[15] Peter van Rooden, 'Dissenters en bededagen. Civil religion ten tijde van de Republiek', *Bijdragen en mededelingen betreffende de geschiedenis der Nederlanden*, 107 (1992), pp. 703–12.

Christian life, and for whom the moral community was no longer identical with their particular religious community, but extended to Christian society as a whole. The search for unity led people to meet in inter-confessional circles like the Rijnsburg Collegiants or the Moravians, to discuss religious topics with kindred spirits.[16] Those who frequented these circles explicitly remained members of their Churches of origin. The idea that all Christians in essence held the same beliefs was only one step further. There were, however, political overtones in the supposition that the confessional divisions were artificial. After all, this division into confessional communities, that each had a special relation towards public authority, had been nurtured and was upheld by this same public authority. Calling this division into question amounted to criticism of the political establishment and its religious policy. It is therefore not surprising to find these ideas appear with greater frequency from about the middle of the eighteenth century, when opposition to the ruling oligarchies gained force.

The standard answer of the establishment to veiled criticism of this nature was to accuse those advocating further unity among at least Protestant Christians of Socinianism, which put a much stronger accent on the Christian life than on points of doctrine.[17] As Socinianism was considered blasphemous, and thus counted as a crime, this accusation enabled magistrates to depose ministers, both in the public Church and in the tolerated Churches. Although there may have been people who privately adhered to the doctrines of Socinus, it seems that these accusations of Socinianism were in many cases a tool to silence criticism of the political elite and its use of the religious diversity within the Dutch Republic.[18]

The confessional diversity in the Dutch Republic and the religious policy of the state regarding this diversity can be used as an

[16] J. C. van Slee, *De Rijnsburger Collegianten: een geschiedkundig onderzoek* (Haarlem, 1895); W. Lütjeharms, *Het philadelphisch-oecumenisch streven der Hernhutters in de Nederlanden in de achttiende eeuw* (Zeist, 1935).

[17] The history of Socinianism in the Netherlands is usually seen exclusively as part of the history of ideas, cf. W. J. Kühler, *Het socinianisme in Nederland* (Leiden, 1912).

[18] Socinianism may well have functioned for Protestant rulers in a way not unlike Jansenism for their Catholic counterparts.

organizing principle for Dutch church history in the early modern period. Much more than the traditional approach from the history of ideas, it allows a reconstruction of the dynamism in religion and society before the separation of church and state. It offers the framework to take account of the incisive changes that marked the period, while presenting it as a continuous development – from the formation of closely knit minority Churches, based on pure doctrine and distinctive piety, that made an end to the traditional undivided Christian society; through the loosening of these tight communities into two wings, one stressing particular confessional identity, the other assimilating to the general Christianity that pervaded public life; to the eventual success of the authorities in using religious diversity as a means to organize society and to assist in maintaining political unity. It also goes some way into explaining the way in which the Dutch Revolutionary governments following the French invasion of 1795, instead of rejecting religion, took great pains to redefine the place of the various Churches in the revolutionary society that marked the beginning of the modern period.

Fryske Akademy, Ljouwert, The Netherlands

# PIERRE DU MOULIN'S QUEST FOR PROTESTANT UNITY, 1613–18

## By W. B. PATTERSON

Pierre Du Moulin was the leading intellectual in the French Reformed Church in the early seventeenth century. His influence within French Protestantism rivalled and complemented that of Philippe Duplessis-Mornay, the prominent nobleman, soldier, and adviser to Henry of Navarre, the Huguenot leader who became Henry IV of France. If Duplessis-Mornay was, as he is sometimes called, the 'Huguenot Pope', Du Moulin, the pastor of the congregation of Protestants in Paris, was the chief cardinal.[1] A prolific writer and a skilful speaker, Du Moulin became noted for his success as a polemicist. Yet during a period of five years, 1613–18, Du Moulin was also the chief spokesman for a plan which would unite the English, Calvinist, and Lutheran Churches. The rather startling final point of the plan called for the reunited Protestants to make a fresh approach to Rome. Du Moulin's *volte-face* in 1613–18 – his sudden emergence as an irenicist – has never been satisfactorily explained.[2]

Du Moulin was a child of the French Religious Wars: the son of a Huguenot pastor who was forced to flee from his church at Mony in 1568 at the beginning of the third of the wars just before Pierre was born. In 1588 his father, Joachim, then a refugee at Sedan, took him to Paris and left him there with a

---

[1] For Du Moulin's life and career, see his autobiography, 'Autobiographie de Pierre Du Moulin, d'après le manuscrit autographe, 1564–1658', *Bulletin de la société de l'histoire du protestantisme français*, 7 (1858), pp. 170–82, 333–44, 465–77; the biography by his son, Peter, in Peter (Pierre) Du Moulin, *The Nouelty of Popery, Opposed to the Antiquity of True Christianity: Against the Book of Cardinal Du Perron, Entituled, A Reply to the Answer of the Most Serene James, King of Great Britain*, tr. Peter Du Moulin (London, 1662), Sig. \*\*3r–\*\*\*\*\*\*2r; Eugène and Emile Haag, eds, *La France protestante*, 9 vols (Paris, 1846–59), 4, pp. 419–33, and 2nd edn, ed. Henri Bordier, 6 vols (Paris, 1877–88), 5, cols 800–24; Lucien Rimbault, *Pierre du Moulin, 1568–1658: un pasteur classique à l'âge classique, étude de théologie pastorale sur des documents inédits* (Paris, 1966); and Brian G. Armstrong, 'The changing face of French Protestantism: the influence of Pierre Du Moulin', in Robert V. Schnucker, ed., *Calviniana: Ideas and Influence of Jean Calvin* (Kirksville, Mo., 1988), pp. 131–49. For Mornay, see Raoul Patry, *Philippe du Plessis-Mornay: un huguenot homme d'état* (Paris, 1933), passim.

[2] The paradox is noted by both Rimbault, *Pierre du Moulin*, p. 75, and Armstrong, 'The changing face of French Protestantism', p. 137. See also W. B. Patterson, 'James I and the Huguenot Synod of Tonneins of 1614', *HThR*, 65 (1972), pp. 241–70, esp. pp. 242–3.

small sum of money to seek his own living.[3] Du Moulin found employment in England as a tutor to Roger Manners, the young Earl of Rutland, a student at Bennet College, Cambridge, and subsequently in the Netherlands as a teacher of logic and philosophy at the University of Leyden.[4] In 1599 he was called to serve the congregation which met just outside Paris, in accordance with the terms of the Edict of Nantes. Du Moulin's intellectual circle continued to include friends in England and the Netherlands. Joseph Hall, the English satirist and theologian, wrote to him in 1611: 'Since your travels here with us, we have not forgotten you . . . your witty and learned travels in the common affairs of religion have made your memory both fresh and blessed.'[5] In the first two decades of the seventeenth century Du Moulin was on close terms with the English and Dutch ambassadors in Paris, especially Sir Thomas Edmondes.

Du Moulin wrote nearly a hundred polemical books and pamphlets, which were published, according to Brian Armstrong, in 'more than 350 editions during his lifetime', including translations into English, Dutch, Italian, and German.[6] Many of the writers whose views he opposed were Roman Catholics, including Cardinal Jacques Davy Du Perron, Cardinal Pierre de Bérulle, Cardinal Richelieu, St François de Sales, the Jesuit Jean Arnoux, and the Dominican Nicolas Coeffeteau.[7] Du Moulin's *Défense de la foy catholique* of 1610, translated into English in the same year, was a defence of the theological views of King James VI and I of Great Britain in his controversy with Pope Paul V and Cardinal Robert Bellarmine over the Oath of Allegiance.[8] The *Défense* pleased King James, who wrote to Du Moulin on 16

[3] 'Autobiographie de Pierre Du Moulin', pp. 171–3; Haag and Haag, *La France protestante*, 2nd edn, 5, cols 797–8.

[4] Du Moulin, *The Nouelty of Popery*, Sig. ★★4r; John Venn and J. A. Venn, eds, *Alumni Cantabrigienses*, pt 1, 4 vols, pt 2, 6 vols (Cambridge, 1924), pt 1, 3, p. 197; John Goldworth Alger on Pierre Du Moulin in *DNB*, 13, pp. 1098–9; 'Autobiographie de Pierre Du Moulin', pp. 180–2; Haag and Haag, *La France protestante*, 2nd edn, 5, col. 801.

[5] Joseph Hall, *The Works of the Right Reverend Joseph Hall, D.D., Bishop of Exeter and Afterwards of Norwich*, ed. Philip Wynter, revised edn, 10 vols (Oxford, 1863), 6, p. 263.

[6] Armstrong, 'The changing face of French Protestantism', p. 136. See also, for a bibliography of Du Moulin's published writings, Rimbault, *Pierre du Moulin*, pp. 242–6.

[7] Rimbault, *Pierre du Moulin*, p. 8.

[8] Pierre Du Moulin, *A Defence of the Catholicke Faith: Contained in the Booke of the Most Mightie, and Most Gracious King James the First, King of Great Britaine, France and Ireland, Defender of the Faith; Against the Answere of N. Coeffeteau, Doctour of Diuinitie, and Vicar Generall of the Dominican Preaching Friars*, trans. John Sanford (London, 1610).

December 1611 that his style of writing was 'appropriate, nervous, and acute', and, in James's opinion, 'inimitable'.[9] The King nevertheless made critical comments on several passages in which he felt that Du Moulin had misunderstood or misinterpreted his views.[10] James and Du Moulin had been in touch several years before, but this was the beginning of a close relationship between the two men which was to last to the end of James's life. Du Moulin had already received a tangible reward for his *Défense*, as Edmondes had recommended. In the autumn of 1610, the King sent Du Moulin a gift of 200 *livres*.[11]

Du Moulin was also a formidable opponent of Protestants with whom he disagreed. On 1 May 1612, King James wrote to Henri de la Tour d'Auvergne, the Duke of Bouillon, to seek the Duke's support in assuaging a dispute between Du Moulin and Daniel Tilenus, a professor at the Protestant academy of Sedan.[12] Despite Bouillon's efforts, the dispute dragged on. On 1 May 1613, Du Moulin wrote to the British King, to set the issues straight as he saw them. Du Moulin claimed that Tilenus had accused him of teaching heterodox doctrine on the incarnation of Christ, especially the relationship between his human and divine natures. Both Tilenus and Du Moulin had written Latin books against the other and had sent them to James. The controversy was to continue for another twelve months before the Synod of Tonneins prescribed a procedure by which it was resolved. King James's efforts to settle this dispute were not simply the result of his concern for Du Moulin as an ideological ally. They were an expression of the role that James had assumed

---

[9] BL, Add. MS 24195, fol. 71r.

[10] Ibid., fols 71v–76v. See also PRO, SP 78/58, fols 270r (Salisbury to Edmondes, 19 Dec. 1611) and 272r–274r ( James I to Edmondes, 19 Dec. 1611). James referred in his letter to Edmondes to Du Moulin's having written skilfully in his defence, but he complained that Du Moulin 'in divers places giveth a cleane contrary interpretacon to the text of Scripture, then that which we give in our booke' (fols 272r–v).

[11] PRO, SP 78/56, fol. 303r (Du Moulin to Salisbury, 17 Oct. 1610). Edmondes had recommended 'some thanckfull acknowledgement' from the King; ibid., fol. 179r (Edmondes to Salisbury, 13 June 1610). That Du Moulin was already known to King James in July 1609 is clear from a note in Pierre de l'Estoile's journal. On 10 July 1609, de l'Estoile wrote that he had received a copy of James's *Apologia pro juramento fidelitatis*, recently published in London; it 'contains notes in the hand of the minister Du Moulin, to whom the king of England had sent it'. Pierre de l'Estoile, *Journal pour le règne de Henry IV*, ed. André Martin, 3 vols (Paris, 1948–60), 2, p. 471.

[12] PRO, SP 78/59, fols 130r–131r.

as the protector of the French Protestants after the assassination of King Henry IV in 1610.[13]

It was in this same letter of 1 May 1613 that Du Moulin introduced what he called 'some means of accord and union among all the Churches which have thrown off the yoke of the Pope.'[14] He submitted them to the judgement of one whom God had seemingly raised up for so excellent a work. These 'Overtures for efforts to achieve the union of the Churches of Christendom and to appease the differences which have emerged already or which will rise in the future' are in twenty numbered paragraphs. The first and, from a practical point of view, most important dealt with the role to be played by the sovereign princes of Protestant Europe. The plan of union, Du Moulin stated, 'can only be carried out successfully with the assistance of the Sovereign Princes of those countries which are not under the subjection of the Pope'.[15] Chief among these, he said, was the King of Great Britain.

According to Du Moulin's plan each prince was to send two theologians to a place 'providing sure and easy access.'[16] These representatives would include two from the Reformed Churches of France, two from the Netherlands, and two from the Swiss cantons, as well as 'one or two each from each prince of Germany of our confession'.[17] Du Moulin also expressed the hope that some German Lutheran princes might be willing to send representatives, especially the rulers of Saxony, Württemberg, and Brunswick. The assembled theologians would not engage in disputes but in a more constructive task. They would lay on the table their various confessions – including those of the Churches of England, Scotland, France, the Netherlands, Switzerland, and the Palatinate – and proceed to draw up a common confession on the basis of these documents. Any future theological disputes were to be settled only with the consent of all the Churches

---

[13] Note, for example, James's instructions to Edward, Lord Wotton, ambassador extraordinary to the Queen Regent of France: '. . . we would not have you make our care of the cause of religion so indifferent or our affection so lukewarme to our friends as not to express unto them that we are resolved to imploy our best means to support those causes which concern the body of the religion in that authority, libertie and safety which they may iustly claime by virtue of their Edicts. . . .' PRO, SP 78/56, fols. 242r–v.

[14] PRO, SP 78/61, fol. 68r.

[15] Ibid.

[16] Ibid.

[17] Ibid.

which had reached this accord. The Churches thus bound together would agree that their differences over ceremonies and ecclesiastical polity would not be any impediment to their 'being in accord in faith and true doctrine'.[18] The next stage, said Du Moulin, would be more difficult. The representatives of these Churches would seek to meet with representatives of the Lutheran Churches.

Du Moulin recognized that a broad range of theological problems threatened to block any agreement between the Reformed and Lutheran Churches, though he spoke favourably of the Confession of Augsburg. Of particular importance were differing interpretations between the two groups on the necessity of baptism and the manner of the reception of the body of Christ in the Lord's Supper. On both subjects, he proposed statements on which both sides could be expected to agree.[19] On the Lord's Supper, for example, he believed that agreement could be reached on the following propositions:

> that the signs are not empty signs nor simple figures destructive of the truth. That in the Lord's Supper we participate really in the body of Christ. That the bread is not transubstantiated and does not cease being bread after the consecration. From which it follows that the sacrament ought not to be adored, and that we ought to lift our hearts on high.[20]

There were also, as he well knew, issues separating the Lutheran and Reformed Churches on the doctrines of the incarnation, predestination, and free will. The clear meaning of Du Moulin's plan was that on all such issues the Lutheran and Reformed Churches would agree to tolerate certain differences. As he said on the contentious issue of the 'ubiquity' of Christ's body: 'If . . . there are different opinions on which there is no agreement: it will be necessary to obtain from the two parties, not to condemn each other on that account and to support one another until God has given more light to those who err.'[21] Du Moulin saw the Lord's Supper as a means of reaching as well as expressing an

---

[18] Ibid.
[19] Ibid., fol. 68v.
[20] Ibid.
[21] Ibid.

accord between the two groups. Before dispersing, the delegates would join in a celebration of the Lord's Supper 'in which the Lutheran pastors and the others would communicate together'.[22]

The coming together of these Churches would only be complete when the agreement had been approved by the 'sovereign princes and ministers and synods' in the various countries.[23] At this point, Du Moulin envisaged that the princes would 'use their authority to the end that the words Lutheran, Calvinist, and Zwinglian may be abolished and that our Churches may all be called Christian Reformed Churches'.[24] It was then that a fresh approach to Rome might be undertaken: 'If it should please God to bless this so holy and praiseworthy work, and one which would crown with praise forever the King of Great Britain and the princes who assist him, then would be the time to seek the accord of the Roman Church.'[25] Du Moulin, whose optimism was considerable on the first two stages, was much less hopeful about this last stage. He expressed doubt that such an accord was feasible, 'because the Pope does not allow any council or conference in which he does not preside'; but, in any case, 'we will be much more considerable and will speak with more authority when we are in agreement'.[26] King James replied on 7 March 1613, giving the plan his cautious support.[27]

This is the document which, in a somewhat revised form, appears in the acts of the national synod of the Reformed Churches of France, which met at Tonneins, in Guienne, from 2 May to 3 June 1614.[28] Lucien Rimbault, the biographer of Du

[22] Ibid., fol. 69r.
[23] Ibid.
[24] Ibid.
[25] Ibid.
[26] Ibid.
[27] Ibid. fol. 88r.
[28] Rimbault, *Pierre du Moulin*, pp. 71–5; John Quick, ed., *Synodicon in Gallia Reformata: or, The Acts, Decisions, Decrees, and Canons of Those Famous National Councils of the Reformed Churches in France*, 2 vols (London, 1692), 1, pp. 434–7; Jean Aymon, ed., *Tous les synodes nationaux des églises réformées de France*, 2 vols (The Hague, 1710), 2 pp. 57–62. For a discussion of the plan as presented at Tonneins, see Patterson, 'James I and the Huguenot Synod of Tonneins of 1614', pp. 254–63. For the presbyterian/synodal polity of the French Reformed Church, including the central role played by the national synod, see Elisabeth Labrousse, 'Calvinism in France, 1598–1685,' in Menna Prestwich, ed., *International Calvinism, 1541–1715* (Oxford, 1985), pp. 285–315, esp. pp. 285–93; Brian G. Armstrong, '*Semper Reformanda*: the case of the French Reformed Church, 1559–1620', in W. Fred Graham, ed., *Later Calvinism: International Perspectives* (St Louis, 1994), pp. 119–40, and Glenn S. Sunshine, 'Reformed theology and the origins of synodical polity: Calvin, Beza and the Gallican Confession', ibid., pp. 141–58.

Moulin, argued persuasively that Du Moulin was the author of the 'Overtures' found there, but he evidently did not know of the letter sent by Du Moulin to James on 1 March 1613.[29] Du Moulin's original plan of 1613 was modified and expanded to twenty-one points on the basis of consultations with Philippe Duplessis-Mornay, chiefly to make clearer the distinction between the first and second stages Du Moulin envisaged. Du Moulin's letter to King James, with the 'Overtures' or plan of union attached, shows definitively that the plan presented to the Synod of Tonneins was his.[30] The first stage, aimed at establishing unity among the Reformed Churches on the basis of a common confession, would not, in the version presented at Tonneins, involve any Lutheran delegates. The Lutheran Churches would only be invited to participate in the second stage, by sending delegates to a meeting at which a broader accord, involving both groups of Churches, would be sought.

Significantly, the revised plan was brought to the Synod of Tonneins by David Home, a Scottish minister who had recently served as a Protestant pastor in France.[31] Home came from England by way of Sedan on a mission from King James to promote a reconciliation between Du Moulin and Tilenus with the help of the Duke of Bouillon.[32] Du Moulin himself did not attend the synod, though he no doubt kept in close touch with proceedings there. In a report on its actions to King James, the synod commented in a positive way on the plan of union. 'As for this Royal overture . . . which has been made to us from your side, in order to procure a stricter correspondence among the Churches of our faith' and to further an accord with those of differing views, the synod was favourable but inclined to be realistic.[33] It endorsed 'so holy and salutary an enterprise, in so far as it will be permissible, in the situation in which we live, under

---

[29] Rimbault, *Pierre du Moulin*, pp. 71–5 and 235–8.

[30] Philippe Duplessis-Mornay, *Mémoires et correspondance*, 12 vols (Paris, 1824–25), 12, pp. 420–3. For Duplessis-Mornay's activities on behalf of Protestant unity, beginning in 1580, see Robert D. Linder, 'The French Calvinist response to the Formula of Concord', *Journal of Ecumenical Studies*, 19 (1982), pp. 18–37, esp. pp. 22–9.

[31] Haag and Haag, *La France protestante*, 2nd edn, 5, p. 518; Quick, ed., *Synodicon*, 1, p. 419; Aymon, *Tous les synodes*, 2, p. 38.

[32] BL, MS Stowe 174, fols 306r–v (Home to James I, 3 April 1614).

[33] PRO, SP 78/62, fol. 53v (Synod of Tonneins to James I, 1 June 1614).

the authority of our Sovereign . . . '.[34] Home reported to King James by way of Edmondes, on 9 June 1614, that he had 'made the overture to the Synod about means of reaching an accord between our Churches and the Lutherans, and of beginning quietly a little assembly of all the sovereignties withdrawn from the yoke of the pope, following the project of Mr du Moulin'.[35] He added that the synod had 'given charge to the deputies of the provinces to think about it carefully for the next national synod'.[36]

Du Moulin wrote to King James in the autumn of 1614 to report on the meeting with Tilenus at Saumur and on the prospects for his plan of union.[37] He was deeply grateful, he said, that his dispute with Tilenus had been settled. On 8 October he had gone to Saumur as the Synod of Tonneins had directed. There a group of seven pastors and professors of Saumur, along with the governor, Duplessis-Mornay, had heard the complaints and explanations offered by Tilenus and himself. The sentence of the theologians was that 'he as well as I declare and protest that on the effects of the hypostatic union we adhere to the decisions of the Councils of Ephesus and Chalcedon . . . [and] that henceforth we will live in peace and concord.'[38] Du Moulin reported that he and Tilenus had 'embraced in a protestation of friendship'.[39] Du Moulin expressed the wish that James, having healed this wound, 'would wish to embrace courageously the general union' which he had sent to the King.[40] He testified that from the reports of various ambassadors in Paris, 'the Estates of the Low Countries and the Princes of Germany' were strongly disposed to it.[41] James's support would have the effect of influencing 'all the Princes and Republics' to follow his example.[42]

[34] Ibid., fol. 54r.
[35] BL, MS Stowe 174, fol. 347r.
[36] Ibid.
[37] PRO, SP 78/58, fols 230r–v, Du Moulin to James I, is undated but filed as 22 November 1611. Based on its contents, the letter seems certain to be from 1614. The procedure Du Moulin describes is that ordered by the Synod of Tonneins and the description which Du Moulin gives of his reconciliation with Tilenus is closely paralleled by Home's description in his letter of 16 October 1614 cited below. I believe that Du Moulin's letter to James should be dated as late October or early November 1614.
[38] PRO, SP 78/58, fol. 230r. Cf. BL, MS Stowe 175, fol. 76r (Home to Edmondes, 16 Oct. 1614).
[39] PRO, SP 78/58, fol. 230r. Cf. BL, MS Stowe 175, fol. 76r.
[40] PRO, SP 78/58, fols 230r–v.
[41] Ibid., fol. 230v.
[42] Ibid.

In the spring and early summer of 1615, Du Moulin spent three and a half months in England as a guest of King James. Du Moulin wrote to Duplessis-Mornay on 5 March 1615 that he intended to consult the King about the implementation of the scheme for union. He evidently did so, though much of his time was spent in helping King James to answer Cardinal Du Perron's oration to the Third Estate of the Estates-General in France in January 1615. Du Perron, in opposing an oath introduced by the Third Estate to require the clergy to deny the papal deposing power, had made disparaging remarks about the English Oath of Allegiance and, by implication, the British King. James's *Declaration*, written with Du Moulin's help, was published in French in 1615 and then in English in 1616 as a *Remonstrance . . . for the Right of Kings*.[43] On 17 August 1615, after his return to Paris, Du Moulin wrote to King James that he had asked Duplessis-Mornay to ask the professors at Saumur 'to draw up one confession comprised of the various confessions of the Reformed Churches of Christendom in simple terms'.[44] Once this had been done, he would send it to James for his comments, after which it could be sent to the Netherlands and elsewhere. He also noted that for the plan to succeed, 'it would be necessary to dispose the German princes [to it] and to invite the Lutherans to enter into some communication'.[45]

The next national synod of the Reformed Churches of France met in 1617 in Vitré, where the deputies heard reports from all the provinces concerning the plan of union. Though the synod believed it was necessary 'to wait for those who made such Overtures to press this Affair further', it did appoint four ministers – André Rivet, Jean Chauve, Daniel Chamier, and Du Moulin himself – to confer with Duplessis-Mornay and to be

---

[43] James I, *Declaration dv serenissime Roy Iaqves I. Roy de la Grand' Bretaigne, France et Irelande, Defenseur de la Foy, povr le droit des rois & independance de leur couronnes, contre la harangve de l'illvstrissime Cardinal du Perron prononcée en la Chambre du Tiers Estat, le XV. de Ianuier 1615* (London, 1615); *Remonstrance of the Most Gratiovs King James I. King of Great Britaine, France, and Ireland, Defender of the Faith, &c. for the Right of Kings and the Independance of Their Crownes against an Oration of the Most Illustrious Card. of Perron, Pronounced in the Chamber of the Third Estate, Ian. 15. 1615* (Cambridge, 1616). For Du Moulin's part in the composition of the book, see David Harris Willson, 'James I and his literary assistants', *Huntington Library Quarterly*, 8 (1944–5), pp. 35–57, esp. pp. 49–51.

[44] PRO, SP 78/63, fol. 269r.

[45] Ibid.

ready to work further towards realizing the plan as opportunities arose.[46] A possible opportunity came in the following year.

In 1618, disputes about predestination in the United Provinces of the Netherlands reached the point that only a national synod there seemed likely to prevent a schism in the Dutch Reformed Church and a civil war in the province of Holland. In the summer of 1618, Maurice, the Prince of Orange, the stadholder of most of the provinces, was disarming militias raised by towns in Holland, which had acted with the support of Johan van Oldenbarnevelt, the chief executive of Holland.[47] The theological dispute was between the followers of Jacob Arminius, who had drawn up a Remonstrance in 1610, dealing with five parts of the doctrine of predestination, and the stricter Calvinists, or Counter-Remonstrants. Oldenbarnevelt was a Remonstrant, along with many of the pastors of the province of Holland, while the Prince of Orange was a Counter-Remonstrant, along with most of the pastors of the other six provinces. The States-General, the representative assembly of the country, invited foreign Churches of the Reformed tradition to meet with a national synod in the city of Dordrecht or Dort.[48] British delegates, led by George Carleton, the Bishop of Llandaff, attended along with delegates from the Rhineland and Switzerland. The Reformed Churches of France were to have been represented by Rivet, Chauve, Chamier, and Du Moulin – the four elected at Vitré the year before to work for the implementation of the plan of union presented at Tonneins in 1614 – but King Louis XIII forbade their attendance.[49] With a Protestant revolt then under way in Bohemia, Louis was unwilling to see members of the

[46] Quick, *Synodicon*, 1, p. 499; Aymon, *Tous les synodes*, 2, pp. 108–9.

[47] Jan den Tex, *Oldenbarnevelt*, 2 vols (Cambridge, 1973), 2, pp. 609–44; Peter Geyl, *The Netherlands in the Seventeenth Century*, 2 vols (London, 1961–4), 1, pp. 51–61.

[48] Geeraert Brandt, *The History of the Reformation and Other Ecclesiastical Transactions in and about the Low-Countries*, 2 vols (London, 1720), 2, p. 388. For the participation of the British delegates at Dort, see Christopher Grayson, 'James I and the religious crisis in the United Provinces, 1613–19', in Derek Baker, ed., *Reform and Reformation: England and the Continent, c1500–c1750* (Oxford, 1979), *SCH.S*, 2, pp. 195–219, and John Platt, 'Eirenical Anglicans at the Synod of Dort', ibid., pp. 221–43; John Platt, 'Les anglais à Dordrecht', in M. Peronnet, ed., *La Controverse interne au protestantisme (XVIe–XXe siècles* (Montpellier, 1983), pp. 109–28; Nicholas Tyacke, *Anti-Calvinists: The Rise of English Arminianism, c.1590–1640* (Oxford, 1987), esp. pp. 87–180; and Peter White, *Predestination, Policy and Polemic: Conflict and Consensus in the English Church from the Reformation to the Civil War* (Cambridge, 1992), esp. pp. 175–214.

[49] Rimbault, *Pierre du Moulin*, pp. 88–9. The king's ordinance forbidding the French delegation from attending the synod was dated 15 October 1618.

religious minority in France in close touch with their co-religionists abroad.

On 8 December 1618, Du Moulin wrote from Paris to Sir Dudley Carleton, the English ambassador at The Hague, about a matter he wished to see introduced at the Synod of Dort. He would, he said, have proposed it himself if he had not been prevented from attending. Du Moulin believed that 'so notable an assembly ought not to content itself with appeasing the troubles of the Church of the Low Countries', but ought to take steps to prevent the outbreak of such ills in the future.[50] The remedy would be to draw up a common confession based on the confessions of England, France, the Netherlands, the Palatinate, and Switzerland, among others. The confession would not deal with ecclesiastical polity and discipline, since practices varied among the Churches.[51] This confession would be sent back to the Churches for their approval, after which doctrinal decisions would only be made with the consent of the Churches which had entered into the agreement. But before the Synod of Dort disbanded, it should 'undertake a project of accord and reconciliation between ourselves and the Lutheran Churches' by inviting them as brothers in Christ to a meeting of theologians from the two traditions.[52] Such a meeting would be held 'not in order to dispute but in order to consult on the means for an accord and mutual toleration'.[53] Du Moulin hoped that King James would 'bring his authority to bear on it', and that these propositions would be made either by the ambassador or by the British theologians at Dort.[54] He urged Ambassador Carleton to write to the King on this subject and to forward his letter to James with the ambassador's.

In his own letter to Sir Robert Naunton, the Secretary of State, on 16 December 1618, Ambassador Carleton said that he had discovered that Du Moulin had corresponded with various delegates at Dort about this plan. Informally, it was already being discussed.[55] He had himself spoken to Maurice, the Prince of

---

[50] PRO, SP 84/87, fol. 111r. See Dudley Carleton, *The Letters from and to Sir Dudley Carleton, Knt. during His Embassy in Holland, from January 1615/16, to December 1620* (London, 1780), pp. 325–6.

[51] PRO, SP 84/87, fol. 111r.

[52] Ibid., fol. 111v.

[53] Ibid.

[54] Ibid.

[55] Ibid., fol. 152r. See Carleton, *Letters*, pp. 318–19.

Orange, and his kinsman Count William, who feared that such a proceeding might hinder the particular business the synod had been convened to consider. But they had no objection to the drawing up of a common confession. If the British King urged that such a confession be drawn up, this could well be done.[56] Count William believed that an approach to the Lutherans would be more successful if made by King James at the request of the synod rather than by the synod directly.[57]

Du Moulin's letter of 8 December thus recapitulated the plan of union on which he had expended a great deal of time and energy in the preceding five and a half years. He saw the Synod of Dort as possibly the first stage in the union of the Reformed Churches described in the plan he had sent to King James in 1613. Du Moulin was convinced that the Synod of Dort could achieve a permanent accord among the Reformed Churches by means of a common confession. He also strongly favoured the synod's extending an invitation to the Lutherans for negotiations aimed at a broader union. The union he envisioned would be a confederation of national Protestant Churches – plus the French Reformed Church – stretching across northern Europe. There would be a large measure of unity, in that the Churches would recognize one another as part of a larger body. But there would not be complete uniformity among them. Differences in discipline and polity among the Churches were expected and were to be considered no impediment to their closer association. Differences over theology would be tolerated. It is clear that Du Moulin's hope was eventually to achieve a broad consensus on fundamental issues of the faith, based on the principles of the Reformation as expressed in the confessions of the various Churches. The proposal was for religious reconciliation and mutual toleration, not for an organic union brought about by merging the various orders of ministry.

The response at Dort to Du Moulin's proposals may be briefly summarized. King James approved Du Moulin's plan in a conversation reported by Naunton in a letter to Ambassador Carleton on 22 December 1618. He joined, wrote Naunton, in the

---

[56] PRO, SP 84/87, fol. 152r.

[57] Ibid., fol. 152v.

'opinion that it will be a matter of great honor to the times and to that Synod, of no lesse importance therein to the Church, if it shall succeede with such an issue as is propounded'.[58] But the project needed to be 'handled with great care, & even temper', lest a failure lead to the ridiculing of the Churches gathered there.[59] When it was appropriate, James was ready 'to interpose himself with and to the Lutheran princes'.[60] On 31 December 1618, Ambassador Carleton reported to Naunton that Bishop Carleton would have 'tryall made' of the proposals at Dort, using 'that caution as your Honor doth recommend'.[61] John Hales, the chaplain to Ambassador Carleton, who wrote to him regularly about the synod's proceedings, reported on 22 January 1619 that Johannes Bogerman, the President of the synod, was willing to consider a common confession and had asked Bishop Carleton and Abraham Scultetus of the Palatinate of the Rhine to draft such a document. But as for approaching the Lutherans, the President 'thinks it not fit that any word at all be made'.[62] The project of a common confession was not ultimately realized, though the delegates all subscribed to the Belgic Confession before the synod ended. The British delegates specifically stated that their assent was to the doctrinal portions only, not to those dealing with polity and discipline.[63]

The Synod of Dort's major work, of course, was to deal with the doctrines then in dispute in the United Provinces. In the course of this task the delegates condemned the Remonstrants. The synod's decrees were a more moderate statement than is generally assumed to be the case, and the British delegation was partly responsible for this result. Du Moulin himself was soon associated publicly with the condemnation of the Remonstrants.

---

[58] Ibid., fol. 174v. This letter is not in Carleton, *Letters.*

[59] PRO, SP 84/87, fol. 174v.

[60] Ibid.

[61] Ibid., fol. 206v. See Carleton, *Letters,* pp. 329–30.

[62] John Hales, *Golden Remains of the Ever Memorable Mr. Iohn Hales of Eton College,* 2 parts in one (London, 1659), Pt 2, p. 71. See also PRO, SP 84/88, fols. 12r–v (Carleton to Naunton, 14 Jan. 1619).

[63] George Carleton, et al., *A Ioynt Attestation, Avowing That the Discipline of the Church of England Was Not Impeached by the Synode of Dort* (London, 1626); Carleton, *Bp Carletons Testimonie Concerning the Presbyterian Discipline in the Low-Countries and Episcopall Government Here in England* (London, 1642). For discussion of this issue, see W. Nijenhuis, 'The controversy between Presbyterianism and Episcopalianism surrounding and during the Synod of Dordrecht', in his *Ecclesia Reformata: Studies on the Reformation* (Leiden, 1972), pp. 207–20.

He published a substantial book in Latin in 1619, translated into English the next year as *The Anatomy of Arminianisme*, which developed at considerable length a refutation of the Remonstrants on the disputed points of predestination.[64] It seems clear that he had begun work on this subject before the synod began. The *Anatomy* was very much in the mode of Du Moulin's other polemical writings: trenchant, vigorous, and learned. His argument was that the Arminians had revived the heresies of the ancient Pelagians and that they adhered to doctrines close to those professed by Roman Catholics. He asserted that the doctrine of reprobation was fully orthodox, if rightly understood, and claimed the support of theologians from Calvin to David Pareus.[65]

What happened in 1613–18 to make Du Moulin, at least temporarily, a Protestant irenicist? One possible answer is that he was seeking favour with King James. The British King was a proponent of a broad union of Christians, as he announced in 1604 to the first Parliament of his reign in England, and he had become publicly identified with this cause through, for example, the writings and activities of Du Moulin's countryman, Isaac Casaubon, during the years 1610–14.[66] It is clear that Du Moulin worked closely with James and received tangible benefits for his services. On the occasion of his visit to England in 1615, Du Moulin was made a prebendary of Canterbury. In late 1624 he received a gift from the King of £200 and soon afterwards, on 11 January 1625, was presented with the living of Llanarmon in the diocese of St Asaph.[67] He visited James early in 1625, shortly before the King died in March.[68] These gifts were, of course, not simply the reward for his services in the cause of ecclesiastical unity. Du Moulin was a prominent supporter of King James in his controversy with the papacy over the Oath of Allegiance. Du Moulin also reported to the King and his Secretary of State on

---

[64] Pierre Du Moulin, *Anatome Arminianismi* (Leyden, 1619), translated into English as *The Anatomy of Arminianisme: Or, The Opening of the Controversies Lately Handled in the Low-Countryes, Concerning the Doctrine of Prouidence, of Predestination, of the Death of Christ, of Nature and Grace* (London, 1620).

[65] Du Moulin, *The Anatomy of Arminianisme*, pp. 82–91 and 498–504.

[66] W. B. Patterson, 'King James I's call for an ecumenical council,' *SCH*, 7(1971), pp. 267–75. For Casaubon, see Mark Pattison, *Isaac Casaubon, 1559–1614*, 2nd edn. (Oxford, 1892), pp. 447–8; Isaac Casaubon, *Epistolae* (Rotterdam, 1709), pp. 441, 447, 452–3; William S. M. Knight, *The Life and Works of Hugo Grotius* (London, 1925), pp. 125–35.

[67] *Calendar of State Papers, Domestic Series, of the Reign of James I, 1611–1618* (PRO, 1858), p. 289; *Calendar . . . 1623–1625* (1859), pp. 373, 385, 444.

[68] 'Autobiographie de Pierre Du Moulin,' p. 474.

current events in France, especially as they concerned the French Protestants.[69] But King James undoubtedly valued Du Moulin highly as an ally in the cause of bringing the Churches together. The final point in Du Moulin's plan of union – *rapprochement* with Rome – seems closer to James's way of thinking than Du Moulin's, and may have been put into the plan to attract the attention and support of the King.

In the final analysis, however, the hope of gaining the favour of the British King cannot be the whole explanation for Du Moulin's actions. The French Protestants had regularly sought closer relations with other Churches in the Reformed tradition as well as with those in the Lutheran tradition. Actions taken by the national synods in France from 1578 to 1607 testify to this effort.[70] The precarious existence of French Protestantism, even under the terms of the Edict of Nantes, made Du Moulin and his co-religionists anxious to secure foreign Protestant encouragement and support.

The most helpful way to understand Du Moulin's plan is to locate it within the context of the international political situation in 1610–14. England, the Netherlands, and the Evangelical Union of princes in Germany were all involved in trying to secure a Protestant succession in Cleves-Jülich, a territory strategically located on the Rhine, just east of the Spanish Netherlands and the United Provinces. Both of the leading claimants, John Sigismund of Brandenburg and Philip-Ludwig of Neuburg, were Lutherans, though the first became a Calvinist and the successor to the second became a Roman Catholic before the territory was finally divided between Brandenburg and Neuburg in 1614.[71] The Evangelical Union formed in 1608 was made up of both

---

[69] In 1615, he reported on the course of the uprising of the Prince of Condé and other nobles and on the meeting of the Protestant Political Assembly. PRO, SP 78/64, fols. 1r–v (Du Moulin to James I, 11 Sept. 1615), 48r (Du Moulin to Winwood, 9 Oct. 1615), 104r–v (Du Moulin to Winwood, 11 Nov. 1615), 146r (Du Moulin to Winwood, 30 Nov. 1615).

[70] Quick, *Synodicon*, 1, pp. 120–2, 153, 239, 263–4; Aymon, *Tous les synodes*, 1, pp. 131–3, 170, 274, 300. For discussion, see Linder, 'The French Calvinist response to the Formula of Concord', pp. 18–37.

[71] Geoffrey Parker, *The Thirty Years' War* (London, 1984), pp. 25–38 (section by Simon Adams). The circumstances referred to in this paragraph are commented on at length in the diplomatic papers in PRO, SP 78/55–62. See also J. V. Polišenský, *The Thirty Years War* (London, 1971), pp. 88–93; J. M. Hayden, 'Continuity in the France of Henry IV and Louis XIII: French foreign policy, 1598–1615', *JMH*, 45 (1973), pp. 1–23; Myron P. Gutmann, 'The origins of the Thirty Years' War,' *Journal of Interdisciplinary History*, 18 (1988), pp. 749–70, esp. pp. 759–63; and N. M. Sutherland, 'The origins of the Thirty Years War and the structure of European politics', *EHR*, 107 (1992), pp. 587–625, esp. pp. 600–10.

Lutheran and Calvinist states in Germany, though not all of the Lutheran states had elected to join. King James allied England with the Union in 1612 and persuaded the United Provinces to enter such an alliance in 1613. He was also closely associated with the Union through the marriage of his daughter Elizabeth early in 1613 to Frederick V of the Palatinate, the leader of the Evangelical Union. Du Moulin's plan would not only provide ideological support for his co-religionists in France, it promised to develop a closer understanding and a stronger alliance among the Protestant states of northern Europe, which was very much in keeping with King James's policies. Du Moulin's plan of union was, in effect, the religious counterpart to the political programme of the Evangelical Union of states. International political considerations were important to Du Moulin, though he was usually discreet enough not to discuss them in letters to King James and the English authorities.[72] International political considerations were certainly important to King James and help to explain why he was receptive to Du Moulin's proposals.

Du Moulin's plan for the union of the Protestant Churches was deeply serious and was rooted in the political realities of the time. By 1619, however, when the Thirty Years' War was beginning to erupt, the time for implementing such a plan was rapidly running out. Remarkably, the plan called for unity to be achieved among the English, Calvinist, and Lutheran Churches by acknowledging the diversity that existed among them in discipline, liturgy, and even in doctrine, while affirming their common foundation on the central tenets of the Christian faith. Moreover, it looked toward an eventual agreement with the Church of Rome. In these ways, it strikingly anticipated the ecumenical movement of three centuries later.

University of the South, Sewanee, Tennessee

---

[72] In 1621, Du Moulin was forced to leave Paris to seek refuge in Sedan under the protection of the Duke of Bouillon when he was discovered to have written to King James by way of the English ambassador, Edward Herbert. See 'Autobiographie de Pierre Du Moulin', pp. 471–2. Du Moulin's explanation to Edmondes is contained in his letter to the former ambassador on 28 February 1621. BL, Stowe MS 176, fols. 177r–v.

# ARGUING FOR PEACE: GILES FIRMIN ON NEW ENGLAND AND GODLY UNITY

## by SUSAN HARDMAN MOORE

Richard Baxter admired the qualities Giles Firmin brought to religious controversy: 'Candor, Ingenuitie, Moderation, Love and Peace'.[1] Firmin, Vicar of Shalford, Essex, 1648–62, argued for peace during the Interregnum, at a time when disputes fractured the churches of his county. Factions of Presbyterians and Independents still fought about the right path to religious reform, in terms dictated by polemic of the 1640s, while sects like the Quakers rattled confidence in a united Church. Firmin devised arguments that crossed party lines, to unite against sectarianism. He wrote from an unusual perspective. He had been to Massachusetts and come home. He had taken part in the colony's bold experiment in Congregationalist church order, which inspired English Independents, but came back into parish ministry in Essex without repudiating his colonial experience.[2] Modern historians, like seventeenth-century Presbyterians, struggle to explain why New England's churches claimed unity with England, but acted differently. Firmin's outlook sets contemporary polemic in a fresh light. Nowadays, he is better known for his anecdotes than for his views, because he scattered his tracts with stories about people he had known in colony and homeland. His opinions tend to escape notice. Yet Firmin used his experience in Old and New England to make a distinctive appeal for unity.

It is ironic that he first came to public attention in the writings of arch-polemicist Thomas Edwards. In the eyes of Presbyterian propagandists like Edwards, New England fomented wrongheaded religious diversity. Edwards was thus delighted to report that 'one out of New-England, one Mr. F.' had started to preach in Colchester; 'an Apothecary Physitian . . . who is not in Orders, nor ever Preached . . . but on Shipboard as he came over'.[3]

---

[1] Richard Baxter, *Rich. Baxter's Apology* (London, 1654), 1, p. 107.

[2] For Firmin (*c*.1614–97), see A. G. Matthews, *Calamy Revised* (Oxford, 1934, reissued 1988) [hereafter *CR*], p. 197; *DNB*; T. W. Davids, *Annals of Evangelical Nonconformity in Essex* (London, 1863), pp. 457–61; J. W. Dean, *A Brief Memoir of Rev. Giles Firmin* (Boston, Mass., 1866).

[3] Thomas Edwards, *Gangraena* (London, 1646), 1, p. 69; for 'Mr. F.' as Firmin, *Gangraena*, 2, pp. 54–5, 63, 99.

Firmin hated 'being branded by Mr. Edwards for an Independent', but would not admit to being Presbyterian either.[4] He refused to fit Edwards' stereotypes of former colonists: he was neither a radical campaigner for the New England Way in church government, nor a disenchanted witness against it. Rather, he wanted to redeem New England from its divisive role, showing Presbyterians that colonial practice was not what propagandists like Edwards made it out to be, and shaming Congregationalists who adopted 'New-England principles' in a such a manner that 'men should now say, and our posterity hereafter believe it, That Independency ruined the Church of England'.[5] The apex of his work came in 1658, when he negotiated a common statement on pastoral ministry for divided Essex clergy to sign, based on the model Richard Baxter put forward in the Worcestershire Voluntary Association. His strategies and motives for healing division in the 1650s, rather than the detail of his views on church government, or his later career, will concern us.[6] Firmin provides a case-study in reconciling unity with diversity, in a setting where ecclesiology and polemic went hand-in-hand.

His instinct for unity sprang from a sense of community, formed among what he liked to call 'old Essex Christians'.[7] To make sense of his conciliatory reading of New England, it is

[4] Giles Firmin, *A Serious Question Stated* (London, 1651), 'To the Courteous Reader'; idem, *The Answer of Giles Firmin* (London, 1689), p. 6. Modern writers tend to classify Firmin as a Presbyterian: see, most recently, Janice Knight, *Orthodoxies in Massachusetts: Rereading American Puritanism* (Cambridge, Mass., 1994); Francis J. Bremer, *Congregational Communion: Clerical Friendship in the Anglo-American Puritan Community, 1610–1692* (Boston, Mass., 1994). He was licensed as a Presbyterian preacher in 1672, but licences often gave inaccurate ascriptions. To borrow a phrase from Nathaniel Ward (*DNB*), Firmin's father-in-law, he was not 'presbyterian nor plebsbyterian but interpendent': Ward, *The Simple Cobler of Agawam in America* (London, 1647), ed. P. M. Zall (Lincoln, Nebraska, 1969), p. 35. Geoffrey Nuttall describes Firmin as 'no more a Classical Divine than he was one of the Congregational Brethren; nor yet was he a new-style Episcopalian': Geoffrey F. Nuttall, 'The Essex Classes (1648)', *United Reformed Church History Society Journal*, 3 (1983), p. 199.

[5] Stephen Marshall (ed. Giles Firmin), *The Power of the Civil Magistrate in Matters of Religion Vindicated* (London, 1657), pp. 22–3.

[6] Geoffrey F. Nuttall, *Richard Baxter* (London and Edinburgh, 1965), pp. 67–70, discusses the Worcestershire Voluntary Association and other county Voluntary Associations of the 1650s. For the Essex Agreement, see note 30. Firmin read Baxter's account of the Worcestershire venture, *Christian Concord* (London, 1653): Firmin to Baxter, 24 July 1654, N. H. Keeble and Geoffrey F. Nuttall, *Calendar of the Correspondence of Richard Baxter*, 2 vols (Oxford, 1991), 1, letter 192 [hereafter *Baxter Calendar*]. Firmin's first call for peace was *Separation Examined* (London, 1652), a response to *A Vindication of the Presbyteriall-Government . . . Published by the Ministers and Elders met Together in a Provinciall Assembly, Novemb. 2nd, 1649* (London, 1650). His views on church order are summarized in *Separation Examined*, 'To the . . . Ministers of London', and 'To the Reader'.

[7] Giles Firmin, *The Real Christian* (London, 1670), p. 270.

important to understand the local context that moulded his outlook. His convictions took shape in a godly community roughly bounded by Dedham, Felsted, Sudbury, and Bishop's Stortford: northern Essex, shading over the borders into Suffolk and Hertfordshire. Defying geography, this community stretched in Firmin's mind from Old England to New; and across the generations, from Elizabethan Puritans to their post-Restoration heirs.[8] Educated at Felsted School and Emmanuel College, Cambridge, Firmin was stirred by the preaching of John Rogers at Dedham, and lived in an area rich with opportunities for hearing eminent ministers.[9] Although Essex Christians were separated by emigration to New England, Firmin's career bridged the divide. He broke off his studies at Emmanuel in 1632, and sailed over with John Wilson, once of Sudbury, Suffolk, by then minister to Boston, Massachusetts. Firmin joined the Boston church in its earliest days. He returned to England for a while, perhaps to study medicine, but went to the colony again in 1637. At this point New England's congregations were on fire with the Antinomian Controversy, an episode that sharpened his prejudice against disunity.[10] In Massachusetts, Firmin kept company with people from his own corner of England: first in Boston, then in Ipswich, where he practised physic. He went to England again in 1644, and though he had not intended to stay there, lived in Essex until his death in 1697.[11] Firmin did not so much emigrate

[8] See, for example, references to the Barrington family, and to the Elizabethan preacher Richard Rogers of Wethersfield and his family, in Firmin, *Real Christian*, 'Epistle Dedicatory' and pp. 67–8, 75–6.

[9] Such as John Wilson, Thomas Hooker, Thomas Shepard, Stephen Marshall, Daniel Rogers and John Norton, who all figure later in his career. For an excellent discussion of this clerical network, see Tom Webster, 'The Godly of Goshen scattered: an Essex clerical conference in the 1620s and its diaspora' (Cambridge Ph.D. thesis, 1992).

[10] R. D. Pierce, ed., *The Records of the First Church in Boston 1630–1868*, Publications of the Colonial Society of Massachusetts, 39 (Boston, 1961), p. 15; Giles Firmin, Πανουργια: *A Brief Review of Mr. Davis's Vindication* (London, 1693), 'To the Reader'. Firmin lived with Governor John Winthrop (to whom he was related), and joined the Boston church before John Cotton arrived. Wilson emigrated in 1630, but had returned home to recruit settlers. Firmin's parents probably came from Sudbury, and also emigrated. Knight, *Orthodoxies in Massachusetts*, reassesses the Antinomian Controversy.

[11] For Ipswich settlers' origins, see D. G. Allen, *In English Ways* (Chapel Hill, NC, 1981), pp. 269–79. The ministers of Ipswich, Massachusetts, were Nathaniel Rogers (*DNB*), son of John Rogers of Dedham, Essex (*DNB*); and John Norton (*DNB*), born in Essex but an emigrant from Bishop's Stortford, Hertfordshire. Nathaniel Ward (see note 4), formerly minister of Stondon Massey, Essex, lived in Ipswich 'out of office'. Firmin's marriage to Nathaniel's daughter, Susanna, made him a kinsman of Nathaniel Rogers in New England, and of Daniel Rogers (*DNB*) of Wethersfield, Essex, in England. Susanna and Nathaniel followed Firmin to Essex in 1646.

and return to his roots, as move within godly circles that nurtured him in Old and New England. He drew constantly on his knowledge of this community to make his case. Plundering his work for godly anecdotes misses the point of these allusions, which was to evoke a sense of unity that spanned the Atlantic.

Emigration to New England strained the community Firmin knew: he deplored the decay of relations between Old and New England, and within his home county. He subscribed to a notion that stood at the heart of godly mentality: truth unites, error divides. Puritan self-fashioning relied as much on arguments for corporate union with Christ as on rhetoric against popery and separatism – images of Rome as the whore of Babylon, the realm of Antichrist, meant little without metaphors of the Church as Bride of Christ, Body of Christ.[12] Ties of communion among the saints proved vital in recruiting settlers, but uneasiness about dividing the Church dogged the venture.[13] Not for the first or last time in Christian history, a quest for purity threatened unity. Firmin never wrote in detail about his decision to leave England, but the tensions can be seen between Samuel Rogers (a near contemporary of Firmin at Felsted School and Emmanuel), and his father Daniel (lecturer of Wethersfield, Essex, later Firmin's close friend and kinsman by marriage). Samuel relished the company of those bound for New England, and saw emigration as part of his search for holiness: 'the more I have of God, the more I sigh after New England, and the more I think of that, I think I find more of God.' His father, however, accused settlers

---

[12] R. Tudor Jones, 'Union with Christ: the existential nerve of puritan piety', *Tyndale Bulletin*, 41 (1990), pp. 186–208; J. C. Brauer, 'Types of puritan piety', *ChH*, 56 (1987), pp. 48–9; Margo Todd, 'Puritan self-fashioning: the diary of Samuel Ward', *JBS*, 31 (1992), p. 254; Peter Lake, 'William Bradshaw, Antichrist and the community of the godly', *JEH*, 36 (1985), pp. 570–89. Puritan interest in Antichrist and union with Christ shows in commentaries written on Revelation and the Song of Songs. Covenants among the godly illustrate the desire for 'embodied' unity: see note 26.

[13] For different readings of the dilemmas emigration posed, see Bremer, *Congregational Communion*; Stephen Foster, *The Long Argument: English Puritanism and the Shaping of New England Culture, 1570–1700* (Chapel Hill, NC, and London, 1991); Susan Hardman Moore, 'Popery, purity and Providence: deciphering the New England experiment', in Anthony Fletcher and Peter Roberts, eds, *Religion, Culture and Society in Early Modern Britain* (Cambridge, 1994), pp. 257–89; Carol Geary Schneider, 'Godly order in a church half-reformed: the disciplinarian legacy, 1570–1641' (Harvard Ph.D. thesis, 1986), pp. 337–407; Webster, 'Godly of Goshen scattered'; Avihu Zakai, *Exile and Kingdom: History and Apocalypse in the Puritan Migration to America* (Cambridge, 1992).

of deserting those left at home: 'All cannot goe, what shall become of such as must stay . . . ?'[14] Stephen Marshall, Vicar of Finchingfield, near Shalford (and like Daniel Rogers, Firmin's friend after his return), opposed New England because its example provoked sectarian behaviour.[15] Emigrants risked schism, which in the Puritans' social view of the Church not only destroyed the unity of Christ's mystical body, but went 'against Charity towards our Neighbour . . . [it] robbes him of a spirituall good'.[16] Firmin's eagerness to heal breaches in charity, within the scattered community of Essex godly, shows even in Edwards' hostile account of him in the 1640s: Firmin 'exhorted to peace', saying 'how near the Independents and Presbyterians were come'.[17] In the 1650s he repeatedly called for peace, with the ingenuity Baxter commended.

To appeal for unity, Firmin brought absent New Englanders into the print and pulpit controversies of Interregnum Essex.[18] He was determined to make present, through anecdote and allusion, the influence of leading figures who had left. New England writers from the area, like Thomas Hooker and John Norton, loom large in his tracts. He also cited John Cotton often, though Cotton came from Lincolnshire: tactically this was essential, because John Owen, whose opinion counted in Essex, claimed Cotton's inspiration for ideas that Firmin thought fragmented the

---

[14] Diary of Samuel Rogers, 1 April [1636], Belfast, Queen's University Library, MS Percy 7, fol. 217; Daniel Rogers, *Naaman the Syrian* (London, 1642), p. 885. See Webster, 'Godly of Goshen scattered', pp. 336–44, and Kenneth W. Shipps, 'The puritan emigration to New England: a new source on motivation', *New England Historical and Genealogical Register* [hereafter *NEHGR*], 135 (1981), pp. 83–97. For the Rogers family, see note 11. Samuel was encouraged to emigrate by John Wilson, with whom Firmin sailed over; however, he stayed in England and died *c*.1643, before Firmin's return.

[15] Marshall's part in the development of competing factions is discussed by Webster, 'Godly of Goshen scattered', pp. 386–409; R. D. Bradley, 'The failure of accommodation', *Journal of Religious History*, 12 (1982–3), pp. 23–47; Schneider, 'Godly order', pp. 408–95.

[16] William Ames, *Conscience and the Cases Thereof* (np, 1639), v, 12, p. 140. Colonial ministers protested that the godly in England were still 'bone of our bone, and flesh of our flesh in Christ, nearer by farre then friends and kindred', but felt shut out of the 'bosomes and inmost affections of their brethren': William Hooke, *New Englands Teares* (London, 1641), p. 17; John Allin and Thomas Shepard, *A Defence of the Answer unto the Nine Questions* (London, 1648), p. 15.

[17] Edwards, *Gangraena*, 1, p. 69. Firmin claimed Edwards attacked him because he challenged Edwards' reports of New England: *Separation Examined*, pp. 101–2.

[18] Ann Hughes illuminates the relation between print and pulpit controversies in 'The pulpit guarded: confrontations between orthodox and radicals in revolutionary England', in Ann Laurence, W. R. Owens and S. Sim, eds, *John Bunyan and his England* (London, 1990), pp. 31–50.

Church.[19] Scholars now distinguish Hooker's moderate ecclesiology from Cotton's radicalism.[20] If Firmin recognized differences between them, he did not admit it. To show how these New England divines kept faith with their English origins, he looked back further in Essex tradition, to the weighty reputation of Alexander Richardson of Barking, 'whom Dr. Ames and Mr. Hooker, honoured much, and follow much'.[21] Firmin's choice of texts reflects his interest in the Essex community and its New England connections: these were the books he chose to buy, on a small budget.[22] His favourite theme was 'had I not lived in New England, and seene the Churches ther . . . I should have been convinced that Independent (as it is here called) Government, was never of Christs institution.' How scandalized 'Holy Hooker' would have been, if he had lived to hear of disruptions in Essex churches near his old parish. Firmin wished 'we had a few . . . Mr. Nortons in England', who could keep 'the peoples liberty' in order; 'if our Congregationall Churches . . . are gone beyond New England, I only say, farewell.'[23]

[19] He turned most often to Thomas Hooker, *A Survey of the Summe of Church-Discipline* (London, 1648); John Norton, *The Answer to the Whole Set of Questions of . . . Mr. William Apollonius* [London, 1648], trans. Douglas Horton (Cambridge, Mass., 1958); John Cotton, *The Keys of the Kingdom of Heaven* (London, 1644); John Cotton, *The Way of the Churches of Christ in New-England* (London, 1645); [Richard Mather], *Church-Government and Church-Covenant Discussed* (London, 1643); and the 'Cambridge Platform' agreed at a synod in Cambridge, Massachusetts, 1648, and first published as *A Platforme of Church Discipline* (Cambridge, Mass., 1649). Firmin wrote against Owen (*CR*) in 1658: see note 30. After his return to England he corresponded with Thomas Shepard, Cotton, Norton and John Winthrop: Firmin, *Real Christian*, p. 214; idem, *Separation Examined*, 'To the Reader'; idem, *Of Schism*, 'To the . . . Associated Ministers in the County of Essex'; *The Winthrop Papers, 1489–1649*, ed. Allyn B. Forbes, 5 vols (Boston, Mass., 1929–47), 5, pp. 88–9.

[20] David D. Hall, *The Faithful Shepherd: A History of the New England Ministry in the Seventeenth Century*, 2nd edn (New York, 1974), pp. 97–105, 110–11; Baird Tipson, 'Samuel Stone's "Discourse" against requiring Church relations', *William and Mary Quarterly*, ser. 3, 46 (1989), pp. 786–95.

[21] Firmin, *Separation Examined*, p. 80. Cotton Mather wrote of 'our most Richardsonian Hooker': *Magnalia Christi Americana*, 2 vols (Hartford, Conn., 1853), 1, pp. 336–7. For Richardson's influence in Essex and beyond, see Webster, 'Godly of Goshen scattered', p. 58; J. C. Adams, 'Alexander Richardson and the puritan ethic', *JHI*, 50 (1989), pp. 227–48.

[22] Firmin's library was limited by his funds and sympathies, and by information that reached him. He did not own Edwards' *Gangraena*; a tract by Cotton on reconciliation seems to have passed him by. Giles Firmin, *A Sober Reply to the Sober Answer of . . . Mr. Cawdrey* (London, 1653), p. 8; idem, *Serious Question Stated*, 'To the Courteous Reader'; John Cotton, *Certain Queries Tending to Accommodation and Communion of Presbyterian and Congregationall Churches* (London, 1654).

[23] Firmin, *Separation Examined*, 'To the . . . Ministers of London', and pp. 68, 98; idem, *Serious Question Stated*, 'To the Courteous Reader'. Firmin criticized New England's Essex divines in print only in 1670, though his reservations about what Hooker and Shepard taught on preparation for grace are apparent in 1654: Firmin, *The Real Christian* (London, 1670); Firmin to Baxter, 24 July 1654, *Baxter Calendar*, 1, letter 192; James W. Jones, *The Shattered Synthesis* (New Haven, Conn., 1973), pp. 32–53; Knight, *Orthodoxies in Massachusetts*, pp. 164–5.

Thus in an area which had sent many settlers over to New England, he tried to persuade two audiences to recognize its example of orderly, harmonious reform: those who believed the colonies had shattered unity (if not by emigration, then by strange innovations when they got there), and those who used New England to justify a quest for purity that set church against church.

Firmin was prepared to argue that the form of the churches in New England might be appropriate over there, but not over here. He made diversity a matter of circumstance. By this argument – an old Puritan strategy, applied in a new situation – he could appeal beyond differences to the fundamental unity of the godly. His contextual ecclesiology relied on colonial apologists' claims that New England had not cast off England's parish churches as false churches.[24] English critics found this defence unconvincing from 3,000 miles away. Firmin, however, came back to Essex to put the principle into practice. This was his rule: 'You must put a difference between Churches new erecting and these in England, which have been Churches for so long; when I raise a house from new from the ground, I may then doe as I please, but if I be mending of an old house, I must doe as well as I can, repair by degrees.[25] He therefore refused to see a covenant as essential to the form of a church, and condemned those near him who separated from parish churches over this. Although he admired the 'order and comelinesse' New England achieved by church covenants – 'if ever I can attaine it I will' – he believed willingness to accept godly discipline constituted an implicit covenant. This, with faith and good conduct, was all he asked of parishioners in Shalford. Firmin tried to show the sincerity of New England's regard for English churches by interpreting, within a parish setting, the affirmations Hooker and company sent back from outside, across the Atlantic. He joined this with a call to imitate the famous covenant of piety made by Richard

---

[24] Firmin found ample support for this in the texts cited in note 19. Peter Lake, *Moderate Puritans and the Elizabethan Church* (Cambridge, 1981), sheds light on Puritan ingenuity in adapting ideology to circumstance.

[25] Firmin, *Separation Examined*, pp. 82, 20; see also Allin and Shepard, *Defence of the Answer*, p. 10; on primordial churches in New England, Theodore Dwight Bozeman, *To Live Ancient Lives: the Primitivist Dimension in Puritanism* (Chapel Hill, NC, and London, 1988), pp. 120–50.

Rogers' parishioners in Elizabethan Wethersfield: 'Excell those Christians if you can'.[26] Firmin heaped up local credibility for his appeal to older ties of custom and affection when he claimed Daniel Rogers and Stephen Marshall, leading lights in the county, and critics of New England, as his closest collaborators in ministry. He presented his co-operation with Rogers as similar to mutual help between neighbour churches in New England. He elaborated Marshall's teaching on magistrates' duties with recommendations based on colonial practice. He was proud to relate that Rogers and Marshall ordained him at Shalford.[27] Like many clergy in the 1650s, he emphasized the authority of ordained ministry to refute sects who 'scorned the blacke-coats' (legitimate diversity had its limits). He even gained a reputation as a Congregationalist who did not shy away from episcopacy.[28] So Firmin held on to what he valued about New England, but nipped and tucked his ideals to accommodate to his English context, and called for a unity beyond 'circumstantiall things'.

This relativism made him ready to exploit ambiguities in the New England Way. He had a keen eye for aspects of colonial life that uncovered common ground between the parties. For example, though New England's theorists argued that the visible Church could exist only in particular churches (the greatest bone of contention between Congregationalists and Presbyterians), Firmin thought New England showed traces of belief in a universal 'Catholick-visible-Church'. Many settlers acted as if being a member of a particular church meant membership of a wider Church. When they moved to a new town, they took letters of recommendation to the minister there, rather than transfer to a new church: they might live 'many miles, twenty or sixty from their owne churches . . . [and] partake of the Sacraments sixe or eight yeeres together in another Congregation';

---

[26] Firmin, *Sober Reply*, pp. 7–8, 24; idem, *Separation Examined*, pp. 81–2; on the Wethersfield covenant, Patrick Collinson, *The Religion of Protestants* (Oxford, 1982), pp. 269–70.

[27] Firmin, *Sober Reply*, 'To the Courteous Reader' and pp. 7–8; Marshall, [ed. Firmin], *Power of the Civil Magistrate*; Firmin, 'A brief vindication of Mr. Stephen Marshall', appended to his *The Questions Between the Conformist and Nonconformist* (London, 1681); idem, *Separation Examined*, p. 27. Nuttall, 'The Essex Classes', p. 199, notes that Firmin was ordained by neighbour ministers, and not by a Presbyterian Classis: the ministers came from different Classis areas, and the Classical structure for the county existed only on paper.

[28] Firmin, *Serious Question Stated*, 'To the Courteous Reader'; Richard Baxter, *Five Disputations of Church-Government, and Worship* (London, 1659), p. 349; Firmin, *Of Schism* (London, 1658), p. 69.

'one Pastor ... might administer the ... Lords Supper to ... members of five or six Churches at one time.' This behaviour has been seen as a sign of separatism in New England, of lay resistance to ministerial interference.[29] But Firmin used this, and other examples of blurred boundaries between churches, to persuade Congregationalists and Presbyterians that they were not so far apart. To sway his English audience, he singled out strands that showed older concerns for discipline and order taking priority over strict practice of the New England Way.

Could shared commitment to godly discipline create a unity that side-stepped fine details of church government? Such a hope inspired Firmin's campaign for a common statement of pastoral policy among Essex ministers, which led to the Essex Agreement.[30] However, to rely on discipline as a strategy for unity has its perils. Perhaps, like Ralph Josselin in nearby Earls Colne, Firmin's story is of 'sectarian defeat snatched from the jaws of puritan triumph' – he seized his chance to bring in discipline, but pressed the issue to a point where it threatened to destroy parochial ministry.[31] On one hand, Firmin believed in the parish community. He thought it schismatic to 'gather true churches from true churches': New England experience confirmed that each community should have one church; while parish should not be equated with church, a minister's care must be bounded somewhere. He was so averse to the sectarian implications of living in one parish but joining a church in another that he advised lay people who had a mind to do that, to move: 'if you thinke it will hinder you a little in your estate ... friend, they who went to New England for true Liberty of Conscience,

---

[29] Firmin, *Sober Reply*, pp. 28–9; idem, *Separation Examined*, p. 63. Firmin remained a church member in Boston long after his move to Ipswich: Pierce, ed., *Boston Church Records*, p. 41. Foster, *Long Argument*, pp. 178–9, interprets this practice as lay resistance to clerical control. Another ambiguous area was the authority of clerical meetings: Robert F. Scholz, 'Clerical consociation in Massachusetts Bay: reassessing the New England Way and its origins', *William and Mary Quarterly*, ser. 3, 29 (1972), pp. 391–414.

[30] *The Agreement of the Associated Ministers of the County of Essex* (London, 1658). Firmin described the process that led to the Agreement, and quotes a letter from John Norton commending it, in a tract which challenged John Owen's ecclesiology: *Of Schism*, 'To the ... Associated Ministers in the County of Essex'. No record survives of the ministers who subscribed, but their agreed statement was to be 'proposed' to their 'particular congregations', and 'to all such in the County that love the Churches Peace': *Agreement*, titlepage. County Voluntary Association statements each have their own character; the Essex Agreement reflects Firmin's concerns.

[31] Patrick Collinson, 'The English conventicle', *SCH*, 23 (1986), p. 256.

payed dearer for it then you doe here.'[32] On the other hand, Firmin's New England experience made him selective in allowing parishioners access to sacraments. He was as rigorous about baptism as communion, and in this went beyond his Presbyterian neighbours, who might exclude more than half the parish from the Lord's Supper, but freely baptized their children. In Shalford, where 'the strongest Party in the Towne is religious', he had enough support to keep up this discipline; but he admitted some in the parish 'come not to heare me . . . nor will owne the Church in this time of reforming'.[33] Firmin's strategy created unity for some at the cost of excluding others. It is riddled with the ambiguities that had long characterized the Puritan quest for holiness in the midst of parish life.[34] Yet the call for a common stance on pastoral discipline, with its debt to pre-Civil War Puritanism, also characterized Richard Baxter's approach to Christian unity during the Interregnum, and captured the imagination of many as a way to heal the harsh divisions over ecclesiology created in the 1640s.

When Firmin's opponents bruised him by taking his books to pieces, he turned to Baxter for advice. Baxter put the heat of argument into perspective:

Have you travailed over so much of the world, & are you yet such a stranger to it? I could never live a contented life till I had learned to suffer from Godly men, & yet unfeignedly to love them & delight in them. The vexatious part is none of Christs; so far as he appeareth in them they are lovely. . . . If therefore it bee not Christ in his Saints that wee admire, but confusedly embrace them as we find them,

---

[32] Firmin, *Separation Examined*, pp. 107–8; idem, *Serious Question Stated*, 'To the Courteous Reader'.

[33] Firmin, *Serious Question Stated*; idem, *Separation Examined*, p. 45; idem, *Sober Reply*, pp. 22, 54. The Worcestershire Voluntary Association debated this issue: Richard Baxter, *Certain Disputations of Right to Sacraments* (London, 1658), pp. 245–349. Firmin claimed Stephen Marshall left his parochial charge because he was 'unsatisfied . . . to baptize all, yet refuse above halfe the Lords Supper. But now he is out of the snare being onely a lecturer': Firmin to Baxter, 24 July 1654, *Baxter Calendar*, 1, letter 192; see also letter 300.

[34] Patrick Collinson, 'The cohabitation of the faithful with the unfaithful', in O. P. Grell, Jonathan I. Israel, and Nicholas Tyacke, eds, *From Persecution to Toleration. The Glorious Revolution and Religion in England* (Oxford, 1991), pp. 51–76.

we shall have the Prickes with the Rose, & sometime much stinge for a little hony.[35]

Like Baxter, Firmin thought conforming after the Restoration was 'quite another thing than before the wars'. He retired from Shalford to nearby Ridgewell, preached three Sundays in the month, and attended the parish church on the fourth.[36] Energetic debates with conformists and nonconformists did not dim his vision of the communion of saints, whatever the fractures in the English Church: 'At that holy Table, where we being many are one bread . . . I do admit Independents, Presbyterians, & Anabaptists, Members of the Church of England, that . . . walk as Christians . . . here Ecclesiastical Union is chiefly seen.'[37]

Firmin reconciled diversity with unity through his sense of godly community, his belief that an ecclesiology right for one place might not be right in another, and his conviction that pastoral godly discipline took priority over details of church order. With his devotion to 'old Essex Christians', and insistence on the authority of ordained ministry, he might be thought conservative. Yet he applied New England experience to his English context in a bold and independent way that defied party rhetoric. Thomas Edwards reviled the colonial venture, and portrayed those who came back as alienated from it, or as radical sectarians. Firmin gives us a different picture, and his view may not be so different from that of other settlers who returned home without drawing attention to themselves as strident supporters or critics of New England. The local character of his perceptions and strategies is striking, all the more so because his localism embraces transatlantic ties. His case illustrates the complexity of local religious politics and controversy in Cromwellian England; his arguments show how 'Candor, Ingenuitie, Moderation, Love and Peace' can tackle a polemical divide.

King's College London

---

[35]  Baxter to Firmin, 13 May 1656, *Baxter Calendar*, 1, letter 306.

[36]  Firmin, *Real Christian*, 'Epistle Dedicatory'; idem, *Questions Between the Conformist and Nonconformist*, 'Epistle Dedicatory', and p. 5; N. H. Keeble, *The Literary Culture of Nonconformity* (Leicester, 1987), p. 39.

[37]  Firmin, *Weighty Questions Discussed*, 'To the Reader', marginal note. This tract shows Firmin's support in the 1690s for the short-lived 'Happy Union' between Presbyterians and Congregationalists.

# 'THE SUREY DEMONIACK': DEFINING PROTESTANTISM IN 1690S LANCASHIRE

by JONATHAN WESTAWAY and RICHARD D. HARRISON

Between 29 April 1689 and 24 March 1690 a number of Dissenting ministers in northern Lancashire conducted a series of meetings at which they examined the eighteen-year-old Richard Dugdale. A gardener by trade, Dugdale had been exhibiting what he and his family claimed were evidences of demonic possession. The Dissenting ministers involved were all convinced of the supernatural origins of Dugdale's strange behaviour, and over the course of the year regularly prayed and fasted in an attempt to exorcise the young man. These meetings ended as abruptly as they began in March 1690, when the ministers claimed to have successfully exorcised him. Seven years after the final meeting a narative of these events was published by two of the Dissenting minsters involved, a step that provoked a hostile exchange of pamphlets. These pamphlets, commonly referred to as the Surey Demoniack pamphlets, form the basis of this article.[1]

---

[1] Anon. [Thomas Jolly enlarged by John Carrington], *The Surey Demoniack or An Account of Satans Strange and Dreadful Actings In and about the Body of Richard Dugdale of Surey, near of Whalley in Lancashire; And how he was Dispossessed by God's Blessing on the Fastings and Prayers of divers Minister and People. The Matter of Fact attested by the Oaths of Several Credible Persons before some of His Majesty's Justices of the Peace in the said County* (London, 1697) [hereafter *The Surey Demoniack*]; Z. Taylor, *The Surey Imposture: Being an Answer to a late Fanatical Pamphlet Entituled The Surey Demoniack* (London, 1697) [hereafter *The Surey Imposture*]; T. J. [Thomas Jolly], *A Vindication of the Surey Demoniack as no Imposture: or, A Reply to a certain Pamphlet Publish'd by Mr. Zach. Taylor, called The Surey Impostor With a further clearing and Confirming of the Truth as to Richard Dugdale's Case and Cure by T. J. One of the Ministers who attended on that Affair from first to last: but replies only to Matters of Fact, and as he therewithal is more especially concerned. To which is annexed a brief Narrative of the Surey Demoniack, drawn up by the same Author, or the satisfaction of such who have not seen the former Narrative* (London, 1698) [hereafter *Jolly's Vindication*]; N. N., *The Lancashire Levite Rebuk'd: Or, A Vindication of the Dissenters From Popery, Superstition, Ignorance, and Knavery, unjustly Charged on them by Mr. Zachary Taylor, in his Book Entituled, The Surey Imposture. In a Letter to Himself By an Impartial Hand With an Abstract of the Surey Demoniack* (London, 1698) [hereafter *The Lancashire Levite*]; Z. Taylor, *Popery, Superstition, Ignorance, and Knavery, Very Unjustly by a Letter In the General pretended: But as far as was Charg'd very fully proved upon the Dissenters that they were concerned in The Surey Imposture* (London, 1698) [hereafter *Popery, Superstition . . . Knavery*]; N. N., *The Lancashire Levite Rebuk'd: Or, A Farther Vindication Of The Dissenters From Popery, Superstition, Ignorance, and Knavery; Unjustly Charged on Them, By Mr. Zachary Taylor, In his Two Books about the Surey Demoniack. In a Second Letter to Himself* (London, 1698) [hereafter *The Lancashire Levite Farther Rebuk'd*]; Z. Taylor, *Popery, Superstition, Ignorance, and Knavery Confess'd, and fully Proved on the Surey Dissenters from the Second Letter of an Apostate Friend, to Zach. Taylor. To which is added, A Refutation of Mr. T. Jollie's Vindication of the Devil in Dugdale; Or, the Surey Demoniack* (London, 1699) [hereafter cited as distinct works, *Knavery Confess'd* and *A Refutation of the Vindication*].

The case of the Surey Demoniack has not been ignored by historians. In his *History of Witchcraft from 1558 to 1718*, Wallace Notestein briefly detailed the events of the exorcism and the ensuing pamphlet debate within the context of the decline of witchcraft in English society in the later seventeenth century,[2] but dismissed the literary works, saying that, 'the controversy . . . degenerated into a sectarian squabble'.[3] The debate was also mentioned, less dismissively, within the same context by Keith Thomas in *Religion and the Decline of Magic*.[4] In the late nineteenth and early twentieth centuries the historians of Lancashire Nonconformity also utilized the pamphlets.[5] More recently Philip Higson's work on Lancashire Nonconformity has also noted the existence of the pamphlets,[6] but he echoes Notestein's sentiments, stating that 'the statements are too violent to be worth quoting'.[7] Arguably however, the violence and sectarian nature of the pamphlets is their most interesting historical quality, shedding light on the religious and political tensions that existed in Lancashire in the 1690s and the tensions that existed within the Dissenting community.

Lancashire was a fertile breeding ground for these tensions. The county contained, as a proportion of the total population, the largest Dissenting population in England,[8] a large and economically significant Catholic minority, and a vibrant strain of popular Anglicanism:[9] a potentially volatile combination in the context of the recent, and controversial, Toleration Act. The religious diversity of the parish in which the exorcism took place was even greater. Whalley parish contained few Presbyterians,

---

[2] W. Notestein, *A History of Witchcraft in England from 1558 to 1718* (New York, 1965), pp. 315–20.

[3] Ibid., p. 318.

[4] K. Thomas, *Religion and the Decline of Magic: Studies in Popular Belief in Sixteenth and Seventeenth Century England* (London, 1971), p. 585.

[5] See B. Nightingale, *Lancashire Nonconformity: Sketches, Historical and Descriptive, of the Congregational and old Presbyterian Churches in the County*, 6 vols (Manchester, 1890–3); idem, *History of the Old Independent Chapel, Tockholes, near Blackburn* (Manchester, 1886); E. Axon, 'Ellenbrook chapel and its seventeenth century ministers', *Transactions of the Lancashire and Cheshire Antiquarian Society* [hereafter *TLCAS*], 38 (1920), pp. 1–34; F. Nicholson and E. Axon, *The Older Nonconformity in Kendal* (Kendal, 1915).

[6] P. J. W. Higson, 'Some leading promoters of Nonconformity and their association with Lancashire chapelries following the Revolution of 1688', *TLCAS*, 75 (1965–6), pp. 123–63.

[7] Higson, 'Promoters of Nonconformity', p. 163, n. 193.

[8] M. R. Watts, *The Dissenters: From the Reformation to the French Revolution* (Oxford, 1978), p. 509.

[9] J. M. Albers, ' "Seeds of Contention": Society, Politics and the Church of England in Lancashire 1689–1790' (Yale Ph.D. thesis, 1988).

but was home to Quaker, Baptist, and Independent meetings. The parish covered 106,000 acres,[10] and contained fifteen chapels of ease, many inadequately funded and poorly supplied.[11] This religious diversity and the political development of Lancashire under James II[12] meant that in the 1690s the relationship between the county's Tory Anglicans and its Dissenters was stormy. Tensions also existed within the Protestant Dissenting community which in many ways mirrored national developments concerning the Happy Union of Presbyterians and Congregationalists. The pamphlets provide a wealth of material that highlights the deep religious tensions within and between Protestant groupings. The first section of this paper seeks to place the pamphlets within the context of the Lancashire Dissenting community and the tensions it experienced in maintaining the County Association in the aftermath of the Toleration Act. The next section analyses the debate in the later pamphlets over the nature of true Protestantism, where a traditional high church-low church dichotomy emerged. The final section relates this debate to the political tension existing in Lancashire between Dissenters and Anglicans. It becomes apparent from this that Lancashire in the 1690s was riven by competing religious ideologies which had rival power bases in different parts of the county. In consequence Protestant disunity became a cause of significant political conflict within the county.

I

The Independent Thomas Jolly[13] was the main proponent of the attempted exorcism, assisted by other Nonconformist ministers.

[10] R. C. Richardson, *Puritanism in North West England: A Regional Study of the Diocese of Chester to 1642* (Manchester, 1972), p. 15.

[11] F. Gastrell, *Notitia Cestrensis, or Historic Notice of the Diocese of Chester*, ed. F.R. Raines, 2 vols in 4, Chetham Society, 1st ser., 8, 19, 21–2 (Manchester, 1845–50), 2/i, pp. 297–347.

[12] L. K. J. Glassey, *Politics and the Appointment of Justices of the Peace, 1675–1720* (Oxford, 1979), pp. 274–7.

[13] Henry Fishwick, *The Note Book of the Rev. Thomas Jolly, AD 1671–1693; Extracts from the Church Book of Altham and Wymondhouses, AD 1649–1725; and An Account of the Jolly Family of Standish, Gorton, and Altham*, Chetham Society, ns 33 (Manchester, 1894); Nightingale, *Lancashire Nonconformity*, 1, passim; A.G. Matthews, *Calamy Revised, being a Revision of Edmund Calamy's Account of the Ministers and Others Ejected and Silenced, 1660–2* (Oxford, 1934), p. 301; A. Gordon, *Freedom after Ejection: A Review (1690–92) of Presbyterian and Congregational Nonconformity in England and Wales* (Manchester, 1917), p. 293.

The case ran from 29 April 1689 until 24 March 1690, ending when the ministers were satisfied with the demoniac's assertion that he was cured.[14] Whilst attracting large crowds at the time, the ministers did not go into print with their version of events until 1697. The intervening period saw the inception and decay of the national union of Presbyterians and Independents under the Heads of Agreement,[15] and the publication of *The Surey Demoniack* must be seen in the light of the increasing tension between the Presbyterians and Independents that wrecked the national union and strained relations within the Lancashire County Association.

Thomas Jolly vigorously promoted county associations in the 1690s as he had promoted regional co-operation in the 1650s.[16] For Jolly union was only part of a more general reformation. There is no doubt that Jolly understood the evangelical potential of the exorcism to facilitate renewal.[17] In its local context the event served many purposes. In succeeding in an exorcism where the local Catholic priests had failed, it would demonstrate the illegitimacy of the Church of Rome, weakening the local priests' hold over plebeian recusants.[18] It gave the Protestant Dissenters the advantage over the established clergy, the English Church having abandoned the priestly office of the exorcist in an ordinal of 1550.[19] A proven crowd puller, the exorcism served in the local context to fix the attention of the laity in a rural and sparsely populated parish on a religious rite with obvious implications for the unrepentant and on the Nonconformist ministers' claims to legitimate spiritual authority. *The Surey Demoniack*

---

[14] *The Surey Demoniack*, p. 1.

[15] Watts, *The Dissenters*, pp. 289–97.

[16] G. F. Nuttall, 'Assemblies and Association in Dissent, 1689–1831', *SCH*, 7 (1971), pp. 298–9 and 302. Minutes for fifteen general meetings of the Lancashire Association, April 1693–August 1700, were published in an appendix to William A. Shaw, ed., *Minutes of the Manchester Presbyterian Classis, 1646–1660*, part 3, Chetham Society, ns 24 (Manchester, 1891), pp. 349–64. They provide evidence that delegates from the Northern District of the Association, especially Jolly, were a fractious element.

[17] *Jolly's Vindication*, p. iv: 'Another great end was, that we might take the opportunity to serve the saving good of those multitudes that resorted to the meetings upon this occassion: However that it might bear a Testimony for God and against the impenitent.'

[18] *The Surey Demoniack*, p. 21: 'Seven Romanists, whereof Two at least seem'd Priests, did one Mid-night undertake Richard in his fit, where Satan, and some of the seven did long talk to one another in a Language unknown.' More generally see B. G. Blackwood, 'Plebeian catholics in later Stuart Lancashire', *NH*, 25 (1989), pp. 153–73.

[19] Thomas, *Religion and the Decline of Magic*, p. 571.

went into print seven years later, however, offered as a proof of a supernatural providence, an attempt to counter not only the generally perceived atheism of the age after the lapsing of the Licensing Act in 1695 but more specifically the threat, perceived by many orthodox Protestant Dissenters, of heterodox tendencies amongst Presbyterians of an Arminian persuasion. The publishing history of the manuscript indicates that it was written and re-written to fit into an international effort to provide evidences of illustrious providences, proofs of the supernatural that would thereby prove the existence of God. One of the contentions of this paper is that *The Surey Demoniack* cannot be understood without reference to Thomas Jolly's epistolatory relationship with one of the main speculators on God's wondrous providences, the Rev. Increase Mather of Boston, Massachusetts.

Presbyterianism had dominated Lancashire Nonconformity during the Interregnum. Independency was consequently weak[20] and this imbalance continued after the passing of the Toleration Act.[21] Michael Watts has argued, however, for the strength of Independent polity through a reliance upon a complicated nexus of national and international ties. Independent churches were 'inheritors of an ecclesiastical system which had been tried and developed in the Netherlands and New England'.[22] The influence of the Mather family on Thomas Jolly was one of the key factors influencing his eventual decision to go into print over the Surey business, and therefore demands a brief preliminary outline.

Jolly had links with both Samuel and Nathaniel Mather. It is, however, the influence of Increase Mather on Thomas Jolly that is the most striking. There is no direct evidence that Jolly and Increase Mather ever met but they did have a number of significant mutual friends.[23] Jolly opened a correspondence with Increase on 2 April 1677 with a letter that cried up the need for a

---

[20] Watts, *The Dissenters*, p. 281, for an explanation of the weakness of Independency in Lancashire.

[21] Ibid., pp. 267–89 and 491–510. Watts's analysis of the Evans List *c.*1715–19 enumerated 42 Presbyterian congregations in Lancashire with 16,630 hearers, representing 8.48% of an estimated county population of 196,120. This was the highest percentage of Presbyterians in any county in England. The Evans List records only 3 Independent congregations in Lancashire, with 1,370 hearers, 0.70% of the population. These 3 were all in sparsely populated upland parishes.

[22] Ibid., pp. 167–8.

[23] Notably Sir Henry Ashurst, Bart (1642–1711): ibid., pp. 220–1; Fishwick, *Note Book*, pp. 27–8. Gary Stuart Krey, *A Fractured Society: the Politics of London in the First Age of Party, 1688–1715* (Oxford, 1985), p. 89.

reformation amongst the reformed Churches, and flattering Increase with the notion that he was the watchman on the walls of
Jerusalem, God's agent for reform.[24] Jolly wrote again in January
1678, suggesting to Increase that a reforming synod be held in
Massachusetts for the revival of religion.[25] Mather was receptive
to the idea, having been preaching covenant renewal since his
year-end sermon in March 1677, and he began working towards
the great reforming synod that convened in September 1679.[26]
After the close of the synod in 1681 a general meeting of ministers
in Massachusetts set in motion a project for the recording of
illustrious providences. Mather took up the task and the scheme
came to fruition in several works,[27] most notably *An Essay for the
Recording of Illustrious Providences*. The evidence is that Jolly read
*Illustrious Providences*[28] and that it had a profound effect on him.
Jolly's own deeply providential view of the world was confirmed
by one of the most eminent scholar-divines of his day, and an
examination of the text of *The Surey Demoniack* suggests that
*Illustrious Providences* became something of a *vade-mecum* for Jolly.
The preface of *Illustrious Providences* ends with an exhortation to
continue the work of amassing the providences that Increase
Mather had begun, and *The Surey Demoniack* must also be seen in
the light of this commission. The flattering relationship with the
pre-eminent New England divine of his day reinforced Jolly's
providentialism, providing him with the intellectual support so
vital to an isolated Independent minister. The example of Increase
Mather showed that it was the task of God's ministers to bear
witness by gathering wonders, and *The Surey Demoniack* was
intended to be read alongside other works of a similar nature.

The publishing history of *The Surey Demoniack* links it with an
international effort to provide evidences of the supernatural.

[24] *The Mather Papers*, Collections of the Massachusetts Historical Society, 4th ser., 8 (Boston, 1868),
pp. 317–19.

[25] Ibid., pp. 319–22. Two further letters are extant, discussing covenant renewal and the synod, pp.
322–7. From Jolly's Note Book we know that Jolly also received a letter from Increase in December
1677, discussing the Half-Way Covenant, Fishwick, *Note Book*, pp. 32–3.

[26] Michael Hall, *The Last American Puritan the Life of Increase Mather, 1639–1723* (Wesleyan, Conn.,
1988), pp. 148–54.

[27] Ibid., pp. 170–4. Increase Mather, *Kometographia, Or a Discourse Concerning Comets* (Boston, 1683);
*The Doctrine of Divine Providence* (Boston, 1684); and *An Essay for the Recording of Illustrious Providences*
(Boston, 1684).

[28] In *Jolly's Vindication*, p. 47, Jolly cites learned sources on the signs of possession: James I, Cudworth
and 'Mr. Mather's Essay as to remarkable providences'.

Richard Baxter, who had just provided the commendatory epistle for Cotton Mather's second edition of *Late Memorable Providences*[29] requested six letters from Thomas Jolly detailing the events of the Surey case[30] for inclusion in his *Certainty of the World of the Spirits* (1691). Jolly claimed that the plan to include his Surey material died upon Baxter's death in December 1691. The manuscripts seem to have been in London in some incomplete form when 'another Reverend London Divine desired that it should be printed, as an Appendix to Mr. Increase Mather's Book; called *A Further Account of the Trials of New England Witches* AD 1693.'[31] Jolly's work not being completed and certified, it failed to be included. It seems most likely that Nathaniel Mather was handling Increase's publishing interests in London at the time,[32] and that it was he who requested Jolly's material. Nathaniel Mather and Thomas Jolly were corresponding throughout 1690 and 1691, Nathaniel outlining his opposition to the Happy Union and explaining his refusal to sign the Heads of Agreement.[33] Nathaniel Mather's fears that Congregational principles were being betrayed and Congregational sovereignty eroded may well have diminished Thomas Jolly's confidence in the Lancashire Association. Jolly already had a stormy relationship with many local Presbyterians, not least for his promotion of the Surey case. As tensions developed nationally between

---

[29] Cotton Mather, *Memorable Providences, Relating to Witchcrafts and Possessions* (Boston, 1689), *Late Memorable Providences Relating to Witchcraft and Possession. The Second Impression. Recommended by the Reverend Mr. Richard Baxter in London, and by the Ministers of Boston and Charlestown in New England* (London, 1691). N. H. Keeble and G. F. Nuttall, eds, *The Calendar and Correspondence of Richard Baxter*, Vol. 2, 1660–1696 (Oxford, 1991), p. 307.

[30] *The Surey Demoniack*, Preface, first page.

[31] *The Surey Demoniack*, Preface, refering to Increase Mather, *A Further Account of the Tryals of the New England Witches* (London, 1693), published with *Cases of Conscience*. It is perhaps ironic that had *The Surey Demoniack* been bound with this edition it would have appeared alongside Increase Mather's *Cases of Conscience Concerning Evil Spirits*. First published in Boston in 1682, it contained Increase's critique of the use of spectral evidence in the Salem witchcraft trials, demanding a stronger basis of evidence in capital cases concerning witchcraft. Therefore by the 1690s even Mather was moving away from simplistic providentialism and was applying a more empiricist approach.

[32] Nathaniel was a keen promoter and contributor to his brother's works. He provided Increase with stories for *Illustrious Providences*; see David D. Hall, *Worlds of Wonder, Days of Judgment: Popular Religious Belief in Early New England* (New York, 1989), p. 85. He contributed a sermon to Increase's *The Doctrine of Divine Providence* and saw into print Samuel's sermons *Iren* (London, 1680), and Samuel's magnum opus, *Figures and Types in the Old Testament*, which went into print in London in 1683 and 1685, reprinting in 1695.

[33] London, Dr Williams's Library, MS 12.78.7, Nathaniel Mather to Thomas Jolly, 3 April 1691: 'Not that I am against communion with Presbyterian churches but this way of proceeding I look on as sinful.'

Presbyterians and Congregationalists the unresolved issues of church government and polity became subsumed in attacks on perceived theological differences. Nathaniel Mather figured prominently in a campaign to counter Arminian tendencies amongst ministers of the Union. By the autumn of 1695 the national Union was in tatters, many Congregationalists having dropped out of the management of the Common Fund.[34] Such was the fear at the time of the dread heresy of Socinianism that many orthodox Protestant Dissenters were willing to campaign against leading Presbyterians, petitioning the King and contributing to the paranoia that ended in the passing of the Blasphemy Act of 1698.[35]

As fears of heterodoxy grew after the lapsing of the Licensing Act, Jolly, in July 1695, showed renewed vigour in promoting the Surey case, getting over thirty people to put their names to depositions as to what they had witnessed at Surey.[36] Jolly, in the preface to *The Surey Demoniack*, made it clear that the work was intended to counter the baneful influence of heterodox theology and free-thinking: 'Many such eminent Divines, Physicians, and others urged the publication hereof as very likely expedient for rooting out Atheism, Debauchery, Sadducism and Devilishness.'[37] Jolly seems to have got little support from eminent divines in Lancashire, however, and apparently generated only hostility from the local Presbyterians. He had often quarrelled with the Presbyterian Richard Frankland who ran the Dissenting Academy at Rathmell in the West Riding, and apparently had a major argument concerning an ordination in Craven early in 1691. Zachary Taylor made much of Jolly's arguing with the Presbyterians,[38] claiming that Henry Pendlebury, one of the ministers loosely associated with the exorcism, changed his mind over whether it was a genuine dispossession and that he had evidence that the local Presbyterians had tried to suppress it.[39]

---

[34] C. G. Bolam, J. Goring, H. L. Short and R. Thomas, *The English Presbyterians: From Elizabethan Puritanism to Modern Unitarianism* (London, 1968), pp. 102–25.

[35] Ibid., p. 122.

[36] *The Surey Demoniack*, pp. 51–64.

[37] Ibid., Preface.

[38] Taylor, *Popery, Superstition, . . . Knavery*, p. 10.

[39] Matthews, *Calamy Revised*, p. 386. R. Halley, *Lancashire, Its Puritanism and Nonconformmity* (Manchester, 1869), pp. 175 and 177–8; Taylor, *Popery, Superstition, . . . Knavery*, p. 17; 'I confes, an ingenious friend of mine, a Dissenting Minister, intimated to me his Endeavours to supress that pamphlet.'

Perhaps most damaging to Jolly were the deep reservations expressed by Oliver Heywood, conveyed in a letter, that the ministers' disputations with the Devil in Dugdale were not sanctioned in Scripture and might prejudice the Dissenters' credibility.[40]

*The Surey Demoniack* thus underwent revisions as Presbyterian and Independent tensions heightened. Jolly's health deteriorated markedly in the 1690s, and most of the writing of *The Surey Demoniack* seems to have been undertaken by another of the ministers who officiated at the exorcism, John Carrington of Lancaster. The case is written up in a manner that seems highly programmatic, for instance fulfilling all of Increase Mather's six indications of a genuine possession outlined in chapter six of *Illustrious Providences*.[41] and reproducing some highly unusual evidences straight out of the literature on John Darrel's supposed exorcisms *c.*1596–9.[42] As with so much of the material on wonders and the supernatural, as David Hall has pointed out, 'experience coincided with the narrative tradition'.[43] The doctrine of divine providence tended to be self-confirming,[44] and the events the Nonconformist ministers witnessed in 1689 confirmed their worldview and were interpreted in the light of other literary evidence. One suspects the years between the event and publication did nothing to diminish this. Their perceptions were governed by the world in which they lived, a providential world where God sent portents to draw men to repentance. Whatever doubts Jolly expressed over the exact nature of the possession, the scholarship of Increase Mather reinforced his belief 'that there are Devils infesting this lower world',[45] and Nathaniel Mather provided him with the opportunity to strike a blow at those who might say it was not so. This view was however on the wane in the 1680s and 1690s, when many old Puritans were waging a last-ditch defence of the doctrine of special providences against the new mechanical philosophy.[46] Even as the *Surey*

[40] London, Dr Williams's Library, MS 12.78.7, Papers of Thomas Jolly.

[41] Increase Mather, *An Essay for the Recording of Illustrious Providences* (New York, 1977), pp. 168–9.

[42] D. P. Walker, *Unclean Spirits: Possession and Exorcism in France and England in the Late Sixteenth and Early Seventeenth Centuries* (1981), pp. 52–73. Thomas, *Religion and the Decline of Magic*. pp. 576–80.

[43] Hall, *Worlds of Wonders*, p. 85.

[44] Thomas, *Religion and the Decline of Magic*, p. 95.

[45] Increase Mather, *Illustrious Providences*, p. 168.

[46] Thomas, *Religion and the Decline of Magic*, p. 128. Perry Miller, *The New England Mind* (New York, 1939), p. 229.

*Demoniack* went into print in 1697 the impetus that brought it to publication waned with the death of Nathaniel Mather in July of that year, and with it much of the fire went out of metropolitan Congregationalism's opposition to Baxterian Arminianism and the Union.[47]

## II

*The Surey Demoniack* prompted a rapid response from Zachary Taylor, a clergyman with strong links with the local Anglican hierarchy, whose previous foray into print journalism had been an important contribution to the Allegiance controversy of the early 1690s.[48] Taylor's *The Surey Imposture* moved the debate on from consideration of the evidences of the possession and exorcism, and with the intervention of the mysterious N. N. into the debate in 1698 the controversy mutated into a consideration of the religious and political divisions of English Protestants, in the nation as a whole, and in Lancashire particularly. Zachary Taylor's critique of Protestant Dissent merits further attention, to examine implications with reference to the relationship of Church and State and the true aims, as Taylor perceived them, of Dissenters, and to explore the relationship between this debate on the nature of true Protestantism and the political and religious divisions that existed in 1690s Lancashire.[49]

---

[47] Bolam et al., *The English Presbyterians*, p. 123.

[48] The relevant pamphlets are [Z. Taylor], *Obedience and Submission to the Present Government Demonstrated from Bishop Overall's Convocation-book* (London, 1690) and [Z. Taylor], *The Vindication of a Late Pamphlet, (Entituled, Obedience and Submission to the Present Government. Demonstrated from Bp. Overal's Convocation-book) from the False Glosses, and Illusive Interpretations of a Pretended Answer* (London, 1691). For the Allegiance Controversy in general see M. A. Goldie, 'The Revolution of 1689 and the structure of political argument: an essay and an annotated bibliography of pamphlets on the Allegiance Controversy', *Bulletin of Research in the Humanities*, 83 (1980), pp. 473–564.

[49] The links between political and religious division in the 1690s have been explored in works by G. V. Bennet, *The Tory Crisis in Church and State 1688–1730: The Career of Francis Atterbury Bishop of Rochester* (Oxford, 1975); 'Conflict in the Church', in G. S. Holmes, ed., *Britain after the Glorious Revolution 1689–1714* (London, 1969), pp. 155–75; 'King William III and the Episcopate', in G. V. Bennet and J. D. Walsh eds, *Essays in Modern Church History in Memory of Norman Sykes* (London, 1966), pp. 104–31. See also G. S. Holmes, *Religion and Politics in Late Stuart England* (London, 1975); idem, *The Making of a Great Power: Late Stuart and Early Hanoverian Britain 1660–1722* (London, 1993); idem, 'Post-Revolution Britain and the Historian', in Holmes, *Britain after the Glorious Revolution*, pp. 1–38.

The tradition of English anti-Catholicism was well established by the 1690s.[50] In the series of Surey Demoniack pamphlets Zachary Taylor attempted to exploit this deep-rooted prejudice and prove that the Dissenters, as a group, were, 'the constant Tools of Popery'.[51] In *The Surey Imposture*, Taylor claimed that the Dissenting ministers involved in the alleged exorcism had naively allowed themselves to be taken advantage of by local Catholic priests.[52] Taylor plainly states that it was the papists who were notorious for fabricating cases of demonic possession which would give them the opportunity to show the superiority of the Catholic faith to Protestantism, and claims that the case of *The Surey Demoniack* was just such an instance.[53] Taylor asserted that the demoniac's father, Thomas Dugdale, was a lapsed Catholic who had recently reconverted and had been persuaded by the Catholics to allow his son to be used to fool the Dissenting ministers. Richard was stubbornly to resist their ministrations, only to be miraculously delivered by local Catholic priests.[54] The picture that emerged from *The Surey Imposture* was that of a hopelessly naive group of Dissenting ministers being taken advantage of by manipulative Catholics attempting to undermine English Protestantism.[55] The other strand of Taylor's argument linked Dissenters' beliefs far more directly to Catholicism. Taylor argued that the Dissenting ministers' vulnerability to the Catholics' deception was rooted in a series of superstitious beliefs that were distinctly popish.[56] This two-pronged argument therefore attempted to undermine both the specific claims of the Dissenting ministers concerning Richard Dugdale, and to attack

---

[50] See C. Z. Weiner 'The beleaguered isle: a study of Elizabethan and early Jacobean anti-Catholicism', *PaP*, 51 (1971), pp. 27–62; P. Lake, 'Anti-Popery: the structure of a prejudice', in R. Cust and A. Hughes, eds, *Conflict in Early Stuart England: Studies in Politics and Religion 1603–1642* (London, 1989), pp. 72–106; R. Clifton, 'The Popular Fear of Catholics during the English Revolution', *PaP*, 52 (1971), pp. 23–55; J. Miller, *Popery and Politics in England 1660–1688* (Cambridge, 1973); J. P. Kenyon, *The Popish Plot* (London, 1972); J. Scott, 'England's troubles: exhuming the Popish Plot', in T. Harris, P. Seaward and M. A. Goldie, eds, *The Politics of Religion in Restoration England* (Oxford, 1990), pp. 107–31; C. Haydon, *Anti-Catholicism in Eighteenth Century England c.1714–1780: A Political and Social Study* (Manchester, 1990).

[51] *The Surey Imposture*, p. 58.

[52] Ibid., p. 1.

[53] Ibid., p. 58.

[54] Ibid., p. 59.

[55] Ibid., pp. 67–9.

[56] Taylor sets this relationship up in the preface to *The Surey Imposture*, and continues to explore it throughout the pamphlet.

the claims of the Dissenting minsters, and by implication Dissenters as a whole, to be called true Protestants. In his reply to this attack Thomas Jolly attempted to rebut this claim, instead pointing out that it was high-church Anglicans who had 'block't up . . . the Cause of Reformation'.[57] This attempt to reverse Taylor's argument so that it was the high-church Anglicans who were seen to be crypto-papists failed, however, to prevent the clergyman elaborating on the link between Dissent and Catholicism in his later pamphlets.

In these pamphlets Taylor confidently asserted many of the traditional high-church arguments of a link between Dissenters and popery. Taylor referred back to what he portrayed as the Puritan execution of Charles I and asked of the Dissenters, 'pray tell me whose Tools they were, when they cut off the Royal Martyr's Head',[58] and revived the theory that by executing Charles the Puritans had been fulfilling, either wittingly or unwittingly, the popish aim of destroying the Anglican Church-State. Taylor was concerned to show that the separation of the Dissenters from the Church of England weakened the Protestant cause in England, and was thus a stage in the re-establishment of Catholicism, calling into question the Protestantism of the Dissenters. Taylor also used more recent history in an attempt to link Dissenters and Catholics as threats to the Church-State. He raised the number of loyal addresses and speeches sent to James II by Dissenters upon the issuing of the Declaration of Indulgence in 1687,[59] and draws particular attention to the visit of Lancashire and Cheshire's Dissenting ministers to Chester in August 1687.[60] Taylor tells his readers, 'you will understand, whose Creatures then they were . . . that they might gad to Chester when King James came there, to complement a Popish King'.[61] The implied criticism of the Dissenters' links to the Catholic and arbitrary James is made explicit in *Popery, Superstition . . . Knavery*, where he openly contrasted the loyalty of the Dissenters to the Catholic James, bent on destroying the legally

[57] *Jolly's Vindication*, p. 43.
[58] *Popery, Superstition, . . . Knavery*, p. 4.
[59] Ibid., p. 5.
[60] See *The Diary of Dr Thomas Cartwright, Bishop of Chester*, Camden Society, 1st ser., 22 (1843), pp. 74–6.
[61] *Popery, Supersition, . . . Knavery*, p. 5.

established church, with the Puritans' treacherous behaviour to Charles I, a monarch whose prime concern was the preservation of the Anglican Church-State.[62] Taylor invites the reader to come to his own conclusions, but clearly intended that the Dissenters should be seen as the Protestant fifth column whose actions would prepare the way for the re-establishment of Catholicism. In *Knavery Confess'd* Taylor's links between popery and Dissent are augmented by his claim that the reasoning N. N. uses in *The Lancashire Levite* and *The Lancashire Levite Farther Rebuk'd* could also be used to justify the Catholic faith. N. N. had argued that although Taylor may be right to question the possession of Richard Dugdale, the Dissenting ministers sincerely believed that they were dealing with a genuine possession, and this excused them from Taylor's charge that they were as superstitious as the Catholics. Taylor gave this argument short shrift, stating that the sincerity of a belief did not stop that belief being superstitious, and pointedly commented that, 'Mr. Pope, and the rest, do not make a superstition of it, but do verily believe that there is a purgatory'.[63]

Taylor also denied the true Protestantism of the Dissenters by arguing that they were an unjustifiable splinter from the true, Anglican, Church. Taylor first made this explicit when he talked of the Dissenters' 'Unchristian division from us,'[64] which he attributed to their 'blind Zeal and the Spirit of division'.[65] In *The Lancashire Levite*, N. N. came to the defence of the Dissenters, pointing out that there was no disagreement between Anglicans and Dissenters on points of doctrine, and that the division was occasioned by disputes over Anglican ceremony which many within the Church of England thought to be too harsh and prescriptive, making compulsory that which should have been optional.[66] N. N. in fact put forward the classic low-church Anglican, comprehensionist perspective,[67] best expressed in his desire that 'there be Unity in all things necessary, Liberty in all

---

[62] *Knavery Confess'd* p. 9.
[63] Ibid., p. 10.
[64] *The Surey Imposture*, p. 69.
[65] Ibid., p. 75.
[66] *The Lancashire Levite*, pp. 12–13.
[67] Bennet, 'King William III and the Episcopate', p. 129 shows that in 1696 and 1697, as the demoniack debate was in progress, Archbishop Tennison floated the idea of reviving comprehension in London circles.

things not necessary, and in both Charity'.[68] In *The Lancashire Levite Farther Rebuk'd*, N. N. elaborated on this when he states that 'The Ch. of E. have it in their Power at any time, to remove the Schism so much complain'd of [if they] Take but away all that Christ hath not commanded, as Terms of Communion, and the Schism ceases'.[69] Taylor however would have none of this. To him all of the articles of the Anglican Church were doctrinal in nature, none of them inessential.[70] Taylor emphasized the duty of loyalty and obedience to church leaders in all things,[71] and stressed this point with reference to the fate of Corah, Dathon, and Abiram as detailed in Numbers 16.[72] He showed how these three separated from Moses over the issue of Aaron's role in church government, while maintaining the same articles of faith that the main body of the Church did, and how this led to God's punishment by the three leaders being swallowed up by the earth and over 250 of their followers being engulfed in fire.[73] He then drew the obvious parallel:

> to avoid the guilt of Corah's Sin, it is not enough to own and admit the Doctrines of a Church, for that Corah did; but they must peaceable submit to its Governours, and not oppose them, by setting up other Minsters, and other Worship against them, for that was Corah's Sin . . . they [the Dissenters] Divide from their Lawful Church-Governours, and consequently by their own Confession, are justly charged with sinful Divisions.[74]

N. N. sought to justify the separation of Dissenters from the Church of England by claiming that it was no different from the Church of England's separation from Rome.[75] This received equally short shrift from Taylor, who stated that there was the world of difference between separation due to the Catholic distortion of true Christianity, through the addition of unbiblical

---

[68] *The Lancashire Levite*, p. 30.
[69] *The Lancashire Levite Farther Rebuk'd*, p. 11.
[70] *Knavery Confess'd*, p. 15.
[71] *Popery, Supersition, . . . Knavery*, p. 8.
[72] *Knavery Confess'd*, pp. 15–17.
[73] Num. 16. 28–35.
[74] *Knavery Confess'd*, p. 17.
[75] *The Lancashire Levite Farther Rebuk'd*, p. 10.

articles of faith, and schism caused by petty disagreements over ceremonies.[76] Taylor was, of course, wilfully ignoring N. N.'s oft-made point that the importance attached by the Church of England to the 1662 Prayer Book and the forms of service laid down there effectively meant that new articles of faith had been imposed, such as kneeling at communion and the use of the cross in baptism,[77] but the fact remains that he was determined to question the claims of Dissenters to be considered a legitimate Church. He attempted to place further doubt upon the Dissenters' legitimacy by calling into question their attitudes towards the 'Glorious Reformers'.[78] Taylor asserted that the Anglican form of service was established at the time of the Reformation, and that the Church of England 'retain'd what we innocently could, and receded no further from the Church of Rome than she had receded from her self and the Primitive Church'.[79] Having stated that the Reformation had established the true Church according to the rites of the primitive Church, it followed from Taylor's argument that the Dissenters had deviated from true Protestantism as it had been established by the Reformers.[80] Taylor needed no encouragement to use this excuse to return to the theme that papists and the Dissenters were cosy bedfellows: 'The Papists cannot but thank you for this, and pray consider whose Tool you are, when you affirm these Glorious Reformers, not only to be Proud and Conceited, but to assume an authority that did not belong to them'.[81]

Therefore, as the pamphlet war went on, Zachary Taylor attempted to deny the true Protestantism of the Dissenters by attacking what he saw as their unjustified schism from the Church of England, the home of true Protestantism. He accepted that the Dissenters may well subscribe the doctrinal articles of Anglicanism, but nevertheless argued that all true Protestants must submit to their lawful church governors in all matters and are not allowed to declare articles concerned with church discipline to be optional. By doing this Taylor stated that

---

[76] *Knavery Confess'd*, pp. 18–19.
[77] *The Lancashire Levite*, pp. 12–13; *The Lancashire Levite Farther Rebuk'd*, pp. 12–17.
[78] *Knavery Confess'd*, p. 27.
[79] Ibid., p. 29.
[80] Ibid., pp. 27–9.
[81] Ibid., p. 27.

the Dissenters were no better than schismatics whose religious legitimacy was therefore greatly undermined.

## III

Taylor's vigorous attack on the Dissenters has to be placed in a local, Lancashire context. In many ways the pamphlet war was a re-run of the debates between high-church Anglicans, low-church Anglicans and Dissenters. To take this view would, however, be short-sighted, as the fierce debate briefly detailed here was given a sharp contemporary edge by the increasingly bitter disputes between Anglicans and Dissenters in Lancashire in the 1690s. By examining disputes over the composition of the local bench,[82] and the possession of Lancashire's chapels of ease, it becomes clear that, far from being an irrelevant anachronism, the debate sparked off by the publication of *The Surey Demoniack* both reflected and exacerbated a tense religious and political climate in Lancashire in the 1690s.

In 1689 Lord Brandon was appointed to be Lord Lieutenant of Lancashire. He had, however, a strong Whig political background, and had assisted James II in his attempts to repeal the penal laws and Test Acts in 1688. This made many of the established Lancashire gentry, especially Tories allied to the Earl of Derby, unwilling to work with Brandon. In consequence he was forced to establish for himself an alternative political base amongst the county's Whig gentry and prominent local Dissenters. Over the next ten years Brandon therefore pursued a policy of gradually excluding political opponents from local office in favour of his supporters, a significant number of whom were Dissenters. Brandon's attempts to include Dissenters on Lancashire's bench became a focus for Anglican resentment. The attempts to exclude Tories,[83] in favour of local Whigs and Dissenters,[84] were most successful in the aftermath of the Assassina-

---

[82] Much of the ground regarding the composition of Lancashire's Commission of the Peace is covered in Glassey, *Politics and Justices of the Peace*, pp. 277–85, and it is only intended to give a brief outline of this admirable analysis here.
[83] Ibid., pp. 277–85.
[84] Ibid., pp. 280–1.

tion Plot of 1696,[85] and it is in this period that we find the most vigorous Anglican exception expressed to the promotion of Dissenters to the bench. For example in 1694 the Anglican gentleman Thomas Marsden commented to the Clitheroe MP Roger Kenyon that 'I have your description of some of our new justices, and it is well our Lord-Lieutenant so frankly exhibits his inclination to undo, at least, our Church government'.[86] In 1696 Roger Kenyon himself felt moved to complain to the secretary of the Chancellor of the Duchy of Lancaster about 'some . . . of the Dissenters, [who] rather than be kept from their office, for a time will come receive the sacrament, though they never come to church againe'.[87] Therefore Brandon's need to form an alternative power base, and its consequent effect on the composition of the commission of the peace, caused conflict between Anglicans and Dissenters. This conflict reached its peak just when Zachary Taylor was launching his offensive against the Dissenting interest. The relevance of Taylor's attempts to undermine the legitimacy of Protestant Dissent to this conflict is unlikely to have been accidental and certainly would not have been lost on his Lancashire readership.

The Lancashire readership would also have had a keen sense of the relevance of Taylor's linking of Dissent and Catholicism, particularly in depicting Dissenters as a Protestant fifth column paving the way for a re-establishment of Catholicism. Lancashire Anglicans still had vivid memories of James II's attempts in 1687 and 1688 to repeal the penal laws and Test Acts, when loyal Anglicans were unceremoniously removed from local office in favour of Lancashire Catholics and Dissenters, in preparation for the calling of a parliament to repeal this legislation. The most dramatic of these purges came in April 1688, when a new commission of the peace removed virtually the entire Lancashire establishment from the bench, replacing them with between twenty-five and thirty-three Catholics and fifteen to eighteen Dissenters and Whig collaborators.[88] Among the new justices was

---

[85] Ibid., p. 282.

[86] *Historical Manuscripts Commission [HMC]: 14th Report, Appendix, Part IV: The Manuscripts of Lord Kenyon* (London, 1894), no. 870, pp. 291–2: Thomas Marsden to Roger Kenyon, 2 April 1694.

[87] Ibid., no. 1034, pp. 411–12: Roger Kenyon to Guicciardini Wentworth, 13 September 1696.

[88] Glassey, *Politics and Justices of the Peace*, pp. 275–7.

Brandon, and he and the recently appointed Catholic Lord Lieutenant, Viscount Molyneux, became the central figures in the attack upon the Tory Anglican elites which had come to dominate Lancashire's incorporated boroughs by the 1680s.[89] Lancaster and Wigan suffered most, with loyal Anglicans being abruptly removed from corporation offices to make way for Dissenters and Catholics prepared to smooth the election of MPs ready to end the Anglican monopoly of office-holding.[90] By the end of 1688, 'virtually the whole of the traditional political establishment in Lancashire was . . . excluded from local office,'[91] in favour of an alliance of Dissenters and Catholics. Lancashire Anglicans had therefore witnessed in the late 1680s what they saw as an attack on the Church-State by this unholy alliance which would, in their opinion, have opened the way for the re-establishment of Catholicism and its political corollary, arbitrary government. The alliance of Dissenters and Catholics to undermine the legal foundations of the Anglican state was not forgotten in the 1690s, and Brandon's attempts to introduce Dissenters to the Lancashire bench in this decade merely revived recent painful memories for Lancashire Tory Anglicans of the way in which Dissenters had aided and abetted the popish and arbitrary James in the 1680s.[92] Taylor's depiction of Dissenters as the cat's-paws of Catholicism would, therefore, have found much sympathy among Lancashire Anglicans, and by reviving memories of the 1680s heightened local concern over Brandon's inclusion of Dissenters on the bench in the 1690s, and the implications of this inclusion.

Taylor's arguments have even greater relevance to a second area of Anglican-Dissent conflict, the battle for possession of the county's chapels of ease. Unlike most counties, where township

---

[89] M. A. Mullett, 'The politics of Liverpool, 1660–1688', *Transactions of the Historic Society of Lancashire and Cheshire*, 124 (1972), pp. 31–56; idem, 'Conflict, politics, and elections in Lancaster, 1660–1688', *NH*, 19 (1983), pp. 61–86; idem, ' "A Receptacle for Papists and an Assilum": Catholicism and disorder in late seventeenth-century Wigan', *CathHR*, 73 (1987), pp. 391–407; idem, ' "To Dwell Together in Unity": the search for agreement in Preston politics, 1660–1690', *Transactions of the Historic Society of Lancashire and Cheshire*, 125 (1974), pp. 61–81.

[90] Preston, Lancashire Record Office [LRO], DDKe/4/9, Remarques upon the change in the Lieftenancy of Lancashire, nd, *c*.1689; Mullett, ' "A Receptacle for Papists" ', pp. 404–7.

[91] Glassey, *Politics and Justices of the Peace*, p. 275.

[92] LRO, DDKe/9/66/11, and *HMC, Kenyon*, no. 813, pp. 273–4: Roger Kenyon to Guicciardini Wentworth, 22 July 1693.

and parish were nearly always synonymous, Anglican parishes in Lancashire often contained several townships spread over a large geographic area, often making the parish church inaccessible to those in the outlying parts of a parish. An Act of Parliament was required to establish a new parish and this was a long, laborious, and expensive procedure. Lancashire therefore developed a system whereby a number of chapels of ease were constructed within the majority of parishes in an attempt to improve Anglican provision.[93] Unfortunately, funding for these chapelries was often inadequate, and this led to significant levels of pluralism and non-provision.[94] In consequence, after the restoration of Anglicanism in 1661 many of these chapels remained in the hands of Protestant Dissenters, and the number claimed by the Dissenters rose in the aftermath of the 1687 Declaration of Indulgence and the Toleration Act of 1689. During the 1690s eighteen Lancashire chapels in fourteen different parishes were claimed by the Dissenters,[95] over twelve per cent of the total number of chapels in the county.[96]

The possession of these chapels of ease became a focal point for Anglican-Dissenting tension.[97] The key point of debate in at least twelve of the disputed chapels was the Dissenters' claim that the chapels in question had either been established by Puritans or had developed a strong Puritan tradition in the course of the seventeenth century, and that as the true heirs of the Puritans the Dissenters were entitled to the possession of these chapels, many of which the Anglican hierarchy had failed to fill. Zachary Taylor was fully aware of these disputes. He had been curate at Wigan parish church since at least 1684,[98] and it was one of

[93] For this phenomenon, which predated the Reformation, see C. Haigh, *Reformation and Resistance in Tudor Lancashire* (Cambridge, 1975), esp. ch. 3, and Richardson, *Puritanism in North West England*, pp. 31–45.

[94] See E. J. Evans, 'The Anglican clergy of northern England', in C. Jones, ed., *Britain in the First Age of Party, 1679–1750: Essays Presented to Geoffrey Holmes* (London, 1986), pp. 221–40.

[95] These figures are extracted from the visitation of the diocese of Chester conducted by the Tory High Anglican Bishop, Francis Gastrell. The Lancashire portion of this visitation is published as Gastrell, *Notitia Cestrensis*, 2 (in three parts, Chetham Society, 1st ser., 19, 21–2). Additional information has been extracted from Nightingale, *Lancashire Nonconformity*.

[96] This is roughly comparable with the 10% of the Lancashire population which the Evans List discovered to be Dissenting hearers in 1718. See Watts, *The Dissenters*, p. 509.

[97] See Higson, 'Promoters of Nonconformity', pp. 123–63 for a consideration of some of the chapels disputed in the 1690s.

[98] Edinburgh, National Library of Scotland, Crawford MSS 47/3/78, List of Wigan In and Out Burgesses 1684.

Wigan's chapels of ease, Hindley, that provided the most notorious battle between Anglicans and Dissenters.[99] Taylor also frequently mentioned the dispute over St Helen's chapel in all of his four pamphlets. It seems fair to say that in his contribution to the debate prompted by *The Surey Demoniack* Taylor was attempting to undermine the legitimacy of Dissenters and question their Protestantism as part of a propaganda attack on a group who were seen to be challenging not only Anglican property rights in terms of the chapel buildings, but the pre-eminence of Anglicanism itself in the county. At a time when Anglicans in Lancashire felt threatened by the expansion of Dissent in the aftermath of the Toleration Act, Taylor's anti-Dissent rhetoric was an important propaganda weapon which reflected, and perhaps exacerbated, the division in Lancashire society between Dissenters and Anglicans.

In this paper we have looked exclusively at the religious and political divisions laid bare by the debate provoked by the publication of *The Surey Demoniack*. What we have been concerned to demonstrate is the way that the event at Surey and its literary interpretation cannot be understood without reference to the contemporary religious and political divisions, both between Anglicans and Dissenters, and within the Dissenting community itself. The debate was a product of these tensions and also a propaganda exercise to reinforce deeply entrenched positions. Any attempt to understand this case divorced from religious and political realities, and to interpret the episode merely in the light of the historiography of witchcraft, will fail to grasp the true importance of the pamphlets, and will deny itself a valuable insight into the bitter religious and political divisions that existed in provincial society in the 1690s.

University of Lancaster

---

[99] J. Lowe, 'The case of Hindley Chapel, 1641–1698', *TLCAS*, 57 (1957), pp. 45–74; Higson, 'Promoters of Nonconformity', p. 180; J. I. Jones, 'The struggle between Conformists and Nonconformists in Hindley Chapel, 1641–1698', *Transactions of the Unitarian Historical Society*, 7 (1939–42), pp. 31–49; Gastrell, *Notitia Cestrensis*, 2/ii, pp. 254–7.

# AFTER THE HAPPY UNION: PRESBYTERIANS AND INDEPENDENTS IN THE PROVINCES*

by DAVID L. WYKES

The Glorious Revolution encouraged Presbyterians to hope for comprehension within the Church of England. The failure of those hopes led them to co-operate more closely with their Congregational brethren. In London the earliest practical outcome of this increased co-operation was the Common Fund, which held its first meeting in June 1690. Controlled by managers drawn from both denominations, the Fund was established to offer financial help to poor ministers, congregations, and students who lived in the provinces. A scheme for uniting the two ministries, the Happy Union, set out in the 'Heads of Agreement', was adopted a year later on 6 April 1691, but within months this union had dissolved amidst bitter dissension. In less than four years all the schemes for co-operation between Presbyterians and Congregationals had collapsed in London. Nevertheless, co-operation between Presbyterians and Independents, and even the ideals of the Happy Union, continued in the provinces long after the failure in London.[1] In part this was because the desire for a union between the two denominations was widely held throughout the country; indeed the earliest agreement was made by an Assembly of West Country ministers at Bristol in June 1690, nearly a year before the 'Heads of Agreement' were adopted in London. Moreover, in many localities following toleration, Presbyterians and Independents still came together in one meeting as a result of the earlier persecution and because of their loyalty to a particular minister. Where dissent was strong, such as in London and the

* I wish to express my thanks to the Revd Dr G. F. Nuttall for his advice and comments on this paper. I am also grateful to the Arts Budget Centre Research Committee of the University of Leicester for a grant in aid of some of the research.

[1] Alexander Gordon, ed., *Freedom after Ejection: A Review (1690–1692) of Presbyterian and Congregational Nonconformity in England and Wales* (Manchester, 1917), pp. 155–8; Roger Thomas, ed., *'An Essay of Accommodation', Being a Scheme for Uniting Presbyterians and Congregationals drawn up c.1680*, Dr Williams's Library [hereafter DWL], Occasional Paper No. 6 (London, 1957), pp. 1–2; Roger Thomas, 'The break-up of Nonconformity', in Geoffrey F. Nuttall, Roger Thomas, H. Lismer Short and R. D. Whitehorn, *The Beginnings of Nonconformity: The Hibbert Lectures* (London, 1964), pp. 35–8; C. Gordon Bolam, Jeremy Goring, H. L. Short and Roger Thomas, *The English Presbyterians: from Elizabethan Puritanism to Modern Unitarianism* (London, 1968), pp. 101–2.

major towns, separate congregations for Presbyterians and Congregationals were likely; but where dissent was weaker, particularly in the countryside, congregations included members from both denominations. In these circumstances, members had to accept a minister who did not necessarily share their own denominational preferences.[2] During the first two decades of the eighteenth century the majority of these joint congregations were to divide, as (in most cases) the smaller body of Congregational supporters withdrew to establish their own meetings. There had, however, been more than twenty years of co-operation in many areas in the period following the collapse of the Happy Union in London, and in a few cases such arrangements even continued until the early nineteenth century. There is evidence from at least two congregations, at Leicester and Chesterfield, of a formal agreement to settle the differences between the two denominations. The Happy Union and its failure in London has been the subject of a number of studies, but by contrast the continuing co-operation between Presbyterians and Independents in the provinces has received little detailed attention.

The desire of Presbyterians and Congregationals for greater union had led to the establishment of a number of ministerial assemblies in the provinces even before the Happy Union in London. All came to adopt the 'Heads of Agreement' as the basis of their association.[3] Ministers from both denominations continued to meet together after the collapse of the Happy Union. Congregational ministers were members of the Western Assembly which met at Bristol, and Thomas Jollie of Altham, an Independent minister, took a prominent part in the work of the

[2] For evidence of the welcome and support given to the Happy Union by both ministers and laity, see Leeds, Yorkshire Archaeological Society, MS 3, 'Original letters, papers, &c collected by the late famous Antiquary Ralph Thoresby', No. 22, Priscilla [Lady] Brooke, Howgrave, to Rev. Richard Stretton, London, 13 Dec. 1690; I[saac] N[oble], *A Funeral Sermon on Occasion of the Death of the Reverend James Forbes, M.A. Preach'd at Glocester, June 3d. 1712* (London, 1713), pp. 27–8; BL, MS Stowe 747, Dering Correspondence, fol. 16r, John Hampden, London, to the Rev. [Francis] Tallents, Shrewsbury, 27 May 1693; Geoffrey F. Nuttall, 'Dissenting Churches in Kent before 1700', *JEH*, 14 (1963), p. 177.

[3] Geoffrey F. Nuttall, 'Assembly and association in dissent, 1689–1831', *SCH*, 7 (1971), pp. 289–90, 296–303; Thomas, '*Essay of Accommodation*', pp. 2, 15–16, n. 11; Alexander Gordon, ed., *Cheshire Classis Minutes, 1691–1745* (London, 1919), pp. 3–4; Allan Brockett, ed., *The Exeter Assembly: The Minutes of the Assemblies of the United Brethren of Devon and Cornwall, 1691–1717*, Devon and Cornwall Record Society, ns 6 (1963), p. vii; Joseph Hunter, *The Rise of Old Dissent, Exemplified in the Life of Oliver Heywood* (London, 1842), pp. 372–7.

northern division of the Lancashire Assembly. Perhaps the longest association involved the Exeter Assembly, where ministers from the two denominations continued to meet together until the mid-eighteenth century, though admittedly the number of participating Congregational ministers was always small. Dr Nuttall identified only seven during the first nine years of the Assembly, while during the same period there were probably more than fifty Presbyterian ministers. Congregrationalists also formed only a small proportion of the ministers belonging to the Cheshire Assembly. This modest level of involvement reflects the small number of Congregational churches in the areas covered by the two Assemblies rather than any reluctance by Congregational ministers to continue as members. Nevertheless, Presbyterian ministers dominated these associations, and Assemblies were not found in areas such as Cambridgeshire and Northamptonshire where Presbyterians were weak. In addition, ministers from both denominations continued to co-operate in the ordination of ministers after the collapse of the Happy Union.[4]

At the congregational level there is also considerable evidence for continuing co-operation, even in the larger towns and cities. In Coventry there was a Congregational meeting dating from the 1650s and a Presbyterian meeting from the late 1660s, of which the latter, known as the Great Meeting, was much the larger. It had two ministers (after 1716 a minister and an assistant) and was said in 1723 to be 'one of the largest dissenting Congregations in England, consisting at least of 1,200 people'. The Congregational meeting by contrast was dependent upon the Congregational Church at Bedworth, five miles from Coventry. As a result of a secession from the Great Meeting in 1724, a new Congregational Church was formed in May 1725 at Vicar Lane by the members of the earlier Congregational Church in Midsfort

---

[4] DWL, MS 12.78, Jollie Papers, p. 141, Copy of a general letter inviting ministers to attend a district meeting at Thomas Jollie's house to discuss the business of the next meeting of the northern division of the United Brethren for Lancashire to be held on 12 April [1692]; 'The minutes of the United Brethren [of Lancashire, 1693–1700]', appendix of W. A. Shaw, ed., *Minutes of the Manchester Presbyterian Classis, 1646–1660*, part 3, Chetham Society, ns 24 (Manchester, 1891), pp. 351–63; Allan Brockett, *Nonconformity in Exeter, 1650–1875* (Manchester, 1962), p. 65; idem, *Exeter Assembly*, p. vii; Nuttall, 'Assembly and association', pp. 293–4; Gordon, *Cheshire Classis*, p. 140. See the Evans List for a survey of the relative strength of the two denominations in these areas, DWL, MS 38.4, 'John Evans List of Dissenting Congregations and Ministers in England and Wales, 1715–29', pp. 12–13, 16–17, 26–9; Hunter, *Rise of Old Dissent*, p. 377.

Street and the secessionists who had left the Great Meeting. The new church called a minister of its own, Patrick Simson of Dundalk.[5] The breach occurred because of the appointment of a new assistant minister at the Great Meeting. According to Philip Doddridge, the senior minister, John Warren, 'has some considerable personal obligations to Mr Smith, and has endeavoured to the utmost to introduce him as Mr R[ogerson]'s successor; but the generality of the people oppose it with a great deal of warmth'. The objection to Smith's appointment was not, it appears, because of his religious sentiments, but as a result of the way in which he was chosen. As a consequence, part of the congregation, 'disgusted at Mr Warren's conduct in the affair of an assistant', 'struck off with a resolution of building another meeting place'. Doddridge refused an invitation from the mayor and several of the aldermen to become minister of the new meeting. When the invitation was renewed, he urged them to act with Warren and not to 'maintain the ground of an angry separation'.[6] Although the breach was over the way in which an assistant had been appointed, and in particular Warren's involvement, there is evidence that the dissidents wanted a Congregational form of church government and that the basis of their quarrel with Warren was that he had ignored the right of the church to appoint its own minister.[7]

Despite the breach which led to the new church being established and the adoption of Congregational principles, the two congregations did co-operate and recognize each other's authority. In September 1727, the Vicar Lane Church agreed to hold a day of solemn thanksgiving for the successful harvest and to

[5] W. B. Stephens, ed., *VCH Warwicks. VIII: The City of Coventry and the Borough of Warwick* (London, 1969), pp. 376, 387, 394; John Sibree and M. Caston, *Independency in Warwickshire: a Brief History of the Independent or Congregational Churches in the County* (Coventry and London, 1855), pp. 27–44, 45–64; DWL, New College MSS, L1/10/2, Philip Doddridge, Hinckley, to Samuel Clark, St Albans, 4 May 1723; Geoffrey F. Nuttall, ed., *Calendar of the Correspondence of Philip Doddridge DD (1702–1752)*, Joint Publications, 26 (London, 1979), p. 11; Coventry, Coventry City Record Office [hereafter CCRO], MS 1184/1/1, Records of the Warwick Road United Reform Church, 'A Church Book Belonging to the New Chappel [Vicar Lane] in Coventry', 22 May 1725–7 Jan. 1804 [unpaginated], see 22 May 1725.
[6] DWL, MS L1/10/2, Doddridge to Clark, 4 May 1723; Letters from Doddridge to John Mason, 14 March 1723/4, to Samuel Clark, 5 May 1724, and to Alderman Richard Poole, Coventry, 29 June 1724, printed in J. D. Humphreys, ed., *Correspondence and Diary of Philip Doddridge*, 4 vols (London, 1829–31), 1, pp. 227, 348, 377, 404; Nuttall, *Calendar*, pp. 11, 19, 21, 23.
[7] CCRO, MS 1184/133/1, 'A Sermon preached at the opening of Vicar Lane Chapel', 14 Oct. 1724, by John Fleming.

invite Warren and the other ministers 'to assist in that work'. In response to the invitation it was reported that Warren was 'disposed to have the two churches to meet together on Such publick occasions for the greater encrease of Brotherly Love & Unity', and that 'Such publick days should be jointly observed by the two Churches alternately in the two places of worship'. A similar day of thanksgiving was held in November 1730, but no other occasions are recorded in the minutes, though Francis Blackmore, assistant minister at the Great Meeting between 1730 and 1742, preached at Vicar Lane the year he left Coventry to become minister at Worcester. Even on the sensitive question of admission to the Lord's Supper the Vicar Lane Meeting was willing to accept members into communion from the Great Meeting and other Presbyterian meetings. In April 1735, the Church agreed to admit Mrs Hancocks to occasional communion during her stay in Coventry on the recommendation of Daniel Mattock, minister of the Presbyterian Old Meeting in Birmingham. Members from the Great Meeting were accepted into communion by the Church apparently without any examination before admission. In June 1743 it was reported that Mrs Fardon, 'a Member of the Old Meeting who in an advanced age is far gone of a Dropsie had an earnest desire of sitting down in Communion with them before she left this World if the Lord may enable her to enjoy that Priviledge; the Church she being well known to many of them readily agreed to it'. The discipline of the church was, however, taken seriously. The decision by the Great Meeting in February 1738 to receive William Jackson into communion 'without any testimony' was censured, because Jackson had previously been suspended from Vicar Lane for swearing and reviling. Co-operation between the two meetings appears to have ceased after Warren's death in 1742.[8]

At Sheffield the appointment of a new minister following the death of Timothy Jollie in 1714 also resulted in a major dispute over the method of choosing a successor and led to a secession and the setting up of a new church on Congregational principles,

---

[8] CCRO, MS 1184/1/1, 'Church Book', Vicar Lane Chapel, see entries under 1, 8, 15, 18 Sept. [1727], 8 Nov. 1730, 3 April 1735, 12 Feb. 1737/8, 3 Aug. 1738, 31 March 1743, 9 June 1743; CCRO, MS 1184/133/1, Sermon preached by the Revd Mr Blackmore, 7 Nov. 1742. The Great Meeting, as the older church, is referred to as Old Meeting in the minutes of the Vicar Lane New Meeting.

later known as Nether Chapel. Jollie had been chosen as minister in 1679, and although he underwent a Presbyterian ordination in April 1681, perhaps to accommodate the Presbyterians in his congregation, the engagement between minister and congregation was clearly made on Congregational principles. After asking those who were not members of the Church to withdraw, an elder addressed Jollie and 'spoke in the name of the people their desires that he would accept of a pastorall office over them, which the rest signified their consent to by lifting up their hands, and he assented, expressing his desires to serve them in the gospel'. According to Oliver Heywood, who was one of the Presbyterian ministers who took part in the ordination, the Church at Sheffield 'was always accounted independent', and he considered the willingness of the Church to 'admit of a pastour ordained by presbiters . . . as an olive-branch of peace amongst gods people'. Heywood also records that when he visited Jollie at Sheffield in May 1700, he found that Jollie admitted to communion some of those who sat under Edward Prime, a Presbyterian minister, and that 'some of his members sit down with Mr Prime, tho' he [Jollie] be congregationall yet of an healing humble spirit – blessed be god for him – these are sweet signall mercies for which I have prayed'.[9]

Unfortunately, after Jollie's death in March 1714, the congregation divided over the appointment of a successor. The dispute reveals the tensions which existed between Presbyterians and Congregationals over fundamental questions of church membership and government. The disagreement centred not only on the particular choice of a new minister but on who had the right to make that choice. There were three separate interests involved: the church, which consisted of the regularly admitted communicants; the trustees, in whom the meeting-house and other property of the congregation were vested; and the seat-holders, by far the largest body, who financed the ministry and the meeting by their subscriptions. The church named John De la Rose, who had been chosen a few years earlier as Jollie's assistant. De la Rose then assumed to himself the office of minister without an invitation from the trustees or the seat-holders.

[9] J. Horsfall Turner, ed., *The Rev. Oliver Heywood, B.A., 1630–1702: his Autobiography, Diaries, Anecdote and Event Books; Illustrating the General and Family History of Yorkshire and Lancashire*, 4 vols (Brighouse, 1881–5), 2, pp. 200–1, 4, pp. 164–5.

Although the elders and the church were for De la Rose, the trustees and the majority of the seat-holders opposed him. The dispute became so heated that the trustees refused the use of the meeting-house to De la Rose after he preached what they saw as a violent and inflammatory sermon. At a general meeting of the congregation, despite stiff opposition from De la Rose's supporters, John Wadsworth, the minister at Rotherham, was invited to be Jollie's successor. Wadsworth at first refused, seeking to persuade the two parties to seek an accommodation. Seeing that the opponents of De la Rose were resolved on another minister, he accepted the call. Thomas Ibbotson, the Independent minister at Chesterfield, reported in a letter that, on the same day that he preached to the separatists,

> Mr Wadsworth accepted the call from the trustees. As I hear his afternoon sermon was upon the qualifications of a bishop, which he shewed in short, and spent most of his time in vindicating himself, and charging the other part of the Church. This is what I hear, so he publicly accepted the call, and when he came into the conference house, he said to some there he thought he had a good call.

Those who formed the church 'felt themselves especially bound to protest against the imposition upon them of Wadsworth, so irregularly chosen, which they called a gross infringement of their Christian privileges'. As a consequence, about a fifth of the meeting withdrew to form a new church established on Congregational principles, and Elias Wordsworth, one of the principal supporters of De la Rose, fitted up a temporary place of worship for them by uniting two houses, until the new meeting-house was completed in November 1715. This was perhaps the earliest and certainly the most important division between Presbyterians and Congregationals in the north of England.[10]

---

[10] Joseph Hunter had use of the correspondence sent by the two parties to William Moult, the Independent minister at Leeds: *Hallamshire: the History and Topography of the Parish of Sheffield* (London, 1819), p. 169; BL, Add. MS 24,437, Collectanea Hunteriana, iii: Collections for an History of the Town and Parish of Sheffield, 1, fols 59r–60r, 'Some account of the dissenters of Sheffield. March 13th 1802'; Add. MS 24,484, 'Britannica Puritanica, or outlines of the history of the various congregations of Presbyterians and Independents which arose out of the schism in the Church of England of 1662', fols 26r–v; James G. Miall, *Congregationalism in Yorkshire: a Chapter of Modern Church History* (London, 1868), p. 352.

At Chester three ejected ministers, William Cook, Ralph Hall, and John Harvey, had gathered meetings in 1672 as a result of Charles II's Indulgence, but the meetings fell as persecution intensified in 1682. The two Presbyterian ministers, Cook and Hall, both died in 1684. 'Those of their Congregations that continued dissenters generally joyn'd with Mr. Harvy, who kept close and preach'd very privately in his own house or elsewhere, and rode out the storm.' Nevertheless, Harvey was a Congregational, and not everyone who belonged to Cook and Hall 'joyned with him in constant Communion'. As a result of the liberty granted by James II's Declaration for the Liberty of Conscience in April 1687, some of Hall's former congregation sent Matthew Henry an invitation to settle as their minister. Henry only accepted after he had gained Harvey's agreement for the establishment of a separate congregation, but attempts by Henry to fulfil the ideals of the Happy Union failed. His suggestion that the two congregations should unite, or at least join for the Lord's Supper, was 'peremptorily refused' by Harvey, he 'saying we would each stand on our own bottom'. Harvey died in November 1699 and was succeeded by his son, Jonathan, who continued preaching until September 1706, when ill-health and a sharp decline in the support he received from his congregation led him to resign his charge and give up preaching. Henry was embarrassed to find members of Harvey's meeting deserting their former minister to join his congregation: 'I have had many searchings of heart about Mr Harvey's congregation who come dropping in to us. As I have endeavoured, in that matter, to approve myself to god, and my own conscience.' Denominational attachments still remained important and some of Harvey's congregation made it clear to Henry that they would have continued with Harvey had he kept up his meeting. The first Independent Church was not established in Chester until 1768.[11]

[11] Chester, Chester City Record Office, D/MH/1, Records of the Matthew Henry Chapel, Chester, Chapel Book, M. Henry, 'A Short Account of the Beginning and Progress of our Congregation' (1710), fols 7r–8v, printed in H. D. Roberts, *Matthew Henry and his Chapel, 1662–1900* (Liverpool, [1901]), pp. 72–100; W[illiam] T[ong], *An Account of the Life and Death of Mr Matthew Henry, Minister of the Gospel at Hackney* (London, 1716), pp. 45, 75; J. B. Williams, *Memoirs of the Life, Character, and Writings of the Rev. Matthew Henry* (London, 1829), p. 181; Roberts, *Matthew Henry*, pp. 78–9, 81, 92–3.

At Nottingham the Presbyterians and Independents had always met separately, but John Barrett, in the funeral sermon for his ministerial colleague William Reynolds in 1698, described the friendly relations which had existed between the two congregations since the time that toleration was first granted. Speaking of the Presbyterian congregation meeting on the High Pavement, 'we had, and still (through much Mercy) have many Week-day Opportunities, and constantly a weekly Lecture, our and our Brother Rythers Congregation joyning in Attendance thereon, and our Brother Ryther and we joyning Harmoniously (blessed be God) in keeping of it up'.[12] John Ryther had been called as minister of the Castle Gate Congregational Church in 1686. There is further evidence of the close relations between the ministers of the two congregations. Ryther's children were baptized by John Whitlock sen., the senior minister of the Presbyterian High Pavement meeting, and on two occasions Ryther joined with his Presbyterian colleagues in ordinations.[13] In 1733 James Sloss was chosen as an assistant minister at Castle Gate. Sloss was a Scottish Presbyterian and as a result had to promise not to attempt any alteration in the congregational mode of church government at Castle Gate. He was ordained in August 1733, when John Wadsworth, minister of the Presbyterian congregation at Upper Chapel, Sheffield, gave the sermon. The long co-operation between the Presbyterians and Independents at Nottingham came to an end in 1736, largely because of Sloss's strict Trinitarian orthodoxy. A communicant at Castle Gate, James Rawson, was suspected of 'having Imbibed the Arrian Notion and Denying the Supream Deighty of Jesus Christ'. After failing to provide a satisfactory answer, Rawson was excommunicated in July 1736. As a consequence a number of members seceded from Castle Gate with Rawson and joined the High Pavement congregation. In December 1739 the Castle Gate Church resolved that 'no person be received from the High Pavement congregation as a member of this congregation without giving in their experience, unless they have been received

[12] John Barrett, *A Short Account of the life of the Reverend Mr William Reynolds, Who slept in Jesus Feb 26th 1697/8 in the 73d Year of his Age* (London, 1698), p. 56.

[13] 'High Pavement baptisms (1690–1723), Nottingham', in *Miscellany*, 1, Nottinghamshire Family History Society, Records Series, 53 (1986), pp. 1, 2, 3, 4; Nottingham, Nottingham University Library Manuscripts Department, Hi 2 M/1, Nottingham Classis Minute Book (at the front of the volume is a list of ordinations, 1675–1703).

members of that Church before the Rev. Mr Hewes left that congregation'.[14]

Not all disputes between Independents and Presbyterians ended in division. In at least two cases an accommodation was reached between the two parties which resolved the differences and enabled the joint congregation to continue. At Chesterfield a meeting-house had been completed for the use of the joint meeting of Presbyterians and Independents in 1694. Under the terms of the trust, ministers were to be chosen by 'the greater number of the usual auditors, being housekeepers'. The right of appointment was therefore vested in the more substantial hearers, and represented a Presbyterian rather than a Congregational form of church government. It is clear that by 1703 differences had arisen between the two parties over the management of the meeting. Although the dispute was between the minister and his 'Audittors att & resorters to the said meeting house who are of the presbyterian perswasion' on one hand, and those of 'the Congregationall perswasion' on the other, the differences involved practical and financial issues rather than doctrinal. Part of the disagreement involved the financial arrangements between the two parties for the upkeep of the meeting-house and manse, but the settlement which was adopted also involved an important change in how ministers were to be chosen. Instead of being determined by a majority of voices, as set out in the earlier trust deed, it was agreed that whenever

> the pastor of either Church shall dye or relinquish [his office] that the said Church related to such pastor shall have full power to choose another pastor in place or stead of such said pastor . . . And that such pastor soe chosen shall have as full power in his respective turne or course to preach & teach as if he had been chosen by the Majority of the voices of the whole Assembly at the said meeting house.

[14] Mr Hewes is Obadiah Hughes, minister of High Pavement Chapel from 1728 to 1735. Nottingham, Nottingham University Library Manuscripts Department, CU/M/1/1, 'An account of the Rise Progress and Proceedings of the Congregational Church of Christ at Nottingham', pp. 14–17 (25 May, 2 and 25 June, 2 July 1736, 28 Dec. 1739); Benjamin Carpenter, *Some Account of the Original Introduction of Presbyterianism in Nottingham and the Neighbourhood* (London, [c.1860]), pp. 152–4; A. R. Henderson, *History of the Castle Gate Congregational Church, Nottingham, 1655–1905* (London, 1905), pp. 139–50.

The reference to 'his respective turne or course to preach & teach' indicates that the two parties met together as a single congregation on Sundays, with each minister having his turn in the service on alternate weeks, though presumably they separated for communion.[15]

A similar agreement was reached at Leicester in 1716. In 1708 the joint congregation of Presbyterians and Congregationals with its minister Edmund Spencer built a substantial brick meeting-house in Parchment Lane (now East Bond Street), which because of its size became known as the Great Meeting. At this time, with the appointment of a second minister, Thomas Gee, there is also evidence of the growing differences between the two denominations. Spencer was a Congregational, but Gee was a Presbyterian. Gee came to Leicester, probably in about 1709, as Spencer's assistant, yet within two years he was the senior minister. Spencer left Leicester in 1711 to become pastor of the Congregational Church at Beccles, which hardly compared in size and importance with the Leicester congregation, of which he had been senior minister for fifteen years in succession to his father-in-law. He was replaced by the Congregational John Greene. The Presbyterian and Congregational parts of the congregation during this period apparently met together for public worship, though they separated for communion, but differences over the management of the meeting and its buildings had to be resolved by arbitration in 1716. This agreement, like that earlier for Chesterfield, was concerned with the practical issues of finance and organization, but the existence of the two parties is clear from the references to 'Mr Gee's friends' and 'Mr Greene's friends'. A major part of the agreement involved apportioning the debts of the meeting between the two parties. Greene left Leicester in about 1722 to be minister of the Congregational Church at Chelmsford. Although after Greene's departure the congregation was served only by Presbyterian ministers, a Congregational Church was not formed at Leicester until 1800, and

---

[15] Chesterfield, Chesterfield Public Library, Records of Elders Yard Unitarian Chapel, Chesterfield, ELD 7–9, Lease and release, 26, 27 Dec. 1695; ELD 11–12, Agreement, 5 Nov. 1703. The Agreement is printed in D. W. Robson, *Origins and History of Elder Yard Chapel, Chesterfield* (Chesterfield, 1921), appendix, pp. 51–5. In 1708 'The Congregational Church of Christ In Chesterfield' invited Thomas Elston to be the minister of their part of the church: see BL, Stowe MS 748, Dering Correspondence, vol. 6, fol. 78r.

then the new Church did not involve a secession from the older congregation but was founded by members of the Church at Market Harborough who had come to live in Leicester. Some loss of members from the Great Meeting did occur as the congregation became avowedly Unitarian under Charles Berry after about 1810.[16]

In the provinces co-operation between Presbyterians and Congregationals clearly continued for many years after the collapse of the Happy Union. In the larger towns where separate meetings existed Presbyterian and Congregational ministers were not only on friendly terms, but, as at Nottingham, they often shared pulpits and other responsibilities. Even in London, where the breach was never healed, there was some formal co-operation between the two denominations which also involved the Baptists. As a result of the growing hostility towards dissenters during Queen Anne's reign, the dissenters in London formed the General Body of Protestant Dissenting Ministers of the Three Denominations to oversee the political interests of dissenters nationally. The Protestant Dissenting Deputies, founded in 1732, also included members drawn from the three denominations. Although joint meetings in the provinces survived the collapse of the Happy Union, most were to break up during the first decades of the eighteenth century. By the early eighteenth century the older ministers who had helped gather and uphold the meetings during the period of persecution had mostly died. Both the choice itself and the method of appointment of a successor proved divisive. The commitment to a meeting that personal loyalty to the original minister had engendered, despite denominational differences which frequently existed between them, rarely survived the minister's death.

Although at the time of the Happy Union the differences between Presbyterians and Congregationals mainly involved church order, these differences were to become increasingly focused on theological issues. The disputes at Coventry and

---

[16] A. Hermann Thomas, *A History of the Great Meeting, Leicester, and its Congregation* (Leicester, 1908), pp. 31–6; London, Public Record Office, C11/898/9 (15 Jan. 1718); J. Wilford, 'Gallowtree Gate Chapel Jubilee', includes a history of the earlier Independent congregation, founded in 1800, later the Bond Street Congregational Church, *Leicester Chronicle*, 20 Dec. 1873, p. xi; Revd Thomas Robinson, Vicar of St Mary's Leicester, to [Revd George Gill, Minister of the Market Harborough Congregational Church], 16 Dec. 1800, in *Congregational Magazine*, ns 2 (1826), p. 191.

Sheffield were essentially the result of fundamental disagreements concerning church government and congregational authority that the appointment of a minister or an assistant raised, though there is evidence that the dislike of De la Rose was in part due to his high Calvinism. Denominational allegiances were also clearly important. Many members of Harvey's former congregation at Chester were reluctant to join with the Presbyterian Matthew Henry. The Presbyterian John Wadsworth was invited to take part in the ordination of James Sloss at the Castle Gate Church in 1733, presumably because Sloss, a Scot, was also a Presbyterian.[17] The controversy at Nottingham in 1736 over the heterodoxy of James Rawson is an unusually early example of the divergence that was growing between the two denominations over doctrine. In truth the 'Heads of Agreement' had succeeded in uniting Presbyterians and Congregationals because, with the exception of ordination, it passed over all the areas of disagreement, leaving such questions as church membership, congregational government and discipline to individual churches to settle. It would be wrong, however, to assume that the break up of the joint meetings of Presbyterians and Congregationals was inevitable. At Chesterfield, the two parties had sought an agreement, 'both parties having a desire that the said differences may be acom[m]odated in order to their livinge together as Christian brethren and Friends'.[18] Matthew Henry, Doddridge, and initially Wadsworth, were all anxious to avoid encouraging schism. Whatever the potential for disagreement between the two denominations, there still remained a heartfelt desire for unity, which was finally broken by pressure of fundamental differences over doctrine.

University of Leicester

[17] Henderson, *History of Castle Gate*, p. 140.

[18] Chesterfield, Chesterfield Public Library, ELD 11–12, Agreement, 5 Nov. 1703. As late as 1730 the Congregational Church in Gloucester was warned that a general appeal for money towards the building of a new meeting-house would not be well received, since many thought they should effect a union with the Presbyterian meeting, from whom they had divided in 1714, and thus 'the Expence of another Place have been sav'd': see Gloucester, Gloucestershire Record Office, Records of Southgate Congregational Church, D6026/6/47, J——. P——., Dursley, to Rev. [Thomas] Cole, [minister of Congregational Church,] Gloucester, 11 May 1730.

# UNITY, PLURALISM, AND THE SPIRITUAL MARKET-PLACE: INTERDENOMINATIONAL COMPETITION IN THE EARLY AMERICAN REPUBLIC

by RICHARD CARWARDINE

I

Following independence, Americans' sense of the special status of their new nation drew succour not merely from their republican experiment but from the unique character of the nation's religious life. Even before the Revolution Americans had witnessed an extraordinary proliferation of sects and churches, to a degree unparalleled in any single European state, as ethnic diversity increased and the mid-eighteenth-century revivals split churches and multiplied congregations. The Congregationalist establishment in New England and Anglican power in the middle and southern colonies uneasily confronted energetic dissenting minorities, including Scotch-Irish Presbyterians, English Baptists, and German Lutheran and Reformed groups. After 1776 it took some time to define a new relationship between church and state. Colonial habits of thought persisted and prompted schemes of multiple establishment or government support for religion in general. The Virginia Act for Establishing Religious Freedom in 1786 and, five years later, the First Amendment to the Federal Constitution did not succeed wholly in eliminating state authority from the sphere of religion; indeed, residual establishments persisted in Connecticut until 1818 and in Massachusetts until 1833. Yet an important shift was under way towards a 'voluntary' system of religious support, in which governmental authority in religion was replaced by increased authority for self-sustaining denominational bodies. After 1790 ecclesiastical institutions grew at an extraordinary pace, shaping the era labelled by historians the 'Second Great Awakening'. As Jon Butler has reminded us, some 50,000 new churches were built in America between 1780 and 1860, sacralizing the landscape with steeples and graveyards and creating a heterogeneous presence that drew streams of European visitors curious to evaluate the effects of America's unique experiment in 'voluntarism'. By 1855 over four million of the country's twenty-seven million people were members of one of over forty Protestant denominations, most of them recognizable by name as churches with an Old World ancestry but with features which made them distinctively American. Additionally, there were over one million Catholics.[1]

The voluntary system meant that church leaders in the early republic were operating in something close to a free market in religion, and the most ambitious of them seized their opportunities to evangelize, and to establish regional and national networks, with an appetite, enterprise, and vision matched by few of their contemporaries. They were energized by a concern to rescue souls from what they saw as a post-revolutionary spiritual decline, to stall the advances of deism and liberal religion, and to cultivate a Christian citizenry as the best defence of republicanism. The era also saw a new style of ministry, one more concerned with making converts and promoting revivals than with theological speculation, and one ever more sensitive to the needs of their congregations in an age of increasing lay self-confidence. Nathan Hatch has shown how, in an era of rapid demographic change, economic transformation and political democratization, the churches which burgeoned were not those which sought to impose from above the ideas of an intellectual elite but rather the more populist denominations, especially Methodists, Baptists, and other New Light churches, which spoke to the people in a language they wanted to hear.[2]

A striking feature of the spiritual market was intense competition amongst Protestant denominations, most sharply expressed in ministers' frequent complaints of 'proselytism', or stealing of converts. The loudest protests emanated from Methodists, who were the most successful of all denominations in generating revivals, targeting penitents, and harvesting members, and were

---

[1] Jon Butler, *Awash in a Sea of Faith: Christianizing the American People* (Cambridge, Mass., 1990), pp. 164–288, esp. 270–1; Timothy L. Smith, *Revivalism and Social Reform: American Protestantism on the Eve of the Civil War* (New York, 1965), pp. 18–21.

[2] Roger Finke and Rodney Stark, *The Churching of America, 1776–1990: Winners and Losers in Our Religious Economy* (New Brunswick, NJ, 1992), pp. 54–108; Nathan O. Hatch, *The Democratization of American Christianity* (New Haven, Conn., 1989); David W. Kling, *A Field of Divine Wonders: The New Divinity and Village Revivals in Northwestern Connecticut 1792–1822* (Philadelphia, 1993), pp. 75–143; Donald M. Scott, *From Office to Profession: The New England Ministry* (Philadelphia, 1978).

consequently the most vulnerable to poaching. Alfred Brunson recalled a camp meeting at Wayne, Ohio, in 1825, where many 'proselyters' at the ground were 'watching for new spoils'. When he objected to converts being 'led away, against their first convictions of duty, by artful maneuvring and false representations', he faced an assortment of threats, which included being ridden on a rail, tarred and feathered, and horse-whipped. A fellow preacher lodged a similar complaint after a revival in the James River district, protesting sourly that 'some professed ministers of the gospel of Christ . . . would rejoice more to gain one Methodist, or Methodist convert to their party, then they would over two sinners brought home as wandering sheep from the Savior's fold. . . . Indeed, . . . what would some other churches do if it were not for the fruit of Methodist labors?'[3]

The character, timing, and intensity of this interdenominational rivalry varied considerably from region to region. Though the whole nation experienced religious competition, the intensely local character and uneven development of American society meant that there was no uniform picture. Where the representatives or heirs of the Standing Order continued to operate they were often able to resist or slow down the inroads of new churches, as did Congregationalists in northwestern Connecticut until the 1820s; only then did Baptists and Methodists successfully lay siege to Hartford and other New Divinity strongholds. In the new settlements of the Cumberland Valley or of western New York, on the other hand, these 'upstart' churches tended to set the pace of denominational advance.[4]

Whatever the context, denominational rivalries were based on more than mere jealousy, though there was some truth in the observation of a renegade Episcopalian that the reason for the

[3] Alfred Brunson, *A Western Pioneer: or, Incidents in the Life and Times of Rev. Alfred Brunson, A.M., D.D., Embracing a Period of over Seventy Years*, 2 vols (Cincinnati, 1972), 1, pp. 295–7; *Christian Advocate and Journal* (Methodist; New York) [hereafter *CAJ* ], 20 Jan., 12 Oct. 1827, 8 Aug. 1828, 25 June 1830.

[4] Kling, *Field of Divine Wonders*, pp. 15, 233–6; Tobias Spicer, *Autobiography of Rev. Tobias Spicer: Containing Incidents and Observations . . .* (Boston, 1851), pp. 84–5; *CAJ*, 28 Dec. 1827; George Claude Baker, *An Introduction to the History of Early New England Methodism, 1789–1839* (Durham, NC, 1941), pp. 7–9 and passim. Cf. Curtis D. Johnson, *Islands of Holiness: Rural Religion in Upstate New York, 1790–1860* (Ithaca, 1989), pp. 21–52; Whitney R. Cross, *The Burned-Over District: The Social and Intellectual History of Enthusiastic Religion in Western New York, 1800–1850* (Ithaca, 1950), pp. 3–24, 252–3; John B. Boles, *The Great Revival, 1787–1805* (Lexington, 1972), pp. 185–6; William Warren Sweet, *Religion on the American Frontier*, 4 vols (Chicago, 1931–46).

great hostility of other Protestants to the Methodist Episcopal Church was '*its continued prosperity*', sufficient to make it the largest denomination in the country by 1830.[5] Antipathies found their most intense expression in discussions over doctrine and the conduct of evangelism, but they could take on an extra edge when reinforced by loyalties of class, ethnicity, and region. The doctrinal fault-line between evangelical Protestants on one side and Universalists, deists, freethinkers, and Catholics on the other was no more divisive (at least before the 1830s) than the fissure within the evangelical world separating Calvinist from Arminian, and more specifically dividing Congregationalists, Presbyterians, and Baptists from the Methodists. In a society where people's daily experience appeared to confirm the reality of human autonomy and capability, and where equality of opportunity in political and economic life was seen as a legitimate goal, Calvinist doctrines of predestination, election, and limited atonement lost favour in the face of Arminian Methodists' stress on human ability and a universal offer of grace. These theological understandings shaped modes of evangelism. The Calvinism of Congregationalists and most Presbyterians and Baptists ensured a chronic questioning of the proper means to be used to secure conversions and sustain revivals. Methodists' understanding of human agency induced fewer scruples. They enthusiastically multiplied camp and protracted meetings, institutionalized a system of itinerant evangelists, and devised new revival practices, including the 'call to the altar', the invitation to seekers to come forward to a place reserved for anxious penitents.[6]

Hostilities often expressed antipathies of class as well as doctrine. Early Methodists and Baptists were generally from the ranks of the poor and unsophisticated, their preachers lacking formal education, and their meeting–places functional but plain. College-trained Presbyterian and Congregationalist pastors ministered, as did Gardiner Spring in New York City's Brick Church, to 'men in the middle ranks of life – thinking, working, independent men' of increasing wealth and social prominence.

[5] *CAJ*, 25 Sept. 1829.
[6] William G. McLoughlin, *Revivals, Awakenings, and Reform: An Essay on Religion and Social Change in America, 1607–1977* (Chicago, 1978), pp. 98–140; Richard Carwardine, *Transatlantic Revivalism: Popular Evangelicalism in Britain and America, 1790–1865* (Westport, Conn., 1978), pp. 4–17; Johnson, *Islands of Holiness*, 33–52.

Such congregations regarded Methodists, according to their minister in Providence, Rhode Island, in 1815, as 'the offscouring of all things'. The judgement was a reaction both to their social make-up (in Providence, they were the church of the poor whites and the blacks), and also to the noise, 'extravagances', 'crudities and excesses' of their meetings, and the 'uncouthness' of their measures. Margaret Bayard Smith complained from Washington in 1822 of the 'excessive' character of Methodist efforts, which offended middle-class sensibilities.

> [T]here is something very repugnant to my feelings in the way in which they discuss the conversions and convictions of the people and in which young ladies and children display their feelings and talk of their convictions and experiences. Dr. May calls the peculiar fever, the *night* fever, and he says almost all cases were produced by night meetings, crowded rooms, excited feelings, and exposure to night air.

Some years later a stalwart Methodist itinerant summarized the era's class and status tensions from his own quite different perspective: 'The Presbyterians, and other Calvinistic branches of the Protestant Church, used to contend for an educated ministry, for pews, for instrumental music, for a congregational or stated salaried ministry. The Methodists universally opposed these ideas; and the illiterate Methodist preachers actually set the world on fire . . . while they were lighting their matches!'[7]

To the aggravations of class must be added the acerbities induced by ethnic, cultural, and regional frictions. In some contexts these operated to reinforce denominational lines of division. In Ohio and other parts of the Old Northwest, for example, the cultural battle between Yankee settlers – that is, those of New England stock – and migrants from the border

---

[7] Shepherd Knapp, *A History of the Brick Presbyterian Church in the City of New York* (New York, 1909), pp. 184–202; W. McDonald, *History of Methodism in Providence, Rhode Island, from its Introduction in 1787 to 1867* (Boston, 1868), pp. 47–8, 53–4; Margaret Bayard Smith to J. Kirkpatrick, 12 Oct. 1822, in Gaillard Hunt, ed., *The First Forty Years of Washington Society: Portrayed by the Family Letters of Mrs. Samuel Harrison Smith (Margaret Bayard)* . . . (New York, 1906), pp. 159–60; Peter Cartwright, *Autobiography of Peter Cartwright: The Backwoods Preacher*, ed. W. P. Strickland (New York, nd), p. 79. Cf. P. H. Fowler, *Historical Sketch of Presbyterianism Within the Bounds of the Synod of Central New York* (Utica, 1877), pp. 176–7.

slave states shaped politics and religion; it gave extra meaning to the conflict between New School Calvinists tied by blood and history to the New England Standing Order, and Methodists, Baptists, and Disciples of Christ whose cultural roots in many cases lay in the back country of the pre-Revolutionary South. The latter feared that these Presbyterians and Congregationalists ('Presbygationalists', as they were known) sought to erect a new, informal theocracy on the ruins of the power their fathers had exercised through the old Standing Order and the Federalist party. In the years following the War of 1812, the few Methodists in the Western Reserve, one of their preachers later recalled, 'were treated as intruders, and with much contempt'. For their part Methodists in the southern part of Ohio were equally contemptuous of the Yankees. Peter Cartwright was sent to Marietta Circuit in 1806, and encountered a colony of New Englanders. 'I had never seen a Yankee, and I had heard dismal stories about them', he reflected years later. 'It was said they lived almost entirely on pumpkins, molasses, fat meat, and bohea tea; moreover, that they could not bear loud and zealous sermons, . . . and were always criticising us poor backwoods preachers.' Further west, an old 'hard-shell' Baptist, 'Daddy' Briggs, maintained that the richness of God's grace 'tuck in the isles of the sea and the uttermost parts of the "yeth." It embraced the Esquimaux and the Hottentots, and some . . . go so fur as to suppose that it takes in these poor benighted Yankees; but *I* don't go that fur.'[8]

The same cultural antipathies could also cut through, as well as between, churches. Alfred Brunson, born into Connecticut Calvinism in 1793, repudiated the Congregational church as an adolescent, became a Methodist exhorter, and after his migration to the Western Reserve was admitted into the travelling ministry. There he faced a double prejudice: Congregationalists' hostility to Methodists, and the unconcealed contempt of southern Methodist preachers from lower Ohio and Kentucky for Yankees, whom they regarded 'as bordering upon the savage state'. Amongst Presbyterians, too, the regional and ethnic mixing of New-School, 'modern' Calvinists from New England and its diaspora with the stern Scotch-Irish from Pennsylvania and the

[8] Brunson, *Western Pioneer*, 1, p. 172; Cartwright, *Autobiography*, p. 98; Joseph Gillespie, *Recollections of Early Illinois, and Her Noted Men* (Chicago, 1880), p. 6.

Appalachian regions proved to be an unstable coalition, and led to a denominational fissure in the mid-1830s.[9]

The principal features, then, of American religion in general, and of Protestantism in particular, in the years between the founding of the Republic and the Civil War were voluntarism, aggressive denominationalism, intense competition, zealous evangelism, and barely checked institutional proliferation and diversity. Yet, paradoxically, the broad thrust of American religious historiography has tended to stress the elements of harmony and the fundamentally tolerant accommodation operating amongst the mainstream Protestant churches. In their denial that the American voluntary system sanctioned 'a disorderly and theologically uninspiring pluralism' or 'sectarian fever', American theologians and historians, as Laurence Moore has cogently pointed out, have simply repeated an orthodoxy first established by nineteenth-century observers.[10]

Especially influential in this process was Robert Baird's remarkable work, *Religion in America*. First published in 1844, the book was the first truly comprehensive and sustained analysis of American religious thought and practice. Baird regarded the essential division in American churches as that between Evangelicals (principally Congregationalists, Regular Baptists, Methodists, low-church Episcopalians, and his own denominational family of Presbyterians) and non-Evangelicals. Though the latter included such fast-growing churches as Roman Catholics and Mormons, Baird was sure that the future lay with the Evangelicals, who ought to be seen 'as branches of one great body'. After all, he reasonably pointed out, they exhibited 'a most remarkable coincidence of view on all important points': a Trinitarian God; the depravity, guilt, and condemnation of all humankind; Christ's atonement, sufficient to procure the sinner's salvation; regeneration by the Holy Ghost; a final judgement resulting in everlasting misery for the wicked and blessedness for the righteous; and, to qualify for admission to full

[9] Brunson, *Western Pioneer*, 1, p. 173; Robert L. Kelley, *The Cultural Pattern in American Politics: The First Century* (New York, 1979), pp. 128, 167; George Marsden, *The Evangelical Mind and the New School Presbyterian Experience: A Case Study of Thought and Theology in Nineteenth-Century America* (New Haven, Conn., 1970), pp. 39–67.

[10] R. Laurence Moore, *Religious Outsiders and the Making of Americans* (New York, 1986), pp. vii–xv, 3–21.

church communion, evidence of a moral life and profession of a personal experience of salvation.[11]

Other antebellum observers concurred with the essence of Baird's analysis. Though Philip Schaff, the German Reformed theologian, could not subscribe to the separation of church and state as an abstract good, he treated the diversity of American sects as the residue of European controversies, not the product of disestablishment; he believed the mainstream Protestant churches in America, and a 'Protestantized' Roman Catholicism would become the engines of Christian unity.[12] James Dixon, too, returning to England after an extensive tour of American Methodism in 1848, concluded that '[n]otwithstanding the number of churches, bearing different names, and adopting diversified forms of service, there is probably as much or more unity in these States than elsewhere. . . . [T]here appeared infinitely less of what is distinctive and sectarian than in this country.' Dixon attributed this unity of spirit to the absence of a religious establishment, so that '[n]o class of ministers, except popish priests and a few hair-brained [sic] Puseyites, ever dream of saying of other ministers that they are "unauthorized," have no "vocation," are "intruders" into other men's folds, and "usurpers" of the priestly office.' He considered true unity to lie not in an enforced outward conformity but in a common belief in the gospel of Christ, even if the *apprehension* of gospel truth would, given the infirmities of human nature, vary from one person to another. Protestant differences in the United States lay 'more on points of discipline and church order, than on questions of truth and faith'.[13]

That this emphasis on unity fed into later nineteenth-century studies of American religion, often written from a providentialist perspective similar to Baird's, is less surprising than that a consensual approach has also dominated scholarly church history since 1900. The work of some of the most influential religious historians this century, including William Warren Sweet, Win-

[11] Robert Baird, *Religion in America; or, An Account of the Origin, Relation to the State, and Present Condition of the Evangelical Churches in the United States, with Notices of the Unevangelical Denominations* (1844; revised ed. New York, 1856), p. 370.

[12] Philip Schaff, *America: A Sketch of Its Political, Social, and Religious Character* (1854), discussed in Moore, *Religious Outsiders*, pp. 7–8.

[13] James Dixon, *Methodism in America . . .* (London, 1849), 140–9. Cf. Smith, *Revivalism and Social Reform*, p. 19.

throp Hudson, and Sidney Mead, as well as of the sociologist Will Herberg, all fall into this category.[14] More recently, however, Edwin Gaustad, Sydney Ahlstrom, and Laurence Moore have sought to come to terms with the emphatic shift in American historiography since the 1960s, and have pointed to the significance for religious history of the depth of ideological and cultural cleavages in American political and social life.[15] Yet we still lack a proper balance of understanding between the harmonizing influences within Protestant diversity on the one hand, and pluralism's function as a source of conflict and instability on the other. There is at least one major area of analysis whose neglect has led us seriously to understate the conflict within competitive evangelicalism: relations between the two largest evangelical forces, the Baptists and Methodists. But before pursuing this it may be instructive to consider ways in which the values and practices of the major Protestant denominations did indeed set limits on contention and encouraged religious convergence.

## II

Baird was right to emphasize the common salvationist, biblicist elements of evangelicals' doctrinal beliefs. Those views formed part of a widely held conviction that, in keeping with the Almighty's special plan for the new republic, the blessings of grace would eventually engulf the whole people. Evangelicals generally shared the profound hopes of most Americans for their nation, signally blessed, as they saw it, with natural resources, human enterprise, and political advantages. As the waves of revival swelled ever higher through the first four decades of the century, they seemed to confirm the new nation's unique

---

[14] Moore discusses these writers in *Religious Outsiders*, pp. 13–20, noting some element of ambivalence in the treatment of American religious homogenization in Will Herberg, *Protestant, Catholic, Jew: An Essay in American Religious Sociology* (Garden City, 1955). Cf. Johnson, *Islands of Holiness*, pp. 94–102, 137–44. In *Revivals, Awakenings, and Reform*, pp. 13–23 and passim, William G. McLoughlin argues that religious divisions were functionally of great importance, for they furnished a way for the vital, core religious culture of each era to reform and survive.

[15] Moore, *Religious Outsiders*; Sydney E. Ahlstrom, *A Religious History of the American People* (New Haven, Conn., 1972); Edwin S. Gaustad, *Dissent in American Religion* (Chicago, 1973). In an earlier era, H. Richard Niebuhr stressed the liberating potential of sectarianism in *The Social Sources of Denominationalism* (New York, 1929).

mission. A minority of unconvinced Protestants despairingly dissected the books of Daniel and Revelation to conclude that schemes of social amelioration were doomed until Christ's second coming inaugurated the millennial reign. But most evangelicals espoused an optimistic postmillennialism that provided the dominant expression of eschatalogical thinking from the turn of the century to the Civil War. During the climactic phase of the Second Great Awakening it seemed, as one Methodist put it, 'that our beloved country will soon become the sanctified, the saved, the redeemed of the Lord, and thus be secure from the terrible convulsions and revolutions which may afflict and terrify other portions of the earth'. Convinced of their duty, thousands of evangelicals threw themselves untiringly into benevolent and missionary projects, many of them interdenominational, through which they would introduce the millennium which would form the prelude to Christ's return.[16]

Millennial aspiration and heightened spiritual intensity often prompted co-operation. Alfred Brunson concluded from his experience in the 1820s as a young Methodist missionary in Detroit that 'the missionary spirit is the millennial spirit', the spirit of fraternity. The Presbyterians having only a licentiate minister, Brunson invited them to his quarterly eucharist, baptizing them and their children when asked. 'In the missionary field', he wrote, 'we met as brethren, laborers with God in one common cause. No controversy between ourselves on non-essential doctrines, and no seeking of the supremacy one over the other [was] . . . apparently thought of. . . . In this is plainly seen the spirit that will prevail in the millennium, when the watchmen of Zion will see eye to eye.' At the height of revivals, too, when missionary aspiration mutated into millennialist joy, Protestant union could become a reality. Methodists, Presbyterians, and Baptists often combined in the turn-of-the-century camp-meetings in the South and West. 'O that this may be the ushering in of a glorious millennium!', Stith Mead prayed in 1802 as union meetings and astonishing revivals swept through Georgia. The great revival that gripped Bristol, Rhode Island, in 1812–13,

---

[16] Ernst Tuveson, *Redeemer Nation: The Idea of America's Millennial Role* (Chicago, 1968); Smith, *Revivalism and Social Reform*, pp. 103–47, 225–37; James L. Moorhead, 'Between progress and apocalypse: a reassessment of millennialism in American religious thought, 1800–1880', *Journal of American History*, 71 (1984), pp. 524–42; *CAJ*, 13 May 1831.

paralysing secular business and setting scores 'at liberty', was pros-
ecuted in union prayer and conference meetings, where Baptists,
Methodists, and Congregationalists worked shoulder-to-shoulder
in unaccustomed harmony. Charles Finney, the shrewdest revivalist
of his generation, wondered 'why persons differing in theory upon
doctrinal points in religion, and belonging to different denominations, will often, for a time, walk together in great harmony and
affection'. It was, he said approvingly, 'because they *feel deeply*, and
feel alike. Their differences are in great measure lost or forgotten,
while they fall in with each other's state of feeling.'[17]

The impact of a revival, whether local or geographically dispersed, was quite rarely limited to a single church or denomination; more commonly it spilt well beyond, sometimes touching
all the community's evangelicals. Lyman Beecher's Congregationalist revival in Boston, in 1826, spread to the Baptists and
even the Unitarians; the three-month Methodist revival in
Rochester, New York, in the following year extended to other
churches; that in New York City in 1831 was 'not confined
to any particular class or denomination of people'; German
Reformed, Presbyterians, and Methodists shared in Philadelphia's religious excitement in 1840 and 1841. The list could be
extended to the point of tedium. Significantly, the acceleration
in rates of annual denominational growth which Methodists
experienced in, for example, the early 1800s, the early 1830s,
and the later 1850s was replicated in Presbyterian, Baptist, and
Congregationalist membership patterns.[18]

The common pulses in growth and the general sharing in the
experience of revival points to the diffusionist, even homogenizing, effects of the spiritual market on evangelical Protestantism. Plainly, churches needed members to survive. Without tax
support or substantial endowments, churches depended on

[17] Brunson, *Western Pioneer*, 1, p. 275; *Wesleyan Methodist Magazine* (London), 25 (1802), pp. 521–3;
36 (1813), pp. 157–8; Madison, NJ, Drew University, Methodist Collection [hereafter DU-MC]Asa
Kent to Abel Stevens, 1 March 1847; Finney's sermon (4 March 1827) is quoted in *Letters of the Rev.
Dr. Beecher and Rev. Mr. Nettleton, on the 'New Measures' in Conducting Revivals of Religion with a Review
of a Sermon, by Novanglus* (New York, 1828), pp. 64–5.

[18] Lyman Beecher, *The Autobiography of Lyman Beecher*, ed. Barbara M. Cross, 2 vols (Cambridge,
Mass., 1961), p. 76; *CAJ*, 28 April 1827, 6 May 1831, 13 Jan. 1841; Carwardine, *Transatlantic
Revivalism*, pp. 45–54. Cf. S. B. Halliday and D. S. Gregory, *The Church in America and Its Baptisms of
Fire* . . . (New York, 1896), p. 598; *New York Observer* (Presbyterian) [hereafter *NYO*], 16 Dec. 1826;
Cross, *Burned-Over District*, p. 254.

voluntary contributions to pay their pastors and meet their other costs. Successful, growing churches became the object of envy and even admiration. As the most effective denomination in the country, increasing dramatically from a little over 60,000 members in 1790 to some 1,500,000 by the mid-1850s, Methodists attracted the greatest attention of all. Whatever doubts their evangelical critics had about Methodist practices, enthusiasm, and doctrines, many came to believe that the best way of countering the Arminians was by 'Methodizing' themselves. Tobias Spicer's experience as a Methodist itinerant in New York state and New England convinced him that 'such had been the success of Methodism that [Calvinist] ministers . . . were obliged to bestir themselves or lose their hold upon their people.'[19]

Amongst Presbyterians, Margaret Bayard Smith noted that in Washington in 1822 the preachers were 'introducing all the habits and hymns of the Methodists into our . . . churches'. From Georgia in 1827 Methodists reported that 'camp meetings, . . . sudden conversions, and sudden admissions into the church, formerly the anomalies of Methodism, are no longer uncommon incidents with our brethren, especially the Presbyterians'; the following year another Methodist smugly noted that though the Presbyterians had 'formerly disapproved of our long established custom of inviting seekers of religion to the altar, or a similar place, that they might be assisted by prayers and exhortation, they have adopted, and are now pursuing the same course'. Charles Finney, the era's most distinguished revivalist, made his reputation by introducing 'new measures' amongst fellow Presbyterians, but there is no doubt about his profound debt to the Methodists' simple and direct style of preaching and to their tools of revival. Protestant Episcopalians in Bristol, Rhode Island, Richmond, Virginia, and elsewhere deliberately used the Methodists' call to the altar to 'keep up with the times'; Congregationalists' widespread adoption of protracted meetings, after initial hostility, equally drew on Methodist practice; Baptists, too, especially through the work of their leading revivalists Jacob Knapp, Jabez Swann, and Emerson Andrews, opened their doors

[19] Spicer, *Autobiography*, pp. 101–2.

to special revival effort of a kind previously deplored and re-sisted.[20]

This diffusion of revival practice was accompanied by a general 'Arminianizing' of Calvinist doctrine. The intellectual jour-neying of the principal denominational theologians and revival-ists towards a 'modern' Calvinism is a familiar story. Amongst Congregationalists and Presbyterians, Nathaniel W. Taylor, Lyman Beecher, Albert Barnes, and Finney himself successfully modified the eighteenth-century 'Consistent Calvinist' doctrines of moral inability, total depravity, and limited atonement; Knapp, Swann, and others battled against 'double-extra Calvin-ism' in the Baptist church, especially repudiating 'views of the sovereignty of the Holy Spirit . . . which led to a practical denial of the necessity of all human agency in bringing sinners to consider the claims of the gospel'. Important in driving Calvinist luminaries in this direction were popular, or market, pressures. These churchmen were acutely aware that ordinary Americans found the stricter Calvinistic formulations increasingly illogical and irrelevant in a world where an ideology of republican equality went hand-in-hand with broadening opportunities for people to make their mark in society. They could see the powerful appeal of Methodist theology, whether to those like Deborah Millet, who 'was a Methodist in sentiment before I knew their doctrines', or to others for whom Methodism acted as a radiant light that helped them make sense of the world and their place in it.[21]

Important to this diffusion of doctrine was the traffic in church members and adherents from one denomination to another. Some-times this followed geographical migration: when people moved it was not unusual for them to join a different denomination,

---

[20] M. B. Smith to J. Kirkpatrick, 12 Oct. 1822, in Hunt, *First Forty Years*, p. 159; *CAJ*, 12 Oct. 1827, 8 Aug. 1828, 5 March 1830, 13 May, 15 July 1831; J. Brockway, *A Delineation of the Characteristic Features of a Revival of Religion in Troy, in 1826 and 1827* (Troy, 1827), p. 59; Charles G. Finney, *The Memoirs of Rev. Charles G. Finney: The Complete Restored Text*, ed. Garth M. Rosell and Richard A. G. Dupuis (Grand Rapids, 1989), p. 90; *NYO*, 24 Aug. 1823; DU-MC, Asa Kent to Abel Stevens, 1 March 1847; Jacob Knapp, *Autobiography* (New York, 1868), pp. 28, 36–41; F. Dennison, ed., *The Evangelist: or Life and Labors of Rev. Jabez. S. Swann: Being an Autobiographical Record of This Far-Famed Preacher . . .* (Waterford, Conn., 1873), pp. 69–107, 181.

[21] Knapp, *Autobiography*, pp. 28, 43–4; George Peck, *The Life and Times of George Peck, D. D.* (New York, 1874), pp. 22–3; Gilbert Haven and Russell Thomas, *Father Taylor, The Sailor Preacher . . .* (Boston, 1872), pp. 73–5; Spicer, *Autobiography*, p. 33.

especially if the range of available choice was limited.[22] Sometimes it resulted from the 'stealing' of revival converts discussed above. Arminians who were induced to join Calvinist churches might serve as catalysts for change in doctrine and practical measures. After the revival in Providence, Rhode Island, in 1815 the Methodists failed to hold on to all their converts because their meeting-house was too small and they were too poor to build a new one; as a result, the Baptists gained many new members, all converted under Arminian preaching. Alfred Brunson, recalling the defection to the Presbyterian church of a hundred camp-meeting converts at Geneva, Ohio, in 1821, believed such events had done much to bring about the growth over the next half-century of Presbyterians' 'liberal feelings toward the Methodists': whatever Presbyterians 'formerly thought of . . . Methodistic conversions, I never knew them to refuse one who offered to join them'. For these reasons many could have echoed the correspondent from Georgia who wrote to the New York *Christian Advocate and Journal* in 1831 that 'the good old doctrines of Methodism' were being 'proclaimed zealously by Presbyterians and Baptists'. Instead of 'talking in the dry old style, about "waiting God's own good time . . ." ' they now insisted that 'Christ tasted death for *every* man', 'All may come', 'If you are damned it is your own fault', and 'All things are *now* ready.' Significantly, the Methodist doctrine of the second blessing, or entire sanctification, also enjoyed a currency well beyond that church, particularly amongst Congregationalists and New School Presbyterians.[23]

Thus by the 1840s and 1850s much of the earlier interdenominational antagonism was yielding to a recognition of what evangelicals held in common. The process was further aided by the profound changes in members' social status within substantial portions of Methodism and the Baptist churches, which narrowed the gap between them and the 'respectable'

---

[22] Kathleen Kutolowski, 'Identifying the religious affiliations of nineteenth-century local elites', *Historical Methods Newsletter*, 9 (1975), pp. 9–10. Cf. Orville V. Burton, *In My Father's House Are Many Mansions: Family and Community in Edgefield, South Carolina* (Chapel Hill, NC, 1985), p. 22.

[23] McDonald, *History of Methodism in Providence*, p. 49; Brunson, *Western Pioneer*, 1, p. 250; *CAJ*, 18 Nov. 1831, 26 Feb. 1857; George Hughes, *Fragrant Memories of the Tuesday Meeting and Its Fifty Years' Work for Jesus* (New York, 1856), p. 38. For cross-denominational influences within families, see Cartwright, *Autobiography*, p. 87; Elizabeth K. Nottingham, *Methodism and the Frontier: Indiana Proving Ground* (New York, 1941), p. 166.

Calvinist churches. From being 'outcast' sects in tension with the established social and ecclesiastical order, by the mid-nineteenth century they had taken on the character of institutionalized denominations that boasted colleges, an educated ministry, fashionable churches, middle-class congregations, community and political influence, and a concern for 'order, method and efficiency' instead of 'extravagant excitements'. By the early 1850s the New York editor George Coles could declare, 'One thing is certain, the *evangelical* sects are more harmonious in their feelings towards each other than they were formerly. The Dutch Reformed, Presbyterians, Baptists, and Episcopal Methodists, are now on a very friendly footing with each other.'[24]

What above all else encouraged co-operation, however, was an increasing sense amongst evangelical Protestants that they faced daunting and common challenges in the form of demographic change, city growth, and the burgeoning of non-evangelical religion. William Hutchinson has written of the 'truly monumental decline' of American Protestantism between the Revolution and the Civil War. It is doubtful if that is exactly how Protestants themselves saw it, for their absolute growth was stunning, as we have seen. But it is true that this was the period of Protestantism's greatest relative decline in the whole of American history, an era when its churches dwindled from almost total command at the end of the colonial period to embracing only sixty per cent of churchgoers in 1860. To a degree that decline reflected the growth of unique American churches, particularly the Mormons, but the principal challenge emerged from the massive influx of Roman Catholics, especially from Ireland and Germany, in the 1840s and 1850s. Those immigrants clung mainly to the rapidly-expanding cities, mainly in the free states, and added to the 'demoralizing' problems that evangelicals had already identified as quintessentially urban ones: lapsed church attendance, free-thought, a corrupting commercial ethic, Sabbath-breaking, drink, prostitution, and generalized 'vice'. This cluster of concerns made Protestants much more attentive to appeals for concerted action. '[T]he times call for

---

[24] Abel Stevens, *Life and Times of Nathan Bangs, D. D.* (New York, 1863), pp. 182–4, 191; George Coles, *My First Seven Years in America*, ed. D. P. Kidder (New York, 1852).

unity of spirit and effort among the evangelical churches', insisted New York City's *Christian Advocate and Journal* in 1842.[25]

To this end, evangelicals could draw on previous experience of co-operation in the face of common adversity, though in each case it had foundered on the more powerful reality of sectarianism. Frontier conditions had at times encouraged a pragmatic pooling of resources: the lack of meeting-houses, for instance, led to a sharing of accommodation, or even to Methodists, Baptists, and Presbyterians worshipping together. But these had been temporary expedients and rarely survived the institutionalizing of churches. In Indiana in 1816 James Finley scornfully rejected a Presbyterian minister's proposal for co-operation: 'Presbyterian union formed for the sole purpose of using the Methodists in advancing Presbyterianism! I plainly told my brethren, I had nothing against the Presbyterians; I loved them, but I loved Methodism more, and, as we had a shop of our own, we would not work journey-work any longer.' Some years later in Illinois, when Peter Cartwright was offered money to build a church provided that he 'would make it a Union Church for all denominations', he firmly declined. All churches built on this principle, he insisted, 'became a bone of contention and created strife, and ended in confusion; . . . a church should always belong to some religious denomination that would take care of it, and I was going to build a church for the Methodists'. Combativeness, schism, and denominational integrity, not union, were the keynotes of the frontier churches.[26]

A more compelling model for mid-century co-operative effort lay in the extraordinary activities of the national benevolent societies which sprang into existence immediately after the war of 1812. This 'evangelical united front' comprised a dozen or so agencies, the most important of which were inter-denominational and included the American Education Society, the American Board of Foreign Missions, the American Bible Society, the American Sunday-School Union, the American Tract Society, and the American Home Missionary Society. Charles I. Foster has shown how these bodies were designed to sustain and enhance the prestige of religion in an era of disestablishment, a time

---

[25] William Hutchinson, ed., *Between the Times: The Travail of the Protestant Establishment in America, 1900–1960* (Cambridge, 1989), p. 304; *CAJ*, 2 June 1827, 14 Dec. 1842.

[26] Nottingham, *Methodism and the Frontier*, p. 153; Cartwright, *Autobiography*, p. 386.

when individual churches were 'too weak, divided, conservative, and lacking in imagination' to achieve these ends on their
own. The united front was just one expression of a post-war
optimistic nationalism and, like that nationalism, drew vigour
from economic boom and a revolution in transport and communications. Driven by an ethic of 'disinterested benevolence'
and commanding a substantial budget, these societies worked
primarily through individual congregations, not the non-sectarian public meeting. Nonetheless many were moved by a vision
of Protestant unity, and a few looked even to create some kind
of non-sectarian suprachurch. Their anxieties derived not just
from the rapid increase in the poorer, disease-ridden, and transient population of the cities, but from the challenge of the new
West. Thus the electoral victory in 1828 of Andrew Jackson,
western hero and antithesis of New England Puritan values,
together with a mounting fear of a Catholic invasion in the
West, turned attention to the Mississippi Valley. Such was the
societies' success in publishing and distributing propaganda, establishing and sustaining Christian education, promoting the
temperance cause, stimulating revivals, and subsidizing missions,
that by the 1830s their hopes of world conquest for Christ
seemed to many Americans no longer a visionary dream but a
practical proposition.[27]

Yet by the late 1830s the evangelical united front had collapsed, a result in part of the movement's own success: the
revitalizing of Protestant religion in general had actually strengthened the individual denominations, now enjoying greater
numbers and prestige than at the turn of the century. Important
here was the societies' determination not to drive sectarian
publishing houses out of business, and their practical assistance to
particular denominations in the form of grants for missionary
activity. But this hardly explains why the good temper of the
early years to the mid-1820s yielded to disputation, schism, and
bitterness. For this we must look to the benevolent societies'
relatively narrow sectarian and regional base. Organized mainly
in the northeast and the middle Atlantic states, their leaders were

---

[27] Charles I. Foster, *An Errand of Mercy: The Evangelical United Front, 1790–1837* (Chapel Hill, NC, 1960), pp. 129, 132–7, 179–207. Some of the most effective non-sectarian enterprises were the mariners' churches strung out along the Atlantic coast from New England to South Carolina. *CAJ*, 26 June, 10 July 1829.

very largely Congregationalists, Presbyterians, and Dutch Reformed. Methodists and Baptists played a role in the united front, but class antagonisms did little to help these denominations look charitably on the 'Presbygationalist' leadership whose call to arms in the 'uncivilized' Mississippi Valley seemed presumptuously to ignore Methodist and Baptist achievements in the West. The efforts of the American Sunday-School Union to secure a charter of incorporation from the Pennsylvania legislature, when seen in conjunction with the call of the Presbyterian minister, Ezra Stiles Ely, for a Christian party in politics, seemed to Nathan Bangs and other Methodists to represent a Presbyterian attack on religious liberty and the voluntary system. Through the later 1820s and 1830s Bangs's efforts for strictly Methodist operations in publishing, home missions, and Sunday-schools gave a lead to Baptists just as angry about 'the practice of some to represent all parts of the country as in almost heathenish darkness, unless some of THEIR *competent ministers* are there. Everything, it seems, must be *Americanized*, or it cannot be other than *sectarian. . . .*' To this inter-denominational antagonism must be added the bitter conflict within the Presbyterian Church which culminated in a separation of New and Old Schools in 1837–8. The fissure within its most energetic force ensured the fragmentation of the evangelical united front.[28]

Despite its fracturing, the benevolent empire provided an organizational model for renewed and energetic evangelical cooperation during the 1840s and 1850s, when the Catholic threat took on new urgency. Evangelicals' concern extended well beyond anxieties over Catholics' creed, liturgy, and ceremonial to alarm over the challenge Rome posed to American republicanism. Catholicism, they were convinced, corroded the high standards of personal behaviour that citizenship demanded in a moral republic, not least because licentious priests condoned in the privacy of the confessional the drunkenness, theft, and sexual immorality that were badges of the Sabbath-breaking, revelling, whisky-swilling, beer-drinking Irish and German immigrants. Unlettered Catholics, controlled by priests and corrupt politicians, perverted the democratic ballot by bloc voting. Papists also

[28] Foster, *Errand of Mercy*, pp. 131–2, 202–3, 214, 239–44; Cross, *Burned-Over District*, pp. 255–7. The campaign in the South achieved relatively little outside the few small urban centres which could function as hubs.

threatened the Protestant spirit of free inquiry by seeking state support for their parochial institutions and opposing the use of the King James Bible in public schools. In New York, Philadelphia, Baltimore, St Louis, Cincinnati, and other cities through the 1840s and early 1850s Protestants organized to resist the Catholic hierarchs' campaign, posing the question: 'Blot out the Bible from the American mind . . . and how long . . . [will] this republic last?'[29]

Protestant leaders who regarded popery as the single greatest threat to the Christian republic were able to exploit a mixture of ideological, political, ethnic, and class antagonism in their efforts to manufacture a cohesive Protestant response. Indeed, by the mid-1840s, as Ray Billington's classic study of American nativism tells us, 'the American churches were able to present a virtually united front against Catholicism.' In this they could draw on a number of agencies from the fractured benevolent empire. The American Bible Society, the least sectarian of the bodies of the former evangelical united front, took a lead in defending the Protestant Bible in common schools; so too did the American Education Society. The American Tract Society also became an anti-Roman organization, operating a system of colportage amongst the Catholic population.[30] At the same time a number of new organizations sprang up to secure Protestant unity against the pope and rebut Catholics' sneers about Protestantism's endemic disharmony. Some of these were spontaneous local coalitions unconnected with national institutions. Evangelicals in Philadelphia, despairing of securing national unity amongst denominational bodies, set about getting individual ministers to co-operate in a Protestant alliance; in 1842 they formed an American Protestant Association with almost one hundred of the city's ministers, representing most denominations, as charter members. A similar conviction that Rome

---

[29] Ray Allen Billington, *The Protestant Crusade, 1800–1860: A Study of the Origins of American Nativism* (New York, 1938); *Western Christian Advocate* (Cincinnati; Methodist), 10 Nov. 1852. Cf. Rufus W. Clark, *Popery and the United States, Embracing an Account of Papal Operations in Our Country, with a View to the Dangers Which Threaten Our Institutions* (Boston, 1847); Horace Bushnell, *Common Schools: A Discourse on the Modifications Demanded by the Roman Catholics* (Hartford, Conn., 1853); Henry Clay Fish, *The School Question: Romanism and the Common Schools: A Discourse* . . . (New York, 1853).

[30] Billington, *Protestant Crusade*, pp. 181–2. An increasing nativist outlook influenced the American Home Missionary Society, too, from the mid-1840s. Ibid., pp. 275–7.

thrived only because of Protestant disunity underpinned American contributions to the World Convention and Evangelical Alliance in London, in August 1846. Most influential of all the new bodies was the Protestant Reformation Society, founded in New York in 1836, and its successors, the American Protestant Society, which by 1849 was publishing over two million pages of tract material a year, and the American and Foreign Christian Union, whose agents found allies in all Protestant denominations. Events confirmed the judgement of the Protestant journal which in 1843 declared that anti-Catholicism now 'becomes the very centre of Christian unity'.[31]

Halting the advance of Catholicism, however, was not to be achieved at any price. Protestant evangelicals harboured serious misgivings over the ugly excesses of working-class nativism – including the burning in 1834 of the Ursuline convent in Charlestown, the deaths and destruction wrought by the Bible riots of 1844 in Philadelphia, and the intolerance of Know-Nothing politics in the 1850s. Many judged that Romanists would succumb to a gospel of love, not to nativist abrasion. Catholics, they believed, had been providentially brought to a land whose moral influences would effect their conversion. As one speaker told the American Home Missionary Society, 'If Protestantism cannot cope with Popery on this free soil, in the midst of Bibles and Sabbaths and schools and seminaries; then I say let us give up the contest, and hasten back to Rome and get absolution as speedily as possible.' Evangelism and revivals, not proscription, were the means of success.[32]

Thus evangelicals' co-operation in revivals came to supplement their involvement in non-denominational anti-Catholic societies. Significantly, the final great revival of the antebellum period and the most dramatic since the great influx of Catholic immigrants, the so-called 'awakening' of 1857–8, was insistently interdenominational. In many respects it marked the high point of Protestant harmony in the period from the Revolution to the

---

[31] Billington, *Protestant Crusade*, pp. 96–8, 166–8, 182–5, 244–56, 264–75. Cf. John Wolffe, 'Anti-Catholicism and evangelical identity in Britain and the United States, 1830–1860' in Mark A. Noll, David W. Bebbington and George A. Rawlyk, eds, *Evangelicalism: Comparative Studies of Popular Protestantism in North America, The British Isles, and Beyond, 1770–1990* (New York, 1994), pp. 179–97.

[32] Richard J. Carwardine, *Evangelicals and Politics in Antebellum America* (New Haven, Conn., 1993), pp. 231–3; Billington, *Protestant Crusade*, p. 280.

Civil War. 'Union' prayer-meetings, especially but not exclusively in urban settings, were the distinctive novelty. These had been prompted by the mid-day interdenominational prayer meetings in New York City's business district, organized to beg God's mercy in a time of financial panic. Some union meetings were held under the auspices of the recently formed, non-denominational YMCA, or in mobile 'union tabernacles' tied to no particular denomination. Controversial topics, theological and political, were avoided. A sense that the revival was 'a great and wonderful day in the Ch[urches] of Christ, and a precursor to some great event', encouraged Christians to forget 'all past alienations and distractions.'[33]

All those elements which for over a generation had made for increasing co-operation amongst American evangelical Protestants operated with special force in 1857–8: millennialist expectation, doctrinal convergence, and concerted response to external challenge and threatening social change. But we should register that the religious events of what contemporary Protestants regarded as an *annus mirabilis* were by definition extraordinary, even unique. This perspective should become all the more compelling once we have explored a strangely neglected area of antebellum Protestant experience, one which reminds us that chronic conflicts continued to operate within evangelicalism even at a time of institutional drives towards Protestant unity.

### III

There is an extraordinary lacuna in the study of popular religion during the early republic: we lack any sustained analysis of the relations between the two giant denominational families of the era, the Baptists and Methodists. The advance of the two movements between the Revolution and the mid-nineteenth century was remarkable by any standards. Representing under twenty per cent of all religious adherents in 1776, they constituted over half the total seventy-five years later. By 1855 they accounted for two

---

[33] E. E. Stuart to her son, 6 April 1858, in Helen S. M. Marlatt, ed., *Stuart Letters of Robert and Elizabeth Sullivan Stuart, 1819–1864*, 2 vols (New York, 1961), 2, p. 862; *NYO*, 5 Aug. 1858; Smith, *Revivalism and Social Reform*, pp. 63–79.

and three-quarter million of the four million Protestant church members, with Methodists comprising thirty-nine per cent and Baptists twenty-seven per cent of the whole body.[34] It is generally recognized that in the early years of the Second Great Awakening relations between the two denominations were marked by aggressive, generally unaccommodating, competition for souls. The reminiscences of the popular preachers of the era are laced with evidence of an intense rivalry in which, as the Methodist minister George Peck noted, 'we looked for no favor'. The preachers' language and metaphors are those of violent battle, and their allusions to explosives, firearms, and blowing adversaries 'sky-high' give credibility to Nathan Bangs's description of the western conflict as a 'sort of warfare'.[35]

Peter Cartwright's celebrated account of his early career as a Methodist itinerant in Tennessee, Kentucky, and Ohio at times seems little more than a string of battles with evangelical rivals, in which Baptists constitute the principal foe. Anti-paedobaptists appear as predators, who would 'rush in, and try to take our converts off into the water' and who 'made so much ado about baptism by immersion, that the uninformed would suppose that heaven was an island, and there was no way to get there but by *diving* or *swimming*'. At Stockton Valley in 1804, as an inexperienced preacher of nineteen, Cartwright delivered a funeral sermon during which several fell to the floor and cried for mercy. He extended the meeting 'night and day for some time', until twenty-three were converted. There was no organized Methodist society in the neighbourhood, so before continuing on his circuit Cartwright left his converts with an invitation to read the Methodist *Discipline* and to join the Church on his return four weeks later. No sooner had he left than the Baptists sent in three of their own preachers to capture the twenty-three for themselves through a so-called 'union meeting'. Cartwright hurried back and listened as each of the twenty-three related their experiences of conviction to the delighted Baptists, who declared them true Christians and offered the hand of fellowship. In desperation, Cartwright gave his experience, too, prompting

---

[34] Finke and Stark, *Churching of America*, p. 55; Smith, *Revivalism and Social Reform*, pp. 20–2.

[35] George Peck, *Early Methodism Within the Bounds of the Old Genesee Conference* (New York, 1860), p. 402; Brunson, *Western Pioneer*, 1, p. 354; Nathan Bangs, *A History of the Methodist Episcopal Church*, 4 vols (New York, 1838–41), 2, p. 351.

'great rejoicing over the Methodist preaching boy'. Baptism by immersion was to follow at the creek the following morning. A large crowd gathered. Cartwright presented himself first and declared himself ready to become a Baptist provided the preachers would accept as a sufficient basis his baptism by sprinkling in infancy. When they inevitably refused, Cartwright seized the occasion to elaborate the 'absurdity' of Baptist doctrine and secure the return of his twenty-three loyal converts.[36]

The general direction of religious historiography has been to treat such contention as a passing phase and to stress rather the likenesses between the two movements.[37] Both were churches of the plain folk. Both were especially strong in the West and South. Both were concerned principally with the individual's direct experience of Christ rather than with the more corporate and abstract aspects of church life. Heart-warming revivals and evangelism were a feature of each denomination's economy, especially as Baptist doctrine acquired an increasingly Arminian tinge. Each prized lay activity. Each knew the value of religious liberty and the cost of its defence. Each had reason to distrust what they perceived as Presbyterian and Congregationalist ambition. They tended to a common political affiliation: under the 'first party system' both were overwhelmingly loyal to the Jeffersonian Republicans, the party of religious toleration and pluralism; under the subsequent party system both have been seen to sustain the Jacksonian Democrats (on one interpretation, the party of 'the common man'; on another, the heirs of Jeffersonian pluralism). In this context the differences over baptismal mode seem largely inconsequential. Baptist Tweedledum, albeit drenched and dripping, mirrored a Methodist Tweedledee, merely sprinkled and slightly damp.

This interpretation seriously understates the chronic and unrelenting antagonism between the two denominations that stretched through to the Civil War, particularly outside New England and the wider northeast. Cartwright, even in his later years, refused to succumb to a more sentimental view of Baptists: 'although I have studied long and hard', he wrote acidly in 1856, 'I have never to this day found out what a Baptist means by a

[36] Cartwright, *Autobiography*, pp. 64–72, 133–4.
[37] See, for example, Smith, *Revivalism and Social Reform*, pp. 24–5.

union meeting.' A North Carolinian, William D. Valentine reflected in 1853: 'The baptists are even now contemned, and hated, indeed they begin to be dreaded.' The great armies of Baptists and Methodists faced one another 'in rivalling and it is feared in threatening mien'. He prayed that they should 'not fall afoul of each other, but unite in battle array . . . , both abjuring error and marching in loving solid phalanx to the advancement of Christ's cause'.[38] Valentine's hopes were doomed, for the festering relations that had prompted his prayer were soon to break out into an extraordinarily rancid and debilitating warfare, one which calls into question the assumption that this was straightforwardly a decade of growing interdenominational harmony. Across the South and Southwest, as well as other parts of the Union, church leaders and publicists were sucked into a conflict, now largely forgotten, between the partisans of two of Tennessee's finest polemicists: the editor of the Nashville *Tennessee Baptist*, the Reverend James Robinson Graves, and the 'fighting parson' of Knoxville, William Gannaway Brownlow.

Graves's newspaper attacks on Methodism, which began in the late 1840s, tapped into a rich vein of Appalachian polemics. For twenty years and more Presbyterians had been churning out anti-Methodist abuse, especially through the pages of Frederick A. Ross's *Calvinistic Magazine*, which had kept up an unremitting attack on Methodism's allegedly tyrannical and debauching influence. After Ross left for Alabama in 1849 Graves, a young man in his twenties, borrowed heavily from his writings, so that when he declared in 1855 'The "Great West" is to-day one great battle-field' and 'the whole South is intensely agitated', the responsibility lay by no means as one-sidedly with the Methodists' Book Concern and circuit-riders as he insisted. In 1856 Graves published his various articles and tracts as *The Great Iron Wheel: or, Republicanism Backward and Christianity Reversed*. Mixing ridicule and vituperation, the 570-page book became an instant success and reached its thirtieth edition by 1860. Not all Baptists approved of its tone, but prominent ministers and lay members in Tennessee and adjoining states readily circulated it, and the North Carolina Baptist Publication Society endorsed it,

---

[38] Cartwright, *Autobiography*, p. 66; University of North Carolina at Chapel Hill, Southern Historical Collection William D. Valentine, 'Diary', 27 June 1853.

as did a range of Baptist newspapers that included the influential *Biblical Recorder*.[39]

The Nashville editor directed the main thrust of an essentially three-pronged attack at the Methodists' centralized system of church government, which he denounced as 'despotic and hierarchical, and . . . antagonistic to all that is republican' and truly American. Ruled by a variant of Wesley's *Discipline* ('a rod of iron' fashioned by a self-declared enemy of American independence and republicanism), the Methodist Episcopal Church had been shaped by unpatriotic 'tory' preachers into a monstrous machine whose wheels ground its powerless church members into submission. Graves took his metaphor from the Methodist minister George Cookman, who had admiringly likened his Church to a lubricated system of wheels within wheels:

> The *great iron wheel* in the system is *itinerancy*; and truly it *grinds some of us tremendously*! the *brazen wheel*, attached and kept in motion by the former, is the *local ministry*; the *golden wheel*, [is] the *doctrine and discipline of the Church*, in full and successful operation. . . . [T]he entire movement depends upon keeping the *great iron wheel of itinerancy* constantly and rapidly rolling round.

Over a million American freemen, mourned Graves, had bowed to Methodism's episcopal absolutism, 'the most fearful Hierarchism on the face of the earth', placed themselves under the control of 'petty spiritual rulers and lordlings', succumbed to 'a perfect system of *passive obedience and non-resistance*', and conspired in their own conscience-destroying regimentation:

> They submit to be controlled in their reading, so that there is a virtual censorship of the press over them. They are drilled to prefer hearing some old hickupping driveler, who has '*got religion*' to listening to [an educated non-Methodist

[39] *Jonesboro Whig*, 12 May 1840, 22, 29 Sept., 20 Oct., 10 Nov. 1847, 14 June, 20 Dec. 1848; E. M. Coulter, *William G. Brownlow: Fighting Parson of the Southern Highlands* (Chapel Hill, NC, 1937), pp. 18–20, 26–34, 53–65; J. R. Graves, *The Great Iron Wheel: or, Republicanism Backward and Christianity Reversed* (Nashville, 1856), pp. vi–vii; William G. Brownlow, *The Great Iron Wheel Examined; or, Its False Spokes Extracted, and an Exhibition of Elder Graves, Its Builder* (Nashville, 1856), pp. xvi, 256–7, 276.

minister]. They submit to being controlled in the cut of
their dress. They are drilled to extraordinary sameness in
expression of face, and tone of voice. They are drilled . . .
to uphold Methodism through thick and thin, right or
wrong. . . . [T]hey are drilled to gather around the preacher
in the pulpit . . . and hurrah over the merest bag of wind. . . .
They are drilled to believe that it is right to hate with
personal, private malignity, every man who speaks against
Methodism . . . .

Brain-washed Methodists had been deluded into believing they
enjoyed religious liberty, though in reality 'deprived of every
governmental right and liberty for which blood was shed on the
battle fields of the Revolution, or the hill of Calvary!'[40]

Graves's second line of attack was to present Methodism as a
fundamentally Romanist movement – as an agent of Antichrist.
Methodists' conception and use of priestly power, he insisted,
equated to the worst form of popery: their bishops, the '*popes* of
Methodism', exercised the same supreme authority as the Jesuits'
'General', compelling ministers to go wherever they were ordered. Once in place, preachers themselves exercised absolute
power over admission and exclusion from the Church, so that
each became 'the absolute Pope, during his short reign, over the
societies in his circuit'.[41]

That power was exerted through band-meetings and classes, in
function and intent no different from the Roman confessional,
where members were encouraged to discuss their sins and temptations in front of others. '[T]he preacher in charge, even if an
unmarried man, is authorized to hear confessions . . . from both
the married and unmarried sisters of his charge! What if some of
their stray thoughts had been concerning himself!' Graves expressed concern for the husband whose wife's confession of
'what she may have done and thought one week' might be made
'the theme of neigborhood gossip the next'. 'What father', he
asked, 'would wish his daughter['s] head made the receptacle of
all the wicked acts, thoughts, and imaginations of a whole band?'
Both Romish and Methodist confessionals sought to submit the

[40] Graves, *Great Iron Wheel*, pp. 153–67, 396–7.
[41] Ibid., pp. 234–5.

mind to priestly control and contrived, by obsessive relating of sins, gradually to harden the conscience and 'break down the natural barriers God has erected in the instinctive shame of human nature, to say nothing of quenching the Spirit'.[42]

Methodists' baptismal practice, too, was a damnable heresy. Baptists had long held that paedobaptist sprinkling of infants was nothing less than a Roman sacrament that had erroneously survived in many Protestant churches. The perceived threat of papal invasion in the Mississippi Valley in the 1830s and subsequent Catholic advances had encouraged Baptists to stress their unique status – the only religious body to demand baptism by complete immersion as a sign and seal of conversion.[43] Graves enthusiastically developed this theme, insisting that 'the mark of the beast, as mentioned in Revelation, which brought the curse of God on some, was the baptism of the Pedobaptists, received by pouring.' '[T]he command to baptize a believer in Christ', he maintained, 'can no more be construed by Methodists into the liberty to baptize unconscious infants and non-believing children of a dozen years, than it can by the Papists into a permission to baptize bells, asses, and locomotives – which they do.'[44]

The third persistent theme of Graves's polemic was the newness and illegitimacy of the Methodist Church. Unlike the Baptists, who traced their ancestry back to John the Baptist, Christ, and the Apostles, Methodists were a 'spurious', 'fraudulent' church descended from those – Thomas Coke and Francis Asbury – unqualified to found a church of Christ. This was not mere name-calling. Graves had already established himself as a leading exponent of 'Landmarkism', a movement of Baptist exclusivism which took its name from James M. Pendleton's tract, *An Old Landmark Re-Set*, which Graves published in 1854. Landmarkers based their position on a doctrine of unbroken Baptist succession which asserted that since the New Dispensation believers had, generation after generation, through the Dark Ages, the medieval world, and the Reformation, passed on the true church by immersing others. Baptists of Graves's persuasion

---

[42] Ibid., pp. 384–402.
[43] Foster, *Errand of Mercy*, pp. 246–7.
[44] Graves, *Great Iron Wheel*, p. 419; Brownlow, *Great Iron Wheel Examined*, p. 264.

insisted that *'the Baptist is the only Church which can claim the apostolic origin'.*[45] Southern Methodists were not slow to reply. In William Gannaway Brownlow, the fifty-year-old editor of the *Knoxville Whig*, they had a polemicist who was more than a match for Graves, at least in vituperative exchange. Brownlow could draw on nearly twenty years' partisan and sectarian combat as an editor and local preacher, including sustained warfare with Frederick Ross. Within the year he had produced a response of over 300 pages, an indication both of his facility with a venomous pen and of Methodists' concern that Baptist acclaim was turning Graves's *'comic almanac'* into 'a *standard work on Methodism'.* In *The Great Iron Wheel Examined; or, Its False Spokes Extracted, and an Exhibition of Elder Graves, Its Builder,* Brownlow began by doing what he did best: assassinating character. Graves, whom he had earlier called in the columns of the *Knoxville Whig* a 'little red-faced, small whiskered dandy' and a 'loathsome blackguard', he now termed 'the dirty *ear-wig* of Baptist exclusiveness', 'a blotch upon the Christian community', 'degraded', 'immoral', 'villainous', 'corrupt', 'licentious', 'an offensive smell', and 'one who eats carrion like the buzzard, and then vomits the mass of corruption upon decent human beings.' Graves was a plagiarist, a plunderer of Ross. He was an unprincipled mercenary: '[h]e would surrender his religion (if he ever had any!) and deny his God, if it would bring him in money, or build him up a faction of which he could remain the acknowledged head.' Brownlow protested – somewhat unconvincingly – that he had been unwilling at first 'to bandy epithets with an inflated *gasometer*, whose brain I believed to be a mass of living, creeping, crawling, writhing, twisting, turning, loathsome vermin', but the time had come for a response to this *'Hindoo leader'* of the warlike wing of his Church'.[46]

Brownlow spent little time on the issue of church government (he could hardly attack a concept – the 'great iron wheel' – which had been coined by a distinguished Methodist), though he

[45] Graves, *Great Iron Wheel*, pp. 138, 142; Brownlow, *Great Iron Wheel Examined*, pp. 61, 91, 184; Ahlstrom, *Religious History of the American People* (New Haven, Conn., 1972), pp. 722–5. Graves drew especially on *A Concise History of Foreign Baptists* (1838) – the work of the English Baptist minister, G. H. Orchard – to sustain his understanding of Baptists' unique historical role; he republished the work, adding his own introduction, in 1855.

[46] Brownlow, *Great Iron Wheel Examined*, pp. xv–xvi, 19–26, 262–5; *Knoxville Whig*, 20 Sept., 4 Oct. 1851, 4 Sept. 1852.

made clear his contempt for Baptists' congregational autonomy. Lacking an organic bond of union, he sneered, their polity was 'a sort of *Indian council-ground form of government*', a botched affair, lacking ' "form and void," as was our earth before the Creator restored it to order'. Local independence resulted in doctrinal and operational inconsistency, with every congregation doing as it chose, 'undoing today what a neighboring congregation may have done on yesterday'. The denomination, he noted sarcastically, was 'held together by the cohesive power and attraction of *water*'.[47]

Instead, Brownlow principally addressed the issues raised by Baptists' doctrine, especially the persisting high Calvinism found in many parts of the rural South, and by their baptismal practices. The watering down of strict Calvinism within sections of the Baptist denomination in the early nineteenth century, and many Baptists' warm response to the missionary and other agencies of the benevolent empire, generated a powerful backlash from 'antimission', 'anti-effort' or 'Hard-Shell' Baptists, who were particularly strong amongst the poorest and least educated of the denomination. Through the 1830s and 1840s these predestin-arians organized themselves into a growing number of 'Primi-tive' Baptist associations, especially in Southern Appalachia and further west. In 1850 fewer than ten per cent of all American Baptists were thus separately organized, but horror of human workmanship, 'craft religion', missions, Bible and tract societies, teetotalism, and 'new measures' revivalism extended well be-yond their ranks.[48] Brownlow played on these internal Baptist stresses, quoting from predestinarians complaining of 'the *Armi-nian* tendency of many of our preachers and churches' and the decline into '*milk-and-cider theology*'. Examining the Baptist Con-fession of Faith of 1742, Brownlow mischievously expressed surprise that Baptists 'believing the number of the *elect* is "so certain and definite that it cannot be either increased or dim-inished," should want to send *missionaries* among the heathen, or elsewhere. . . . What good can missionaries do, if this doctrine be correct?' Indeed, he asked, what was the purpose of baptism in a

---

[47] Brownlow, *Great Iron Wheel Examined*, pp. 71–2, 88, 284, 303–4.

[48] Ahlstrom, *Religious History of the American People*, pp. 719–20; Bertram Wyatt-Brown, 'The Antimission movement in the Jacksonian South and West: a study in regional folk culture', *Journal of Southern History*, 36 (Nov. 1970), pp. 501–29; B. C. Lambert, *The Rise of the Anti-Mission Baptists: Sources and Leaders, 1800–1840* (New York, 1980).

predestinarian cosmos? If men are unconditionally elected 'they will be saved if they never see water, and die drunk in the bargain'; and if unconditionally reprobated, 'to immerse a man seventy times seven in the veritable *Jordan* would be of no avail'. Graves, sneered Brownlow, was inconsistent, even accusing Methodists themselves of Calvinism while dodging the implications of his own creed.[49]

Brownlow's principal target was the Baptist doctrine of believer's immersion. For Methodists, water baptism was 'the *initiating* rite into the Church'; it entitled a person 'to the privileges of the Church on earth'; but it was not essential to salvation itself, unlike 'the baptism of the Holy Ghost', which was. Baptism was 'the external and visible badge of Christianity' and 'the seal of a new covenant' of grace in the way that circumcision had been the seal of the Abrahamic covenant under the Mosaic law. Thus Methodists readily baptized three classes of persons: '*converted* believers, *unconverted* believers [penitents], and *infants*'.[50] Baptists' doctrine, restricting baptism to believing adults, was not only an abominable heresy but, Brownlow added slyly, the product of a Popish cast of mind:

The Romanists . . . consider baptism, administered by a priest, as *of itself* applying the merits of Christ to the individual baptized. The Baptists and Romanists differ as to the *mode* . . . of baptism, but not as regards the *efficacy* of the sacrament of baptism. According to Romanists, baptism is absolutely necessary to salvation. . . . The Baptists hold that baptism by *immersion* is absolutely necessary to salvation, but deny its validity when administered by any one but a *Baptist preacher*, who has himself been *immersed* by some one who was *immersed before him*. . . .[51]

According to Brownlow, Baptists' insistence on complete immersion as the only scriptural form of baptism wholly misunder-

[49] Brownlow, *Great Iron Wheel Examined*, pp. 55–6, 166–74, 305–8; Graves, *Great Iron Wheel*, pp. 500–13.
[50] Brownlow, *Great Iron Wheel Examined*, pp. 193–203, 219–23.
[51] Ibid., p. 194. Whether deliberately or not, Brownlow here misleadingly conflated the doctrinal position of the Regular Baptists, for whom baptism was not essential for the remission of sins, with that of the Campbellites, for whom it was.

stood the purifying, consecrating sense of the Greek word *bap-tizo*, which implied no particular mode. The scriptural evidence was as weak as the semantic case. Even assuming that John the Baptist was a legitimate subject for investigation (which was doubtful, Brownlow maintained, since his was a Jewish not a Christian ordinance), it was implausible that he practised complete immersion.[52] By a less than rigorous historical method Brownlow concluded that John had baptized some three million people during a ministry of nine months. Complete immersion would have been impossible.

> [N]o mortal man . . . could have stood in three feet [of] water *six* hours in the day, for 220 days, with only an occasional rest day . . . ; moreover, he had no more than 1,300 hours for the act of baptizing, giving him 'a fraction over *two thousand* [people] to the hour, *thirty* to each minute, or *one* to every two seconds! This, then, is baptizing with too great speed. . . . No man on earth could pass along a row of mortals, and pat one on the shoulders for every two seconds, much less plunge him under water and raise him up again.[53]

Brownlow conceded that Christ, at his own baptism, might have 'waded into the water up to his waist, "yea, he might have gone in up to his arm-pits" ' but he had not been totally immersed; nor were any of the New Testament subjects of Christian baptism. In knockabout style, Brownlow noted that the Jordan was a bold and dangerous river with a rapid current. 'Wonder how many females could be induced to encounter "bold Jordan" with a Baptist preacher who acknowledges himself that he *can't swim!* What would one of these, fleshy, overgrown women do, with her several garments on, in such a rapid current? Or, forsooth, what would a female *in a peculiar fix* do in such a scrape?'[54]

For much of the century Methodists had attributed to this mania for immersion and Calvinistic doctrine what they perceived as an uncommonly lax moral code amongst Baptists. When Graves charged that Wesley's followers themselves were

---

[52] Ibid., pp. 204–7, 227, 242.
[53] Ibid., pp. 210–11.
[54] Ibid., pp. 231 and 271.

morally deficient, not least because Methodist ministers admitted 'unregenerate and unbaptized seekers' to the Lord's Supper, Brownlow energetically picked up the challenge. Graves, he charged, would 'take into his fellowship a prostitute, and hug to his bosom a burglar, if they have been baptized by immersion!' Proofs of conversion were inadequately rigorous. Brownlow proffered a scurrilous catalogue of converts' testimonies to make his point, including those of a woman in a Jonesboro revival who stated that '*Christ first appeared to her while she was in bed with a man!*', and of another at Fall Branch, who 'had attended the preaching of Elder Riggs . . . and was taken sick at the *stomach* – said she soon learned it was *conviction for sin* – engaged earnestly in prayer to God – soon after *vomited copiously* – thereupon obtained immediate relief, and felt her load of sin removed!' (Brownlow ruminated, 'This is changing the *seat* of human depravity, which has hitherto been regarded as the *heart*. I would like to have seen the discharge!') By telling such superficial converts that they 'may *lie, cheat, steal*, and get *drunk*, and do any other wickedness, without falling from grace', and that 'once under the water' they were beyond the reach of temptation, Baptist preachers ensured that their churches were more populated with 'bad men and hypocrites' than any other in the land.[55]

The controversy over *The Great Iron Wheel* amounted to much more than personal pugilism between Graves, the Baptist Bruiser, and Brownlow, the Methodist Mauler. The conflict was warfare on a royal scale, but perhaps because it occurred well beyond New England and its cultural diaspora, and originated in the unfashionable southern highlands, its deeper significance has suffered undeserved historical neglect. Until quite recently a 'Puritan-Calvinist synthesis' has shaped writings on American religious development. The religious culture of New England, the wider northeast and the Yankee diaspora has been generally better served than that of the South and southwest. From the perspective of Boston, New York, or Philadelphia, and especially from within the Congregationalist and Presbyterian traditions, the story of Protestantism in the 1840s and 1850s is one of increasing co-operation and even supra-denominational unity,

55 Graves, *Great Iron Wheel*, pp. 366–77; Brownlow, *Great Iron Wheel Examined*, pp. 21, 27–47, 73–4, 96–100, 256, 282–3.

through the Evangelical Alliance and the early YMCA. But the further we retreat from urban and metropolitan America into certain parts of the rural hinterland, the more a different picture emerges, one of persisting religious exclusivism and disdain for apparently false and sentimental notions of church unity. The Baptist-Methodist antagonism in the South and West has to be seen in this light. It related to two fundamentally antagonistic outlooks on the world, not to nuanced, minor differences between two essentially similar denominations.

First, Baptists have to be seen as intense individualists whose rejection of 'organic Christianity' (as the Presbyterian minister David Riddle put it) indicated a deep attachment to protecting individual autonomy through local independence.[56] Most southern and southwestern Baptists represented the poorer elements of a rural society which from the late colonial period feared and resisted the centralization of power, whether by the British imperial authorities or by Hamiltonian Federalists and their successors. These Baptists were likely to be Antifederalist, Jeffersonian or Jacksonian defenders of republican liberty against potentially tyrannical concentrations of power in the hands of a nationalist federal government or an overweening church. Antimission feeling fed on fear of 'meddling' ecclesiastical autocrats who would centralize power in agencies controlled by Yankee outsiders. Methodists, by contrast, blended the Protestant celebration of individual conscience and personal salvation with growing involvement in a world beyond the locality. Methodist congregations were connectionally tied into an ecclesiastical structure which encouraged members to see themselves as part of a wider universe. The system of Methodist itinerancy introduced a new minister to the church every year or two, one who often brought a perspective that transcended the local community. The denomination's expanding publishing empire connected ordinary members through its newspapers to a sophisticated, even cosmopolitan, world. Whereas Baptists' polity encouraged centrifugal provincialism and intense localism, Methodism tended to integrate its members into the region and even the nation.

---

[56] *North Carolina Presbyterian* (Fayetteville), 24 July 1858.

Secondly, Methodists seem to have been more consistently supportive of energetic schemes of social and material improvement than their religious rivals. Methodists' Arminian 'effort' and enterprise in spiritual affairs was entirely consonant with the entrepreneurialism of the advancing market economy. We should not regard Methodists as champions of the old subsistence order struggling to resist the advances of the national market;[57] rather their theology and outward-looking church culture encouraged them to seize the opportunities of the transport revolution, the commercializing of agriculture, the expansion of commerce, and early industrialization. Significantly, Brownlow himself was one of southern Appalachia's most outspoken economic improvers and along with other Methodists of the mountain region energetically promoted educational opportunity, temperance, and other moral reforms. Amongst Baptists, on the other hand, at least those of the anti-mission tendency, there were many who feared commercial advance and the 'steam religion' of a 'money-hunting' priesthood. Unlike Christ and his disciples, who did not 'make gain by godliness', modern improvers – temperance men, foreign and home missionaries, tract publishers, Sunday-school promoters, and their printing establishments – based their projects on 'beggars and money'.[58]

Thirdly, Methodists' concern for improvement seems to have made them more sensitive to notions of refinement and propriety. Though Graves taunted Methodists with lack of decorum and restraint in the '*sanctified row*' of their revival meetings, claims such as Brownlow's, that 'there is as much of wealth, talents, respectability, and of influence in the Methodist . . . as any Church can boast of', were customary in mid-century Methodism.[59] There is no doubt that Methodists were convinced of their social superiority over Baptists. Brownlow and others commonly portrayed Baptists, lay and clerical, as hicks whose speech confirmed their public boast that 'they have no "*edecation*" or "*human larnin*" '; when Leonard Smith, a young Methodist itinerant in central Illinois, attended a gathering of Baptist ministers

[57] For a stimulating but ultimately unpersuasive statement of this view, see Charles Sellers, *The Market Revolution: Jacksonian America, 1815–1846* (New York, 1991), pp. 137–8, 157–61, 164–5, 178, 299–300.

[58] *Primitive Baptist* (Tarborough, NC), 5 (1840), pp. 70–1, 77–8, 120–1.

[59] Graves, *Great Iron Wheel*, pp. 531–3; Brownlow, *Great Iron Wheel Examined*, pp. 62, 160.

in 1860 he despaired of their ignorance, remarking: 'Believe a man should be educated as well as holy to be useful.' The practice of total immersion allowed Brownlow not only to ridicule his rivals (the Baptists' conventions, he sneered, meant that they entered the Church of God '*backwards*, or . . . *wrong end foremost*') but also to point to the 'indecent personal exhibition[s]' involved in total immersion, where male preachers were known to change their clothes in the presence of females. Christ had

> never intended *females* should submit . . . after that notoriously vulgar fashion of the Baptist denomination. . . . The usual custom throughout the South and West is to bandage the forehead of a delicate and beautiful female, and tie a handkerchief round her waist, as a sort of *handle* for an awkward Baptist preacher to fasten upon; and thus she is led into the water, step by step, in the presence of a mixed multitude, who are making their vulgar remarks and criticising her steps as she *fights down her clothes*, which rise to the top of the water, and float round her delicate and exposed limbs! She is taken by the preacher, who fastens one hand in her *belt*, and the other on the back of her head; and after planting his big feet firm upon the bottom of the stream, and *squaring himself* as though he were about to knock a beef in the head, he plunges her into the water! . . . [R]espectable females com[e] out of the water with their thin garments sticking close to their skin, and exhibiting their *muscles* and *make* in so revolting a manner, that ladies present have felt constrained to surround them, so as to hide their persons from the gaze of the vulgar throng. I witnessed this disgusting sight several times in the spring of 1842, at the edge of Green's Mill-pond, in Jonesborough.[60]

These antithetical world-views of Baptists and Methodists seem to have fed into divergent political allegiances. Though the two denominations were largely bound together in the ranks of the Jeffersonian Republicans at the turn of the century, in union against the ecclesiastical tyranny of a Standing Order, their

---

[60] Brownlow, *Great Iron Wheel Examined*, pp. 99–100, 191, 202–3, 214–15; Springfield, Illinois State Historical Society, Leonard F. Smith, 'Diary', 1 Sept. 1860.

political loyalties by no means remained yoked in the subsequent party alignments of the 1830s and 1840s. In North Carolina, for instance, there seems in the poorer western countries to have been a strong correlation between the Baptists and Jacksonian Democracy on one side and between Methodism and Whiggery on the other.[61] It is probable that Baptists rallied to the party of *laisser-faire*, weak government, and ambivalence towards the forces of the national market, whereas Methodists, as economic and moral improvers, turned to the Whigs – the party of government activism in the cause of progess. When Frank Richardson, a young Methodist itinerant, took up his appointment in Anderson County, Tennessee, in the mid-1850s he found the conflict between the two denominations so intense that as well as meeting-places each had their own schools, taverns, stores, and even ferries across the river. 'Like the Jews and Samaritans', he recalled, 'they had no dealings with each other whatever. . . . Most of the Methodists were Whigs, and most of the Baptists were Democrats.'[62] It is noteworthy that Brownlow himself was as bellicose a Whig as he was Methodist; Graves, a Democrat.[63]

These Baptists and Methodists, then, were launched on diverging social trajectories. While antebellum Methodists moved into finer churches, dressed more fashionably, rented their pews, replaced their circuit-riders with a stationed, seminary-trained ministry, and generally rose in society, Baptists (at least in the South) clung much more tenaciously to their unlettered, unpaid, part-time preachers and resisted the secularizing forces. By mid-century Methodism had made significant social advances in the cities and the eastern states, while Baptists, apart from their

---

[61] Gary R. Freeze, 'The ethnocultural thesis goes south: religio-cultural dimensions of voting in North Carolina's second party system' (unpublished paper delivered at the Southern Historical Association Convention, Nov. 1988), pp. 2–18.

[62] Frank Richardson, *From Sunrise to Sunset: Reminiscence* (Bristol, Tenn., 1910), pp. 107–8.

[63] Both Graves and Brownlow were drawn to the anti-Catholic Know-Nothing party when it burst into being in the mid-1850s, but Graves quickly backed off when he realized how deeply involved were his Methodist adversaries in a party that quickly came to resemble the hated Whigs. Brownlow, *Great Iron Wheel Examined*, p. 292. The warfare in New Jersey between John Q. Adams (Baptist minister and Democrat) and John Inskip (Methodist preacher and Know-Nothing) took on the same religio-political aspect: *Biblical Recorder* (Raleigh, NC), 15 Jan. 1857. Adams's short tract, *Episcopal Methodism Anti-American in Its Spirit and Tendency* (1854), depicted Methodist 'despotism' as enfeebling American republicanism, and opening the way for a Romanist take-over. Michael F. Holt, *The Political Crisis of the 1850s* (New York, 1978), pp. 4–6, 8, 16–17, and passim, regards Americans in that decade as particularly fearful for the security of republican institutions.

strength in New York and Massachusetts, remained mainly a poor rural and southern denomination. After the Civil War, as Sydney Ahlstrom tells us, '[p]overty, agrarian backwardness, and terrible educational deficiencies prevented the Baptists, even more severely than the Methodists, from coming to terms with the main intellectual currents.' Significantly, though, southern Baptists – unlike their northern co-religionists and the Methodists, who relatively lost ground to other churches – more than held their share of the total church population. Baptists became the vehicle whereby an impoverished and defeated population could sustain its conservative social values and sacralize the 'lost cause'.[64]

## IV

This analysis of Baptist-Methodist rivalry confirms that those historians who have built on Robert Baird to emphasize the co-operative and unifying impulses within American religious diversity in the early republic have seriously underestimated the depth of cultural conflict between evangelical Protestant churches. It might be tempting to see the combatants' robust language as merely a matter of style, camouflaging an essential unity; that would be to understate both Baptists' determined exclusiveness and Methodists' sense that their opponents had broken the rules by which mutual evangelical tolerance might be maintained. Brownlow acknowledged that 'Divine love', when untrammelled, could create 'an entire union of sentiment, affection, and design' and put an end to religious disputes. But the conditions of human society – marked by 'error and bigotry' – made religious controversy both inevitable and necessary. Religious disputation, Brownlow judged, advanced the cause of Christ, by eliciting truth and exposing error: 'had it not been for *controversy*, Romish priests would now be feeding us all with *Latin masses* and with their *wafer gods!*' As Christ himself had controverted the Pharisees and Saducees and other heretics, so

---

[64] Finke and Stark, *Churching of America*, pp. 145–78; Ahlstrom, *Religious History of the American People*, p. 721. For the tension between 'New School' Baptists, especially in New England, on the one hand, and those of an anti-mission orientation, hostile to ministerial education and voluntary association, on the other, see Foster, *Errand of Mercy*, pp. 101–2, 190–1, 253–4.

latter-day defenders of orthodoxy had to stand up to Graves the Baptist, Ross the Presbyterian, and other 'unregenerate adversaries'. Brownlow's convictions were reinforced the more that Graves's school of Close Baptists insisted that paedobaptist societies were '*not gospel Churches in any true sense*', that their preachers were not real gospel ministers, and that Baptists, as members of the only apostolic Church, should not share in the sacrament of the Lord's Supper with paedobaptist Christians, on pain of expulsion.[65]

Such 'rigid sectarian proscription' gave rise to stereotyping tales which reflected popular perceptions throughout the South and West. In one of these a Baptist minister at a revival meeting recounted a dream in which he had died and gone to hell. Satan escorted him through all the apartments of the infernal region, where he saw quite a number of Methodists, Episcopalians, Presbyterians, and Catholics, but not a single Baptist. This, said the preacher, showed they had gone to heaven, because of their scriptural correctness over adult immersion. A Methodist preacher then reported a similar dream. He too was conducted by the Devil through his dominions; he too saw Catholics and all denominations of Protestants except Baptists. Asking anxiously if there were no Baptists, he was taken to a large trap-door which was opened to reveal a multitude in 'a lower deep'. 'These', Satan exclaimed, 'are all Baptists holding *close communion!*'[66]

James Dixon, the English Methodist, knew little of such antagonisms when he offered the judgement at mid-century that American 'society is not convulsed, nor the state put in jeopardy, by religious contentions, claims and projects. If religion . . . does not allay human passions, neither does it exasperate them.'[67] He could not have been more wrong. Not only did he fail to encounter the cultural divisions discussed here, but he did not fathom the connections between evangelical antagonisms and the gathering sectional quarrel over slavery. The animated discussion of the churches' proper relationship to the peculiar institution clearly increased the diversity and disunity within

---

[65] Brownlow, *Great Iron Wheel Examined*, pp. xiii, 164, 192 (quoting *Tennessee Baptist*, 22 Dec. 1855). For similar unsentimental understandings of the Christian's duty to promote church harmony, see, e.g., *CAJ* 9 Nov. 1829, 17 Dec. 1830.

[66] Brownlow, *Great Iron Wheel Examined*, pp. 94–5, 217.

[67] Dixon, *Methodism in America*, pp. 148–9.

American Protestantism. It did so by fracturing denominations into southern and northern branches, and producing a legacy of litigation, violence, and bloodshed. That is another story, which I have dealt with elsewhere.[68] The ensuing cataclysm of Civil War, however, helped to draw each section's Christians together in unparallelled unity to defend their own conception of a Christian republic. Yankee Protestants co-operated to sustain a Union which was a vehicle of both religious and political values, especially after Lincoln's Emancipation Proclamation; Confederate Christians, in defence of a conservative Christian orthodoxy, similarly pulled together.[69] But this unprecedented co-operation should not obscure the prior reality of which the Baptist-Methodist conflict is a neglected symptom. The Protestant landscape of the American republic between the Revolution and the Civil War presented not smooth terrain but a crazed arrangement of deep fault-lines created – in Brownlow's phrase – by 'rigid sectarian proscription'.

University of Sheffield

---

[68] Carwardine, *Evangelicals and Politics*, pp. 133–74, 245–8, 285–92.

[69] The relationship between loyalty to church, section and nation deserves attention in its own right. Useful starting points are provided by James Moorhead, *American Apocalypse: Yankee Protestants and the Civil War, 1860–1869* (New Haven, Conn., and London, 1978); Drew Gilpin Faust, 'Christian soldiers: the meaning of revivalism in the Confederate army', *Journal of Southern History*, 53 (1987), pp. 63–90; James W. Silver, *Confederate Morale and Church Propaganda* (Tuscaloosa, Ala, 1957).

# 'FRIENDS HAVE NO CAUSE TO BE ASHAMED OF BEING BY OTHERS THOUGHT NON-EVANGELICAL':[1] UNITY AND DIVERSITY OF BELIEF AMONG EARLY NINETEENTH-CENTURY BRITISH QUAKERS

*by* SIMON BRIGHT

One of the most remarkable features in the history of British Quakerism is its ability rapidly to change its theological orientation – changing in succession from an outward looking mass movement, to an inward-looking sect, to an evangelical ecumenically-minded denomination, to a theologically liberal association of like-minded individuals. This paper considers the third of these transitions, the move from sectarianism to evangelicalism. This period of transition provides a useful case study of how the beliefs of a pan-denominational movement (in this case *evangelicalism*) interact with the existing beliefs of a sect (in this case the corpus of traditional Quaker beliefs known as *Quietism*). In this case study, particular attention will be focused on Joseph John Gurney (1788–1847), the individual most closely associated with the rise of evangelicalism within British Quakerism.

Some scene setting is necessary to explain why British Quakerism during this period provides such a useful field for studying how pan-denominational and sectarian beliefs interact. During the early part of the nineteenth century, a significant group of Friends adopted evangelical beliefs. Even a brief survey of their writing shows their preoccupation with the central tenets of evangelicalism, including fear of damnation and the need for salvation. Samuel Tuke informed his readers that 'There can be, and there ought to be, no subject as interesting to us as our interest in eternity' and called attention to the 'great doctrine of the sacrifice of Christ for sin'.[2] These Friends combined their sympathy for evangelicalism with a willingness to associate with non-Quaker evangelicals (something which would have been unheard of among an earlier generation of Friends). This is

---

[1] 'The Evangelical Alliance', *The British Friend*, 4 (1846), p. 45.
[2] Charles Taylor, *Samuel Tuke, His Life, Works and Thoughts* (London, 1900), pp. 33, 83.

demonstrated by the evangelical Friends' willingness to hold evangelistic services in churches belonging to other denominations, most commonly Methodist, but also Anglican, Baptist, and Presbyterian.

Joseph John Gurney, the pre-eminent member of this group, was acknowledged as such even by contemporary non-Quakers – with whom he freely associated. *The Christian Observer* described him in 1835 as 'an apostle among his own people'.[3] Gurney himself was educated by Anglican clergymen[4] and several of his siblings married Anglicans who would establish themselves as leaders of the evangelical movement within the Church of England.[5] Four bishops feature in a list which Gurney drew up of 'persons of superior mind or talent' with whom he had a close friendship (with another fourteen bishops appearing on a 'reserve' list of persons whom he was 'partially acquainted with').[6] Gurney also co-operated with non-Quakers in philanthropic and evangelistic causes, especially (but by no means exclusively) the British and Foreign Bible Society.[7]

Gurney's involvement in British Quakerism during this period is made all the more interesting due to the ambiguities inherent in his own membership of the Society of Friends. He came from a family which had strayed very far from Quakerism's traditional lifestyle of simplicity. One Quaker visitor to the Gurney family's home noted that it was 'very large and magnificent, far from being of a piece with our profession'.[8] If Gurney's wealthy lifestyle was uncharacteristic of traditional Friends, so also were his doubts about the authority of early Quaker authors. On one occasion he declared that some of the early Friends had been 'carried off their centre by a warm imagination' and that he was 'by no means prepared to justify all they did, or all that they said'.[9]

[3] 'Review of works connected with the controversy among members of the Society of Friends', *The Christian Observer*, 33 (1835), pp. 629–42.

[4] David E. Swift, *Joseph John Gurney, Banker, Reformer, and Quaker* (Middletown, Conn., 1962), pp. 28–36 and London, Library of the Society of Friends [hereafter LSF], MS vol. 532, Joseph John Gurney, 'Autobiography Addressed to his Nephew John Gurney' [hereafter 'Autobiography'], p. 21.

[5] Michael Hennell, *Sons of the Prophets* (London, 1979), pp. 16–18.

[6] London, LSF, MS vol. 185, Joseph John Gurney, 'Persons of Superior Mind or Talent with whom I have had a Familiar Acquaintance' and 'Persons of Eminent Talent or Reputation, with whom I have Conversed, and been Partially Acquainted'.

[7] J. B. Braithwaite, *Memoirs of Joseph John Gurney*, 2 vols (Philadelphia, 1854), 2, p. 72.

[8] Francis R. Taylor, *Life of William Savery of Philadelphia, 1750–1804* (New York, 1925), p. 346.

[9] Joseph John Gurney, *Observations on the Distinguishing Views and Practices of the Society of Friends* (Norwich, 1842), p. 504.

Gurney, who in many ways was typical of evangelical Quakers as a whole, found his membership of the Society of Friends fraught with ambiguities. These ambiguities might not have caused problems if these evangelical Friends were a small or insignificant group in early nineteenth-century Quakerism. However, these evangelical Friends were at the very centre of Quakerism during this period and had a profound influence on the Society of Friends. An 1831 article in *The Congregational Magazine* contrasted Friends' isolation from members of other denominations at the beginning of the century with their current participation in the British and Foreign Bible Society and also commented on the growing biblical concern apparent among contemporary Quakers.[10]

While *The Congregational Magazine* was clearly delighted by the Society of Friends' move towards evangelicalism, many traditionalist Friends (Quietists) opposed this doctrinal sea-change and argued that Quakers should maintain their sectarianism. This attitude is clearly expressed in the quotation which provides the title for this paper, which originally appeared in *The British Friend*, a pro-Quietist magazine founded in 1843. The Quietists regarded the development of evangelicalism as a sign of Quakerism slipping back into the old, unreformed Church, with the most vocal of them, Sarah Grubb, declaring that 'We are fast going back to Episcopalianism.'[11] One evangelical Friend in particular was picked out for criticism, with one leading Quietist stating that: 'I declare that J[oseph] J[ohn] G[urney] is an Episcopalian, not a Quaker.'[12] Other Quietists were equally critical of Gurney. For example, John Barclay found fault with Gurney's preaching, claiming that the inspiration for the latter's sermons came from his intellect rather than the leadings of the Spirit and claimed that this was a 'sort of new gift that has sprung up these days'.[13]

It is not surprising that the Quietists' criticisms of Gurney made reference to his apparent unwillingness to follow the direction of the Spirit during his preaching, as the most

---

[10] 'Review of Biblical Notes and Dissertations', *The Congregational Magazine*, 12 (1831), pp. 553–4.

[11] J. Grubb and H. Grubb, *A Selection from the Letters of the Late Sarah Grubb* (Sudbury, 1848), p. 299.

[12] John Wilbur, *Journal of John Wilbur, A Minister of the Society of Friends* (Providence, RI, 1859), p. 546.

[13] Ibid., p. 199.

significant area of theological disagreement between the evangelicals and the Quietists was over the role and authority of the Spirit. For the Quietists the Spirit's influence in the life of the believer was the sum of Quaker theology, arguing that 'our first Friends were raised up as a people, to bear testimony to the sufficiency of this pure principle of light and life in all mankind.'[14] The Quietists placed that Spirit above the historical revelation contained in the New Testament.[15] They therefore regarded the evangelical Friends' apparent attempts to substitute the authority of the Scriptures for that of the Spirit as 'Episcopalian'[16] or, more dramatically, the 'work of the Devil'.[17]

Through their opposition to the evangelicals' emphasis on the Scriptures and their savage criticism of the latter's apparent 'backsliding' into the unreformed Church, the Quietists drew attention to the divisions that existed within British Quakerism during the early part of the nineteenth century. Subsequent historical study of this period has also emphasized these divisions and often cast evangelicalism as an invading force in British Quakerism. This is because, as ever, history was written by the winners. The birth of Quaker historical study coincided with the eclipse of evangelicalism within London Yearly Meeting and its replacement with a liberalism which doubted whether evangelical doctrine represented the true beliefs of Friends. Elizabeth Isichei has identified the links that existed between the main motor of Quakers' study of their own past, the Friends Historical Society, and the rise of liberalism within British Quakerism.[18] The liberal Quaker historians could be as scathing of the evangelicals as their Quietist predecessors had been. For example, Edward Grubb (a descendant of Sarah Grubb) remarked that 'Just as J. H. Newman, in despair of human reason, took refuge in an infallible church, so J. J. Gurney sought it in an infallible Bible.'[19] Non-Quaker historians studying Friends during this period have also emphasized the differences between evangelical and Quietist

---

[14] Thomas Shillitoe, *An Address to Friends in Great Britain and Ireland*, 1st edn (London, 1820), p. 3.

[15] John Wilbur, *A Few Remarks on the Controversy Between Good and Evil* (Boston, 1855), p. 36.

[16] Henry Martin, *The Truth Vindicated* (London, 1835), pp. 5–12.

[17] Wilbur, *Journal*, pp. 150–1.

[18] Elizabeth Isichei, *Victorian Quakers* (London, 1970), p. 14; idem, 'From sect to denomination among English Quakers', in Bryan Wilson, ed., *Patterns of Sectarianism* (London, 1967), pp. 161–3.

[19] Edward Grubb, *Separations Their Causes and Effects* (London, 1914), p. 70.

Friends. For example, David Bebbington notes the conflict between traditional Quaker spirituality and evangelicalism and argues that the former was forced 'underground' by the latter.[20]

While both Quietists who were contemporaries of Gurney and later historical studies of this period are right to note that there were significant differences between evangelical Quakerism and Quietism, it must be asked whether the two schools of thought were really so far apart, and whether there were areas of common ground where these two sets of beliefs concurred or could complement each other. The Quietists (and to a lesser extent historians such as Edward Grubb) seem to have prejudged this question. However, if instead of seeking areas of conflict coincidences of ideas between the two schools of thought are sought, a radically different picture emerges.

Many of these coincidences of ideas between Quakerism and evangelicalism can be identified through studying Joseph John Gurney's life in the period 1811–12. During these years he moved from nominal membership of the Society of Friends to serious commitment to both Quakerism and the evangelical movement. He was clearly influenced by both of these schools of thought during this period – his record of his studies shows that, as well as works by Quaker apologists such as Job Scott and Isaac Pennington, he read evangelical fare such as Philip Doddridge and Bishop Butler.[21] As well as literary influences, during this period he came into close contact with both serious-minded evangelicals and devout Quakers, meeting many of the former at the inaugural meeting of the Norwich Auxiliary Bible Society in 1811, an event which had a profound influence on him.[22] Of equal significance was his attendance at the 1812 sessions of London Yearly Meeting. This clearly had a significant effect on him, as he noted that it 'transplanted me from my old cares and distractions, turned me to myself, and I humbly hope brought me nearer to my Gracious master'.[23]

---

[20] D. W. Bebbington, *Evangelicalism in Modern Britain* (London, 1989), pp. 155–6.

[21] London, LSF, MS vol. 185, Joseph John Gurney, 'Examined Copy of Joseph John Gurney's Journal of His Readings, Studies and Literary Labours'.

[22] Augustus J. C. Hare, *The Gurneys of Earlham*, 2 vols (London, 1845), 1, pp. 229–30.

[23] London, LSF, MS vols. 181–5, Joseph John Gurney, 'Examined Copy of the Private Journal of Joseph John Gurney' [hereafter 'Journal'], 6 June 1812.

This desire to turn himself away from his own cares toward God is one of the key themes which evangelicalism and Quakerism held in common. Both called upon their members to lead serious lives. Ian Bradley argues that the evangelicals were prone to excessive seriousness and the shunning of apparently innocent pleasures.[24] Equally, Thomas Clarkson's study of pre-evangelical Quakerism published in 1806 observed that Friends were required to refrain from a variety of apparently harmless pleasures, including games of chance, music, dancing, and novel reading.[25] Gurney's own concern to lead a serious and worthy life is highlighted by his fears about devoting too much time to sleep – writing in 1814 of his fears that excessive sleep was 'creeping too close to the fire' and in 1819 that sleeping had for too long been a 'successful enemy'.[26] Gurney's habit of committing his fears about oversleeping to paper is indicative of another of the distinctive features of the evangelical movement – an almost obsessive self-examination.[27] This rigorous self-examination was also apparent in Quakerism, as Friends were required to give serious (and often self-deprecating) thought to their actions. For example, Gurney wrote during a quarterly review of his spiritual and moral progress in 1811 of his 'deep humiliation for past faults, & continued imperfections'.[28]

Gurney's anxieties about his shortcomings drove him into a commitment to serious religion. The manner in which he expressed his commitment, by adopting the Friends' dress code, once again shows a coincidence of ideas between Quakerism and evangelicalism. In his autobiography he noted that at the age of twenty-one he felt the need to adopt the Quaker practices 'of "plainness of speech, behaviour and apparel" ',[29] which included refusing to doff the hat in greeting (an action which, while having serious egalitarian and radical overtones during the seventeenth century, had perhaps become a little absurd by the nineteenth). Gurney's journal describes his first public engagement where he refused to give 'hat honour':

[24] Ian Bradley, *The Call to Seriousness* (London, 1976), pp. 22–8.

[25] Thomas Clarkson, *A Portraiture of Quakerism*, 2 vols, 4th edn (London, 1806), 1, p. 246.

[26] Gurney, 'Journal', 30 October 1814 and 18 April 1819.

[27] Bradley, *The Call to Seriousness*, p. 23.

[28] Gurney, 'Journal', 6 January 1811.

[29] Ibid., 27 February 1815.

I was engaged to a dinner party at the house of S. J. Sothwell, one of our first county gentlemen – three weeks before the time I was engaged . . . [with] the apprehension of which I could not dispose myself that I must march into his drawing room with my hat on! . . . From this sacrifice – strange and unaccountable as it appeared, I could not escape. I was caught like a fish on a hook . . . , I made my entrance at the dreaded moment – Shook hands with the mistress of the house – went back to the hall, deposited my hat, joined the dinner party. Spent a rather comfortable evening and returned home with some degree of peace. I had afterwards the same to do at the Bishop's – the result was that I found myself the decided quaker [sic] – was perfectly understood to have assumed that character – and to dinner parties, except in the family circle, was asked no more![30]

This incident, as well as having profound implications for Gurney's social diary, draws out some of the elements of lifestyle which were held in common by Quakers and evangelicals. It is important to acknowledge the significance which Friends attached to their dress code. Clarkson noted that Friends rejected all 'the ornaments of the fashionable world', and were 'also particular in the choice of the colour of their clothes', with grey being de rigueur.[31]

This concern with the appearance presented to the world would have some parallels in evangelicalism. As David Newsome notes, evangelicals believed that outward appearance was very important and a sign of conversion.[32] More significantly, Gurney's account of his refusal to give hat honour, with its linkage of distinctive dress with social ostracism, is indicative of another theme held in common by Quakers and evangelicals: their desire to be a separate (and holy) people. Indeed Isichei notes that this Quaker dress code played an important part in giving Friends a sense of being separated from the world.[33] Evangelicals shared this sense of being to a degree separated from the world.[34]

---

[30] Gurney, 'Autobiography', p. 39.

[31] Clarkson, *A Portraiture*, 1, p. 258.

[32] David Newsome, *The Parting of Friends* (London, 1966), p. 49.

[33] Isichei, *Victorian Quakers*, p. 146.

[34] Bradley, *The Call to Seriousness*, p. 22.

As significantly, Gurney's decision to make his Quakerism known by orthopraxis rather than by an assertion of orthodoxy is again indicative of an attitude to life which was held in common by Quakerism and evangelicalism. Both schools of thought were forms of experiential religion – in that they were more concerned with belief and action rather than doctrine. As Elliott-Binns observes, the main concern of evangelical theology was the application of the gospel rather than the construction of an elaborate doctrinal system.[35] Quaker apologists were equally impatient with theological speculation as a substitute for belief, so much so that Friends' theology radically separated the intellect from the spiritual life, suggesting that 'the former cannot enter into the province of the latter. As water cannot penetrate the same bodies as fire can, so neither can reason the same subjects as the spiritual faculty.'[36]

The coincidences of thought between evangelicalism and Quakerism go some way to undermining the Quietists' (and subsequent historians') assertion that evangelical doctrine and Friends' theology were incompatible. More interesting than these coincidences of thought, however, were the creative tensions that sometimes appeared during Gurney's attempts to remain true to both Quakerism and evangelicalism. In many instances Quaker and evangelical beliefs complemented each other; and through combining elements of these two schools of thought Gurney and his supporters were able to produce a unique theology.

Ironically, the theological question which caused the evangelical Friends most difficulties with their Quietist brethren was also to provide Gurney with the most fruitful opportunity to combine elements of evangelicalism and traditional Quaker beliefs. This theological question was the relative authority of the Scriptures and the Spirit. To begin with, it should be noted that Gurney's critics over-emphasized the degree to which he disparaged the Quietist doctrine of the Spirit guiding and instructing the believer (referred to in traditional Quaker parlance as 'immediate revelation'). Indeed, on one occasion he referred to immediate revelation as the 'grand practical characteristic' of Christianity.[37]

[35] L. E. Elliott-Binns, *The Evangelical Movement in the Church of England* (London, 1928), p. 383.
[36] Clarkson, *A Portraiture*, 2, p. 124.
[37] London, LSF, vol. 344, Joseph John Gurney, 'Letter from Joseph John Gurney to Dr Hancock, 8 June 1835 (Printed Privately)'.

Perhaps more significant than such intellectual accidence to this doctrine was his practical application of it during his evangelistic missions. The autobiographical accounts of these tours assign an almost Montanist role to the Spirit as the source of inspiration for the preacher, with Gurney claiming that he could neither stop nor start his ministry.[38] As an example of this use of immediate revelation in his preaching tours, in 1819 during a meeting at Beccles he believed for a long time during the service that he would have nothing to say to his audience, then he rose to make a few remarks concerning worship which was followed by a flow of ministry lasting for over an hour.[39] Clearly Gurney accepted the doctrine of immediate revelation. Where he differed from the Quietists was that he also recognized the absolute authority of the Scriptures. He argued that the authority of the scriptures was sufficient and final;[40] and also claimed that the Bible had greater authority than the Spirit, although the latter had wider authority and had pre-dated the former.[41]

Was there any way in which he could simultaneously claim that both sources of instruction (immediate and historical) had absolute authority? Certainly Gurney tried to reconcile these two forces; indeed his theology was a lifelong quest to achieve this goal. In this quest to reconcile the Scriptures and the Spirit he did not seek to place one higher than the other, believing that they should not be compared in order to establish a preference.[42] Instead he was concerned to show how these two forces worked in tandem and did this most successfully through his Christology. One of the most surprising features of his theology (and one which many of his critics seem to have overlooked) is that he developed a comprehensive doctrine of the incarnation. Gurney writes at length on the Jesus of history, declaring that the latter was really and absolutely human, being one of God's creatures with the body and soul of a human. This picture of the human Jesus (which he tempered with the assertions of Christ's divinity)

---

[38] Joseph John Gurney, *Sermons and Prayers, Delivered by Joseph John Gurney, in the Friends' Meeting House, Liverpool, 1832*, 1st edn (Liverpool, 1832), pp. 2–3.

[39] London, LSF, Gurney MSS 3/338, Letter from Joseph John Gurney to Elizabeth Fry, 29 June 1819.

[40] Joseph John Gurney, *Friendly Letters to Dr Wardlaw* (Norwich, 1836), p. 89.

[41] Ibid., p. 4.

[42] Joseph John Gurney, *Strictures on Certain Parts of an Anonymous Pamphlet, Entitled the Truth Vindicated* (London, 1836), p. 11.

gave Gurney considerable scope to describe how the Spirit operated in Jesus's life. Gurney (without subscribing to adoptionism)[43] argued that it was through the Spirit that Jesus was conceived, anointed,[44] and made prophet and king.[45] This description of Christ allowed Gurney to show historical revelation and the action of the Spirit working in tandem and with equal value. This picture focused on the historical revelation of Jesus and, as the records of the Gospels were the source of this description, thereby indicated the pre-eminent value of the Scriptures. Simultaneously, as the motive force in this Christology was the Spirit, this picture of Christ's life gave equal standing to the work of immediate revelation. This Christology therefore allowed Gurney the intellectual satisfaction of being able to see the doctrines of historical and immediate revelation operating in unison; equally importantly, it had a profound influence on Gurney's attitude to contemporary society. In focusing both the work of the Spirit and the Scriptures on the human life of Jesus, his spirituality also centred on the physical world and, most significantly, on philanthropy as a means to help Christ's 'near kinsman'.[46]

Gurney's philanthropy itself was empowered and shaped by his combination of Quietist and evangelical beliefs, particularly the two camps' differing ideals of progress. From Quakerism, Gurney inherited an emphasis on individual moral progress which was based on Friends' insistence that sanctification was *a priori* justification. He argued that 'no man can be saved while he continues in his carnal state – in his original, fallen condition'[47] and that the believer was prepared for heaven by gradual, yet complete, purification.[48] This doctrine of sanctification was one of the main motivating forces behind his philanthropy, with his participation in the voluntary causes of his era being driven by a

---

[43] Joseph John Gurney, *Essays on the Evidence, Doctrines and Practical Operation of Christianity*, 2nd edn (London, 1826), pp. 175, 206, 115, 120.

[44] Joseph John Gurney, *On the Scripture Doctrine of the Operation of the Holy Spirit for the Salvation of Man, Selected from the Writing of Joseph John Gurney* (Newcastle-upon-Tyne, 1843), pp. 26–7.

[45] Joseph John Gurney, *Essay on the Habitual Love of God*, 2nd edn (London, 1835), p. 51.

[46] Joseph John Gurney, *Biblical Notes and Dissertations*, 1st edn (London, 1830), p. 51.

[47] Gurney, *On the Scripture Doctrine of the Operation of the Holy Spirit*, p. 14.

[48] London, LSF, vol. 344, Joseph John Gurney, Letter from Joseph John Gurney to Isaac Crewdson, 27 April 1835, no. 2 (Printed Privately), pp. 27–8.

desire to promote sanctification by removing abuses and social ills which would hinder individuals' moral advancement.

Alongside this concern for promoting individual moral progress, Gurney's understanding of philanthropy was shaped by evangelicalism's belief in universal progress in society. That belief that society would reach a utopian state through gradual progress (rather than through Christ's premillennialist return) has been examined by a number of authors.[49] Gurney accepted this belief in universal progress, arguing that society could advance as well as individuals – with each generation morally and intellectually outshining its predecessor.[50] He accepted that technological breakthroughs would have great benefits for humanity. In an example of preaching to the converted, he told the Mechanics' Institute of Manchester that 'Machinery is one means of immensely increasing the powers of man for useful purposes; and that it is our duty in the sight of God and our fellow creatures, to make the most of our capacities for such purposes, no sound moralist can deny.'[51]

Gurney combined this belief in universal progress with his Quakerish concern for removing barriers to individual moral progress. Between them, these two ideas motivated and shaped his philanthropy. This is of significance as Gurney made a major contribution to virtually every major philanthropic cause of his period and did as much as anyone else to establish the Friends' reputation as philanthropists. The manner in which this philanthropic work was shaped by these two ideas of progress is clearly demonstrated in his work in relation to the anti-slavery cause and his support for the Society for the Promotion of Permanent and Lasting Peace (hereafter the Peace Society).

Gurney's involvement in the anti-slavery cause clearly demonstrates the manner in which he united Quakerism's concern to remove barriers to individual progress and the evangelical movement's desire to promote universal progress. He clearly believed that the institution of slavery morally corrupted individuals. He claimed that a 'society in which one large proportion of the population is the absolute property of another, must have a

---

[49] For example, Bebbington, *Evangelicalism in Modern Britain*, pp. 60–3.

[50] Joseph John Gurney, 'The triumph of Christianity over infidelity', *The Amethyst: or Christian's Annual*, 1 (1832), p. 241.

[51] Joseph John Gurney, *The Minor Works of Joseph John Gurney* (London, 1839), p. 196.

tendency to corrupt, degrade and harden the heart',[52] and elsewhere drew attention to the spiritual captivity of the slave
trader.[53] Alongside this fear that slavery would morally degrade
individuals, Gurney expressed concerns that the institution
would impede economic progress in society. He argued that
'slavery and waste are twin sisters, whereas freedom is married to
economy',[54] and suggested that Jamaica's economy would pros-
per and outperform its rivals after its abolition of slavery.[55]
Gurney's campaign against slavery therefore shows how his interest, as a Quaker, in freeing individuals from sin was united
with his desire, as an evangelical, to promote economic progress
in society.

Gurney's participation in the Peace Society similarly shows
how he united Quakerism's commitment to removing barriers to
individual progress and to evangelicalism's desire to encourage
universal progress. Gurney was alarmed by the collateral damage
which wars caused to individuals' morality. He claimed that war
was accompanied by the 'destruction of moral and pious feeling'.[56] Gurney found this particularly distressing, as war (after
lowering the moral state of individuals) sent them beyond hope
of redemption: 'What countless multitudes of persons, full of
angry and violent passions – persons who we cannot reasonably
believe to have been prepared for death – have been suddenly
consigned to judgement and eternity, by the "red right hand" of
war!'. Gurney would have been equally anxious to remove war
from the world as he believed that it hurt society as much as
individuals. He argued that cessation of war would lead to 'rapid
improvement . . . in the wealth, comforts and intellectual conditions of the nations of Europe'. It should, however, be noted that
Gurney saw something more than mere economic gain from the
cessation of war. Instead he drew the abolition of war into a
vision of a postmillennialist utopia, arguing that 'the nations of
the earth, succumbing to the spectre of the Prince of Peace, will

---

[52] Joseph John Gurney, *Substance of a Speech . . . on the Subject of British Colonial Slavery* (London, 1824), p. 1.

[53] Joseph John Gurney, *Thoughts on Habit and Discipline* (London, 1845), p. 44.

[54] Joseph John Gurney, *A Winter in the West Indies*, 2nd edn (Norwich, 1840), p. 58.

[55] Joseph John Gurney, *Reconciliation, Respectfully Recommended to all Parties in the West Indies* (London, 1840), p. 4.

[56] Joseph John Gurney, *An Essay on War, and its Lawfulness Under the Christian Dispensation*, 1st edn (London, 1835), p. 7.

repose together under the banner of love. The word of prophecy is express and unquestionable. "NATION SHALL NOT LIFT UP SWORD AGAINST NATION, NEITHER SHALL THEY LEARN WAR ANY MORE".'[57]

Gurney's involvement in these two philanthropic causes indicates that he was able successfully to combine elements of the two schools of thought and therefore did not have to abandon Quakerism to adopt evangelicalism. It must, however, be noted that he never found this combination of beliefs truly comfortable, and throughout his life he felt that he was caught between Scylla and Charybdis (to use a phrase which he himself used).[58] This can be seen in the way that he always described himself as being caught between two opposing forces. During the Beaconite controversy (a theological dispute within British Quakerism which culminated in 1836 with many evangelicals resigning from the Society of Friends), Gurney claimed that 'Extreme opinions on either side appear increasingly to manifest themselves.'[59] Gurney clearly regarded himself as holding the middle against these contending forces, declaring in 1836 that 'I am truly thankful to find myself still in the centre of the boat of the Society'.[60]

That there was tension in Gurney's dual commitment to Quakerism and evangelicalism cannot be denied; but it was always a creative tension. Therefore Gurney's theology deserves something better than the often repeated claims that he deserted one set of beliefs to adopt another. Instead, the manner in which his Quaker and evangelical beliefs interacted shows a dialectical process under way, with the emergence of a revived Society of Friends which was both Quaker and evangelical. It is only through understanding this dialectical process that historians of the Quaker movement can understand its development during the nineteenth century, and the best tool for such a study is an examination of the life of Joseph John Gurney.

University of Keele

---

[57] Joseph John Gurney, *An Address to Ministers of the Gospel, and to all Professors of Christianity, on the Subject of War and Peace* (Norwich, nd), pp. 23, 1. 8.

[58] Anna Braithwaite Thomas, 'The Beaconite Controversy', *Bulletin of the Friends' Historical Society of Philadelphia*, 3 (1912), p. 76.

[59] Gurney, 'Journal', 26 April 1835.

[60] Ibid., 10 April 1836.

# DIVERSITY AND STRIVINGS FOR UNITY IN THE EARLY SWISS *RÉVEIL*

## by TIMOTHY C. F. STUNT

About thirty years ago, Dr John Walsh observed that 'the comparative history of the many evangelical or pietistic revivals of the nineteenth century remains to be written'[1] and on this particular front we can hardly claim today to have made very much progress. Any such study could well start with the French-speaking Swiss awakening or *réveil*, in the second decade of the century, which was soon to have a considerable impact on both French-speaking Protestants in general and, a little later, on British Evangelicals. Reacting against the conservative rationalism of the establishment many of the *réveillés* turned to a more romantic and experimental form of pietism which was liable to bring them into conflict with the ecclesiastical authorities and sometimes caused them to hive off into secession. The young men whose aims and ideals led to these divisions had nevertheless some genuinely ecumenical aspirations and a real concern for some visible expression of the Church's unity. The movement in French-speaking Switzerland is therefore a good field of enquiry in which the tensions between strivings for unity and separatist diversification can be explored.[2]

A significant number of those involved in the French-speaking Swiss *réveil* were students or recent graduates of the universities of Geneva and Lausanne, but had been nurtured in the cradle of Moravian devotion. While they attached special importance to the authority of Scripture, and in particular to the doctrines associated with the eighteenth-century evangelical revival, their enthusiasm tended to lay great stress on the *experience* of salvation. Neither of these characteristics was likely to endear them to the ecclesiastical establishment and there was little chance of

---

[1] John Walsh, 'Religion: Church and State in Europe and the Americas', in C. W. Crawley, ed., *New Cambridge Modern History*, 9 (Cambridge, 1965), p. 164.

[2] For the Swiss *réveil* see H. de Goltz, *Genève religieuse au dix-neuvième siècle* (Geneva, 1862); E. G[uers], *Le premier réveil et la première église indépendante à Genève* (Geneva, 1871); Leon Maury, *Le réveil religieux dans l'église réformée à Genève et en France (1810–1850)* (Paris, 1892); J. Cart, *Histoire du mouvement religieux et ecclésiastique dans le Canton de Vaud pendant la première moitié du XIX^e siècle*, 6 vols (Lausanne, 1870–80); Henri Meylan, *Notre Église* (Lausanne, [1958]), pp. 69–96; Paul Perret, *Nos Églises dissidentes* (Nyon, 1966), pp. 33–54; Alice Wemyss, *Histoire du réveil, 1790–1849* (Paris, 1977).

their pious yearnings finding recognition, let alone opportunities for expression in the Genevan Established Church whose virtual monopoly of Protestant worship had in effect gone unchallenged for many years.

There were of course some Genevan pastors whose piety was sympathetic to the movement. But Cellerier of Satigny and the somewhat mystically inclined Moulinié and Demellayer were far from typical of the *vénérable compagnie* of pastors whose first concern was usually with social morality and the need for vigilant opposition to the sort of licence and disorder associated in their minds with the French Revolution. In the neighbouring canton of Vaud, many more pastors were sympathetic to the doctrinal orientation of the *réveil*, but there was a similar anxiety about informal or unauthorized gatherings where enthusiastic lay participation might become the norm.

One reason for the survival of the almost unchallenged authority enjoyed by the Establishment was the valuable safety-valve provided by the Moravian Brethren. Ever since Zinzendorf's visit in 1741 there had been Moravian gatherings in Geneva which had been a useful outlet for pious enthusiasm, but their leaders always insisted that they were *not* a separatist movement, and that their meetings were only a supplement to those of the Establishment and in no way intended to replace them. The Moravian ideal of *ecclesiolae in Ecclesia* (little churches within the Church) has perhaps been underestimated as a significant factor in the avoidance of secession in eighteenth-century Europe.

This non-separatist tradition was maintained by a significant element in the Swiss *réveil*. In the 1820s Genevans like Louis Gaussen, Merle d'Aubigné, and Antoine Galland managed to weather the disapproval of the older and more traditional pastors without breaking away. In the case of Gaussen, his survival was the result of a judicious avoidance of contentious issues until he was established securely as pastor in Satigny, formerly the parish of the aged Cellerier and therefore one in which Gaussen's own piety was not unacceptable. More often, however, newly ordained ministers were on probation as *suffragans* (assistant ministers), and therefore vulnerable if their devotions seemed too enthusiastic or if their preaching concentrated unduly on such favourite themes of the *réveil* as the need for conversion and assurance of salvation. To avoid a confrontation several of them spent the first years of their careers abroad, serving congregations which were less critical of their enthusiasm. D'Aubigné's early ministry was in Hamburg and later in Brussels, while Galland served as pastor of the French-speaking church in Bern and then became Director of the Missionary Institute in Paris.[3]

Gaussen, like most of the *réveillés*, was very doubtful about the orthodoxy of the Genevan pastors who by their notorious edict of 3 May 1817 sought to prohibit any preaching on the subjects of Christ's deity, original sin, the workings and efficacy of grace, or the doctrine of predestination.[4] Gaussen protested at the pastors' apparent Arianism by republishing the Second Helvetic Confession – an action which was seen as a direct challenge to the rationalist catechism which the pastors had authorized to replace the older one. By 1830 Gaussen had reluctantly decided that he could no longer be identified with the official body of pastors who seemed to have abdicated their position as the spiritual pilots of the ship of state which, in consequence, 'had lost its anchors and lacked both cables and rudder . . . [and] was now left to be swept by every wind of doctrine',[5] but this did not mean that he wanted to secede from the Established Church. Gaussen now took a leading part in the foundation of the *Société Évangélique de Genève* and of its *École de Théologie*, both of which were intended to be institutions functioning (in theory at least) *within* the National Church. When D'Aubigné and Galland returned to Geneva they were associated with the venture, teaching in the theological school and preaching in the *Oratoire* where the Society held its meetings.[6] Galland insisted that the *Oratoire* was merely a 'preaching hall' supplementing the services of the Established Church[7] but in time it assumed the character

---

[3] Cf. Charles Rieu, who ministered to a French congregation at Fredericia in Denmark. Similarly soon after his dismissal as *suffragan* at Orbe (Vaud) in 1825, Charles François Recordon became the pastor of the Swiss Church in Florence though he later seceded and joined the Brethren; Cart, *Histoire*, 2, p. 376; G. Spini, *Risorgimento e Protestanti* (Naples, 1956), p. 125.

[4] The complete edict is in H. Heyer, *L'Église de Genève 1535–1909* (Geneva, 1909), pp. 119–20. For an unconvincing defence of the edict see Wemyss, *Histoire*, pp. 79–80, 86–8.

[5] S. R. L. Gaussen, *Mémoires adressés au conseil d'état de la république de Genève* (Geneva, 1832), p. 82. Cf. Gaussen, *Lettres à la vénérable compagnie des pasteurs de Genève* (Geneva, 1830); 'Memoir of the author' in Gaussen, *Parables of the Spring or the Resurrection and the Life* (London, nd), pp. 5–20.

[6] B. Biéler, *Un fils du Refuge: Jean-Henri Merle d'Aubigné* (Geneva, 1934), pp. 126–31.

[7] For an early account of the *Oratoire* (when Galland's claim was still valid) see the letter written by Rodolphe de Rodt (a young French-speaking aristocrat from Bern, teetering on the brink of secession), to J. Wenger (March 1834) in *Calcutta Christian Advocate* (11 November 1843), p. 342.

of a church where baptism and the Lord's Supper were regularly administered. Nevertheless the *Oratoire* was in principle what may be called the Genevan home of the 'Established' or 'National' wing of the *réveil*. In the canton of Vaud, where the Establishment was doctrinally uncompromised in the eyes of the *réveillés*, many more ministers continued to serve in the pulpits of the National Church for two more decades until the secession of 1845 and the establishment of the *Église libre vaudoise*.

In contrast to this accommodation with the Establishment was the *dissidence* (or dissent) in Geneva of men like Henri-Louis Empaytaz, Henri Pyt, Émile Guers, Jean-Guillaume Gonthier, and others who founded the *Assemblée de Bourg-de-Four* or (as it was known in its earliest days) *La Petite Église*. Like their less radical contemporaries they were young romantics who had grown up in unsettled times when Swiss life was scarred by economic distress and foreign occupation.[8] Similarly it is true that some of them had experienced domestic upheaval, but Mme Wemyss exaggerates when she repeatedly dismisses them as 'une bande de jeunes exaltés', 'traumatisé[s]' or 'les jeunes frustrés'.[9] Certainly they were enthusiasts; but their earliest experience of evangelical piety had been in the context of Moravian non-separatism and they were reluctant to secede. The ordinands among them in 1817 could reasonably claim that this course was forced upon them by the decree of an Established Church which required an undertaking from them to refrain from teaching some of the truths that they cherished and valued most dearly. Guers's final exams were due to begin the day after the edict was issued. To his father's grief he refused to subscribe and by so doing was barred from ordination.[10] Henri Pyt's reaction was to abandon his studies in the theological faculty where he still had two more years to go before his exams, but neither he nor Guers became separatists by conviction overnight, as they still had in mind the possibility of ordination in France or another part of

---

[8] Henri Dubief, 'Réflexions sur quelques aspects du premier Réveil et sur le milieu où il se forma', *Bulletin de la société de l'histoire du protestantisme français*, 114 (1968), pp. 384, 376–8.

[9] Wemyss, *Histoire*, pp. 50–2.

[10] Guers's father had previously abandoned the Roman communion and become a Protestant but now reverted to Catholicism because, 'Despotisme pour despotisme, il préférait encore celui de Rome.' Guers, *Premier réveil*, p. 92. He had taken refuge in Geneva from the revolutionary upheavals in Savoy; Francis Chaponnière, *Pasteurs et laïques de l'église de Genève* (Geneva, 1889), pp. 88–9.

Switzerland where the attitude of the Genevan pastors was by no means the norm.

On the other hand the edict did confirm their earlier feelings that there was scant hope of finding in the services of the National Church the spiritual sustenance for which they were looking. Not only would they have to listen to numerous sermons in which the name of Jesus would probably go unmentioned, but all too often communion would be administered by men who scorned any emphasis on the experience of conversion and indeed were now identified with an *official* ban on a substantial part of orthodox Christian teaching. Ultimately these children of the *réveil* had either to find or to found an ecclesiastical community to which they could belong and which would provide what they felt was lacking elsewhere. 'Although we were well on the way to *dissidence*, we were in no hurry to found a separate church. . . . We would have been only too happy to serve the Church of our country if we had been able to do so with complete freedom of conscience.'[11] It was thus their inability to carry out their duties, as they understood them, within the National Church, that caused these men to separate from it. At heart they were Moravians still, and had no wish to secede. At this stage they apparently had no quarrel with the idea of an Established Church as such.

It was therefore force of circumstance which transformed their previously discrete meetings for mutual edification at *La Tête-Noire*[12] into rather more formal occasions, and barely a fortnight after the edict of 3 May the participants took steps to form a Christian Association composed of believers 'in so far as we could recognize them'.[13] Although the arrival, in 1817, of the Scots evangelist Robert Haldane and his meetings with some of the students of divinity at the University had played a significant part in what may be called the visible launching of the *réveil* in Geneva,[14] the initiative to form the community which in due

---

[11] Cf. 'Le fait de la dissidence avait par la force même des choses, précédé pour nous la théorie.' Guers, *Premier réveil*, pp. 98–9.

[12] This was the school-room of Julien-François Privat, another member of the earlier Moravian circle.

[13] Guers, *Premier réveil*, p. 99.

[14] For Haldane's earlier career see Deryck W. Lovegrove, 'Unity and separation: contrasting elements in the thought and practice of Robert and James Alexander Haldane', in Keith Robbins, ed., *Protestant Evangelicalism: England, Ireland, Germany and America, SCH.S*, 7 (Oxford, 1990), pp. 153–77.

course would become the Bourg-de-Four Assembly, had come principally from men whose faith was established before Haldane came to Geneva. Indeed, it can be argued that at first there was little to distinguish the new association from any of the other Moravian groups to which most of its members had previously belonged.[15]

One enthusiast, associated with them at this early stage, must be categorized rather differently. César Malan had been ordained in 1810, but his evangelical conversion had led him in March 1817 to deliver a highly critical sermon which was probably a decisive factor in provoking the decree of 3 May. When, four months after the formation of their association, Guers and his friends took holy communion together for the first time, it was Malan who officiated,[16] but the next day (22 September) he refused their request for him to be their pastor. If he had accepted, they might just have been able to claim that they had not separated from the Established Church. Instead they chose three of their number, Gonthier, Pyt, and a young French pastor, Pierre Méjanel, to form a joint pastorate. When Pyt distributed the bread at the first communion service at *La Tête-Noire* on 5 October they were finally crossing the Rubicon, as Pyt was not ordained and was therefore breaking the law. It had taken five months for their dissent to become a reality.

The direction of the *Petite Église* was in the hands of the pastors together with two elders, Guers and Empaytaz,[17] the latter of whom had returned to Geneva at Guers's invitation. One of their tasks was to arrange a rota of those who would preside over meetings at *La Tête-Noire* and the little Moravian meeting at Saint-Gervais which had asked one of them to be responsible on Sundays, Thursdays, and Fridays. By February 1818 the 'little Church' had preaching responsibilities in three private houses, in a meeting room at Bourg-de-Four, and in the school room at *La*

---

[15] Haldane's activities in Geneva greatly irritated the pastors who stigmatized the *réveil* as an import from abroad. The accounts of the movement's early historians, de Goltz and Maury, are often unduly coloured by this criticism.

[16] This took place in the home of Henry Drummond, another visitor to Geneva whose interest seemed to suggest foreign origins.

[17] Empaytaz had studied for ordination but left Geneva in 1814 when his continuing association with a community established by the rather unstable Mme de Krüdener had incurred the wrath of the pastors who ordered his name to be struck off the roll of ordination candidates. See E.G[uers], *Notice sur Henri-Louis Empaytaz, ministre de l'évangile, mort dans le Seigneur, le 23 avril 1853* [Geneva, 1853]. For a less charitable account of Empaytaz, see Wemyss, *Histoire*, p. 52.

*Tête-Noire.* In the course of the next few years this activity expanded and assumed a missionary dimension, with members of the assembly evangelizing in the canton of Vaud and other French-speaking parts of Switzerland as well as in France. Some of the members of this newly established church undoubtedly were or soon became strongly separatist – perhaps by way of reaction to the hostility and indeed persecution which they experienced at the hands of the Establishment. For example, when Jean-Nicolas Coulin and Antoine Porchat were preaching in and around Ste Croix in Vaud in 1818 and 1819 they upset a number of the Moravians by their aggressive criticisms of the Establishment. It was said that Porchat had dismissed the worship of those in the National Church as 'nothing but an act of hypocrisy; their attendance at communion was sacrilege and their clergy were a group of mercenaries'.[18] Nevertheless it is clear that the Moravians remained on good terms with the *Petite Église* in Geneva. That this stridency was by no means typical of the assembly's preaching is well illustrated by two of its better known workers.

Ami Bost, in whose home Moravians had gathered as far back as 1810 and who had been ordained as a Genevan minister in 1814, became an independent evangelist and at times was critical of members of the Establishment; but his *Mémoires* make quite clear that whenever possible he co-operated and tried to maintain good relations with the Moravians.[19] Similarly Félix Neff, whose indefatigable labours in southeastern France led to his being known as the 'apostle of the Alps', insisted that the National Church should not be confused with the true Church. His letter to one of the 'awakened' Vaudois ministers, Marc Fivaz, was uncompromising: 'The People of God must be *a people of free will*; these religious forms in which they are more or less tightly bound – whether worldly or Christian – do not constitute the People of God.' He was not however advocating secession. His words in an earlier letter were very emphatic when he wrote in 1820 from Lausanne: 'The Lord seems to have opened a wide

---

[18] E. A. Senft, *L'Église de l'unité des frères* (Neuchâtel, 1888), pp. 242–3. Cf. Cart, *Histoire*, 6, p. 521. There is no mention of the episode in [Mme. Porchat and A. Cadier], *Vie de Porchat* (Pau, 1866). See also D. Robert, *Les Églises reformées en France* (Paris, 1961), pp. 358–60.
[19] A. Bost, *Mémoires pouvant servir à l'histoire du réveil religieux des églises protestantes de la Suisse et de la France*, 3 vols (Paris, 1854–5), 1, pp. 128–31.

door in this canton for the preaching of the Gospel; neither will it be shut, so long as prudence is exercised, and care is taken to agitate no secondary question, which, not relating directly to salvation, might raise an alarm and excite apprehension of a schism.' His sentiments were similar when writing to the Vaudois minister Auguste Rochat: 'I entreat you in the name of the Lord's Church, that nothing in the shape of separation may be thought of, it would be grasping a shadow and losing the substance.'[20] While the members of the new assembly in Geneva accepted ecclesiastical diversity many of them were anxious to avoid the charge of schism.

Such a conciliatory spirit was not characteristic of the later position of their fellow *dissident*, César Malan, whose patriarchal appearance and unbending insistence on the need for assurance was seen by many British observers as the very quintessence of the *réveil*.[21] Malan's refusal to serve as a pastor of what soon became the Bourg-de-Four assembly was related to the fact that he hoped to remain within the State Church. In fact he was temporarily reconciled to the pastors, but soon found in 1818 that he could not suffer the restraints imposed on his ministry. If he wished to preach on the subjects closest to his heart he would not have access to the pulpits of the Establishment. For a while he preached with the *dissidents* but later gathered a congregation in his own home at Pré-l'Evêque, in the garden of which he later built a chapel. He still claimed to be a faithful member of the National Church, insisting that his services were in accordance with the original regulations and liturgy of the Establishment.[22]

In 1821, however, he published an inflammatory booklet which could only exacerbate the situation in Vaud where the Doyen Curtat had issued an extraordinary pamphlet stating that household meetings were 'contrary to the laws of God and the

[20] A. Bost, *Letters and Biography of Felix Neff, Protestant Missionary in Switzerland and the Department of Isère and the High Alps* (trans. M. A. Wyatt) (London, 1843), pp. 17–18, 41. The original French of the second letter is cited in L. Burnier, *Notice sur Auguste Rochat, ministre de l'évangile* (Lausanne, 1848), p. 109, where the last sentence is rather less poetic: 'Ce serait tout perdu pour un rien.' These quotations should dispose of Mme Wemyss's repeated dismissal of Neff as a divisive sectarian; Wemyss, *Histoire*, pp. 128–30. Grudgingly she allows that in 1822, 'il commençait à se détacher du sectarisme': ibid., p. 155. In reality his position displays an interesting blend of principle and tact.
[21] T. C. F. Stunt, 'Geneva and British evangelicals in the early nineteenth century', *JEH*, 32 (1981), pp. 36, 40, 43–5. See also [S. C. Malan], *La Vie et travaux de César Malan* (Geneva, 1869); G. Sabliet, *Un Gagneur d'âmes* (Dieulefit, 1943).
[22] César Malan, *Déclaration de fidelité à cette église* (Geneva, 1821).

laws of men', suggesting in passing that the fate of Eutychus (Acts 20.10) was confirmation of divine disapproval.[23] Instead of providing an irenic reply, Malan gave an account of just such a meeting in the home of a Bernese aristocrat at Rolle (in Vaud) to which he, a Genevan minister, had been invited. In his tract he gave full expression to his high Calvinism and made some far from charitable references to the widely respected Curtat. Many, including the young Alexandre Vinet who was sympathetic to some aspects of the *réveil*, were particularly infuriated by a prayer in which Malan asked God to enlighten Curtat and 'endow him with the gift of love'.[24] Not surprisingly, in 1823 Malan was finally suspended from his ministry in Geneva, and reluctantly he had to recognize that he was now a *dissident*. It was shortly after this in 1824 that he founded the *Église du Témoignage*.

Malan's position now became increasingly isolated and intractable – all the more obviously so when the Bourg-du-Four assembly was engaged in a daring experiment in ecclesiastical accommodation.[25] In matters of discipline the elders of the *Petite Église* sought to use admonition rather than excommunication, and their regular meetings for discussion with the members of the Church meant that their ecclesiology was as much congregational as presbyterian. In the matter of reception at communion *any* believer was welcome at the Lord's Table. At first some of their number apparently wanted to exclude those who were less separatist in their views, but by a resolution of 24 October 1819 it was decided that all Christians, whether members of the State Church or not, would be received. While the Zwinglian view of the communion service was widely held it was by no means the assembly's official teaching. Even more original was their success in containing different views on baptism – a subject which was notoriously liable to be a point of division. While the majority of

---

[23] L. A. Curtat, *De l'Établissement des conventicules dans le canton de Vaud* (Lausanne, 1821); the sequel, *Nouvelles observations sur l'établissement des conventicules et sur les missions en pays chrétiens* (Lausanne, 1821), was rather less extreme but also reflected Curtat's deep fear of popular piety unrestrained by clerical control. Cf. Meylan, *Notre Église*, pp. 67–8.

[24] [C. Malan], *Conventicule de Rolle, par un témoin digne de foi* (Geneva, 1821), p. 53. Vinet's anonymous reply to Malan was entitled, *Lettre aux jeunes ministres qui figurent comme interlocuteurs dans la brochure intitulée: Conventicule de Rolle* (Basel, 1821); cf. Alexandre Vinet, *Lettres*, ed. Pierre Bovet, 4 vols (Lausanne, 1947–9), 1, p. 133.

[25] For the rest of this paragraph see Guers, *Premier Réveil*, pp. 159–81.

the congregation were paedobaptists like Empaytaz, there were some like Guers who were baptists.

They were soon to discover that Malan had very little time for such inexactness. In their quest for a visible expression, at the Lord's Table, of the unity of the Church universal, and in their anxiety to avoid any semblance of schism, the leaders at Bourg-de-Four initiated more than one attempt to amalgamate their assembly with Malan's congregation but were repeatedly re-buffed by his insistence that 'union leads to communion but fusion leads to confusion.'[26] What de Goltz described as Malan's 'absolute monarchy'[27] at Pré-l'Evêque was in sharp contrast to the flexible and conciliatory arrangements negotiated by the multiple pastorate at Bourg-de-Four. While the Bourg-de-Four assembly may be said to have thrived on diversity, Malan's outlook was rigid and monolithic and there was more than one occasion when Malan broke off relations with his unprincipled fellow *dissidents*. It was during one such rupture in 1828 that Neff felt the need in his forthright way to write to Malan rebuking him for his narrow authoritarianism:

> N'exposez plus l'Évangile à l'opprobre au milieu des hommes donnant lieu si largement aux reproches de présomption, d'ambition, et d'orgueil qu'ils vous addressent de toutes parts. Cessez d'asservir et de vous approprier en quelque sorte les brebis de Christ, cessez d'attirer et d'affaiblir le christianisme de beaucoup d'âmes par l'influence de votre exemple, et de vos principes tout-à-la-fois étroits et relâchés, cessez enfin d'affliger vos frères et de diviser l'église de Christ par votre esprit d'intolérance, d'exclusion & de domination.[28]

The path of the *réveil* was never a smooth one and the attempt to accommodate diversity was often misunderstood by those who confused union with uniformity.

I have suggested elsewhere that the Swiss *réveil* was a seminal influence on such radical ecclesiologies as those of the Irvingites and Plymouth Brethren,[29] and the early outlook of these move-

---

[26] J. A. Bost, *César Malan, impressions, notes et souvenirs* (Geneva, 1865), p. 48.

[27] De Goltz, *Genève religieuse*, p. 339.

[28] Geneva, University Library, D.O. autogr, F. Neff to C. Malan, 27 June 1828. It is possible that the letter was not in fact sent.

[29] Stunt, 'Geneva and British evangelicals', pp. 42, 44.

ments does have some features corresponding to what we have observed in the Swiss *réveil*. In the case of the Brethren, Charles de Rodt in August 1836 wrote from Plymouth to his friends at Bourg-de-Four in Geneva, enthusiastically describing 'une chère Église constituée largement selon nos principes', whose leaders were trying to persuade him to attend the conference of Brethren at Powerscourt in Ireland.[30] Although the Brethren were later to become almost a by-word for exclusive isolation, in their earliest phase they arranged their services for the breaking of bread at a time which would not clash with the communion services of other denominations.[31] A similarly conciliatory note from the early days of the movement can be found in the plea of John Synge when he insisted that their meetings should be seen as providing a nutritional supplement to the meagre fare of the Anglican Established Church rather than replacing their services.[32] A similar parallel between the Brethren and the Bourg-de-Four assembly is their successful accommodation of both infant and adult baptism.[33]

In the case of the Catholic Apostolic Church (popularly known as Irvingites), established by Henry Drummond and others in the early 1830s, the more appropriate parallel is with Malan, to whom Irving and his companions looked with respect in their early years.[34] Irving, like Malan, had no quarrel with the idea of a National Church,[35] but unfortunately for him, the Establishment rejected both his christology and his compulsive desire to make room in his church for charismatic manifestations, and in consequence he found himself driven into isolation. The later ecclesiastical structures of the community were an unfortunate cul-de-sac from which there was no way out, but even so

---

[30] *Feuille de la Commission des églises associées pour l'évangelisation* (Geneva, 1837), 1, p. 147. For the Powerscourt conferences see H. H. Rowdon, *The Origins of the Brethren* (London, 1967), pp. 86–8.

[31] The process by which this was abandoned in Limerick in 1832–3, causing J. N. Darby himself some anxiety, can be traced in J. N. Darby, *Letters*, 3 vols (London, nd), 1, pp. 11, 15–16, 18.

[32] J. Synge, *Observations on 'A Call to the Converted' as it relates to Members of the Church of England* (Teignmouth, 1831), p. 8. For the context of this pamphlet see T. C. F. Stunt, 'John Synge and the early Brethren', *Journal of Christian Brethren Research*, 28 (1976), pp. 45, 50–7.

[33] H. H. Rowdon, 'The early Brethren and baptism,' *Vox Evangelica*, 11 (1979), pp. 55–63.

[34] Stunt, 'Geneva and British evangicals', p. 45.

[35] M. Oliphant, *Life of Edward Irving*, 2nd edn (London, 1862), 1, p. 383. In this respect Sheridan Gilley's portrayal of Irving as an 'other-worldly' sectarian is perhaps misleading: S. Gilley, 'Edward Irving: prophet of the millennium', in J. Garnett and C. Matthew, eds, *Revival and Religion since 1700: Essays for John Walsh* (London, 1993), pp. 96–8.

it is noteworthy that in later years there were many in the Catholic Apostolic community who regarded themselves as an order within Anglicanism.[36]

All too often, new ecclesiastical bodies have been labelled as schismatic, destroying the unity of the body of Christ, when in fact they could claim with some reason that the inability of the existing institutions to accept diversification was the more divisive factor in the situation. The protests of seceders that they had no wish to create yet another denomination should not be dismissed as disingenuous, bearing in mind how often the process by which they detached themselves from the establishment was painfully slow and hesitant.

Stowe School, Buckingham

---

[36] See E. Miller, *History and Doctrines of Irvingism*, 2 vols (London, 1878), 1, pp. 343–4. Cf. R. A. Davenport, *Albury Apostles* (London, 1974), p. 215. This bond with Anglicanism is reflected in their occasional gifts to the Church of England Clergy Sustentation Fund. See David Tierney, 'The Catholic Apostolic Church: a study in Tory Millenarianism', *HR*, 63 (1990), p. 310.

# UNITY IN DIVERSITY? NORTH ATLANTIC EVANGELICAL THOUGHT IN THE MID-NINETEENTH CENTURY

*by* JOHN WOLFFE

L eonard Bacon, minister of the First Congregational Church at New Haven, preaching before the Foreign Evangelical Society in New York in May 1845, found in the Atlantic Ocean a vivid image of an underlying unity which he perceived in the divided evangelical churches that surrounded it. Separated though they were, still influences upon them operated like 'the tide raised from the bosom of the vast Atlantic when the moon hangs over it in her height, [which] swells into every estuary, and every bay and sound, and every quiet cove and sheltered haven, and is felt far inland where mighty streams rise in their channels and pause upon their journey to the sea'.[1] The choice of metaphor betrayed an aspiration that the North Atlantic itself should become an evangelical lake. Such hopes, Bacon appreciated, would be worse than fruitless if they were driven by a model of Christianity as 'one and indivisible'. No, the model should be the American, not the French Republic, *e pluribus unum*, unity in diversity.[2]

A view of the Atlantic as a uniting rather than dividing factor in evangelical history is currently receiving increasing attention from scholars,[3] but, one might ask, does this tell us as much about the predilections of late twentieth-century academics as about the reality of the eighteenth and nineteenth centuries? A related issue is the problem of defining and understanding the limits and scope of Protestant evangelicalism, a movement which professed a strong overall identity but often seemed highly fissiparous in practice.[4] A consideration of the theological and ideological

---

[1] Leonard Bacon, *Christian Unity* (New Haven, Conn., 1845), p. 25.

[2] Ibid., p. 28.

[3] For a bibliography see Larry Eskridge, 'An introductory guide to the literature of comparative evangelical history', in George A. Rawlyk and Mark A. Noll, eds, *Amazing Grace: Evangelicalism in Australia, Britain, Canada and the United States* (Grand Rapids, 1993), pp. 401–9.

[4] D. W. Bebbington, *Evangelicalism in Modern Britain* (London, 1989), pp. 1–19; John Wolffe, 'Anti-Catholicism and evangelical identity in Britain and the United States', in David W. Bebbington, Mark A. Noll and George A. Rawlyk, eds, *Evangelicalism: Comparative Studies of Popular Protestantism in North America, the British Isles and Beyond, 1700–1990* (New York, 1994), pp. 179–97.

context of the concept of 'unity in diversity', as advocated by Bacon and others in the early Victorian period and associated with the formation of the Evangelical Alliance in 1845–6, will illuminate both debates.[5]

A major factor in prompting mid-nineteenth-century evangelicals to articulate their perceptions of unity was a sense of a growing challenge from Roman Catholicism, which needed to be met not only on the pragmatic level of joint action, but also on the ideological level of asserting the catholicity (with a small 'c') of Protestantism. Thus in 1828 Baptist Noel (despite his Christian name an Anglican clergyman until 1848) followed a sermon on the right of private judgement with one on Protestant unity in fundamental doctrines. Both were part of a series delivered in London 'on the points in controversy between Roman Catholics and Protestants'. Noel denied the Roman charge that insistence on the authority of Scripture meant that each 'may affix his own interpretation without fear of reproof'. Rather, a sound understanding of biblical authority implied that each doctrine should be valued and asserted in proportion to the certainty and prominence which it received in Scripture. Hence for example, Protestants accepted the deity of Christ, but not transubstantiation. Where Scripture was unclear, dogmatism was inappropriate and unnecessarily divisive; but where it was plain, 'bold and unhesitating maintenance of truths' was required. The unity of true Christians lay not in their membership of divided visible churches, but in their shared acceptance of 'one Lord, one Faith, one Baptism'.[6]

The Roman Church's right to call itself 'Catholic' was vehemently denied by evangelicals, notably in the pages of the Birmingham-based *Protestant Journal*, which from 1832 subtitled itself 'the true catholic's protest against the modern Church of Rome'. It was true that some erstwhile evangelicals such as John Henry Newman and Richard Waldo Sibthorp were drawn to Rome by the appearance of unity, but their fellow-Anglican Edward Bickersteth saw them as misguided. 'The unity of the Roman Church', he maintained, 'is a mere outside unity covering every-

---

[5] The present chapter complements my account of the institutional expression of this concept in John Wolffe, 'The Evangelical Alliance in the 1840s: an attempt to institutionalise Christian unity', *SCH*, 23 (1986), pp. 333–46.

[6] Baptist W. Noel, *On Protestant Unity in Fundamental Doctrines* (London, 1828).

thing that is most discordant to Christ and his Gospel'.[7] Others, notably but not only in America, gave such views an additional cutting edge by branding the unity of Rome as a false unity imposed by spiritual despotism.[8] In the United States the link between evangelical unity and anti-Romanism was well expressed in the very names of organizations such as the Christian Alliance and the American and Foreign Christian Union. These were in fact primarily concerned with the struggle against 'popery'.

The model of 'unity in diversity' was explicitly contrasted with a model of unity through 'uniformity' which was associated with the Roman Catholic Church.[9] For example, in his book *Religion in America* (1844), Robert Baird repudiated the charge that the multiplicity of denominations in the United States implied a lack of harmony among evangelical Christians. On the contrary, Baird maintained, the reality was one of considerable 'mutual respect and brotherly love' which was much greater than if they had all been coerced into one denonomination. He alleged that the apparent unanimity of Rome concealed divisions, heartburnings and hatreds.[10]

Thus anti-Romanism was not merely a negative prejudice, but rather a key stimulus to positive thinking about the common ground shared by evangelicals. It was part of a wider cluster of concerns for the spread of the gospel. A widely-cited biblical text was John 17.20–1, implying as it did that the unity of Christians was a prerequisite for the conversion of the world. The achievements of interdenominational bodies on both the home and foreign mission fields were acknowledged and held up as an indication of how much more might be achieved through deeper and more far-reaching unity: 'Let the different Denominations, retaining their preferences as to modes and forms, be one in Fellowship; and will not the world, beholding the sight, feel and confess the truth and divinity of our common Religion?'[11] Hopes

---

[7] Oxford, Bodleian Library, Bickersteth Papers, Box 25, Edward Bickersteth to R. W. Sibthorp, 2 Oct. 1843.

[8] See for example T. H. Skinner in *Evangelical Christendom*, 1 (1847), p. 68.

[9] For general analysis of these two models of Christian unity see Ruth Rouse and S. C. Neill, eds, *A History of the Ecumenical Movement, 1517–1948* (London, 1967).

[10] Robert Baird, *Religion in the United States of America* (Glasgow, 1844), p. 610.

[11] *Evangelical Christendom*, 1 (1847), p. 69. Cf. Samuel Farmer Jones, *Christian Unity Necessary for the Conversion of the World* (New York, 1837); Robert S. Candlish, 'Christian union in connection with the propagation of the Gospel', in *Essays on Christian Union* (London, 1845), pp. 106–34.

of this kind were fuelled by the revivalistic excitement of the early 1840s, which was current on both sides of the Atlantic: in 1845 the *New York Evangelist* asserted its full persuasion 'that our blessed Lord will take care of the unity of his Church by pouring out his Spirit upon it'.[12] A further stimulus came from the Disruption of the Church of Scotland in May 1843, which seemed both to release considerable evangelistic energies and to point the way to a radical reshaping of existing denominational structures. Its impact was felt far outside Scotland. Such events heightened millennial expectation:[13] certainly many believed that real unity among Christians would only come with the return of Christ, and this conviction could lead, especially among those of a futurist outlook, to a feeling that human efforts to bring it about were premature and even impious. On the other hand, among those whose historicist understanding of biblical prophecy led them to interpret contemporary events as signs of the end, unity was indeed an idea whose time had come. J. W. Massie, the English Congregationalist chronicler of the Evangelical Alliance, perceived it as potentially ushering in the restoration of Zion.[14]

Americans with their strong sense of denominational pluralism found 'unity in diversity' a particularly attractive slogan, but British writers did much to substantiate its biblical and theological credentials. A pioneering statement was made by Baptist Noel in 1837 in his pamphlet *The Unity of the Church*, pointedly subtitled 'Another Tract for the Times'. Noel began by citing the biblical passages which identified 'those in whom marks of regeneration appear' and asserted that 'All such persons, by whatever other peculiarities they may be marked, are the children of God.'[15] Accordingly, they should all be loved as brothers. Error was to be condemned if it involved 'a perversion of the plain statements of revelation', but not if it arose merely 'from

---

[12] *New York Evangelist*, 18 Sept. 1845.

[13] In a letter to Thomas Chalmers (Oxford, Bodleian Library, Bickersteth Papers, Box 25, 17 June 1843) Edward Bickersteth related the Scottish Disruption to his speculations on the fulfilment of biblical prophecy. T. R. Birks published the letter in his biography of his father-in-law (*Memoir of the Rev. Edward Bickersteth*, 2 vols [London, 1852], 2, pp. 233–4) but suppressed the paragraph in question.

[14] J. W. Massie, *The Evangelical Alliance: its Origins and Development* (London, 1847), p. ii; Donald M. Lewis, *Lighten their Darkness: The Evangelical Mission to Working-Class London* (Westport, Conn., 1986), pp. 101–3.

[15] B. W. Noel, *The Unity of the Church* (London, 1837), pp. 3–5.

the obscurity of the subject, and from the infirmities of our understandings'.[16] Noel went on to maintain that differences over infant baptism or episcopacy fell into the latter rather than the former category. On such matters all true Christians should respect each other's integrity. This did not mean abandoning disputed doctrines, but it did imply avoiding hasty judgement and the imputation of unjustified inferences and corrupt motives, and the furthering of united action wherever possible.

Noel's tract was stronger in pious exhortation than in logical argument: in particular his emphasis on respect for the right of private judgement gave rise to the charge that the eventual outcome of his prescriptions would be that 'every man, who in conscience chooses, becomes a church to himself'.[17] However, Edward Norris Kirk, an American Presbyterian, was to revel in the apparent paradox that such ultimate assertion of diversity was the basis of true unity: 'there is one thing at least, in which all Protestants are united . . ., that is the . . . earnestness of our attachment to the right of private judgement in matters between God and the soul. And he who differs from us there is no Protestant.'[18]

In the meantime others attempted more nuanced statements of the position put forward by Noel. A notable collaborative statement came with *Essays on Christian Union*, published in 1845 and containing pieces by several leading Scottish Presbyterians as well as one by the prominent English Congregationalist, John Angell James. Thomas Chalmers contributed the opening essay in which he emphasized that, in the short term at least, union did not mean the incorporation of all Christians in one society, but rather 'their harmonious co-operation for the fulfilment of one or more objects which they shall agree in thinking and feeling to be desirable'. There was a need for mutual forbearance on matters which were not central doctrines of the faith: to insist on keeping up fine points of distinction and so postponing the attainment of the preconditions for the conversion of the world

---

[16] Ibid., p. 9.

[17] *Schism: An Examination of the Principles contained in the Hon. and Rev. B. W. Noel's Tract 'On the Unity of the Church'* (London, 1838), p. 17.

[18] *Addresses of Rev. L. Bacon, D. D. and Rev. E. N. Kirk at the Annual Meeting of the Christian Alliance* (New York, 1846), p. 22.

was 'truly to strain at so many gnats, and to swallow a most enormous camel'.[19]

In the same volume Robert Balmer, professor of systematic theology in the United Secession Church, examined the scriptural basis of unity. It did not mean absolute uniformity, as this would imply the extinction of free enquiry: those who sought such an end would produce results worthy only of the Tacitean tag, 'solitudinem faciunt, pacem appellant'.[20] Rather, 'all true christians ought to walk together in all things in which they are agreed; and as the points on which they differ, though some of them may be very important, cannot be essential to salvation, they ought to make these points matters of forbearance.'[21] This, Balmer maintained, was by no means a 'latitudinarian' position. It was sanctioned by Scripture, as indicated by the readiness with which the early Church admitted those whose conversion had been attested (Acts 10.47–8); in St Paul's recognition that Christians did hold varying views (Rom. 14.1–3); and in his exhortations to walk together and show forbearance (Phil. 3. 15–16, I Cor. 13.4, 7).[22] Balmer subsequently addressed the objection that the distinction between essential and non-essential truth was unwarranted and impossible to apply in practice. To say something was non-essential was not the same as to regard it as unimportant: forbearance did not mean a neglect of legitimate attempts to change the views of others. However, if all specific doctrines were essential for salvation then no-one could ever be saved; in practice black and white could be clearly distinguished while the acknowledged existence of shades of grey was a providential safeguard against wholesale abandonment of the beneficial but non-essential.[23]

In a series of letters to *The Record*, published in July and August 1845, Edward Bickersteth imbued such arguments with the gloss of his own distinctive and profound spirituality. His starting point was that 'Only truth, drawn from the word of God and tried in living experience can unite the souls of Christians.' Strife

---

[19] Thomas Chalmers, 'How such a union may begin and to what it may eventually lead', in *Essays on Christian Union*, pp. 3–17.

[20] 'They make a desolation and call it peace' (Tacitus, *Agricola*, c. 20).

[21] Robert Balmer, 'The scriptural principles of unity', in *Essays on Christian Union*, p. 37.

[22] Ibid., pp. 40–8.

[23] Ibid., pp. 84–92.

and dissension had their root cause in error, and in order to combat them the Christian needed to pray for the spirit of truth and for a deeper knowledge of God. The next step was to hold truths in due proportion, given that they were not all equally vital. Lesser truths should not be sacrificed but they must not be given excessive weight. Moreover all should be set in the perspective of eternity, transcending 'the petty circle' of the flesh and focusing on 'the salvation of the precious and never dying soul'. In a second letter Bickersteth examined the teaching of Scripture on Christian unity. Its final attainment was promised (John 17.20–1; Eph. 4.1–16; Rev. 21.2) and even though present achievement inevitably fell short of eschatological expectation, the knowledge of the ideal should be a spur to 'draw us now nearer to each other'. Scripture urged forbearance: the Church was a gathering of sinners not seraphs, and others had to be accepted even when their understanding was deficient and their practice wanting (Gal. 6.1–5; Phil. 1.15–19). Moreover, Christian union was the progressive construction of a heavenly building (I Pet. 2.5), so the limited extent of current achievements and even the appearance of serious obstacles should not be allowed to frustrate the vision. In his third letter he considered some of the hindrances to union, which included confusing the forms of a Church – such as the nature of its ministry, or its relationship to the state – with its essence. A further obstacle was clericalism which filled the clergy with pride and the laity with apathy. Christians too needed to be more aware of the objective existence of diversity. Making explicit comparisons between Britain and the United States, Bickersteth observed that 'the forms may vary and yet the inward spiritual life, the inner man, as the Apostle speaks, be the same. And on the other hand the outward forms may be similar or resemble each other and yet the inward life be an entire contrast.' Finally, while there were times when contention for the faith was called for, there were many others when 'a false fire' and 'the wrath of man' led to unnecessary division, notably over 'Calvinism and Arminianism, Nationalism and Voluntaryism, Paedobaptism and Antipaedobaptism, Presbytery and Episcopacy'.[24]

---

[24] Oxford, Bodleian Library, Bickersteth Papers, Box 25.

For an example of how such ideas were developed in America, we turn to a sermon by T. H. Skinner, a Presbyterian minister in New York. Skinner posed the question as to whether the prayer of John 17.20–1 implied 'outward Uniformity' or 'practical Communion or Fellowship'. Any aspirations to uniformity, he argued, would be at odds with the objective existence of great diversity within, as well as between, denominations. Moreover as the New Testament did not contain any equivalent of the Levitical law, it was evident that Christ and the Apostles had not expected or required uniformity. It was theoretically possible that God might have made a particular Church a repository of authoritative truth, but he would then have ensured that its identity was unmistakable. Given that no such body existed – repudiation of the claims of Rome being axiomatic – it followed that fellowship was the only viable route to Christian unity. Fellowship he defined as

> a holy line of conduct which practically acknowledges and proclaims others besides ourselves to be component parts of the Christian Church. . . . [It] assumes that claims to Churchship are not invalidated by diversities of form or government. It rests upon agreement in other and weightier matters: such an agreement as is comprised in union with Christ: agreement in the faith of the Gospel, in the spirit of Christianity, in Christian experience, in the great elements of Christian life and character.

Just as mankind was providentially divided into different nations rather than living under a universal monarchy, so diversity among Christians should be seen as the ordinance of God, and an expression of positive freedom rather than of negative disunity.[25]

A further line of argument was an appeal to history, more often used to legitimate exclusive and dogmatic interpretations of evangelical Christianity. According to Leonard Bacon, the sixteenth-century Reformers had initially seen themselves as partners in a work that transcended sect and nationality. The subsequent period of codification of credal statements was asso-

[25] *Evangelical Christendom*, 1 (1847), pp. 65–9.

ciated with disunity and the loss of a living spirit. This process was only reversed by the eighteenth-century revivals. These were again characterized by warm sympathy between diverse and geographically-separated participants, and by renewed aspirations towards unity which Bacon saw as reaching their culmination in his own time.[26] In similar vein, Massie preceded his account of the formation of the Evangelical Alliance with an historical survey. He claimed that the Reformers were initially reluctant to leave Rome because of their belief in the visible unity of the Church, and that subsequently they were essentially united among themselves. He traced a cross-denominational line of advocates of unity without compulsory conformity, from John Jewel to Robert Hall, by way of Jeremy Taylor, Isaac Watts, John Wesley, and others.[27]

A considerable weight of argument was thus arrayed behind the concept of 'unity in diversity', but especially as its advocates sought to further their vision through the formation of the Evangelical Alliance in 1845–6, its weaknesses also became very much apparent. A key difficulty was the conclusive identification of the 'true Christians' whose private judgement on disputed matters must be respected. Implicitly the advocates of 'unity in diversity' preferred an experiential rather than doctrinal definition: 'true Christians' were those who had undergone an authentic conversion and were enjoying a living relationship with Christ under the guidance of the Holy Spirit. How, though, did one reliably test the professions of others? As one of Noel's critics put it, 'we are not called to unite with everyone who calls HIMSELF a Christian'.[28] Accordingly, in practice, a doctrinal approach became inescapable. Even in his 1845 'Letters on Christian Union', Bickersteth seemed to be moving in that direction:

> We should then first gain deeper and deeper impressions of those truths which most real Christians feel to be the most weighty and have received – such as the greatness and power, the righteousness and love of God the reality of his

---

[26] Bacon, *Christian Unity*, pp. 22–8.

[27] Massie, *Evangelical Alliance*, pp. 3–62.

[28] *Anti-Schism: A Review of the Principles contained in the Hon. and Rev. B. W. Noel's Tract 'The Unity of the Church'* (London, 1838), p. 7.

Providence, the grace and glory of Christ our Divine Saviour, the promise of the Holy Spirit; the work of Christ the only foundation of every hope; the only means of salvation simple faith, the need of holiness and its heart reality, the duty of mutual love, of forbearance to believers and of compassion to those dead in sins, with the resurrection, the judgment to come and the life everlasting.[29]

It was a revealing irony that the Evangelical Alliance, having set out to be as inclusive as possible, was in fact the first evangelical organization to produce an explicit basis of faith, which inevitably had the effect of excluding some who might otherwise have joined, notably because of the article requiring belief in eternal punishment. This course of action was defended on the grounds that it was necessary in order to distinguish the 'friends of truth': without such a doctrinal statement the organization would have been so lacking in focus that no-one would have thought it worth supporting. It was admitted that the price which had to be paid for such definition was a rendering of the Alliance less than 'absolutely Catholic', but such a sacrifice was judged to be inevitable 'as things are in the kingdom of God on earth'.[30]

A more specific problem was the tendency of many to treat the matter of the relationship between church and state as an 'essential' rather than 'non-essential' matter. For example, Bacon maintained that

The 'voluntary principle' – the principle of perfect and absolute religious freedom – the principle that without compromise or evasion gives to Caesar the things that are Caesar's and to God the things that are God's – that principle, thoroughly carried out, and every where established, is essential to the universal and complete manifestation of the living unity of Christ's disciples.[31]

Such a viewpoint was understandable and indeed unproblematic when held in an American context, but when applied to Britain it set obvious limits to the extent of comprehension possible.

[29] Oxford, Bodleian Library, Bickersteth Papers, Box 25.
[30] *Evangelical Christendom*, 1 (1847), p. 69.
[31] Bacon, *Christian Unity*, p. 31.

Moreover unqualified rejection of 'uniformity' as a basis for unity presented a problem not only for the Church of England with its Prayer Book and Thirty-Nine Articles, but also for the Presbyterian churches with their professed adherence to the Westminster Confession. In Scotland one Free-Church critic of the Evangelical Alliance felt its appeal to the authority of the Westminster Assembly to be thoroughly specious.[32]

It was true that the events of the 1840s – minor secessions from the Church of England as well as the Disruption of the Church of Scotland – provided some vindication of the voluntaryist perception that in due course 'true Christians' in the Established Churches would all come to find the yoke of state connection intolerable. Had the judgement of the Privy Council in the Gorham case in 1850 proscribed rather than allowed an evangelical view of baptismal regeneration it was indeed possible that the trickle of evangelical departure from the Church of England would have become a flood. In the event, however, American Voluntaryists, Scottish Free Churchmen and English Nonconformists all failed to appreciate the depth and integrity of Anglican evangelical attachment to the principle of Establishment. Within the Church of England, professed evangelicals might stop short of urging the converse argument, current among High Churchmen, that Dissent was incompatible with 'devoted piety'.[33] However, many of them did feel that the basis on which the ideal of 'unity in diversity' was being urged placed them unfairly on the defensive and that the only appropriate course was to hold themselves aloof from the movement.[34]

A more unexpected, but highly revealing, example of the practical difficulties that arose in implementing the ideal was the matter of slavery. In late August 1846 the Evangelical Alliance's international founding conference found itself sharply divided as a result of a demand by some British participants that slaveholders be excluded from membership. The Americans strongly objected. This was not because the delegation, predominantly from the northern states, itself included slaveholders, but because its members did not want to cut themselves off from

---

[32] *The Evangelical Alliance the Embodiment of the Spirit of Christendom* (Edinburgh, 1847), pp. 83–97.

[33] *Anti-Schism*, p. 15.

[34] *The Christian Observer*, 45 (1845), pp. 722–61; 46 (1846), pp. 29–60 and passim; *The Record*, 22 Dec. 1845.

fellow-evangelicals in the south. To them the question of slavery was a 'non-essential' matter which did not impinge on doctrine and spiritual authenticity and was subordinate to the maintenance of evangelical and national unity. In the eyes of the British anti- slavery lobby, however, such a standpoint suggested unacceptable compromise and spiritual declension. The result was a deadlock in which the different national organizations agreed to differ in setting their own terms for membership and the unity of North Atlantic evangelicalism appeared seriously fractured.[35] It was indeed difficult for evangelicals to accept diversity when it seemed to stand in the way of their own crusading moral and evangelistic zeal.

There is accordingly some justice in regarding the vision of 'unity in diversity' as a kind of mirage, an attractive ideal on the horizon that tended to dissolve in conflict and recrimination when the visionaries attempted to make it an actuality. Such a judgement is true but partial. Achievement might be limited, as with other models of Christian unity, but this did not undermine the credibility of the objective, especially when its most thoughtful advocates, such as Bickersteth, had never minimized the difficulties and had hinted that the goal could only fully be attained with the coming of the millennium. The Evangelical Alliance, it was suggested, did not so much represent the achievement of Christian unity, as the initial awakenings of faith that such unity would eventually be attained. In the meantime a sense of evangelicalism as a spiritual ocean touching all the varied cultures of the North Atlantic world continued a powerful legitimating force. It gave rise to such assertions as the following:

One wide impulse from God's Spirit and from the current of Providential events, like the wind before which wave the forests and fields of a whole landscape, seems to have imparted a momentum towards union to a widely extended body of believers, whose sectarian barriers forbid us to ascribe it to human concert and contrivance. . . . Here the genius of Republicanism from the New World, overleaping

[35] *Evangelical Alliance. Report of the Proceedings of the Conference, held at Freemasons' Hall, London* (London, 1847), pp. 292–3, 401–7 and passim; Robert Baird, *The Progress and Prospects of Christianity in the United States of America* (London, 1851), pp. 40–9.

the wide waste of intervening ocean, blends in thought and feeling with the time-hallowed monarchism of Europe, Asia and Africa to attain the common ends of brotherly love and Christian philanthropy.[36]

More recent analysts have understandably eschewed such ontological confidence. However they too have been faced with the tension between a perception of evangelicalism as a broad coherent movement and the tendency for this impression to dissolve as soon as precise questions of definition and detail are faced. At the same time, in the face of institutional, geographical, cultural, and even doctrinal variation, currents of simultaneous discovery and change can readily be discerned, as in the initial revivals of the mid-eighteenth century, in the Second Great Awakening two generations later, and in the mid-nineteenth-century aspirations for unity surveyed in this paper. The concept of 'unity in diversity', for all its obvious paradoxes and limitations, thus serves as an important clue to historical understanding of evangelicalism.

The Open University

---

[36] *Evangelical Christendom*, 1 (1847), p. 194.

# FROM DIVERSITY TO SECTARIANISM: THE DEFINITION OF ANGLICAN IDENTITY IN NINETEENTH-CENTURY ENGLAND

by FRANCES KNIGHT

The purpose of this paper is to investigate the subject of Anglican identity in the period from about 1800 to about 1870. This is a complex topic, and it will be possible here only to highlight a few themes. It will be suggested that the understanding of who was and who was not a 'real' Anglican underwent several important shifts during the period, until by the 1870s the definition had become increasingly narrow and exclusive. The result was not unity, but an atmosphere of increasingly narrow sectarianism, which had the effect of repelling those who were on the fringes of Anglican allegiance, and thus narrowing the base of lay support for the Church of England in the country at large.

According to the classical theory of Anglicanism, the Church was co-extensive with the nation, and therefore every citizen was automatically a member. By the beginning of the nineteenth century, rising numbers of Nonconformists and Roman Catholics meant that this theory ceased to have much practical credibility; but the Church was only just beginning its transition from national to denominational status, and so it would have been premature for the idea to be dispensed with entirely. For many Protestant Christians, the concept of a rigid denominational allegiance, adhered to throughout life, remained alien for much of the century. There were several reasons why this was so. Anglican evangelicalism blended with accessible forms of Nonconformity, with the result that many who regarded themselves primarily as church people had some experience of chapel activities, and many who regarded themselves primarily as Nonconformists, and particularly if they were Wesleyan Methodists, continued to maintain some contact with their parish church. Indeed, an evangelical Anglican or a Wesleyan Methodist might well have been seen as lacking in religious seriousness if he or she did not take advantage of the spiritual opportunities provided by both communities. Among historians, there has been a tendency to assume that people who attended chapel to any extent were dissenters. But examination of contemporary sources reveals numerous examples of individuals, and in some cases whole communities, who moved easily between church and chapel, as at Stretham near Ely in 1825, where although the parson provided two Sunday services, it was understood by all concerned that the people would attend the meeting-house if he merely read prayers, but church if he preached a sermon.[1] Double allegiance to church and chapel, rather than implying indifference, as Henry Pelling suggested,[2] in fact seems to indicate an underlying seriousness about religious matters. 'What must I do to be saved?' was the question which was formulated, and reformulated, and which echoed throughout the century. When people went to both church and chapel, it was because both were available. For some, it was their first experience of choice in matters of religion. Almost everybody had an alternative to the Established Church within a convenient distance of their doorstep. In the confusion of an increasingly plural religious culture, it was not unnatural for those concerned about their souls to take advantage of the variety of religious opportunities available, particularly if the paths to salvation offered appeared intriguingly different.

As the theory which linked Anglican identity to national identity became finally redundant in the period from 1800 to 1830, a new emphasis began to be placed on the significance of Anglican baptism. Before the implementation of the Civil Registration Act in 1837, an Anglican baptism certificate had functioned very much as a birth certificate has done subsequently, conveying definitive information about age, parentage and place of birth. It was difficult therefore to attribute a distinctive religious meaning to it. After 1837, those who found the rite objectionable were able to opt out of it completely. Anglican baptism did not, however, become in any sense restricted to those with an exclusive commitment to Anglicanism; Methodists, and Wesleyans in particular, continued to look to the parish church as the place where baptism and the other rites of passage should be observed, and to use it as a means of registering a continuing sense of loyalty. The attitude of a Dissenter in East

[1] CUL, E.D.R. C1/6 1825.
[2] Henry Pelling, *Popular Politics and Society in Late Victorian Britain* (London, 1968), pp. 19–25.

Dereham in Norfolk, who had his children baptized in the parish font in 1862, seems to have been typical. 'Oh,' said the man, when questioned by the vicar, 'I ollus say *begin and end* with the Church whatever you do between-whiles.'[3] The vicar of Lockington in Leicestershire said in 1872 that all were baptized, married, and buried in the parish church, though there was a Methodist chapel available.[4] Despite the superior strength of Methodism in Cornwall, Cornish Methodists also expressed a preference for being married in the parish church, and it remained usual for them to be buried in Anglican churchyards.[5] Until as late as the 1930s, Nonconformists at Staithes in North Yorkshire seem to have preferred to have their children baptized in the parish church. David Clark remarks that although Anglicanism had always remained remote from village life in Staithes, the attitude seems to have been that the rites of passage were more effectively validated by the Established Church.[6]

Anglican confirmation was another of the rites of passage which seems to have enjoyed widespread support among Nonconformists. The large numbers of candidates coming forward in the period up until 1860 suggest that many who were not Anglicans in an exclusive sense were presenting themselves.[7] The clergy were also under pressure to demonstrate to their bishops their ministerial effectiveness by sending the largest possible number of youngsters to the confirmation, and some may have dispensed tickets to the candidates rather indiscriminately. Alternatively, they may have seen it as perfectly reasonable for youngsters with fairly tenuous Anglican connections to wish to be confirmed. A confirmation ticket was withheld from one candidate because she would not promise never to attend a meeting-house service. Two days before the confirmation, the clergyman changed his mind and issued a ticket, though he was still uncer-

---

[3] Herbert B. J. Armstrong, *Armstrong's Norfolk Diary: Further Passages from the Diary of The Reverend Benjamin John Armstrong, Vicar of East Dereham, 1850–88* (London, 1963), p. 96.

[4] David M. Thompson, 'Baptism, Church and Society in Britain since 1800', University of Cambridge Hulsean Lectures, 1983–4, p. 50. A copy of the lectures is deposited at CUL.

[5] Thomas Shaw, *A History of Cornish Methodism* (Truro, 1967), pp. 31, 44.

[6] David Clark, *Between Pulpit and Pew: Folk Religion in a North Yorkshire Fishing Village* (Cambridge, 1982), p. 118.

[7] Frances Knight, 'Bishop, Clergy and People: John Kaye and the Diocese of Lincoln, 1827–1853' (University of Cambridge Ph.D. thesis, 1990), pp. 285–9.

[8] Peter J. Jagger, *Clouded Witness: Initiation in the Church of England in the Mid-Victorian Period, 1850–1875* (Allison Park, Penn., 1982), p. 167.

tain whether he was right to do so.[8] In 1839, George Wilkins, the Archdeacon of Nottingham, wrote to his bishop asking advice on what to do with confirmation candidates who attended Dissenting places of worship.[9] Confirmation could hardly be withheld from those who had been baptized as Anglicans, if they fulfilled the other criteria and could give an adequate rendition of the catechism, the creed, the Lord's Prayer and the ten commandments.

The findings of the 1851 religious census reveal that the practice of Anglicans and Methodists worshipping together in each others' churches was still continuing at mid-century. The rector of Swaby, Lincolnshire commented in his census return that

> What is all but universal, in this part of Lincolnshire at least, [is] the attendance of members both at church and the Wesleyan chapels. In most churches, the practice has been to have the one service in the church alternately morning and afternoon and the service (or preaching as it is at the chapels) is regulated accordingly, so that but few attend the church or chapel exclusively. Therefore no accurate estimate can be made of the relative number of attendants at each.[10]

This tendency was confirmed by the vicar of Elsham in Lincolnshire. He said: 'The congregations vary very much in this parish owing to there being many Dissenters, who at times come to church.'[11] It was corroborated also from the Wesleyan side; the chapel steward at Kelstern wrote: 'No service in church hours, the congregation attends the church also.'[12] The incumbent of St Mary Magdalene in the city of Lincoln summed up the tendency when he answered the enquiry about average attendance by writing, 'Very uncertain. They go from church to church, from chapel to church, and from church to chapel.'[13] In Nottinghamshire, the Anglican clergy at Treswell, Morton, and Kirton noted

---

[9] Lincolnshire Archives Office [hereafter, LAO], CorB5/8/22, George Wilkins to John Kaye, 29 July 1839.

[10] R. W. Ambler, ed., *Lincolnshire Returns of the Census of Religious Worship, 1851*, Lincolnshire Record Society, 72 (1979), p. 172.

[11] Ibid., p. 236.

[12] Ibid., p. 189.

[13] Ibid., p. 109.

in their census returns that on 30 March their congregations had been diminished because a proportion of their parishioners had gone instead to Wesleyan love feasts or other gatherings.[14] In this case, when faced with a choice between a love feast and Anglican evening prayer, people opted for the love feast. Furthermore, the clergy seem to have accepted this as inevitable. Perhaps, however, by 1851 this level of toleration on the part of the clergy may have been more or less restricted to more rural areas. There is no evidence of it in Nottingham itself, a city where Anglicans were outnumbered by Nonconformist worshippers, and as a result had adopted a rather embattled mentality, seeing themselves as a faithful remnant fighting against an incoming tide of infidelity. Joshua Brooks, vicar of St Mary's Nottingham, was so distrustful of Dissenters that he insisted on forwarding his census returns direct to the Registrar General, 'in order to prevent any improper use being made of them by the officers appointed to receive them, the majority of whom in Nottingham are Dissenters'.[15] In urban areas, denominational boundaries had hardened, and people had ceased to flit between church and chapel.

How is this evidence to be understood in the light of Alan Gilbert's theory of urban religion – that a decision for church or chapel represented a choice between two very different social and religious belief systems?[16] Gilbert's theory may well explain the workings of the religious culture of more highly politicized urban areas, like Nottingham, where Nonconformity was more frequently harnessed to political radicalism, and where Baptists and Congregationalists might outnumber Methodists. It may also shed light on predominantly rural counties like Hampshire and Sussex, where in 1851 Independency was stronger than Wesleyan Methodism, and where the census returns do not allude to Anglicans and Nonconformists attending each other's services.[17] It does not, however, seem possible to transpose Gilbert's theory into those rural areas where Methodism was the chief rival to the

---

[14] Michael Watts, ed., *Religion in Victorian Nottinghamshire: The Religious Census of 1851*, 2 vols (Nottingham, 1988), vols 1 & 2, pp. 36, 202, 221.

[15] Ibid., p. 183.

[16] Alan D. Gilbert, *Religion and Society in Industrial England: Church, Chapel and Social Change, 1740–1914* (London, 1976), p. 69.

[17] John A. Vickers, ed., *The Religious Census of Sussex, 1851*, Sussex Record Society, 75 (1989); idem, *The Religious Census of Hampshire, 1851*, Hampshire Record Series (1993).

Church of England, or where relations with an older body of Dissenters were good. In these parts of the countryside, there existed the people David Hempton describes as a 'band of denominational gypsies of no fixed abode'.[18] Glimpses may be caught of such communities at Stretham in the example cited above, and at Melton Mowbray in 1839. The parishioners there were 'highly offended' when Mr La Trobe, the parish lecturer, was given notice to leave by the new vicar, on account of his supposedly evangelical opinions. The worried archdeacon reported: 'The Church-People talk of building a new Church, and the Dissenters, who went to hear him, are gone back to their Chapels: The Independent-Chapel, which was by no means full, has now only 2 pews unoccupied.'[19]

Alan Gilbert concluded that Anglicanism became little more than a 'cultural expression of national identity . . . an obvious if merely nominal concomitant of being English'.[20] Besides failing to recognize that it was in the process of being exported all over the world, this does not seem to do justice to the complex motives in lay religion. There remained something about the Church of England which the mushrooming meeting-houses appeared to be unable to rival. In the minds of Methodists, the Church was associated with citizenship and loyalty to the crown and Englishness; and it gave a reassuring sense of being legal – 'by law established' – which lingered even after full civil rights had been granted to Dissenters. It had a clear appeal to the temperamentally conservative. The Newark father who, as late as 1851, angrily demanded baptism as his child's legal right, and claimed that if the curate refused it, his child would be subject to 'certain civil disabilities' when mature, was clearly articulating this sense of the need for legal security.[21] Yet Anglican baptism also conveyed a spiritual meaning, as it did to the parents of infants in Whaplode, Lincolnshire, who protested that if they were forbidden to bring their children to be baptized at the vicarage three days after birth, and the children should die prematurely, they would be committed to the earth 'like dogs'

---

[18] David Hempton, *Methodism and Politics in British Society, 1750–1984* (London, 1984), p. 12.

[19] LAO, CorB5/5/17/4, T. K. Bonney to Kaye, 25 Nov. 1839.

[20] Gilbert, *Religion and Society*, p. 207.

[21] LAO, CorB5/8/34, R. J. Hodgkinson to Kaye, Sept. 1851.

without Christian burial.[22] The Whaplode parents were displaying a concern for the eternal welfare of their offspring which was a predominant element in the lay religion of the period. The Church of England's links with the political and social order, strong though they remained, did not preclude it from also being capable of conveying religious meaning to a broad spectrum of society.

In the second half of the nineteenth century, the pattern of double allegiance to Methodism and Anglicanism began to come under new pressure, as the worlds of church and chapel became more sharply delineated. There were reasons for this development from both the Methodist and the Anglican sides. Methodists increasingly found that the full range of their religious needs could be met within Methodism. The parish church at St Just in Cornwall had contained many Methodists in the 1860s, but a marginal note in the burial register in 1889 described Betsy Bottrall as the last one who regularly attended communion services there.[23] Members of almost all denominations were less inclined to spend as many hours at church at the end of the century as they had at the beginning, and this led to their developing a loyalty to a single place of worship. Furthermore, what was perhaps an increasing incidence of off-hand treatment by the parish clergy caused Methodists to reflect on the wisdom of maintaining their close links with the Church. Back in 1839, the incumbent of Everton in Nottinghamshire received a request to preach and celebrate the sacrament for the centenary of the Wesleyans in his parish. He asked the bishop to give a ruling on the legitimacy of acceding to the request. Bishop Kaye responded by suggesting that any service held to mark the occasion should be advertised without reference to the Methodists, or their centenary, although it would be permissible to preach a sermon 'on Brotherly Love, or on the necessity of co-operation against the encroachments of Romanism'.[24] It was rebuffs like this which led Methodists to conclude that it was more appropriate to invite a Methodist preacher to celebrate a Methodist centenary, and not to allow an Anglican bishop to determine how the service should be conducted.

[22] LAO, CorB5/4/54/1, T. Tunstall Smith to Kaye, 17 Jan. 1845.
[23] Shaw, *Cornish Methodism*, p. 122.
[24] LAO, CorB5/8/28/13, R. Evans to Kaye, 10 Oct. 1839; Kaye to Evans, 12 Oct. 1839.

Another important factor which led to double allegiance becoming markedly less common in the second half of the century was the growth in the numbers of Anglican clergy who were residing in their parishes for the first time, often as a result of being compelled to do so by the Pluralities Acts of 1838 and 1850. From the perspective of lay people, perhaps the most obvious sign that the Church of England was changing was the disappearance of the band of transitory, sometimes non-resident curates – which had been so familiar a part of the ecclesiastical landscape in the first half of the century – and the arrival of the permanent resident incumbent. Although this was generally assumed to be a desirable development – both by church reformers at the time, and by church historians subsequently – the benefits for the laity were much dependent on the character and attitudes of the clergyman who arrived. Given an attentive clergyman, parishioners could expect a higher standard of pastoral care, and also the reassurance that the revenues which the incumbent derived from their parish would be used in their parish, whether in the form of charitable donations, or as support for local trade. Unfortunately, however, the state of pastoral relations after the arrival of the resident parson has been little documented from the perspective of lay Anglicans. What is clear, however, is that his arrival coincided with a hardening of denominational divisions, and the introduction of a largely clerically-imposed narrowing of the definition of Anglican identity. The newly-resident incumbent set the tone of the worship and ethos of Anglicanism within his parish, where previously it had been less sharply defined. He was in a position to provide more services than his non-resident predecessors, and if he chose he could time them to coincide with chapel worship, thus forcing his religiously-inclined parishioners to make a choice. Faced with the need to carve out and defend his territory, and feeling under threat from the proliferation of Nonconformist chapels, he was likely to be less tolerant of Dissent, and to be perceived as hostile by the Nonconformists themselves. Church identity and chapel identity were no longer easily compatible, and people began to choose one or the other, or neither. As co-operation gave way to hostility, religious life in the countryside began to fragment along denominational faultlines in the way that it had done a few decades earlier in the towns.

Anglicans in the nineteenth century had no formal definitions of membership, and were not therefore in a position to compile membership statistics in the way that the Nonconformists did. This did not, however, prevent the clergy from drawing up their own informal definitions. The most liberal understanding equated membership of the Church with citizenship, or with baptism – even when the individual seldom or never came near the church again. An Anglican could be defined almost equally liberally as one who looked to the Church to validate the significant moments in life, or who attended Sunday worship in church on an occasional basis. A narrower definition demanded an exclusive commitment to Anglican services and the shunning of all other denominations. By the end of the period, the clergy were beginning not merely to make a sharper distinction between Anglicans and Nonconformists, but also between those parishioners who had some sort of general affiliation to Anglicanism, perhaps extending no further than participation in Anglican rites of passage, those who were nominally communicants, and those who attended the sacrament on a regular basis. Visitation articles began to make distinct enquiries about all three groups. The visitation returns for the archdeaconry of Bedford in 1873 reveal that out of an estimated population of 138,000 people, 46,447 were seen as being 'church people' rather than 'chapel people' or 'nowhere people', but only 7,235 were perceived as communicants, and only 3,878 were seen as regular communicants who could normally be expected to be present when the sacrament was celebrated.[25] As precise figures, these underestimate the true situation, for not all incumbents provided the information requested on the visitation form. Nevertheless, a general trend of very low level participation in the eucharist seems incontrovertible. Bedfordshire, it may be noted, was not a notably irreligious county, and on K. S. Inglis's calculations it had registered the highest index of attendance of any county in the Census of 1851. On the basis of the figures available for 1873, it appears that a mere three per cent of the entire population of the county were regular communicants, five per cent were occasional communicants and thirty-four per cent were

---

[25] CUL, E.D.R. C3/40, Archdeaconry of Bedford visitation returns, 1873.

nominally Anglican. Of those whom the clergy defined as nominally Anglican, only eight per cent were regular communicants, which is perhaps the most significant figure. James Obelkevich's examination of the visitation returns for South Lindsey in the same year reveals a similar picture. Twelve per cent of the entire population were communicants in parishes of under a hundred people, but only two per cent in parishes with a population of more than 600. In parishes with a population of between 400 and 499, the figure was three per cent.[26] If statistics such as these had been available to contemporary clergymen, they might have paused to reflect on the wisdom of trying to transform their parishes into eucharistic communities. By the 1870s, devotion to the eucharist was becoming the clergy's index to measure the commitment of lay Anglicans; it was a definition of Anglican identity which permitted none of the diversity of the past. The result may have been a certain degree of unity within the newly-formed communicants' guilds, but for the great mass of those who for whatever reason chose not to participate, it was a definition which left them to some degree unchurched.

University of Wales, Lampeter

[26] James Obelkevich, *Religion and Rural Society: South Lindsey, 1825–1875* (Oxford, 1976), p. 139.

# THE POLITICS OF THE BIBLE: RADICALISM AND NON-DENOMINATIONAL CO-OPERATION IN THE BIRMINGHAM POLITICAL UNION*

*by* EILEEN L. GROTH

In May 1832, as emissaries from the Birmingham Political Union sought to gain support for the Reform Bill in Staffordshire, the editor of the pro-Reform *Birmingham Journal*, W. G. Lewis,[1] exhorted 'Our cause is a holy cause, – it is the cause of religion, – it is the cause of humanity, – it is the cause of the Bible.'[2] This is but one of many declarations by radical Christian figures of the intrinsic connection they saw between religion and politics. They not only confirmed that it was right for Christians to be involved in the political sphere, but asserted that the teachings of Scripture demanded fundamental changes to the socio-political order and the principles upon which it was founded.

Elsewhere, I have argued that radical formulations of Christianity were more prevalent and distinct than has heretofore been suspected. It has been demonstrated that throughout Britain there was a thriving culture of Christian radicalism composed of activists from a wide range of denominational backgrounds and social circumstances.[3] This characteristic of Christian radicalism raises the question of the extent and nature of non-denominational co-operation among political radicals. A study of the Birmingham Political Union provides some particularly revealing insights on this issue because of its importance at a national level in the movement for the Reform Bill of 1832 and the beginnings of Chartism as well as the availability of membership lists and reports of meetings. In these sources, one can see perhaps the clearest evidence of individuals explicitly referring to their religious differences and self-consciously overcoming

---

* I am grateful to David M. Thompson and Alison Winter for their suggestions on this paper.

[1] *Reports of the Staffordshire Reform Meetings, Held on the 14th of May, 1832* (Birmingham, 1832), p. 2. Carlos Flick, *The Birmingham Political Union and the Movements for Reform in Britain 1830–1839* (Hamden, Conn., 1978), p. 46.

[2] *Reports of the Staffordshire Reform Meetings*, p. 2.

[3] Eileen L. Groth, 'Politicians in the pulpit: Christian radicalism in Britain, 1830–1850' in Richard Fulton, ed., *A British Studies Sampler* (Vancouver, Washington, 1994), pp. 93–108; idem, 'Christian radicalism in Britain, 1830–1850' (Cambridge Ph.D. thesis, 1993).

them. This paper will describe the nature of Christian radicalism and the threat it posed to church and state alike, and then highlight three of the leading clerical figures in the BPU – Arthur Savage Wade (Church of England), Hugh Hutton (Unitarian), and Thomas McDonnell (Roman Catholic) and the ways in which they contributed to common objectives.

Wade, Hutton, and McDonnell belong to a fairly large grouping of individuals which I have termed 'Christian radicals'. Broadly speaking, Christian radicals focused on the rights of the poor. They argued that numerous gifts had been given by God in creation and careful provision had been made should an unequal distribution of those gifts arise. They pointed to the Levitical and Deuteronomic codes which emphasized the right of the poor to relief. It was not as an expression of magnanimity or good will that sustenance was provided for the poor, but a sacred obligation.

One of the most successful ways in which radicals sought to gain the Christian ground was to present their views as being sanctioned by God – whether implicity or explicitly. They made frequent reference to the deliverance of the Israelites from oppression, and consistently put forward the view that God would avenge such wrongs committed against the poor of Britain. Perhaps the climactic appeal in Christian radical argument arose when they looked to the example of Christ and those aspects of his behaviour toward the poor which seemed to confirm their special place. The Church of Scotland minister Patrick Brewster exclaimed to his congregation in Paisley, 'The Son of God came especially to the poor. He came to preach his gospel to the poor. He came emphatically, – literally as well as figuratively, temporally as well as spiritually – to "loose the bands of wickedness, and to undo the heavy burden." '[4] Brewster pointed to the special responsibility which all Christians bore for the poor in accordance with the example of Christ. He asserted that 'after the love of God,' it was the 'highest duty' of Christians 'to aid and sustain each other, during their brief and painful journey; to INSTRUCT THE IGNORANT; to RELIEVE THE DESTITUTE; to COMFORT THE AFFLICTED; to DELIVER

---

[4] Patrick Brewster, *Chartist Sermon I* in *The Seven Chartist and Military Discourses Libelled by the Marquis of Abercorn, and Other Heritors of the Abbey Parish* (Paisley, 1843), pp. 11–12.

THE OPPRESSED'.[5] For, he concluded, 'This is the practical part of Christianity.'[6] To many of Brewster's auditors, this sort of appeal provided the truest resonances with their understanding of the gospel. In response to this attention to 'practical' Christianity, a number of Christians became prominent agitators in the campaigns for parliamentary and factory reform, the Anti-Poor Law Movement, and Chartism.

Interpretations of the 'politics of the Bible' have often brought a split between those who asserted the traditional texts concerning obedience – texts which asserted that 'every soul be subject to higher powers' and instructed Christians to 'submit yourselves to every ordinance of man for the Lord's sake'[7] – and those who felt that some circumstances demanded aggressive action to fight against evil and uphold the weak. This split was strikingly obvious in the period under consideration. Those who joined the BPU were described by one reporter as some 'of the most respectable inhabitants of the place'[8] who 'have not been in the habit of taking a part in politics, but they now see the necessity, to use the expression of one of them, of buckling on their armour'.[9] Among the new subscribers to the Union, the reporter noted 'persons of all creeds' including '4 Catholic Priests' and 'about 20 quakers'.[10] It is also clear that even among those individuals who believed aggressive action was justified in some circumstances, opinions varied as to how aggressive that action should be. Most reformist organizations in this period suffered divisions on this issue, and the BPU was no exception. For instance, in the end, McDonnell seemed to take a more radical line on the issue of parliamentary reform than that advocated by the BPU and resigned his position on its Council.[11] His reputation for radical activity endured well into the Chartist period. It was claimed by his nephew, William McDonnell, that he was

[5] Ibid., p. 25.

[6] Ibid., p. 25.

[7] Rom. 13.1–7; I Pet. 2.13–18.

[8] *Report of the Proceedings of the Public Meeting of the Inhabitants of Birmingham. Held at Newhall-Hill, May 10, 1832* . . . (Birmingham, 1832), p. 3.

[9] Ibid., p. 3.

[10] Ibid., p. 3.

[11] Judith F. Champ has pointed to the vociferous opposition that McDonnell received from a powerful faction within his congregation which may well have contributed to his decision to resign from the Council of the BPU: Champ, 'Priesthood and politics in the nineteenth century: the turbulent career of Thomas McDonnell', *Recusant History*, 18 (1987), p. 296.

involved in hosting Chartist meetings concerned with the movement of weapons around the country.[12]

Riots, strikes, and demonstrations by large crowds demanding
changes in government policies brought a frightened response
from many quarters. While the civil authorities responded by
arresting and imprisoning radical leaders, the churches sought to
help quell the disturbed state of the country through the preaching of sermons and publication of tracts reminding individuals of the dictates of Scripture concerning submission and
obedience.[13] Several sermons, like those of John Scott, incumbent of St Mary's Church, Hull, exhorted working men to
'labour truly to get their own living and to do their duty in that
state of life into which it shall please God to call them'.[14] They
were urged to place their trust not in 'patriots preaching political
freedom in chains of moral bondage',[15] but solely in Jesus Christ.
For he was the means not only to 'secure final happiness hereafter, but find unspeakably greater happiness now, than you can
ever hope for from indulging rebellious passions, from tur-
bulence and disorder'.[16] While the Church of England was most
prominent in disseminating sermons and tracts on these themes,
particularly in the opportunities occasioned by the four 'political
feasts/fasts' in the Book of Common Prayer (Gunpowder Plot
Day and the arrival of William III; Martyrdom Day; Restoration
Day; and the anniversary of the Accession of the current mon-

---

[12] William McDonnell tried to solicit payment from the Home Office for information about his
uncle's activities. (It is not clear whether such an offer was taken up.) PRO, HO 45/264A fols 27–9:
William McDonnell to the Home Office, Sheffield, 15 December 1842.

[13] For examples see: William Gale Townley, *A Sermon Occasioned by the Late Chartist Movements,
Preached at Upwell, St. Peter, In the County of Norfolk, and the Diocese of Norwich, On Sunday, the 17th of
November 1839* (London, 1839); James Francis, *Sermon, to the Working Classes, Preached in St. Paul's
Church, Newport, On Sunday Evening, April 21st, 1839* (Newport, 1839); J. Casebow Barrett, *The
Christian Patriot's Duty at the Present Crisis. A Sermon Preached at St. Mary's Chapel, Birmingham, On
Sunday, August 4, 1839* (London, 1839); J. Rawlings, *Animadversions Upon a Sermon Preached by Mr.
John Warburton, Minister of the Gospel, At Zion Chapel, Union Street, Trowbridge, Sunday Morning, May
26, 1836 upon The Doctrine of Non-resistance to the Higher Powers* (Bath, [1839]).

[14] John Scott, *Popular Delusions Exposed by Scripture. A Sermon Preached Before the Corporation of Hull, in
Holy Trinity Church, October 21, 1832, On Occasion of the Mayor's Entrance Upon Office* (Hull, 1832), p.
27. The sermon was regarded as a paradigm of conservative exegesis and was reviewed in *The Bristol
Job Nott; or Labouring Man's Friend* (LVII, 10 Jan. 1833, pp. 225–6; LVIII, 17 Jan. 1833, p. 232, LIX,
24 Jan. 1833, pp. 235–6), a newspaper published 'to try the power of TRUTH against FALSE-
HOOD, of LOYALTY against SEDITION, and of RELIGION against INFIDELITY' (V, 12 Jan.
1832, p. 17) in the wake of the riots in Bristol (1831).

[15] Ibid., p. 22.

[16] Ibid., p. 23.

arch) and sermons before the assizes and universities, other Christians strongly supported the same premise. Differing interpretations and approaches to Scripture by Roman Catholics, Anglicans, and other Protestants did not manifest themselves in the explication and denominational teaching concerning these crucial texts. The only exception came from Unitarians, who denied an active role in instituting government; however, they still urged acquiescence to civil authorities.[17]

The degree to which the churches felt especially threatened by a Christian radical exegesis is seen through the move to censure or expel ministers and laypeople who promoted such views. Patrick Brewster was one of many called by church leaders to answer for his radicalism. His fervour in championing the cause of the poor was deemed disorderly to the proceedings of the Presbytery meeting on a number of occasions.[18] The publication of a series of his sermons was one of the major factors in the decision to suspend Brewster from his pastorate for one year.[19] And his continued involvement in political radicalism was also without doubt a major factor in his failure to be appointed to the Chair of Church History at Glasgow University,[20] and in the Marquess of Abercorn's refusal to appoint him to the First Charge of Paisley Abbey when the position became vacant and the congregation strongly supported his candidature.[21]

Another response of the churches to the challenge of Christian radicalism was the development of a defence of government policies through an appeal to Scripture. A strong conservative

---

[17] Robert Hole, *Pulpits, Politics and Public Order in England, 1760–1832* (Cambridge, 1989), pp. 12–31, 34–6.

[18] E.g. Edinburgh, Scottish Record Office [hereafter SRO], CH2/2/294/15, fols 309–10.

[19] SRO, CH1/2/186 Assembly Papers, Main Series 1842 (1); CH1/3/35 Record of the Commission of the General Assembly from 1841–1848, fols 155–9; CH2/294/15, fols, 342–61, 364–7, 371–2, 399–435, 474; CH2/294/16, fols 5–6, 10, 41.

[20] *Testimonials in Favour of the Rev. Patrick Brewster, One of the Ministers of the Abbey Parish, as a Candidate for the Chair of Church History in the University of Glasgow* (April 1851).

[21] Edinburgh, National Library of Scotland, broadside [pressmark: 6.1699 (8)]: *The Rights of a Christian Congregation. Mr. Brewster of Paisley and His Congregation versus Patronage and Clerical Subserviency. Appeal of the Paisley Abbey Congregation Committee to the People of Great Britain*; SRO, CH2/490/47 [Brewster's protest at not being appointed to the First Charge – erased by order of the Presbytery], fols 349–51; CH2/490/48 [description of the stricken portion may be surmised by the order for erasure], fol. 175; CH2/294/17, fols 279, 282–4, 288–90, 310–35; Paisley, Paisley Abbey MS: Andrew Wilson, Minister in the First Charge to James Murray, Paisley, 17 December 1852; *Report of the Proceedings in the Case of the First Charge of The Abbey of Paisley. With an Appendix Containing the Sermons Charged with Heresy* (Paisley, 1853).

exegesis was particularly apparent during the period of debate over the New Poor Law. A. M. C. Waterman, Boyd Hilton, and others have given valuable insight on those who formulated a Christian political economy.[22] Sumner's *Treatise on the Records of the Creation*[23] was seen in the eyes of many as having achieved a successful synthesis of assent to Malthusian population theory with a fervent belief in the goodness and power of the Creator.[24] One result of the Sumnerian adjustments to some aspects of political economy was that the essentially secular formulations of the Poor Law Commissioners and others were given a form of religious sanction by several clerical writers.

Responses of this nature had important implications for the ways in which Christian radicals interacted with the churches and with each other. There were of course some who severed their existing church connections and became involved with independent congregations such as the Chartist churches. For example, the Unitarian Isaac Barrow urged his hearers to above all things 'deal exclusively with parsons'.[25] If no suitable ministers could be found, he recommended that they 'become your own parsons; meet in your own private homes, conduct religious service amongst yourselves, and let him who is taught of God teach his brethren freely, fervently, purely.'[26] However, it seems to have been more common for radicals to work within their churches. And to work within meant some amount of negotiation of the degree to which one espoused a radical position.

---

[22] A. M. C. Waterman, *Revolution, Economics and Religion. Christian Political Economy, 1798–1833* (Cambridge, 1991); idem, 'The ideological alliance of political economy and Christian theology, 1798–1833', *JEH*, 34 (1983), pp. 231–44; Boyd Hilton, *The Age of Atonement. The Influence of Evangelicalism on Social and Economic Thought, 1785–1865* (Oxford, 1988); Peter Mandler, 'Tories and paupers: Christian political economy and the making of the New Poor Law', *HistJ*, 33 (1990), pp. 81–103; Salim Rashid, 'Richard Whately and Christian political economy at Oxford and Dublin', *JHI*, 38 (1977), pp. 147–55.

[23] John Bird Sumner, *A Treatise on the Records of the Creation, And on the Moral Attributes of the Creator*, 2 vols (London, 1816).

[24] Ibid., 2, Part 3; for further remarks on Sumner's thought, see Robert S. Dell, 'Social and economic theories and pastoral concerns of a Victorian archbishop', *JEH*, 16 (1965), pp. 196–208. For examples of the endorsement of Sumner's synthesis by other leading churchmen see R. A. Soloway, *Prelates and People. Ecclesiastical Social Thought in England, 1783–1852* (London, 1969), pp. 101–6.

[25] PRO, HO 45/55 fol. 46v; Isaac Barrow, *A Standard Lifted for the People. A Sermon Delivered on Castle Hill, Hindley, On Sunday, August 14, 1839* (Bolton, 1839), p. 14.

[26] Ibid., p. 14.

Of the three clerics in the BPU highlighted in this paper, Hugh Hutton (1795–1871), Minister of the Old Meeting House in Edgbaston, was perhaps the most successful in steering a path between commitment to radical political action and careful consideration of the wishes of their flocks. Hutton's congregation was small but economically powerful and influential.[27] His efforts to promote their religious tenets through his published sermons and discourses[28] along with a moderate degree of political involvement[29] met with warm approval.[30] While Hutton was attentive to the needs of his own congregation,[31] he believed that a minister's duties extended far beyond. It was also the minister's responsibility to help bring forth the best quality of life for all in the community and the nation.[32] To this end, he became involved with the BPU. While he took part in many of the Union's activities, he is best remembered for the part he played in the celebrations at Newhall Hill following the recall of Earl Grey (May 1832), when he offered a short prayer which set the stage for the proceedings which followed.[33] The Chairman of the Union, Thomas Attwood, responded to the prayer by saying, 'Be assured, when our just cause is supported in this spirit – when patriotism, religion and courage are combined, we must be successful. When these form the combined principle of our

---

[27] Birmingham, Birmingham Central Reference Library, Local Studies Department [hereafter, BCRL, LSD]: 'Death of Hugh Hutton, M.A.' in *Newspaper Cuttings, Birmingham Biography*, 1, pt 1, p. 2.

[28] E.g. Hugh Hutton, *Unitarian Christians Distinguished From Unbelievers in Christianity* . . . (London, 1832); idem, *An Appeal to Scriptural Principles in Support of the Claims of Unitarian Christians* (London, 1829).

[29] Hutton put very clear limits on his level of involvement in politics as was seen by the considerable effort he made to correct a report in the radical press which indicated that he supported trade unionism: Hugh Hutton, *Gathered Leaves of Many Seasons* (London, 1858), preface.

[30] *Address Presented to the Rev. Hugh Hutton, M.A., April 1, 1839. By a Deputation from the Congregation assembling in the Old Meeting House, Birmingham* (printed at the request and for the use of the Congregation, 1839).

[31] London, Dr Williams's Library, MSS 38.123 (7–10): Hugh Hutton to T. E. Lee [Chairman of the Vestry Committee. Old Meeting House, Birmingham], 7, 15 Dec. 1821; 20 Jan. 1822; 14 Feb. 1822. At the time of writing, Hutton was still minister to a congregation at Warrington. The correspondence was occasioned by the desire for Hutton to 'supply' the Old Meeting. Hutton clearly placed the congregation at Warrington above all other engagements. We may assume that he felt this same sort of responsibility toward all the congregations to which he ministered.

[32] Hutton, *Gathered Leaves*, pp. 73–6.

[33] *Report of the Proceedings of the Public Meeting of the Inhabitants of Birmingham Held at Newhall-Hill, May 16, 1832* . . . (Birmingham, 1832), p. 4.

actions, we cannot but secure the liberty and happiness of our country.'[34]

Perhaps it was in part Hutton's ability to work with people within his congregation who held different political and economic views that prompted him to turn his attention to co-operation between Christians. In one of many fervent appeals, he spoke of 'the simplicity of the gospel, when Christians loved each other; when each felt a brother's concern for the temporal and spiritual welfare of every fellow-disciple'.[35] The co-operation and return to primitive Christianity of which he spoke was the fellowship of those who 'disclaim the authority of . . . Human Creeds, Either as a Test of Christian Truth, or as a Bond of Christian Communion, and who practically maintain the sufficiency of the Scriptures to make men wise unto salvation'.[36]

It is extremely unlikely that Wade or McDonnell would have 'disclaimed the authority' of the traditional creeds of their churches; however, both clearly saw something in the appeal to the Scriptures. Wade, seeking to defend himself particularly after he had been ostracized by his congregation and more moderate reformers and forbidden to preach by his bishop, said: 'I am a minister of the Church of England, a servant of Christ and I wish to follow the Saviour's example in standing up for the poor and oppressed.'[37] McDonnell likewise interpreted his role as a priest in a way that encompassed the spiritual as well as the secular welfare of the people. He said: 'The essential duties of the priest are to labour for the sanctification of his soul, and to endeavour to promote the salvation of the people entrusted to his care.'[38] Political action was a necessary corollary to this call and was 'sanctioned by the Divine Word'.[39]

Such principles won support from Christians of all denominations. The Chairman of the First Annual Meeting of the BPU, lauding McDonnell, said that he belonged 'to an ancient and

---

[34] Ibid., p. 4.

[35] Hugh Hutton, *The Duty and Benefits of Co-operation Among the Friends of Scriptural Christianity; A Sermon Preached in the Meeting House of the Second Presbyterian Congregation, Belfast* . . . (Belfast, 1827), p. 2.

[36] Ibid., inscription.

[37] BL, Add. MS 27,820, fol. 119.

[38] *The Case of the Rev. T. M. McDonnell, Late of St. Peter's Mission, Birmingham, Stated by Himself in a Series of Letters* (London, 1842–4), p. 27.

[39] Ibid., p. 27.

venerable church, from whence we drew the best principles of our religion; and from whose mouth he had often heard sentiments and expressions which did honour to his character as a man, a gentleman, and a christian.'[40] By the following year McDonnell had so impressed his Protestant colleagues in the Union that George Edmonds, a local attorney, proposed him to the Council. Edmonds was the son of a Baptist minister[41] and had been a fierce opponent of Catholic Emancipation. In proposing McDonnell, he 'begged to remind the Meeting, those very men who had extorted from the odious tyrant, John, the blessings of the Magna Charta, were Catholics also. It was not for men, in the present day, to split themselves into sects: whether Catholics or Protestants he trusted that they should all know what were the blessings of Liberty.'[42]

McDonnell's exertions on behalf of the poor made him one of the most popular clergymen in the city. Following McDonnell's removal from Birmingham, petitions with over 7,000 signatures from both Catholic and Protestants pleading for his return were drawn up within three days and presented to the Bishop of Cambysopolis, Vicar Apostolic of the Midland District. And in a subsequent petition to Pope Gregory XVI, it was stated that McDonnell 'commended himself to those, who are without the fold, by the charity, which accompanied his zeal, and by advocating the cause of the poor and the oppressed, so as to have acquired, in the words of the Vicar Apostolic himself, "the noble appellation of the poor man's friend" '.[43]

These striking instances of co-operation or 'unity in the church' raise several questions, such as why was this co-operation possible, and was it an isolated case? John Bossy has argued that Catholicism may be placed within the broader context of Nonconformity. He asserts that in the 1820s the alliance between Catholics and other Nonconformists was more than 'a tactical alliance' in the quest to achieve specific political

---

[40] *Report of the Proceedings of the First Annual Meeting of the Birmingham Political Union, On Monday July 26, 1830* (Birmingham, 1830), p. 14.

[41] BCRL, LSD: 'Death of Mr. George Edmonds' in *Newspaper Cuttings relating to Birmingham Obituaries*, p. 34.

[42] *Report of the Proceedings of the Second Annual Meeting of the Birmingham Political Union, On Monday, July 4, 1831* (Birmingham, 1831), p. 7.

[43] *Case of McDonnell*, p. 194.

objectives: 'it represented a similarity of status and background and a genuine approximation of views about the practical implications of Christianity and the means to be adopted for achieving them'.[44] McDonnell and Hutton had been involved in the campaigns for the abolition of church rates and other dissenting causes in the earlier period. Their involvement in the BPU may be seen as the continuation of their commitment to liberal causes. Surely aspects of this co-operation continued into the 1830s and 1840s. If anything, the practical aspects of Christianity came much more to the fore in the 1830s and 1840s in the discussions about the poor and poor relief. While co-operation between Catholics and Nonconformists became less prominent because of the intensification of Protestant feeling which John Wolffe's work has illustrated,[45] co-operation between members of the Established Churches in England and Scotland and Nonconformists grew dramatically. This is clearly illustrated in the anti-Poor Law Movement and Chartism. In some sense, the BPU may be seen as an organization where new models of co-operation were supplanting the old.

One might argue that it was possible for radicals of different religious backgrounds to co-operate because their religious differences became less important as they focused primarily on the achievement of particular political objectives. This can only be a part of the explanation. Despite significant doctrinal differences, Christian radicals shared certain agenda which were derived from a cluster of common religious concerns. As emphasized earlier, these primarily concerned a commitment to the principle of the rights of the poor and the obligations of the rich to honour these rights. Moreover, this commitment was grounded in a shared attention to a specific set of scriptural texts which made it possible for the Bible, read in vastly different places of worship, to have the same political message for the individuals like Wade, Hutton, and McDonnell. For all Christian radicals, the poster displayed in the window of Samuel Cook's drapery shop summed up their creed. It announced, 'The Bible is the Best

---

[44] John Bossy, *The English Catholic Community, 1570–1850* (London, 1975), p. 352.
[45] John Wolffe, *The Protestant Crusade in Great Britain, 1829–1860* (Oxford, 1991).

Political Book in the World! When you Read the Bible, or Hear it Read in Churches or Chapels, Attend to its Politics!'[46]

Florida State University

[46] Dudley, Dudley Archives, Samuel Cook Broadsides SC4[4c]: Samuel Cook, *The Bible is the Best Political Book in the World!*, Dudley, 1 September 1836.

# THE RESHAPING OF CHRISTIAN TRADITION: WESTERN DENOMINATIONAL IDENTITY IN A NON-WESTERN CONTEXT

## by BRIAN STANLEY

In August 1841 George Spencer, great-grandson of the third Duke of Marlborough and second Bishop of Madras, entertained two house guests in his residence at Kotagherry. Both were seeking admission into the Anglican ministry. One was an Indian, a former Roman Catholic priest who had begun to question the catholicity of the Roman communion, had joined himself for a while to the American Congregational mission in Madura, but had eventually reached the conclusion, in Spencer's words, that 'evangelical doctrine joined to Apostolic Government were only to be met with in indissoluble conjunction with the Church of England'. Bishop Spencer, while keen to employ the Indian as a catechist, felt it premature, 'in a matter of such importance', to receive him as a presbyter, even though the validity of his orders was unquestionable. The Indian is not named in the records, and it would appear that he never became an Anglican priest.[1]

Bishop Spencer's other guest, Robert Caldwell, was a missionary of the London Missionary Society (LMS), born in Ulster to Scottish Presbyterian parents, but who had received his theological education in Glasgow at the hands of the Congregationalists Greville Ewing and Ralph Wardlaw. Caldwell had been accepted by the LMS in 1834 and ordained into the Congregational ministry, even though his mind was already moving, through his reading of Hooker and Waterland, in the direction of episcopalian principles. As an outward dissenter, 'whilst in mind more or less a church man', Caldwell sailed for India in 1837, hopeful that he was leaving behind the battle-ground of ecclesiastical partisanship and that, in joining himself to the

---

[1] Oxford, Rhodes House, United Society for the Propagation of the Gospel archives [hereafter USPGA], CLR 2, pp. 254–9, Bishop of Madras to A. M. Campbell, 14 Aug. 1841. I am grateful to the USPG for permission to cite material from their archives. Frank Penny, *The Church in Madras*, 3 vols (London, 1904–22), 3, pp. 405–11, lists all native clergy ordained in Madras diocese during Spencer's episcopate, but none of those listed were former Roman Catholic priests.

professedly non-denominational LMS, his feet would be on neutral ground.[2]

In point of fact, Caldwell found Madras at the close of the 1830s to be no less subject to ecclesiological ferment than was Britain. The Anglican Church in the presidency was still recovering from the damaging controversy between C. T. E. Rhenius, the German Lutheran employed by the Church Missionary Society (CMS), and the CMS authorities which had led to the secession of numerous congregations from the Anglican Church.[3] Rhenius had been influenced by Anthony Norris Groves of the Christian (or Plymouth) Brethren, whose distinctive quest for primitive apostolicity continued to exert a powerful appeal on the minds of the most devoted Anglicans during Caldwell's early years in Madras.[4] Many of those who were held back from Brethrenism owed their fidelity to the Church of England to the magnetic hold on English society in Madras exercised by John Tucker, secretary of the CMS corresponding committee. According to Caldwell, the 'real Bishop' of Madras was not the amiable yet 'somewhat feeble' Spencer, but rather Tucker, who indeed might properly have been called 'not the Bishop, but the Pope of Madras'.[5] As a Calvinistic High Churchman and personal friend of John Keble, Tucker was able to trump the Brethren card with the claim that the search for true evangelical catholicity need look no further than the Church of England.

The effect on Robert Caldwell of imbibing this heady brew of ecclesiological controversy was to bring him, fortified by a course of theological reading that ranged from the Ante-Nicene Fathers to the Cambridge Platonists, to the conclusion that he should join the Church of England as 'the best representative in our time both of the catholicity and of the freedom of thought of the earliest ages'.[6] He began by introducing Anglican baptis-

---

[2] J. L. Wyatt, ed., *Reminiscences of Bishop Caldwell* (Madras, 1894), pp. 3–8, 23, 64.

[3] See Hans Cnattingius, *Bishops and Societies: A Study of Anglican Colonial and Missionary Expansion, 1698–1850* (London, 1952), pp. 167–73; Stephen Neill, *A History of Christianity in India, 1707–1858* (Cambridge, 1985), pp. 218–22.

[4] Wyatt, *Reminiscences of Bishop Caldwell*, p. 54; on Groves see [M. B. Groves], *Memoir of the Late Anthony Norris Groves, . . . compiled by his widow* (London, 1856), and G. H. Lang, *Anthony Norris Groves: Saint and Pioneer* (London, 1939).

[5] Wyatt, *Reminiscences of Bishop Caldwell*, pp. 54–5; on Tucker see Eugene Stock, *The History of the Church Missionary Society*, 4 vols (London, 1899–1916), 1, pp. 328–9.

[6] Wyatt, *Reminiscences of Bishop Caldwell*, pp. 62–3.

mal and eucharistic liturgy to the LMS churches, with predictably divisive effects amongst the membership.[7] On 1 April 1841
he gave the LMS district secretary three months' notice of his
impending resignation.[8] The response of the Society was to
suggest that Caldwell's change of denominational allegiance was
no reason for severing his connection with the LMS.[9] Reference
was apparently made to the 'Fundamental Principle' enshrined in
the constitution of the LMS since 1796:

> As the union of Christians of various denominations in
> carrying on this great work is a most desirable object, so, to
> prevent if possible, any cause of future dissension, it is
> declared to be a Fundamental Principle of the Missionary
> Society, that our design is not to send Presbyterianism,
> Independency, Episcopacy, or any other form of Church
> Order and Government, (about which there may be dif-
> ference of opinion among serious persons) but the Glorious
> Gospel of the blessed God, and that it shall be left (as it
> ought to be left) to the minds of the persons whom God
> may call into the fellowship of His Son to assume for
> themselves such form of Church Government as to them
> shall appear most agreeable to the Word of God.[10]

Caldwell had in fact already considered the possibility that, in
the spirit of the Fundamental Principle, he might remain within
the Society as an Anglican, but had rejected it as a recipe for
disharmony. He noted that the LMS had conceded that Baptists
could not be expected to co-exist harmoniously with Independents within the same organization. It was surely equally
apparent that churchmen and Independents could not successfully paper over their fundamental differences on questions of

---

[7] London, School of Oriental and African Studies, Council for World Mission archives [hereafter CWMA], LMS South India Tamil Incoming Letters, Box 8, J. Bilderbeck to A. Tidman and J. J. Freeman, 23 Sept. 1841. Bilderbeck himself became an Anglican and joined the CMS in 1843. I am grateful to the Council for World Mission for permission to cite material from their archives.

[8] CWMA, LMS South India Tamil Incoming Letters, Box 8, R. Caldwell to A. Tidman, 30 June 1841.

[9] USPGA, X1085, MS Memoirs of Bishop Caldwell.

[10] CWMA, LMS Board Minutes, 9 May 1796, cited in I. M. Fletcher, 'The Fundamental Principle of the London Missionary Society', *Transactions of the Congregational Historical Society*, 19, 3 (Oct. 1962), p. 138.

church order. With some justice, Caldwell complained that in reality the Fundamental Principle meant that Congregationalists were free to act on their ecclesiological principles while everyone else had to keep theirs in abeyance.[11] He therefore determined, not to join the CMS, which was the dominant Anglican force in Madras, but the much weaker Society for the Propagation of the Gospel. The SPG, as he was prepared to admit, was almost at 'the last stage of inanition', but at least its principles seemed to reflect the catholicity of the Church of England, in contrast to the CMS, whose voluntaryism and theological partisanship 'appeared to set up a Church within a Church, with principles and doctrines of its own'.[12]

Thus it was in August 1841 that Caldwell found himself in Bishop Spencer's residence, seeking Anglican ordination. Spencer had a higher opinion of Caldwell than Caldwell had of him, and informed the SPG in London that he intended to ordain him without delay.[13] A little over a month later, on 19 September, Caldwell was admitted to the Anglican diaconate. Subsequently Arthur Tidman, the LMS Foreign Secretary, wrote to him asking for a reimbursement of the £400 the Society had spent on his theological education and passage money. Caldwell indignantly refused the request as unreasonable, arguing in response that he had supposed that the 'Fundamental Principle' would enable him to act as a churchman with as much consistency as the Independents were able to observe in fidelity to their Congregationalism. If, even at this stage, the LMS were prepared to offer him such freedom, he would gladly re-transfer his allegiance.[14] This was a bluff that Caldwell knew would not be called, not least because it was logically incoherent. Whatever was meant by acting consistently with church principles, it certainly could not mean one isolated priest in a Nonconformist

---

[11] USPGA, X1085, MS Memoirs of Bishop Caldwell; Wyatt, *Reminiscences of Bishop Caldwell*, p. 65. There is evidence that in its early years the LMS had been prepared to accept Baptist missionary candidates, and at least one such served with the Society; see R. H. Martin, *Evangelicals United: Ecumenical Stirrings in Pre-Victorian Britain, 1795–1830* (Metuchen, NJ, and London, 1983), pp. 47–8. In Caldwell's own day, William Young, a member of a Baptist church in Calcutta, served with the LMS in Batavia and China; see James Sibree, *London Missionary Society: A Register of Missionaries, Deputations, etc., from 1796 to 1923* (London, 1923), pp. 29–30.

[12] Wyatt, *Reminiscences of Bishop Caldwell*, p. 63.

[13] USPGA, CLR 2, p. 254, Bishop of Madras to A. M. Campbell, 14 Aug. 1841.

[14] CWMA, LMS South India Tamil Incoming Letters, Box 8, Caldwell to Tidman, 13 Feb. 1842.

mission being given a free hand to do his own thing. More fundamentally, Caldwell had come to the conclusion that Independency, whatever its merits might be in Britain, was simply not suited for India. The apostolic context of the Indian mission field demanded adherence to an apostolic model of church order.[15]

Robert Caldwell was followed into the Anglican Church by four other LMS missionaries and six missionaries or assistant missionaries from the Wesleyan Methodist Missionary Society.[16] A gratified but slightly embarrassed Bishop Spencer felt it necessary to assure the SPG that he was not in the business of poaching missionaries, and that there was no other explanation than that the evangelical and catholic truths of the Church of England were exercising their rightful drawing power.[17] Caldwell himself went on to become a distinguished assistant bishop of Madras in Tirunelveli from 1877 to 1891, and a leading architect of the Anglican Church in South India. None the less, he maintained friendly relations with the LMS missionaries, indeed so much so that in 1844 he married the daughter of Charles Mault, the senior LMS missionary at Nagercoil.[18] Furthermore, he retained some of the distinctive emphases of his Nonconformist past throughout his episcopate. Addressing the Centenary Conference on the Protestant Missions of the World held in London in 1888, Caldwell stressed that it had been a governing principle of his entire missionary career 'to make the congregation the centre round which all work revolved'. The key element in his strategy to make the South Indian churches self-supporting and self-governing had been the introduction of church councils in each district, elected by each congregation and wielding substan-

[15] Wyatt, *Reminiscences of Bishop Caldwell*, p. 65.

[16] The four LMS missionaries were John Bilderbeck, Henry Bower, William Howell and J. A. Regel. I have identified five of the six WMMS missionaries or assistant missionaries with reasonable certainty as James Kershaw Best, Robert Carver, John Guest, Peter Percival and George Uglow Pope. Wyatt, *Reminiscences of Bishop Caldwell*, p. 64; G. G. Findlay and W. W. Holdsworth, *The History of the Wesleyan Methodist Missionary Society*, 5 vols (London, 1921–4), 5, pp. 33, 194; Penny, *The Church in Madras*, 3, pp. 366–70; Sibree, *London Missionary Society: A Register*, pp. 23, 31, 39, 44; C. F. Pascoe, *Two Hundred Years of the S. P. G.: An Historical Account of the Society for the Propagation of the Gospel in Foreign Parts* (London, 1901), pp. 916–19.

[17] USPGA, CLR 2, p. 259, Bishop of Madras to A. M. Campbell, 14 Aug. 1841.

[18] M. E. Gibbs, *The Anglican Church in India, 1600–1970* (New Delhi, 1972), p. 149; Penny, *The Church in Madras*, 3, p. 279; Sibree, *London Missionary Society: A Register*, p. 20.

tial financial and administrative power.[19] For all of his dissatisfaction with evangelical voluntaryism, Caldwell took with him into Anglicanism something of the Congregational insistence that responsible power in the church proceeds upwards from the gathered congregation of Christ's people.

Robert Caldwell's change of denominational allegiance introduces some of the central themes of this paper. Our discussion of denominational identity will be limited primarily to the British Protestant tradition. Nevertheless, the contrast between Caldwell's indecently rapid acceptance by the Anglican Church and the obstacles which were placed in the path of the former Roman Catholic priest highlights, in the first place, the fact that the distance separating Congregationalist from Anglican in 1841 was as nothing in comparison with the gulf that divided the churches of the Reformation from the Roman communion. However profound the effect of the missionary context on Western denominational divisions, the chasm between Protestant and Catholic remained almost as wide in the non-Western world as in Europe until after the Second Vatican Council.

Secondly, Caldwell's story might appear to illustrate the extent to which the pan-evangelical ecumenism which characterized the missionary awakening at the end of the eighteenth century had, by the 1840s, worn painfully thin under the pressure of heightened sensitivities to church order among both churchmen and dissenters.[20] That interpretation, though plausible, underestimates the extent to which the pioneers of the missionary awakening in the 1790s held in tension genuine enthusiasm for interdenominational co-operation and a hard-nosed appreciation of what was possible in, to use William Carey's famous phrase, 'the present divided state of Christendom'.[21] It might be more accurate to suggest that cases such as Caldwell's uncover the ambiguity that had been latent in the LMS Fundamental Principle from the very beginning. As David Thompson has pointed out, the contention within the Principle that church order is a 'thing indifferent', of secondary importance to 'the Glorious

[19] James Johnston, ed., *Report of the Centenary Conference on the Protestant Missions of the World, Held in . . . London, 1888*, 2 vols (London, 1888), 2, pp. 350–1, 356.

[20] See Martin, *Evangelicals United*, pp. 194–203.

[21] William Carey, *An Enquiry into the Obligations of Christians to Use Means for the Conversion of the Heathens* (Leicester, 1792; new edn, ed. E. A. Payne, London, 1961), p. 84.

Gospel of the blessed God', was arguably one that no-one of High-Church principles, whether those principles were Anglican or Presbyterian or even Independent, could easily accept.[22] The Fundamental Principle was drafted by Alexander Waugh, minister of the Scots Secession Church in London. Although described by Norman Goodall as 'a staunch Presbyterian', Waugh came from that strand of Scottish Presbyterianism which was closest to Congregationalism in its *de facto* church polity.[23] Nevertheless, he did not regard questions of church order as unimportant. The Principle, claimed Waugh, was not intended to 'confound all distinctions of religious opinion, or to deride and insult with names of ill repute the honest scruples of a tender and inquiring mind'. Rather it sought to draw a distinction between the 'word of life' in Scripture, in which there was no darkness at all, and the decrees passed by human assemblies on questions of church order, which mixed truth and error and were no part of the divine deposit to be transmitted to the heathen.[24]

It was the questioning of that distinction that lay behind the secessions to Anglicanism of Caldwell and others in the early 1840s. The issue at stake was whether each gathered congregation of heathen converts must be left to make its own judgement on questions of church polity, as the Fundamental Principle laid down, or whether there was an apostolic pattern of church order whose transmission was an integral part of the missionary task. In practice this tended to boil down to a choice between a modified form of congregational independency and episcopacy. For, as Professor Walls has observed, the clause lurking in parenthesis in the Principle — 'as it ought to be left' — can be interpreted as introducing congregationalism by the back door, since it asserted that the determination of church order was properly a matter for each identifiable unit of heathen converts to decide, and if no particular system of church organization were to be

[22] David M. Thompson, *Denominationalism and Dissent, 1795–1835: A Question of Identity*, Friends of Dr Williams's Library 39th Lecture (London, 1985), pp. 11–12.

[23] Norman Goodall, *A History of the London Missionary Society, 1895–1945* (London, 1954), p. 4; see Andrew L. Drummond and James Bulloch, *The Church in Victorian Scotland, 1843–1874* (Edinburgh, 1975), pp. 43–4, 48–9.

[24] James Hay and Henry Belfrage, *A Memoir of the Reverend Alexander Waugh, D.D.* (London, 1830), p. 216.

imposed on them, what other unit could there be than the gathered congregation?[25] Missionary agencies from a wide variety of denominational backgrounds shared a strong theoretical commitment to the goal of establishing a self-governing church. However, even those whose historic ecclesiology was antipathetic to independency tended in the missionary context to extol the virtues of the congregational insistence on the autonomy of newly planted churches. Peter Williams has pointed out that Henry Venn, the CMS secretary who is regarded as one of the two architects of the Three-Self Theory of the autonomous church, drew considerable inspiration from the example of Nonconformist missions which sought to implement on the mission field the church polity that they had long practised at home.[26]

A third question raised by Caldwell's case is that of the relationship between the voluntary society – that characteristically eighteenth-century product which became the predominant model for Protestant missionary agency – and the institutional church. Minds of high ecclesiological principle have always found missionary societies exasperating. To quote Professor Walls again, 'The voluntary society is one of God's theological jokes, whereby he makes tender mockery of his people when they take themselves too seriously.'[27] Caldwell did not appreciate the divine sense of humour, preferring the SPG to the CMS on the grounds that the former was not so obviously a church within a church. This is more than a little ironic in view of the fact that the SPG had made rapid strides since 1838 in transforming itself from a colonial church society dependent on parliamentary grants to a missionary society prepared to compete for support in the market place of popular Christian philanthropy.[28] The prime mover in that transition was Bishop John Inglis of Nova Scotia, who had come to realize that, as the props of establishment privilege were knocked away from the colonial

---

[25] Andrew F. Walls, 'Missionary societies and the fortunate subversion of the church', *Evangelical Quarterly*, 88 (1988), p. 149.

[26] C. Peter Williams, *The Ideal of the Self-Governing Church: A Study in Victorian Missionary Strategy* (Leiden, 1990), pp. 25–6, 50–1. The other generally recognized architect of the Three-Self Theory is Rufus Anderson, senior secretary of the American Board of Commissioners for Foreign Missions from 1832 to 1866.

[27] Walls, 'Missionary societies', p. 147.

[28] Brian Stanley, 'Home support for overseas missions in early Victorian England, c.1838–1873' (Cambridge Ph.D. thesis, 1979), pp. 76–91.

Anglican churches, they had no alternative but to 'learn the ways of voluntaryism'.[29] The SPG was fast approximating itself to the ways of its more successful evangelical rival. As a result, colonial bishops were beginning to voice the same complaints about the threats to their authority posed by SPG diocesan committees as they frequently did about the CMS.[30]

A fourth question raised by Caldwell's case comes close to the primary concern of this paper. Although one suspects that Caldwell would eventually have become an Anglican even if he had not gone to India, part of his justification for his change of allegiance was the claim that Independency was not suited for the cultural context of India. Mid-nineteenth-century mission strategists were not afraid to ask the question of whether some forms of ecclesiology were better fitted than others for transplantation to the mission field, although they were far from unanimous in their answers. The issue was specifically discussed during the 1850s at one of the monthly meetings of the secretaries of the principal evangelical societies.[31] At the Liverpool missionary conference in 1860 much of the discussion on the subject of native churches focused on the question of whether *any* Western system of church organization ought to be transmitted to mission converts. Joseph Mullens, an LMS missionary in Calcutta, stirred up considerable disagreement by his exposition of the conventional LMS line that missionaries ought not to export British denominational peculiarities to the mission field. William Shaw, the Methodist pioneer in South Africa, raised much the same objection as Caldwell – that this was in effect to opt for congregationalism. Several other speakers agreed with Shaw that the substantial reproduction of Western denominational forms was inevitable, if somewhat regrettable. The conference resolution on the subject was an obvious compromise, conceding that missionaries would naturally begin by organizing churches on the system with which they were familiar, but urging them to retain only the 'essential features' of such systems, and to abandon 'mere technicalities' and accidental historical accretions.[32]

---

[29] Ibid., pp. 81–2; Robert T. Handy, *A History of the Churches in the United States and Canada* (Oxford, 1976), p. 236.

[30] Cnattingius, *Bishops and Societies*, pp. 211–20.

[31] *Conference on Missions Held in 1860 at Liverpool . . . Edited by the Secretaries to the Conference* (London, 1860), p. 279.

[32] Ibid., pp. 283–303, 312.

The debate at Liverpool in 1860 was concerned with a supposedly simple choice between either the acceptance or the conscious minimalization of Western denominational distinctiveness. Few speakers were prepared to give more than a theoretical acknowledgement that denominational principles had been forged in particular historical circumstances that did not apply on the mission field. There was also little or no awareness of the fact that transmission of any Christian tradition across a cultural barrier and by means – whether missionary or indigenous – that were quite different from the patterns familiar to the domestic church, carried with it the inevitable implication that the tradition itself would be changed. Bishop Bengt Sundkler very properly began his history of the road to church union in South India with these words:

> The day when a church becomes a sending church, a missionary church, is among the most fateful in its history. When it moves across the seas to be transplanted in other soil, it does of necessity change, either by conscious and willing adaptation or else through its very resistance to change. The factors of growth and change are set out in sharper relief by the situation in a mission field than by the situation within the older churches of Europe and America. Transplantation means mutation.[33]

As the modern missionary movement moved from its pioneer evangelistic stage to an increasing preoccupation with the nurture of indigenous churches towards the goal of autonomous life, the issue of the reshaping of Christian tradition came into sharper relief. The nature, limits, and implications of that process of reshaping will form the predominant theme of the remainder of this paper.

From the 1880s onwards, a growing number of missionary spokesmen began to display a readiness to see the relativity of their own denominational tradition which contrasts with the defensiveness evident at Liverpool in 1860. For some, this increased openness was partially attributable to the corrosive effect

---

[33] Bengt Sundkler, *Church of South India: The Movement Towards Union, 1900–1947*, rev. edn (London, 1965), p. 11.

of modern historical and biblical scholarship on previously in-
flexible dogmatic positions. At the Centenary Conference on
Protestant Missions in 1888, one Anglican speaker, C. C. Fenn,
a CMS secretary who was firmly in the Venn tradition of
commitment to an autonomous church,[34] showed an extremely
loose adherence to episcopacy. Drawing directly on J. B. Lightfoot's recently published *Apostolic Fathers*, Fenn conceded that
the transition in the second century from presbyterian to episcopal patterns of church order was in harmony both with the
evolution of a more structured understanding of the operation of
the Holy Spirit and with the generally monarchical pattern of
civil government at the time. On the same principle, however,
the contrary trend in the nineteenth century from monarchical
to democratic forms of government suggested that episcopacy
might be on the way out. Fenn confidently looked forward to a
future united church in India which would embrace a variety of
forms of government, and predicted that Anglicans in India
would have little hesitation in laying aside 'the fact or the theory
of the so-called Apostolical succession', if it stood in the path of
church union.[35]

Fenn's views were, perhaps, not so surprising for a disciple of
Henry Venn, for whom episcopacy was a goal for the young
church to aspire towards rather than a pre-condition of church
order. Anglo-Catholic questioning was less radical but no less
significant in its ultimate implications. The most notable
example is supplied by Henry Whitehead, principal of Bishop's
College, Calcutta, who in 1899 was consecrated fifth Bishop of
Madras. At the Madras meeting on Faith and Order in 1910
Whitehead appealed to the non-episcopal churches of South
India to 'accept *the fact* of the Historic Episcopate, without in any
way committing themselves to any particular theory about it'.[36]
That appeal stood in obvious harmony with the emphasis placed
by Lambeth Conferences from 1888 onwards on the historic
episcopate as one of the essential ingredients of reunion.

---

[34] See Williams, *The Ideal of the Self-Governing Church*, pp. 55, 59–60, 73–80.

[35] Johnston, *Report of the Centenary Conference*, 2, pp. 474–7; Fenn cites J. B. Lightfoot, *The Apostolic Fathers. Part II*, 2 vols (London, 1885), 1, p. 382.

[36] Sundkler, *Church of South India*, pp. 62–3. A similar distinction between the fact and the theory of episcopacy was introduced into Anglican–Free Church discussions in England from 1922; see G. K. A. Bell, ed., *Documents on Christian Unity: A Selection from the First and Second Series 1920–30* (London, 1955), p. 46.

Whitehead found immediate support for his principle in the criticisms of mechanical theories of the transmission of grace through the apostolic succession of the episcopate published in 1912 by A. C. Headlam and W. H. Frere.[37] However, the origins of Whitehead's separation of fact and theory in relation to episcopacy lay, at least in part, in the recent contention of American Protestant liberals that the findings of critical scholarship placed the question of church reunion, and specifically the status of episcopacy, in a wholly new light. Thus Whitehead was influenced by the Congregationalist Newman Smyth's argument in his *Passing Protestantism and Coming Catholicism* (1908) that episcopacy held the key to the door to the larger Catholicism of the future, not because of any theory of apostolic succession, which Smyth regarded as highly dubious, but simply because episcopacy offered factual evidence of the continuity and universality of the Church.[38] Similarly, Whitehead drew upon C. A. Briggs's *Church Unity* (1909), with its iconoclastic insistence that all *jure divino* theories of church government – whether Anglo-Catholic, Presbyterian or Congregational – must be reckoned as inanimate corpses, slain by historical criticism.[39]

The significance for our purposes of these critical questionings lies in the fact that they perceived the historical contingency of ecclesiology on the cultural context. Thus J. H. Wyckoff, a missionary from the American Dutch Reformed Church, and one of the South India United Church representatives at the

[37] H. Whitehead, 'The next step towards unity', *The Harvest Field* [hereafter *HF*], 33 (1913), pp. 45, 48. Whitehead refers in particular to A. C. Headlam's article on apostolic succession in G. Harford and M. Stevenson, eds., *The Prayer Book Dictionary* (London, 1912), pp. 38–43, and W. H. Frere's review of Headlam's article in *CQR*, 75 (1912–13), pp. 150–3. Whitehead's distinction between fact and theory is not made explicitly by the relevant sections of the Lambeth documents from 1888 or 1908; see R. T. Davidson, ed., *The Six Lambeth Conferences, 1867–1920* (London, 1920), pp. 156–61, 431–4.

[38] Newman Smyth, *Passing Protestantism and Coming Catholicism* (London, 1908), pp. 154–5, 161; Sundkler, *Church of South India*, pp. 56, 63–4, 365. Smyth had been in touch with William Reed Huntington, the author of the Chicago-Lambeth Quadrilateral, as early as 1882, and their contact was renewed after 1908 in the context of Episcopal-Congregational discussions in Connecticut. These discussions suggested that a functional approach to episcopacy might be a fruitful way forward in church union. See Newman Smyth, *A Story of Church Unity Including the Lambeth Conference of Anglican Bishops and the Congregational-Episcopal Approaches* (New Haven, Conn., and London, 1923).

[39] Charles Augustus Briggs, *Church Unity: Studies of its Most Important Problems* (London, 1910), pp. 79–84; Sundkler, *Church of South India*, p. 365. Briggs, professor at Union Theological Seminary, had left the Presbyterian Church for the Protestant Episcopal Church following his suspension from the ministry in 1893 for heterodoxy.

Madras conference in 1910, had in the previous year used Lightfoot's demonstration that the organization of the early Church took on different forms in imperial Rome, democratic Greece, and Palestine to claim that the organization of an indigenous Indian church ought to mirror as closely as possible the traditional Hindu system of self-government by village communities. Perhaps surprisingly, Wyckoff went on to argue that episcopacy need not contradict this principle, provided that centralizing tendencies were resisted.[40] G. Sherwood Eddy, the American Congregationalist who contributed so much to the process of church union in South India, advanced similar views. While using Lightfoot and an assortment of other scholars to rebut theories of apostolic succession and a monarchical episcopate, Eddy argued in the Madras interdenominational publication *The Harvest Field* in 1911 that episcopacy rather than congregationalism was the system best adapted to the 'genius of the Orient'. Asian peoples, claimed Eddy, had 'no genius for democracy'. Congregationalism was unsuitable for 'depressed and ignorant people'. India was used to government by the *rajah* and the *panchayat* (the village council of elders); what the Indian church required, therefore, was a combination of bishop and presbytery as the nearest approach to *rajah* and *panchayat*.[41] Here, from the pen of an American Congregationalist, was the case for that 'constitutional' episcopacy which subsequently became the basis of the plans for church union in both South and North India.

Arguments based on appropriateness to the Indian cultural context did not all point in the same direction. Eddy's case for an episcopal united church in South India was attacked by a Presbyterian missionary who drew from the *panchayat* model precisely the opposite conclusion, namely that a democratic form of church government was more in harmony with 'the genius of the people' than the autocratic rule of a bishop could ever be.[42] A year later, the LMS missionary Bernard Lucas, a dyed-in-the-wool Congregationalist and a self-diagnosed sufferer from 'congenital episcopophobia',[43] listened with amazed delight to

[40] J. H. Wyckoff, 'The Indian church', *HF*, 30 (1910), pp. 128–30.

[41] G. S. Eddy, 'A national church for India', *HF*, 31 (1911), pp. 213–19; cited in Sundkler, *Church of South India*, pp. 66–7.

[42] A. Andrew, 'An Indian national church', *HF*, 31 (1911), pp. 260–1.

[43] Sundkler, *Church of South India*, p. 109.

Whitehead's confession to the National Missionary Conference in Calcutta that he regarded as untenable the theory of the historic episcopate as a necessary channel of sacramental grace, only to be dismayed by the bishop's subsequent assertion that episcopacy was nevertheless to be recommended as the only safeguard of unity, a claim which Lucas regarded as historical nonsense. Whitehead had suggested that the only alternative to the Anglican position was for each body of Christians to be free to make their own decisions of church order, and alleged that, in the context of a caste society, this would mean total capitulation to the inequalities of caste. Lucas's published reply retorted that the LMS had been working on that very principle in India for over a century, and that the LMS churches had a better claim than any to be free of caste distinctions.[44]

The argument in South India over which form of church government corresponded most closely to that indefinable entity – 'the genius of the Indian people' – rumbled on into the 1930s and beyond. Advocates of the scheme for a united Church of South India, such as Bishop V. S. Azariah, claimed that their distinctive 'episcopresbygational' hybrid, as defined by the Tranquebar Manifesto of 1919, was just what the Indian national soil required.[45] Critics of the proposals, notably D. M. Devasahayam of the Bangalore *Christo Samaj* group, countered that the scheme was in fact an importation of a Western institutional model of church union to a religious culture which prized spirituality more highly than organization, and insisted that the only authentic pattern for Indian Christianity would be a network of independent *ashram*s, with virtually no superstructure – in other words, a far purer form of congregationalism than that which obtained in the West.[46]

What made the church union process possible in South India and subsequently in North India was thus the growing convergence between the ecclesiologies of Anglicans and Nonconformists, even though significant voices among missionaries and

[44] B. Lucas, 'The next step towards unity', *HF*, 33 (1913), pp. 85–9. Whitehead's address is printed in ibid., pp. 45–51.

[45] Sundkler, *Church of South India*, pp. 99–100.

[46] D. M. Devasahayam, *The South India Church Union Movement* (np, nd [Madras, 1938]), pp. 25–6. On Devasahayam see Sundkler, *Church of South India*, pp. 194–6, 205, 225–6, 399, and CWMA, LMS India Odds Box 11, Goodall Deputation 1937 File, A. H. Legg to A. M. Chirgwin, 27 Nov. 1939.

national Christians resisted the homogenizing trend. That convergence was the product of the gradual redefinition of their respective denominational traditions, which took place, both consciously and unconsciously, within the Indian context.

In Bishop Whitehead's case, what placed his Tractarian principles under increasing question was not so much the transition from England to India as the move south from Calcutta to Madras. In Bengal Christianity had made little progress, and Whitehead's educational role as principal of Bishop's College offered few challenges to existing patterns of thought. In the south, on the other hand, Whitehead found the church in the Telegu country on the brink of a mass movement towards Christianity which held out the prospect of the conversion of two million *pariahs*, as well as many of higher caste.[47] Furthermore, he found the SPG mission woefully disunited and disorganized in comparison with the CMS Telegu mission.[48] The result was that Whitehead threw his whole weight behind the effort to reap the evangelistic harvest among the rural poor and endeavoured, to the dismay of many SPG missionaries and Bishop Montgomery at SPG headquarters in London, to close Bishop Heber College at Trichinopoly.[49] More fundamentally, his ecclesiological thinking moved into an evangelistic and consequently pragmatic mode. As an old man in 1935, Whitehead confessed to Godfrey Phillips of the LMS that the chief axiom of his thinking on matters of ministry and church order from 1912 onwards had been the paramount importance of determining what was best calculated to foster the unity of the Church in the particular historical and cultural circumstances in which it was set. That, in his understanding, was the prime determinant of the growth of the ministry in the apostolic and sub-apostolic age. This too was the nub of Whitehead's case for constitutional episcopacy. In 1935 the very same principle inclined him to oppose any provision for lay administration of the eucharist in the church union scheme. Lay celebration was not wrong in

[47] USPGA, CLR 56, pp. 370–2, Bishop Whitehead to Bishop Montgomery, 21 Dec. 1904; Sundkler, *Church of South India*, p. 52.

[48] USPGA, CLR 55, p. 507, Bishop Whitehead to H. W. Tucker, 5 June 1900.

[49] USPGA, CLR 57, inserts between pp. 289 and 290, T. H. Dodson to Bishop Montgomery, 22 and 27 Dec. 1907, and A. D. Limbrick to T. H. Dodson, 2 Dec. 1907; see also D. O'Connor, *Gospel, Raj and Swaraj: The Missionary Years of C. F. Andrews, 1904–14* (Frankfurt, 1990), pp. 160–3.

principle, but dangerous in practice, for decidedly Protestant reasons: unless accompanied by sound theological teaching, celebration of the holy communion among ignorant people who had only recently been rescued from superstition ran the danger of confusing sacrament and magic. Whitehead's favoured solution was, however, scarcely less radical than lay celebration: he suggested creating within the Indian church a new order of ministry by ordaining school teachers with powers to celebrate the eucharist.[50]

Henry Whitehead is not the only case of a missionary thinker within the Catholic tradition of Anglicanism being willing to refashion ecclesiastical order in response to missionary opportunity and by appeal to early Christian precedent. William Tozer, second missionary bishop in Central Africa, revived the ancient order of the subdiaconate in 1870 as an essential first step towards preparing Africans for the priesthood; he also advocated a radical simplification of the liturgy for the African context.[51] Tozer's successor, Edward Steere, though an uncompromising High Churchman by background, did not toe the party line in central Africa. Concerned, like Whitehead later in India, that uneducated people would direct their adoration at the eucharist more to the Presence than to the Person of Christ, he taught and practised a plain doctrine of the sacrament which caused fervent Catholic spirits to doubt whether their bishop believed in the Real Presence at all. Steere also strongly favoured lay preaching, then illegal, as a means of undercutting the appeal of evangelical dissent.[52]

All such examples need to be seen against the backcloth of the fundamental changes in Anglicanism consequent upon its removal from the peculiar historical circumstances of the Church of England. Until 1927 the Anglican Church in India remained legally part of the Church of England, and hence partook of the character of establishment. In the light of the upsurge of Indian nationalism from 1905, established status came to be seen by the

---

[50] CWMA, LMS India Odds 20, Church Union, S. India, Whitehead to Phillips, 7 May 1935; see Sundkler, *Church of South India*, pp. 283–95.

[51] J. T. Moriyama, 'The evolution of an African ministry in the work of the Universities' Mission to Central Africa in Tanzania, 1864–1909' (London Ph.D. thesis, 1984), pp. 54–5.

[52] R. M. Heanley, *A Memoir of Edward Steere, D.D., LL.D., Third Missionary Bishop in Central Africa* (London, 1888), pp. 179–81, 393–3, 432.

most perceptive Anglican observers, such as C. F. Andrews, as an evangelistic liability.[53] As a result, the Indian Church in 1927 was finally able to follow the advice which W. E. Gladstone had offered to the colonial churches in the mid-nineteenth century 'to organise themselves on that basis of voluntary consensual compact which was the basis on which the Church of Christ rested from the first'.[54] Anglicanism outside England thus found it both necessary and possible to integrate many of the assumptions of religious voluntaryism into its spiritual tradition to an extent that the Church of England itself still refuses to do. Perhaps the most significant consequence of the adoption of voluntary status has been the emergence of synodical government, pioneered by the Episcopal churches of Scotland and the USA, and adopted by the colonial churches from 1844 onwards. Bishops deprived of the constitutional checks of establishment were found to possess degrees of power which they themselves, let alone others, regarded as dangerous. The institution of diocesan and provincial synods, given general legitimacy at the first Lambeth Conference in 1867, brought into Anglicanism elective principles of representation, and above all gave a guaranteed place to the power of the laity.[55] The trend was not welcomed by all. Mark Napier Trollope, consecrated third Bishop of Korea in 1911, though firmly committed to establishing a diocesan synod as a means of creating a Korean Catholic church in communion with Canterbury, resisted the inclusion of the laity in decision-making. He argued that the increasingly prevalent pattern of government by bishop, priests, and laity in synod owed more to the British constitutional model of King, Lords, and Commons than it did to primitive catholic tradition.[56] Trollope, however, remained a minority voice.[57] Lay representation

---

[53] O'Connor, *Gospel, Raj and Swaraj*, p. 166.

[54] J. McLeod Campbell, *Christian History in the Making* (London, 1946), p. 310. For the background to the Indian Church Measure and Act of 1927 see Cecil John Grimes, *Towards an Indian Church: The Growth of the Church of India in Constitution and Life* (London, 1946).

[55] Campbell, *Christian History in the Making*, pp. 309–12; G. R. Evans, *Authority in the Church: A Challenge for Anglicans* (Norwich, 1990), pp. 48–56; William L. Sachs, *The Transformation of Anglicanism: From State Church to Global Communion* (Cambridge, 1993), pp. 190–201; Alan M. G. Stephenson, *The First Lambeth Conference, 1867* (London, 1967), pp. 66–77, 256–66, 330–1.

[56] Constance A. M. Trollope, *Mark Napier Trollope: Bishop in Corea, 1911–1930* (London, 1936), pp. 52–9. Trollope objected to using the term 'Anglican' outside of the Church of England.

[57] Campbell, *Christian History in the Making*, p. 311.

within synodical organization became a normal feature of global Anglicanism well before the Church of England accepted the principle to its full extent in 1969.

Anglicanism in the missionary context was compelled increasingly to become a believers' church, committed to structures and principles that promoted mission and autonomous life. Nonconformity, at least in the renewed form that emerged from the Evangelical Revival in Britain, was already so committed. Yet the impact of the mission field on Nonconformist church order was no less profound. In 1805 the Baptist missionaries of Serampore adopted a 'Form of Agreement' as a statement of the principles to which their covenanted mission community was bound. In that document it was prescribed that native ministers must be allowed to preach the word and administer the ordinances

> as much as possible, without the interference of the missionary of the district who will constantly superintend their affairs, give them advice in cases of order and discipline, and correct any errors into which they fall; and who, joying and beholding their order, and the stedfastness of their faith in Christ, may direct his efforts continually to the planting of new churches in other places, and to the spread of the gospel in his district, to the utmost of his power.[58]

Here was a fine distinction between legitimate 'superintendence' and illegitimate 'interference'. For William Ward, the author of the Form of Agreement,[59] and his colleagues William Carey and Joshua Marshman, the distinction was more than a linguistic nicety, since they were committed to the view that foreign missions should, as far as possible, be financially independent of the sending country. 'Control', they wrote in 1817, 'originates wholly in Contribution, and is ever commensurate

---

[58] *Periodical Accounts Relative to the Baptist Missionary Society*, 3 (1804–9), p. 206, cited in Brian Stanley, 'Planting self-governing churches: British Baptist ecclesiology in the missionary context', *Baptist Quarterly*, 34 (1991–2), p. 381.

[59] Ward's authorship is clear from Joshua Marshman, ed., *Letters from the Rev. Dr Carey . . .* , 3rd edn (London, 1828), p. 56; J. C. Marshman, *The Life and Times of Carey, Marshman, and Ward*, 2 vols (London, 1859), 1, p. 229. See also Oxford, Regent's Park College, Angus Library, Baptist Missionary Society archives [hereafter BMSA], transcript of Ward's journal for 19 Oct. 1805, pp. 443–5. I am grateful to the Baptist Missionary Society for permission to cite material from their archives.

therewith; control indeed follows contribution, as the shadow the substance.'[60] The contention that direction of policy should lie, not in an elected committee in London responsible to a body of subscribers, but in the hands of the community of expatriate and indigenous Christians actually engaged in mission, lay at the heart of the Serampore Controversy which ultimately led Carey and his colleagues to separate from the Baptist Missionary Society (BMS) in 1827.[61] In terms of the subsequent development of the missionary movement, the Serampore missionaries must be judged to have lost that crucial argument, although their case was later to be revived by such strange bedfellows as Bishop Steere in central Africa and James Hudson Taylor of the China Inland Mission.[62] For Nonconformist missions, the ecclesiological implications of the victory of committee rule were immense.

According to the Form of Agreement, European missionaries were to be discouraged from assuming the pastorates of native churches. Their functions were to be apostolic and episcopal, planting new congregations and exercising superintendence and discipline over existing churches. Although many Baptist missionaries, no less than those of other societies, subsequently found it impossible to resist the temptation to become pastors of indigenous congregations, the quasi-episcopal role which the Form of Agreement laid down for them was one that the successors of the Serampore Trio fulfilled to the letter, but with the major proviso that, with financial control firmly vested in London, the distinction between superintendence and interference was now almost impossible to maintain. Missionaries from Baptist and Congregational churches in Britain that would have strongly resisted any attempt to curtail their domestic ecclesiastical autonomy increasingly accepted the necessity and legitimacy of exercising control over indigenous churches. In 1867 the BMS Committee confessed to its shame that in the whole of its India field, it was not aware that, in a single church presided over by a native pastor, 'the Members have been instructed to elect

---

[60] Serampore missionaries to BMS sub-committee, 4 Sept. 1817, in Joseph Ivimey, ed., *Letters on the Serampore Controversy, Addressed to the Rev. Christopher Anderson* (London, 1831), p. 123.

[61] See Brian Stanley, *The History of the Baptist Missionary Society, 1792–1992* (Edinburgh, 1992), pp. 57–67.

[62] See Heanley, *Memoir of Edward Steere*, pp. 208, 240, 294–5, 302; Andrew Porter, 'Evangelical enthusiasm, missionary motivation and West Africa in the late nineteenth century: the career of G. W. Brooke', *Journal of Imperial and Commonwealth History*, 6 (1977), pp. 26–9.

Deacons, or permitted to exercise the full discipline of the Church, or that the Pastor has enjoyed the uncontrolled administration of the ordinances of the Gospel, apart from the immediate supervision of the Missionary.'[63] By the 1880s some Nonconformists were admitting openly that their historic polity was not workable on the mission field. Thus at the Centenary Conference in 1888 Robert Craig, a director of the LMS, asserted that, of all forms of church polity, the congregational system was the weakest, unless a high level of moral purity could be sustained among the members, a condition which he judged to be difficult to meet on the mission field without the firm hand of European superintendence.[64] At the same conference a representative from the Friends' Foreign Mission described the close relationship that existed in Madagascar between his own mission and the LMS, characterized the Malagasy church that was emerging as neither Independent nor Quaker nor episcopalian, though in some way it resembled all of these, and concluded by confessing that 'the Missionary is like a little Bishop', dispensing fatherly advice to the many congregations under his care.[65]

Nevertheless, objective missionary assessments of how far congregational church order was being modified by the dynamics of mission-church relationships remained rare. At Edinburgh in 1910 the report of Commission II on the Church in the Mission Field presented to the World Missionary Conference began by surveying the various forms of church organization being implemented on the field. The section on congregational polity held up the Serampore Form of Agreement (which was printed as an appendix) as a model of how missionaries adhering to congregational order exercised 'fostering parental influence, but do not officially govern'. There was only a limited recognition that the power of the mission, and specifically the power of the purse, sometimes 'obliterates for a time the line of demarcation between influence and control'.[66] The report did acknowledge that amongst churches of all denominations dependence on the

---

[63] BMSA, Sub-Committee Reports, Miscellaneous, 1863–7, circular letter dated 10 July 1867, p. 2; cited in Stanley, 'Self-governing churches', p. 382.

[64] Johnston, *Report of the Centenary Conference*, 2, pp. 365–6.

[65] Ibid., 2, pp. 361–2.

[66] World Missionary Conference 1910, 2, *Report of Commission II: The Church in the Mission Field* (Edinburgh and London, nd), pp. 15, 284–5.

advice of the missionary was in places strengthening, but saw this as a temporary consequence of the organic development of autonomous congregations towards organized regional or national churches.[67] The report often failed to penetrate beneath the surface appearance of a formal continuing fidelity to the historic polity of the sending church. Thus on the crucial question of admission to church membership it reproduced the answers of Baptist and Congregational missionaries that admission to church membership was, as in Britain, by the vote of the church meeting. Yet it also recorded an account by a Baptist missionary in the Congo of how applicants for baptism had to spend at least six months attending a Christian Endeavour class and pass weekly examinations, before their names could even be considered by the church meeting in the light of reports from the out-station teacher, native district superintendent, and, crucially, the visiting missionary. It also observed that Wesleyan Methodist missionaries, rather than adhering to the domestic practice of admitting new members on the vote of the leaders' meeting, conformed more closely to an episcopal rule, by vesting the right of admission in the native ministers and themselves, in consultation with the local evangelist.[68]

The Edinburgh Commission report exhibited a serene confidence that an autonomous church on the mission field was no longer a distant ideal, but a prospect already being realized.[69] It was assumed that the exercise of pastoral discipline was rapidly passing from mission to church, and that the days of missionary control wielded through the power of the purse were numbered.[70] This was an optimistic judgement, though undoubtedly rather more true of missions in Asia than of those in Africa; it is noteworthy that of the correspondents whose evidence was summarized by Commission II, 156 were serving in Asia, and only thirty-six in Africa.[71] Yet the report's confident assumptions about autonomous churches were belied by its candid admission that the organization of churches on the mission field still reflected Western patterns more closely than indigenous cultural

---

[67] Ibid., pp. 32–3.
[68] Ibid., pp. 52–3, 75.
[69] Ibid., p. 38.
[70] Ibid., pp. 95–6, 203–4.
[71] Ibid., pp. ix–xix.

norms: 'It is, we think, disappointing that the native mind in the countries concerned has not made a deeper mark on Church organisation.'[72] It was characteristic of the mood of Edinburgh that the fault was seen to lie, not with missionary dominance and inflexibility, but with the inadequate development of native spiritual and mental energy. Hence the indignant reaction of many of the conference delegates to V. S. Azariah's famous and impassioned complaint that the prevailing relationship of missionary to Indian worker was still one of paymaster to servant rather than one of friend to friend.[73]

The appropriate conclusion to draw from such evidence as that supplied by Edinburgh 1910 might, therefore, appear to be that the reshaping of Christian tradition consequent upon its missionary transmission from West to East was of a minor and relatively superficial kind. It can be conceded that Anglicans were becoming more voluntaristic while Free Churchmen were inclining towards functional episcopacy. Equally there is no doubt that it was this convergence that made church union on the basis of a constitutional episcopate possible in both South and North India.[74] But it could be objected – as indeed it has been by such diverse critics as D. M. Devasahayam in South India and John Kent in Britain – that the resulting amalgam had more to do with Western denominational politics than with authentic Indian aspirations.[75] It is easy for the mission historian to forget the truism that denominational traditions were evolving in Europe and the USA as well as on the mission field. In Britain the logic of the Evangelical Revival had impelled Baptists and Congregationalists in the direction of more coherent national organization for the sake of mission, with significant long-term implications for their ecclesiology.[76] Similarly, in the USA both Episcopalians and Congregationalists had moved some way from

---

[72] Ibid., p. 12.

[73] World Missionary Conference 1910, 9, *The History and Records of the Conference* (Edinburgh and London, nd), pp. 306–15; W. H. T. Gairdner, *'Edinburgh 1910': An Account and Interpretation of the World Missionary Conference* (Edinburgh and London, 1910), pp. 109–11; Williams, *The Ideal of the Self-Governing Church*, p. 228.

[74] For North India see the comments of the chief Baptist negotiator from 1955 to 1964, Leslie Wenger, in *Church Union News and Views*, Feb. 1956, p. 6.

[75] See n. 46 above, and John Kent, *The Unacceptable Face: The Modern Church in the Eyes of the Historian* (London, 1987), pp. 208–9.

[76] See Thompson, *Denominationalism and Dissent*, passim.

the historic polities of their British denominational parents in the direction of a Presbyterian model.[77] It was no accident that the most vocal Nonconformist advocates of episcopacy in South India were New England Congregationalists who were very far from seeing themselves as a beleaguered dissenting minority and whose denomination was among the first to respond to the statements on reunion made by the 1908 Lambeth Conference.[78]

These qualifications are weighty and not to be ignored. From the standpoint of present-day concerns in the Two-Thirds World to develop authentic indigenous expressions of Christian life and theology, the remoulding of Western denominational traditions in the missionary era may appear insubstantial. The first impression made on a British visitor to many Baptist churches in modern Zaire, for example, is that their patterns of worship are a depressingly faithful reflection of those that obtained in British Baptist life in the 1940s or 1950s. However, too glib a dismissal of the impact of the mission process on the character of non-Western Christianity is perilous, for it is liable to miss three points of abiding and fundamental importance.

The first is to underline the significance of the increasing scepticism apparent within Nonconformist circles by the end of the nineteenth century about the viability of traditional congregational polity on the mission field. In the period before the First World War, fears similar to those that caused Anglicans in the aftermath of the Bishop Crowther affair on the Niger to hang back from the cultivation of an indigenous episcopate inclined Nonconformist missionaries to retain control of the crucial functions of church discipline and ordination, and to restrict the implementation of forms of church order that gave ultimate power to the gathered congregation.[79] Sherwood Eddy's remarks in 1911 on the unfitness of Asians for democracy provide one articulated instance of views that were more often implicit: non-Western people who were still young in the faith simply could not be trusted to manage their own affairs without the

---

[77] Briggs, *Church Unity*, pp. 78–9.

[78] Sundkler, *Church of South India*, pp. 63–4; see Ruth Rouse and Stephen Charles Neill, eds, *A History of the Ecumenical Movement, 1517–1948* (London, 1954), p. 408.

[79] For the Anglican case, see Williams, *The Ideal of the Self-Governing Church*, chs IV to VI; for two Nonconformist examples see Stanley, 'Planting self-governing churches', pp. 381–5, and Goodall, *History of the LMS*, pp. 95–100.

guiding hand of one who had the office, if not also the name, of a bishop, and one suspects that Eddy assumed that the bishop would normally be an expatriate for the foreseeable future. What is abundantly clear is that many of those who became Christians in Congregational and Baptist churches in Asia and Africa in this period perceived power to flow downwards from missionary society to missionary to church officers to native congregation, rather than upwards from the congregation to its elected leaders. This perception has inevitably affected the ecclesiology of the autonomous churches that have emerged from the missionary era. In Mobutu's Zaire, the Baptist churches founded by the BMS have since 1972 formed one Baptist community within a single national Protestant church, the *Église du Christ au Zaire*.[80] Within the context of a large and disparate nation held together by the cult of an autocratic leader, it is clear that for local Baptist members the leaders of the Baptist community and Protestant church in distant Kinshasa have come to play the role formerly occupied by the BMS committee in even more distant London.

A similar pattern has been observed even in cases where a modern African church owes its origins to a secession from missionary control. Donald Mackay has argued that the Kimban-guist movement in Bas-Zaire, progenitor of the largest inde-pendent church in modern Africa, derived its structures of power substantially from the model supplied by the Baptist mission, as interpreted through the lens of the cosmological beliefs of the Bakongo people.[81] Power over the local Baptist congregation was exercised by the local deacon; he was in turn responsible to the central mission church, where the word of the missionary was law; yet the missionaries themselves were subject to the power of the BMS committee in London, whose authority to do the work of God was believed to be bestowed by God himself. W. Holman Bentley, the leading BMS missionary on the lower Congo, noted in 1899 that the Bakongo Christians felt that 'the majority of the missionaries have the power of the keys and can bind or loose eternally'.[82] Even though the missionaries them-

---

[80] See Stanley, *History of the BMS*, pp. 447–50, 458–9.

[81] D. J. Mackay, 'Simon Kimbangu and the B. M. S. tradition', *Journal of Religion in Africa*, 17, 2 (June 1987), pp. 113–71.

[82] Cited in ibid., p. 116.

selves disclaimed such a theory of absolute apostolic power, they were unable to rid their people of such an un-Baptist perception. Thus, when in 1921 their young convert from Nkamba, Simon Kimbangu, found his claims to a supernatural ministry of healing and raising from the dead repudiated by the BMS missionaries, his followers within the Baptist churches of the lower Congo transferred to the prophet that unique apostolic authority which hitherto they had vested in the missionary tradition. The majority of the Baptist church membership of the Ngombe Lutete district now found in the person of Kimbangu a substitute for the BMS committee as a proximate authority to God, and moved into schism.[83]

A second point to emphasize in conclusion is that overseas mission experience did compel at least some Western observers to acknowledge the momentous possibility that their whole thinking on church order, whether Catholic or Protestant, was partial because it was contingent upon a particular historical and cultural tradition. Within the Roman Catholic Church, the most notable first step in this direction was the serious attention given at the Second Vatican Council to the figure of the catechist, so central to Catholicism in Africa, and to the question of whether some catechists should be admitted to a restored permanent diaconate.[84] But the status of catechist or evangelist is only one example of the widening of the ecclesiological agenda. One of the most prescient statements on ecumenical affairs made in that *annus mirabilis* of 1910 came from the lips of the SPG missionary, Herbert Pakenham-Walsh, when addressing the Bangalore missionary conference in November. Pakenham-Walsh predicted that one of the issues that would have to be addressed in the future if progress towards unity were to be sustained was the question of charismatic or irregular ministries.[85] Pakenham-Walsh made approving reference to Charles Gore's work on *Orders and Unity*, with its emphasis on the importance and legitimacy of the prophetic ministry of the Spirit in the early centuries.[86] This was a theme which was sporadically taken up by

---

[83] Ibid., pp. 131–6, 153–6; Stanley, *History of the BMS*, pp. 343–4.

[84] *Ad Gentes Divinitus*, 16–17, in Austin Flannery, ed., *Vatican Council II: The Conciliar and Post Conciliar Documents* (Leominster, 1975), pp. 832–4; see Aylward Shorter and Eugene Kataza, eds, *African Catechists Today* (London, 1972), pp. 78–82, 103–18.

[85] H. Pakenham-Walsh, 'Some problems of unity', *HF*, 31 (1911), p. 29.

[86] Charles Gore, *Orders and Unity* (London, 1909), pp. 135–40.

other Anglo-Catholic spokesmen in India, notably by Bishop E. J. Palmer of Bombay. Although more consistent in his continuing adherence to Catholic principles than Henry Whitehead, Palmer was insistent that a future united church in India ought to include provision for the ministry of prophets as a distinct order.[87]

These fragmentary perceptions of what might be an appropriate pattern of church order for a future Indian church were not translated into reality, any more than was Whitehead's advocacy in 1935 of a ministerial order of teachers. It was, of course, in Africa rather than India that these questions were to become most insistent, as both Evangelical and Catholic missions attempted to respond to the challenge of independent churches which accorded prophetic and charismatic ministries a centrality rarely seen in Christendom since the days of the Montanists. The reaction of missionaries to phenomena that had no parallel in their own experience was not so universally hostile as might be supposed. The BMS missionary at São Salvador, just over the border into Portuguese Congo from Ngombe Lutete, was a staunch Ulster Calvinist trained at Spurgeon's College, Robert Haldane Carson Graham.[88] Graham's response to the host of 'minor prophets' who sprang up in Kimbangu's wake in 1921 was initially to welcome their apparent biblical orthodoxy and evangelistic power, even though he remained sceptical about the validity of the signs and wonders which were being attributed to them.[89] Only when it became clear that the prophets were usurping Baptist ecclesiology by claiming direct spiritual authority to admit to church membership, exercise church discipline, appoint church officers, and to perform marriages did Graham influence the São Salvador church to take a firm, but still sympathetic, stand against the prophets.[90]

In modern times it was the church on the mission field which first had to grapple seriously with the theological and ecclesio-

[87] See Sundkler, *Church of South India*, pp. 118, 162.

[88] See Thomas Lewis, *These Seventy Years: An Autobiography* (London, 1930), pp. 127–8. The Angolan nationalist leader, Holden Roberto, was named after Graham.

[89] For Graham's initial assessment see *Missionary Herald*, Oct. 1921, pp. 192–3; BMSA, São Salvador church meeting minutes, 7 June 1921.

[90] BMSA, São Salvador deacons' meeting minutes, 29 June 1921; church meeting minutes, 5 July 1921.

logical issues raised by charismatic phenomena, issues that now face many of the Western churches as what was once Christendom emerges from the age of the Enlightenment to the new mission context of postmodernity. For this reason, amongst others, it would be profoundly misleading to conclude from the evidence we have surveyed that the sole or even the primary effect of the mission process on Christianity has been to homogenize it, making Catholics more evangelical and Evangelicals more catholic. Whilst that statement seems to me to hold as a useful generalization about trends within the European missionary tradition, it needs to be balanced by a contrary emphasis which, although not my primary concern on this occasion, is of such importance that it must sound the final note of this discussion.

The transmission of Christianity from West to East and North to South was always a far broader and more variegated process than the story of what European missionaries did, said and believed. As Richard Gray has stressed in relation to Africa, the Christianity that was planted in the non-Western world was never synonymous with the missionaries' understanding of the faith.[91] In Africa above all, missionary personnel were never numerous enough to hog the process of evangelization to themselves. Even in India, where missionaries were more heavily concentrated than anywhere else, there were in 1941 only 1,266 ordained missionaries serving a non-Roman Christian community of approximately four million.[92] The crucial agents in the propagation of Christianity in both Asia and Africa were neither missionaries nor indigenous priests and ministers – whose numbers in the Protestant churches were extremely small throughout the colonial period – but rather those described in the Catholic tradition as catechists and in Protestantism more often as evangelists and teachers.[93] Many of those had little or no formal theological training, and only minimal Christian literature beyond a vernacular Bible (in part or in whole) and perhaps a

---

[91] Richard Gray, *Black Christians and White Missionaries* (New Haven, Conn., and London, 1990), p. 84.

[92] C. W. Ranson, *The Christian Minister in India: His Vocation and Training* (London and Redhill, 1945), pp. 67, 71.

[93] Gray, *Black Christians and White Missionaries*, pp. 80–1. For a detailed study of a notable case see M. Louise Pirouet, *Black Evangelists: The Spread of Christianity in Uganda, 1891–1914* (London, 1978).

vernacular hymnbook. They have been the crucial actors in that process of vernacularization, and hence cultural diversification, which Lamin Sanneh has identified as the hallmark of Christian, as opposed to Islamic, expansion in modern Africa.[94] The evidence of rapid and continuing church growth in the post-colonial era in Africa and significant parts of East Asia would suggest that, contrary to the pessimism of many theological commentators, Christianity is being indigenized in the Two-Thirds World to an extent that would have gladdened the hearts of Alexander Waugh and his LMS colleagues. The reshaping of Christian tradition in the non-Western world may yet turn out to be infinitely more significant than the convergence of early twentieth-century missionary minds on the question of a constitutional episcopate.

Trinity College, Bristol

[94] See Lamin Sanneh, *Translating the Message: The Missionary Impact on Culture* (Maryknoll, NY, 1990).

# MOTHER CHURCH AND COLONIAL DAUGHTERS: NEW SCOPE FOR TENSIONS IN ANGLICAN UNITY AND DIVERSITY

by ROBERT S. M. WITHYCOMBE

Nova Scotia and Quebec were the only two overseas Anglican bishoprics in 1800, besides the eleven in the USA. By 1900 there were ninety-three overseas Anglican bishops, as well as the seventy-two in the home and missionary dioceses of the USA Church.[1] Rapidly expanding colonial and missionary work was an essential element in the life of all nineteenth-century British Churches. Each by 1900 supported denominational and interdenominational missionary societies and encouraged local congregational missionary activities. Here and in fostering emigration to colonies, each British Church willingly took its part in fulfilling British imperial ideals.

This overseas dimension of recent British religious life is still arguably a relatively unexplored historical terrain.[2] There have been histories of the missionary societies, some critical, others more triumphalist.[3] Most general histories of British religious or church life make overseas activities appear as peripheral as the church bazaars which their need for support proliferated.

Some general Anglican histories focus on the Lambeth Conferences, often in a search for a common Anglican identity. The agenda of these Conferences, however, like early Tridentine sessions, were often unduly governed by the preoccupations of those who could afford to attend. The interests of more remote

---

[1] See *Crockford's Clerical Directory*, 1900 and 1901.

[2] S. C. Carpenter, *Church and People, 1789–1889* (London, 1933), refers briefly to Anglican colonial churches in Part 3, pp. 428–63; W. O. Chadwick, *The Victorian Church*, 2 vols (London, 1966–70), recognizes the overseas dimension in his introduction to vol. 1 (p. 6), but chooses not to examine it; Roger Lloyd, *The Church of England, 1900–1965* (London, 1966), refers to Anglican feats in missionary conferences and in their Church in South Africa (e.g., chs 20 and 24); and Adrian Hastings's more recent *A History of English Christianity, 1920–1985* (London, 1986) makes brief reference to 'missionary enterprise' (p. 714). They are more histories of the Christianity in England than of English Christianity. William L. Sachs's recent *The Transformation of Anglicanism* (Cambridge, 1993) is a welcome advance in mapping this terrain.

[3] Compare, e.g., Eugene Stock, *The History of the Church Missionary Society*, 3 vols (London, 1899), or Gordon Hewitt, *The Problems of Success: A History of the Church Missionary Society, 1910–1942* (London, 1971), and Mary Geraldine Taylor, *The Story of the China Inland Mission*, 2 vols (London, 1893–4).

427

colonial and missionary churches were under-represented in proportion to the numerical dominance of the British and US episcopate. No history of Lambeth Conferences is a substitute for comparative studies of the experience of the colonial church leaders themselves. This paper is a plea that this be done. Such studies will supply ample instances of the tensions of unity and diversity. Here are some.

Colonial and missionary churches faced from their earliest days an inevitable task of acclimatization: adapting British religious traditions to survive in unfamiliar physical, social, and political circumstances – a Darwinian process for diversity! Colonial and missionary churches adapted while being still largely dependent for funds and human resources on the home churches, with whom they prudently affirmed a close and fundamental unity. Missionaries did not always distinguish their gospel from British civilization; and their diverse activities and priorities were often governed by meeting the expectations of the one home board or committee who paid them.

Religion is an important part of the nexus of all migrant communities with their mother culture. Religion was (and still is) an essential part of ethnic identity in Australian, New Zealand and Canadian settlements. Religion defined and sustained cultural identity. Nevertheless, pastoral experience had often contradicted this. Colonial church leaders were appalled at the religious apathy of many immigrants, an indifference perceived even earlier by chaplains on emigrant ships, and by those wishing to retain the religious allegiance of emigrants after arrival and dispersal.[4] Such experiences in turn offer an interesting perspective on home religious allegiance. Most early residents in Australian and Canadian colonies were not 'Mayflower' religious refugees.

Have Commonwealth Studies (or whatever they are now called) always paid sufficient attention to this religious strand in the multicore cable of the home–colonial nexus? The transfer of the Westminster political system, of the British legal traditions, and of systems of education at all levels, have all been surveyed, as have imperial defence and the imperial economy. Why the

---

[4] For the experience of some early chaplains, see extracts from their letters in *Occasional Papers from St Augustine's College, Canterbury*, especially nos 6 and 9; and in London, Lambeth Palace Library [hereafter 'LPL'], Papers of Archbishop Howley [hereafter 'Howley Papers'], 1, fols 705–19, 819–27, and LPL, Papers of Archbishop Tait [hereafter 'Tait Papers'], 270, fols 217–355.

religious strand seems to have received less attention itself warrants examination.

Most Anglican colonial bishops (those in Australia and New Zealand at least) expressed the strong desire to stand as one with their home Church in England – in doctrine and worship, if not in discipline. Throughout the later nineteenth century there was continual debate about *how* this unity was best achieved. Bishops, senior clergy, and laity all differed over how to sustain a common identity against forces for greater political and ecclesiastical independence.[5]

Controversy over how far home traditions of church discipline could be sustained in colonial churches erupted under Bishop Gray in South Africa. From there matters were taken on appeal to the Judicial Committee of the Privy Council. Its decisions in Long *vs* the Bishop of Capetown (in 1863) and the related Colenso Judgement (in 1865) brought to prominence issues of the unity and independence of home and colonial Churches, and accelerated diverse responses. The decision to uphold Bishop Colenso's appeal against his metropolitan Bishop Gray's attempt to remove him from office indicated that the powers conferred on colonial bishops under Royal Letters Patent on consecration were no longer legally valid in those colonies possessing a degree of legislative independence. Such powers needed to be redefined in relation to the new local legislatures.[6] In a later judgement that established Bishop Colenso's legal rights to the income of the endowments of his Bishopric of Natal, Lord Romilly, the Master of the Rolls, argued strongly for the supremacy of statute and court-interpreted law, commending it as the basis and bond of Anglican Church unity.[7]

Home Church members disagreed, however, over the authority of the Judicial Committee and its decisions, and over the dominance Parliament had exercised over the Church of England – since 1688, if not since the Henrician Reformation 150 years earlier. Such sensitivities were inflamed by the High-Church or Catholic revivals associated with the Oxford

---

[5] See, e.g., LPL, Tait Papers, vol. 160 *passim*, and below.

[6] The Judicial Committee's Colenso judgement, dated 20 March 1865, is quoted in *Law Journal Reports for the Year 1867*, 45, ns 36, Part 1, pp.9–10.

[7] *Law Reports: Equity Cases before the Master of the Rolls and the Vice Chancellors*, 3, 1866–7 [30 Victoriae], pp. 33ff.

Movement. So, while some colonial bishops, conservative in church forms and practice, sought security and unity in obedience to a very legal Royal Supremacy, as expressed and defined in English courts,[8] others sought opportunities to challenge home church practices they considered 'Erastian', 'Reformation', or 'Protestant' and to approximate colonial church practices to more 'Catholic' norms. Accordingly Bishop Gray of Capetown, with the support of a majority of the bishops in the Canterbury Convocation, proceeded in apparent schism to consecrate a successor to Bishop Colenso in defiance of the Judicial Committee's decision.[9] In New Zealand, following the Colenso Judgement, the Anglican bishops offered to resign their Letters Patent, and (under Selwyn's more Tractarian leadership) asserted their inherent right and power to function as a branch of the Christian Church without the sanction of the state.[10] Bishop Tyrrell, of Newcastle in New South Wales (NSW), seemed in 1867 to follow a similar line of argument, as did Bishop C. H. Bromby of Tasmania, though more cautiously.[11] Diversity of opinion at home often took more concrete form in the colonies.

The Colonial Office also fostered diversity in home and colonial Church life. Successive Secretaries of State for the Colonies (and especially their Colonial Office advisers) appear to have developed their own policies on British chaplaincies and colonial churches. Neither the Bishop of London nor the Archbishop of Canterbury were in early years widely consulted on candidates for episcopal appointment.[12] When Edward Cardwell in 1865

[8] See letters in LPL, Tait Papers of Charles Perry, Bishop of Melbourne [1866], 160, fols 55–8; of Frederick Barker, Metropolitan and Bishop of Sydney [1866], ibid., fols 20–1; [1868] 169, fols 5–6; and of William Macquarie Cowper, Dean of Sydney [1866], 160, fols 24–7.

[9] For Gray's initiatives, see P. Hinchliff, *The One-Sided Reciprocity: a Study in the Modification of the Establishment* (London, 1966), pp. 155–6, and ch. 6, *passim*. Archbishop Longley supported Gray; Bishop Tait of London did not: see LPL, Tait Papers, 144, fols 322–6, Tait to Sir George Grey, 3 May 1866.

[10] See opinions of G. A. Selwyn in 1866, LPL, Papers of Archbishop C. T. Longley [hereafter 'Longley Papers'], 7, fols 199–202; of C. J. Abraham, Bishop of Wellington, and of his diocesan synod in July 1867, in ibid., 4, fols 322–3, 331–6, and in LPL, Tait Papers, 160, fols 151–2; of W. Williams, Bishop of Waiapu (1867), ibid., fols 160–1; H. J. C. Harper, Bishop of Christchurch (1867), ibid., fols 138–41; and of Octavius Hadfield, Archdeacon of Otaki (1867), ibid., fols 153–4.

[11] For Tyrrell see LPL, Tait Papers, 160, fols 28–9, and 170, fols 74–5; and for Bromby, LPL, Tait Papers, 160, fols 15–18.

[12] See LPL, Longley Papers, 3, fol. 5, Duke of Newcastle, Secretary of State for the Colonies, to E. Hawkins, Secretary, Colonial Bishoprics Council, 24 February 1863, and PRO, 30/6/138, fols 76–8, Earl of Carnarvon, Colonial Secretary, to Lord Derby, Prime Minister, 20 August 1866 (copy, among Carnarvon Papers).

drafted a Bill to resolve *inter alia* the uncertainties about the powers of colonial bishops that the Colenso Judgement had uncovered, his efforts aroused vigorous opposition and further bouts of mid-Victorian religious anxiety in home and colonial Church leaders. Some were alarmed that the initiative should be his, others at the solutions his draft legislation proposed. The Lambeth Palace archives record much diversity amongst the alternatives that were proposed.[13]

Hitherto, responsibility within the Church of England for colonial churches had been assumed by the Bishop of London. (This is reflected in the Fulham Palace archives and in the Lambeth papers of Howley and Tait, for example.) The Archbishops of Canterbury at first related to the home government, not to colonial churches directly. That was to change. Howley and then Tait had been active Bishops of London before appointment to Canterbury. Both continued to express an active personal interest in colonial churches.[14] Responsibility for convening the Lambeth Conferences after 1867 further contributed to the elevation of the Archbishop of Canterbury as the Patriarch of a world-wide Anglican Communion. Not all archbishops were willing or able to sustain these quasi-patriarchal expectations. Archbishop Benson (1883–96) was more reluctant or ambivalent, and this may have led some to see the Lambeth Conferences as a more conciliar and alternative point of focus and authority.

Further tensions in unity and diversity are reflected in the way English bishops shared their archbishops' conservative and paradoxical reluctance to relinquish their influence over the policy and leadership of daughter colonial churches. Appointment to colonial sees was often delegated formally to certain English bishops by colonial churches, and after 1870 by Colonial Secretaries informally to the Archbishop.[15] These bishops intervened

---

[13] For the content of Cardwell's Bill, see UK *Hansard*, 3rd ser., 183, 1032–4 (15 May 1866), and for its fate, 187, 761–2 (20 May 1867). For colonial responses, see LPL, Tait Papers, 160, *passim*.

[14] See LPL, Tait Papers, 144, fols 322–6.

[15] At Bishop Barker's suggestion, Longley nominated Mesac Thomas to the Colonial Secretary for appointment by the Crown as first Bishop of Goulbourn, NSW: LPL, Tait Papers, 129, fols 396–7. Similarly, Barker recommended S. E. Marsden for Tait to recommend to the Colonial Secretary for nomination to the Queen as first Bishop of Bathurst, NSW: LPL, Tait Papers, 171, fols 284–5. Nelson Diocese in 1864 delegated to Tait, as Bishop of London, the power to nominate Bishop Hobhouse's successor to the Colonial Secretary: LPL, Tait Papers, 158, fols 42–4. On principle, Cardwell looked increasingly to the Archbishop of Canterbury and the Bishop of London for nominees for colonial bishoprics: see LPL, Tait Papers, 158, fols 91–2, Cardwell, CO, to Tait, 27 August 1865.

in support of Gray of Capetown, and in support of Jenner as first Bishop of Dunedin.[16] With some show of humility, Tait wrote as Bishop of London to all Anglican diocesan bishops in October 1866 requesting their views on certain questions about critical issues of preserving Anglican unity and diversity. Matters of dispute were often referred to the English episcopate for decision.[17] The financial power of the Society for the Propagation of the Gospel, and of the Colonial Bishoprics Fund, further augmented home church controls over colonial church life.

The policies of these home bishops were also governed by local political expediencies. The initiative of the state, which reduced the episcopate in the Irish Church Establishment in 1833, entirely disestablished that Church in 1869–70. The Liberation Society's clamorous activities in and out of Parliament in this period (and later the ambiguity of the Liberal Party's platform in 1881 on disestablishment) converted every colonial disestablishment, or move towards greater constitutional autonomy, into a potential model for political action at home. The cessation of funding for Church of England chaplains in Crown colonies like Hong Kong, Malacca, the Straits Settlements, and also in Ceylon (like the earlier treatment of clergy reserves in Canada and in NSW, and the extension of public funding to other denominations, as in the NSW Church Act of 1836), were often read by those so minded as ominous harbingers of what radical Parliamentary dominance might achieve at home.[18] On the other hand, the capacity of the colonial churches to achieve a greater degree of constitutional autonomy – often, as in New Zealand's case, with an eye to the model of the Protestant Episcopal Church of the USA (PECUSA) – added to the frustrations of those who sought similar rights and liberties at home, and strengthened the arguments of those who believed the church healthier by separation from state control. In England the legal legacies of the Reformation Settlements, like the suspicions of Dissent, were a political reality that the English archbishops

---

[16] On Capetown see Hinchliff, *The One-Sided Reciprocity*; idem, *The Anglican Church in South Africa* (London, 1963), pp. 48ff., 91ff., on the H. L. Jenner case, see LPL, Tait Papers, 170, fols 1–38; 178, fols 305–50; 195, fols 233–63; 201, fols 203–44; 214, fols 161–4.

[17] See, e.g., LPL, Tait Papers, 194, fols 5–10, Charles Perry, Melbourne, to A. C. Tait, Lambeth, 19 April 1873, on colonial ecumenical relationships.

[18] For correspondence on the Straits Settlements, see LPL, Tait Papers, 288, fols 206–32.

did not wish to ignore, divisive and frustrating to many as they were. Archbishop Sumner's attempts to pass an Imperial Bill allowing colonial churches powers of self-government were frustrated in 1853. When he proceeded very cautiously to revive his own Canterbury Convocation in 1855–6, the Archbishop of York refused to sanction any debates in his. Diocesan synods were, however, already being held in New Zealand after 1844 and in South Africa by 1857 (without state sanction), and in Canadian and Australian colonies after 1856, some by 'consensual compact', others with some statutory recognition.[19]

Studying the processes of episcopal appointment to colonial churches reveals how each colony had its own variation on home–colonial church relationships, and shows how home and colonial bishops themselves entertained differing views on how unity and diversity were best maintained.

There were usually two distinct viewpoints. The first affirmed the integral unity and legal identity of the Church of England in the colonies with the United Church of England and Ireland, as it then was, in Britain. Holders of this view sought to reinforce this union in several ways: (i) through ultimate recourse to a home court of final appeal, if only to enforce contracts negotiated between church officers in the colonies; (ii) through seeking to retain as necessary the Crown's Mandate for the consecration of each new colonial bishop (however selected); and (iii) through each metropolitan (if not each bishop) receiving mission from, and pledging allegiance to, the see of Canterbury. Several who espoused this viewpoint also called on the home church and government to preserve this union through imperial or local colonial legislation designed to bestow or restore those powers (which the Royal Letters Patent were hitherto believed to convey) on colonial bishops as Church of England bishops now resident in self-governing colonies.

The second basic viewpoint foresaw an emerging pattern of daughter churches taking the initiative to become more

[19] For J. B. Sumner's Colonial Church Regulations Bill, see *Colonial Church Chronicle*, 6 (1853), p. 81; and for debates on it, see UK *Hansard*, 3rd ser., 129, 512–33 (21 July 1853), 1207–14 (2 August 1853). For the growth of colonial synodical self-government, see H. L. Clarke, *Constitutional Church Government* (London, 1924). Australian issues are well discussed in J. T. R. Border, *Church and State in Australia, 1788–1872* (London, 1962), pp. 190ff. On the later constitutional history of the Church of England in Tasmania and the Australian colonies, John Davis, *Australian Anglicans and their Constitution* (East Brunswick, 1993) is illuminating.

independent branches of the Church of England, bound to the mother church not by state-imposed law but by affection, sound commonsense, and loyalty, each voluntarily adopting in its constitution as fundamental provisions, and agreeing to be governed by, the doctrinal and liturgical standards of the Church of England. They would also then adopt and subscribe to her disciplinary traditions, so far as they were applicable in varied colonial circumstances.

How the Colonial Office distanced itself from these processes and consequently changed them is well illustrated by the Metropolitan Bishop of Montreal's 1868 account of the transition in the Canadian Church: 'The first impression here was that the powers vested in the Synods in the Election of Bishops only went as far as giving a right of nomination – but that the sanction of the Crown was necessary, and a Royal mandate to enable the Bishop-Elect to obtain Consecration . . .'[20] Accordingly, when Benjamin Cronyn became the first Anglican Bishop elected in Canada (for the new diocese of Huron) in 1857, the election was notified to the Governor-General asking him to forward it to the Queen, requesting that she license the consecration. Doubts about the Canadian Church's autonomy were still sufficient for Cronyn to be sent to England for consecration, with Letters Patent and Royal Mandate, at Lambeth, on 28 October 1857. When the diocese of Ontario was formed in 1862, and Dr Lewis elected by the Synod, the Governor-General was similarly notified. The Queen issued a Patent in the normal way, establishing and defining the diocese of Ontario, and appointing Lewis as first Bishop. In 1860, however, the Queen had formally constituted these five dioceses into a province, appointing Montreal as Metropolitan See. When Royal authority was given to the Archbishop of Canterbury to secure Lewis's consecration, he on this occasion transmitted it to Fulford as Metropolitan. Dr Lewis was then consecrated at Kingston by Fulford and his suffragans. When Bishop Mountain of Quebec died in 1863, the Quebec Diocesan Synod elected Dr J. W. Williams, and wrote to Fulford (then in England) to arrange for his consecration. A petition was again sent to the Queen notifying her of the election and seeking

[20] LPL, Tait Papers, 170, fols 411–16, F. Fulford, Bishop of Montreal, to Tait, Bishop of London, 31 July 1868.

434

as usual her Mandate and Letters Patent. The Crown Law Officers advised Her Majesty, however, not to issue Letters Patent, as they were deemed (by recent Privy Council decisions) no longer to have any force for bishops located in self-governing colonies. Nevertheless a Royal Mandate was issued, but to Fulford and not to the Archbishop of Canterbury. Fulford complied in Quebec on 21 June 1863 acting, that is, under Royal Mandate but without Letters Patent since (as he believed) it was for diocesan synods (under the Canadian Synod Acts) to define and provide the powers of coercive jurisdiction.

Finally, when in 1866 Archdeacon Bethune was elected Coadjutor Bishop of the diocese of Toronto, the Synod again petitioned the Queen (on Fulford's advice) for a Royal Mandate to consecrate, as they had done with Bishop Williams of Quebec. When Fulford had applied to the Colonial Office for this, Lord Carnarvon told him the Crown Law Officers were all of the opinion that there were no longer means of enforcing such a mandate and that the Provincial Synod already possessed sufficient powers to proceed without one. Fulford reported that this had not been his own nor his Diocesan Chancellor's view, and concluded his report regretfully: 'Our present independence, so far as it exists, was never contemplated or sought for by us – it has gradually been developed and we accept it – and try to make the best of it.'[21]

Many colonial dioceses in Australia and New Zealand (such as Nelson in 1865) chose to delegate the appointment of their bishops to a panel of English bishops. Others were content to ensure each bishop was consecrated by Canterbury and believed that if each bishop swore an oath of canonical obedience to him that would strengthen and secure Anglican unity.[22] The New Zealand Church ordained its own bishops when occasion demanded. Selwyn told Tait in 1870 that where English bishops appointed, 'they ought to show their full approval by consecrating' a bishop, as they had in the case of Bishops Harper and Hobhouse.[23] Was he tongue-in-cheek? Abraham of Wellington

---

[21] Ibid.

[22] As with the new NSW dioceses of Goulbourn (1863), Bathurst (1869–70), and Grafton and Armidale (1868–70).

[23] LPL, Tait Papers, 171, fols 29–31, G. A. Selwyn, Bishop of Lichfield, to Archbishop Tait, 12 December 1870.

had been elected in New Zealand, but consecrated in England while on sick leave. William Williams had only lately returned from England when elected to Waiapu, so was consecrated in New Zealand. Selwyn himself had already, along with his suffragans, previously used his 'inherent power' in 1858 to consecrate Patteson as first Missionary Bishop of Melanesia.[24]

Following the Colenso Judgement, therefore, the Colonial Office no longer equipped colonial bishops with Letters Patent. This had strange results in New South Wales. When Dr Sawyer, the first Bishop of Grafton, drowned crossing the shoals at the entrance of a coastal river in his NSW diocese, twelve months after his arrival in that colony, he had never been officially installed in his see. In the absence of Letters Patent no agreed alternative procedure existed that defined his territorial responsibilities and his relationship to his Metropolitan. Until these were clarified from England, his Metropolitan had refused to install him.[25]

Gradually Archbishop Tait helped devise new processes for appointing colonial bishops, observing due form at home and securing local colonial approval.[26] It was a delicate and precarious arrangement between home and colonial churches, where not preserving the dignity as well as the legal processes of each threatened division. The hazards were real, as the sad case of Bishop Jenner of Dunedin demonstrated.[27]

Following his usual unilateral practice in creating new bishoprics, Bishop Selwyn of New Zealand asked Archbishop Longley to find a bishop for the new diocese Selwyn was anxious to establish in Otago and Southland at Dunedin. Distance increased

---

[24] LPL, Longley Papers, 7, fols 199–202, G. A. Selwyn, Bishop of New Zealand, to C. T. Longley, Archbishop of Canterbury, 4 January 1866 (Abraham was consecrated [as Selwyn had been] at Lambeth, on 29 September 1858; Williams at Wellington, N.Z., on 3 April 1859.)

[25] LPL, Tait Papers, 170, fols 59–60, F. Barker, Metropolitan and Bishop of Sydney, to H. E. the Earl of Belmore, Governor of NSW, 24 January 1868 (copy). Sawyer had been consecrated by Longley on 2 February 1867, by Royal Mandate but without Letters Patent.

[26] See correspondence in LPL, Tait Papers, 170, fols 70–5, 84–5; 171, fols 282–316.

[27] The Jenner case is well discussed in W. P. Morrell, *The Anglican Church in New Zealand: a History* (Dunedin, 1973), pp. 91–6, more sympathetically to Jenner's cause in John H. Evans, *Southern See* (Dunedin, 1968), esp. chs 1–3, and more recently in John Pearce, ed., *Seeking a See: Journal of the Rt Revd Henry Lascelles Jenner, DD, of his Visit to Dunedin in 1868–69* (Dunedin, 1984).

delays. The new New Zealand Provincial Constitution of 1865 was unfamiliar to Canterbury and (it seems) to Selwyn. Amidst the usual delays in gaining legal approval of H. L. Jenner's nomination and consecration, Archbishop Longley was outraged to discover the encouragement Jenner was giving to those 'ritualist' practices then being made so sensitive by English Ritual Commission Reports and by the English bishops' attempts to contain them. News of Jenner's supposed 'Romanizing' proclivities was communicated by Longley to representatives of the Church in Dunedin and Southland, set amidst a vigorously Presbyterian colony.[28] This, and tenuous and uncertain financial arrangements for funding a new see, together with assertions of New Zealand Church independence, led to the unhappy outcome of Jenner's rejection by the New Zealand Church. When a New Zealand Synod shortly afterwards selected S. T. Nevill as their first Bishop of Dunedin, the English bishops rushed to avoid another schism, affirming the validity of Jenner's earlier consecration as Bishop of Dunedin, and recognizing Nevill as second Bishop. New Zealand church leaders adamantly opposed this unilateral judgement by the English bishops, whose opinion reflected as much their respect and admiration for Selwyn (now Bishop of Lichfield and no neutral party) as their sense of natural justice towards Jenner.[29] Jenner thereafter remained a bishop without a see, sad, obdurate, and driven toward eccentricity. His partisan supporters still remain within the New Zealand Church. The New Zealand Church, however, did not experience schism as did the contemporary Church in South Africa.

A sense of colonial independence and self-identity emerged in these complex processes, whether in making episcopal appointments for the colonies, in securing proper approval by diocesan and national synods and the local episcopate, or in the difficulties in finding good men in England willing to leave the *cursus honorum* for less glorious colonial service. This sense co-existed with a more conservative desire to maximize wherever possible their identity with the Church at home, as much in teachings and practices as in dress, décor, and architecture. Asserting common

---

[28] LPL, Longley Papers, 4, fols 237–40, C. T. Longley, Archbishop, to H. L. Jenner, Bishop of Dunedin, 19 December 1867.
[29] See correspondence in LPL, Tait Papers, 170, fols 2–38; 178, fols 305–50; 195, fols 233–63; 201, fols 203–44; 214, fols 161–4.

identity could also reflect motives of expediency and self-interest: close unity reinforced Anglican Church status amidst the competitive religious pluralism of colonial social and political life.[30]

Along with a sense of growing colonial independence and identity, most colonial churches' lay and clerical leaders still shared a growing sense of pride by the 1870s in being part of the glory of one rapidly expanding Empire. Advocacy of imperial destiny, along with warnings of the *hubris* this fostered, were part of a colonial ethos articulated by several church denominations. Some, such as the predominantly Irish Roman Catholics, did not share in this enthusiasm. Their scepticism about the benefits of English imperialism fed local Protestant anxiety (after 1900) about the way local Roman Catholic bishops encouraged these newly federated colonies to regard the USA as their social, religious, and political model. Identification with the ethos of empire became a source of local division and conflict. Not surprisingly, therefore, the early twentieth-century observances of British Empire Day on 25 May, the formation of Lord Meath's League of the Empire and Baden Powell's scouting movement, found an active advocacy in Anglican Church leadership in Australia, New Zealand, and Canada.[31] In the short term World War I partly resolved the issue. Religion had a divisive role in the search for a common Australian national identity. In Canada and in South Africa, equally, it was no less important, though operating in different ways.

Rapid growth in number and extent of colonial churches during the nineteenth century created new agenda for tensions in unity and diversity in the Church of England. Similar tensions had surfaced in the relationship of other colonial denominations to their central or mother churches, all providing (for another occasion) further colonial and missionary variations on the theme of 'unity and diversity in the church'.

Among the Anglicans, new bishops, clergy, and laity continued to arrive from 'home' with views freshly sharpened by religious controversy in England over the issues of church and

---

[30] See, e.g., LPL, Tait Papers, 160, fols 38–53; 171, fols 302, M. Thomas, Bishop of Goulburn, to A. C. Tait, Bishop of London, 22 December 1866 and 19 May 1869; or 287, fols 32–3, A. Short, former Bishop of Adelaide, to Archbishop Tait, 7 July 1882.

[31] See correspondence of 1905–6 in LPL, Davidson Papers, 115, fols 177–262.

state. They gave new colonial forms to home divisions. Many chose to show their close identity with the Church in England by scrupulous conformity to its supposed laws. This policy appears to have been especially attractive amongst bishops and synods where Low and Evangelical traditions were paramount; Tractarian disciples were generally more impatient for change, exploiting their colonial freedom to approximate colonial church life to their ideals and acting as independently of the state as continued access to trust property and endowments would allow.

Furthermore, the emergence of provinces with metropolitans, and the uncertain powers of colonial metropolitans and primates, both within provinces and adjacent colonies, and in their relationship to the Primacy of Canterbury, raised, as in Canadian, South African, Australian, and New Zealand Churches, new issues of unity and diversity within a world-wide Anglicanism. The colonial daughters' very success in achieving greater self-sufficiency and independence created new family tensions.

St Mark's National Theological Centre,
Canberra, A C T, Australia

# DIVERSITY OR APOSTASY? THE CASE OF THE JAPANESE 'HIDDEN CHRISTIANS'*

*by* STEPHEN TURNBULL

When Christian missionaries returned to Japan in 1859, after having been excluded from that country for over two centuries, they hoped that there might be some possibility of making contact with descendants of Japan's original evangelized communities, and locating some folk memory of the so-called 'Christian Century', which had ended with the expulsion of European priests in 1614, and the persecution of native Christians.[1] None of the newly arrived missionaries, however, had been prepared for the discovery of active secret communities who had maintained the Christian faith as an underground church for seven generations. Yet this was the revelation experienced by Father Bernard Petitjean of the French Société des Missions Étrangères in the porch of the newly consecrated church at Ōura in Nagasaki, on 17 March 1865:

> Urged no doubt by my guardian angel, I went up and opened the door. I had scarce time to say a *Pater* when three women between fifty and sixty years of age knelt down beside me and said in a low voice, placing their hands upon their hearts: 'The hearts of all of us here do not differ from yours.'[2]

They were the first of several thousand 'Hidden Christians' to disclose themselves to the European priests, whose reaction was at first one of unbounded joy, yet changed shortly to two very serious considerations. The first was to ensure the safety of the newly revealed secret believers. Even though the Japanese authorities had been aware of the existence of pockets of secret Christianity for at least fifty years, whenever such a group was discovered the resulting suppression had been little more than a token gesture. The Christian threat, perceived as a serious

* Research for this paper was carried out as part of a Winston Churchill Memorial Trust Travelling Fellowship, which is gratefully acknowledged.

[1] For the history of Japan's 'Christian Century' see C. R. Boxer, *The Christian Century in Japan*, 2nd edn (Berkeley, Cal., 1967); George Elison, *Deus Destroyed: The Image of Christianity in Early Modern Japan* (Harvard, 1973).

[2] From the most detailed account of the incident in J. Marnas, *La Religion de Jésus, Iaso Ja-Kyō ressucitée au Japon dans la seconde moitié du XIXᵉ siècle* (Paris, 1896), pp. 487–91.

challenge to state security during the seventeenth century, appeared to have faded into obscurity. This liberal attitude had, however, totally changed with the return of the Europeans and, unknown to the French missionaries, eighty Christians had already been arrested in 1859, though most were released. The Hidden Christians' disclosure to the priests, and their new-found determination to proclaim their faith and cast off their forced allegiance to Buddhism, placed them in grave danger.[3] Thousands of Christians from the Urakami area of Nagasaki were rounded up and exiled, producing a furious response from the diplomats of the Western nations, whose concerted pressure was enough to make the Japanese government include religious toleration in the 1873 constitution of the Meiji government.[4]

The second issue confronting the missionaries was the question suggested by the title of this paper, because the covert Christianity displayed by these people was of a strange and unexpected variety, an echo of sixteenth-century Catholicism blended in with elements from Buddhism and Shintō.[5] Were these Hidden Christians therefore an example of the extremes of Christian diversity, or had they 'slipped over the edge' into apostasy? This paper attempts to answer this question by studying the history of the emergence from secrecy of one of the communities with whom Petitjean and his colleagues first made contact. At the time of the missionaries' return this particular community was located in Zenchō-dani (the Zenchō valley), five miles along the coast to the south of Nagasaki, and an offshoot by emigration of the secret Christian groups of Kashiyama on the western Sonogi peninsula.[6] Kashiyama, with its

[3] Otis Cary, *Christianity in Japan, a History of Roman Catholic, Protestant and Orthodox Missions* (Rutland, Vermont, 1976), p. 277.

[4] John L. Breen, 'Heretics in Nagasaki: 1790–1796' in Ian Nish, ed. *Contemporary European Writing on Japan* (Tenterden, 1988), p. 597.

[5] The most important studies of the nature of the underground church in Japan as revealed at the time of their rediscovery by the Europeans are Masaharu Anesaki, *Kirishitan shūmon no hakugai to senpuku* [*The Persecution and Underground Activity of the Christian Faith*] (Tokyo, 1925) and Wasaburō Urakawa, *Kirishitan no Fukkatsu* [*The Resurrection of Christianity*] 2 vols (Tokyo, 1928). Japanese names are given here with the surnames last.

[6] The community of Zenchō-dani has been little studied in comparison with other Hidden Christian groups. There are accounts in Kōya Tagita, *Shōwa-jidai no Senpuku Kirishitan* [*Secret Christians of the Present Age*] (Tokyo, 1954), pp. 74–5, 333–4; Yakichi Kataoka, *Kakure Kirishitan* [*The Hidden Christians*] (Tokyo, 1967), p. 272; and the most detailed account in Chizuko Kataoka, 'Nagasaki Hantō no Kirishitan-shi' ['A history of Christianity in the Nagasaki peninsula'] in *Sanwa-chō Kyōdoshi* [*Local History of Sanwa Township*] by various authors (Nagasaki, 1986), pp. 702–25.

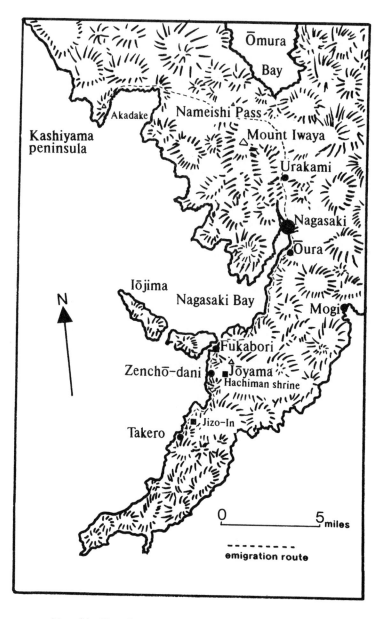

Map of the Nagasaki area, showing places mentioned in the text.

dramatic red cliffs rising sheer out of the sea, had achieved great symbolic value among the Hidden Christians because it was believed to point towards Rome.[7] Christians from Nagasaki would climb nearby Mount Iwaya and pray with their eyes fixed on Kashiyama, which indicated the direction from which the European priests had once arrived, and from where, one day, they would return.

To make a closer visit to Kashiyama, which was also the site of death of several Christian martyrs, was well nigh impossible, for a journey would have entailed crossing the border between the *han*, or territories, of two different *daimyō*, the feudal war lords who were entrusted by the Japanese government with keeping the local peace, including the total suppression and control of Christianity. The distribution of territories around Nagasaki was a patchwork of interlocking fiefs, and one border ran from north to south down the middle of the Kashiyama peninsula, placing its western half, Nishi-Kashiyama, within the Ōmura-*han*, the territory which included Nagasaki itself. The eastern half, Higashi-Kashiyama, where the Christian holy places lay, was owned by the *daimyō* of Saga. By and large, the persecution of Christianity in the Saga territories was much less severe than in the Ōmura lands, the inhabitants being spared the annual ordeal of trampling on a Christian image to demonstrate their continued rejection of the faith.[8] However, the anti-Christian zeal displayed by the *shōya* (village headman) of Higashi-Kashiyama in 1823 largely negated the effects of this leniency, and a number of families petitioned the Saga *daimyō* to be allowed to move elsewhere within the han where they would not experience such harassment. Permission was granted, and eight families and two single males were transferred round Nagasaki bay to the slopes of the Zenchō valley.[9] According to well-established rules, they were assigned to the local Buddhist temple, the Jizō-In, which was of the same sect (Zen) as the one they had left in Higashi-Kashiyama. Here all births and deaths would be registered, and the local Buddhist priest would ensure that funerals and memorial services were

---

[7] Diego Yuuki, 'The Crypto-Christians of Nagasaki', *Japanese Religions*, 19 (1994), p. 123.

[8] For the *fumi-e* see Yakichi Kataoka, *Fumi-e: Kinkyō no Rekishi* [*Image Trampling: a History of Prohibition*] (Tokyo, 1969).

[9] Kataoka, 'Nagasaki', p. 713. There appears to have been some theatrical posturing around mock expulsion to save the *shōya*'s face.

carried out in accordance with Buddhist requirements. They also became *ujiko* (parishioners) of the local Shintō shrine, which was dedicated to Hachiman, the god of war, and lay on top of Jōyama, the mountain beneath which Zenchō-dani nestled.[10] The requirements of the Shintō shrine were monthly offerings of purificatory sand and water.[11] All the families involved were secret Christian believers, and took with them their clandestine traditions which they practised in tandem with the requirements of the indigenous Japanese religions.

The leader of the group was their *mizukata* or baptizer, called Hasegawa Saya. He would baptize newborn infants, thus continuing the one sacrament of the Catholic Church which the underground Christians had been able to preserve. His house became the centre of community life in Zenchō-dani, and at dusk on the twelfth and fifteenth days of every lunar month the heads of household would put on their best clothes and gather there, mounting a guard on each side of the house. They would pray until midnight with their eyes on a certain spot on the inner wall, where was concealed an image of the Virgin Mary. They would also listen to a sermon, and discuss matters of community interest, and the proceedings would finish with a simple communal meal.[12] Saya died on the thirteenth day of the third lunar month of 1838, with the heads of households gathered at his bedside. His dying words are said to have been, 'I believe in my heart that the black ships will return', words that echoed the four predictions of Bastian, the catechist of Higashi-Kashiyama martyred in 1659.[13]

From 1854 onwards, 'black ships' were increasingly seen in Japanese waters, and the renewed wave of active suppression of Christianity reached Zenchō-dani in 1856. In that year a raid was carried out on the Hidden Christians of Urakami. A certain

---

[10] The temple registration system had been introduced deliberately to suppress Christianity. See Kenneth Marcure, 'The Danka System', *Monumenta Nipponica*, 40 (1985), pp. 39–67. For most of Japan's history the indigenous religion of Shintō, and Buddhism, introduced from abroad, have coexisted peacefully with much intermingling.

[11] Kataoka, *Kakure*, p. 272. Shintō is a religion that lays great stress on purification, the most important ritual elements being water and salt. The purificatory sand would have been spread beneath the shrine building as described in Jean Herbert, *Shintō: At the Fountain-Head of Japan* (London, 1967), p. 82.

[12] Kataoka, 'Nagasaki', p. 713.

[13] For the predictions of Bastian, who saw 'confessors returning in huge black ships', see Stephen Turnbull, 'From Catechist to Kami: martyrs and mythology among the Kakure Kirishitan', *Japanese Religions*, 19 (1994), p. 73.

Mojū had buried some Christian images in a box at the foot of the mountain in Higashi-Kashiyama. He was apprehended and the objects discovered. Because of the family links with Zenchō-dani vigorous searches were carried out there, but nothing was found.[14] Such a recent first-hand experience of government suppression carried out against a hitherto undisturbed community probably explains why it took three years from Petit-jean's discovery of the Hidden Christians in 1865 before anyone from Zenchō-dan dared venture to Ōura church to reveal themselves to the missionaries. Two young men made the first contact, and returned with prayer-books and medals, which they shared among the community. Catechetical instruction continued secretly for the next few years, and, as in all examples of contact between the French priests and the Hidden Christians, some rejoined the Catholic Church amid great enthusiasm, others were more cautious, while some were never to be reconciled. Fear of renewed persecution was an important consideration, but once this danger was lifted in 1873 other factors came into play. To the missionaries there could be no accommodation with the paganism they perceived to have contaminated the secret Christians' beliefs. With little recognition of the achievement of these people in preserving any trace of the Christianity taught to their ancestors, any deviation from Catholic doctrine was consigned to the realm of error and criticized.[15] Father Renaut refers to them in his diary of 1875 quite simply as 'bad Catholics'.[16] Another missionary wrote in 1893: 'Those who remain to be converted seem to be so obstinate in their blindness that it would take a miracle to open their eyes.'[17] Evangelization was carried out as if the Hidden Christians were followers only of Buddhism and Shintō, and sometimes more rigorously, as shown by the comment of one priest who reckoned that the

---

[14] Mojū was tortured in prison and executed. See Turnbull, 'From Catechist to Kami', p. 75, and full accounts in Wasaburō Urakawa, *Urakami Kirishitan-shi* [*A History of Christianity in Urakami*] (Tokyo, 1943), p. 32, and Yakichi Kataoka, *Nihon Kirishitan Junkyōshi* [*A History of Christian Martyrdom in Japan*] (Tokyo, 1979), p. 555.

[15] For a good discussion of the attitude of the French missionaries see Ann M. Harrington, *Japan's Hidden Christians* (Chicago, 1993), pp. 113–23, which is based on the original records and diaries of the priests.

[16] Harrington, *Japan*, p. 113.

[17] Ibid., p. 120.

Hidden Christians were 'further away from conversion than the pagans'.[18]

The most dramatic illustration of the different attitudes which could be engendered by the priests concerns the question of funerals. It had been the practice among the Hidden Christians to perform their own brief funeral rites before the arrival of the officiating Buddhist priest.[19] With the granting of religious toleration in 1873 they began to conduct all of the ritual themselves, but in 1884 a ministerial directive laid down that all funerals should be conducted by appropriate clergy, either Buddhist or Catholic. The inhabitants of the island of Iōjima, in Nagasaki bay near Zenchō-dani, settled the matter by returning to Catholicism *en masse*.[20] Their reconciliation was most strongly marked by the destruction of their family *kamidana* and *butsudan* (Shintō and Buddhist altars respectively), found in Japanese homes. On the *butsudan* were displayed the *ihai*, the black-lacquered memorial tablets for the family ancestors. These *ihai* are very precious objects. For about fifty years after the person's death memorial services are held in front of the *ihai*, and through the *ihai* the ancestors are petitioned and engaged in conversation as if they were still living family members.[21] The burning of *ihai* and *butsudan* horrified those among the Hidden Christians who had doubts about being reconciled with Catholicism, and, as Furuno notes for the island of Ikitsuki, the beginning of the *Kakure Kirishitan*, or 'Hidden Christian', faith as a religion distinct from the Catholicism it believed it had preserved, may be said to date from these incidents of destruction.[22]

Many other communities, like Iōjima, became completely Catholic. In others, particularly the outlying islands, the new Catholics were to remain in the minority, and to this day the

---

[18] Ibid., p. 116.

[19] Secret Christian funerals are described by Kiyoto Furuno in *Kakure Kirishitan* [*The Hidden Christians*] (Tokyo, 1959), p. 143 and Kataoka, *Kakure*, pp. 287–9.

[20] Marnas, *La Religion*, p. 433.

[21] Robert J. Smith, *Ancestor Worship in Contemporary Japan* (Stanford, 1974), p. 84, notes newspaper reports of *ihai* being rescued from burning buildings at great personal risk.

[22] Furuno, *Kakure*, p. 106. The destruction of *butsudan* and *ihai* had been a prominent feature of the great zeal shown by the first Christian converts during the sixteenth century, as noted in Cary, *History*, p. 59. It is now conventional to use the term *Kakure Kirishitan* (literally 'Hidden Christians') only for the communities who chose to remain separate subsequent to the missionaries' return, to distinguish them from the *Senpuku Kirishitan* (secret Christians) of the time of persecution, who are often referred to simply as 'Christians'.

447

separated *Kakure Kirishitan* still outnumber Catholics on Ikitsuki, and continue their own distinctive version of Christianity. Inevitably, tensions grew between those who had chosen the different paths. The Ikitsuki Christians continued to live together quite amicably, but this was not to happen in Zenchō-dani. For reasons which are now impossible to determine, but which probably have their roots in the tightly-knit nature of Japanese communities, those who had decided to stay separate felt that they could no longer live alongside their Catholic neighbours, and in 1884 they followed the example of their ancestors in moving to another district. They transferred themselves only five miles further down the coast to the little village of Takero, but this was far enough to ensure a separation, and here they continued to practise the *Kakure Kirishitan* faith.[23]

Zenchō-dani was thus left completely Catholic. A little wooden church was built in 1895, providing a local focus for the allegiance the new Catholics had transferred from their previous enforced affiliation to the Buddhist Jizō-In and the Shintō Hachiman shrine. In 1918 a certain house was re-roofed, disclosing a trunk filled with Hidden Christian artefacts, which were transferred to Urakami cathedral, only to be lost in the atomic bombing of Nagasaki in 1945. In 1933 a monument was erected on the site of Saya's house, and the nearby wooden church was replaced by the present building in 1952.[24]

By contrast, the *Kakure Kirishitan* who had moved to Takero stayed as a completely separate and secretive group until 1931, when they were visited by the researcher Tagita Kōya. Tagita was the pioneer of the study of the *Kakure Kirishitan*, and made a brief inspection of Takero as part of his wide-ranging field work which took in Ikitsuki and Kashiyama. He was particularly struck by the ritual performed by the inhabitants of Takero on the fifteenth day of each lunar month. Even though sixty years had passed since the granting of religious freedom and the removal of any compulsory affiliation to shrines or temples, on that day the *Kakure* of Takero still carried on their shoulders buckets of sand from the beach at Takero to the Hachiman shrine above the Zenchō valley, a distance of five miles in each direction along

---

23 Kataoka, 'Nagasaki', p. 717.
24 Ibid., p. 716.

mountain paths.[25] It was a tradition that could not be explained
away as Christian camouflage, which is often the case with
*Kakure* rituals associated with the anonymous sites of Christian
martyrdom,[26] because the martyred ancestors of the Takero community were buried in distant Higashi-Kashiyama, which their
forefathers had left in 1823. In his book (finally published in
1954) Tagita concluded that the Takero *Kakure* had abandoned
the essentials of Christianity:

> among eighty households there was not one *chōkata* (calen-
> dar official) or *mizukata* (baptiser). There were probably a
> number of *Maria Kannon*, but no one said prayers, *sawari*
> (days of rest) were unknown, as was baptism. There was a
> consciousness among the villagers that the images were to
> be worshipped, but those who practised were few in num-
> ber. Only visits to shrines and graves were important to
> them.[27]

In 1986 Tani Jūbei, a member of the Takero community then
aged seventy-one, shared his recollections of boyhood with
Sister Kataoka Chizuko of Junshin University, Nagasaki, and
challenged Tagita's findings on several points. Days of *sawari*
were indeed kept on the twelfth and twenty-fifth days of the
lunar month, when trees and grass could not be cut, manure was
not to be handled, and for women sewing was forbidden, thus
placing a taboo on most activities of a rural community. There
was also a monthly religious gathering, but Tani agreed with
Tagita's general observation that the traditions of Takero had
been in decline.[28] The ritual of carrying sand to Jōyama was
abandoned in about 1932, and, in common with other *Kakure
Kirishitan* communities, other traditions suffered from the enforced absence of menfolk during the Second World War.

[25] Tagita, *Shōwa*, p. 333.
[26] For examples see Stephen Turnbull, 'The veneration of the martyrs of Ikitsuki (1609–1645) by the "Hidden Christians" of Japan,' *SCH*, 30 (1993), pp. 295–310; idem, 'Martyrs and Matsuri: The massacre of the Hidden Christians of Ikitsuki in 1645 and its relationship to local Shintō tradition', *Japan Forum*, 6 (1994), pp. 159–74.
[27] Tagita, *Shōwa*, p. 75. The *Maria-Kannon* is so called from the use of Kannon, the Buddhist goddess of mercy, as a disguise.
[28] Kataoka, 'Nagasaki', p. 718.

Tagita's conclusion that the Takero *Kakure* had effectively apostasized was based also on his observations of their attitude to the two Shintō shrines in the village. Both were known as the Minami-jinja. One was next to the beach, and the other, which Tagita does not appear to have visited, was on elevated ground about a quarter of a mile away. It consists of an arrangement of natural stones in the shape of an open-fronted box. There is a figure inside, half-buried in the deep sand from the beach with which the site is carpeted. This makes an attractive setting, and is a striking link with Takero's former tradition of carrying sand to the Hachiman shrine. According to Tani's account, when the community moved from Zenchō-dani, the home of the leader was established next to this shrine, and when shrine visits were made it was customary to go to his house also to pray, just as in the days of persecution. By 1932 the house had changed hands and become decrepit, so it was demolished, and is now the site of another Shintō shrine called the Takero-jinja which consists of a *hokora* (a small carved stone shrine with a sloping roof).[29] It is likely that this house is the one indicated by Tagita when he refers to 'a certain house on the hillside', where, according to the villagers, there was enshrined a *go inkyō-sama* (literally 'retired god') which had been brought from the other Minami shrine on the beach.[30] Tani however suggested that Tagita's informants may well have been confusing this image with accounts they had heard of the image of the Virgin concealed within the double wall of Saya's house in Zenchō-dani. Kataoka also notes that when the old house in Takero was demolished nothing was found.[31]

The belief that the image at Takero was of the Virgin and had come from the other Minami shrine on the beach indicates an important role for this site, suggesting perhaps that it was a Christian martyr's grave disguised as a Shintō shrine. This was a possibility entertained by Tagita, whose detailed description is similar to my own observations.[32] The site is a grove of trees on

[29] Ibid., p. 719.

[30] Tagita, *Shōwa*, p. 333. The term *go inkyō-sama* refers to the practice by the *Kakure Kirishitan* of preserving old images and holy pictures when they have worn out and have been replaced by new ones, as noted in Yakichi Kataoka, *Kinsei no chika shinkō* [*Underground Faiths of the Present Day*] (Tokyo, 1974), p. 50.

[31] Kataoka, 'Nagasaki', p. 719.

[32] Tagita, *Shōwa*, p. 333. I visited the shrine in 1993.

a hillock immediately adjacent to the beach. The two dying pine trees mentioned by Tagita have been replaced. There is a stone *torii* (Shintō gateway), bearing the date Meiji 25 (1892), and two *hokora*, one of which contains the figure that replaced the one now enshrined on the hillside. Once again the ground surface is covered with a carpet of neatly brushed sand, and a broom rack gives evidence of the immense care still taken to preserve the site. Tagita's account of the shrine begins the chapter in his book which includes descriptions of the martyrs' sites of Ikitsuki and Higashi-Kashiyama, but unlike these well-defined Christian sites Tagita was unable to find any link with a named Christian martyr, or indeed any concrete evidence of a definite Christian connection other than its adoption by the Takero *Kakure* when they moved there in 1884. Tani said that he still visited the Minami-jinja on the beach at New Year and *Bon* (the Shintō festival of the dead), but that the old custom of removing one's shoes before entering had long since been discontinued.[33] While it is clearly a Shintō shrine, neither Tagita nor Tani could identify the Shintō *kami* enshrined there.[34] Tagita concluded, perhaps optimistically, that the Minami-jinja is an example of Christian camouflage, but one, surely, taken to its ultimate degree, where the camouflage was no longer needed, and even the identity of the camouflage had been forgotten! Tani suggested to Kataoka that the shrine may simply be to an unknown victim of drowning washed up on the beach, a process of memorialization that is by no means uncommon in Japan.[35]

The community of Takero has managed to keep itself isolated until the present day. Tani stated that marriage outside the community was unknown until 1941, while over the years the separation was made more acute by the transfer of family graves from Zenchō-dani down to Takero.[36] Father Diego Yuuki, the

---

[33] Kataoka, 'Nagasaki', p. 719.

[34] Tagita, *Shōwa*, p. 334. *Kami* are the numinous entities that are the focus of worship in Shintō.

[35] Kataoka, 'Nagasaki', p. 719. There are numerous folk-beliefs among Japanese fishing communities regarding drowned men. According to Ōtō Tokohiko, 'The taboos of fishermen', in Richard Dorson, ed., *Studies in Japanese Folklore* (Bloomington, Ind., 1963), p. 112: 'drowned men, often called *nagare-botoke* (floating Buddhas), are used in supplicatory rites aimed at increasing catches of fish, after their corpses are encountered floating at sea.' Drowning victims washed ashore are not employed in this fashion, but like all victims of disaster throughout Japan they may be deified as a means of placating their spirits, lest they prove violent or revengeful.

[36] Kataoka, 'Nagasaki', p. 720.

Director of the Twenty-Six Martyrs Museum in Nagasaki, visited Takero during the early 1970s, and was able to confirm that the *Kakure* tradition was still alive. In a conversation in October 1993, he explained how his visit had come about as a result of an invitation from the Catholic priest of Zenchō-dani, who was a friend of the then community leader of the *Kakure* of Takero. Unfortunately they arrived at the time of the funeral of the leader, who had died just a few days before. Yuuki reports that as they joined the company in their communal meal, a *Maria Kannon* statue in the corner was covered in a cloth, and that every question he asked produced a claim of ignorance. Eventually one man began to talk to them, but was immediately asked to leave the room, and Yuuki was assigned to a lady to continue his conversation, but she proved not to be from Takero, and could tell him nothing about the *Kakure* life.

In 1986 more details of Takero became known through Tani Jūbei's conversation with Sister Kataoka Chizuko, and in 1992 Yuuki returned to Takero at the invitation of a Catholic lady living nearby, and had a meeting with the community leaders. He found that much had changed. Unlike twenty years before, they were willing to share their recollections with him, but the paucity of information led Yuuki to conclude that the *Kakure* faith had now almost completely died out. The leader told him that the reason the Takero people had the reputation for not talking to outsiders was simply that they no longer had anything to say. All now belonged to the Buddhist temple, and their once feigned ignorance about the *Kakure* faith was now genuine. All the man could tell him was that he remembered many years ago being told that no work should be done on the twenty-fourth day of December, but that he had not known why until Catholics had told him that it would have been because the *Kakure* had chosen that day as Christmas. During this man's boyhood *Kakure Kirishitan* was the religion of the village, but it was a religion that required them to say and show nothing. Secrecy thus became its own legitimator, and little by little they began to forget the content. A similar point has been made by Nosco in a thoughtful article on the history of the Japanese underground church. He comments, 'It is only within an open society that the members ever enjoy the luxury of asking why a practice is upheld, or what meaning underlies an action, whereas in an underground community the secrecy itself has become a self-sufficient source of meaning.'[37]

The greatest motivation for any of the *Kakure Kirishitan* groups has been, and still is, a desire for fidelity to what they believe are the traditions of their ancestors. Thus the communities on Ikitsuki still sing the *Laudate Dominum* in recognizable Latin, transmitted orally since 1639, and pray at the island's sites of martyrdom. When the French missionaries arrived in Japan the community that was later to move to Takero was still one of these secret societies, maintaining as best it could an underground faith believed to be the authentic Catholicism taught by St Francis Xavier. The missionaries' rapid conclusion of apostasy was both premature and harsh, but a judgement that was to become progressively true as the years of separation went by, and this inward-looking community moved further and further from even their own original extreme of Christian diversity. Takero's *Kakure* problems were more acute than those of Ikitsuki, for their tradition had been weakened by two instances of emigration, so that there were no longer any Christian holy places within reach to link them physically to the past. Instead their sole link to their community's history was focused on Zenchō-dani, by maintaining their ancestors' tradition of arduous service by coercion to a Shintō shrine with no Christian connection, and the adoption of an anonymous shrine on the beach as their own.

Thus one extreme example of Christian diversity has faded away into a virtual abandonment of the faith, but to use the word apostasy for what happened would imply an act of rejection. There was no rejection of Christianity by the *Kakure* other than that of the unfamiliar, suspect, and exclusive version preached by the French missionaries. Living within a closed society that had chosen physical separation in addition to religious schism, their fidelity to their Christian ancestors was mediated through a tradition that valued secrecy above transmission, until the content of their faith itself became forgotten. As Yuuki put it in our conversation about Takero, 'When the old men died there was nothing left to transmit. They knew nothing, and they consider

---

[37] Peter Nosco, 'Secrecy and the transmission of tradition: issues in the study of the "Underground" Christians', *Japanese Journal of Religious Studies*, 20 (1993), p. 26.

themselves now to be Buddhists. The big secret of Takero now is that there are no secrets.'

University of Leeds

# ANGLICAN RECOGNITION OF PRESBYTERIAN ORDERS: JAMES COOPER AND THE PRECEDENT OF 1610

*by* DOUGLAS M. MURRAY

One of the foremost advocates of union between the Anglican and Presbyterian Churches at the beginning of this century was James Cooper, Regius Professor of Ecclesiastical History in the University of Glasgow from 1898 to 1922. Cooper was the best-known representative within the Church of Scotland of the Scoto-Catholic or high-church movement which was expressed in the formation of the Scottish Church Society in 1892. One of the 'special objects' of the Society was the 'furtherance of Catholic unity in every way consistent with true loyalty to the Church of Scotland'.[1] The realization of catholic unity led high churchmen to seek what Cooper termed a 'United Church for the British Empire'[2] which would include the union of the Church of Scotland and the Church of England. This new unity would require a reconciliation of differences and the elimination of diversities: on the one hand an acceptance of bishops by the Scottish Presbyterians; on the other an acceptance of the validity of Presbyterian orders by Episcopalians and Anglicans.

Cooper had no difficulty in accepting episcopacy. His native Morayshire was a strongly Episcopalian area, his grandmother was an Episcopalian, and as a boy he worshipped in the local chapel when there was no evening service in the parish church.[3] As a student at Aberdeen, Cooper agonized over whether he should enter the ministry of the Church of Scotland or the Church of England.[4] Among the attractions of Anglicanism was that the episcopal form of government was 'as at least as

---

[1] The Constitution of the Scottish Church Society IV.21, 22, in *Scottish Church Society Conferences*, 1st series (Edinburgh, 1894), p. 199. Cf. Douglas M. Murray, 'The Scottish Church Society, 1892–1914: the High Church Movement in the Church of Scotland' (Cambridge Ph.D. thesis, 1975).

[2] James Cooper, *A United Church for the British Empire* (Forres, 1902). Cf. G. W. Sprott, in Scottish Church Society, *Annual Report 1901–2*, p. 17.

[3] H. J. Wotherspoon, *James Cooper: A Memoir* (London, 1926), pp. 39, 50.

[4] Ibid., pp. 75–6. Cf. Douglas M. Murray, 'James Cooper at Glasgow (1898–1922): presbytery and episcopacy', in William Ian P. Hazlett, ed., *Traditions of Theology in Glasgow 1450–1990* (Edinburgh, 1993), pp. 68–9.

455

agreeable to Scripture as Presbyterianism, as more expedient, as more likely to be the primitive (so far as there was one at all), and also as more Catholic'. From his historical studies Cooper would later conclude that the period from 1610 to 1638, when bishops acted as permanent moderators of Scottish presbyteries, witnessed greater progress than any other similar time.[5] In addition to recognizing that the Kirk had previously experienced a modified form of episcopacy, Cooper saw the value of a superintendent or bishop in relation to the pastoral care of ministers and congregations.[6] Cooper did not wish to replace one type of church government with another, or to impose Presbyterianism south of the border as had been attempted by the Solemn League and Covenant of 1643. Rather he wished to combine the best features of both systems, the collective nature of presbyteries with the personal ministry of bishops.

The other prerequisite of a united Church for the British Empire was the Anglican recognition of Presbyterian orders. In Cooper's view the ministry of the Church of Scotland belonged to an apostolic succession, although it was one of presbyters rather than of bishops. To support his view Cooper turned again to the episcopate of the early seventeenth century. When three Scottish ministers were consecrated bishops in London in 1610 they were not first of all required to be ordained as presbyters. On their return to Scotland ordinations were carried out by bishops and presbyters together, ministers were not required to be episcopally ordained, and no bishops were reordained before their consecration.[7]

Cooper was pleased to note, too, that this precedent had been mentioned by the Lambeth Conference of 1908 as a possible approach to union between the Anglican and Presbyterian Churches.[8] Prior to the Conference Cooper had set out his historical arguments in two articles he had written for *The Glasgow Herald*

[5] Wotherspoon, *James Cooper*, p. 2.
[6] Ibid., pp. 23, 340. Cf. James Cooper, *The Historical Side of the Reunion Question* (Dublin, 1914), p. 7; idem, 'The problem of reunion in Scotland', *CQR*, 68 (1909), pp. 180–1.
[7] James Cooper, *Church Reunion: the Prospect in Scotland*, reprinted from the *Irish Church Quarterly*, April 1910 (Dublin, 1910), p. 9, *Reunion: A Voice from Scotland* (London, 1918), pp. 33, 43.
[8] Cooper, *Church Reunion: the Prospect in Scotland*, p. 10; *Conference of Bishops of the Anglican Communion 1908* (London, 1908), Resolution 75, p. 65. Cf. Norman Sykes, *Old Priest and New Presbyter* (Cambridge, 1956), pp. 221–2.

on the proposed reunion in Australia.[9] The precedent of 1610 was a recurrent theme in Cooper's writings[10] and received detailed treatment in one of the papers he contributed to the Christian Unity Association of Scotland.[11]

The consecrations of 1610 took place as part of James VI's programme to restore the episcopate to the Church of Scotland. Following an Act of Parliament in 1606 titular bishops were appointed, but they did not receive the full recognition of the Church until the General Assembly agreed to the King's proposals in 1610.[12] Since there were no surviving consecrated bishops in Scotland, Archbishop John Spottiswoode of Glasgow, Bishop Andrew Lamb of Brechin, and Bishop Gavin Hamilton of Galloway were summoned by the King to Westminster to receive spiritual authorization. They were consecrated by the Bishops of London, Ely, Rochester, and Worcester.[13] The only hesitation raised by the Scottish ministers was that by this act the Church of Scotland might be held to be subject to the Church of England. To avoid this implication, neither of the two English archbishops took part in the rite.[14]

According to Spottiswoode, Bishop Lancelot Andrewes of Ely raised the question of the orders of the men about to be consecrated. Should they not first of all be ordained deacon and priest? Archbishop Richard Bancroft replied: 'that thereof there was no necessity, seeing where Bishops could not be had the ordination given by the presbyters must be esteemed lawful, otherwise that it might be doubted if there were any lawful vocation in most of the Reformed Churches'.[15] Andrewes acquiesced when the other bishops agreed with Bancroft. According to a later account

[9] *The Glasgow Herald*, 3 and 6 July 1908 (published as *Australian Reunion* [Glasgow, 1908] ). Cf. 'The Lambeth Conference', *CQR*, 67 (1909), p. 21.

[10] Cooper, *Church Reunion: the Prospect in Scotland*, p. 9; *Reunion: A Voice from Scotland*, p. 33.

[11] James Cooper, ' "The first episcopacy" ', in *Historical Papers submitted to the Christian Unity Association of Scotland*, Privately Printed (Edinburgh, 1914), pp. 59–81.

[12] Gordon Donaldson, *Scotland: James V to James VII* (Edinburgh, 1965), pp. 205–6; David George Mullan, *Episcopacy in Scotland: The History of an Idea, 1560–1638* (Edinburgh, 1986), pp. 105–13.

[13] Archbishop Spottiswoode mentioned Bishop James Montague of Bath and Wells as one of the consecrators, but it would appear that he was unable to attend and that the Bishop of Rochester took his place. See Leonel L. Mitchell, 'Episcopal ordinations in the Church of Scotland, 1610–1688', *Historical Magazine of the Protestant Episcopal Church*, 31 (1962), p. 143 n. 1; George R. McMahon, 'The Scottish Episcopate, 1600–1638' (Birmingham Ph.D. thesis, 1972), p. 34.

[14] John Spottiswoode, *History of the Church of Scotland*, ed. M. Russell, 3 vols (Edinburgh, 1851), 3, p. 209.

[15] Ibid.

by the Anglican historian Peter Heylyn,[16] Bancroft put forward another view, that consecration to the episcopate might be *per saltum*: 'There was no such necessity of receiving the order of Priesthood, but that Episcopal Consecration might be given without it, as might have been exemplified in the cases of Ambrose and Nectarius.' As Cooper pointed out, Bancroft stated only that the consecrations *might* be seen in that way.[17] The *per saltum* theory would have accorded more exactly with Heylyn's outlook and it may be that he was simply crediting the Archbishop with his own position.[18] It may be, too, that Bancroft expressed one view to the Scottish ministers and another to his more conservative episcopal colleagues. It would be possible to hold both views together. A. J. Mason has pointed out that there is nothing in Spottiswoode's account that 'does violence to what we know of the opinions of Bancroft or of Andrewes', and that there is no reason 'why the same man should not have used both arguments ascribed to Bancroft, or why Andrewes should have been compelled to choose between them'.[19]

It is of more significance that the Anglican Church at that time would appear to have recognized the ministry of other Reformed Churches. Norman Sykes has shown that Anglicans who asserted the developing view of the divine right of episcopacy in the early seventeenth century 'generally stopped short of unchurching the foreign reformed churches and of denying the validity of their ministry and sacraments'.[20] Indeed it could be argued that a much more doctrinaire view of church order was held by Presbyterians in both England and Scotland.[21] For example, the Scottish *Second Book of Discipline* of 1578 set out what it considered to be the only biblical pattern of church polity, one which was valid for all times and places.[22] Its attempt to base the government of the Church upon biblical precedent

[16] P. Heylyn, *The History of the Presbyterians, 1563–1647* (Oxford, 1670), p. 387, quoted in Sykes, *Old Priest and New Presbyter*, p. 102 n. 1.

[17] Cooper, ' "The first episcopacy" ', p. 75.

[18] Mitchell, 'Episcopal ordinations in the Church of Scotland', pp. 143–4, n. 2.

[19] A. J. Mason, *The Church of England and Episcopacy* (Cambridge, 1914), p. 72.

[20] Sykes, *Old Priest and New Presbyter*, p. 69.

[21] Ibid., pp. 60–1. Cf. Patrick Collinson, *The Elizabethan Puritan Movement* (London, 1967), pp. 101–8.

[22] James Kirk, ed., *The Second Book of Discipline* (Edinburgh, 1980), II, xi, p. 177, n. 40.

provides a marked contrast to the more limited and pragmatic approach of the *First Book of Discipline* of 1560.[23]

What is not in dispute is that the new bishops proceeded to consecrate others to the episcopate in Scotland without ordaining them first of all as deacons and priests. In addition no Scottish ministers were required to be reordained. The office of deacon is also not found in the Scottish Church in this period, except for an isolated instance in 1637 as part of the ill-fated ecclesiastical policy of Charles I.[24] As to the practice of ordination, it would appear that a variety of forms were in use. A Scottish Ordinal was not issued until 1620, and it is not clear how widely it was employed. Ordinations seem to have been carried out either according to the new Ordinal, or following the English Service Book, or according to the previous practice supplemented by the laying on of hands.[25] What is clear is that the bishop would always be associated with the presbytery, the word 'priest' was carefully avoided, and there was no provision for the celebration of the eucharist. It would appear, too, that purely Presbyterian ordinations continued to take place.[26] In spite of the variations in practice, the Church of Scotland seems to have been regarded as a sister Church by the Church of England.

When bishops were appointed in Scotland following the Restoration, however, the precedent of 1610 was not followed. Of the four ministers who went to London to be consecrated in 1661, two had not received ordination from a bishop: James Sharp, Archbishop of St Andrews, and Robert Leighton, Bishop of Dunblane. They were first of all ordained deacon and priest. Sharp at first objected and referred to the precedent of 1610. The English bishops replied:

for then the Scots were only in an imperfect state, having never had bishops among them since the Reformation; so

---

[23] George Yule, 'Continental patterns and the Reformations in England and Scotland', *Scottish Journal of Theology*, 22 (1969), pp. 305–23.

[24] Mitchell, 'Episcopal ordinations in the Church of Scotland', pp. 152–3. Cf. William McMillan, *The Worship of the Scottish Reformed Church, 1550–1638* (London, 1931), p. 357.

[25] Mitchell, 'Episcopal ordinations in the Church of Scotland', p. 148; G. W. Sprott, ed., *Scottish Liturgies of the Reign of James VI* (Edinburgh and London, 1901), pp. 111–31.

[26] Stewart Mechie, 'Episcopacy in post-Reformation Scotland', *Scottish Journal of Theology*, 8 (1955), pp. 28–9.

in such a state of things in which they had been under a real necessity, it was reasonable to allow of their orders, how defective soever: but that of late they had been in a state of schism, had revolted from their bishops, and had thrown off that order; so that orders given in such a wilful opposition to the whole constitution of the primitive church was a thing of another nature.[27]

Yet when the newly consecrated bishops returned to Scotland they did not first of all ordain those whom they raised to the episcopate, nor were the clergy compelled to receive episcopal ordination.

It was clear to James Cooper in the early twentieth century that the consecrations of 1610 provided a more favourable precedent for the acceptance of Presbyterian orders. The question remained, however, as to whether the Church of England of his day regarded the Church of Scotland as a sister Reformed Church as had happened in 1610. The lack of an Anglican recognition of the ministry of the Kirk implied that such was not the case. It is also significant that contemporary Scottish Episcopalians saw the consecrations of 1661 as providing a safer precedent.[28]

The Lambeth Conference of 1908 cited the precedent of 1610 as an example of how consecrations to the episcopate might be carried out in a future reunion. It was a suggestion rather than a principle.[29] The relevant Resolution stated that 'in the welcome event of any project of reunion between any Church of the Anglican Communion and any Presbyterian or other non-episcopal Church it might be possible to make an approach to reunion on the basis of consecrations to the episcopate on lines suggested by such precedents as those of 1610.'[30] In the Report of the Committee on Reunion and Intercommunion it was noted that if these precedents involved consecration to the

[27] Gilbert Burnet, *The History of My Own Times*, 2 vols (London, 1838), 1, p. 92. Cf. Sykes, *Old Priest and New Presbyter*, pp. 118–20; Mechie, 'Episcopacy in Post-Reformation Scotland', p. 30.

[28] T. I. Ball, 'The reunion problem: a "Scottish Episcopal" view', *CQR*, 68 (1909), p. 370; Thomas Hannan, 'The reunion problem: another Scottish Episcopal view', *CQR*, 69 (1910), pp. 316–7; idem, 'The Scottish consecrations in London in 1610', *CQR*, 71 (1910–11), p. 413. Cf. Beatrice M. Hamilton Thompson, 'The post-Reformation episcopate in England', in Kenneth E. Kirk, ed., *The Apostolic Ministry* (London, 1946), pp. 420–1.

[29] 'The Lambeth Conference', pp. 20–1; 'Presbyterianism and Reunion', *CQR*, 67 (1909), pp.320–1.

[30] *Conference of Bishops 1908*, p. 65.

episcopate *per saltum*, 'the conditions of such consecration would require careful investigation and statement'.[31] The reference to the precedent of 1610 was thus not such a clear indication of the possible Anglican recognition of Presbyterian orders as Cooper might have wished.

The Report of the Committee also pointed out that the Presbyterian Churches possessed the first three of the four conditions which had been laid down by the Lambeth Conference of 1888 as a possible approach to reunion: the Scriptures, the sacraments, and the creeds. While Presbyterians had not retained the fourth, the historic episcopate, they had nevertheless insisted upon a definite ordination to the holy ministry with the laying on of hands and prayer 'by those who have themselves been ordained and are authorised to ordain others'.[32] In addition many leading Presbyterian divines 'maintained the transmission of Orders by a regular succession through the presbyterate'.[33] An appendix included extracts on the doctrine of ordination from the Kirk's standard authorities as well as from more recent unofficial statements. The view of a ministerial succession of presbyters held by Cooper's fellow high churchman George W. Sprott was included, but it was also pointed out that Principal Robert H. Story of Glasgow in his Baird Lectures had spoken 'rather lightly' of the importance of succession as a fact.[34]

The Lambeth Conference had recognized a difference of opinion among leading Scottish churchmen regarding the importance of ministerial succession. Cooper's argument in favour of the precedent of 1610 was based on the view that the Church of Scotland possessed a succession which could be recognized by the Anglican Church.[35] Yet he was not always convinced that such a claim could be made. The question of the validity of his Presbyterian orders had caused a crisis early in his ministry. In 1879 he wrote to George Sprott to say that he contemplated leaving the service of the Church of Scotland as he had torturing

---

[31] Ibid., p. 184 n.

[32] Ibid., p. 183.

[33] Ibid.

[34] Ibid., pp. 190–1. G. W. Sprott, *The Worship and Offices of the Church of Scotland* (Edinburgh and London, 1882), pp. 187–8; R. H. Story, *The Apostolic Ministry in the Scottish Church* (Edinburgh, 1897), pp. 5, 248.

[35] Cooper, *Church Reunion: the Prospect in Scotland*, pp. 8–9.

doubts about his ordination.[36] Cooper described the difficulty as a 'thorn in the flesh' and said that 'the whole neighbourhood of it is inflamed and sore'. The problem had been aggravated by a statement he had read which said that ordination had been omitted in the Kirk for thirty years after the Reformation and that the succession 'hangs on nothing'. Sprott's reply to this cry for help has not been preserved, but shortly afterwards Cooper wrote again to say that he would not do anything rashly. His anxiety, he said, was not so much about the validity of Presbyterian orders but about the continuity of the succession. Cooper remained within the Church of Scotland and along with other high churchmen would seek to argue that there had been no significant break in the succession of presbyterial ordination at the time of the Reformation.

The difficulty arose because ordination with the laying on of hands was rejected in the *First Book of Discipline*. The Scots reformers stated: 'Other ceremonie than the publick approbation of the people, and declaration of the chiefe minister . . . wee cannot approve, for albeit the Apostles used imposition of hands, yet seeing the miracle is ceased, the using of the ceremonie we judge not necessarie.'[37] High churchmen went to great lengths to minimize the significance of that statement. They said, for example, that the omission of the imposition of hands was because those offering themselves for the ministry would have been ordained already as priests.[38] Their arguments in favour of the continuing practice of ordination by the laying on of hands after the Reformation have for the most part failed to convince other scholars.[39] To seek to discount the outright repudiation of the 'miracle' of ordination by the reformers is to fail to understand the radical nature of their position. The previous succession had failed and it was therefore rejected. A new way of

---

[36] Wotherspoon, *James Cooper*, pp. 105–6.

[37] James K. Cameron, ed., *The First Book of Discipline* (Edinburgh, 1972), p. 102.

[38] Sprott, *Worship and Offices*, pp. 196–7; Scottish Church Society, *Presbyterian Orders* (Edinburgh, 1926), p. 13.

[39] Only William McMillan, in *The Worship of the Scottish Reformed Church*, pp. 343–4, has agreed with this contention. Those who have challenged this view are: Duncan Shaw, 'The inauguration of ministers in Scotland: 1560–1620', *Records of the Scottish Church History Society*, 16 (1969), pp. 35–62; James L. Ainslie, *The Doctrines of Ministerial Order in the Reformed Churches of the 16th and 17th Centuries* (Edinburgh, 1940), pp. 173–4; and W. D. Maxwell, *The Liturgical Portions of the Genevan Service Book* (Edinburgh, 1931), p. 171. See also Murray, 'The Scottish Church Society, 1892–1914', pp. 208–15.

appointing ministers was adopted which would seek to ensure, in the words of the *Scots Confession*, 'the true preaching of the Word of God' and 'the right administration of the sacraments'.[40] High churchmen were right to point out that other statements in this period favoured ordination by the laying on of hands, and that the practice was set out in the *Second Book of Discipline*, but there was great variation in practice until the early seventeenth century.[41] The General Assembly in 1597, for example, found it necessary to state that ordinations were to be carried out with the imposition of hands, which would imply that the practice could not be assumed.[42]

Cooper noted that the succession was assured from the consecrations of 1610 onwards when any irregularities of the previous period would have been corrected. That line of bishops would have ordained the majority of those who in each presbytery transmitted the gift after 1637. Since then, he said, 'no break in the chain can be alleged'.[43] In view of this consideration Cooper came to view the question of whether or not there had been a break in ministerial succession following the Reformation as of no 'practical importance'.[44] Yet it was of the utmost importance if the precedent of 1610 was to be taken seriously. According to Cooper the bishops of the Church of England consecrated Scottish presbyters to the episcopate on the basis of their existing orders, that is, because they shared in a ministerial succession. Yet there is no evidence that either side held that such a view of succession was crucial in relation to the ministry of the Scottish Church. It cannot be certain, either, that those who received consecration in 1610 had been ordained by the laying on of hands.[45] Cooper could not argue in both ways. Anglican recognition of Presbyterian orders could proceed either on the basis of

[40] *The Scots Confession of 1560*, a modern translation by James Bulloch (Edinburgh, 1984), XVIII, p. 16. Cf. Mechie, 'Episcopacy in post-Reformation Scotland', pp. 24–5.

[41] Gordon Donaldson, 'Scottish ordinations in the Restoration period', *ScHR*, 33 (1954), p. 170.

[42] Shaw, 'The inauguration of ministers', pp. 57–8.

[43] James Cooper, *The Revival of Church Principles in the Church of Scotland* (Oxford, 1895), p. 11. Cf. Thomas Leishman, 'The ritual of the Church', in R. H. Story, ed., *The Church of Scotland, Past and Present*, 5 vols (Edinburgh, 1890), 5, p. 350; Gordon Donaldson, *The Scottish Reformation* (Cambridge, 1960), pp. 117–18.

[44] Edinburgh, New College Library, Church Service Society Papers, James Cooper to G. W. Sprott, 17 July 1900.

[45] Hannan, 'The Scottish consecrations in 1610', pp. 404–5, 410.

the precedent of 1610, in which case ministerial succession was not the issue, or on the basis of an unbroken succession of presbyters. If the latter argument was used then, according to Cooper's own position, the precedent of 1661, rather than that of 1610, was the one which should be followed.

University of Glasgow

# UNITY, UNIFORMITY AND DIVERSITY:
## THE ANGLICAN LITURGY IN ENGLAND AND
## THE UNITED STATES, 1900–1940

### *by* MARTIN DUDLEY

'Uniformity', declared Sir John Nicholl, one of the greatest of Anglican ecclesiastical lawyers, 'is one of the leading and distinguishing principles of the Church of England – nothing is left to the discretion and fancy of the individual.'[1] At the Reformation the English Church was distinguished not by the decisions of councils, confessional statements, or the writings of particular leaders, but by one uniform liturgy.[2] This liturgy, 'containing nothing contrary to the Word of God, or to sound Doctrine' and consonant with the practice of the early Church, was intended to 'preserve Peace and Unity in the Church' and to edify the people.[3] It was also opposed to the 'great diversity in saying and singing in Churches within this Realm' and, abolishing the liturgical uses of Salisbury, Hereford, Bangor, York, and Lincoln, it established that 'now from henceforth all the whole Realm shall have but one Use'.[4] This principle of liturgical uniformity was enshrined in the several Acts of Uniformity from that of the second year of King Edward VI[5] to that of the fourteenth year of Charles II,[6] amended, but not abolished, in the reign of Queen Victoria.[7] It was a principle conveyed to the churches in the colonies so that, even if they revised or abandoned the Book of Common Prayer in use in England, as the Americans did in 1789, what was substituted was called '*The Book of Common Prayer*' and declared to be 'the Liturgy of this Church' to be 'received as such by all members of

---

[1] *Newbury v. Goodwin* (1811), 1 Phillimore 282; quoted by G. W. O. Addleshaw, *The High Church Tradition* (London, 1949), p. 23.

[2] M. J. Hatchett, 'Prayer Books', in S. Sykes and J. Booty, eds, *The Study of Anglicanism* (London, 1988), p. 121.

[3] The Preface to the Book of Common Prayer, 1662.

[4] Ibid., 'Concerning the Service of the Church'.

[5] 2 & 3 Edw. 6, c. 1.

[6] 14 Car. 2, c. 4.

[7] Act of Uniformity Amendment Act, 1872 (35 & 36 Vict. c. 35).

the same'.[8] The principle of uniformity was modified during the Anglican Communion's missionary expansion. The Lambeth Conference of 1920 considered that liturgical uniformity throughout the Churches of the Anglican Communion was not a necessity,[9] but the 1930 Conference held that the Book of Common Prayer, as authorized in the several Churches of the Communion, was the place where faith and order were set forth,[10] and so implied a degree of uniformity maintained by the use of a single book.

The Anglican Churches also accepted the principle of liturgical change. It was embodied in the first line of the Preface to the Book of 1662. The Church of England set a mean 'between the two extremes, of too much stiffness in refusing, and of too much easiness in admitting' any variation from the Church's liturgy. The two principles were unevenly applied. The English Book had only been revised in small ways since 1662 and the pressure for a major revision was growing. The American Book, by contrast, had been revised first in 1789 and then again in 1892. The General Convention of that year had been exceedingly timid and there were strong calls for a further examination of the liturgy in which everything would be 'open to consideration, and possible amendment or revision'.[11] The principles of uniformity and openness to change were to be much tested in the following years.

The English revision came first and the immediate reason for its initiation was the need to resolve a problem that dogged the late nineteenth-century Church, clerical lawlessness or what Archbishop Randall Davidson called 'Ritual restlessness'. In 1898 T. A. Lacey, a noted Anglo-Catholic apologist, described in an Alcuin Club Tract entitled *Liturgical Interpolations* the way in which the face of the Church of England had changed in the previous sixty years. The change was, he argued, not of nature but of aspect; the actual rites of the Church remained unaltered but the way in which they were performed was very different

---

[8] 'The Ratification of the Book of Common Prayer by the Bishops, Clergy, and the Laity of the Protestant Episcopal Church in the United States of America', 16 October, 1789. Printed in the Prayer Book.

[9] Resolution 36; text in *The Lambeth Conferences (1867–1948)* (London, 1948), p. 45.

[10] Resolution 49; text in *The Lambeth Conferences*, p. 173.

[11] J. W. Suter and C. M. Addison, *The People's Book of Worship* (New York, 1919), p. 28.

from that which had formerly prevailed.[12] Though the Alcuin Club itself promoted the practical study of ceremonial 'in accordance with the rubrics of the Book of Common Prayer', it managed to interpret those rubrics in a distinctly pre-Reformation way.[13] Archbishop Lang called the ritualist approach to the liturgy a process of 'unauthorised revision by way of alterations and additions carried on by individual clergy, or groups of clergy, to meet their own desires'. Though he greatly deprecated these individual initiatives he saw that the 'excessive straitness of the letter of the law [had] rendered this kind of arbitrary and irresponsible revision both inevitable and extremely difficult to control.'[14] Controlled it had to be, if unity and a degree of uniformity were not to be entirely lost, and in England these principles were enshrined in law and hence the concern of Parliament. In February 1904 Archbishop Davidson was faced with the likelihood that Parliament would enquire into the worship of the Church and the degree to which it conformed to the law. Davidson's biographer, Bishop Bell, calls Prayer Book revision a drama in five acts – this was the first act.[15] The Archbishop persuaded Balfour, the Prime Minister, to appoint a Royal Commission on Ecclesiastical Discipline. The Commission was not welcome but it was better than a Parliamentary Select Committee. It would inquire 'into the alleged prevalence of breaches or neglect of the Law relating to the conduct of Divine service in the Church of England' and would also consider ornaments and fittings, and the powers and procedures needed to bring about compliance.[16] Davidson's evidence to the Commission emphasized that 'from the days of Queen Elizabeth to our own, notwithstanding very definite rubrics and stern Acts of Uniformity and searching Episcopal injunctions . . . wide varieties [prevailed] in the mode of conducting Divine service.' He made the point that, in his view, there had never been a period

[12] T. A. Lacey, *Liturgical Interpolations*, 3rd ed. (London, 1912), p. 1. The tract, which first appeared in 1898 and was reprinted in 1903, appeared in its third edition as the first of the Alcuin Club's Prayer Book Revision Pamphlets.

[13] As in the Club's first tract, *The Ornaments of the Rubric*, by J. T. Micklethwaite (London, 1897). The Club's aims and objectives are set out on the end-pages.

[14] *The Prayer Book Measure: Speeches delivered by the Archbishops of Canterbury and York to the Convocations at the Church House, Westminster, Monday, February 7th, 1927* (London, 1927), p. 29.

[15] G. K. A. Bell, *Randall Davidson* (London, 1938), p. 462.

[16] Ibid., p. 462.

in the Church of England 'when what is called uniformity had not to be interpreted by a very wide elasticity'.[17] The Commission submitted its report in June 1906. It delivered itself of one of the most significant statements in liturgical history since the Restoration when it declared that

> the law of public worship in the Church of England is too narrow for the religious life of the present generation. It needlessly condemns much which a great section of Church people, including many of her most devoted members, value; and modern thought and feeling are characterised by a care for ceremonial, a sense of dignity in worship, and an appreciation of the continuity of the Church, which were not similarly felt at the time when the law took its present shape.[18]

The Commission thought it reasonable to expect that revision of the strict letter of the law would secure the obedience of many who wanted to be loyal but could not be within the present constraints, and that it would also justify the Church insisting on the obedience of all.[19] Prayer Book revision was therefore initiated in 1908 – this is the second act – and it continued until the third act, the Great War. The limitations of the Church's worship became clearer during the War and new needs were revealed.[20]

The fourth act was the long process of legislation in the Church Assembly. The proposals, embodied in the Deposited Book of 1927, were intended to provide the flexibility that would resolve the ritual crisis and meet the needs of a new age. Neither Archbishop really wanted it, however, and their lack of real enthusiasm was a factor in the Book's failure. It was merely the means to an end, a resolution of the ritual crisis. Archbishop Davidson told the Convocations in 1927 that the new book would 'maintain unity without irksome uniformity'. He spoke of 'increased elasticity' for the liturgy but also stressed that the proposals were permissive only, and that those who found in the

---

[17] Ibid., p. 463.
[18] Ibid., p. 471. *Report of the Royal Commission on Ecclesiastical Discipline* (London, 1906), § 399.
[19] Ibid.
[20] Donald Gray, *Earth and Altar*, Alcuin Club Collections, 68 (Norwich, 1986), pp. 35–62.

old Prayer Book all that they desired could 'rest content in those pastures still'.[21] The *Spectator*, in an article whole-heartedly supporting the new book, adopted the slogans of the Archdeacon of Chesterfield:

Diversity without Division.
Unity without Uniformity.
Discipline without Servility.[22]

In the final act of the drama, the Book was rejected in the House of Commons in December 1927 and again in June 1928. Between the two debates Davidson published an apologia – *The Prayer Book: Our Hope and Meaning*[23] – in which he frankly acknowledged that if the Measure was again rejected then 'the prospect of confusion and of the spread of lawlessness looms large and ugly'.[24] It was not possible, he said, to adhere strictly to the rules of 1662 but what the Church wanted was 'the liberty of departing from them to be a liberty which is authorised and regulated, lest in some direction or another the liberty become licence and abuse'.[25] When rejection came, the Church was in crisis. Lang suggested that the bishops should fall back on their inherent authority and allow use of most of the amended Book.[26] In September 1928 the English bishops agreed, though not with total unanimity, to the use of 1662 or most of the 1928 Book, except, for legal reasons, the Ordinal and the alternative Marriage Service. They issued a statement to that effect, printed in *The Times* on September 29, 1928:

During the present emergency, and until further order be taken, the Bishops, having in view the approval given by the Houses of Convocation and the Church Assembly to the proposals for deviations from and additions to the Book of 1662 set forth in the Book of 1928, cannot regard as inconsistent with loyalty to the principles of the Church of

---

[21] *The Prayer Book Measure*, p. 18.

[22] *The Spectator*, 21 May 1927; reprinted as a pamphlet, *Unity without Uniformity* (London, 1927).

[23] London, 1928.

[24] *The Prayer Book: Our Hope and Meaning*, p. 39.

[25] Ibid., p. 13.

[26] Robert F. Schmidt, *Prayer Book Revision in the Church of England, 1906–1929: Liturgy, Doctrine, and Ecclesiastical Discipline* (Ann Arbor, 1984), p. 309.

England the use of such additions or deviations as fall within the limits of those proposals . . . . Accordingly the Bishops, in exercise of their legal or administrative discretion, will be guided by the proposals approved in 1928 . . . , and will endeavour to secure that practices which are consistent neither with the Book of 1662 nor with the Book of 1928 shall cease.[27]

In 1929 Lang asserted that the bishops 'now possess a norm or standard by which to determine what usages may or may not be regarded as in accordance with the principles of the Church of England.'[28] In general the bishops followed the same line in every diocese. Bishop Headlam of Gloucester gave his Diocesan Conference instructions for the use of the 1928 Book.[29] In one line he summed up the new position: 'the standard of loyalty is set for us by the two Prayer Books'. The principle of uniformity had been officially abandoned in England.

The American Church had also suffered from ritual restlessness; but Protestant principles were not there maintained by law or upheld through the civil courts. Evangelical opposition had brought the liturgical revision that was begun in 1880 to an unhappy conclusion. The General Convention wanted to move 'in the direction of liturgical enrichment and increased flexibility' following the mood of the times. The 1883 Convention approved *The Book Annexed*, which was mainly the work of William Reed Huntington, but it was rejected by the 1886 Convention as liturgically, historically, and doctrinally unsatisfactory. The growing catholic party had to wait until 1913 for a revision that was largely based on Huntington's work.[30]

In 1928 the new American *Book of Common Prayer* was given final authorization by the General Convention. On October 23 that year the House of Bishops received a revised copy of the Message to the Clergy drafted by the Bishop of Central New

---

[27] *The Times*, 29 September 1928, p. 10; Schmidt, *Prayer Book Revision*, p. 311.

[28] *Chronicle of Convocation, 1929*, 131; Schmidt, *Prayer Book Revision*, p. 315.

[29] 8 October 1929.

[30] R. W. Albright, *A History of the Protestant Episcopal Church* (New York, 1964), pp. 296–7. Credit is also given to H. B. St George of Nashotah House by E. R. Hardy, Jr, 'The Catholic Revival in the American Church, 1722–1933', in N. P. Williams and C. Harris, *Northern Catholicism* (London, 1933), p. 113.

York. 'After fifteen years of careful study', the letter began, 'the Church is authorising for use in public worship a revised and enriched Book of Common Prayer. This book is now the only authorised manual set forth by this Church for acts of corporate worship.' The bishops went on to note the peril, conspicuous in American life, of placing undue emphasis upon personal liberty and of paying little respect 'to what has been set forth by duly constituted authority', and they called for 'a loyal recognition of our common obligation to render generous obedience in observing in their integrity the provisions of our enriched Book of Common Prayer'.

> Such loyalty does not, of course, preclude, as occasions may require, special services as provided for in the rubrics of the Prayer Book or authorised by the Bishops; but it does demand of the authorised Ministers of the Church obedience to rubrical directions of its authorised book of worship, as at all times binding upon priest and people. These rubrics and the various offices of the book are the solemn expression of the mind of the Church. To ignore or disregard them, or to set them aside and substitute other forms for them, is an obvious violation of the Church's law and order. We protest against the tendency towards an exaggerated individualism and eccentricities in devotional practice.

The Bishops themselves accepted some responsibility for 'permitting irregularities and in adopting a policy of undue toleration' but were quite clear that the 'liberty of experimental usage allowed during the period of Revision should now cease.'[31]

This call for loyalty and obedience was reinforced by the Pastoral Letter issued on the last day of the General Convention. The bishops gave a summary account of the Anglican inheritance – 'Catholic in our unbroken continuity with the Christian ages and in the fullness of our Christian heritage, Protestant in our participation in the great 16th century movement of reformation and freedom.' They also pointed to the tensions created by the extremes. 'If Catholic and Protestant cannot find a way to live

---

[31] *Journal of the General Convention of 1928* (New York, 1928), p. 107.

together, and to worship together the one Lord' whom both adore, 'then is our faith vain. We are yet in our sins.'[32] They then moved to practical considerations:

> There is little or no excuse for individualistic extremes such as often disturb the peace of the Church and its normal life. Let us have prophets, let us have life and initiative, but let us remember that there is a norm of teaching and of worship in the Prayer Book. The ordination vows of the Clergy pledge them to loyalty to the 'doctrine, discipline and worship' of this Church. These great words are nowhere accurately defined, but for a loyal priest desirous of doing his work honestly, not obscure in meaning! Loyalty does not consist in meticulous obedience to the letter of rubrics and canons. Such obedience may be rendered accompanied by real disloyalty to the spirit of the Church. Loyalty means the honest attempt to understand, to enter into and to express in one's ministry that spirit. It means the use of Prayer Book language, and the careful distinction between what is Church law or doctrine and what is merely the individual's wish or opinion. It does not forbid reaching out to the best in Christian experience wherever found. It does forbid the submerging of established usage in alien rites. It does not forbid freedom of criticism. It does forbid subversive conduct.[33]

Charles Lewis Slattery, Bishop of Massachusetts, was Chairman of the Commission on the Revision and Enrichment of the Book of Common Prayer and wrote an introduction to the new Book. In it he pointed to the House of Bishops address and stressed that the 'directions and rubrics of the Prayer Book guard the freedom of the laity'.[34] He explained what it means to be the Book of Common Prayer, belonging to all people, and denied that any special liturgical power belonged to the bishops so far as the book was concerned; the Presiding Bishop was as much bound by its laws as the least important person in the Church.[35] The rubrics

---

[32] Ibid., p. 148.

[33] Ibid., p. 149.

[34] C. L. Slattery, *The New Prayer Book: An Introduction* (New York, nd but presumably 1928 or 1929), p. 37.

[35] Ibid., p. 37.

of the services of Holy Communion, Baptism, Confirmation, Marriage, and Ordination set the limits of the liturgical freedom of any loyal servant of the Church.[36]

For the ritualists, the stricter Anglo-Catholics, the position in England had hardly changed after 1928. Neither the Prayer Book nor the additions or deviations proposed in 1927 and 1928 met their needs. They continued to practice 'advanced ceremonial' drawn either from the prevailing rites of the Roman Church or from a meticulous and scholarly reconstruction of the medieval English use. The *English Missal* and the *Anglican Missal* were still to be found on their altars and their ceremonial was ordered according to *Ritual Notes* and *The Parson's Handbook*.[37] As Kenneth Kirk put it, 'two new documents had been added to the library of English liturgical literature, but that was all.'[38] Bishop Frere, in Truro, told Archbishop Lang that the opportunity of calling the clergy and people to order in liturgical matters was gradually slipping away.[39] Yet the Book of 1928 gained some respect and adherence. The Alcuin Club revised its *Directory of Ceremonial* (first published in 1921) in 1931 to take account of the 1928 Book, calling it 'the most authoritative expression of the mind of the Church of England in current circumstances'.[40] W. K. Lowther Clarke, writing for the English Church Union in 1932, was unclear what he should make of it: lacking synodical authority it seemed to be of only academic interest, yet in so far as it represented the judgement of the Church of England on reform of the liturgy it would be pedantic to ignore it.[41] Ten years later he noted that much of the new material was in regular use.[42] The 1928 Prayer Book had institutionalized diversity rather than promoting a new standard of uniformity.

In America, though the Episcopal Church's 1928 Book of Common Prayer was widely accepted, it was supplemented in

---

[36] Ibid., p. 39.

[37] J. M. M. Dalby, 'Anglican Missals', *CQR*, 168 (1967), p. 212. *Ritual Notes* first appeared in 1886 and *The Parson's Handbook*, compiled by Percy Dearmer, in 1899. Both were regularly revised. The last editions appeared in 1964 and 1965 respectively.

[38] E. W. Kemp, ed., *Beauty and Bands* (London, 1955), p. 60.

[39] Letter of 30 March 1929 in *Walter Howard Frere: His Correspondence on Liturgical Revision and Construction*, ed. R. C. D. Jasper, Alcuin Club Collections, 39 (London, 1954), p. 182.

[40] Alcuin Club Tracts XIII, *A Directory of Ceremonial*, Part 1, 3rd edn (London, 1931).

[41] W. K. Lowther Clarke, ed., *Liturgy and Worship* (London, 1932), p. 2.

[42] W. K. Lowther Clarke, *The Prayer Book of 1928 Reconsidered* (London, 1943), p. 1.

1931 by an *American Missal*. There was a notable growth of 'High Church' liturgical practices, widely sanctioned or at least tolerated by bishops, and, in the struggle between the Western and Sarum uses there were as many versions of correctness as there were shades of churchmanship.[43] Despite the strong words of the American House of Bishops in 1928, when the Standing Liturgical Commission reported to the General Convention of 1940 it felt bound 'to call the attention of the Church to increasing lawlessness in the conduct of worship'.[44] It stressed that it was not calling for uniformity; great diversity within the limitation of the law of the Church was both possible and desirable, but, said the Commission, 'that freedom does not include freedom to alter rubrics or disregard constitutional provisions upon the part of either Bishop or Priest'.

During the period of Prayer Book revision, 1890–1930, the Anglican Church was strongly affected by the great advances in liturgical knowledge made during the nineteenth century. The work of revision itself promoted deeper knowledge of the Prayer Book liturgy and made Anglicans aware of the strengths and weaknesses of what they had inherited. Above all things, in the words of the American liturgical scholar Massey Shepherd, it 'put a seal of acceptance upon a comprehensive diversity in Anglican worship: unity in essentials, permissible liberty in non-essentials'.[45] Liturgical revision later in this century has provided a much greater variety of liturgical options than that allowed by any prayer book hitherto. Uniformity, in any sense, is no longer seen as a necessary condition for unity. The reformed liturgies reflect and reinforce a flexibility in belief which may go well beyond Shepherd's idea of unity and permissible liberty. The experience of the period which has been our concern here is that no amount of liturgical revision, canonical prohibition, or episcopal exhortation can enforce the principle of liturgical unifor-

---

[43] H. Boone Porter, 'Toward an unofficial history of episcopal worship', in Malcolm C. Burson, ed., *Worship Points the Way: A Celebration of the Life and Work of Massey Hamilton Shepherd, Jr.* (New York, 1981), p. 107.

[44] *Journal of the General Convention of 1940* (New York, 1940), p. 472.

[45] Massey Hamilton Shepherd, Jr, 'The history of the liturgical renewal', in M. H. Shepherd, ed., *The Liturgical Renewal of the Church* (New York, 1960), p. 48.

mity in the modern church and the principle of unity must be found elsewhere.[46]

## St Bartholomew the Great, Smithfield, London

[46] See W. Taylor Stevenson, 'Lex Orandi-Lex Credendi', in Sykes and Booty, *Study of Anglicanism*, pp. 174–88.

# ECUMENISM OR DISTINCTIVENESS? SEVENTH-DAY ADVENTIST ATTITUDES TO THE WORLD MISSIONARY CONFERENCE OF 1910

*by* KEITH A. FRANCIS

For the Seventh-day Adventist Church, whose doctrines are rooted in eschatological and apocalyptic theology, ecumenism is problematic. While the Church sees itself as one heir of the historic tradition of Christianity[1] and so welcomes recognition as part of the mainstream,[2] it also claims to be the organization through which God proclaims a special message to the modern age. Put simply, sometimes Seventh-day Adventists are happy to be part of the universal Church and at other times they claim to be members of the only true Church. Obviously, the latter, exclusivist attitude is in contradiction to the ethos of the ecumenical movement.

If it were simply the case that Seventh-day Adventists rejected the ecumenical movement out of hand, ecumenism could hardly be described accurately as a 'problem'. Rather, ecumenism would be an issue of no interest to Seventh-day Adventists. However, it is the Church's 'Jekyll and Hyde' attitude to the ecumenical movement that is intriguing. Seventh-day Adventists are interested in the ecumenical movement: first, because of the Church's strong interest in missions; and second, because the progress of ecumenical movement is an important component of the Church's apocalyptic theology.

The Seventh-day Adventist Church's ambivalent attitude towards ecumenism highlights one of the problems facing the modern ecumenical movement. If ecumenism implies 'unity' – whether structural, doctrinal, or simply co-operative – then the question of who is involved in this unity is of some importance. Does 'unity' mean that all Churches participate in ecumenism – an eventuality which seems highly unlikely? Is it impossible for some Churches to be involved in the ecumenical movement

---

[1] See Bryan W. Ball, *The English Connection: The Puritan Roots of Seventh-day Adventist Belief* (Cambridge, 1981), for an example of a book which argues that Seventh-day Adventist doctrine has antecedents in earlier Christianity.

[2] The willingness of Seventh-day Adventists to work with other Christians in collecting money for charities such as Christian Aid, for example, has aided the perception of the Seventh-day Adventist Church as 'mainstream'.

because of the nature of their theology? And, furthermore, even if a Church is involved in ecumenism is it feasible – or wise – to expect a majority of its members to be 'ecumenically-minded'? An examination of the Seventh-day Adventist attitudes to ecumenism will help to shed light on the answers to these questions.

In a paper of this length it is not possible to provide a summary of Seventh-day Adventist attitudes to the modern ecumenical movement from the late nineteenth century to the present day;[3] it will, therefore, focus on the beginnings of the ecumenical movement and the implications of Seventh-day Adventist attitudes for the future of ecumenism. In particular, it will examine the attitudes to the event generally considered to have had a major impact on the development of modern ecumenism, the World Missionary Conference held at Edinburgh in 1910.[4]

In order to understand the rationale underpinning Seventh-day Adventist attitudes to ecumenism it is necessary to explain why Seventh-day Adventists consider missions so important and to explain, briefly, the exclusivist apocalyptic theology referred to earlier.

The Seventh-day Adventist Church was organized officially in 1863, having its headquarters in Battle Creek, Michigan.[5] The majority of its members had been Millerites, that is, in agreement with the ideas of William Miller, a millennialist preacher who had predicted that the Second Advent would occur around 1843. The predictions of Miller had, obviously, not come true but some Millerites who had survived this 'disappointment'[6] man-

---

[3] A simple introduction to the modern ecumenical movement from a Seventh-day Adventist perspective is Bert Beverly Beach's *Ecumenism: Boon or Bane?* (Washington, DC, 1974).

[4] Justo L. Gonzàlez, *The Reformation to the Present Day*, vol. 2 of *The Story of Christianity* (San Francisco, 1984), pp. 388–92; Kenneth Scott Latourette, 'Ecumenical bearings of the missionary movement and the International Missionary Council', in Ruth Rouse and Stephen Charles Neill, eds, *A History of the Ecumenical Movement, 1517–1948*, 2nd edn (London, 1967), pp. 355–63; Stephen Neill, *A History of Christian Missions* (London, 1965), p. 393; Alec R. Vidler, *The Church in an Age of Revolution (1789 to the Present Day)* (Harmondsworth, 1971); pp. 257–65.

[5] For a general introduction to the history of Seventh-day Adventism see: Richard W. Schwarz, *Light Bearers to the Remnant* (Boise, Idaho, 1979) and Gary Land, ed., *Adventism in America* (Grand Rapids, Mich., 1986). More apologetic histories include: Le Roy Edwin Froom, *Movement of Destiny* (Washington DC, 1971) and Arthur Whitefield Spalding, *Origin and History of Seventh-day Adventists*, 4 vols (Washington DC, 1962).

[6] 'The Great Disappointment' was a term used by Millerites – and later by Seventh-day Adventists – to describe the failure of Christ to appear in 1844. See Ronald L. Numbers and Jonathan M. Butler, eds, *The Disappointed: Millerism and Millenarianism in the Nineteenth Century* (Bloomington, Ind., 1987) for a good introduction to the Millerite movement.

aged to maintain a loose affiliation with each other, bound by a common belief in Sabbatarian adventism. When these Sabbatarian adventists organized themselves as the Seventh-day Adventist Church they chose the particular name of their organization because they wanted to draw attention to their most distinctive doctrines – their acknowledgement of the Sabbath as the seventh day of the week, Saturday, instead of the first; and their belief in an imminent Second Advent.

More interesting than the doctrines themselves was the Seventh-day Adventist understanding of how these doctrines would be propagated. Based on their interpretation of texts such as Revelation 12.17,[7] Seventh-day Adventists believed that God had given them the special task of proclaiming the twin doctrines of the Sabbath and the imminent Second Advent to everyone, including other Christians.[8] For this reason, members of their Church were 'the Remnant' and maintaining this distinctiveness, and exclusivity, was vital if Seventh-day Adventists were to accomplish their mission successfully.[9]

Perhaps this thinking would be of no interest to anyone concerned about the future success of the ecumenical movement were it not for the fact that Seventh-day Adventists took their understanding of their special mission to what they considered was its logical conclusion. Not only was the Seventh-day Adventist Church special, but other Christian Churches espousing spurious doctrines, particularly the Roman Catholic Church, were 'Babylon', evil opponents of true Christianity.[10] Furthermore, in the period just before the Second Advent, these 'apostate Churches' would persecute believers loyal to true Christianity.[11] Clearly such an attitude meant that Seventh-day Adventists would show little interest in ecumenism but, more importantly, if other Christian Churches adopted a similar

---

[7] 'And the dragon was wroth with the woman, and went to make war with the remnant of her seed, which keep the commandments of God, and have the testimony of Jesus Christ.'

[8] This belief in the special mission of Seventh-day Adventists is highlighted by the title of one of the histories of the Church: C. Mervyn Maxwell's *Tell It to the World: The Story of Seventh-day Adventists* (Mountain View, Cal., 1977).

[9] The best study of the development of Seventh-day Adventist doctrinal ideas is P. Gerard Damsteegt's *Foundations of the Seventh-day Adventist Message and Mission* (Grand Rapids, Mich., 1977).

[10] Ibid., pp. 179–81.

[11] Ibid., pp. 208–20.

exclusivist attitude there would be no future for the ecumenical movement.

However, the desire of Seventh-day Adventists to propagate their message meant, ironically, that they were interested in other Churches; or, to be more precise, the evangelistic efforts of other Churches. The membership of the Seventh-day Adventist Church had grown from 5,440 in 1870 to 90,736 in 1910, and the Church was now becoming international rather than merely American.[12] Considering Seventh-day Adventists' understanding of their mission, there would be no 'resting on their laurels'; there was a whole world 'waiting' to be converted. Obviously any discussion of developments in missiology, as would occur at the World Missionary Conference, was of interest.

The World Missionary Conference was an attempt by leaders in a number of Protestant Churches to generate more interest in missions and to advance a more scientific approach to the conduct of missionary activity.[13] The stated objective of the Conference was 'to consider missionary problems in relation to the non-Christian world'.[14] This included discussion of topics such as 'The Church in the Mission Field' and 'The Missionary Message in Relation to Non-Christian Religions'.

The committee responsible for organizing the Conference – called the International Committee – believed that participation by representatives from as many missionary societies as possible was vital if the Conference was to be a success. For this reason, it encouraged its three executive committees – in Britain, continental Europe, and the United States respectively – to send invitations to every missionary society. The only restriction was that the society had to be spending at least £10,000 on missionary activity among non-Christians; the first £2,000 allowed the society to send one delegate and an additional delegate could be sent for each sum of £4,000 above the initial £2,000.[15]

---

[12] Land, *Adventism in America*, pp. 252–3.

[13] The definitive history of the Conference, including reports of the various preparatory commissions and the text of some of the major speeches, is in *The World Missionary Conference, 1910*, 9 vols (Edinburgh, 1910).

[14] This objective was placed at the beginning of each report from the preparatory commissions. See *History and Records of the Conference* (Edinburgh, 1910), vol. 9 of *The World Missionary Conference, 1910*.

[15] W. H. T. Gairdner, *Edinburgh 1910*, 2nd edn (Edinburgh, 1910), p. 48.

The World Missionary Conference was held from 14 to 23 June 1910 and it is likely that the American Executive Committee sent an invitation to the Seventh-day Adventist missionary society, known as the Foreign Mission Board, sometime in 1909. But, taking into account the major tenets of Seventh-day Adventist theology described earlier, what was the likelihood of Seventh-day Adventists being receptive to the idea of attending a conference which, while its main focus was on missions and missiology, had as a topic for discussion 'Co-operation and the Promotion of Unity'? If some of the contemporary praise for the World Missionary Conference is used as the standard to judge it by then the Conference would have been difficult to ignore. A Methodist delegate, F. B. Turner, described it as 'a conference great beyond the power of description'. Another Methodist delegate, J. Pickett, enthused that the Conference 'will be considered by future historians as the most remarkable assemblage of the people of God that this world has yet seen'.[16]

The first mention of the Conference in Seventh-day Adventist records suggests mild interest rather than the antagonism which might be expected. The executive committee of the Church – the General Conference Committee – met in January 1910 and suggested that L. R. Conradi, the leader of Seventh-day Adventists in Central Europe, and 'whoever may go over from America to the summer meetings in Europe' should attend the World Missionary Conference.[17] This was hardly a ringing endorsement; rather than opposition, the official position of the Church seemed to be that the Conference was unimportant.[18]

By March the official position had changed. The official Church journal, the *Adventist Review and Sabbath Herald*, proclaimed that the Conference would be 'one of the greatest world's missionary conferences ever held'. The editorial further

[16] 'The World Missionary Conference', *United Methodist*, 23 June 1910, p. 478 and 'The Mighty Missionary Conference', *Primitive Methodist Leader*, 30 June 1910, p. 449

[17] E. G. White–SDA Research Centre Europe, Newbold College, Bracknell, Berkshire, General Conference Committee Minutes [hereafter 'Bracknell, GC Minutes'], 17 Jan. 1910. The 'summer meetings in Europe' were meetings of the executive committees responsible for running the Seventh-day Adventist Church in various European countries such as Denmark, Germany, France and England.

[18] There is no mention of the World Missionary Conference in any other Seventh-day Adventist publications nor in any private correspondence. This seems to confirm the lack of importance Seventh-day Adventists attached to the Conference.

advised Seventh-day Adventist workers to attend the subsidiary meetings of the Conference in order to 'avail themselves of this opportunity for studying mission problems'.[19]

The reason for the change of attitude is not clear. No reason is given in Seventh-day Adventist publications and the delegates who attended the World Missionary Conference do not comment on the change either. (Perhaps the American Executive Committee of the World Missionary Conference prevailed upon the Foreign Missions Board.) Nevertheless, this change of attitude resulted in the General Conference Committee voting to send three men, A. G. Daniells, L. R. Conradi, and W. J. Fitzgerald, to the main meetings in the Assembly Hall and three more, W. H. Anderson, H. C. Lacey, and M. A. Altman, to the parallel meetings held in the Synod Hall.[20] A month later the General Conference Committee voted to substitute W. A. Spicer for A. G. Daniells and Guy Dail for W. H. Anderson.[21]

The status of the men sent to the World Missionary Conference is further evidence that there had been a change of thinking among the leaders of the Seventh-day Adventist Church. Spicer, for example, was the secretary of the Foreign Mission Board and the General Conference Committee as well as the editor of the *Adventist Review and Sabbath Herald*. The other delegates included the leader of the Seventh-day Adventist Church in Britain, Fitzgerald, and the secretary of the executive committee for the Seventh-day Adventist Church in Europe, Dail. The Seventh-day Adventist delegates were men of importance in the Church; somewhat akin to bishops such as Randall Davidson and Charles Gore who represented the Church of England at the Conference.[22]

A list of the Seventh-day Adventist delegates at the World Missionary Conference seems to suggest that the Church had given up some of its exclusivist ideas: in fact, this was not the case. One scholar suggests, probably correctly, that Seventh-day

---

[19] *Adventist Review and Sabbath Herald*, 87/14 (April 1910), p. 24. As well as the meetings for delegates, there were meetings held in the Tollbooth Parish Church, Edinburgh, and St George's Church, Glasgow, which anyone could attend.

[20] Bracknell, GC Minutes, 6 March 1910.

[21] Ibid., 20 April 1910.

[22] Tissington Tatlow, 'The World Conference on Faith and Order' in Rouse and Neill, *History of the Ecumenical Movement*, p. 406; and 'The World Missionary Conference', *Church Times*, 17 June 1910, p. 800.

Adventists were engaging in a 'trial marriage' with inter-Church co-operation.[23] Statistics from Seventh-day Adventist financial records show that the Foreign Missions Board had a fund of about $450,000 – about £90,000 by the day's exchange rate – but the Church only sent six official delegates.[24] It is possible that the budget of the Foreign Missions Board included money spent on evangelizing Christians, but unlikely that this activity accounted for seventy per cent of the budget. The number of Seventh-day Adventist delegates suggests that the Church was 'putting its toes in the water'. Perhaps the thinking of the General Conference Committee members was that if the experience confirmed their fears about 'Babylon' not too much would be lost by a few Seventh-day Adventists listening to speeches and discussions on missions.

Furthermore, there is no evidence to suggest that the Seventh-day Adventist delegates participated in the debates and discussions. An examination of the Conference records shows that not all of the 1,200 delegates had the opportunity to speak, but it is a little surprising that none of the six men, all of whom were experienced in missionary work, said anything. Again it seems that the Seventh-day Adventists engaged in what could be called 'observer ecumenism' rather than 'participatory ecumenism'.

Another way to gauge the Seventh-day Adventist reaction to the World Missionary Conference is by examining comments about the Conference in Church journals. Two men reported on the Conference: Spicer, who wrote for the *Adventist Review and Sabbath Herald*; and W. T. Bartlett, who wrote for the other major Church journal, the *Signs of the Times*. (Bartlett's comments are interesting because he was not listed in General Conference Committee minutes as an official delegate; he either followed the advice in the *Adventist Review and Sabbath Herald* mentioned earlier,[25] or he went to Edinburgh as a correspondent for *Signs of the Times*.) In summary, the reaction of these men to

---

[23] Borge Schantz, 'The Development of Seventh-day Adventist Missionary Thought: A Contemporary Appraisal' (Fuller Theological Seminary Ph.D. Thesis, 1983), p. 389.

[24] General Conference Statistical Report quoted in Schantz, 'Development of Seventh-day Adventist Missionary Thought', pp. 388–9. The Foreign Missions Board could have sent another twenty delegates.

[25] See p. 481–3.

the Conference was positive on the subject of missions and suspicious about anything that resembled ecumenism.

In his two articles, Spicer stated his belief that the modern missionary movement, as exemplified by the World Missionary Conference, was the successor of the Protestant Reformation. The Reformation had resulted in many people being able to hear the gospel and the same was true of the contemporary missionary movement. Spicer also stated his belief that the World Missionary Conference affirmed the Seventh-day Adventist efforts at evangelism; he noted, 'It is of deep significance that the key note of this great congress, representing so diverse and even conflicting views, should be that now, just now, is the time to strike for the evangelization of the world.'[26]

Spicer was much less positive on the question of co-operation. While he agreed with the consensus view that a weakness of the Conference was the lack of participation by the Roman Catholic and Orthodox Churches, he thought that any moves by Christian Churches towards unifying their missionary efforts was dangerous. Spicer suggested that such a change would result in the missionary movement mirroring the church federation movement in the United States: in an attempt to promote unity, minority opinions were ignored or rejected too readily.[27]

Bartlett, on the other hand, was much more suspicious of the Conference; he perceived the events in Edinburgh as a fulfilment of his eschatological expectations. He admitted that the World Missionary Conference was 'a remarkable and important occasion' but thought that the emphasis on missions illustrated the imminence of the Second Advent. As for the calls for Church unity, to Bartlett these were simply malevolent signs that the world would soon come to an end. The gathering of important Church dignitaries and the large number of Churches represented demonstrated that there would be a time when 'the remnant' would be persecuted by 'apostate Christians'.[28]

Perhaps the most interesting Seventh-day Adventist reactions to the World Missionary Conference are found in two almost

---

[26] Spicer, 'Notes from the World's Missionary Conference', *Adventist Review and Sabbath Herald*, 87/29 (July 1910), p. 9.

[27] Spicer, 'More Notes from the World's Missionary Conference', *Adventist Review and Sabbath Herald*, 87/32 (August 1910), pp. 11–12.

[28] Bartlett, 'The World Missionary Conference', *Signs of the Times*, 37/29 (July 1910), pp. 10–11.

incidental references in the journal *Liberty*.[29] The comments suggest that not all Seventh-day Adventists were willing to become involved in inter-Church co-operation.

In an article entitled 'Rome Applauds the Conference', the editor of *Liberty*, C. M. Snow, commented on the letter sent to Silas McBee, the editor of *The Churchman*, by Monsignor Bonomelli, the Bishop of Cremona. In this letter, which he allowed to be read to the delegates, Monsignor Bonomelli congratulated the representatives on their unity of effort and purpose.[30] Reflecting on what the letter meant, Snow said, 'a united Christendom, to the Catholic mind, means the whole world acknowledging spiritual and temporal allegiance to the Pope. . . . The Church of Rome sees plainly that the confederation of Christian churches will yet lead the world to the feet of "the vicar of Christ".'[31]

If Snow was suggesting that the Roman Catholic Church – and, by implication, Protestant ecumenism – was not to be trusted, another writer, C. E. Holmes, suggested that the Roman Catholic Church was actually dangerous. In an article entitled 'A Determined Attack Upon Protestant Missions', Holmes suggested that the Roman Catholic Church was preparing a determined attack on American Protestantism. Towards the end of his article Holmes quoted part of a speech by John Mott, the Chairman of the World Missionary Conference, in which he said that the Christian Church must be ready to meet the 'present world crisis'.[32] It is highly unlikely that Mott was referring to the progress of Roman Catholicism in the United States when he talked about a world crisis, but for Holmes Mott's words helped to illustrate his thesis that contemporary events were leading to the end of the world.

What conclusions about the future of the ecumenical movement can be drawn from this episode in Seventh-day Adventist history? One deduction is that *mentalité* is a major barrier to ecumenism. Even though the World Missionary Conference

---

[29] *Liberty* was a Seventh-day Adventist journal which focused on religious toleration; it particularly informed its readers about developments in church and state relations.

[30] Latourette, 'Ecumenical Bearings of the Missionary Movement', pp. 361–2; and *Co-operation and Unity*, vol. 8 of *The World Missionary Conference, 1910*, pp. 220–3.

[31] *Liberty*, 5 (Third Quarter, 1910), p. 27.

[32] Ibid., p. 40.

focused on a subject dear to Seventh-day Adventists, the world view of the group – which was derived from their theology – made acceptance of the Conference and full participation in it an unlikely occurrence. It was not their actual theology – ideas about the Sabbath or the Second Advent – that was the barrier to co-operation but the 'suspicion' of Seventh-day Adventists that their fellow-Christians would turn against them eventually and so should not be trusted.

If the Seventh-day Adventist Church of 1910 was one example of Christian reaction to ecumenism – and it was probably not alone in its suspicions – then clearly 'Church unity' cannot mean the uniting or even the co-operation of every Church. There may be Churches who are constitutionally unable to stomach ecumenism.

And what of the future? Is it possible for these Churches to change? The problem with the Seventh-day Adventist Church of 1994 is that it is still exclusivist – in a word, anti-ecumenical – in the main. They may no longer be 'Seventh-day Door-shutters',[33] a name given to Sabbatarian adventists in the 1850s because they believed that after a particular date no-one else could obtain salvation – the door of probation was shut, as they put it – but the exclusivist mentality is still very much part of the Seventh-day Adventist psyche.[34] This is certainly true of the proverbial Seventh-day Adventist person-in-the-street. The expression of the Church's distinctiveness is certainly couched more carefully in official publications of the Seventh-day Adventist Church in the modern era – Seventh-day Adventists are members of 'the remnant' but so are other Christians – but, nevertheless, the emphasis in these publications is on distinctiveness rather than ecumenism.[35]

There is, however, a possibility that Seventh-day Adventist attitudes will change. The Church has observer status on the World Council of Churches[36] and the Council of Churches for

---

[33] Schwarz, *Light Bearers*, pp. 94–5.

[34] Good discussions of Seventh-day Adventist mentality are found in Malcolm Bull and Keith Lockhart, *Seeking a Sanctuary: Seventh-day Adventism and the American Dream* (San Francisco, 1989), esp. pp. 95–175, and Edwin S. Gaustad, ed., *The Rise of Adventism* (New York, 1974), esp. pp. 154–206.

[35] See, for example, *Seventh-day Adventists Believe . . .* (Hagerstown, Maryland, 1988), pp. 152–69.

[36] The World Council of Churches meeting in Canberra, Australia, in 1991 was reported in some detail in the Church Journal *Adventist Review* (the renamed *Adventist Review and Sabbath Herald*). See 168, 11 April 1991, pp. 8–10; 18 April 1991, pp. 14–16; 2 May 1991, pp. 8–10.

Britain and Ireland – the reconstituted British Council of Churches. On the local level there is even more involvement; Seventh-day Adventists have acted as chairmen of local councils of churches and the present treasurer of Churches Together in Bracknell is a Seventh-day Adventist.

Clearly co-operation between Christian Churches, whether 'fundamentalist' or 'mainstream' is possible. It happened in 1910 and is happening at the present. However, it is not possible to ignore what might be considered 'sociological' factors.[37] Whether one group of Christians 'feels comfortable' with another may be just as important as any theological questions. Seventh-day Adventism was founded on the idea of a separate community and this idea still pervades the thinking of its members.[38] It may not be – perhaps is not – possible to convince every Seventh-day Adventist of the efficacy of ecumenism. Perhaps the best that can be hoped for, as in 1910, is that some Seventh-day Adventists will be 'converted'. And maybe this is true of the ecumenical movement in general: not every Church nor all Christians can be persuaded to participate. To steal a line from Jesus, 'many are called but few are chosen'.[39]

Pacific Union College

---

[37] See Vidler, *Church in an Age of Revolution*, pp. 267–8.
[38] See Bull and Lockhart, *Seeking a Sanctuary*, pp. 1–15.
[39] Matt. 22. 14.

# 'AN ARTISAN OF CHRISTIAN UNITY': SIR FRANK WILLIS, ROME AND THE YMCA

by CLYDE BINFIELD

I have always most earnestly desired that Christians should meet in Associations, such as will meet on Thursday, with this conviction, that their common Christianity ought to form a bond far more powerful to unite them to their one Lord, and Master, and Head, and in brotherhood one to another, than that their conscientious differences of opinion should form cause or excuse for hostile separation. I am glad to know that some of my brethren in the ministry of the Church of England will be with you.[1]

YMCA is a household acronym. Throughout the world people are sure that they know what it means. In 1926 two well-connected Labour politicians, the Wedgwood Benns, were in Moscow. There the head of the Bureau for Cultural Relations with Foreigners, Olga Kamenev, who was also well-connected, since she was Trotsky's sister, told them about one of the Russian capital's most serious problems: the street children. These youngsters, homeless since the civil war, slept under bridges and robbed railway trains:

'We tried putting them in institutions but they kept running away. So we have called in the help of our splendid League of Godless Youth'. This turned out to be the Young Men's Christian Association – without religion. 'How did one join this League?' we asked. She showed us, pinned to her wall, pictures of what had to be given up: a glass of vodka, a pack of cards, young women. In addition, complete atheism had to be declared and several nights a week had to be given to welfare work. 'Our youth are absolutely godless', she often repeated.[2]

[1] Dean Elliott of Bristol, regretting his inability to chair Bristol YMCA's first annual meeting, 1853, quoted by Sir F. Willis and adduced as confirming his view that from its earliest days the YMCA was not just 'very largely a Nonconformist (or Free Church) organisation' but 'was supported by quite a number of Anglicans who were what was generally called Low Churchmen'; Geneva, World Alliance Archives [hereafter WAA], Sir F. Willis to Dr Paul Limbert, Hampstead, 12 March 1962.
[2] Margaret Stansgate, *My Exit Visa* (London, 1992), p. 106.

489

That is an eerie recollection. Seventy years on, street children have returned to Moscow. They are a world-wide phenomenon, engaging the concern of the YMCA which is a world-wide movement. The YMCA has returned to Russia, where it existed before the Bolshevik Revolution. In his youth William Wedgwood Benn had been a member of one of the London Congregational Churches most closely associated with the founding in 1844 of what is regarded as the prototype YMCA.[3] Origins like that might explain the movement's tenacious reputation for puritanical heartiness. Less easily explained, since its history repeatedly contradicts it, is the movement's reputation for a benign, because contentless, secularism. Much more justifiable would be a reputation for sustained and developing ecumenism. Here most certainly is a diversity of unity.

In 1963 Sir Frank Willis, formerly YMCA National Secretary for England, Wales and Ireland, prepared a report for the Geneva-based World Alliance of YMCAs on the first session of the Second Vatican Council. With characteristic caution he marked it: 'Confidential. For limited circulation only.'[4] Willis was having the time of his life. The Vatican had issued invitations to 'Delegate-Observers' from fifteen world Church bodies as well as the World Council of Churches and the Friends' World Committee. It had also invited some 'Guests of the Secretariat'. The YMCA featured neither among observers nor guests. Willis turned this to good account. Observers and guests were by definition non-Catholics. Willis firmly believed that the YMCA should not be regarded as non-Catholic. Its possibly hurtful absence from the Council's guest-list was thus providential. Besides, the YMCA was at the Council, for Willis had turned up in Rome as the accredited press representative of the World Alliance's house journal, *World Communiqué*, a glossy bi-monthly modelled on *Picture Post*. Willis was no journalist. He was seldom content with one word unless twenty more could be found to qualify it (and each other). Nonetheless his bulletins from the

---

[3] In 1895, with his parents, a brother and two sisters, he joined F. B. Meyer's Christ Church, Westminster Bridge Road, the heir to Rowland Hill's famous Surrey Chapel. I am indebted to the Revd Ian Randall for this information.

[4] WAA: F. Willis, *Report of the First Session of the Second Vatican Council* (Geneva, 1963). Willis was famous for his confidential reports, most notably that on the YMCA and sex, marked 'Confidential: not for reproduction.' He was quite without a sense of humour.

Vatican duly appeared in *World Communiqué*, distilled and streamlined from the reports for the World Alliance's secretariat, which were his real business, and the interviews and conversations on which those reports were based. His was a corridor-filled mind and Vatican ways fascinated him. He was also a man with a mission: to facilitate, even to achieve, Vatican recognition of the YMCA. An early conversation captures both that mission and its almost impenetrable context. Willis had taken the Italian YMCA's National Secretary, Olindo Parachini, who was a Roman Catholic, to meet an American bishop, Curtis of Bridgeport, Connecticut. The Italian movement was small, America's was the world's largest. The Italian asked the American what he felt about Roman Catholics joining the YMCA. '[T]hough the Bishop could not have been more friendly and sympathetic, he smilingly replied, "But they oughtn't to do so at all, ought they?" '[5] Yet within twenty-five years the President of the World Alliance of YMCAs would be a Peruvian Catholic and within thirty years its Secretary-General would be an Irish-American from Chicago who had graduated from a Jesuit university having trained at a seminary with the priesthood in mind. In most countries YMCA members were as likely to be Catholic as Protestant and in many that would also apply to YMCA leaders. Indeed, within six years there would be official Catholic participation at a YMCA World Council. That would have been inconceivable without Vatican II but it owed something at least to the relentless diplomacy of Sir Frank Willis, determinedly interpreting Rome and Geneva to each other.

The motor of that diplomacy is best expressed by Willis's account of a sermon delivered at the Council press corps' weekly mass by another American bishop, Sheen of New York. Sheen's sermon took the form of press reports from Jerusalem, the first Council of them all. He focused on that Council's four-fold tensions – between the centralists and the federalists (Pope Peter against Bishops John and James), between the westerners and the easterners (Pope Peter against Bishops Philip and Andrew), between conservatives and liberals (here it was Bishops Matthias and Simon Zelotes in tension with bishops from the new and underdeveloped areas of Asia and Africa who were backed by the

---

[5] Ibid., p. 7.

one leading Father who had never been part of the Jerusalem Curia, Bishop Paul), between the Scripture mystics (Bishop John) and the modernists (Bishop Thomas, who would only accept what was scientifically established). And then he asked:

> Did the pre-Council press reports of conflicts, blocs and groups ever materialise? Not a one! And why? Because Bishops outside a Council are quite different from Bishops inside a Council. In the Council the two thousand five hundred Bishops under the power of the Holy Spirit are 'changed' (though not in the same way as the bread and wine in the Mass) into the Teaching Body of the Church. Their individual appearances remain the same: they have the national and linguistic traits, but under the white fire of the Holy Spirit, as at Pentecost, they unite for the good of the Church. The Peter who denied Our Lord to a maid servant at the Court of Caiaphas, was not the same Peter who, after the descent of the Spirit, told Caiaphas that he had crucified the Lord. We go in as two thousand five hundred fallible men. But add two elements to this two thousand five hundred, namely the Holy Spirit and the Vicar of Christ, and you have infallibility.[6]

Such a sermon, heard by such a man as Willis, whose first name was Zwinglius, who had been training for the Congregational ministry when the Great War deflected him into the YMCA and the Church of England, was irresistible. If this was Roman Catholicism, it was also Presbyterianism, even Congregationalism, of purest essence. Here might be grounded an official transformation of attitudes which were already changing unofficially.

From the World Alliance's point of view such a transformation would ratify carefully cherished myth. Its centennial history, described by its chief author, C. P. Shedd of Yale, as a 'comprehensive and authoritative record of the origin and development of the oldest ecumenical organisation, next to the Evangelical Alliance organized in 1846, and without exception the oldest

---

[6] Ibid., pp. 5–6.

international Christian body with a federative type of organization', had received the imprimatur of that ecumenist extraordinary, John R. Mott.[7] Mott's 'Foreword', which had been written by Shedd, was presented as his last message to the movement which he had dominated for sixty years and presided over for twenty.[8] In Mott's life the YMCA, that ecumenical serving agency 'sensitive to the needs of the common man', joined the World Student Christian Federation (WSCF) and, at the last, the World Council of Churches (WCC), but it was the YMCA which had provided his first key international contacts and shaped a career of unparalleled missionary advocacy.

When he died Mott was buried in the crypt of Washington Cathedral beneath the chapel of St Joseph of Arimathea. An old YMCA warhorse, Darius Davis, explained the circumstances to Geneva: 'Many are curious to know how Dr. Mott came to be buried in the Cathedral. As you know he was an Honorary Canon of the Cathedral. Last summer the Bishop raised the question with Dr. Mott at Evanston.'[9] The ecumenical undertones of that delicate negotiation are unmistakable. When the WCC first assembled at Amsterdam in 1948, one historian of the ecumenical movement reflected that 'Four-fifths of those assembled on these platforms probably owed their ecumenical inspiration to some connection with the YMCA, with the YWCA, or with the closely connected Student Christian Movement.'[10] After the WCC's second assembly at Evanston in 1954, a year before the World Alliance's centennial conference at Paris, the Alliance's new Secretary-General, Paul Limbert, was careful both to point the way forward and to sound a warning note. He called to witness a Swiss-Frenchman, an Englishman, and an American – Roger Schutz of Taizé, Edwin Barker, and Edwin Espy. Schutz furnished the rationale for ecumenism:

[7] C. P. Shedd et al., *History of the World's Alliance of Young Men's Christian Associations* (London, 1955), pp. xvii, ix–x.

[8] Mott died on 3 January 1955. The previous December Shedd had travelled to Orlando, Florida, to hammer out the Foreword: 'As we read our suggestions to him sentence by sentence, he would break out and in his characteristic way with fire and enthusiasm say "That's right. That's what I mean. That's what I want to say . . .".' Then, early in the new year, 'I found from Dr. Mott the following wire. "Approve use of my name to manuscript submitted. Would decidedly prefer that manuscript be not reduced, signed John R. Mott." ' WAA: C. P. Shedd to Paul Limbert, Yale, 1 Feb., 1 Jan. 1955.

[9] WAA: Dr D. A. Davis to Paul Limbert, Westwood, NJ, 12 Feb. 1955.

[10] Ruth Rouse, quoted in T. Strong, 'The World's Alliance in a changing world', in Shedd, *History*, p. 464.

Sin separates, divides that which was originally in union and communion with God. This work of division is the work of the devil ('diabolos' – the divider). Christ is come to reassemble that which is dispersed, to unite that which is divided, that all may be one . . . and He has based the work of union on the uniting power of love in the heart of His Church.

Barker drew a necessary moral:

Unless we take steps to come into the heart of the new Ecumenical Movement we are in danger of becoming merely a part of its early history. . . . An Ecumenical Movement without a Youth Wing is in a dangerous position, and there may be much to be said for the YMCA, the YWCA, and the SCM becoming this part of the total Movement.

Espy underlined the urgency: Evanston had 'stressed with renewed clarity the role of the laity in relation to the Church. . . . Little if any specific place was given to the role of lay movements of Christians under non-ecclesiastical auspices, such as the YMCA. . . . Both the YMCA and the Churches stand to gain from a serious wrestling with this issue.'[11]

There was little such wrestling between Evanston and the WCC's third assembly at New Delhi in 1961, but there was a great deal of interconfessional excitement. Two months before New Delhi the Pan-Orthodox Conference in Rhodes had gathered more representatives of Orthodox churches than had been seen for three hundred years. And it was now almost certain that twelve months after New Delhi a Second Vatican Council would meet in Rome. Paul Limbert was alert to the implications of this new ecumenical setting. The WCC retained the Eastern European (and therefore Orthodox) links which the YMCA had largely lost since the fall of the Iron Curtain. The YMCA had a growing, if unofficial, Roman Catholic membership, which the WCC lacked. There was a further dimension: 'Hindu, Buddhist and Muslim youth are not outsiders to the YMCA; they take part freely in many kinds of YMCA activity. The problem of the

[11] *World Communiqué* [hereafter *WC*], May/June 1955, 66, No. 3, pp. 3–9.

YMCA, unlike that of many churches, is not *contact* but *impact.*'
In short, the YMCA was still strategically placed for ecumenical
action at its broadest – and yet 'One might very well ask therefore whether the day of the lay Christian movements like the
YMCA is over. What is the future for the YMCA when the
churches themselves see their function more and more in terms
of lay activity? This is a question to be taken seriously by YMCA
leaders.'[12] Sir Frank Willis's presence among Vatican II's press
corps was part of Limbert's strategy for answering this question.

The YMCA's ecumenical credentials were thus impeccable,
perhaps inevitable and yet surprising. John R. Mott had known
the movement's English founder, Sir George Williams, whom he
had first met in Amsterdam in 1891.[13] That made for a power-
fully apostolic succession, but it was a very Protestant succession.
Williams's evangelicalism was never in doubt. His London young
men of the 1840s were those for whom the Evangelical Alliance
was a beacon and the Exeter Hall a temple. Their word spread
through the evangelical and commercial bush telegraph, its
rhetoric unimpeachable and yet elastic with opportunity. Thus
by 1926 there were YMCAs in sixty-three countries, twenty of
them mainly Protestant, seventeen of them mainly Catholic, five
mainly Orthodox, and the rest non-Christian.[14] Tensions were
inevitable. The rapid popularity of the Red Triangle, as the
newest Y symbol, fuelled the suspicions of those who knew that
Jesuits, Freemasons, and Theosophists, as well as Orthodox, used
a similar symbol.[15]

At an official level relations varied. In 1928 a consultation of
Orthodox and YMCA leaders at Sofia agreed 'that in predominantly Orthodox countries the work of the YMCA should be
conducted in harmony with the principles of the Orthodox
Church and in consultation with its leaders'.[16] That was also what
happened in practice with the Catholic Church in Poland where
work had developed apace after 1922. For Catholics, however,

---

[12] Ibid., March/April 1962, pp. 4–6.
[13] Shedd, *History*, p. ix. For Williams see C. Binfield, *George Williams and the YMCA: A Study in Victorian Social Attitudes* (London, 1973).
[14] Shedd, *History*, p. 492.
[15] Ibid., p. 489.
[16] Z. F. Willis, 'That they all may be one', in Shedd, *History*, p. 701.

the situation had been formally blocked since November 1920 when Cardinal Merry Del Val, Secretary of the Holy Office, had issued a categorical warning against 'certain newly-formed associations of non-Catholics'.[17] That warning remained in force for over forty years, notwithstanding the success of the 'Polish option', or the World Alliance's growing consciousness of its 'place . . . as a lay movement in the ecumenical task of the Church',[18] or the unimaginable pressures and displacements of the Second World War, or the increasing attempts of Catholics in the movement from Latin America to the Philippines to get the Church to relax its stance. This explains the Bishop of Bridgeport's amiable rebuke to Olindo Parachini. It also explains Sir Frank Willis's sense of mission.

The Vatican Council was due to open on 11 October 1962. Late in August Willis was writing about 'the suggestion that I should spend some four or five weeks in Rome during the initial period', perhaps as an accredited press correspondent. Financially he would be covered by 'the lay friend to whose generous help I have been so indebted since my retirement'.[19]

Willis's press work consisted, when he was not buttonholing important priests in sacred corridors or waylaying the long suffering Monsignor Willebrands, of invaluably Willisian (and therefore confidential) despatches to Geneva and more upbeat bulletins to *World Communiqué*. *Communiqué's* first significant piece on the Council noted the formation under Cardinal Bea and Monsignor Willebrands of the Secretariat for Promoting Christian Unity. 'We may expect', wrote Father George Tavard,

a new departure of Catholic ecumenism as it has taken shape in the course of the last 80 years. There is every reason to believe that Catholic ecumenism in its intellectual as well as its spiritual aspect, is not a transient phenomenon in the history of the Church. It is called to continue. The Protestant Ecumenical Movement will therefore be well advised to study its conclusions seriously.[20]

[17] Ibid., p. 698.

[18] Ibid., p. 707.

[19] Since that unnamed benefactor had, however, died, Willis was careful to point out the implications for any further attendance. WAA: Sir F. Willis to Paul Limbert, Hampstead, 27 Aug., 11 Sept. 1962.

[20] 'The Second Ecumenical Council of the Vatican', *WC*, Nov./Dec. 1962, p. 13.

Willis was not in St Peter's for the opening ceremonies. He watched them on television in Rome's YMCA. This was another exclusion which he turned to good account when he learned how badly placed the press seats in St Peter's were. Carefully he balanced the good, bad, and indifferent points of the momentous happenings. He found himself haunted as so often before in Rome by the 'superstition in practice if not in belief'. He deprecated the absence of laity: notwithstanding the unprecedented Commission on the Lay Apostolate, of 833 members of the various preparatory bodies only eight were laypersons, there were none in the Council itself and the few lay advisers were by their very nature sorts of honorary ecclesiastic. He deprecated too the unrepresentative structure. The Pope might well declare that he had 'shown to all the world the holy liberty that the sons of God enjoy in the Church', and the presence on the ten Conciliar Commissions of 160 fathers from forty-two countries might well represent universality in action but they also represented the fact that under a tenth of the Council was directly involved in the official discussions taking place outside it. This was a recipe for division. It was a most serious procedural defect.[21]

On the other hand Willis warmed to the Council's language. Its notices were issued in French, Spanish, English, German, and Arabic, thus revealing 'the universality of Christendom, capable even in its unchangeability, of assuming the values and traditions of the individual peoples, of all latitudes and all times, of the present and of the future'. Its debates, of course, were in Latin and this

> because of its logical precision and of its concrete phraseology of legal terms . . . is particularly suited for theology and dogma. Latin also has considerable psychological and ascetical values since it tends to make one speak in a logical and rational manner and prevents abandonment to sentimentalism and romantic evasions. It tends to give its user discipline of expression and of life.[22]

---

[21] Willis, *Report*, pp. 14–17.
[22] 'In Measured Stride', *WC*, Jan./Feb. 1963, p. 14.

There spoke an Edwardian King's man. And the issues? Willis seized on the change of emphasis from '*separated* brethren' to 'separated *brethren*'. He stressed the question of who has what authority in the Church and was (almost) sure that 'what may be termed the "Divine Right" of Bishops will, I think, be stressed' and infallibility seen as the infallibility of the Church-in-Council. He was sure that Catholics would emerge more aware of their Church's glory and unity and more determined to pursue its mission. He picked up the word '*aggiornamento*'.[23]

Ever the press man, Willis attended each of the Council's four sessions as well as the third World Congress for the Lay Apostolate and the first Synod of Bishops, which met in Rome in the Council's wake in autumn 1967. The second session (14 September to 21 November 1963) was to be relished. Willis trained his sights on the amenable Willebrands. 'I made sure in more than one way that he knew that I was again in Rome.' He made himself known to Archbishop Heenan, new to Westminster. He made it painfully clear to Lukas Vischer, the WCC observer, how important it was that the World Alliance, which 'has a more comprehensive ecumenical reference than has the World Council of Churches', should not be seen to shelter under any WCC umbrella 'or indeed under any label which might imply that we are non-Catholic'. And he became positively conspiratorial about the continued status of the 1920 Warning. So keen was he to secure the movement's implicit inclusion in a sort of general Vatican directory of ways in which bishops might properly exercise their discretion, that 'I ventured to point out that in my judgement it would be both naive and unwise to make any suggestion that the 1920 Warning should be withdrawn or cancelled, or that any reference should be made to the YMCA by name in any document which may emanate from the Vatican Council'.[24] Willis was out-Roming Rome in his discretion.

Certainly the world had changed excitingly. There was a new Pope in Rome (Montini of Milan) and a new Secretary-General in Geneva (Fredrik Franklin, a Swedish Baptist who had been a missionary in India). There were more Observers and Guests,

---

[23] In the sense of 'updating' or 'renewal' rather than 'adjournment' or 'postponement'. Willis, *Report*, pp. 22–7.
[24] WAA: Sir F. Willis to Fredrik Franklin, Hampstead, 6 Dec. 1963.

notably from the Church of South India, and there was, at last, a group of lay 'Auditores' in the Council itself. All augured well:

> The First Vatican Council was clearly the Council of the Pope. The Second Vatican Council may from this point of view well go down in history as the Council of the Bishops, though it may confidently be hoped that it will be best known as the Council of Unity, or, more precisely, of preparation for Unity.[25]

Willis listened carefully to the speeches. He reported exhaustively on those of men like Cardinal Ruffini of Palermo for whom 'ecumenism' was a Protestant artefact. Others, like Cardinal Suenens, threw out lifelines of hope. Thus, Bishop Hannon of Washington DC, 'The Laity should be urged to join the organizations which can influence daily life: associations of parents interested in educational activities, and organizations with professional, charitable, and civic aims, not excluding participation in politics. Men cannot be led to Christ unless associations of this kind are marked with the spirit of Christ.' Thus Cardinal Bea himself, 'The role of authority is not to replace individual members in what they can do by themselves but only to supply what they cannot provide. This is true of any authority but particularly of authority in the Church. . . .'[26]

Willis summed all their words up with what for him was rare succinctness: 'The problem confronting the present Council is how to combine Church and Pope and Bishops into a single vehicle of the Holy Spirit for the maintenance of the purity of the revelation made by Jesus Christ and for its further apprehension, and thus to complete, as it were, the main unfinished business of the First Vatican Council.'[27] For *World Communiqué* he was more decisive: 'Gone, and we may thank God, gone for ever, is the old climate of distrust, of hostility, and of diatribe between the Roman Church and other Christian Communions. . . . Gone likewise are many wrong conceptions of the nature and meaning of the Papacy and of the functions and authority of

---

[25] WAA: F. Willis, *Report of the Second Session*, p. 16.

[26] Ibid., pp. 29, 25, 21.

[27] Ibid., p. 18.

the Curia'.[28] And in his reports he stressed the new Pope's emphasis on the centrality of Christ, his gaze 'beyond the confines of the Christian horizon', his insistence on the place of the laity – all of them key factors in YMCA thinking if only that antithesis of Roman catholicity, the local YMCA association, could be trained to acknowledge its high and rigorous calling. Willis, the present Anglican and past Congregationalist, was understandably uneasy about that.

He was back in Rome for the autumn of 1964 and the Council's third session. It was a time when 'so often my mind and my heart have not been in accord'.[29] Of the Council's creativity there was now no doubt. He painstakingly rehearsed its statements on the Mystery of the Church, on the People of God, on the Bishops, on the Laity, culminating in the Decree on Ecumenism.[30] He delighted in their careful wording. He dwelt on the moments of 'DOUBT, TENSION, DRAMA'. Had the Curia won? Had the Pope lost his commitment? He noted the 'high survival potential' of 'Curial power and juridical and monarchical conceptions of the Church' and wondered about the Pope's reference to the spreading ('a little everywhere') of 'the mentality of Protestantism and Modernism, denying the need for and the legitimate existence of an intermediate authority in the relationship of the soul with God'. He wondered even more at the papal sleight of hand when, the Council having opposed a request from the Polish, Belgian, and Brazilian bishops to proclaim Mary 'Mother of the Church', the Pope did so himself in his concluding address, and one Observer felt that 'It will take three generations to regain the ground lost in the last three days.'[31]

On the other hand the Observers and Auditors had grown apace and now they included fifteen women whom the Pope greeted as 'our beloved daughters in Christ, the first women in history to participate in a conciliar assembly'. There was another first, when a layman, England's Patrick Keegan, President of the International Federation of Movements of Christian Workers,

[28] F. Willis, 'The Vatican Council: Decisive Days for Christian Unity', *WC*, March/April 1964, p. 10.

[29] WAA: F. Willis, *Report of the Third Session*, p. 2.

[30] Ibid., pp. 8–20.

[31] Ibid., pp. 29–38.

addressed the Council. His theme was the Lay Apostolate.[32] These were revolutionary happenings with profound implications. 'The idea of the laity as those who only "pay and obey" is gone for ever', and 'Dogmatism and Doctrinalism . . . and Literalism and Immobilism have given way to Pastoralism, Mobilism and Dynamism': all of it in the course of this drawing together, this 'watersmeet of no return', of the four great Christian streams, Roman, Orthodox, Anglican, and Protestant.[33] And if 'the fundamental conception of the nature and structure of the Church and of the power and primacy of the Pope still stand, and are indeed strengthened by what has now been added regarding the authority of the Bishops and their power when acting under and with the Pope', then how could or should it have been otherwise?[34] All in all the Vatican Council had been curiously like a YMCA World Council in its display of the 'occupational hazards of large deliberative bodies', or so his 'considerable experience behind the scenes of world gatherings' had taught him.[35]

'What many already regard as the greatest event in the history of the Roman Church' ended with the Council's fourth session on 8 December 1965.[36] For Willis the three last excitements lay in the Decree on the Apostolate of the Laity ('the laity had completely arrived in the very heart of the Church . . . another point of no return'), the Dogmatic Constitution on Divine Revelation, which covered the Bible and biblical research (a 'remarkable and creative Decree'), and the Declaration on Religious Freedom ('A long-standing ambiguity has finally been cleared up: . . . the dignity of man consists in his responsible use of freedom').[37] A YMCA layman could rest his case. Here in Rome the papacy had been presented as service not power and the episcopate as a fellowship with a common and not just a localized responsibility. The Church as people of God had been stressed. The laity had arrived 'as welcome and indispensable

---

[32] Ibid., p. 6.

[33] Ibid., pp. 48–50.

[34] 'The Bishop will in future share directly with the Pope, in ways to be determined by him and always subject to his unique and unquestioned primacy, in the government of the Church.' F. Willis, 'The Vatican Council: a "creative and historical session"', *WC*, Jan./Feb. 1965, p. 10; Willis, *Report of the Third Session*, p. 43.

[35] Willis, *Report of the Third Session*, p. 39

[36] F. Willis, 'The Vatican Council', *WC*, March/April 1966, p. 12.

[37] WAA: F. Willis, *Report of the Fourth Session*, pp. 30, 28, 22.

collaborators with the clergy in the fulfilment of the Mission of the Church in Salvation History'. The Bible had a central place, with its scholarly examination proclaimed as duty not whim. 'The supremacy of the informed conscience and the inalienable dignity of every individual are fully recognized and unequivocally acknowledged'.[38] Willis felt that if he could not yet call Rome's 'the one *true Church*' yet it was 'in many respects the *one Church of Truth*'.[39]

Two years later he was back in Rome to report on the Congress for the Lay Apostolate and the Synod of Bishops. From his press box he noted the four official YMCA observers to the former, two of them Catholics,[40] and the assembly's 'impatient and progressive views' (which 'astonished and sometimes almost shocked' the observers) and the Pope's response that the 'normal instrument of the divine designs and the spiritual guide is the hierarchy. Anyone who attempts to act without the hierarchy or against it could be compared to a withered branch, because it is no longer connected with the sap.' There was less to note about the synod, largely because 'conditions of considerable secrecy prevailed . . . members . . . were asked — some would say instructed — not to give interviews'. But he was sure that it had been a successful experiment and that its future was secure.[41]

Willis's former colleagues in England were convinced that the Vatican had taken over his life. No conversation with him was ever Vatican-free. His new contacts delighted him: Willebrands, of course; Father Stransky, whose brother, 'I think, in Milwaukee, . . . has received considerable help from the YMCA . . .'; and, best of all, Archbishop Pignedoli, Secretary of the Congregation for the Propagation of Faith and a friend of the Pope. Pignedoli 'made very clear that he attached little importance to the 1920 Warning which he evidently regarded as no longer relevant'. Then, 'Just as I was taking leave of him he said, with a delightful twinkle and smile, that in his present position he is in constant touch with Bishops throughout the world and that if at

---

[38] *WC*, March/April 1966, p. 12.

[39] Willis, *Report of the Fourth Session*, p. 45.

[40] F. Carrera, an engineer from Concepción, Chile, and Italy's Olindo Parachini, with the Lutheran German Dr Jentsch and the Swedish Baptist Fredrik Franklin. Other observers included Dr Klaus von Bismarck, Dietrich Bonhoeffer's brother-in-law.

[41] F. Willis, 'Roma: two historical ecumenical events', *WC*, March/April 1968, pp. 8–9.

any time I had some problem or difficulty with a bishop I could let him know and he would write to him.' To each one Willis repeated his hope that the YMCA would figure in no official statement, however well-meaning, as a *Protestant* organization, and his further hope that if any development were to be 'on the lines of episcopal discretion . . . the discretion should be that of bishops individually and not of National Episcopal Conferences, as the latter could well contain unfavourable minorities . . .'[42] Willis's terrier-like persistence was ineradicable, even by Rome.

In January 1969 Geneva once more sought his advice. That summer there was to be a World Council in Nottingham. Should Rome be invited to send an official fraternal delegate? Willis wrapped himself in qualification but 'I have devoted very considerable thought and prayer to the question . . . and . . . I have become convinced that . . . the time is *not yet* opportune.' He wrote of 'confusion, uncertainty, tensions, and . . . the "conservative backlash", now almost everywhere prevalent in the Roman Church, and in many ways particularly at the Vatican.' He feared lest dear Willebrands ('exceedingly prudent, and by nature, I think, somewhat timid') be embarrassed. He pondered the diplomacies appropriate to the English bishops who might be involved: Heenan 'would be positive and friendly' but the Bishop of Nottingham (according to 'exceptionally reliable inside sources') was 'very conservative and only hesitatingly ecumenical'.[43] He had, however, reckoned without the Vatican's Associate Secretary of the Consilium de Laicis, Rosemary Goldie, a 'small, able, humorous and resourceful' woman.[44] Geneva had appealed to her as well as to Willis, with additional queries about a Papal Greeting to the Council and a Catholic chaplain. When Willis wrote to Geneva it was to 'Dear Franklin'. When Miss Goldie wrote it was to 'Dear Fred'. She saw no problem about a delegate-observer, rather more about a greeting. As for a chaplain, the ideal source was Portsmouth's Bishop Worlock, whom Willis himself readily acknowledged as 'one of the wisest of the progressives and extremely friendly to us'.[45]

[42] WAA: Sir F. Willis to F. Franklin, Hampstead, 11 Nov. 1967.

[43] Ibid., 1 Feb. 1969.

[44] F. Willis, 'Roma', *WC*, March/April 1968, p. 8.

[45] WAA: Rosemary Goldie to F. Franklin, Vatican, 18 March 1969.

That was at the beginning of March. 'There seems to be a special Providence watching over the preparation of your World Council', Miss Goldie reported on 18 March. The Bishops of Nottingham and Portsmouth had met in Rome. They found no difficulty about the principle of a Catholic chaplain or his sharing in an ecumenical act of worship, indeed they had two men in view. As to the fraternal delegate, who better than Patrick Keegan, now OBE? Even the Holy Father's greeting seemed less of an impossibility: 'The whole programme of your Council deals with questions of such deep concern to the Holy Father that I personally feel a favourable response might be expected if it was presented to him, and if he was informed of the fully ecumenical character of the meeting, the R.C. participation, the agreement of the local R.C. authorities. . . .'[46]

Willis was still dubious. No doubt he felt vindicated when Willebrands, who was now a Cardinal, intimated that they might have to make do with a greeting from him instead. That came on 25 July: 'Please accept the assurance of our close attention to and fraternal interest in your meeting also promise of prayers for mature guidance and for decisions according to Christ's will for growing Unity'.[47]

Surely, with such a message, such a chaplain, such a fraternal delegate, indeed such a World Council (for Nottingham 1969 made some momentous decisions for the movement), the 1920 Warning could be laid to rest? It was at this time that the Chilean YMCA layman, Fernando Carrera, had been writing to the Bishop of Concepción about this very matter. Naturally Willis, whose health was now failing and who was preparing for two cataract operations, was kept in the picture. Willis was ever predictably unpredictable. An optimistic letter would elicit a most gloomy response; gloom would send him straight to the bright side. Carrera's approach to his bishop had reached Rome and landed on the desk of Cardinal Seper who had replied in what Carrera felt was an 'extremely cold and cautious' way. Willis could not agree. A busy man like Seper had probably delegated the whole business. Besides, such letters were always

---

[46] Ibid.
[47] WAA: John, Cardinal Willebrands to F. Franklin, Vatican, 11 July 1969; Telegram, Willebrands, Secretariat for Christian Unity, Vatican, 25 July 1969.

'restrained by traditional caution'. In any case, Seper's reply amounted 'to a clear abandonment' of the 1920 Warning as an Instruction, 'though this is, of course, implicit rather than explicit which could hardly be expected. Furthermore and positively, it substantially confirms the position assumed by the National Episcopal Conferences in the United States and Canada, that decision about the YMCA is now fully within the discretion of such Conferences and of Bishops within their Dioceses.'[48] And he wrote hearteningly to Carrera:

> It is difficult for me to find words in which to express the measure of my thankfulness to Almighty God for this most encouraging and memorable outcome of all the splendid efforts which you have made with such patience during the past few years. The YMCA Movement throughout the world is deeply indebted to you for what you have thus accomplished.[49]

Of course, Willis, being Willis, retained considerable doubts as to what had in fact been accomplished. The Warning was, after all, still officially on the record.[50] Perhaps he should have paid more attention to his own conclusion to his confidential reports on Vatican II: 'Adversaries, difficulties, obstacles are not to be a condition of our passing through the doors God opens before us, but just incidental facts at any given time. Surely, the YMCA is now before such another opened door . . .'.[51]

University of Sheffield

---

[48] WAA: Sir F. Willis to F. Franklin, Hampstead, 10 Nov. 1969.
[49] Ibid.: copy sent to F. Franklin.
[50] WAA: Sir F. Willis to F. Franklin, Hampstead 29 Nov. 1971.
[51] Willis, *Report on the Fourth Session*, p. 55.

# THE UNITY OF THE CHURCH IN TWENTIETH-CENTURY ENGLAND: PLEASING DREAM OR COMMON CALLING? (*PRESIDENTIAL ADDRESS*)

*by* DAVID M. THOMPSON

How diverse can the Church be and yet still be one? This way of posing the issue is very different from the way in which several historians and sociologists have treated the twentieth-century ecumenical movement. John Kent has de-scribed the ecumenical movement as 'the great ecclesiastical failure of our time'.[1] That may be a back-handed compliment, if it implies that there was at least an initial chance of success. Nevertheless he is right to point out that 'attempts at historical description and analysis have been few',[2] and this address is a small attempt to redress the balance. I confess that I approach the topic out of a significant involvement in the ecumenical move-ment at local, national, and international level for the last thirty years. Over ten years ago I attended a meeting in Geneva to consider the publication of a third volume of the *History of the Ecumenical Movement*,[3] and the reasons for the failure of that project to materialize would be worth several paragraphs on another occasion.

John Kent affirmed that the historian should not give the Church privileged status in seeking to explain its historical devel-opment. Like Peter Berger, he also noted that between the end of the First World War and the 1960s there developed a new theological emphasis on the Church despite (or perhaps because of?) its institutional decline – 'the idea of the "church" as a corporate necessity, supernaturally founded and endowed, with a right to claim obedience from each individual member, and assured of historical survival and final triumph'.[4] Essentially Kent

---

[1] John Kent, *The Unacceptable Face. The Modern Church in the eyes of the Historian* (London, 1987), p. 203.
[2] Ibid., p. 204.
[3] Ruth Rouse and Stephen Charles Neill, eds, *A History of the Ecumenical Movement, 1517–1948* (London, 1954); Harold E. Fey, ed., *The Ecumenical Advance: A History of the Ecumenical Movement*, vol. 2, *1948–1968* (London, 1970).
[4] Kent, *The Unacceptable Face*, p. 7; cf. Peter Berger, *The Sacred Canopy* (New York, 1969), pp. 162–4.

regarded the key to understanding ecumenism as the search for the political power appropriate to social influence. Thus many years ago, he described the work of Hugh Price Hughes, one of the main architects of the Free Church unity movement of the 1890s in England, as an attempt to impose evangelical pietism on the country – a kind of late nineteenth-century Nonconformist imperialism.[5] Similarly Tissington Tatlow once remarked that the whole Faith and Order movement was regarded in Europe, and particularly in Germany, as Anglican imperialism, because of its Anglo-American origins in the Protestant Episcopal Church.[6] Roman Catholic involvement in the ecumenical movement from the time of Pope John XXIII and the Second Vatican Council (which some have even tended to regard as the *beginning* of the movement) has often been seen as Roman Catholic imperialism. In each case, however, explicit statements of motivation have been reinterpreted. Clearly statements of intention must always be scrutinized: ecclesiastical politics do not cease to be politics by being ecclesiastical. But the hermeneutics of suspicion can go too far.

Another approach to the ecumenical movement has been sociological.[7] Here contemporary movements towards unity have been seen as a sign of the loss of original vitality and distinctiveness. They are a response to decline – actual, threatened, or perceived. Thus in Bryan Wilson's view the sect is the truly vital religious grouping in the secular world, though always tending to follow the path of institutionalization and become a denomination or even a church.[8] Robert Currie's analysis of nineteenth-century Methodism suggested that movements toward reunification were a response to the difficulties of division as growth rates tailed off.[9]

Sociological insights have undoubtedly been very helpful, but they do have an implicit reductionist tendency. The identification of religious vitality with the sect rather than the church, or

---

[5] John Kent, 'Hugh Price Hughes and the Nonconformist Conscience' in G. V. Bennett and J. D. Walsh, eds, *Essays in Modern English Church History in memory of Norman Sykes* (London, 1966), p. 185; John Kent, *The Age of Disunity* (London, 1966), p. 199.

[6] Rouse and Neill, *History of the Ecumenical Movement*, p. 417.

[7] See David M. Thompson, 'Theological and sociological approaches to the motivation of the ecumenical movement', *SCH*, 15 (1978), pp. 467–79.

[8] Bryan R. Wilson, *Religion in Secular Society* (London, 1966), p. 179

[9] Robert Currie, *Methodism Divided* (London, 1968), p. 314.

(to borrow Weber's terminology) with charismatic rather than bureaucratic leadership, is an assumption or a value-judgement. Furthermore, the related argument that different churches represented or served particular social, class or interest groups in society, whilst very fruitful for certain purposes, can often be deployed as though this was the primary intention of the churches. That is also an assumption, but it tends to entail the view that division, as distinct from diversity, is normal. It is reflected in the populist (rather than technical) use of the term 'broad church' to describe the Church of England (and indeed political parties on occasion) when the ability of a group to contain differences, perhaps even wide differences, of view is being emphasized. The hidden implication is that normally the church will not be broad, in other words that diversity is incompatible with unity, or even that religious diversity is best protected by a divided church. This is a fundamental question which needs to be examined, not assumed.

How true are some traditional notions of unity and diversity anyway? If we leave on one side the Orthodox Churches for a moment (whilst noting the significance of the fact that we speak of the Orthodox Churches rather than the Orthodox Church), we might ask whether the Reformation was novel, or perhaps the continuation of diversity by other means. The assumption so often is that the Reformation was a decisive turning-point at which a united Church ceased to be the norm and a divided Church took its place. Bryan Wilson even claimed that 'the concept of the Church, as it has been understood in the social sense, is one which acquired its full meaning and realization in European feudal society.'[10] Does that represent an uncritical acceptance of Troeltsch's ecclesiology, which then becomes a sociological norm? How do we decide what needs to be explained, or what is 'natural'? Is it unity, or disunity? Clearly certain naive images have to be abandoned – any uncritical idea of a primitive unity of the Church, for example,[11] or even the idea that a divided Church is inevitably unbelievable. The latter argument has been popular amongst missionary apologists, who have seen the division of the Church as an obstacle to faster

[10] Wilson, *Religion in Secular Society*, p. 221.
[11] See the discussion in James D. G. Dunn, *Unity and Diversity in the New Testament* (London, 1977).

growth. But it is at best an unproven hypothesis, since there is relatively little evidence to suggest that the periods of most rapid growth for the Church have been when it has been united. Even so, is that the most illuminating way of approaching the subject? Does it fix our attention on the right issues?

This paper concentrates on a single issue: the relations between the Church of England and the Free Churches, particularly in the period 1920–5. In many ways it is a well-known story. Following the Appeal to all Christian People by the Lambeth Conference of 1920, discussions took place between representatives of the Church of England and the Federal Council of Evangelical Free Churches. These reached a considerable agreement on the shape of a future united Church in a relatively short space of time. Despite this, it proved impossible to reach an agreement which changed anything; and indeed the agenda remained substantially the same down to the abortive negotiations over a Covenant for Unity in England which failed in 1982. Why did so much apparently change so quickly, and why did so little in the end change at all?

In some ways what happened was a delayed acceptance of the fact that the breakaway groups in the Church were not actually going to die out, however much that may have originally been hoped. The bishops of the Church of England undoubtedly expected Nonconformity gradually to die out in the later seventeenth century, and in the early eighteenth century it nearly did. But when it was revived by the Evangelical Revival, and accompanied by a new force in Methodism, the bishops had to lengthen their expectations and change their tactics. Some pessimists in the 1830s like Thomas Arnold thought that comprehension was the only answer – it had after all been on the agenda for two hundred years. Others put their faith in church reform, hoping to beat Nonconformity by superior efficiency, and there is some evidence to suggest that this did have an effect, sufficient to stimulate greater self-consciousness on the part of Nonconformity in its rural strongholds. In the towns, however, the chances of the Church of England bringing about the decline of Nonconformity simply by more effective performance had already passed, because effective performance had become a problem for all churches. By the end of the century, therefore, Anglicans were gradually accepting that the Free Churches were there to stay; and the question became what difference if any this made to Anglican self-perceptions.

A good illustration of this was the Anglo-Catholic Edward Talbot's reaction to the approaches of local Nonconformist ministers when the diocese of Rochester was divided in 1899 and he moved to Southwark. The Revd F. B. Meyer, minister of Christ Church, Westminster Bridge Road, invited him to attend the centenary of the Sunday School begun by Rowland Hill. 'It would be a noble act of Catholicity', Meyer wrote, 'and would strike a keynote which would ring through your diocese.' Talbot replied that he would be doing harm in order to do good. Although he respected Nonconformists and was ready to co-operate with them, he could not on principle support their organizations. 'For in one aspect their *raison d'être* is the fault and error as they deem it of the Church, and therefore opposition to her on points of doctrine and practice.'[12] He also declined an invitation from the Revd John Scott Lidgett, Warden of the Wesleyan Bermondsey Settlement, to attend a picture exhibition which was to be opened by Princess Louise, on the same grounds. By the time he left Southwark for Winchester in 1911, however, he had changed his mind and consented to open the Settlement's picture exhibition.[13] Anglo-Catholics like Talbot and Charles Gore gradually moved before the First World War to a position where they were prepared to concede the title of 'church' to the Nonconformist bodies, though the reappraisal of high Anglican ecclesiology involved was uneven and incomplete. Thus Talbot wrote in 1920 that Anglo-Catholics were called to reconsider the language which had confined the Church to those churches which retained the apostolic ministry as well as the creeds and sacraments and to acknowledge that all communions were fragments of the one true Church, sharing alike in the sin of schism.[14]

The traditional view of the significance of the Lambeth Appeal of 1920 was largely shaped by the biographies of Davidson and Lang. It was also affected by emphasis on its consequences rather

---

[12] Gwendolen Stephenson, *Edward Stuart Talbot, 1844–1934* (London, 1936), pp. 114–15.

[13] J. Scott Lidgett, *My Guided Life* (London, 1936), pp. 230–1.

[14] The Bishop of Winchester, 'The Lambeth Appeal', *Contemporary Review*, 118 (Oct. 1920), p. 469, quoted Newman Smyth, *A Story of Church Unity* (New Haven, Conn., 1923), p. 48; cf. Alfred E. Garvie, *Memories and Meanings of My Life* (London, 1938), p. 193.

than its origins. The origins were inauspicious. Because the previous three Lambeth Conferences had all dealt with the question of reunion, it was expected that the 1920 Conference would deal with it as well. But there was a domestic Anglican agenda arising from the Kikuyu controversy, and Lang, as Chairman of the Reunion Committee, did not approach its task in a very hopeful spirit.[15] A conference at Kikuyu in 1913 had proposed a scheme of federation between seven different missions in British East Africa. The conference had concluded with a communion service in the Church of Scotland church, at which the Bishop of Mombasa presided, using the Anglican Prayer Book, a Presbyterian had preached, and all the delegates except the Friends had received the sacrament. Upon hearing of this, the Bishop of Zanzibar, Frank Weston, indicted the Bishops of Mombasa and Uganda to the Archbishop of Canterbury on the ground that they had propagated heresy and committed schism. Randall Davidson, having laid the matter before the Consultative Body of the Lambeth Conference, declined to condemn the proposals for a federation of missions, but said that a more than local sanction was needed for them. He also declined to condemn the communion service, which provoked the ironic comment that 'The Commission comes to the conclusion that the Service at Kikuyu was eminently pleasing to God, and must on no account be repeated.'[16] A revised constitution for the Alliance of Missionary Societies in British East Africa was approved in 1918, which made it clear that intercommunion between episcopal and non-episcopal bodies was impossible at present.[17]

Much of the discussion in the Reunion Committee was taken up with the issues relating to intercommunion and episcopacy which Kikuyu had raised. Lang's idea of an Appeal 'to all Christian People' neatly sidestepped the ecclesiological issue of giving formal recognition as churches to what were at the time customarily called 'non-episcopal bodies'. Moreover, to the surprise of many Weston was conciliatory and popular, and the general

---

[15] J. G. Lockhart, *Cosmo Gordon Lang* (London, 1949), p. 267.

[16] G. K. A. Bell, *Randall Davidson*, 3rd edn (London, 1952), pp. 690–708; W. J. Noble and others, *Towards a United Church, 1913–1947* (London, 1947), pp. 15–63. Talbot had been one of the leading English bishops to warn of the problems caused by Kikuyu: see Stephenson, *E. S. Talbot*, pp. 240–1.

[17] *Documents Bearing on the Problem of Christian Unity and Fellowship, 1916–1920* (London, 1920), pp. 37–47.

principles underlying the revised constitution for the Alliance of Missionary Societies were approved – though obviously Weston and his friends secured the main points they wanted.[18]

Hensley Henson provided one of the fullest and most entertaining accounts in print of the Reunion Committee's deliberations. Henson had an hour's private conversation with Davidson on the opening day of the Conference, and noted that the Archbishop was apprehensive of a deadlock. When Henson said that the conflict on first principles was reaching a point within the Anglican communion which threatened disruption, Davidson responded that he *would not be the Archbishop in whose time the High Church party was driven out of the Church of England*, a remark which Henson put in italics. Henson noted in his journal at the time that the Archbishop would probably give in to a threat of secession. In his *Retrospect* he wrote that Davidson's 'generous heart could not tolerate the possibility of a secession which would repeat in the twentieth century the disastrous precedent of the Non-juring schism in the seventeenth'; and he added, 'his temperamental dislike of conflict was strengthened by his personal friendship with the Anglo-Catholic leaders, and his opportunist habit inclined him to overrate the effectiveness of delay and the practical value of discussion'.[19] Whether there was ever any serious threat of secession, one may doubt, though at one point Henson suggested an implied threat of schism by the bishops of St Albans and Zanzibar if J. H. Shakespeare's request for the two small steps of exchange of pulpits and admission of Nonconformists to communion where their own churches were inaccessible was conceded.[20] Of course, the circumstances of Henson's appointment as Bishop of Hereford in 1917 still made him *persona non grata* in Anglo-Catholic circles.

Bell's own role in the Reunion Committee is also not apparent from his own account. He described how the idea of gathering the non-episcopal denominations within a larger communion, sketched by Weston in the opening week, was taken up by others and how 'with the Archbishop of

---

[18] Bell, *Davidson*, p. 1012; Lambeth Conference 1920, resolutions 10–12, *The Six Lambeth Conferences, 1867–1920* (London, 1929), Appendix, pp. 29–31.

[19] Herbert Hensley Henson, *Retrospect of an Unimportant Life*, 2 vols (London, 1942–3), 2, p. 4.

[20] Ibid., p. 10.

Canterbury's connivance, a group of kindred episcopal souls met by themselves in Lollard's Tower to see whether anything might come from that'.[21] He did not say that he suggested the idea to Davidson and acted as the group's secretary: as his wife wrote, 'I remember coming upon the group *very* late one evening in Lollard's Tower – Jimmy Bombay sitting crossed-legged on the floor like an Indian Buddha, Neville Talbot draped along the mantelpiece, cups of tea everywhere, and George, pen and notebook in hand, correlating all the words of wisdom'.[22]

The emphasis on the consequences of the Lambeth Appeal, which certainly up to the Second World War and possibly into the 1960s seemed generally positive, has meant that analysis of the origins has been pushed into the background. Moreover until the 1960s when access to the relevant papers at Lambeth Palace became possible, the story was inevitably told in terms of the published material, which lays more emphasis on the consequences. Perhaps Bell's own role in the drafting of the Appeal is responsible for this emphasis, together with his succinct account of it and the discussions with the Free Churches in his life of Davidson.[23] In this view the initiative is represented as coming from the Church of England (or the Anglican Communion) in the Lambeth Conference, and the Free Churches are placed in the position of respondents. It reflects the Anglican-centred nature of much of our modern British church history. This is not so much wrong, as skewed. The story can also be told in a way which makes the Church of England the respondent. Bell also provided the material for this view in the collection of documents from the period 1916–20 which he edited as background material for the Committee on Reunion.[24]

The most important initiative here was the work of the English Sub-Committee appointed in connection with the proposed World Conference on Faith and Order. Its consequences have probably been underestimated, because everyone remembers 1927 as the date when the Lausanne Conference convened,

[21] Bell, *Davidson*, p. 1011.

[22] Ronald C. D. Jasper, *George Bell, Bishop of Chichester* (London, 1967), p. 57.

[23] Bell, *Davidson*, pp. 1007–15, 1115–24.

[24] *Documents on Christian Unity and Fellowship*. This volume was edited by Bell (although his name does not appear on the title page), which is acknowledged in the British Library catalogue, but not, for example, in the Cambridge University Library catalogue.

rather than 1910 when the initiative was taken, or 1920 when the preliminary conference was held in Geneva. In 1912 a deputation from the Protestant Episcopal Church of the USA crossed the Atlantic to seek the support of the Anglican Churches in Great Britain and Ireland for the proposed World Conference on Faith and Order. Davidson and Lang with nine others met the group and agreed to set up a representative committee to keep in touch with the arrangements for the conference. Tissington Tatlow, General Secretary of the Student Christian Movement, became the Committee's secretary.[25] In 1913 at the first meeting in New York of representatives of the Commissions appointed by the various Churches, it was decided to send another deputation, this time of non-episcopal ministers, to meet with the English Free Churches and the Presbyterian Churches in Scotland. This deputation, led by the Congregationalist, the Revd Newman Smyth, arrived in Britain in January 1914, and met with members of the Swanwick Free Church Fellowship at Whitefield's Tabernacle in London, and with another thirty official groups. As a result all the main non-Anglican Churches (apart from the Roman Catholics) agreed to take part in the World Conference, and a joint Anglican–Free Church group was appointed in May 1914.[26] This group prepared two significant reports in 1916 and 1918, which paved the way for the Free Church response to the Lambeth Appeal after 1920.

At the same time the movement for a greater measure of unity among the Free Churches themselves was gaining momentum. In 1916 the Revd J. H. Shakespeare, Secretary of the Baptist Union, was President of the Free Church Council when it met at Bradford. In his presidential address he made a passionate plea for a United Free Church of England. He had first proposed this in 1910; and he told Hensley Henson in 1917 (when the latter preached at the City Temple to the discomfiture of Winnington Ingram, Bishop of London) that he first conceived the idea when he heard Henson address the autumn meeting of the Congregational Union.[27] There had already been some work done in

[25] Rouse and Neill, *History of the Ecumenical Movement*, pp. 409–10.

[26] Ibid., pp. 411–12; 'Bulletin of the Commission of the Protestant Episcopal Church, no 5', reprinted in K.-C. Epting, *Ein Gespräch beginnt* (Zürich, 1972), p. 332.

[27] Henson, *Retrospect of an Unimportant Life*, 1, p. 202; Albert Peel, *These Hundred Years* (London, 1931), p. 395, indicates that the autumn assembly in 1910 was held at Hampstead, rather than Portsmouth as Shakespeare told Henson, so Shakespeare's memory may have been at fault.

1913–14 by special committees on Free Church co-operation, following Shakespeare's earlier initiative, but not surprisingly the war had brought things to a halt. His presidential address re-kindled enthusiasm, and three meetings, consisting of eighty-one officially appointed representatives of the Churches, were held in 1916–17. Two methods were considered: corporate union and federation. The former, based on the models of the United Free Church of Scotland (1900) and the United Methodist Church (1907), was felt to be premature at that time. So proposals were prepared for a Federal Council of the Free Churches. (It needs to be remembered that the basis of representation at the existing National Council of the Evangelical Free Churches was through local Free Church councils: the Churches as such were not represented.) All the major Free Churches accepted the propo-sals in 1918, though the Wesleyan Conference delayed until 1919.[28] A Declaratory Statement of Common Faith and Practice for the Federal Council was drafted by Dr Carnegie Simpson, Professor of Church History at Westminster College, Cam-bridge.[29]

The Faith and Order discussions involved several of the same people on the Free Church side. The 1916 interim report con-tained statements of agreement on matters of faith and on matters relating to order; the third part listed differences in relation to matters of order which required further study and discussion.[30] The second interim report was published in March 1918, from a slightly enlarged group. They did not claim to be formulating a basis for the reunion of Christendom, but said they were guided by two convictions: first, that believers in Christ should be one visible society, and secondly, that such visible unity was not adequately expressed in the co-operation of churches for moral influence and social service, but 'could only be fully realised

---

[28] E. K. H. Jordan, *Free Church Unity* (London, 1956), pp. 127–35; J. H. Shakespeare, *The Churches at the Cross-Roads* (London, 1918), pp. 118–20; Arthur Black et al., *Pathways to Christian Unity* (London, 1919), pp. 148–51, where the Federal Council of the Churches of Christ in America, formed in 1905, was cited as a model.

[29] P. Carnegie Simpson, *Recollections* (London, 1943), p. 75; the statement is in Black, *Pathways to Christian Unity*, pp. 222–6.

[30] *Documents on Christian Unity and Fellowship*, pp. 5–9: the differences were the extent of uniformity or variety in the visible society of the Church; the conditions in the ministration and reception of the sacraments on which their validity depends; and the question of whether the authority of the ministry was derived through episcopal or presbyteral succession or through the community of believers, or by a combination of them.

through community of worship, faith and order, including common participation in the Lord's Supper', a community which they believed to be 'quite compatible with a rich diversity in life and worship'. Whilst eschewing the abstract discussion of the origin of the episcopate historically or its authority doctrinally, they agreed to acknowledge two facts: first, the position of episcopacy in the greater part of Christendom, such that members of Episcopal churches ought not to be expected to abandon it; and secondly, 'that there are a number of Christian Churches not accepting the Episcopal order, which have been used by the Holy Spirit in His work of enlightening the world, converting sinners, and perfecting saints'. Hence they suggested that the conditions of reunion involved the effective preservation of continuity with the historic episcopate, the episcopate should re-assume a constitutional form, both in the method of election and the manner of its exercise, and that 'acceptance of the fact of Episcopacy and not any theory as to its character should be all that is asked for'.[31]

Scott Lidgett noted that whilst the committee (which included both Edward Talbot and Charles Gore) had little difficulty in reaching a unanimous agreement on matters of faith, no agreement was reached on the relationship of church order to faith:

> The prevailing Anglican view was that Church Order as they understood it was part of the essentials of the Faith, and therefore inseparable from it, whereas the Free Church members held that ecclesiastical Order was subordinate to the Faith, and that it had been developed by successive stages in response to practical needs as they arose throughout the early history of the Church.[32]

Nevertheless the Congregationalist theologian, Alfred Garvie, attributed the crucial point about the fact, rather than the theory, of the episcopate to a declaration of Bishop Gore.[33]

There were also two other more informal sets of meetings between Anglicans and Free Churchmen. The two Mansfield conferences in January 1919 and January 1920 had Anglican

---

[31] Ibid., pp. 11–13.
[32] Scott Lidgett, *My Guided Life*, pp. 243–4.
[33] Garvie, *Memories and Meanings*, p. 193.

members who were predominantly evangelical, though William Temple and H. D. Major attended the second. Scott Lidgett wrote that the Anglican evangelicals held the same view of the relation between faith and order as the Free Churchmen. The Mansfield conclusions differed from those of the Joint Faith and Order Committee in the call for intercommunion, exchange of pulpits, and joint work in mission and social work.[34] The second conference, whilst expressing the view that a reunited Church must be episcopal in constitution, not only called for interchange of pulpits and mutual admission to the Lord's Table under due authority, but also suggested the

> acceptance by ministers, serving in any one denomination, who may desire it, of such authorisation as shall enable them to minister fully and freely in the churches of other denominations; it being clearly stated that . . . this authorisation . . . is not to be taken as reordination, or as repudiation of their previous status as ministers in the Church Catholic of Christ'.[35]

The other informal meeting was that at Swanwick in December 1919 (which, unlike any of the other groups, included fourteen women out of a total of sixty-two). There was a strong SCM presence, but the group also included three of Davidson's past or future chaplains – Mervyn Haigh, J. V. Macmillan, and Oliver Quick – and Neville Talbot, son of the Bishop of Winchester and about to become Bishop of Pretoria. This group called for the Churches to authorize intercommunion and for the forthcoming Lambeth Conference to make the question of unity the central issue. Unlike the others the meeting linked the pressing need of reunion to 'the furthering of foreign missionary enterprise, the promotion of the League of Nations, the re-ordering of society – in a word the establishing of the Kingdom of God'.[36] This not only reflects the SCM involvement but also reminds us that in the minds of many of those involved in this

---

[34] *Documents on Christian Unity and Fellowship*, pp. 54–6.

[35] Ibid., pp. 81–6; quotation from p. 84. (It should perhaps be noted that contemporary references to this conference, e.g. *Contemporary Review*, 117 [March 1920], pp. 364 ff. refer to this as the *third* Oxford conference.)

[36] Ibid., pp. 73–6; quotation from pp. 74–5.

movement, there was nothing of the later distinction between Faith and Order, and Life and Work. Shakespeare emphasized the importance of the Kingdom of God in *The Churches at the Cross-Roads*, and Bell himself was deeply influenced by the meeting of the first post-war meeting of the International Committee of the World Alliance for promoting International Friendship through the Churches at Oud Wassenaar in autumn 1919. Edward Talbot had become President of the British Council of the Alliance in 1918 and was an enthusiastic supporter. At Oud Wassenaar Archbishop Söderblom of Uppsala first floated his idea of an ecumenical council of the Churches. He was impressed by Talbot, whom the Scottish theologian, David Cairns, described as 'the foremost man in the Church of England', and also by Bell. Subsequently Söderblom wrote that 'no man means more for the ecumenical awakening than this silent Bell. This Bell never rings unnecessarily. But when it sounds . . . it penetrates more than many boisterous voices. He does not speak without having something to say.'[37] This close identity in Britain between advocates of Faith and Order issues and those involved in what became the Life and Work movement is also illustrated by the speakers at the Mürren Conference of Church Leaders, organized by the Wesleyan veteran, Sir Henry Lunn, in September 1924.[38]

The Council of the English Church Union rejected the Mansfield Conference findings in March 1920, wishing to adhere to the practice of the Catholic Church in regard to the avoidance of communion with schismatics, and feeling that the statement could be interpreted as obscuring the necessity of episcopal ordination.[39] A group of ninety Anglo-Catholics also issued a reply to the resolutions of the second Mansfield Conference in April 1920. The reply was largely drafted by Gore and Darwell Stone and suggested that the Mansfield proposals involved a violation of the understanding of the succession of episcopal ordination, which would lead to disaster for the Church of England. 'To purchase reunion with those with whom we are not now in communion at the price of disruption within the

---

[37] Bengt Sundkler, *Nathan Söderblom* (London, 1968), pp. 220, 226; Jasper, *George Bell*, pp. 57–60; quotation from p. 60.

[38] See the Report of the Mürren Conference in *The Review of the Churches*, ns 2 (Jan. 1925).

[39] *Documents on Christian Unity and Fellowship*, p. 87.

Church of England is the disaster which we fear.'[40] This is probably the threat of disruption which worried Davidson and which Henson regarded as implausible. That the extreme Anglo-Catholics were on the defensive is indicated by their hostility to A. C. Headlam's Bampton Lectures on *The Doctrine of the Church and Reunion*, published on the eve of the Conference, and Stone's annoyance with T. A. Lacey, whom he regarded as having persuaded Frank Weston to support the Lambeth Appeal. Stone was hesitant even to acknowledge the baptism of members of heretical and schismatical bodies.[41] Headlam, by contrast, defended the episcopate as the best basis for Christian unity, but rejected the Anglo-Catholic understanding of apostolic succession as mechanical in practice, untrue to the facts of contemporary church life and untrue to church history.[42]

The reason it was possible for the Church of England and the Free Churches to reach agreement so quickly, therefore, is that the essential common ground had already been cleared before the Lambeth Conference met. In an article in the *Contemporary Review* for May 1920, Scott Lidgett declared that the interim reports on Faith and Order had 'shown complete agreement in regard to the Faith' and had outlined a policy of reconstruction as to Order which, whilst not having the same theoretic agreement, at least supplied 'a workable plan by which reunion could be effected without imposing any intolerable, or even serious, strain upon the conscience' of those involved. It was up to the Anglican bishops to take decisions which would either encourage the movement towards reunion or bring despair to it.[43] Even Gore thought that the Faith and Order interim reports offered a basis superior to the Lambeth Appeal because they recognized the need of common faith.[44]

In the discussions between the Church of England and the Free Churches, therefore, the main problem from an Anglo-Catholic point of view was how to avoid the Anglican Commu-

[40] Ibid., pp. 88–93; quotation from p. 89; F. L. Cross, *Darwell Stone* (London, 1943), pp. 140–1.

[41] Cross, *Darwell Stone*, pp. 141–7.

[42] A. C. Headlam, *The Doctrine of the Church and Christian Reunion*, 3rd edn (London, 1929), pp. 242–7, 261–9.

[43] J. Scott Lidgett, 'The Anglican Church and Evangelical Nonconformity', *Contemporary Review*, 117 (May 1920), pp. 643–4.

[44] G. L. Prestige, *The Life of Charles Gore* (London, 1935), p. 453.

nion committing suicide. The issues on which the discussions came to grief were those of the status of the existing Free Church ministry and the necessity of episcopal ordination. It was clear from the resolutions of the various Free Churches welcoming the Lambeth Appeal in 1921 that they were likely to be the stumbling blocks. The Joint Conference report of May 1922 recorded agreement on the nature of the Church, the ministry, and the place of the creed. The section on the ministry included acceptance of the episcopate for the united Church of the future, together with the council of presbyters and the congregation of the faithful, and noted that 'the acceptance of Episcopal Ordination for the future would not imply the acceptance of any particular theory as to its origin and character, or the disowning of past ministries of Word and Sacraments otherwise received, which have, together with those received by Episcopal Ordination, been used and blessed by the Spirit of God'.[45] This echoed the phraseology of the Second Interim Report of the joint Faith and Order Committee.

The Anglican memorandum on the status of the existing Free Church ministry of July 1923 began promisingly by saying that they found it impossible to regard Free Church ministries as invalid and that they considered that they were entitled, 'by manifest tokens of Divine blessing which these ministries possess, and also by the spirit and terms of the Lambeth Appeal about them, to go further, and to say that we regard them as being within their several spheres real ministries in the Universal Church'.[46] (The phrase 'within their several spheres' was inserted by Talbot.)[47] Unfortunately the next section began, 'Yet ministries, even when so regarded, may be in varying degrees irregular or defective', and concluded that the Church of England could not authorize anyone to exercise his ministry among them who had not been episcopally ordained without imperilling relations with other episcopal Churches in East and West or even causing schism in their own communion.[48] This conclusion reflected keen debate within the Anglican group. Headlam's original

---

[45] G. K. A. Bell, *Documents on Christian Unity 1920–4* (London, 1924), pp. 146–51; quotation from p. 150.
[46] Ibid., p. 158.
[47] Stephenson, *E. S. Talbot*, p. 261.
[48] Bell, *Documents 1920–4*, pp. 159–60.

memorandum had proposed mutual recognition of orders. Bishop Gibson had insisted that all ministers should submit to episcopal ordination, and Lang had argued that, since section VIII of the Lambeth Appeal specifically referred to 'a commission through episcopal ordination', the Anglican group were not free to go beyond what the Appeal laid down.[49]

The Free Church members drew attention to the seventeenth-century exceptions to the rule which the Anglicans claimed to have been consistent throughout their history, and also pointed out that the union movement could not live 'entirely on private conferences and their reports' – especially in the minds of the people – and renewed its appeal for acts of unity between the Churches.[50] It took two years for a further and final response to come from the Church of England. A second memorandum of June 1925 suggested that the problem in relation to Free Church ministries was not spiritual efficacy but due authority. Two possible solutions were suggested: the first was a solemn authorization conferred by the laying on of hands by a bishop; the second was conditional ordination. They expressed a preference for the second, because the first was open to the objection that it was unclear whether the authority conferred was one of order or only of jurisdiction.[51] The Free Church representatives indicated that conditional ordination was unacceptable, and the conversations came to an end by mutual agreement. Anglican confusion over the matter was illustrated by the way the first alternative was posed; since if spiritual efficacy really was independent of order, the Anglo-Catholic position collapsed. It was therefore disingenuous to suggest that the problem was due authority. Headlam had already recognized this in his original memorandum, but his second attempt to persuade Lang to accept mutual recognition also failed.[52]

From a political point of view the Anglicans played their cards badly. By insisting on a narrow view of the ministry as tied to episcopal ordination, they allowed the Free Churches to claim the moral high ground. Thus the Free Churches were never called upon to test out their members as to whether an episcop-

[49] Ronald Jasper, *Arthur Cayley Headlam* (London, 1960), pp. 151–2.

[50] Bell, *Documents 1920–4*, pp. 166–8.

[51] G. K. A. Bell, *Documents on Christian Unity: Second Series* (London, 1930), pp. 82–4.

[52] Jasper, *Headlam*, pp. 153–4.

ally-ordered Church really was acceptable for the future. It may be thought controversial to suggest that the Anglican view on ordination was narrow; but there was a certain pride among Anglo-Catholics of the Oxford type about their narrowness. It was seen in Henry Scott Holland's letter to Talbot after the formation of the Christian Social Union in 1889 on its sacramental basis: 'You see how narrow we are!'[53] Some might call this attitude typically sectarian. Since the Anglicans used conditional baptism as a justification for conditional ordination, another analogy from the baptismal debate may be illuminating. Those who believe that only believers' baptism is right and claim the right to baptize those already baptized as infants on the grounds that what they have received already is not really baptism stand in exactly the same position as the Anglo-Catholics who claim that only episcopal ordination is ordination and therefore claim the right to ordain those who have already received ordination on the grounds that what they have received already is not really ordination.[54] In the ecumenical debate the first position is more generally condemned than the second. In my judgement neither position is tenable if ecumenical progress is to be made. The crucial point is a difference of view over whether conditional ordination implies the disowning of ministries of Word and Sacrament otherwise received. Many Anglicans seem unable to understand the point expressed trenchantly during the English Covenant negotiations by the Revd Arthur Macarthur, General Secretary of the United Reformed Church, when he said, 'I will not legitimise myself by bastardising my parents!'

There was, of course, opposition to the idea of episcopal government among Nonconformists. T. R. Glover, who also opposed the introduction of Baptist Area Superintendents at the same time, attacked the proposals root and branch, arguing for the priesthood of all believers, and questioning the sacramental role of the ministry in the light of a critical approach to the Gospels. He even questioned whether Jesus intended his Church to be one in the way usually supposed.[55] Bernard Manning, as a

---

[53] Stephen Paget, ed., *Henry Scott Holland* (London, 1921), pp. 170–1.

[54] Carnegie Simpson wrote in 1920 that 'the only two people in England who make reunion impossible are the exclusive Anglican and his brother the close Baptist': 'Some Steps towards Reunion', *Contemporary Review*, 117 (March 1920), p. 369.

[55] T. R. Glover, *The Free Churches and Reunion* (Cambridge, 1921), *passim*, especially p. 53.

representative of high-church Congregationalism in the 1930s, said that the essential issue was that of a new legalism. Congregationalists had no particular quarrel with government of the Church by bishops, he wrote. 'It is with salvation by bishops, not with government by bishops, that we quarrel. When it is admitted that government by bishops is not essential for the full and regular exercise of the grace of God, we will consider that system of government on its merits.'[56]

The Lambeth Appeal was actually narrower in scope than the Lambeth Quadrilateral of 1888, despite the apparent openness of putting the claim for the episcopate as a question (albeit rhetorical) rather than as a statement. The origin of the Quadrilateral lay in the USA with William Reed Huntington, a New England rector, who first expounded the idea in his book, *The Church Idea – an Essay toward Unity* in 1870. He persuaded the bishops of the Protestant Episcopal Church to adopt it at their Convention in Chicago in 1886, and that was how it came to the Lambeth Conference of 1888. In 1890 Huntington said that posterity would thank the bishops for taking 'the Historic Episcopate rather than the Apostolical Succession for the key-note of their appeal'; and the reason he gave was that apostolical succession would have 'committed them hopelessly to a particular philosophy of the ministry' whereas the historic episcopate expresses 'a fact without insisting upon any interpretation of the fact'.[57] It is striking that this way of putting the matter emerges in the Second Interim Report of the Joint Faith and Order Commission in 1918 and from there passes into the Report of Anglicans and Free Churchmen of 1922. Newman Smyth, the New England Congregationalist who led the non-episcopal delegation to Britain in 1914, was a long-standing friend of Huntington, and in his *Passing Protestantism and Coming Catholicism* of 1908 expounded an understanding of the fourth article of Lambeth 1888 in terms of fact rather than theory.[58]

The continuation of the Anglican–Free Church debate about episcopacy was carried on not in England but in South India.

---

[56] Bernard Lord Manning, *Essays in Orthodox Dissent* (London, 1939), p. 142.

[57] W. R. Huntington, *The Peace of the Church* (London, 1891), pp. 204, 206.

[58] Newman Smyth, *Passing Protestantism and Coming Catholicism* (London, 1908), pp. 154–5; cf. Newman Smyth, *Story of Church Unity*, pp. 7–13. Dr Brian Stanley's paper (pp. 399–426) also draws attention to the significance of Smyth's book.

There is no time now to recount the story of those discussions as they moved forward from 1919 to the inauguration of union in 1947. But, as Bengt Sundkler pointed out, 'the struggle over South India was not really fought over South India at all. Fundamentally and theologically it was concerned with building a replica of the early Church on Indian soil.' The question then was, what was the early Church like? and different answers were given to this question. To quote Sundkler again, 'the main contestants in this debate were not to be found in the assemblies of South India. They were sitting in their studies in Oxford and in Cheltenham.'[59] (The reference is to the Congregationalist, Vernon Bartlet, and Bishop Palmer.) The Church of South India is the only union between episcopal and non-episcopal churches which has taken place on the basis of acceptance of episcopacy for the future and mutual acceptance of existing ministries at the point of union. John Kent suggested that in retrospect the creation of the Church of South India seems to have been a disaster, but it is not clear whether he thought this was so mainly because no-one else has followed, or because it led to the long agony over Anglican-Methodist union, or because it was not good for the Church in India.[60] What certainly was unfortunate was the unwillingness of the Anglican Communion as a whole to be in communion with ministers of the Church of South India other than those who had been episcopally ordained. It was another triumph for the Anglo-Catholic spikes.

Why has it not been possible to make further progress on unity? One oft-repeated explanation is that the leaders were ahead of the people.[61] Bryan Wilson suggested that ministers and professional theologians speak a common language which separates them from the laity; hence the former support unity and the latter do not.[62] Peter Berger has written of the shared attitudes of church bureaucrats, and has drawn attention to the importance of church organization.[63] It is certainly true that uniting churches today is much more complex than it would have been two hundred years ago because of the sheer expansion of central

[59] B. Sundkler, *Church of South India: the Movement towards Union, 1900–1947* (London, 1954), p. 178.

[60] Kent, *The Unacceptable Face*, p. 203.

[61] E.g. Jordan, *Free Church Unity*, p. 174.

[62] Wilson, *Religion in Secular Society*, pp. 163–9.

[63] Berger, *Sacred Canopy*, pp. 139–44.

organization. Much of this began in the evangelical revival with the new forms of organization for home and foreign missionary work, which shifted the burden of support for ministerial payment from the localities to the centre. It is noteworthy that such organization generally does not fit easily into traditional ecclesiologies and is usually ignored in theological discussions. (Interestingly, in the preface to the third edition of his life of Davidson, Bell referred to the urgent need to relieve the pressure of administration on the Archbishop of Canterbury and to provide space for unhurried reflection on strategy – something which has increasingly happened since 1952.)[64] The problem with these arguments, however, is that the evidence does not immediately suggest that the laity are the problem in church union, but rather the ministers and bureaucrats – precisely those people whom the sociologists suggest should be most in favour.

More important perhaps is the policymakers' fear of division in the quest for unity. In the nature of the case this is a gamble, and most church leaders are inclined to be cautious. Hence, as Henson noted, Davidson was reluctant to press the Anglo-Catholics to the test, even though Henson thought that the threat would be empty. One might indeed argue that the threat of Anglo-Catholic schism has hung over the Church of England for the whole century until the decisive vote on the ordination of women in 1992, exercising a stranglehold over national (though not local) Anglican initiatives for unity.

This is a reminder that in today's world unity depends on consent: it cannot be imposed from above as, for example, King Frederick William III did in 1817 when he decreed the union of Reformed and Lutheran Churches in Prussia to commemorate the tercentenary of the Protestant Reformation. In the Anglo-American world, unions require votes in church assemblies (and in every congregation for congregationally-organized churches). Moreover since the Free Church of Scotland case of 1904, when the House of Lords awarded the property of the former Free Church to those congregations which did not enter the union of 1900, it has been necessary to secure parliamentary assent in the form of a bill to modify trust deeds relating to property. The assumption has been that a seventy-five per cent majority in

---

[64] Bell, *Randall Davidson*, pp. xvi–xviii.

favour should be secured, since this was required in the Act of Parliament which made the formation of the United Methodist Church lawful in 1907.[65] Both the unions which produced the Church of Scotland in 1929 and the United Reformed Church in 1972 and 1981 left minorities behind. Nevertheless in view of all the talk about ecumenical failure, it is worth recalling that all the union schemes debated in Britain since the war have had majority support: it was the required majority (now usually two-thirds) that they lacked, often by only a few percentage points. It is very difficult in practice to put Humpty-Dumpty together again.

These legal requirements have significant implications. They necessarily involve widespread discussion if the issues are felt to be controversial. It is then relatively easy for congregations, particularly small ones, to be swayed by local rather than national arguments. They also focus the worries of church leaders about possible divisions. The hazards of the private bill procedure in Parliament make it relatively easy for particular MPs to influence the course of discussion. All this produces a weariness with the political technicalities that puts off all but the strong-minded. The fact is that it is very much easier not to make any changes.

In summary, therefore, how can what happened and what failed to happen be explained? First, there is the argument about the Free Church search for legitimation and social power. Ironically the period after the First World War was one in which the decline of the Free Churches first became apparent, and they realized that the golden dream that the twentieth century would be their century was beginning to fade. But for those involved in the conversations this was probably unimportant. Carnegie Simpson remarked that Anglicans and Free Churchmen got to know one another and began to talk *to* one another, instead of talking *at* one another. 'Moreover,' he added, 'they came to look on one another with friendly and, I will add, level eyes; Anglicanism shed much of its superiority, and the Free Churches outgrew their inferiority complex.'[66] It is clear that genuine and significant personal friendships developed – Scott Lidgett's friendship

---

[65] United Methodist Church Act, 1907 (7 Edward VII, c. lxxv), clauses 6 and 7: see W. J. Townsend, H. B. Workman and G. Eayrs, eds, *A New History of Methodism*, 2 vols (London, 1909), 2, p. 570. Later clauses in the Act required the same majority for changes in the constitution and deed poll.

[66] Carnegie Simpson, *Recollections*, p. 81.

with Randall Davidson, for example.[67] In fact, it proved easier for different church leaders to make friends among themselves than for them to bring their Churches together to a similar friendship. This has been true of formal institutional links from the earliest conversations between the Church of England and the Free Churches in 1920–5 to Michael Ramsey's unsuccessful efforts to persuade the Church of England to accept the Anglican-Methodist unity proposals in 1972.

It may also be that some of the social distinctions which separated the Churches in the nineteenth century were disappearing in the twentieth as a result of Nonconformist upward social mobility – though this often meant that Nonconformists became Anglicans. Michael Ramsey's father was a Congregationalist, in contrast to the impeccable Anglican pedigree of Temple and Fisher (although the fathers of Lang and Davidson were from the Church of Scotland). The changed political contours of twentieth-century Britain reduced the significance of the Churches in legitimating different social groups, though the exceptional position of Northern Ireland in this respect always needs to be remembered. For those concerned with a 'social gospel', however crude and misleading that term is, the differences between Anglicans and Free Churchmen were less important: this is the particular significance of COPEC (Conference on Politics, Economics, and Citizenship) and the Life and Work movement generally in the English context.

Secondly, there is the impact of war. There is no doubt that the First World War did have an impact on those involved in the post-war discussions, and particularly on the next generation down. One of Bell's preparatory documents for Lambeth was a set of resolutions on Christian unity adopted by eighteen chaplains and YMCA workers in France in March 1918 – including the Deputy Chaplain-General, Llewellyn Gwynne, who was of Anglo-Catholic persuasion, Edward and Neville Talbot, B. K. Cunningham, later Principal of Westcott House, and J. V. Macmillan.[68] But in my view the significance of the Faith and Order Joint Committee, which was established as a result of pre-war initiatives, shows that progress was independent of the war. Little

[67] Scott Lidgett, *My Guided Life*, pp. 251–8; Rupert E. Davies, ed., *John Scott Lidgett* (London, 1957), pp. 199–201.
[68] *Documents on Christian Unity and Fellowship*, pp. 57–8.

was eventually agreed that was not presaged in the 1918 report. The war may have made people more receptive to the ideas, but it did not create the possibility of reaching the agreement in the first place.

Thirdly, there is the role of theology. In the end the critical factor in determining success was the Anglo-Catholic attitude. If the Anglican response had been different, for example, along the lines of Headlam, the crucial factor could have been the Free Church response to the agreement that an episcopal order was appropriate for a united church. Anglo-Catholic intransigence on how one got within sight of that goal meant that the Free Churches did not have to answer, and indeed have never had to answer that question directly. The nearest they came to it was in the Church of South India scheme, where the Free Churches did accept bishops. Anglicans also accepted those ministers ordained in the Free Churches prior to union without further ceremony. Despite constant Anglo-Catholic niggling in England, the scheme received significant support from high Anglicans in India, and also had the backing of Westcott (B. F. Westcott's son), who was Metropolitan of the Province of India, Burma, and Ceylon.[69] However, Anglo-Catholics prevented any repetition of the Church of South India model: thus the Church of North India was different, Anglicans pulled out of the discussions in New Zealand in the 1970s, and crucially the model was avoided in the Anglican-Methodist scheme. In so far as it is possible to explain ecumenical failure in terms of Anglo-Catholic attitudes, it does not seem necessary to invoke the explanations of Kent or Wilson.

Sadly, the Anglo-Catholic justification for their hard line was their hope for catholic unity, especially with Rome. But the progress that has been made between the Anglican Communion and Rome has depended scarcely at all on the Anglo-Catholics. Indeed it was inevitable that their influence should be least, since it was not their opinions which needed to be changed. In the work of the first Anglican-Roman Catholic International Commission, for example, it was those from the evangelical side who made the most significant contribution. Moreover the Second Vatican Council, which was the main stimulus for the change in

[69] Sundkler, *Church of South India*, pp. 233, 236, 329.

Roman Catholic attitudes, swept away some of the doctrines Anglo-Catholics like Darwell Stone wished to defend. The acknowledgement by the Decree on Ecumenism of a real though imperfect communion between Roman Catholics and those Christians separated from Rome, and the willingness of *Lumen gentium* to affirm that the Universal Church subsists in (rather than is) the Roman Catholic Church indicate the first steps away from the former position. It is salutary to reflect that the issues which so annoyed the Anglo-Catholics of 1920 – the exchange of pulpits and admission of Nonconformists to Anglican communion services – have been commonplace since the 1960s and are now legal under the Church of England's ecumenical canons.

Finally, there is the question of motivation. Peter Berger advanced a sociological explanation of ecumenicity, admittedly in the North American context, in terms of cartelization within a religious free market economy. He regarded monopoly as an unlikely outcome of such moves. He suggested that the degree of rationalization which organizational merger implies would have happened regardless of theological arguments, though he also says that this does not threaten the integrity of theological intentions.[70] From a historical point of view that does not seem to be satisfactory. The element of inevitability in Berger's sociological argument must marginalize the significance of the theological argument if one is to be consistent. Different layers of explanation can only coexist if all of them are openended. The historian cannot be satisfied with inevitability-type arguments, since the significance of the contingent is vital for historical explanation. That contingency may be sociological, or theological, or political; but it is the contingency that makes people important, and the attitudes of people are in the end crucial to the questions of unity and diversity in the Church. It is difficult to see the unity issue going away and it will not be resolved without some acknowledgement of necessary diversity. In the English context that means that the shadows of the failure of comprehension between 1660 and 1662 are long indeed. Until the Church of England as a whole is prepared to acknowledge in principle the diversity which it recognizes empirically,

---

[70] Berger, *Sacred Canopy*, pp. 143–4.

and even glories in from time to time, it will be impossible for it to unite with any other Church. So long as that is so, unity will be the 'pleasing dream', which was Andrew Fuller's description of William Carey's idea for missionary co-operation, rather than the 'common calling', which the constitution of the World Council of Churches declares it to be.

Fitzwilliam College, Cambridge

# INDEX

# Index

# Index

Bell, G. K. A.   467, 513–14, 519, 526, 528
Bellarmine, Robert   236
Benedict, *Rule*   62–3, 80, 85
Benedict of Aniane   68–9, 121
Benedict Biscop   45, 49
Benedict XII, Pope   117
Benedict XIII, antipope   146, 147
benevolent societies, American   312–14
Benjamin of Tudela   119
Benson, Edward White   431
Bentley, W. Holman   422
Benz, Karl   86
Berger, Peter   507, 525, 530
Bernard, St   194
Bernardino, St   190, 194
Berry, Charles   294
Bérulle, Pierre de   236
Bethune, Archbishop   435
Bible
  and Carolingian reforms   63–4, 70, 80
  and English Reformation   171, 189
  and evangelicalism   364
  and Quakers   339, 340, 344–6
  and radicalism   388–9, 391–2, 394, 396–7
  and Second Vatican Council   501–2
  and unity   368–9
*Biblia pauperum*   194, *198*, *199*, 201
Bickersteth, Edward   364–5, 366 n.13, 368–9, 371–2, 374
Bilderbeck, J.   401 n.7, 403 n.16
Billington, Ray   315
Birmingham Political Union xx, 387–97
Bischoff, Bernard   74–5, 79
Blackmore, Francis   287
Blas of Pamplona   104
Bobbio Missal   22, 24–5, 49, 54
Bogerman, Johannes   247
Bonaventure, St   109

Boniface IX, Pope   147
Boniface, St
  and Bavaria   74, 78
  and Gregory the Great   32
  and liturgy   50, 56, 57, 78
Bonomelli, Mgr   485
*Book of Common Prayer*
  American   470–4
  and Dissent   277
  and diversity and unity   8, 176, 373, 465–6
  and medieval Catholicism   181–2, 186
  revision   466–70, 473–4
Bossy, John   395–6
Bost, Amy   357
Bouillon, Henri Duc de   237, 241, 250 n.72
Bradford, John   193
Bradley, Ian   342
Braga, Council   27
Brandon, Charles Gerard, 2nd baron   278–80
Brechter, Suso   31, 32
Brewster, Patrick   388–9, 391
Briggs, C. A.   410
Briggs, 'Daddy'   302
British and Foreign Bible Society
  and Quakers   338, 339
Bromby, C. H.   430
Brooks, Joshua   381
Brown, Peter   3–4
Brownlow, William Gannaway   320, 324–8, 330–2, 333–5
Brunson, Alfred   299, 302, 306, 310
Bucer, Martin   212
Buddhism and Hidden Christians   442, 444–8, 452, 454
Bull, John   193
Bullinger, Heinrich   184–5, 223
Bunny, Edmund   204 n.68
Burchard of Worms, *Decretum*   91 n.46
Burgos, Council   105
Butler, Jon   297–8
Butler, Joseph   341

# Index

# Index

# Index

# Index

# Index

# Index

# Index

John III Doukas Vatatzes 133–5, 139, 142–4
John V Palaeologus 117, 127
John X, Pope 96
John X Camaterus 132
John XXIII, antipope 146
Jollie, Timothy 287–9
Jolly ( Jollie), Thomas 265–72, 274, 284–5
Jonas of Orléans 41–3
Josselin, Ralph 259
Jouarre, monastery 52–4
Julius II, Pope 150, 162–4

Kamenev, Olga 489
Kataoka Chizuko 449, 450–2
Kaye, John 383
Keegan, Patrick 500–1, 504
Kent, John 420, 507–8, 525, 529
Kenyon, Roger 279
Kerver, Thielman 194, *195*
Kimbangu, Simon 422–3, 424
Kirk, Edward Norris 367
Kirk, Kenneth 473
Knapp, Jacob 308, 309
Know-Nothing party 316, 332 n.63
Knox, John 193

La Rose, John de 288–9, 295
Labadie, Jean de 224–5
Lacey, H. C. 482
Lacey, T. A. 466–7, 520
Lainez, Diego 218
laity
  and administration of eucharist 413–14
  and chalice xviii, 207–19
  and ecumenism 525–6
  and exorcism 266–7
  and Second Vatican Council 497, 499–502
  and Swiss *réveil* 352, 356
  and synodical government 415–16
  in Tudor England 168, 171–5, 182–3, 187–98
Lamb, Andrew 457

Lambeth Conference
  1867 415
  1888 409, 461, 524
  1908 421, 456, 460–1
  1920 xxi, 466, 510, 511–15, 518, 520–4, 528
  1930 466
  and colonial churches 427–8, 431
Lancashire
  and appointment of justices 278–82
  and Dissenters 264–82
Lancashire County Association 265, 266, 269, 285
*The Lancashire Levite* 275–6
*The Lancashire Levite Farther Rebuk'd* 275–6
'Landmarkism' 323–4
Lang, Cosmo Gordon 467, 469–70, 473, 511–12, 515, 522, 528
Langmuir, Gavin 109–10, 111–12
language in fourth-century Church 8–10
Lateran Council
  Fifth 164
  Fourth 110, 111, 113, 114
Latin 9, 81
Latin Church
  and Carmelite order xviii, 117–29
  and Greek tradition 83–6, 90
  and imperial political structures xvii, 1–17
  and mission to Nicaea xviii, 131–44
Latomus, Bartholomew 212
Leclerq, Jean 87 n.24
lectionaries
  Bavarian 74, 76
  Carolingian 71, 76
  Merovingian 21, 22, 23, 24–5
Lectionary of Luxeuil 22, 24–5
Leicester, interdenominational co-operation 284, 293–4
Leighton, Robert 459
Leo I, Pope 214 n.23

544

# Index

# Index

Massie, J. W. 366, 371
Mather, Cotton 256 n.21, 269
Mather, Increase 267–9, 271
Mather, Nathaniel 267, 269–70, 271–2
Mather, Samuel 267
Mattock, Daniel 287
Mault, Charles 403
Maurice, Prince of Orange 244, 245–6
Mayr-Harting, H. 51
Mead, Sidney 305
Mead, Stith 306
media, influence 2–3
Méjanel, Pierre 356
Mennonites in Netherlands 222, 223, 226, 227–8, 231–2
menstruation and ritual purity 33–4, 36, 39–42
Merovingians and liturgical diversity xvii, 19–30, 31, 53
Methodism
  and Arminianism 300, 308, 330
  and Church of England 377, 378–84, 510, 528–9
  and evangelical co-operation 306–7, 311–14
  growth in numbers 317–18
  and interdenominational competition xx, 298–302, 306, 308–10, 314, 318–35
Methodius, St 9, 60
Meyer, F. B. 511
Meyvaert, Paul 31–2, 33
Mézières, Philippe de 128
Michael Keroullarious 136
Middle Ages
  and papacy xviii–xix, 145–69
  and unity of Church xix, 107–16
millennialism and evangelical revival 306, 317, 348–9, 366
Miller, William 478
Millet, Deborah 309
Miltiades, Pope 13
ministry, prophetic 423–4
*Missale Francorum* 53–5, 57
missionary societies

and church 406–7, 427
and church order 401–2, 404–6, 407–24
and denominational identity xx, 399–426
Molyneaux, Caryll, 3rd viscount 280
monasticism
  and Basil 84–5, 88–9, 121–2, 127
  Benedictine 62–3, 72, 80, 85, 118
  Cluniac 96, 98, 105
  Greek/Latin 83–5, 94, 117–29, 132
  and liturgy 26, 45–7, 52–3, 56–7
  Spanish 96, 98–9, 101–2, 104–5
  and unity 81
Montecassino and Nilus and Romuald 83–5
Montgomery, Bishop 413
Moore, Laurence 303, 305
Moravia, Christianization 59–60, 78
Moravian Brethren and Swiss *réveil* 351, 352, 354–7
More, Thomas 159–60, 172–6, 178
Moreton, M. B. 57, 67
Morrison, Karl 82
Mott, John R. 485, 493, 495
Moulinié 352
Moult, William 289 n.10
Mullens, Joseph 407
Musaeus 20–1
music and Roman rite 29 n.54, 47–8, 61, 71–2, 82

Nantes, Edict of 236, 249
nativism, American 315–16
Naunton, Sir Robert 245, 246–7
Navarre 96, 100, 104–5
Neff, Félix 357, 360
Nelson, Janet 59
Neophyus of Cyprus 126
nepotism and papacy 163–4

546

# Index

549

# Index

# Index

# Index

Index compiled by Meg Davies (Society of Indexers)